TERRORISM

Documents of International and Local Control

VOLUME 98

TERRORISM

Documents of International and Local Control

VOLUME 98

TERRORISM IN INDIA

Douglas C. Lovelace Jr., Esquire
Senior National Security Strategist

Oceana®
NEW YORK

OXFORD
UNIVERSITY PRESS

Oxford University Press, Inc., publishes works that further Oxford University's objective of excellence in research, scholarship, and education.

Published by Oxford University Press, Inc.
198 Madison Avenue, New York, New York 10016

Cataloging-in-Publication information is available from the Library of Congress.

ISSN 1062-4007
Terrorism: Documents of International and Local Control

ISBN: 978-0-19-538308-9 (v. 98)

Note to Readers:

This publication is designed to provide accurate and authoritative information in regard to the subject matter covered. It is based upon sources believed to be accurate and reliable and is intended to be current as of the time it was written. It is sold with the understanding that the publisher is not engaged in rendering legal, accounting, or other professional services. If legal advice or other expert assistance is required, the services of a competent professional person should be sought. Also, to confirm that the information has not been affected or changed by recent developments, traditional legal research techniques should be used, including checking primary sources where appropriate.

(Based on the Declaration of Principles jointly adopted by a Committee of the American Bar Association and a Committee of Publishers and Associations.)

TABLE OF CONTENTS

VOLUME 98

TERRORISM IN INDIA

DOCUMENTS

A. INDIAN GOVERNMENTAL REPORTS AND STATEMENTS

DOCUMENT NO. 1: India's Country Report, 2005, D. K. Pathak 1

DOCUMENT NO. 2: Social Network Analysis of Terrorist Organizations in India, Institute for Defence Studies and Analysis, India, IDSA Report, 2004, Aparna Basu, Institute for Defence Studies and Analysis (IDSA) 13

DOCUMENT NO. 3: An Overview on India-Pakistan Relations, Indian Ministry of External Affairs, April 21, 2008. 23

DOCUMENT NO. 4: Kashmir: The True Story, Indian Ministry of External Affairs, January 2004 29

DOCUMENT NO. 5: Brief on India-Sri Lanka Relations, Indian Ministry of External Affairs, February 26, 2007 41

DOCUMENT NO. 6: Speech of Union Home Minister Shivraj Patil, November 22, 2008 45

DOCUMENT NO. 7: Speech of Prime Minister Dr. Manmohan Singh, November 23, 2008 55

DOCUMENT NO. 8: Prime Minister's Address to the Nation on the Mumbai Attacks, November 27, 2008 61

B. INDIAN LEGISLATION

DOCUMENT NO. 9: The Armed Forces (Special Powers) Act, Act 28 of 1958, September 11, 1958 63

DOCUMENT NO. 10: The Unlawful Activities (Prevention) Act, 1967, Act No. 37 of 1967, December 30, 1967. 67

DOCUMENT NO. 11: Terrorist and Disruptive Activities (Prevention) Act, 1987, September 3, 1987 79

DOCUMENT NO. 12: The SAARC Convention (Suppression of Terrorism) Act, 1993, No. 36 of 1993, April 26, 1993 99

DOCUMENT NO. 13: Parliament Resolution on Jammu and Kashmir, February 22, 1994 105

DOCUMENT NO. 14: The Prevention of Terrorism Ordinance, 2001, No. 9 of 2001, October 24, 2001 107

DOCUMENT NO. 15: The Prevention of Terrorism Act, 2002, Act No. 15 of 2002, March 28, 2002 141

DOCUMENT NO. 16: The Prevention of Terrorism (Repeal) Ordinance, 2004, September 21, 2004 175

DOCUMENT NO. 17: The Unlawful Activities (Prevention) Amendment Act, 2004, No. 29 of 2004, December 29, 2004. 177

DOCUMENT NO. 18: Weapons of Mass Destruction and Their Delivery Systems (Prohibition of Unlawful Activities) Act, 2005, No. 21 of 2005, June 6, 2005. 195

C. INTERNATIONAL AGREEMENTS

DOCUMENT NO. 19: Agreement Between India and Pakistan on Bilateral Relations (Simla Agreement), July 2, 1972 207

DOCUMENT NO. 20: The Lahore Declaration, February 21, 1999 . . .211

DOCUMENT NO. 21: India, European Union Joint Declaration against International Terrorism, November 21, 2001 213

D. INDIA'S REPORTS TO THE UN

DOCUMENT NO. 22: India's 2001 Counter-Terrorism Report to the UN, UN Security Council Resolution, S/2001/1278, December 27, 2007 215

DOCUMENT NO. 23: India's 2002 Counter-Terrorism Report to the UN, UN Security Council Resolution, S/2002/883, August 7, 2002. . . .283

DOCUMENT NO. 24: India's 2003 Counter-Terrorism Report to the UN, UN Security Council Resolution, S/2003/452, April 21, 2003 311

DOCUMENT NO. 25: India's 2004 Counter-Terrorism Report to the UN, UN Security Council Resolution, S/2003/452, June 3, 2004 . .321

DOCUMENT NO. 26: India's 2007 Counter-Terrorism Report to the UN, UN Security Council Resolution, S/2007/196, April 11, 2007 . . .347

DOCUMENT NO. 27: Report of India's Mission to the UN on Small Arms and Light Weapons, June 11, 2007. 367

E. US PERSPECTIVES

DOCUMENT NO. 28: International Terrorism in South Asia, CRS Report, RS21658, K. Alan Kronstadt, Analyst in Asian Affairs, Foreign Affairs, Defense, and Trade Division, November 3, 2003 377

DOCUMENT NO. 29: India: Chronology of Events, CRS Report, RS21589, K. Alan Kronstadt, Analyst in Asian Affairs, Foreign Affairs, Defense, and Trade Division, December 3, 2003 385

DOCUMENT NO. 30: Typologies and Open Source Reporting on Terrorist Abuse of Charitable Operations in Post-Earthquake Pakistan and India, U.S. Treasury, March 9, 2007 393

DOCUMENT NO. 31: India and Pakistan Engagement: Prospects for Breakthrough or Breakdown?, United States Institute of Peace (USIP) Special Report 129, January 2005 405

DOCUMENT NO. 32: Quickstep or Kadam Taal?: The Elusive Search for Peace in Jammu and Kashmir, United States Institute of Peace (USIP) Special Report 133, March 2005 427

F. OTHER NON-INDIAN PERSPECTIVES

DOCUMENT NO. 33: International Commission of Jurists' Report, 1995 443

DOCUMENT NO. 34: Muslims, Terrorism and Rise of The Hindu Right in India, The Australian National University: Strategic and Defence Studies Centre, Working Paper No. 389, Sandy Gordon, May 2004 449

DOCUMENT NO. 35: Lashkar-e-Tayyiba, Australian Attorney General, September 11, 2007 491

DOCUMENT NO. 36: The Kashmir Conflict and its Global Reach, Intelligence and Terrorism Information Center (ITIC) at the Center for Special Studies (C.S.S), June 21, 2006 497

SUBJECT INDEX 505

A. INDIAN GOVERNMENTAL REPORTS AND STATEMENTS

DOCUMENT NO. 1

INDIA'S COUNTRY REPORT

2005

D. K. Pathak*

I. Terrorism Defined

Before we proceed on any deliberation on the subject it would be desirable to know what is terrorism. It is believed that social scientists are yet to agree on a clear cut definition of terrorism. However, the so called academic consensus definition written by A. P. Schmid and widely used by social scientists and within the UN itself is—

Terrorism is an anxiety-inspiring method of repeated violent action, employed by (semi) clandestine individuals, groups or state actors, for idiosyncratic, criminal or political reasons, whereby—in contrast to assassination—the direct targets of violence are not the main targets. The immediate human victims of violence are generally chosen randomly (targets of opportunity) or selectively (representative or symbolic targets) from a target population, and serve as message generators. Threat and violence based communication processes between terrorists (organisation), (imperilled) victims, and main targets are used to manipulate the main target (audience(s)), turning it into a target of terror, a target of demands, or a target of attention, depending on whether intimidation, coercion or propaganda is primarily sought.

In India section 15 of the Unlawful Activities (Prevention) Amendment Ordinance, 2004 defines terrorist act as "whoever, with intent to threaten the unity, integrity, security or sovereignty of India or to strike terror in the people or any section of the people in India or does any act by using bombs, dynamite or other explosive substances or inflammable substances or firearms or other substances (whether biological or otherwise) of a hazardous nature, in such a manner as to cause or likely to cause death of or injuries to any person or persons or loss of or damage to or destruction of property

* Insepetor General of Police (Law & Order) Assam Police Headquaters, India.

or disruption of any supplies or services essential to the life of the community in India or causes damage or destruction of any property or equipment used or intended to be used for the defence of India, any State government or any of their agencies or detains any person or threatens to kill or injure such person in order to compel the government of India or any other person to do so or abstain from doing any act, commits a Terrorist act".

II. Terrorism in India

India has been among the major victims of terrorism—mostly cross border state sponsored Terrorism—for over two decades. Despite the intolerably high cost in terms of human lives, people and material, India has steadfastly pursued a counter strategy which gives primacy to dialogue, democratic political processes and the rule of law.

Armed counter actions are based on the doctrine of "minimum use of force" within the framework of the constitution which guarantees human rights. The magnitude of the problem of terrorism in India could be gauged by the violence statistics as given in *Appendix A*.

III. Indian Initiatives

To deal with the problems of terrorism India has taken several initiatives at various levels.

A. At the International Level

- India has been supportive of all efforts, particularly in the UN to combat terrorism and has played a leading role in shaping international opinion and urging the international community to prioritize the fight against terror. Its consistent and basic stand before the international community has been that—
  - There could be no justification for terrorism on any grounds: religious, political, ideological or any other.
  - The fight against terrorism must be given the highest priority
  - To be effective, the fight against terrorism has to be long term, comprehensive and sustained.
  - Strengthening of international cooperation is vital to ensure that action is not restricted simply to the perpetrators but also encompassed states, which sponsor, support, or provide safe haven to terrorists.
  - Ad hoc and selective actions have limited chances of success and compartmentalization of actions in terms of regions, religions or organizations is bound to be counterproductive.

B. Multi-Lateral Arrangements and Agreements

- It welcomed UN Security Council Resolution 1373 and is fully committed to implement it. It has submitted its national report on measures taken to implement UN Security Council Resolution 1373 in December 2001 and also submitted a supplementary report on specific queries by the Counter Terrorism Committee under the Security Council.
- It is signatory to all the thirteen UN Sectoral Conventions on Terrorism. It has been supportive of all measures within the UN General Assembly, the sixth Committee and the UN Security Council. It has supported UN Security Council Resolution 1269 and 1368, which clearly identify terrorism as a threat to international peace and security. In addition, India has supported and fully implemented Resolutions 1267, 1333 and 1363 relating to terrorism by the Taliban Regime in Afghanistan.
- It has piloted the comprehensive Convention on International Terrorism (CCIT) in the UN with the objective of providing a comprehensive legal framework to combat terrorism.

C. Regional Arrangements

- At the regional level, India is a party to the SAARC Regional Convention on Suppression of Terrorism 1987 and has enacted the enabling legislation in the form of the SAARC Conventions (Suppression of Terrorism Act) 1993.
- The ASEAN Regional Forum (ARF) was set up in 1994 as a regional security dialogue platform with ten ASEAN countries of which India is also a member.

D. Bilateral Arrangements

India has entered into three types of bilateral treaties to combat international terrorism

- **Agreements** to combat terrorism and organized crimes, drug related offences, etc. such agreements are essentially framework agreements to facilitate the exchange of operational information and development of joint programmes to counter organized crimes and terrorism.
- **Extradition Treaties** to facilitate transfer of fugitive offenders and suspected terrorists. Such treaties have been signed with seventeen countries, signed but not exchanged with eight countries in addition to extradition arrangements with eleven countries.
- **Bilateral Treaties on Mutual Legal Assistance (MLATs)** in criminal matters to facilitate investigation, collection of evidence, transport of witnesses, location and action against proceeds of crime, etc. Such

MLATs have been signed with ten countries in addition to those signed but not exchanged with nine countries.

E. Mechanism of Interpol

- In addition to the above, cooperation on matters relating to terrorism is also effected through the mechanism of Interpol, of which India has been a member since 1946; there is an Indian member on secondment to Interpol. The nodal point for coordination with Interpol at the central level is the CBI.

IV. Legal Regime in India

In keeping with the requirement of dealing with the menace of terrorism, India has put in place a comprehensive legal infrastructure. There are several pieces of legislation, of which some of them are listed below—

(i) The Unlawful Activities (Prevention) Act, 1967

(ii) The Armed Forces (Special) Powers Act, 1967

(iii) The National Security Act, 1980

(iv) The Arms Act, 1959

(v) The Explosives Act, 1884

(vi) The Explosives Substance Act, 1908

(vii) The Indian Penal Code, 1860

(viii) The Code of Criminal Procedures, 1973

(ix) The Anti-Hijacking Act, 1982

(x) The Prevention of Money Laundering Act, 2002

It would be relevant to highlight some of the penal provisions of one or two pieces of legislation dealing with the acts of terrorism.

A. The Unlawful Activities (Prevention) Act, 1967

This Act was enunciated by the Indian Parliament in 1967 to make powers available to the law enforcement agencies for dealing with unlawful activities directed against the integrity and sovereignty of India. It provides for effective prevention of certain unlawful activities of individuals and associations including terrorist organizations. It extends to the whole of India.

Sec. 3—Power of the Government of India to declare an association as unlawful. (The list of the terrorist organizations banned under this Act is given under Appendix B)

Sec. 16—Punishment for terrorist acts—death or imprisonment for life as the case may be and liable to a fine.

Sec. 17—Punishment for raising funds for terrorist acts—imprisonment for life and also liable to a fine.
Sec. 18—Punishment for conspiracy—imprisonment from five years to imprisonment for life and liable to a fine.
Sec. 19—Punishment for harbouring, etc.—imprisonment from 3 years to imprisonment for life and liable to a fine.
Sec. 33—Forfeiture of property of certain persons during trial and conviction.
Sec. 40—Offence of raising funds for a terrorist organization—imprisonment up to fourteen years or with a fine or both.

B. The National Security Act, 1980

The Act came into force in 1980 with a view to providing power to the Central Government and State Governments to make orders to detain certain persons including foreigners whose action may be prejudicial to the defence of India, security of India, prejudicial to the maintenance of public order and maintenance of supplies and services essential to the community.

Sec. 3-(3)—Detention period—in the first instance exceed three months but the State Government may, if satisfied as aforesaid that it is necessary so to do, amend such order to extend such period from time to time by any period not exceeding three months at any one time.
Sec. 9—Constitution of Advisory Boards.
Sec. 11—Procedure of Advisory Boards.
Sec. 13—Maximum period of detention: 12 months.

C. Prevention of Money Laundering Act, 2002

Sec. 2—Whosoever directly or indirectly attempts to indulge or knowingly assists or knowingly is a party or is actually involved in any process or activity connected with the proceeds of crime and projecting it as untainted property shall he guilty of the offence of money laundering.
Sec. 4—Punishment for money laundering.
Sec. 5&8—Deals with provisional attachment and confiscation.
Sec. 19—Power of arrest.
Sec. 24—Puts the burden of proof on the accused.
Sec. 45—Offences cognizable, non-bailable and limitation on granting bail.
Sec. 72—Provides for continuance of proceedings in the event of death or insolvency.

D. Armed Forces (Special) Powers Act, 1967

(Salient features—without replicating the wording in the Act)

Sec. 3—The whole or any part of the country/state can be declared as a disturbed area by the central government or the governor of the state

Sec. 4—* Special powers can be utilized by any commissioned officers, non-commissioned officers, warrant officers or any other person of the equivalent rank
- * Authorizes use of force, even causing death against any person who is acting in contravention of law or carrying weapons
- * Authorizes the destruction of any arms dumps, prepared or fortified positions from which armed attacks are made or likely to be made
- * Authorizes arrest without warrant of any person who is suspected to have committed or likely to commit any cognizable offence. May even use such force as necessary to effect the arrest
- * Enter and search without warrant any premises suspected to be used for any illegal purposes as defined under the Act
- * Arrested person to be handed over to the officer in charge of the nearest police station with the least possible delay

The above provisions confer sweeping powers on the members of the armed forces and since they are likely to be misused the Supreme Court of India has issued eleven commandments regulating the exercise of powers under this Act.

V. Suggested Measures to Combat Terrorism

A. It must be understood fully that while anti-terrorism is a philosophical anti-thesis that emerges from a painstaking examination of the concept of terrorism as well as an attempt to understand and articulate what constitutes terrorism, counter terrorism refers to the practices, tactics, and strategies that governments, the military and other groups adopt in order to combat terrorism. A few of the strategies, apart from the legal recourse, which may be adapted to combat insurgency are:

1. A clearly defined policy and no compromise with terrorism
2. Dialogue with insurgents only within the ambit of the Constitution
3. Pro-active measures, including (if necessary) pre-emptive strikes on anti-terrorist camps and bases
4. Strengthening of existing anti-terror laws

5. Punitive action against sympathizers, beneficiaries of terrorism and funding sources

6. Strengthening of mechanisms such as psychological warfare in order to combat terror. Such mechanisms must be decidedly pro-active

7. Creation of and the joining in anti-terror cooperative groups in the region such as Shanghai Cooperation Organisation

8. Spearhead a global denouncement and alienation of states sponsoring or not acting against terror. Non-distinction of terror perpetrated by religious groups

B. Talking of the legal regime to combat insurgency, a decision needs to be taken at all levels, including under the UN mandate, as to the extent to which the personal liberties of citizens can be compromised vis-à-vis the implementation of the various legal provisions already in vogue. Most of the time the war on the legal count against the *Ultras* is lost because of extreme sensitivity of our system to the alleged violation of personal liberties. A balance has to be arrived at between both aspects.

C. At the end, what is required is a will to win the war over terrorism backed up by strict enforcement of existing laws at the National and International level. Any system as it marches ahead reveals certain lacunae and loopholes, which in the instant case affords the terrorists an advantage and ultimately in getting away rather mildly. There should be parity in the norms to be adopted by different countries at the international level when it comes to protecting the national interest.

Appendix A
Violence Statistics (2001–2005)

- *Total Number of Incidents*

J & K	16394
LWE	7290
NE	6294
Punjab	4
Total	**29982**

- *Attacks on Security Forces*

J & K	3439
LWE	830
NE	1728
Punjab	Nil
Total	**2879**

- *Total Persons Killed*

J & K	13404
LWE	2752
NE	5387
Punjab	5
Total	**21548**

- *Civilians Killed*

J & K	4253
LWE	1457
NE	2345
Punjab	5
Total	**8060**

- *Security Forces Killed*

J & K	2098
LWE	545
NE	612
Punjab	Nil
Total	**3255**

- *Terrorists Killed*

J & K	7053
LWE	750
NE	2430
Punjab	Nil
Total	**10233**

- *Weapons Recovered*

J & K	9427
LWE	2765
NE	2640
Punjab	256
Total	**15088**

Abbreviations used:
J & K Jammu and Kashmir
LWE Left Wing Extremism
NE North Eastern States of India

Note: The above statistics are not complete for 2005 and hence, they are only indicative.

Appendix B
Terrorist Organisations Banned in India

1. Babbar Khalsa International
2. Khalistan Commando Force
3. Khalistan Zindabad Force
4. International Sikh Youth Federation
5. Lashkar-E-Taiba/Pasban-E-Ahle Hadis
6. Jaish-E-Mohammad
7. Harkat-Ul-Mujahideen/Harkat-Ul-Ansar/Harkat Ul-Jehad-E-Islami
8. Hizb-Ul-Kujahideen
9. Al-Umar-Mujahideen
10. Jammu and Kashmir Islamik Front
11. United Liberation Front of Assam (ULFA)
12. National Democratic Front of Bodoland (NDFB)

13. Peoples Liberation Army (PLA)
14. United National Liberation Front (UNLF)
15. Peoples Revolutionary Party of Kangleipak (PREPAK)
16. Kangleipak Communist Party (KCP)
17. Kanglei Yaol Kanba Lup (KYKL)
18. Manipur Peoples Liberation Front (MPLF)
19. All Tripura Tiger Force
20. National Liberation Front of Tripura
21. Liberation Tigers of Tamil Elam (LTTE)
22. Students Islamic Movement of India
23. Deendar Anjuman
24. Communist Party of India (M-L)—Peoples War Group and all its formations and front organizations
25. Maoist Communist Centre (MCC) and all its formations and front organizations
26. Albadr
27. Jamiat-Ul-Mujahideen
28. Al-qaida
29. Dukhtaran-E-Millat (DEM)
30. Tamil Nadu Liberation Army (TNLA)
31. Tamil National retrieval Troops (TNRT)
32. Akhil Bharat Nepali Ekta Samaj (ABNES)

Appendix C
Summary of Counter-Insurgency Operations in Assam From 1 January 2000 to 2005 (Up to 25 December)

Year	Insurgent Killed	Insurgent Captured	Arms/Ammn./ Cash Recovered		Security Personnel Killed	Civilians Killed	No. of Incidents	Surrendered
2000	328	1535	Arms	371	80	412	643	1834
			Ammn.	5266				
			Rs.	17,70,256				

Year	Insurgent Killed	Insurgent Captured	Arms/Ammn./ Cash Recovered		Security Personnel Killed	Civilians Killed	No. of Incidents	Surrendered
2001	308	912	Arms	410	86	261	485	438
			Ammn.	6842				
			Rs.	4,36,664				
2002	322	715	Arms	365	36	218	454	139
			Ammn.	6686				
			Rs.	9,07,138				
2003	276	1024	Arms	456	15	260	474	3067
			Ammn.	20488				
			Rs.	11,21,184				
2004	135	1080	Arms	349	25	202	349	1050
			Ammn.	9623				
			Rs.	8,92,494				
2005 (up to 25. Dec)	75	784	Arms	196	9	63	294	217
			Ammn.	6150				
			Rs.	10,92,544				
TOTAL	**1444**	**6050**	**Arms**	**2147**	**251**	**1416**	**2699**	**6745**
			Ammn.	**55055**				
			Rs.	**6219270**				

DOCUMENT NO. 2

SOCIAL NETWORK ANALYSIS OF TERRORIST ORGANIZATIONS IN INDIA

Institute for Defence Studies and Analysis, India
IDSA Report

2004

Aparna Basu
Institute for Defence Studies and Analysis (IDSA)
JNU Old Campus, New Delhi 110067, India
aparnabasu.dr@gmail.com

Abstract

In this study we have tried to derive a linkage map of terrorist organizations in India, using the methods of Social Network Analysis. The presence of links between terrorist organizations has been inferred from media reports of terrorist violence, where the frequency of co-occurrence of names of terrorist organizations has been used as a basis for inferring intensity of links. The groupings effected by SNA based on textual links alone correctly displayed ideological and regional groupings of the terrorist organizations. Our analysis correctly identified the major groups of terrorist organizations operating in the country and their linkages to international terrorist organizations. Using betweenness centrality we were able to mark out key players such as the ISI of Pakistan, in spite of its having a relatively low intensity of links. The role of ISI in terrorism in India is well known and borne out by conventional analysis. Other prominent organizations were the Lashkar-e-Tayyiba and Jaish-e-Mohammed. The methodology used in this paper is likely to be useful for strategic analysis based either on open source or intelligence (classified) data.

Contact:
Dr. Aparna Basu
Fellow, GN Ramachandran Genome Informatics Knowledge Centre
Institute of Genomics and Integrative Biology (at TCGA)
254 Okhla Industrial Estate - Phase 3
New Delhi 110020, India

Tel: +91 9818405134
Fax: +91 11 51708321
E-mail: aparnabasu.dr@gmail.com

Key Words: Terrorism, Social Network Analysis, India, co-occurrence, bibliometrics, scientometrics

Support: The author acknowledges a 6 month consultancy on the Project on Terrorism at the Institute of Defence Studies and Analysis (IDSA), India from December 2003 to May 2004, during which this study was done.

In recent times Asia has taken the lead in world incidences of terrorism. By 2000, Asia already accounted for 75 percent of all terrorism casualties worldwide.[1] From Afghanistan and Pakistan on the West to Bangladesh and Burma on the East, India is at the geographical center of a belt of terrorist, insurgent and separatist violence.[2] Internally, India is faced with terrorist violence in Jammu and Kashmir, in the North East and the South. Militant organizations have links to external agencies, and these links can be surprisingly long. For example, one of the terrorists freed by India in the Kandahar hijacking of a commercial jetliner in 1999 was suspected to have financed a hijacker in the Sep. 11th bombing of the World Trade Towers.[3]

Increase in global terrorism in recent years, and heightened threat perception by governments and the public has, of necessity, focused keen interest in this area. With the advent of the internet, there is a growing volume of text on the net that relates to terrorist activity, mostly media reports of terrorist incidents, apprehension of terrorists, etc., posted on portals and other sites, such as those maintained by newspapers. Once the reliability of a source is established, this information in the open domain becomes a valuable resource that can be tapped for an understanding of the operations of terrorist organizations. As a first step terrorism information needs to be captured and organized in a usable form as a database. This involves automated search, capture, data cleaning to eliminate multiple reports of the same incident, and storage in a searchable database/GIS system. The ongoing

[1] U.S.Department of State, Patterns of Global Terrorism—2000 (Washington, D.C.: Office of the Coordinator for Counterterrorism, Department of State, April 2001).
[2] Chellany, Brahma (2001) Fighting Terrorism in Southern Asia, International Security, Vol. 26, No. 3 (Winter 2001/02), pp. 94–116.
[3] CNN, "Suspected Hijack Bankroller Freed by India in '99," http://www.cnn.com/2001/US/10/05/inv.terror.investigation/index.html.

exercise at IDSA to populate the Terrorist Tracker database with data on terrorist organizations in was used to generate data for the present study.

Together with an overall increase in militancy, ties are emerging between globally widely dispersed militant organizations, characterized by flows of funds, personnel, ideological and military support. Terrorist and criminal organizations use network forms of organization[4] that tend to be intrinsically more stable and less liable to be disrupted by simple measures. Being covert organizations, with largely invisible membership, it can be extremely difficult to obtain accurate information of their ties and linkages. Textual analysis of open source information[5] provides a possibility of using scientometric tools such as co-occurrence analysis in mapping links between terrorist organizations. The existence of textual links may be considered as indicative of covert **collaboration** or association between the entities.

Study of the linkage patterns of terrorist networks can usefully draw upon the academic perspectives provided by Social Network Analysis[6,7] and modern statistical and visualization tools. SNA uses **graph theoretic** calculations to study the behaviour of networks and **multivariate analysis** to create visual displays. The idea of using SNA to study covert networks is not new.[8] In some form or other these methods have been used to track and uncover associations of criminals. SNA has a long history of application to evidence mapping in both fraud and criminal conspiracy cases.[9,10,11] Once investigators have a suspect they can build a network by looking at various sources of relational information such as telephone logs, credit card transactions, etc.[12]

For the hijackers of the planes in the Sep 11 World Trade Center bombing in USA, networks have been traced using media reports after the event.[13]

---

[4] Ronfeldt, David and John Arquilla (2002) Networks, Netwars and the Fight for the Future http://www.firstmonday.dk/issues/issue6_10/ronfeldt/index.html

[5] For an account of open source use in Scotland Yard, see SO11 Open Source Unit Presentation, (undated); Belgium see *OSS '96*: Captain Patrick George, Head, Criminal Analysis Bureau, Central Bureau of Investigation, Belgium, for establishing an open source intelligence analysis unit and an open source intelligence network across all of Belgium, *OSS '95*: Institute for Scientific Information, for its extraordinary overnight support of "The Burundi Exercise" that was instrumental in persuading the Aspin/Brown Commission that open source intelligence is a discipline in its own right.; *OSS '96*: Commission on the Roles and Missions of the U.S. Intelligence Community, for its documented finding that U.S. Intelligence Community access to open sources is severely deficient and should be a top priority for funding and a top priority for DCI attention, http://www.oss.net

[6] Scott, John (1991) Social Network Analysis: A Handbook, Sage Publications.

[7] Wasserman, Stanley and Katherine Faust (1994) Social Network Analysis: Methods and Applications, Structural Analysis in the Social Sciences, Vol. 8, Cambridge University Press.

[8] Sparrow, M.K. (1991) The application of network analysis to criminal intelligence: An assessment of the prospects. Social Networks 13: 251–274.

[9] Baker, W.E. and R.R. Faulkner (1993) The social organization of conspiracy: Illegal networks in the heavy electrical equipment industry. American Sociological Review 58(6): 837–860.

[10] Defense Intelligence Agency (2000) Criminal Network Analysis Training Course.

[11] Klerks, P. (2001) The network paradigm applied to criminal organizations, Connections 24(3): xx-yy.

[12] Krebs, Valdis E. (2002) Mapping Networks of Terrorist Cells, CONNECTIONS 24(3): 43–52.

[13] http://www.orgnet.com/tnet.html

More recently network methods have formed a successful part of intelligence work. According to Bruce Berkowitz, former CIA analyst, research fellow at the Hoover Institution and senior analyst at the RAND Corporation, detailed networks were apparently drawn to trace the kinship network of Saddam Hussein prior to his capture.[14]

In this paper, using textual links as a proxy for real links we derive a network of terrorist organizations operating in India over the last two years. The roles and positions of different organizations within the network are analyzed using graph theoretic indicators and displayed visually using multivariate techniques. Our findings are summarized in the concluding section. The same methodology has been used by us in our earlier work on incidences of terrorism in Jammu and Kashmir.[15,16,17]

Social Network Analysis: "Collaboration" Network of Terrorists

The data selected for analysis of terrorist linkages are reports of terrorism in the Terrorist Tracker database (termed category 1 incidents) from 2001 to 2003. The "collaboration" or nexus between terrorist organizations has been inferred from the data by using the co-occurrence of different organizations in a report of a single incident. (Similar methods have been used in co-word analysis in bibliometrics/scientometrics.) Based on the frequency of these co-occurrences an adjacency matrix of 61 organizations with organization-to-organization links is created. This data is noisy in that every co-occurrence may not represent a real or meaningful link. Some errors are also introduced through different names or variants for the same organization or conversely the same name (or acronym) being used for different organizations. To reduce the noise, very infrequent occurrences suggesting spurious or unimportant linkages have been filtered out, using the principle of "thresholding".

In Table 1 we have listed the first few organizations with the largest number of links, totaling 85% of all links between organizations. This demonstrates the applicability of the 80-20 Rule to terrorism (the rule states that 20 percent of the entities account for 80 percent of the activity).

---

14 Berkowitz, Bruce (2003) Learning to Break the Rules, Commentary, NY Times, Dec. 19 http://www.rand.org/commentary/121903NYT.html

15 Basu, Aparna and Sudhir Saxena (2004) Network Analysis of Terrorist Organizations in India: An Analysis of Terrorist Outfits in Jammu and Kashmir, in International Workshop on Webometrics, Informetrics and Scientometrics & 5th COLLNET Meeting, Roorkee, India, March 5–8, 2004.

16 Saxena, Sudhir, K. Santhanam, Aparna Basu (2004) Application of Social Network Analysis (SNA) to Terrorist Networks in Jammu & Kashmir, Strategic Analysis Vol. 28 No.1, Jan–Mar (pp. 84–101) http://www.idsa-india.org/SA-2004.HTM (abstract).

17 Santhanam S., Aparna Basu, Sudhir Saxena (2004) in Indo-U.S. Science and Technology Forum Workshop on "Science and Technology to Combat Terrorism" Goa, India, January 12, 2004.

Table 1. Twenty organizations with the highest links

Rank	Organisation	Percent links
1	Jamiat Ulema-e-Hind	11.26%
2	J&K Jamiat-e-Islami	8.85%
3	Taliban	8.09%
4	Sipah-e-Sahaba	6.98%
5	Jamiat-e-Islami	6.84%
6	Jamiat Ulema-e-Islam	4.57%
7	Jamiat-e-Ullemah-e-Islami	4.57%
8	Central Military Commission	4.06%
9	Lashkar-e-Tayyiba	3.85%
10	Maoist Communist Centre	3.73%
11	Inter Service Intelligence	2.76%
12	Al Badr	2.64%
13	Al Qaida	2.60%
14	People's War Group	2.34%
15	All Tripura Tiger Force	2.13%
16	United Liberation Front of Asom	2.04%
17	Islamia Students League	2.00%
18	Jaish-e-Mohammad	1.86%
19	National Liberation Front of Tripura	1.83%
20	Hizbul Mujahideen	1.51%

Network Visualization: Multidimensional Scaling

The terrorist network is mapped using the Multidimensional Scaling routine in UCINET.[18] Each organization is mapped as a node in a connected graph, grouping together structurally similar organizations (having a similar pattern of linkages) on the map. Fig. 1 shows the linked graph of 61 terrorist organizations operating in India. A clear picture does not emerge at this stage, but linkages to geographically distant and foreign organizations can be seen.

After "thresholding" by eliminating ties with link strength less than 5 co-occurrences in two years, we are left with 35 linked nodes shown in Fig. 2.

[18] Borgatti, S.P., Everett, M.G. and Freeman, L.C. (2002) Ucinet for Windows: Software for Social Network Analysis. Harvard: Analytic Technologies.

Figure 1: MDS Map of Terrorist Network of 61 organizations operating in India

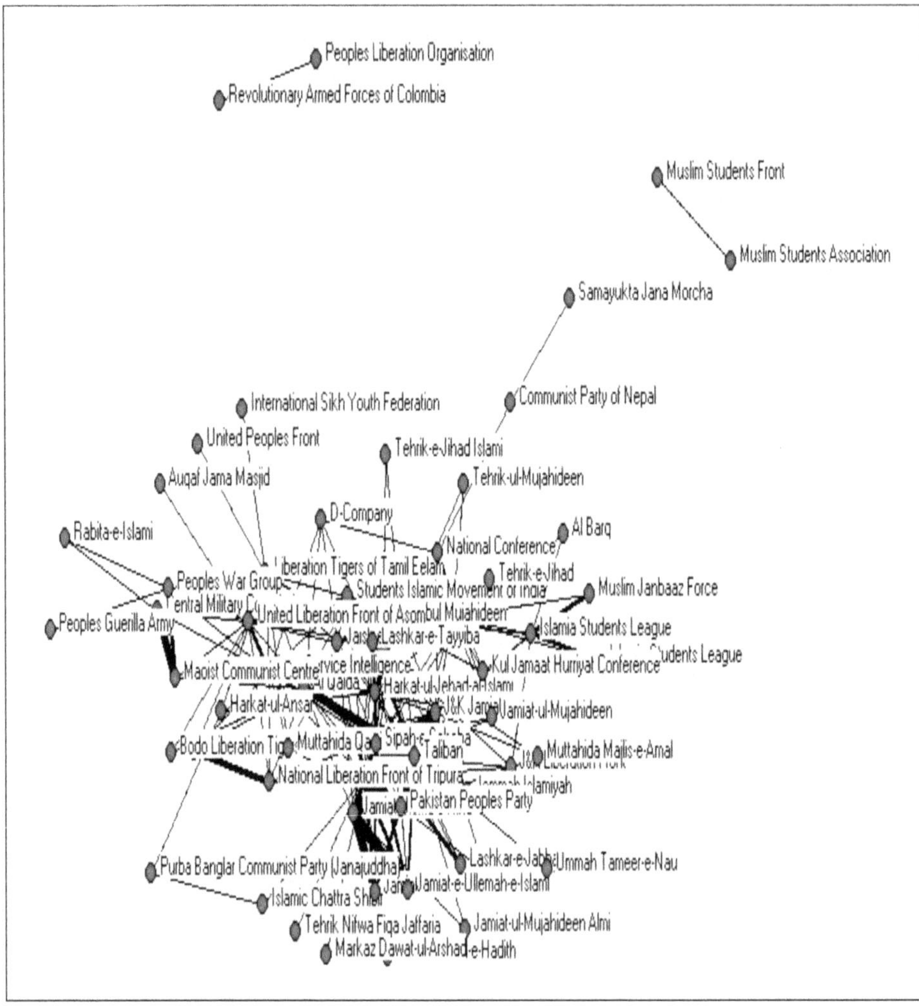

Note the vertical dotted line clearly separating the Islamic groups on the right from the non-islamic groups on the left. In the quadrants marked 1–4 in Fig. 2, we find terrorist organizations operating in the J&K region in the first and second quadrants, organizations in Assam and the North East in quadrant 3, and the left wing organizations in quadrant 4; along with international organizations such as the Taliban and Al Qaida. The thickness of the lines is proportional to the link frequency. Isolated small groups seen at the base of the figure are not included in the analysis.

The high frequency of links and the large number of Islamic organizations reflect the preponderance of terrorist activity and groups in J&K. The groupings effected by SNA based on textual links correctly display ideological

Figure 2: Network of the more central terrorist organizations (link strength >5)

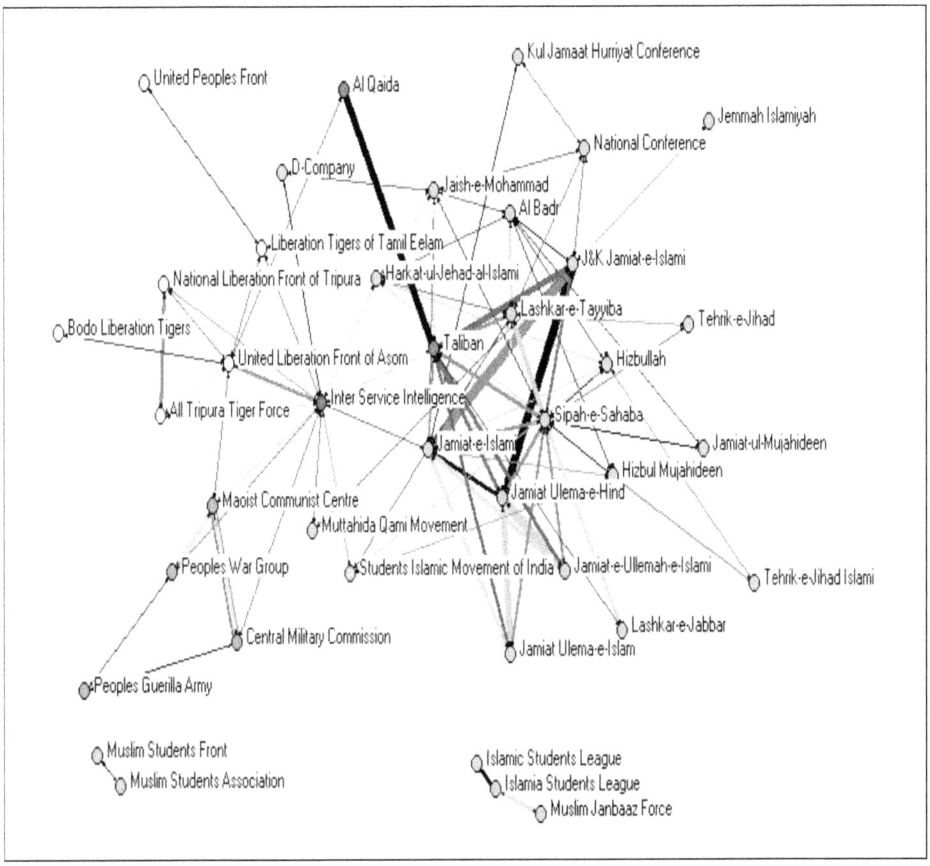

and regional groupings. Further information can be gleaned about the individual roles of organizations in the network based on their network positions and interlinkages.

Indicators: Centrality and Betweenness

The role and positions of different organizations in the network can be investigated using concepts from graph theory such as **centrality** and **betweenness**. Out of several measures of centrality, we have focused on organizations with high betweenness index. The betweenness index is an indicator of a "brokerage" role, signifying an organization that has links with diverse unrelated groups of organizations.

We note that the organization with the highest BI is the Inter Services Intelligence (ISI) of Pakistan (Table 2). In Fig. 3 we show the network visualization with node size proportional to BI. This marks out the ISI of Pakistan as a key player in the Indian terror network.

Table 2. Betweenness index for Terrorist organizations

Organization	Betweenness
Inter Service Intelligence, Pakistan	12.60
Jamiat-e-Islami	5.25
Taliban	4.34
Sipah-e-Sahaba	4.14
Jaish-e-Mohammad	3.00
J&K Jamiat-e-Islami	2.96
United Liberation Front of Asom	2.69
Liberation Tigers of Tamil Eelam	2.35
Harkat-ul-Jehad-al-Islami	1.74
Lashkar-e-Tayyiba	1.64
Hizbul Mujahideen	1.35
Hizbullah	1.35
Al Badr	1.09
Students Islamic Movement of India	0.91
Peoples War Group	0.90
Central Military Commission	0.90
Jamiat Ulema-e-Hind	0.83
National Conference	0.76
Al Qaida	0.66

Conclusions

The main question in this analysis was whether and to what extent open source data and textual links could be used as a proxy for information on real links, and whether without going into details of the content of the database, a datamining exercise could be performed to yield meaningful results. It would appear from the results obtained that SNA would be suitable in a first cut analysis of the links between terrorist organizations. Our analysis of textual data on terrorist incidents identified the major groups of terrorist organizations operating in India and their linkages to international terrorist organizations. The groups are known to share ideological and regional links. The statistical analysis of a very large number of links brings out latent patterns while suppressing noise. Complex interlinkages are readily perceived though the visualization techniques. Computation of graph theoretic indices helps identify key players with different kinds of

Figure 3: Terrorist Network with Node Size proportional to High Betweenness Index

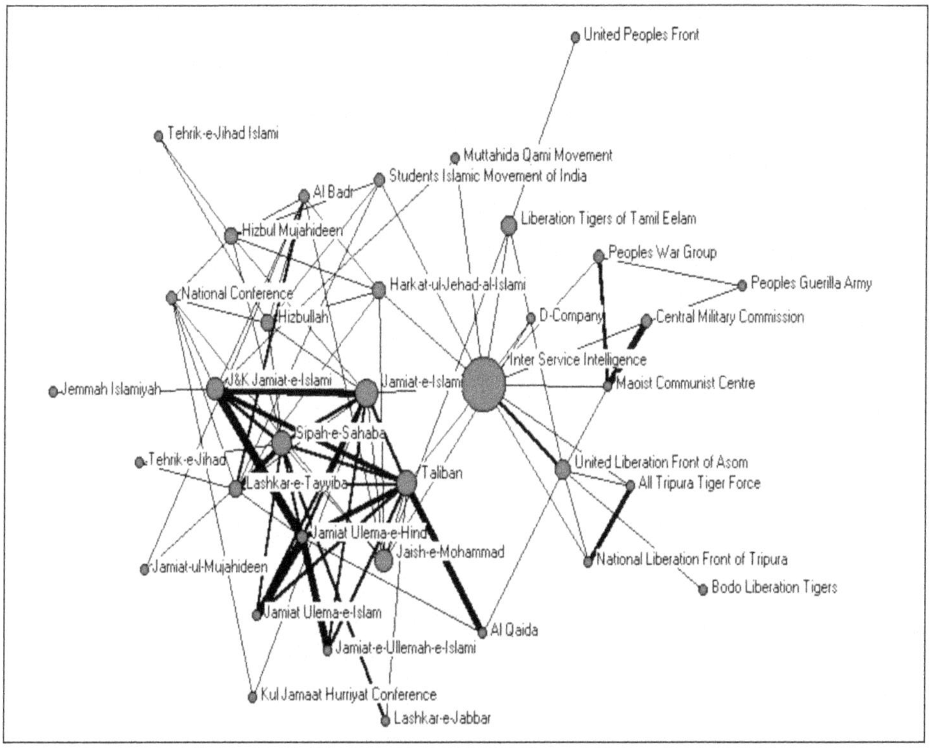

roles. Using the centrality and betweenness centrality indices we were able to mark out the key players such as the ISI of Pakistan. An important point to note here is that the ISI was correctly identified in spite of the fact that it did not have a large number of links. Its rank in terms of link frequency was 12 (Table 1), well below some of the J&K organizations. The role of ISI in terrorism in India is well known and borne out by conventional analysis (Fig. 2). Our list also identifies prominent organizations like the Lashkar-e-Tayyiba and Jaish-e-Mohammed. Some caution in interpretation is necessary as centrality indices are sensitive to slight changes in nodes and links (Krebs, 2002).

We also conclude that it is possible to derive interesting results based on **open source** data. While much of the results here may already be known through conventional intelligence, it is significant that the method of using open source data collected in databases, coupled with recent advances in datamining methods now provide challenging opportunities for computer based analytical techniques to sift through large volumes of terrorist related information that would be difficult for humans to process in a reasonable amount of time. "Essentially, the art and science of pattern analysis from signals intelligence must now be brought over to the open source world, both in print and broadcast media monitoring".[19] Finally, while analyzing networks after an event is fairly easy for prosecution and other purposes, mapping covert networks to prevent criminal or terrorist activity is much more difficult and has some special problems.[20] This is an issue that needs to be addressed in the future.

[19] Steele, Robert David (2002), The New Craft of Intelligence: Personal, Public, & Political—Chapter 15 (OSS International Press, 2002).

[20] Erickson, B.H. (1981). Secret societies and social structure. Social Forces 60(1): 188–210.

DOCUMENT NO. 3

AN OVERVIEW ON INDIA-PAKISTAN RELATIONS

Indian Ministry of External Affairs
(PAI Division)

April 21, 2008

The Composite Dialogue and its technical-level meetings and the Joint Commission and the Eight Working groups set up by it form the basis for the structured official dialogue in India Pakistan bilateral interaction.

2. The Composite Dialogue Process was set into motion from June 2004 in pursuance of a decision taken during the visit of former Prime Minister, Shri Atal Bihari Vajpayee to Pakistan in January 2004. It is predicated on the assurance given by Pakistan that it will not permit any territory under Pakistan's control to be used to support terrorism in any manner. The commitment is contained in a joint press statement issued after meeting between the PM of India Dr Manmohan Singh and the President of Pakistan General Musharraf.

3. The Composite Dialogue deals with eight issues: Siachen, Sir Creek, Tulbal Navigation Project, Terrorism & Drug Trafficking, Economic & Commercial Cooperation, Promotion of Friendly Exchanges, Peace & Security, including CBMs and Jammu & Kashmir. So far Four Rounds of the Composite Dialogue have been completed. Each round of dialogue is initiated and reviewed by Foreign Secretaries and the overall progress is reviewed at EAM level. The fourth round was started in March 2007 and completed in August 2007. This is now due for review at FS and EAM level.

4. Technical and expert level talks on Nuclear CBMs, Conventional CBMs, Cross LOC CBMs, Cooperation between Coast guards, Narcotics control Agencies, Civil Aviation etc., are also being held regularly.

5. The most significant achievement of the Composite Dialogue so far has been the successful continuation of the ceasefire on the International Border, LoC and AGPL, which came in to effect in November 2003. The Composite Dialogue process has also been strengthened by the intensification and expansion of

people-to-people interaction, as a result of the establishment of several transport linkages between the two countries and people-centric Confidence Building Measures. A tabular list of specific achievements of the four rounds of Composite Dialogue is attached in Annexure I.

6. The Joint Commission was revived after a gap of 16 years (the third session held in 1989) with the fourth session held on 4 October 2005 in Islamabad under the co-chairmanship of the two Foreign Ministers. It was decided then to set up Technical Level Working Groups on Agriculture, Health, Science & Technology, Information, Education, I.T. & Telecommunications, Environment and Tourism. The fifth meeting of the Joint Commission was held on 21 February 2007 in New Delhi.

7. Humanitarian issues related to **prisoners and fishermen** are high on the agenda of Government. There are presently 372 Indian fishermen, 342 boats and 199 (estimated) prisoners in Pakistani custody. According to our information there may also be about 73 Indian **Missing Defence Personnel** in Pakistan including 53 from the 1971 war. The Pakistan government has consistently denied their presence. There are no Pakistani POWs in India. Indian Nationals in jails in Pakistan include many who have not been produced for Consular Access. During EAM's visit to Pakistan in January 2007 a decision was taken to form a **Judicial Committee on Prisoners** to ensure humane treatment of prisoners; both sides have exchanged lists of retired judges comprising the committee and its first meeting was held on 26 Feb 2008. The committee made recommendations to the two Governments, which inter alia includes immediate release and consular access of fishermen and exchange of consolidated list of nationals in each others' jails on 31 Mar 2008.

8. **Status of Cross Border Terrorism:** The ceasefire of 25 November 2003 along the IB, LOC and the Actual Ground Position Line (AGPL) has largely held. However terrorist attacks, including outside J&K, have continued. There have been a number of terrorist attacks in Mumbai, Srinagar, Varanasi, Delhi and Bangalore. Pakistan has so far not taken any significant action to dismantle the infrastructure of support to terrorism, such as communications, launching pads, training camps, funding, etc. India has continuing and serious concerns on cross-border terrorism and has repeatedly reiterated the importance of Pakistan fulfilling its commitment outlined in the Joint Press Statement of 6 January 2004 against terrorism.

9. A **Joint Anti-Terrorism Mechanism (JATM)** was put in place during the meeting of PM with President Musharraf in Havana on 16 September 2006 to identify and implement counter-terrorism initiatives and investigations. The first meeting of the mechanism took place on 6 March 2007 in Islamabad. This was in the backdrop of the terrorist bombings on suburban trains in Mumbai. The two sides agreed that specific information will be exchanged for (i) helping investigations on either side related to terrorist acts and

(ii) prevention of violence and terrorist acts in the two countries. The second round of JATM was held in October 2007 in New Delhi to exchange further information. In these meetings, the position taken by Pakistan was disappointing. However, the Government of India attaches importance to this mechanism and believes it could be useful instrument if implemented effectively.

10. **Trade and Commerce:** Total bilateral trade stood at US$ 1.66 billion in the Financial Year (FY) 2006–07 as compared to US$ 859.33 million of FY 2005–06, $ 616 million for 2004–05 and US$ 344.29 million in 2003–04. In FY 2006–07 India's export to Pakistan was valued at US$ 1.34 billion and India's import at US$ 0 .32 billion. In FY 2007–08 (April–Dec 2007) total bilateral trade stood at US$ 1.53 billion. This is 34% more than the corresponding period in previous year. The trade is expected to cross the mark of US$ 2 billion during 2007–08. Unofficial trade through third countries is also of significance which increases the transaction costs for end users in Pakistan. While India has accorded MFN status to Pakistan, Pakistan continues to restrict items of import from India to a positive list of 1075 items. On SAFTA, Pakistan has refused to extend the negotiated tariff concessions to items outside the positive list to India thereby negating the letter and spirit of the agreement as exports are limited only to items on the positive list. Both countries agreed in August 2007 to allow each other's trucks to cross at Wagha/Attari border up to designated points on either side and the agreement is being implemented with effect from 1 October 2007. Efforts are underway to start the Srinagar-Muzaffarabad truck service across the Line of Control (LoC) for trade in agreed items.

11. **Transport Links:**

- The **Delhi-Lahore bus service** that was started on 20 February 1999 was stopped on 1 January 2002 after the attack on Parliament. The service resumed from 11 July 2003 following the re-establishment of transport links. The frequency of this service was increased from two to three trips per week in the meeting of India-Pakistan Standing Committee on Bus Services held on 21 Feb 2008. During EAM's visit to Pakistan on February 15–17, 2005, an agreement was reached to start a bus service between Amritsar and Lahore and to Nankana Sahib. It was also agreed to begin cross LOC transport services by way of bus service between Srinagar and Muzaffarabad. The **Amritsar-Lahore weekly bus** service commenced on 24 January 2006. PM Manmohan Singh flagged off the **Amritsar-Nankana Sahib bus** service on 24 March 2006. The **Srinagar-Muzaffarabad bus** service started on 7 April 2005. A second cross LOC service-**Poonch-Rawalakot bus service**—commenced on 20 June 2006.
- The bi-weekly Delhi-Attari-Wagah-Lahore **Samjhauta rail** resumed service on 14 January 2004. During the visit of President Musharraf

in April 2005, it was agreed to establish the **Munabao-Khokrapar rail** link. The link known as the 'Thar Express' commenced service from 18 February 2006.

- With the signing of MoU on 15 Feb 2008 to revise the Air Services Agreement between India and Pakistan there is an increase of frequencies (each way) from 12 to 28, designated air lines from 1 to 3 and addition of Islamabad and Chennai to the existing four points of call viz. Mumbai, Delhi, Karachi, and Lahore.

12. **Energy sector cooperation:** The Cabinet approved on 9 February 2005 a proposal to discuss the **Iran-Pakistan-India gas pipeline** between Iran, Pakistan and India with Pakistan in the framework of security and assured supplies. Our concerns regarding the security of the pipeline in transit, particularly through the disturbed areas of Balochistan, and guarantee of assured supplies remain. Minister of Petroleum & Natural gas visited Pakistan on June 3–8, 2005, when a Secretary-level Joint Working Group to discuss financial, technical, commercial and legal related issues on IPI pipeline was set up. The Pakistani Petroleum Minister visited India on February 16–20, 2006. Issues relating to gas pricing, project structure, transit fees and framework agreement are being discussed and are yet to be finalized.

13. During the Foreign Secretary level meeting in June 2004 the two Governments had agreed, in principle, to the **reopening of the Consulates General** in Mumbai and Karachi. In April 2005, Pakistan High Commission had identified a plot of land in Santa Cruz to build their Consulate but have not been able to find a property to rent *ad-interim* so far. India is ready to open its Consulate in Karachi but Pakistan insisted on simultaneous opening of the both Consulates in Karachi and Mumbai. Pakistan's inability to locate suitable premises in Mumbai has delayed the reopening of the consulates in both countries.

14. India provided substantial **earthquake relief material to Pakistan** announcing official assistance of $ 25 million. India also participated at the Ministerial level in Donors' Conferences in Geneva (October 2005) and Islamabad (November 2005). The official assistance granted on emergency basis was about 1300 tonnes of relief material. Pakistan High Commission was allowed to open a bank account to receive cash donations. Prompt over-flight clearances were accorded for relief planes and Pakistan's rescue helicopters were allowed to fly in the 'no-fly' zone close to the LoC. Pakistan, however, showed hesitation in receiving aid, and declined our offer of helicopters, medical teams, repair of telecom infrastructure and cross-LoC joint relief operations, on grounds that it had sensitivities with respect to Indian soldiers operating on Pakistani soil. An MOU was signed on 11 July 2006 to facilitate the utilisation of the assistance of $ 25 million

offered by India. This is yet to be utilised by Pakistan, although the Pakistan High Commission is believed to be making efforts to do so.

Summary

15. Government is committed to continue with the present process of confidence building, cooperation and dialogue in an atmosphere free from terror and violence.

16. India is committed to peace, friendship and good neighbourly relations with Pakistan. In pursuit of this goal, a number of policy initiatives have been taken by the Government of India with emphasis on enhancing people-to-people contacts. A wide-range of bilateral issues is being discussed within the framework of the Composite Dialogue under eight subjects including Terrorism & Drug trafficking and Jammu & Kashmir. This dialogue had commenced in 2004 following a commitment made by President Musharraf that territory under control of Pakistan would not be allowed to support terrorism in any manner. Four rounds of the dialogue process have been completed.

17. India has nevertheless continuing and serious concerns on cross-border terrorism and has repeatedly reiterated the importance of Pakistan fulfilling its commitment outlined in the Joint Press Statement of 6 January 2004 against terrorism. The dialogue process hinges on an atmosphere of trust and confidence.

18. India has avoided to the extent possible being prescriptive vis-à-vis Pakistan particularly in the charged domestic situation which developed subsequent to the dismissal of the Chief Justice of Pakistan in March 2007. Our history with Pakistan has been a difficult one. We have our own assessment of terrorism emanating from within Pakistan. However, our effort for the past 4 years has been to try to insulate our bilateral relationship from the vagaries of Pakistan's domestic politics.

19. We have consciously refrained from any extensive comment in the recent developments in Pakistan. On the 3 November 2007, the Official Spokesperson of the Ministry of External Affairs had stated on the news of the declaration of emergency that: "We regret the difficult times that Pakistan is passing through. We trust that conditions of normalcy will soon return permitting Pakistan's transition to stability and democracy to continue." After CHOGM's decision to suspend Pakistan from the Councils of Commonwealth, our Official Spokesperson on 23-11-2007 stated that "We have noted the decision of the CMAG. Our hope remains that Pakistan will return to stability and democracy as soon as possible." On Elections in Pakistan, MEA spokesperson said "The recent elections in Pakistan are Pakistan's internal affair. The Government of India welcome the fact that the people of Pakistan have been able to express themselves clearly and in a democratic manner on their

own future. As ever, the Government of India stands ready to resume the composite dialogue process as soon as a duly constituted government is in place in Pakistan. It remains our hope that we will be able to resolve outstanding issues and build a mutually beneficial relationship with Pakistan in an atmosphere free of violence and terrorism. India wishes to see Pakistan develop and prosper within a stable democratic order."

. . .

21 April 2008

DOCUMENT NO. 4

KASHMIR: THE TRUE STORY

Indian Ministry of External Affairs

January 2004

Jammu & Kashmir is an integral and inalienable part of India. Basic facts pertaining to this issue are well established. However, there has been a concerted dis-information campaign that presents a distorted historical account of the developments that led to the irrevocable accession of the state of Jammu & Kashmir to India; the subsequent wars inflicted by Pakistan on India and the unleashing of terrorist violence in the once tranquil and beautiful Kashmir Valley. The involvement of Pakistan in fomenting insurgency and terrorism in various parts of India, especially Jammu & Kashmir, has been well documented and accepted by all impartial observers. Following the cataclysmic events of 9/11 the international community also accepts that there can be no justification for acts of terrorism. Nevertheless, the historical perspective on Jammu & Kashmir needs to be put in the correct, factual light. The following pages attempt to do so.

The Jammu and Kashmir Issue

Accession to India

1. The Accession of the State of Jammu and Kashmir to India, signed by the Maharaja (erstwhile ruler of the State) on 26th October, 1947, was completely valid in terms of the Government of India Act (1935), Indian Independence Act (1947) and international law and was total and irrevocable. The Accession was also supported by the largest political party in the State, the National Conference. In the Indian Independence Act, there was no provision for any conditional accession. The Instrument of Accession executed by the Maharaja was the same as the ones executed by over 560 princely states in India. There has been no complication in any of the other cases. There would have been none in this case either, except for Pakistan's action in sending in tribal invaders first (in October 1947) and its own regular troops later (May 1948).

2. Lord Mountbatten's acceptance of the Instrument of Accession was unconditional. He said: "I do hereby accept this Instrument of Accession". The Instrument of Accession was complete with the offer and acceptance.

3. There can, therefore, be no question of negotiating on the question of accession of the State of Jammu & Kashmir to India.

Reference to UN

4. India made a reference to the United Nations on 1st January 1948 under Article 35 of the Charter, which permits any member state to bring any situation, whose continuance is likely to endanger international peace and security, to the attention of the Security Council. The intention behind this reference was to prevent a war between the two newly independent countries, which would have become increasingly likely if the tribal invaders assisted first indirectly and then actively by the Pakistan army had persisted with their actions against India in Kashmir. The Government of India requested the Security Council "to put an end immediately to the giving of such assistance which was an act of aggression against India".

5. Pakistan consistently misled the world regarding its involvement in Kashmir: (a) It claimed initially in 1947 that it was not in any way assisting the tribal invaders and was only not actively opposing their passage out of fear that they may turn against the local Pakistani population. It was, however, clearly established that these invaders were being looked after in Pakistan territory fed, clothed, armed and otherwise equipped and transported to J&K with the help, direct and indirect, of Pakistani officials, both military & civil. The first Governor General of Pakistan, Mohammad Ali Jinnah claimed in a meeting with the then Governor General of India Lord Mountbatten that he was in a position "to call the whole thing off" subject to some of his demands being met. (b) Pakistan later claimed that its own forces were not involved directly in operations in Kashmir. But the UN Commission that visited India in July 1948 found Pakistani forces operating in Pakistan occupied Kashmir. The UNCIP Resolution of August 1948 documented the Pakistani aggression when it stated: "The presence of troops of Pakistan in the territory of the State of Jammu and Kashmir constitute a material change in the situation since it was represented by the Government of Pakistan before the Security Council". The UN sponsored mediator, Owen Dixon, was also constrained to record in his report of 15.9.1950 that "I was prepared to adopt the view that when the frontier of the State of J&K was crossed, on I believe 20 October 1947, by hostile elements, it was contrary to international law, and that when, in May 1948 as I believe, units of the regular Pakistan forces moved into the territory of the State that too was inconsistent with international law".

Non-implementation of UN Resolutions by Pakistan

6. India had made it clear that full implementation of the UN resolutions would be conditional upon Pakistan fulfilling Parts (I) & (II) of the UNCIP resolutions of 13 August, 1948, which inter alia, required that all forces regular and irregular under the control of both sides shall cease fire; Pakistan would withdraw its troops, it would endeavour to secure withdrawal of tribesmen and Pak nationals and India will withdraw bulk of its forces once the UNCIP confirms that the tribesmen and Pak nationals have withdrawn and Pak troops are being withdrawn. India was also to ensure that the State government takes various measures to preserve peace, law and order. Indian acceptance of these UNCIP resolutions was also subject to several conditions and assurances given by UNCIP including that Pakistan would be excluded from all affairs of Jammu & Kashmir, "Azad J & K Government" would not be recognised, sovereignty of J & K government over the entire territory of the State shall not be brought into question, territory occupied by Pakistan shall not be consolidated, and Pakistani troops would be withdrawn completely. Pakistan never fulfilled these assurances.

Preconditions for Plebiscite Never Fulfilled by Pakistan

7. The Government of Pakistan wrecked any possibility of plebiscite being conducted by not implementing Part II of the resolution, perhaps because it was fully aware of what the result of such an exercise would be. The Pakistani troops, which were to withdraw from the State, did not do so. As a result normal conditions under which a plebiscite could be held were never created.

8. India had accepted these resolutions, subject to assurances, (mentioned in para 6) and in the hope of having the matter resolved quickly. Pakistan, however, wrecked the implementation of the resolutions at that time by not fulfilling the preconditions. As V.K. Menon stated in the Security Council (763 Meeting, 23 January, 1957): "If an offer is made and it is not accepted at the time it is made, it cannot be held for generations over the heads of those who made it". With Pakistan's intransigence, and passage of time, the offer lapsed and was overtaken by events. In fact, the representative of India (M.C. Chagla) had stated in the Security Council as far back as 1964 (1088 meeting, 5 February 1964): "I wish to make it clear on behalf of my Government that under no circumstances can we agree to the holding of a plebiscite in Kashmir".

9. In a statement in New York on March 31, 1966 the then Prime Minister of India had said that "any plebiscite today would by definition amount to questioning the integrity of India. It would raise the issue of secession—an issue on which even the United States fought a civil war not so very

long ago. We cannot and will not tolerate a second partition of India on religious grounds. It would destroy the very basis of the Indian State." Today, thirty-seven years later, the Pakistani position is even more untenable.

Non-Applicability of 'Self-determination' to Integral Parts of States

10. Under the UN Charter, the principles of self-determination are meant to apply to colonial territories and not to integral parts of countries. Pakistan's harping on "self-determination" today, against the principles advocated by the founders of Pakistan, are only a cover for territorial ambitions. The principles being espoused by Pakistan pose severe dangers to several countries in the world where multi-ethnic and multi-religious societies co-exist.

Solution Proposed by Resolutions: Time and Context Specific

11. Since 1957 there have been no UN resolutions on the substantive aspects of the Jammu and Kashmir issue. Time and circumstances have not stood still. More than four and a half decades have lapsed since the original proposals were made as a possible solution. They can no longer be considered valid. In fact, in his report (dated 29th April, 1957), the UN Representative, who was then President of the Security Council, Gunnar Jarring, after completing his mission to India and Pakistan in 1957, took note of larger realities of the subcontinent including in Jammu and Kashmir and stated: "The Council will, furthermore, be aware of the fact that the implementation of international agreements of an ad hoc character, which has not been achieved fairly speedily, may become progressively difficult because the situation with which they were to cope has tended to change".

12. Dr. Frank Graham, the UNCIP representative stated in March 1958: "... the execution of the provisions of the resolution of 1948 might create more serious difficulties than were foreseen at the time the parties agreed to that. Whether the UN representative would be able to reconstitute the status quo which it had obtained ten years ago would seem to be doubtful...".

13. Over fifty five years after Partition, the ground situation in the state to which the resolutions referred to has considerably changed. Pakistan unilaterally ceded a part of the state to China in 1963. There has been a demographic change on the Pakistani side with generations of non-Kashmiris allowed to take residence in the parts of J&K occupied by Pakistan. Pakistan sponsored terrorism into J&K has also forced the minority Kashmiri Pandits to migrate out of the Kashmir valley to Jammu and to other parts of India. If the resolutions had begun to lose relevance in 1957, they have far less relevance now.

14. The above position is increasingly being acknowledged by the world today. Highlighting the fact that the UNCIP resolutions did not come under Chapter VII, and were therefore not self enforcing, the UN Secretary General stated at a press conference in Islamabad in March 2001, that "the

two parties discussing these issues and finding a peaceful way out, is the route I recommend".

15. It is now widely acknowledged that bilateral dialogue, in accordance with the Simla Agreement, reiterated in the Lahore Declaration, is the only way to address all bilateral issues between India and Pakistan, including the issue of J&K. UNSG's view was categorically supported by EU Commissioner, Chris Patten, during his visit to Pakistan in May 2002. UK's Secretary of State for Foreign and Commonwealth Affairs, stated in the British Parliament on 10th June 2002, that "if United Nations resolutions could have solved the matter, it would have been solved more than 50 years ago". Speaking for the British Government, he said: "We think that there is not a huge amount of point in getting in a historiographical exercise about which position is correct. We have to deal with the here and now", adding that a solution to this issue could be found only "by looking forward and by a direct dialogue between those two sovereign nations, India and Pakistan". The US Government has also made its stand clear that in keeping with the Simla Agreement of 1972, this issue should be addressed by India and Pakistan bilaterally.

Choice Made by the People of J&K and Elections in Kashmir

16. The people of Jammu and Kashmir could not wait indefinitely to decide their future. In any case the UN resolutions did not recognise or grant any role to Pakistan in the conduct of the plebiscite. "If Pakistan, therefore, has no part in the plebiscite, it really became a domestic matter for India". (V.K. Krishna Menon, UNSC, 800th meeting, 11 November, 1957). India waited several years for Pakistan to fulfil the preconditions. When that did not happen, the people of Jammu and Kashmir then convened a Constituent Assembly in 1951, which once again reaffirmed the Accession of the State to India in 1956 and finalised the Constitution for the State. The Jammu and Kashmir Constitution reaffirms that "the State is and shall be an integral part of the Union of India."

17. The people, therefore, were consulted. "We did not consult them privately; we did not consult them by selecting the people who were to be consulted. We consulted them by a normal process of democratic election - not even for a Parliament which we established, or the existing Government of Kashmir established, but for a Constituent Assembly". (V.K. Krishna Menon, UNSC, 800 Meeting, 11 November, 1957). In several subsequent local, state and national elections the people of Jammu and Kashmir have repeatedly exercised their democratic choice.

India Pakistan Discussions on J&K

18. India has always been willing to discuss all issues, including the issue of Jammu & Kashmir, with Pakistan. In fact, in the decades of the '50s and

'60s, several rounds of bilateral discussions took place between India and Pakistan over 1950–51, 1953–54, 1956–57 and 1962–63, to resolve the differences over Kashmir. J&K is also one of the eight subjects identified for dialogue under the Composite Dialogue set up at India's initiative in 1998. A perusal of the records of these meetings makes it clear that they failed in their endeavour only because of Pakistan's intransigent, unrealistic, and on occasions, unifocal approach, which did not take into account either the moral and juridical aspects of the issue or the existing realities.

19. As in the UNSC, during these bilateral discussions, Pakistan has sought parity with India in terms of locus standi in Kashmir. This is untenable since the erstwhile ruler of J&K had duly acceded to India, the largest popular party had endorsed the Accession, and the people had subsequently ratified the earlier decisions. Pakistan, as the aggressor could not have parity with India, with which the accession of Jammu and Kashmir was complete and final.

1965 War: Its Implications

20. Pakistan tried to impose a military solution on J&K yet again in 1965, by instigating a war against India. The people of J&K resisted this new invasion. Pakistan's failure to impose this military solution and the efforts of the people of Kashmir to thwart the aims and designs of the Pakistani invaders are well documented.

21. By imposing a war, Pakistan negated the very reason for which a reference had been made to the UN in 1948. All the arrangements that were arrived at with Pakistan through the instrumentality of the Security Council were based on the integrity and inviolability of the cease-fire line established after the 1947–48 skirmishes. By violating this line in 1965, Pakistan rendered obsolete and dead the resolutions of 1948 and 1949, in the context of which the Cease-Fire Line had been established through the Karachi Agreement of 1949.

Simla Agreement—Its Implications

22. Pakistan imposed yet another war on India in 1971. After this conflict, bilateral talks were held in June–July 1972 and the 'Simla Agreement' signed on 2 July 1972. In terms of this Agreement, which was duly ratified by the two Governments in 1972 itself, the two countries undertook to resolve all differences bilaterally and peacefully. Pakistan, through its commitments enshrined in this Agreement, accepted the need to shift the J&K issue from the UN to the bilateral plane.

23. India's stand has been clearly enunciated. Jammu and Kashmir is an integral part of India. While India is prepared to resolve all differences with Pakistan through bilateral talks as envisaged in the Simla Agreement, there

can be no compromise on India's unity and sovereignty. The issue that remains to be resolved is the vacation by Pakistan of territory illegally occupied by it.

24. For meaningful bilateral negotiations, Pakistan must create the right climate by stopping its support to terrorism. There must be tangible and credible evidence of this on the ground. The Simla Agreement, reiterated in the Lahore Declaration, expressly forbids hostile propaganda, interference in internal affairs and encouragement of any acts detrimental to maintenance of peaceful and harmonious relations. It also enjoins respect for each other's territorial integrity and sovereignty Pakistan is violating all these provisions.

The Lahore Visit of the Prime Minister

25. Prime Minister A.B. Vajpayee took a historic initiative and visited Lahore from February 20–21, 1999. The visit was aimed at conveying India's deep desire to establish peaceful, co-operative and friendly ties with Pakistan. Prime Minister Vajpayee proclaimed from the Minar-e-Pakistan that a stable, secure and prosperous Pakistan was in India's interest. The Lahore Declaration, which committed the two countries to build trust and confidence and develop mutually beneficial co-operation to resolve outstanding issues including J&K through bilateral negotiations, provided a blue print for India-Pakistan relations into the 21st Century

Kargil

26. However, the ink had barely dried on the Lahore Declaration that the Pakistani Army manifested its compulsive hostility towards India by launching a military operation in May 1999 across LOC in an attempt to occupy dominating heights along a 140-Km long stretch of Srinager-Leh Highway. Its aim was to create a situation by which Pakistan would dominate the strategically important Kargil heights. India's firm response forced Pakistani troops to retreat to their side of LOC. India's policy of maintaining the sanctity of the LOC and the tremendous restraint shown by India in its firm action aginst the intruders without crossing the LOC found wide international support and endorsement.

Agra Summit

27. Notwithstanding the continued sponsorship of cross border terrorism, on May 23, 2001 India again took the initiative to establish a high level political dialogue with Pakistan by inviting General Musharraf to visit India. The Pakistani President General Musharraf visited India from July 14–16, 2001 and had talks with Prime Minister Vajpayee in Agra. However, during the Summit, Pakistan demonstrated a unifocal approach, fixated entirely on one question, and sought to make any improvement in

relations conditional on prior resolution of the Kashmir issue. Pakistan was also reluctant to address India's concerns relating to cross border terrorism. The hopes of forward movement in bilateral relations thus remained largely unattained.

December 13, 2001 and Its Aftermath

28. The December 13 attack on the Indian parliament by Pakistan-based terrorists constituted the last straw in the threshold of India's tolerance for Pakistan's continued sponsorship of cross border terrorism. A number of concrete and firm steps were taken by India in response. These included—severing of diplomatic and other links with Pakistan, mobilisation of the armed forces on the LOC and international border with Pakistan, and apprising the world community about Pakistan's continued sponsorship of cross border terrorism and infiltration, especially in the State of Jammu and Kashmir. This led President General Pervez Musharraf to make a commitment on January 12, 2002, that "no organization will be allowed to indulge in terrorism in the name of Kashmir. . ..strict action will be taken against any Pakistani individual, group or organization found involved in terrorism within or outside the country, (and) Pakistan will not allow its territory to be used for any terrorist activity anywhere in the world."

MORI Poll

29. Pakistan's persistent claim that the people of Jammu & Kashmir have no desire to live in democratic India and that the terrorist acts in the State are a part of a "freedom struggle" received a further jolt when the findings of a survey conducted in J&K by the respected London-based independent market research company, MORI International, were unveiled on May 30, 2002. The survey revealed, inter alia, that on the issue of citizenship, overall 61% of Kashmiris said that they felt that they would be better off politically and economically as citizens of India and only 6% expressed a preference for Pakistani nationality. The survey also clearly brought out the popular disenchantment of the people of J&K against terrorist violence in the Valley. Over 2/3rd of the respondents in J&K took the view that Pakistan's involvement in the region had been "bad" and the presence of foreign militants in the State had been damaging.

J&K State Assembly Elections, October 2002

30. It is a tribute to the people of Jammu & Kashmir that, in spite of facing not only terrorist threats but bullets, and notwithstanding open calls from across the border for boycott of the polls, they came out in large numbers in exercise of their right to vote in the free, fair and transparent elections for the J&K Legislative Assembly conducted in September-October 2002. The heavy turn out of about 44% confirmed that the people of Jammu & Kashmir

were tired of the oppressive activities of the terrorists and sought a way out through the democratic process.

New Government in J&K

31. Based on its electoral promises of providing a 'healing touch', the new government in Jammu & Kashmir announced fresh policy initiatives that included release and reintegration of militant elements and attempting to initiate a dialogue with them. Government of India also appointed an interlocutor to talk to the elected representatives as well as others.

32. The measures taken by the new government to reach out to all sections of Kashmiri society and to ensure the return of the minority Kashmiri Pandits, who had migrated out of the Valley, back to their homes, received tremendous popular response from the people of the State. The positive response was manifest in the enthusiastic welcome given to Prime Minister Vajpayee during his visit to J&K in April 2003. The public rally addressed by the Prime Minister in Srinagar on April 18 was attended by more than 20,000 people.

33. During his visit to J&K, Prime Minister Vajpayee announced measures designed to improve the economic situation of the State. He said that at least one-lakh new jobs would be created in J&K in the next two years. He also said that a comprehensive plan would be drawn to tackle the unemployment problem confronting the state youth. He also laid the foundation of two major infrastructure projects in the state—the Udhampur-Baramulla railway project, and the section of North-South superhighway corridor falling in J&K.

34. The successful elections and installation of the new government despite attempts to disrupt the democratic process by Pakistan sponsored terrorist groups and their proxies had increased the frustration within the Pakistani establishment and the terrorist groups sponsored by Pakistan. Their frustration had been manifest in the sinister nature of acts of terrorism committed by the terrorists, and attempts to obstruct the movement of the newly installed government towards restoration of peace and normalcy. Terrorists also targeted more vulnerable sections of the society, including women and children. By targeting the minority community (the attack on the Kashmiri Pandits in Nadimarg on March 23, 2003 and killing of the pilgrims to the Vaishno Devi shrine in Jammu on July 21, 2003), the terrorists and their backers across the LOC wanted to further drive away the minority community from the state and frustrate the plans of the State government to bring the Pandits back to their homes, and pressurise the new government to re-examine its policy of releasing and reintegrating alienated sections of Kashmiri society. Terrorists had also targeted the free press in Jammu & Kashmir with an aim to stifle the important instrument of freedom of speech and democracy

35. The buoyant mood in the Valley, reflected in increasing tourist arrivals, overwhelming response to Amarnath Yatra and pilgrimage to Vaishno Devi, record number of pilgrims for the Kheerbhawani Mela, and holding of a large number of conferences in Srinagar including a meeting of the Inter State Council and of Chief Ministers of Congress-ruled states, led the Hurriyat Conference to moderate its stance on dialogue with the Centre. In desperation, Pakistan engineered a split in the coalition. On October 22, 2003 the Government of India offered to have a meeting with the Hurriyat Conference at the level of Deputy Prime Minister. The Hurriyat, led by Maulvi Abbas Ansari, announced its decision to accept the offer of dialogue. Despite the best efforts of the ISI and militant outfits, the hardline Geelani faction remains marginalized with the major constituent parties either in favour of dialogue or neutral at best.

Pakistan: Epicentre of International Terrorism

36. The present situation in Kashmir has been created by Pakistan's support to terrorism. This support to cross border terrorism is not only an attempt to unilaterally alter the status quo on the ground but also to undermine India's secular fabric. Following the terrorist incidents of 9/11, there is a widespread consensus in the international community that there can be no justification for terrorism. There is also a growing realisation amongst the international community about Pakistan being the epicentre of terrorism in the world today. Many countries have repeatedly called upon Pakistan to end cross border infiltration; dismantle the infrastructure of support to terrorism; and to stop acting as a platform for international terrorism. Mr. Jack Straw, UK Foreign Secretary, stated in the British Parliament on June 10, 2002: "A number of terrorist organisations-including Lashkar-e-Toiba, Jaish-e-Mohammed and Harkat-ul-Mujahideen . . . have been at the forefront of violent activity in the region. India has long charged that such terrorism has had the covert support of successive Pakistani Governments and, in particular, of the main intelligence agency in Pakistan, the Inter-Service Intelligence Directorate-ISID. Her Majesty's Government accept that there is a clear link between the ISID and those groups". He added: "Successive Governments of Pakistan have, through their Inter-services Intelligence Directorate, encouraged and funded terrorists. . . to make incursions across the Line of Control as outsiders in that dispute, and to engage in mayhem and terrorism." Ms. Condoleezza Rice, US National Security Adviser said on October 30, 2003: "It is absolutely the case that the infrastructure of terrorism has to be dismantled. It is absolutely the case that everybody needs to do more, and Pakistan needs to do more to make sure that there cannot be terrorist acts taken in - from Pakistan or from Kashmir against targets there". The US Ambassador to Pakistan Nancy Powell said at the Pakistan American Business Council Meeting in Karachi

on January 23, 2003: "The Government of Pakistan must ensure that its pledges are implemented to prevent infiltration against the LOC and end the use of Pakistan as a platform for terrorism." Russian President Vladimir Putin said on June 7, 2002: "We must call upon the leadership of Pakistan in the first place to put an end to the terrorist activities being carried out from its territory in India, in Kashmir and to do everything to ensure that society in Pakistan becomes transparent, democratic, predictable and understandable." Dominique de Villepin, the French Foreign Minister, reminded his Pakistani counterpart on March 29, 2003 of the necessity of completing the implementation of the commitments undertaken by his authorities in regard to the ending of terrorist operations in Kashmir and the strict respect of the Line of Control. On June 10, 2002 the European Union called upon Pakistan "to take visible, decisive and verifiable steps to seal the Line of Control, stop the supply of militant groups, help restrain the violent activities of these groups in Kashmir, close the militant training camps on Pakistan's side of the Line of Control."

The ceasefire in J&K

37. On October 22, 2003, India announced a series of measures aimed at promoting people to people contacts with Pakistan. The measures, inter alia, included the offer to start a bus link between Srinagar and Muzaffarabad. On November 23, 2003, Prime Minister Jamali of Pakistan offered a ceasefire on the LOC. India welcomed the proposal and extended the offer of ceasefire to Siachen as well. Subsequently the DGMOs of the two countries agreed to observe ceasefire on the International Border, LOC and the Actual Ground Position Line (AGPL), with effect from the midnight of November 25, 2003. This is the first time that a formal ceasefire is being observed in Jammu and Kashmir extending from the International Border and LOC up to the AGPL in Siachen. It is hoped that Pakistan will take a lesson from the tremendous positive response generated by the ceasefire and end its support to cross border infiltration and terrorism on a permanent basis so that the ceasefire can also become a permanent one.

Developments in J&K—An Internal Matter for India

38. In a diverse country like India, disaffection and discontent are not uncommon. Indian democracy has the necessary resilience to accommodate genuine grievances within the framework of our sovereignty, unity and integrity. Government of India has expressed its willingness to accommodate the legitimate political demands of the people of the state of J&K. However, Pakistan sponsored terrorists have terrorised the population and hindered political dialogue by intimidating or silencing voices of moderation that wish to engage in dialogue. The human rights of the people of J&K have been systematically violated by such terror tactics and the kidnappings and killings of innocent people by terrorists.

39. Jammu & Kashmir is an integral part of India. There can be no compromise on India's unity and integrity. We remain determined and totally committed to resist terrorism and violence until it is decisively eliminated. Clearly, in Jammu & Kashmir, we have met the challenges posed by terrorists and have succeeded in defeating their designs. Through consistent efforts and commitment we have been able to bring about normal conditions in J&K. We have a duly elected Government in J&K through a credible electoral process and are confident that we would move forward in reviving the economy, accelerating development activities and addressing other issues and problems of the people of J&K.

DOCUMENT NO. 5

BRIEF ON INDIA-SRI LANKA RELATIONS

Indian Ministry of External Affairs
(BSM Division: Sri Lanka)

February 26, 2007

Background

India-Sri Lanka relations have undergone a qualitative and quantitative transformation in the recent past. Political relations are close, trade and investments have increased dramatically, infrastructural linkages are constantly being augmented, defence collaboration has increased and there is a general, broad-based improvement across all sectors of bilateral cooperation. India was the first country to respond to Sri Lanka's request for assistance after the tsunami in Dec 2004. In July 2006, India evacuated 430 Sri Lankan nationals from Lebanon, first to Cyprus by Indian Navy ships and then to Delhi & Colombo by special Air India flights.

There exists a broad consensus within the Sri Lankan polity on the primacy of India in Sri Lanka's external relations matrix. Both the major political parties in Sri Lanka, viz., the Sri Lanka Freedom Party and the United Nationalist Party have contributed to the rapid development of bilateral relations in the last ten years. Sri Lanka has supported India's candidature to the permanent membership of the UN Security Council.

Exchange of Visits

The institutional framework for the relationship is provided by frequent contact at political level, including the highest one. President Mahinda Rajapaksa made his first visit abroad after his victory at the Nov 2005 elections to India on Dec 27–30, 2005. His second visit to India was on Nov 25–29, 2006. On Apr 1–4, 2007 he visited India for the 14th SAARC Summit. His recent visit to India was on Oct 12–14, 2007. Prime Minister Ratnasiri Wickremanayake visited India on Jan 28–30, 2007. Foreign Minister Rohitha Bogollagama visited India on a number of occasions, most recently on

Dec 7–8, 2007 for SAARC Council of Ministers Meeting. Leader of Opposition Ranil Wickremesinghe also visited India on a number of occasions, most recently on Dec 28, 2007. From our side, EAM visited Sri Lanka on Jan 9–10, 2007. The 6th meeting of the Joint Commission, co-chaired by EAM, took place in Colombo on June 10, 2005. A Parliamentary delegation headed by Lok Sabha Deputy Speaker Charanjit Singh Atwal visited Sri Lanka on Mar 28–Apr 3, 2006 to participate in the 4th Conference of the Association of SAARC Speakers and Parliamentarians.

There is regular contact at the official level including Foreign Secretary led Foreign Office Consultations (last held in Colombo in May 2005) *{Last FS level visit to Sri Lanka was on Nov 23–24, 2006}*, Commerce Secretary level talks (last held in Delhi in Jan 2006), talks between Customs authorities, fisheries officials, the Navy/Coast Guards etc.

Agreements Reached

The juridical framework for the relationship is provided by a Free Trade Agreement (FTA), a Double Taxation Avoidance Agreement (DTAA), a Bilateral Investment Protection & Promotion Agreement (BIPPA) and agreements/MoUs on Air Services, Small Development Projects, Cooperation in Small Scale Industries, Tourism, IT, Space, Agriculture and Education. Work on augmenting this framework is being undertaken through negotiations for Comprehensive Economic Partnership Agreement (CEPA) *{11th round was held on Jan 2–4, 2008}*, MoU on Fisheries, agreement on Cooperation on Counter-Terrorism & Prevention of Illicit Drug Trafficking, agreement on Mutual Legal Assistance in Criminal Matters and agreement on Transfer of Sentenced Persons.

Ethnic Conflict in Sri Lanka

India's consistent position has been that there is no military solution to the ethnic problem in Sri Lanka, and that the way out is a negotiated, political settlement based on credible devolution of powers within the framework of united Sri Lanka and acceptable to all communities in Sri Lanka, including Tamils. It is with this in mind that we have welcomed as a first step the intention of the Government of Sri Lanka to fully implement the 13th Amendment to their Constitution. However, we have emphasized to the Government of Sri Lanka the need to put forward a 'credible' devolution package at the earliest which can form the basis for a lasting political settlement of the ethnic issue. In May 2006, India extended the ban on LTTE for two years. The Norwegian facilitation in Sri Lanka is currently stalled. More recently, there is a great escalation in violence with the air attacks by the LTTE on Government establishments. With the termination of the Ceasefire Agreement in January 2008 after both the sides violated it with impunity for almost two years since the beginning of 2006, security situation in Sri Lanka has been worsened and there is little hope for resumption of peace talks. With the deterioration of the security situation in North & East of Sri Lanka since the beginning of 2006, there is a fresh influx of Sri Lankan Tamil refugees into India. Since January 12, 2006 till March 20, 2008, a total of 20,944 refugees have arrived in India.

Fishermen Issue

There have been several incidents of firing on Indian fishermen fishing in Palk Bay. Government has always taken up the issue of safety of Indian fishermen on a priority basis with the Government of Sri Lanka. We have impressed on the Sri Lankan Navy to act with restraint and for our fishermen to be treated in a humane manner. Presently there is no bona fide Indian fisherman in the Sri Lankan custody. A Joint Working Group (JWG) has been constituted to deal with the issues related to Indian fishermen straying in Sri Lankan territorial waters, work out modalities for prevention of use of force against them and the early release of confiscated boats and explore possibilities of working towards bilateral arrangements for licensed fishing. The JWG last met in Jan 2006.

Economic Cooperation

Since the entry into force of the FTA in March 2000, trade has grown rapidly. Sri Lanka is India's largest trade partner in the SAARC region. India is the largest trade partner of Sri Lanka. Bilateral trade rose to US$ 3.299 billion in 2007. Exports from India to Sri Lanka amounted to US$ 2.782 billion, while exports from Sri Lanka to India amounted to US$ 516.5 million. India is the biggest source of Sri Lankan imports and the 3rd largest destination for Sri Lankan exports. With FDI approvals of US$ 200 million, India is the 4th largest investor in Sri Lanka. Indian Oil Corporation (running 170 petrol pumps as well as managing the Trincomalee Oil Tank Farm), Taj Hotels, L&T, Ambujas, Tatas and Ashok Leyland are among the prominent Indian companies operating in Sri Lanka. In Sept 2006, Indo-Lanka Chamber of Commerce and Industry was inaugurated by our Finance Minister. Connectivity between the two countries is at an all time high with close to 120 flights per week including by Indian private airlines and tourist arrivals from India are the largest. Other important projects in bilateral economic cooperation are: a 500MW coal-based thermal power plant at Trincomalee by NTPC, oil & gas exploration in Mannar blocks of Sri Lankan waters by OVL and upgradation of the Colombo-Matara railway by RITES-IRCON.

With regard to the Sethusamudram Ship Channel Project, it has been agreed that an exchange of views on the environmental aspects in relation to Sri Lanka would be arranged between the technical experts of the two countries. The last such meeting took place in April 2006.

Development Cooperation

India is active in a number of areas of development activity in Sri Lanka. About one-sixth of the total development credit granted by GOI is made available to Sri Lanka. Lines of credit: In the recent past three lines of credit were extended to Sri Lanka: US$ 100 million for capital goods, consumer durables, consultancy services and food items, US$ 31 million for supply of 300,000 MT of wheat and US$ 150 million for purchase of petroleum products. All of these lines of credit have been fully utilized. Another line of credit of US$ 100 million is now being made available for rehabilitation of the Colombo-Matara railway.

A number of development projects are implemented under 'Aid to Sri Lanka' funds. In 2006–07, the budget for 'Aid to Sri Lanka' was Rs 28.2 Crs. Small Development Projects: A MoU on Cooperation in Small Development Projects has been signed. Projects for providing fishing equipments to the fishermen in the East of Sri Lanka and solar energy aided computer education in 25 rural schools in Eastern Sri Lanka are under consideration. Health Projects: We have supplied medical equipments to hospitals at Hambantota and Point Pedro, supplied 4 state of the art ambulances to the Central Province, implemented a cataract eye surgery programme for 1500 people in the Central Province and implemented a project of renovation of OT at Dickoya hospital and supplying equipment to it. The projects under consideration are: Construction of a 150-bed hospital at Dickoya, upgradation of the hospital at Trincomalee and a US$ 7.5 million grant for setting up a Cancer Hospital in Colombo. Education Projects: Upgradation of the educational infrastructure of the schools in the Central province including teachers' training, setting up of 10 computer labs, setting up of 20 e-libraries (Nenasalas), Mahatma Gandhi scholarship scheme for +2 students and setting up of a vocational training centre in Puttalam. India also contributes to the Ceylon Workers Education Trust that gives scholarships to the children of estate workers. Training: A training programme for 465 Sri Lankan Police officers has been commenced in Dec 2005. Another 400 Sri Lankan Police personnel are being trained for the course of 'Maintenance of Public Order'.

Defence Cooperation

A major part of the training of Sri Lankan Armed Forces is carried out in India. There has been a significant increase in the number of training slots for Sri Lankan armed forces personnel in recent years. These were: 977 for 2005–06, 870 for 2006–07; and 1058 for 2007–08 with 637 for Army, 316 for Navy and 105 for Air Force. Besides this, there is continued cooperation in terms of exchange of visits and cooperation between Navies. Indian Coast Guard extended assistance to Sri Lanka in containing oil spill off Galle in Sept 2006.

DOCUMENT NO. 6

SPEECH OF UNION HOME MINISTER SHIVRAJ PATIL

November 22, 2008

Text of the inaugural speech of the Union Home Minister at the two-day conference of Directors General of Police and Inspectors General of Police at New Delhi on November 22, 2008.

"I am happy to declare, at the outset only, that this Conference is inaugurated. I wish the Conference all the best.

I wish to salute the memory of all those, who have laid down their lives, in the service of the nation and for protecting the lives and properties of others and to see that law and order is protected and preserved.

This is for the fifth time in five years, I am attending this Conference. It is always a pleasure to attend it and hear the views and concepts put forth by the participants. I hope that, this year also, the Conference would prove to be equally useful and interesting.

I would like to congratulate the officers and men of Intelligence Bureau, who have been awarded the Indian Police Medal for their meritorious service, on the occasion of Independence Day of 2007 and the Republic Day of 2008. The Governments and the people have highest regard for the sincerity and dedication exhibited by these officers, who have been discharging their duties in a low key manner and with-out direct and instantaneous public recognition. I am confident that these awards would motivate and encourage other I.B. personnel to excel in their field work.

Since we met last year, Assembly Elections have been held in six States, including Gujarat, Himachal Pradesh, Karnataka, Meghalaya, Nagaland and Tripura. It is a matter of great satisfaction that the elections were conducted peacefully in all these States. Substantial credit for the smooth completion of the election process goes to our Police and Central Para-Military Forces. I have no doubt in my mind that the current phase of Assembly Elections in the States of Chhattisgarh, Delhi, Jammu and Kashmir, Madhya Pradesh, Mizoram and Rajasthan will also be conducted peacefully with your cooperation.

You, who are participating in this Conference, are Senior officers of our police forces. You know the laws of the country, the strength of the forces, the problems they have to face, the expectations of the people, the complications involved in the issues that have to be faced and solved, the trends in the fields of technologies and the kinds of crimes that are likely to be committed in the days to come, the psychologies of the victims and the criminals and the people at large. The fund of knowledge you have acquired through your experiences is very valuable and is going to help you to advise the Governments and the people to deal with the issues relevant to the security. This Conference provides you a national forum which can be used by you to exchange your notes and views and enrich your understanding of the situations and solutions to be found out and to use.

As explained by DIB in his speech, it is proposed to concentrate on a theme which is being discussed very widely and the theme is Terrorism. You have done well in selecting this theme for your discussion.

There was a time when the countries of the world discussed the problems and issues, relevant to war and as to how to avoid it, control it and save the humanity from it. Fortunately, it appears that the countries of the world have succeeded in achieving the objectives of avoiding war, to a great extent and that has given a big relief to the peace loving people of the world. However, unfortunately, it appears that some people who are narrow minded, interested in protecting their greed, who are misinformed about the basic issues of culture and religion, who have wrong notions about the sovereignty of states and given to separatism of all kinds, have begun to use modern technologies, equipments, weapons, explosives, transport and communication facilities, the power of disseminating information, to terrorize the innocent, the weak, the non-suspecting human beings and are destroying valuable properties, lives and limbs of human beings. This is happening in almost all countries of the world and in India also, and is being perpetrated in the name of religion, culture, community, caste, political and economic ideologies and such other concepts. Therefore, the countries of the world have to join hands to defeat these kinds of ideologies, in the interest of peace and tranquility everywhere. However, it is found that in some countries, it is resorted to, to weaken other countries and advance and protect their own nefarious designs. If the countries of the world show willingness to exchange information regarding the terrorists designs and to refuse to provide shelter in their countries to terrorists and decide not to allow the funds to flow from one part of the world to the other and also to refuse to give small arms and explosives to the terrorists, terrorism can be controlled in a better manner.

In India, terrorism is visible in Jammu & Kashmir, in the North Eastern States, in some States which are covered with thick forests and which are not developed as other parts of the country are, in hinterland and in some cities of importance, for trading and industrial activities. These days, the terrorism is discussed a great deal in the media and is highlighted on a very large scale, creating awareness about it and alerting us all to take steps to control and nip it in the bud. We have, therefore, to pay adequate attention to it and counter it effectively. Fortunately, the number of incidents and casualties that have occurred in the last four and half years is much less than those that occurred in the four and half years, before the present period. Yet, the impression created is that terrorism has increased and is not reduced. Even if one incident occurs or one person becomes a casualty, it should cause us concern and should make us alert. However, it should not demoralize us and give wrong impression to the uninformed section of the society. What is happening in our country should be studied by us to find effective solutions to the existing problems.

The questions that require our immediate attention are: What can be done? What should be done? Where and by whom, the steps should be taken? In what fashion, the matters should be dealt with? What should be our short, medium and long term plans prepared for this purpose? How the Governments should cooperate with one another? How should they obtain the cooperation of the people? What are the deficiencies? How should they be removed?

On these issues, decisions are taken by the Governments. Directors General and other officers can help in taking the necessary decisions.

The Governments have to provide more funds in their plans and budgets, for strengthening the forces, for having more police stations, for establishing more training centres, for modernizing the transport and communication facilities. Once that is done, the Heads of the Forces have to see that the funds provided to them are utilized in time. If the funds given by the Union or State Governments remain unutilized, the purpose of strengthening the forces cannot be fulfilled. In the forces, there are many vacancies which have remained unfilled for many years. If the number of vacancies is around one lakh, we need to take immediate actions to fill them. In this respect, the Directors General of the Forces can help. It is not possible to discuss all the details and deficiencies relating to vacancies. They should be discussed and overcome, by the Heads of the Forces in cooperation with their Governments.

The Police-Population ratio in India is not very comfortable. In order to improve upon the ratio, some other schemes and methods should be invented and used. In order to overcome the deficiencies of officers and men, it should be possible to have schemes, to have on contract the retired officers and men, to help the forces. The schemes for these purposes can be made by the concerned Governments on the basis of advice given by the members of the Forces.

Terrorist activities are perpetrated in the areas which are close to international borders, in the areas covered with thick forests, in the areas which do not have good transport facilities and in cities. It is necessary to have plans and schemes to deal with them in these areas. The speedy means of transport should be provided for this purpose. Helicopter and planes can be made available to the forces to reach the places where they are needed in time.

In big cities, different methods need be used. In mega cities, large number of CCTV cameras should be used. The big cities should have Control Rooms, Mobile Police Stations and the cooperation of the Unions and Associations of the employees, traders, industrialists and professionals to get the necessary information and other help in time. The cities are being attacked and are likely to be attacked more in future. So, plans to provide special kind of security arrangements for cities should be made and used.

Terrorists have begun to use military tactics. The police use police methods and strategies to deal with the criminals. It has, therefore, become necessary to impart knowledge in tactics to the police, which can help in countering terrorists in an effective manner.

The Union Government has decided to raise COBRA Battalions. The State Governments are also expected to have a portion of their forces trained for countering the terrorist activities. We know that the States, which have trained their police for countering terrorist activities have succeeded in giving better results. It would be useful if all States, at least all states which are affected by terrorist menace, do take special steps to raise special kind of forces for countering terrorism.

Terrorists depend upon their ability to create fear psychosis. They are choosing the targets which can lead to the disturbance of bigger and more complicated nature. That is why they appear to be attacking the places of religious nature, so that conflicts between the people belonging to different religions or communities can be created. The Police have to bear this aspect in their minds, while dealing with terrorists, while investigating the incidents and while informing the people about their activities and investigations, which are not completed. If care is not taken in this respect, terrorists may succeed in achieving their nefarious objectives.

Religions or cultures do not preach terrorism. Terrorism is nothing but a kind of violent cowardice. It is different from taking a firm stand with respect to that on which you have full confidence and firm belief. But, terrorists want to use the psychology of unsuspecting and innocent persons to flare up communal disturbances. The police should never forget this and should take proper action.

At present, terrorists are using sophisticated small weapons and explosive devices to perpetrate terror. In future, they are likely to use nuclear, biological and chemical devices and other mechanical and psychological devices. The police forces should be trained to cope up with these kinds of problems and incidents. If they are not trained and prepared before such incidents begin to occur, the loss caused to the lives, limbs and properties of the innocent persons would be of enormous nature. It is, therefore, necessary to have plans and projects prepared for this purpose in advance.

Cooperation between the states and their forces to control terrorism is necessary. Each State can have a nodal officer, who can deal with his counterparts in other states. If laws are needed to be amended for facilitating cooperation between the states, that should be done. The neighbouring states can prepare plans to control terrorism in cooperation with one another.

The cooperation between the Union and its forces and the states and their forces is also needed. In fact, fortunately, they are cooperating with one another.

The Union guards international borders of our country. It gives forces to States to deal with incidents that occur every now and then. The Union helps the States to raise IR Battalions, which should be raised without delays. At present, that is not happening. It gives funds to the states to modernize their forces, prisons and strengthen their criminal justice system. The funds given should be utilized. The forces sent to the States should be returned after the period for which they are given. If this has to happen, the states have to strengthen their forces. In fact, the States should have more officers and men for this purpose and should not think of saving money by allowing vacancies to remain unfilled.

The best weapon, which can be used to counter terrorism, is intelligence. No other device or weapon can be as useful as intelligence can be. Unfortunately, the machinery, which is with the States, is not strong enough to collect the intelligence. Their Special Branches and the CID are not fully manned, and provided with modern devices. It is, therefore, necessary to strengthen them without delays. The Union Intelligence agencies are stronger and better equipped. But, they also need be strengthened further. Steps are being taken to strengthen them.

The States and the Union help one another, in sharing the intelligence. What is given by the Union to the States is not always of operational nature. Some times, misunderstanding develops when such matters are discussed publicly. In fact, the terrorists choose the time and place of their choice to attack. The operational intelligence is not always easy to obtain. However, it is necessary to develop the capability for this purpose.

Many other persons who are not in government services can also help in collecting intelligence. If the people are sensitized to discharge their duties in this respect, it would be very helpful.

It is seen that terrorists live in one State, perpetrate terror in another State and hide themselves in other States or other countries. They can be prevented from perpetrating terror or investigating crimes committed by them without delays and in an effective manner, if a Central agency for this purpose is created and allowed to act, by amending laws, if necessary. Such a central agency need not be allowed to take charge of ordinary criminal cases. It can be permitted to act in special kinds of cases, with the approval of some bodies, created to decide which kind of cases or which cases should be tackled by it. For this purpose, the cooperation of the States would be needed. Let us hope that it would become available sooner than later.

We have laws, which have provisions to deal with terrorism. They should be used properly. It is suggested by some in the country that a special law may be enacted for this purpose. POTA was such a law. It was enacted and used. When it was repealed, some relevant chapters in it were transferred into the Unlawful Activities Prevention Law, lock, stock and barrel. The chapters have provisions useful to control terrorist activities, free flow of funds to the terrorist groups and relating to the admissibility of certain kinds of evidence collected with the help of electronic equipments and some such other matters.

There were provisions in POTA which went against the basic principles of criminal jurisprudence relating to the onus of proof and admissibility of the confessions, not made according to the principles adopted in the Criminal Procedure Code.

It is not possible to have a law like POTA on the statute book. The relevant provisions in POTA, needed to control terrorism have been introduced and retained in the Unlawful Activities Prevention Act.

If some other kinds of provisions are required to facilitate investigation of the cases relating to terrorism and which do not go against the basic principles of criminal justice system and the Human Rights, there may not be any difficulty in having them in the existing laws. The matter is being looked into for appropriate decision. Anything done in this respect should not solve only a few problems and create many more problems. The experts and experienced persons are looking into the needs of the investigating agencies, to make the laws more helpful in finding out real culprits and preventing their activities. Law making is a balancing act, which should aim at doing real justice which means punishment of the culprits and the protection of the innocent, solve problems and not creating more problems. If real culprits are punished, terrorism will be controlled. If innocent persons are punished, terrorism may find justification to exist, which should be avoided. The Union Government would definitely help the investigating agencies to do their duties in the best possible manner, without jeopardizing liberty, life and property of the innocent.

It seems that you are going to discuss terrorism in J&K, North Eastern States, in States affected by Naxalism. Information regarding the situations in different parts of the terrorism affected States, the policies that are used to tackle it, in brief, and the funds provided by the Union to the States to tackle it and to modernize the forces, is given in the booklets that are given to you. If you go through them and compare the facts and figures of the last eight years, you would find that the situations in these states have not worsened, but in some States it has improved. This fact should be borne in mind, while trying to make correct assessment and to find correct solutions.

In J&K, the situation has improved a great deal. It has happened because of the policies of the Union and the State Governments, the efforts done by the State Police, Para-Military Forces, the Military and the People and the fence erected on the borders between India and our western neighbour and also because of the fatigue developed in the minds and hearts of the persons responsible for bloodshed and destruction.

In the North Eastern region, Sikkim, Arunachal Pradesh, Meghalaya, Mizoram are quite normal and peaceful as other states are. Tripura has improved by nearly forty per cent. Assam, Nagaland and Manipur continue to suffer as they used to do in the past. Nagaland and Manipur situations indicate slight improvement. Assam does not indicate satisfactory improvement. All the three states have common international border.

Andhra Pradesh, Chhattisgarh, Jharkhand, Orissa, Maharashtra, Bihar have been suffering because of naxal activities. In Andhra Pradesh, the situation has improved by nearly sixty percent, because of the efforts done by the police and the training given to the members of their forces and the policies of the State. Nearly, more than sixty percent of naxal activity is found in two states alone i.e., Chhattisgarh and Jharkhand. Even in each of these two states, only two districts contribute to nearly sixty percent of terrorism. In Bihar, the situation has improved by nearly more than forty percent. In Orissa, the situation has deteriorated. In Maharashtra, the graph of terrorism has gone up a bit. If we take the total number of incidents and casualties in these states, it appears that the graph has remained at the same level.

Naxalism in India is presented by some, in a manner which does not give the correct picture. On occasions, it is said that ten states in India, nearly 180 districts in States, are affected. It means that one third of the country is affected. If one village in a district is affected, it is treated that one district is affected. It does not mean that all the villages in that district are affected. If one or two districts of a State are affected, it does not mean that all districts in the State are affected. Crimes committed by Naxalites cannot certainly be compared with the ordinary crimes and need extraordinary attention. Yet, they should not be presented in such a manner that they would create a fear psychosis in the society.

To control the terrorism in the hinterland, we have to see that infiltration of terrorists from other countries do not take place through sea routes and through the borders between India and friendly countries. The coast lines also have to be guarded through Navy, coast guard, coastal police. The States' Special Branches and the CID should identify the persons forming part of the sleeper cells and lodging in cities and towns and studying in educational institutions and working in industries and professions.

It should also be seen that others from the country do not join them, who come from outside. It need also be seen that no retaliatory actions are taken by persons from the country. Unless that is done, the menace of terrorism cannot fully be controlled. While doing this, action to be taken against such persons should not be motivated by any other aspects. Unless we are just and correct and unless we act only with a view to curb terrorism of any kind, perpetrated by any person, belonging to any section of the society or any kind of ideology or culture, the purpose of controlling it effectively would not be served.

At the national level, we have tried to pay attention to policy making and developing systems to achieve the objective of controlling terrorism and helping the states to deal with the incidents and individuals as per their perceptions and assessments. We have issued directions and given suggestions as per the constitutional provisions and laws and rules, only to see that no aberrations in these matters are allowed to occur and no injustice is done to any section of the society. We have tried to understand the difficulties of those in the states and in the fields and to help them with funds, intelligence, equipments and such other things, which we would continue to do in future also, without allowing the situations to develop in an incorrect and unacceptable manner. Our approach of this nature should not be wrongly interpreted, as dictatorial or being soft on terror, for it is nothing but balanced and just, legal and constitutional, and helpful to the Union and the States, and the innocent individuals and the country as a whole. Our efforts have been to help one and all, at all levels, the international, national and the state level. This policy will continue in future also.

Terrorism need be tackled by using multi-pronged approach. Police forces can help. But, other methods to deal with it are also required. Less developed areas should be better developed. People should be helped to live better lives. No social, cultural, political and economic injustice should be done to any individuals or section of the society. In the neighbourhood, understanding and amity should be developed. That violence does not help should be understood and appreciated by one and all. That, to be happy, others should be made happy, should be understood. Wars and designs for committing crime and terrorism first occur in the minds of culprits. They should be tackled and controlled there too. When all these methods do not help, the collective might of the people, represented by the State, should be used to control the human aberrations, terrorist and criminal tendencies. These are things, which are also being done and would be done on a larger scale and in a better manner.

Well, I have made some points, which occurred to me. You may also give your suggestions. Finding solutions to the problems is more important than identifying deficiencies and just complaining against them. We are placed in positions, which can help us to find solution and solve problems.

I need say no more. I thank you for your attention. Jai Hind!"

Source: ***Press Information Bureau, Government of India***

DOCUMENT NO. 7

SPEECH OF PRIME MINISTER DR. MANMOHAN SINGH

November 23, 2008

Text of the speech of the Prime Minister at the two-day conference of Directors General of Police and Inspectors General of Police at New Delhi on November 23, 2008.

At the outset, I would like to congratulate the recipients of the highly coveted President's Police Medal for Distinguished Service. Their consistent and excellent performance in a difficult sector of policing has earned them this medal. I am sure that they would continue to strive harder to achieve still greater heights in their profession.

In October last year, I had an opportunity to address the Conference of Directors-General of Police. The international environment is in far greater turmoil to-day than it was a year ago. This has major consequences for us, for in a globalised world, what affects one part of the globe often affects the other parts as well. The current international financial crisis is a good index of the inter-active nature of to-day's globalised world. Likewise, in the realm of security, globalisation has produced a whole new range of interactive threats and risks. Globalisation has also led to a blurring of the distinction between external and internal threats.

It is appropriate that the theme of this year's Conference of Directors-General of Police should be Terrorism. The advent of many non-state actors has greatly increased our vulnerabilities. Terrorism is now recognized as the main scourge of the modern world. To-day's terrorists—whether they be non-state actors or others—use modern communications and exploit cyber space to carry out their disruptive activities, and I hope that this Conference will find ways and means not only to deal with the terrorist problem but also improve the techniques needed for this purpose.

I only wish to emphasise here that time is not on our side. We cannot afford a repetition of the kind of terrorist attacks that have recently taken place in Delhi, Hyderabad, Bangalore, Mumbai, Ahmedabad, Surat, Guwahati and some other urban centers. Every time a terrorist attack takes place there is a public outcry over the failure of the Government, accompanied by criticism of the police and the intelligence agencies. I am aware that many terrorist attacks have been prevented, thanks to the vigil of the police and intelligence agencies, but a single incident of reasonable magnitude causes repercussions, and calls into question the capability and capacity of the Government and its agencies. The globalisation of terror has made Terrorism an all—encompassing danger. We should anticipate that the scale of such terrorist incidents would only grow in the future and this would then become a major test of your capacities. You must be prepared for such an eventuality.

Alongside this, we need to guard against the new danger posed by the spread of fundamentalist and extremist ideas. We have, of late, been witnessing the emergence of such pernicious tendencies and trends, and there are elements in our society who are actively pursuing such programmes. We are a nation of over a billion people, belonging to different religions, communities, castes and speaking different languages who have lived peacefully together for hundreds of years. Our inclusive society must be preserved for posterity.

The virus of communal violence that threatens the secular fabric of our country needs to be checked in time, otherwise our multi-religious, multi-ethnic and multi-caste society could well unravel. This cannot be done by the police and law & order agencies alone, but the Police are often the first responders and have, hence, a critical role to play. Many years ago, our first Prime Minister, Pt. Jawaharlal Nehru had remarked: "All of us, of whatever religion we belong to, are equal children of India with equal rights, privileges and obligations. . . . No nation can be great whose people are narrow in thought or in action." Sixty years and more after Independence, this remains the leit motif of our liberal pluralistic democracy. Whatever be the circumstances, the police must not remain passive spectators, when deliberate efforts are made by communal elements or others to disturb the peace.

It is important that you have a proper understanding of the complex forces that are at work to-day in the country. You will need to avoid stereotypes that might wittingly, or unwittingly, enlarge the fault lines in our society. As the most visible symbol of our pluralistic democracy and national identity, you must create an image of the police as a fair and impartial entity. You will come under attack from those sections of society who are determined to undermine India's liberal ethos, but this challenge will have to be met. You may rest assured that in carrying out your responsibilities and duties you will have the fullest support of our Government.

Another major challenge before the Police will be restoring the faith of the people—specially those belonging to religious and ethnic minorities and the weaker sections—in the impartiality and effectiveness of the police.

To-day, aspersions are being made regarding police impartiality and capabilities, and while I recognize that much of this is motivated, you must face up to the reality that many are convinced that the police is less than fair. This is so even when policemen die in the line of duty.

You must introspect deeply why this is happening. An adverse image of the police undermines its efficiency. It makes your task much more difficult. Your work is with, and amongst, people, and you require their support and help. You need to win the trust of civil society. You need understanding from and rapport with the media. Above all you must carry conviction to one and all about your impartiality and honesty of purpose. This is fundamental if the police has to succeed in a democracy. An appropriate media policy, which could assist the police in gaining public confidence, through informing the public about what it needs to know and avoiding random or baseless speculation, is thus important.

In his address yesterday, the Home Minister would have covered the broad trends in the prevailing security scenario. I do not, hence, propose to enlarge upon this. All I would like to add is that while no one is questioning the professional competence of individual members of the Police Force, some misgivings do exist as to whether the police is adequately geared to deal with to-day's complex security problems. The contours of internal security have changed fundamentally over the years, and the basic character of threats has become greatly enlarged and also more complicated. A question that is often posed is whether the police have adequately upgraded their skills, have an indepth understanding of to-day's security problems, are technologically qualified, and have honed their abilities in every direction. In my interaction later to-day, I hope to hear from you what progress has been achieved in these areas.

This is particularly true of the threat posed by Left Wing Extremism—perhaps the most serious internal security threat that we face. It is evident that despite the efforts that have, and are being made, the measures taken so far have not yielded desired results. The police need to demonstrate greater resourcefulness and strengthen in term of both their intelligence machinery and their response capacity. This is equally true in some measure in regard to the threat from terrorist outfits. The inability of the Intelligence—Agencies and the police to obtain pinpointed and actionable intelligence and in time—has enabled these outfits to carry out some high-profile attacks.

There could be several reasons for this, and I am aware of some of them. The resources at the disposal of the police are often inadequate. The strength of personnel in police stations clearly needs to be augmented. There are far too many vacancies, and much larger numbers need to be recruited into the police, particularly into the civil police. The intelligence machinery at both the State and Central levels needs to be upgraded and should be more sophisticated.

Police training has not kept pace with requirements. A quantum increase in the Police Budget across the country is also called for.

There is a great deal, notwithstanding all these limitations, that you could still do as leaders of the police force. To begin with, closer supervision at every level of the police hierarchy would yield better results. There is scope for effective connectivity between a policeman on duty and his headquarters through an effective and advanced communication system that could result in a 2-way flow of messages and data. With more senior level appointments in the Police, it should be possible to innovate better and create new instrumentalities for more effective policing. Training, in particular, can receive greater attention. Efforts can also be concentrated as much on the lowly beat constable as on members of Specialized Forces such as the Greyhounds in Andhra Pradesh and the COBRA battalions of the CRPF.

I am aware that some work is already in place and the Ministry of Home Affairs and the various agencies under the MHA, including the Bureau of Police Research & Development, are engaged in this task. Yet, as I just stated, when it comes to high-tech crimes, terrorist situations, insurgent problems, or complex law & order matters, the perception remains that the police have a great deal of leeway to make up. This is something that has to be taken up urgently.

There is thus a great deal of pressure to re-energise and re-vitalise the police force. In 2005, while addressing the Conference of Directors-General of Police, I had recommended a 'Police Mission' approach with a view to achieving focused attention on different police related tasks. The intention was to create an image of the Indian Police as a professionally competent and technologically advanced force, one that would be an agent of socio-economic change endowed with a spirit of humanism. I am told that some steps have been taken in this direction and meetings of the 'Micro Missions' that were established have been held. On the ground, however, tangible results are yet to be seen. I think a Committee of the Directors-General of Police should assess what needs to be done so that the original spirit with which the idea of the 'Police Mission' was initiated, is re-created.

I believe that in the dynamic environment that we find ourselves, in which the pace, scale and complexity of changes are unprecedented, we need and should evolve a networked security architecture. Risks are often unforeseen in to-day's work. Threats are often hidden. This has made the work of law and order professionals far more challenging than previously. We need to be able to anticipate better. To ensure a proper networked security architecture, I suggest the establishment of a Task Force which would initiate a 100-day plan to:

- Develop an integrated capability to address emerging challenges in areas such as Left Wing Extremism, Terrorism and Insurgency;

- Improve the ability to anticipate and prevent surprises, through closely networked intelligence collaboration and upgradation of both human and technological intelligence;
- Create an awareness regarding the critical importance of strategic foresight in regard to social and political developments;
- Develop a net-centric information command structure that enables State and Central agencies to access and exploit information in a secure manner;
- Strengthen inter-State and inter-agency collaboration;
- Ensure innovation and technological leadership.

In a period of 100 days, the Task Force should come out with a road map regarding the detailed steps to be taken immediately, as also the subsequent steps to be taken over the next several months so as to translate this vision of an integrated net-centric capability into reality. The Task Force could be chaired by the National Security Adviser with suitable representation from the Central and State agencies.

I also suggest the setting up of a Standing Committee of State DGPs to advise the Government on police and police-related legal matters. This institutional mechanism could comprise five State DGPs taken on a rotation basis. Side by side with this, it would be advantageous if the MHA could devise a scheme by which a certain number of Executive level police personnel could be inducted into the Ministry to help with policy formulation and induce a degree of field experience into various formulations involving police matters.

I am sure the DIB and the DGPs and other delegates would work towards these objectives.

In conclusion, I would like to congratulate you and through you the members of the Police Force for the selfless and untiring work that you have been performing. The Police are seldom praised and are almost always the butt of criticism. Nevertheless, the work done by the Police is invaluable and our nation has every reason to be thankful to the two million strong Police Force of the country.

Thank you.

Source: ***Prime Minister's Office, Government of India***

DOCUMENT NO. 8

PRIME MINISTER'S ADDRESS TO THE NATION ON THE MUMBAI ATTACKS

November 27, 2008

In the aftermath of the multiple terrorist attacks in Mumbai, Prime Minister Dr. Manmohan Singh addressed the nation on November 27, 2008. Presented below is the full text of the speech:

PM's address to the Nation

Dear Citizens,

The dastardly terror attacks that took place in Mumbai last night and today leading to the loss of many precious lives and injuries to many others have deeply shocked the nation. I strongly condemn these acts of senseless violence against innocent people, including guests from foreign countries. I offer my deepest condolences to the bereaved families and sympathies to those injured. The Government will take all necessary measures to look after the wellbeing of the affected families, including medical treatment of injured.

The well-planned and well-orchestrated attacks, probably with external linkages, were intended to create a sense of panic, by choosing high profile targets and indiscriminately killing foreigners.

I salute the courage and patriotism of the police officers, including the Chief of the Anti-Terror Squad, Shri Hemant Karkare and men who have laid down their lives in fighting these terrorists. I assure the country that we will attend in an urgent and serious manner to police reform so that the law and order authorities can work unitedly, effectively and in a determined manner to tackle such threats to national integrity.

We are not prepared to countenance a situation in which the safety and security of our citizens can be violated with impunity by terrorists. It is evident that the group which carried out these attacks, based outside the country, had come with single-minded determination to create havoc in the commercial capital of the country.

We will take the strongest possible measures to ensure that there is no repetition of such terrorist acts. We are determined to take whatever measures are necessary to ensure the safety and security of our citizens.

Instruments like the National Security Act will be employed to deal with situations of this kind. Existing laws will be tightened to ensure that there are no loopholes available to terrorists to escape the clutches of the law. Most importantly, it is essential to immediately set up a Federal Investigation Agency to go into terrorist crimes of this kind and ensure that the guilty are brought to book.

We will take up strongly with our neighbours that the use of their territory for launching attacks on us will not be tolerated, and that there would be a cost if suitable measures are not taken by them. We will take a number of measures to strengthen the hands of our police and intelligence authorities. We will curb the flow of funds to suspect organizations. We will restrict the entry of suspects into the country. We will go after these individuals and organizations and make sure that every perpetrator, organizer and supporter of terror, whatever his affiliation or religion may be, pays a heavy price for these cowardly and horrific acts against our people.

In this hour of tragedy, I appeal to the people to maintain peace and harmony so that the enemies of our country do not succeed in their nefarious designs. All concerned authorities are on alert and will deal sternly with any attempts to disturb public order.

I am confident that the people of India will rise unitedly to face this grave challenge to the nation's security and integrity.

Jai Hind !

Source: *Prime Minister's Office, Government of India*

B. INDIAN LEGISLATION

DOCUMENT NO. 9

THE ARMED FORCES (SPECIAL POWERS) ACT, 1958

Act 28 of 1958

September 11, 1958

An Act to enable certain special powers to be conferred upon members of the armed forces in disturbed areas in the State of [1][Arunachal Pradesh, Assam, Manipur, Meghalaya, Mizoram, Nagaland and Tripura].

Be it enacted by Parliament in the Ninth Year of the Republic of India as follows:

1. Short Title and Extent—

(1) This Act may be called [2][The Armed Forces (Special Powers) Act, 1958].

[3][(2) It extends to the whole of the State of [4][Arunachal Pradesh, Assam, Manipur, Meghalaya, Mizoram, Nagaland and Tripura].

2. Definitions—In this Act, unless the context otherwise requires:

(a) "armed forces" means the Military forces and the air forces operating as land forces, and includes any other armed forces of the Union so operating;

(b) "disturbed area" means an area which is for the time being declared by notification under section 3, to be a disturbed area;

(c) all other words and expressions used herein, but not defined and defined in the Air Force Act, 1950 (45 of 1950), or the Army Act, 1950 (46 of 1950) shall have meanings respectively assigned to them in those Acts.

---

[1] Subs. By Act 69 of 1986, sec. 43, for "Assam, Manipur, Meghalaya, Mizoram, Nagaland and Tripura and the Union Territory of Arunachal Pradesh" (w.e.f. 20-2-1987).

[2] Subs. By Act 7 of 1972, sec. 3, for "the Armed Forces (Assam and Manipur) Special Powers Act., 1958" (w.e.f. 5-4-1972).

[3] Subs. By Act 7 of 1972, sec. 4 (w.e.f. 5-4-1972).

[4] Subs. By Act 69 of 1986, sec. 43, for "Assam, Manipur, Meghalaya, Mizoram, Nagaland and Tripura and the Union territory of Arunachal Pradesh" (w.e.f. 20-2-1987).

[3][3. **Power to Declare Areas to be Disturbed Areas**—If, in relation to any State or Union territory of which the Act extends, the Governor of that State or the Administrator of that Union territory or the Central Government, in either case, if of the opinion that the whole or any part of such State or Union territory, as the case may be, is in such a disturbed or dangerous condition that the use of armed forces in aid of the civil powers in necessary, the Governor of that State or the Administrator of that Union territory or the Central Government, as the case may be, may, by notification in the Official Gazette, declare the whole or such part of such State or Union territory to be a disturbed area].

4. Special Power of the Armed Forces—Any commissioned officer, warrant officer, non commissioned officer or any other person of equivalent rank in the armed forces may, in a disturbed area—

(a) if he is of opinion that it is necessary so to do for the maintenance of Public order, after giving such due warning as he may consider necessary, fire upon or otherwise use force, even to the causing of death, against any person who is acting in contravention of any law or order for the time being in force in the disturbed area prohibiting the assembly of five or more persons or the carrying of weapons or of things capable of being used as weapons or of fire-arms, ammunition or explosive substances;

(b) if he is of opinion that it is necessary so to do, destroy any arms dump, prepared or fortified position or shelter from which armed attacks are made or are likely to be made or are attempted to be made, or any structure used as a training camp for armed volunteers or utilised as a hide-out by armed gangs or absconders wanted for any offence;

(c) arrest, without warrant, any person who has committed a cognisable offence or against whom a reasonable suspicion exists that he has committed or is about to commit a cognisable offence and may use such force as may be necessary to effect the arrest;

(d) enter and search without warrant any premises to make any such arrest as aforesaid or to recover any person believed to be wrongfully restrained or confined or any property reasonably suspected to be stolen property or any arms, ammunition or explosive substances believed to be unlawfully kept in such premises and may for that Purpose use such force as may be necessary.

5. Arrested Persons to be made over to the Police—Any person arrested and taken into custody under this Act shall be made over to the officer-in-charge of the nearest police station with the least possible delay, together with a report of the circumstances occasioning the arrest.

6. Protection to Persons acting under Act—No persecution, suit or other legal proceeding shall be instituted, except with the previous sanction of the Central Government, against any person in respect of anything done or purported to be done in exercise of the powers conferred by this Act.

7. Repeal and Saving—[Repealed by Amending and Repealing Act, 1960 (58 of 1960), First Schedule, sec. 2 (26-12-1960)]

DOCUMENT NO. 10

THE UNLAWFUL ACTIVITIES (PREVENTION) ACT, 1967

Act No. 37 of 1967

December 30, 1967

An Act to provide for the more effective prevention of certain unlawful activities of individuals and associations and for matters connected therewith.

BE it enacted by Parliament in the Eighteenth Year of the Republic of India as follows:—

Chapter I
Preliminary

1. Short title and extent.

1. (1) Short title and extent. This Act may be called the Unlawful Activities (Prevention) Act, 1967.

[1*][(2) It extends to the whole of India:

Provided that it shall come into force in the State of Jammu and Kashmir on such date as the Central Government may, by notification in the Official Gazette, appoint.]

2. Definitions.

2. Definitions. In this Act, unless the context otherwise requires,—

(a) "association" means any combination or body of individuals;

(b) "cession of a part of the territory of India" includes admission of the claim of any foreign country to any such part;

(c) "prescribed" means prescribed by rules made under this Act;

[1] Subs. by Act 24 of 1969, s. 2, for sub-section (2).

The Act comes into force in the State of Jammu and Kashmir on 1.9.1969, vide Notifn. No. G.S.R. 2098, dated 30.8.1969, Gazette of India, Exty., Part II, Sec. 3(i), page 615.

(d) "secession of a part of the territory of India from the Union" includes the assertion of any claim to determine whether such part will remain a part of the territory of India;

(e) "Tribunal" means the Tribunal constituted under section 5;

(f) "unlawful activity", in relation to an individual or association, means any action taken by such individual or association (whether by committing an act or by words, either spoken or written, or by signs or by visible representation or otherwise),—

(i) which is intended, or supports any claim, to bring about, on any ground whatsoever, the cession of a part of the territory of India or the secession of a part of the territory of India from the Union, or which incites any individual or group of individuals to bring about such cession or secession;

(ii) which disclaims, questions, disrupts or is intended to disrupt the sovereignty and territorial integrity of India;

[2*][(g) "unlawful association" means any association—

(i) which has for its object any unlawful activity, or which encourages or aids persons to undertake any unlawful activity, or of which the members undertake such activity; or

(ii) which has for its object any activity which is punishable under section 153A or section 153B of the Indian Penal Code (45 of 1860), or which encourages or aids persons to undertake any such activity, or of which the members undertake any such activity:

Provided that nothing contained in sub-clause (ii) shall apply to the State of Jammu and Kashmir.]

2A. Construction of references to laws not in force in Jammu and Kashmir.

[3*][2A. Construction of reference to laws not in force in Jammu and Kashmir. Any reference in this Act to a law which is not in force in the "State of Jammu and Kashmir shall, in relation to that State, be construed as a reference to the corresponding law, if any, in force in that State.]

Chapter II
Unlawful Associations

3. Declaration of an association as unlawful.

3. Declaration of an association as unlawful. (1) If the Central Government is of opinion that any association is, or has become, an unlawful association,

[2] Subs. by Act 31 of 1972, s. 4, for cl. (g).
[3] Ins. by Act 24 of 1969, s. 3.

it may, by notification in the Official Gazette, declare such association to be unlawful.

(2) Every such notification shall specify the grounds on which it is issued and such other particulars as the Central Government may consider necessary:

Provided that nothing in this sub-section shall require the Central Government to disclose any fact which it considers to be against the public interest to disclose.

(3) No such notification shall have effect until the Tribunal has, by an order made under section 4, confirmed the declaration made therein and the order is published in the Official Gazette:

Provided that if the Central Government is of opinion that circumstances exist which render it necessary for that Government to declare an association to be unlawful with immediate effect, it may, for reasons to be stated in writing, direct that the notification shall, subject to any order that may be made under section 4, have effect from the date of its publication in the Official Gazette.

(4) Every such notification shall, in addition to its publication in the Official Gazette, be published in not less than one daily newspaper having circulation in the State in which the principal office, if any, of the association affected is situated, and shall also be served on such association in such manner as the Central Government may think fit and all or any of the following modes may be followed in effecting such service, namely:—

(a) by affixing a copy of the notification to some conspicuous part of the office, if any, of the association ; or

(b) by serving a copy of the notification, where possible, on the principal office-bearers, if any, of the association ; or

(c) by proclaiming by beat of drum or by means of loudspeakers, the contents of the notification in the area in which the activities of the association are ordinarily carried on ; or

(d) in such other manner as may be prescribed.

4. Reference to Tribunal.

4. Reference to Tribunal. (1) Where any association has been declared unlawful by a notification issued under sub-section (1) of section 3, the Central Government shall, within thirty days from the date of the publication of the notification under the said subsection, refer the notification to the Tribunal for the purpose of adjudicating whether or not there is sufficient cause for declaring the association unlawful.

(2) On receipt of a reference under sub-section (1), the Tribunal shall call upon the association affected by notice in writing to show cause, within thirty days from the date of the service of such notice, why the association should not be declared unlawful.

(3) After considering the cause, if any, shown by the association or the office-bearers or members thereof, the-Tribunal shall hold an inquiry in the manner specified in section 9 and after calling for such further information as it may consider necessary from the Central Government or from any office-bearer or member of the association, it shall decide whether or not there is sufficient cause for declaring the association to be unlawful and make, as expeditiously as possible and in any case within a period of six months from the date of the issue of the notification under sub-section (1) of section 3, such order as it may deem fit either confirming the declaration made in notification or cancelling the same.

(4) The order of the Tribunal made under sub-section (3) shall be published in the Official Gazette.

5. Tribunal.

5. Tribunal. (1) The Central Government may, by notification in the Official Gazette, constitute, as and when necessary, a tribunal to be known as the "Unlawful Activities (Prevention) Tribunal" consisting of one person, to be appointed by the Central Government:

Provided that no person shall be so appointed unless he is a Judge of a High Court.

(2) If, for any reason, a vacancy (other than a temporary absence) occurs in the office of the presiding officer of the Tribunal, then, the Central Government shall appoint another person in accordance with the provisions of this section to fill the vacancy and the proceedings may be continued before the Tribunal from the stage at which the vacancy is filled.

(3) The Central Government shall make available to the Tribunal such staff as may be necessary for the discharge of its functions under this Act.

(4) All expenses incurred in connection with the Tribunal shall be defrayed out of the Consolidated Fund of India.

(5) Subject to the provisions of section 9, the Tribunal shall have power to regulate its own procedure in all matters arising out of the discharge of its functions including the place or places at which it will hold its sittings.

(6) The Tribunal shall, for the purpose of making an inquiry under this Act, have the same powers as are vested in a civil court under the Code of Civil Procedure, 1908 (5 of 1908), while trying a suit, in respect of the following matters, namely:—

(a) the summoning and enforcing the attendance of any witness and examining him on oath;

(b) the discovery and production of any document or other material object producible as evidence;

(c) the reception of evidence on affidavits;

(d) the requisitioning of any public record from any court or office;

(e) the issuing of any commission for the examination of witnesses.

(7) Any proceeding before the Tribunal shall be deemed to be a judicial proceeding within the meaning of sections 193 and 228 of the Indian Penal Code (45 of 1860) and the Tribunal shall be deemed to be a civil court for the purposes of section 195 and Chapter XXXV of the Code of Criminal Procedure, 1898 (5 of 1898).

6. Period of operation and cancellation of notification.

6. Period of operation and cancellation of notification. (1) Subject to the provisions of sub-section (2), a notification issued under section 3 shall, if the declaration made therein is confirmed by the Tribunal by an order made under section 4, remain in force for a period of two years from the date on which the notification becomes effective.

(2) Notwithstanding anything contained in sub-section (1), the Central Government may, either on its own motion or on the application of any person aggrieved, at any time, cancel the notification issued under section 3, whether or not the declaration made therein has been confirmed by the Tribunal.

7. Power to prohibit the use of founds of an unlawful association.

7. Power to prohibit the use of founds of an unlawful association. (1) Where an association has been declared unlawful by a notification issued under section 3 which has become effective under sub-section (3) of that section and the Central Government is satisfied, after such inquiry as it may think fit, that any person has custody of any moneys, securities or credits which are being used or are intended to be used for the purpose of the unlawful association, the Central Government may, by order in writing, prohibit such person from paying, delivering, transferring or otherwise dealing in any manner whatsoever with such moneys, securities or credits or with any other moneys, securities or credits which may come into his custody after the making of the order, save in accordance with the written orders of the Central Government and a copy of such order shall be served upon the person so prohibited in the manner specified in sub-section (3).

(2) The Central Government may endorse a copy of the prohibitory order made under sub-section (1) for investigation to any gazetted officer of the Government it may select, and such copy shall be a warrant whereunder

such officer may enter in or upon any premises of the person to whom the order is directed, examine the books of such person, search for moneys, securities or credits, and make inquiries from such person or any officer, agent or servant of such person, touching the origin of any dealings in any moneys, securities or credits which the investigating officer may suspect are being used or are intended to be used for the purpose of the unlawful association.

(3) A copy of an order made under this section shall be served in the manner provided in the Code of Criminal Procedure, 1898 (5of 1898), for the service of a summons, or, where the person to be served is a corporation, company, bank or other association, it shall be served on any secretary, director or other officer or person concerned with the management thereof, or by leaving it or sending it by post addressed to the corporation, company, bank or other association at its registered office, or where there is no registered office, at the place where it carries on business.

(4) Any person aggrieved by a prohibitory order made under subsection (1) may, within fifteen days from the date of the service of such order, make an application to the Court of the District Judge within the local limits of whose jurisdiction such person voluntarily resides or carries on business or personally works for gain, to establish that the moneys, securities or credits in respect of which the prohibitory order has been made are not being used or are not intended to be used for the purpose of the unlawful association and the Court of the District Judge shall decide the question.

(5) Except so far as is necessary for the purposes of any proceedings under this section, no information obtained in the course of any investigation made under sub-section (2) shall be divulged by any gazetted officer of the Government, without the consent of the Central Government.

(6) In this section, "security" includes a document whereby any person acknowledges that he is under a legal liability to pay money, or whereunder any person obtains a legal right to the payment of money.

8. Power to notify places for the purpose of an unlawful association.

8. Power to notify places for the purpose of an unlawful association. (1) Where an association has been declared unlawful by a notification issued under section 3 which has become effective under sub-section (3) of that section, the Central Government may, by notification in the Official Gazette, notify any place which in its opinion is used for the purpose of such unlawful association.

Explanation.—For the purposes of this sub-section, "place" includes a house or building, or part thereof, or a tent or vessel.

(2) On the issue of a notification under sub-section (1), the District Magistrate within the local limits of whose jurisdiction such notified place is situate or

any officer authorised by him in 'writing in this behalf shall make a list of all movable properties (other than wearing-apparel, cooking vessels, beds and beddings, tools of artisans, implements of husbandry, cattle, grain and foodstuffs and such other articles as he considers to be of a trivial nature) found in the notified place in the presence of two respectable witnesses.

(3) If, in the opinion of the District Magistrate, any articles specified in the list are or may be used for the purpose of the unlawful association he may make an order prohibiting any person from using the articles save in accordance with the written orders of the District Magistrate.

(4) The District Magistrate may thereupon make an order that no person who at the date of the notification was not a resident in the notified place shall, without the permission of the District Magistrate, enter, or be on or in, the notified place:

Provided that nothing in this sub-section shall apply to any near relative of any person who was a resident in the notified place at the date of the notification.

(5) Where in pursuance of sub-section (4), any person is granted permission to enter, or to be on or in, the notified place, that person shall, while acting under such permission, comply with such orders for regulating his conduct as may be given by the District Magistrate.

(6) Any police officer, not below the rank of a sub-inspector, or any other person authorised in this behalf by the Central Government may search any person entering, or seeking to enter, or being on or in, the notified place and may detain any such person for the purpose of searching him:

Provided that no female shall be searched in pursuance of this sub-section except by a female.

(7) If any person is in the notified place in contravention of an order made under sub-section (4), then, without prejudice to any other proceedings which may be taken against him, he may be removed therefrom by any officer or by any other person authorised in this behalf by the Central Government.

(8) Any person aggrieved by a notification issued in respect of a place under sub-section (1) or by an order made under sub-section (3) or sub-section (4) may, within thirty days from the date of the notification or order, as the case may be,, make an application to the Court of the District Judge within the local limits of whose jurisdiction such notified place is situate—

(a) for declaration that the place has not been used for the purpose of the unlawful association; or

(b) for setting aside the order made under sub-section (3) or sub-section (4), and on receipt of the application the Court of the District Judge shall, after giving the parties an opportunity of being heard, decide the question.

9. Procedure to be followed in the disposal of applications under this Act.

9. Procedure to be followed in the disposal of applications under this Act. Subject to any rules that may be made under this Act, the procedure to be followed by the Tribunal in holding any inquiry under sub-section (3) of section 4 or by a Court of the District Judge in disposing of any application under sub-section (4) of section 7 or sub-section (8) of section 8 shall, so far as may be, be the procedure laid down in the Code of Civil Procedure, 1908 (5 of 1908), for the investigation of claims and the decision of the Tribunal or the Court of the District Judge, as the case may be, shall be final.

Chapter III
Offences and Penalties

10. Penalty for being members of an unlawful association.

10. Penalty for being members of an unlawful association. Whoever is and continues to be a member of an association declared unlawful by a notification issued under section 3 which has become effective under sub-section (3) of that section, or takes part in meetings of any such unlawful association, or contributes to, or receives or solicits any contribution for the purpose of, any such unlawful association, or in any way assists the operations of any such unlawful association, shall be punishable with imprisonment for a term which may extend to two years, and shall also be liable to fine.

11. Penalty for dealing with funds of an unlawful association.

11. Penalty for dealing with funds of an unlawful association. If any person on whom a prohibitory order has been served under subsection (1) of section 7 in respect of any moneys, securities or credits pays, delivers, transfers or otherwise deals in any manner whatsoever with the same in contravention of the prohibitory order, he shall be punishable with imprisonment for a term which may extend to three years, or with fine, or with both, and notwithstanding anything contained in the Code of Criminal Procedure, 1898 (5 of 1898), the court trying such contravention may also impose on the person convicted an additional fine to recover from him the amount of the moneys or credits or the market value of the securities in respect of which the prohibitory order has been contravened or such part thereof as the court may deem fit.

12. Penalty for contravention of an order made in respect of notified place.

12. Penalty for contravention of an order made in respect of notified place. (1) Whoever uses any article in contravention of a prohibitory order in

respect thereof made under sub-section (3) of section 8 shall be punishable with imprisonment for a term which may extend to one year, and shall also be liable to fine.

(2) Whoever knowingly and wilfully is in, or effects or attempts to effect entry into, a notified place in contravention of an order made under sub-section (4) of section 8 shall be punishable with imprisonment for a term which may extend to one year, and shall also be liable to fine.

13. Punishment for unlawful activities.

13. Punishment for unlawful activities. (1) Whoever—

(a) takes part in or commits, or

(b) advocates abets, advises or incites the commission of, any unlawful activity, shall be punishable with imprisonment for a term which may extend to seven years, and shall also be liable to fine.

(2) Whoever, in any way, assists any unlawful activity of any association, declared unlawful under section 3, after the notification by which it has been so declared has become effective under sub-section (3) of that section, shall be punishable with imprisonment for a term which may extend to five years, or with fine, or with both.

(3) Nothing in this section shall apply to any treaty, agreement or convention entered into between the Government of India and the Government of any other country or to any negotiations therefor carried on by any person authorised in this behalf by the Government of India.

14. Offences to be cognizable.

14. Offences to be cognizable. Notwithstanding anything contained in the Code of Criminal Procedure, 1898 (5 of 1898), an offence punishable under this Act shall be cognizable.

Chapter IV
Miscellaneous

15. Continuance of association.

15. Continuance of association. An association shall not be deemed to have ceased to exist by reason only of any formal act of its dissolution or change of name but shall be deemed to continue so long as any actual combination for the purposes of such association continues between any members thereof.

16. Bar of jurisdiction.

16. Bar of jurisdiction. Save as otherwise expressly provided in this Act, no proceeding taken under this Act by the Central Government or the District

Magistrate or any officer authorised in this behalf by the Central Government or the District Magistrate shall be called in question in any court in any suit or application or by way of appeal or revision, and no injunction shall be granted by any court or other authority in respect of any action taken or to be taken in pursuance of any power conferred by or under this Act.

17. Prosecution for offences under this Act.

17. Prosecution for offences under this Act. No court shall take cognizance of any offence punishable under this Act except with the previous sanction of the Central Government or any officer authorised by the Central Government in this behalf.

18. Protection of action taken in good faith.

18. Protection of action taken in good faith. (1) No suit or other legal proceeding shall lie against the Government in respect of any loss or damage caused or likely to be caused by anything which is in good faith done or intended to be done in pursuance of this Act or any rules or orders made thereunder.

(2) No suit, prosecution or other legal proceeding shall lie against the District Magistrate or any officer authorised in this behalf by the Government or the District Magistrate in respect of anything which is in good faith done or intended to be done in pursuance of this Act or any rules or orders made thereunder.

19. Power to delegate.

19. Power to delegate. The Central Government may, by notification in the Official Gazette, direct that all or any of the powers which may be exercised by it under section 7, or section 8, or both, shall, in such circumstances and under such conditions, if any, as may be specified in the notification, be exercised also by any State Government and the State Government may, with the previous approval of the Central Government, by order in writing direct that any power which has been directed to be exercised by it shall, in such circumstances and under such conditions, if any, as may be specified in the direction, be exercised by any person subordinate to the State Government as may be specified therein.

20. Effect of Act and rules, etc., inconsistent with other enactments.

20. Effect of Act and rules, etc., inconsistent with other enactments. The provisions of this Act or any rule or order made thereunder shall have effect notwithstanding anything inconsistent therewith contained in any enactment other than this Act or any instrument having effect by virtue of any enactment other than this Act.

21. Power to make rules.

21. (1) Power to make rules. The Central Government may, by notification in the Official Gazette, make rules to carry out the purposes of this Act.

(2) In particular, and without prejudice to the generality of the foregoing power, such rules may provide for all or any of the following matters, namely:-

(a) the service of notices or orders issued or made under this Act and the manner in which such notices or orders may be served, where the person to be served is a corporation, company, bank or other association;

(b) the procedure to be followed by the Tribunal or a District Judge in holding any inquiry or disposing of any application under this Act;

(c) any other matter which has to be, or may be, prescribed.

(3) Every rule made by the Central Government under this section shall be laid, as soon as may be after it is made, before each House of Parliament while it is in session for a [4]*total period of thirty days which may be comprised in one session or [in two or more successive sessions, and if, before the expiry of the session immediately following the session or the successive sessions aforesaid], both Houses agree in making any modification the rule or both Houses agree that the rule should not be made, the rule shall thereafter have effect only in such modified form or be of no effect as the case may be; so, however, that any such modification or annulment shall be without prejudice to the validity of anything previously done under that rule.

Source: http://mha.nic.in/acts-rules/The%20Unlawful%20Activities%20Prevention%20Act,%201967.pdf

Downloaded: May 14, 2007

[4] Subs. by Act 4 of 1986, s.2 & Sch. (w.e.f.15.5.1986).

DOCUMENT NO. 11

TERRORIST AND DISRUPTIVE ACTIVITIES (PREVENTION) ACT, 1987[1]

September 3, 1987

Commonly known as TADA, the act was the first and only legislative effort by the Union government to define and counter terrorist activities. It was formulated in the back drop of growing terrorist violence in Punjab which had its violent effects in other parts of the country too, including capital New Delhi. The Act, which was criticised on various counts by human rights organisations and political parties was permitted to lapse in May 1995 though cases initiated while it was in force continue to hold legal validity. The full text of the Act follows.

(Act No. 28 of 1987)
(Amended by Act 43 of 1993)

[3rd September, 1987]

An Act to make special provisions for the prevention of, and for coping with, terrorist and disruptive activities and for matters connected therewith or incidental thereto.

Be it enacted by Parliament in the Thirty-eighth year of the Republic of India as follows :—

Part I
Preliminary

1. Short title, extent, application, commencement, duration and savings.—

(1) This Act may be called the Terrorist and Disruptive Activities Prevention) Act, 1987.

(2) It extends to the whole of India, and it applies also,—

a. to citizens of India outside India;

[1] Received the assent of the President on 3rd September, 1987; published in the Gazette of India, (Extra.), Part II, Section 1, pp. 1 to 15, dated 3rd September, 1987.

b. to persons in the service of the Government, wherever they may be; and

c. to persons on ships and aircraft registered in India, wherever they may be.

(3) Sections 5, 15, 21 and 22 shall come into force at once and the remaining provisions of this Act shall be deemed to have come into force on the 24th day of May, 1987.

(4) It shall remain in force for a period of [2][eight years] from the 24th day of May, 1987, but its expiry under the operation of this sub-section shall not affect,—

a. the previous operation of, or anything duly done or suffered under this Act or any rule made thereunder or any order made under any such rule, or

b. any right, privilege, obligation or liability acquired accrued or incurred under this Act or any rule made thereunder or any order made under any such rule, or

c. any penalty, forfeiture or punishment incurred in respect of any offence under this Act or any contravention of any rule made under this Act or of any order made under any such rule, or

d. any investigation, legal proceeding or remedy in respect of any such right, privilege, obligation, liability, penalty, forfeiture or punishment as aforesaid.

and any such investigation, legal proceeding or remedy may be instituted, continued or enforced and any such penalty, forfeiture or punishment may be imposed as if this Act had not expired.

2. Definitions—

(1) In this Act, unless the context otherwise requires,—

(a) *"abet"*, with its grammatical variations and cognate expressions, includes,—

i. the communication or association with any person or class of persons who is engaged in assisting in any manner terrorists or disruptionists;

ii. the passing on, or publication of, without any lawful authority, and information likely to assist the terrorists or disruptionists, and the passing on, or publication of, or distribution of, any document or matter obtained from terrorists or disruptionists;

---

[2] Subs. by Act 16 of 1989, Section 2, for the words "two years", re-subs. by Act 35 of 1991, for "four years", (w.e.f. 2-5-1991) and again subs. by Act 43 of 1993, Section 2, for "six years".

iii. the rendering of any assistance, whether financial or otherwise, the terrorists or disruptionists;

(b) "*Code*" means the Code of Criminal Procedure 1973 (2 of 1974);

(c) "*Designated Court*" means a Designated Court constituted under Section 9;

(d) "*Disruptive activity*" has the meaning assigned to it in Section 4, and the expression "disruptionist" shall be construed accordingly;

(e) "*High Court*" means the High Court of the State in which a judge or an additional judge of a Designated Court was working immediately before his appointment as such judge or additional judge;

(f) "*notified area*" means such area as the State Government may, by notification in the official Gazette, specify;

(g) "*public prosecutor*" means a Public Prosecutor or an Additional Public Prosecutor or a Special Public Prosecutor appointed under Section 13, and includes any person acting under the directions of the Public Prosecutor;

[3][(gg) "*property*" means property and assets of any description, whether corporeal or incorporeal, movable or immovable, tangible or intangible and deeds and instruments evidencing title to, or interest in, such property or assets, derived or obtained from the terrorist Act and includes proceeds of terrorism;]

(h) "*terrorist act*" has the meaning assigned to it in sub-section (1) of Section 3, and the expression "terrorist" shall be construed accordingly;

(i) words and expressions used but not defined in this Act and defined in the Code shall have the meaning respectively assigned to them in the Code.

(2) Any reference in this Act to any enactment or any provision thereof shall, in relation to an area in which such enactment or such provision is not in force, be construed as a reference to the corresponding law or the relevant provision of the corresponding law, if any, in force in that area.

Part II
Punishments for, and Measures for Coping with, Terrorist and Disruptive Activities

3. Punishment for terrorist acts.—

(1) Whoever with intent to overawe the Government as by law established or to strike terror in the people or any section of the people or to alienate

[3] Ins. by Act 43 of 1993, Section 3.

any section of the people or to adversely affect the harmony amongst different sections of the people does any act or thing by using bombs, dynamite or other explosive substances or inflammable substances or lethal weapons or poisons or noxious gases or other chemicals or by any other substances (whether biological or otherwise) of a hazardous nature in such a manner as to cause, or as is likely to cause, death of, or injuries to, any person or persons or loss of, or damage to, or destruction of, property or disruption of any supplies or services essential to the life of the community, or detains any person and threatens to kill or injure such person in order to compel the Government or any other person to do or abstain from doing any act, commits a terrorist act.

(2) Whoever commits a terrorist act, shall,—

(i) if such act has resulted in the death of any person, be punishable with death or imprisonment for life and shall also be liable to fine;

(ii) in any other case, be punishable with imprisonment for a term which shall not be less than five years but which may extend to imprisonment for life and shall also be liable to fine.

(3) Whoever conspires or attempts to commit, or advocates, abets, advises or incites or knowingly facilitates the commission of, a terrorist act or any act preparatory to a terrorist act, shall be punishable with imprisonment for a term which shall not be less than five years but which may extend to imprisonment for life and shall also be liable to fine.

(4) Whoever harbours or conceals, or attempts to harbour or conceal, any terrorist shall be punishable with imprisonment for a term which shall not be less than five years but which may extend to imprisonment for life and shall also be liable to fine.

[4][(5) Any person who is a member of a terrorists gang or a terrorist organisation, which is involved in terrorist acts, shall be punishable with imprisonment for a term which shall not be less than five years but which may extend to imprisonment for life and shall also be liable to fine.

(6) Whoever holds any property derived or obtained from commission of any terrorist act or has been acquired through the terrorist funds shall be punishable with imprisonment for a term which shall not be less than five years but which may extend to imprisonment for life and shall also be liable to fine.]

4. Punishment for disruptive activities.—

(1) Whoever commits or conspires or attempts to commit or abets, advocates, advises, or knowingly facilitates the commission of, any disruptive

[4] Ins. by Act 43 of 1993, Section 4.

activity or any act preparatory to a disruptive activity shall be punishable with imprisonment for a term which shall not be less than five years but which may extend to imprisonment for life and shall also be liable to fine.

(2) For the purposes of sub-section (1), "disruptive activity" means any action taken, whether by act or by speech or through any other media or in any other manner whatsoever,—

(i) which questions, disrupts or is intended to disrupt, whether directly or indirectly, the sovereignty and territorial integrity of India; or

(ii) which is intended to bring about or supports any claim, whether directly or indirectly, for the cession of any part of India or the secession of any part of India from the Union.

Explanation—For the purposes of this sub-section,—

(a) "cession" includes the admission of any claim of any foreign country to any part of India, and

(b) "secession" includes the assertion of any claim to determine whether a part of India will remain within the Union.

(3) Without prejudice to the generality of the provisions of sub-section(2), it is hereby declared that any action taken, whether by act or by speech or through any other media or in any other manner whatsoever, which—

a. advocates, advises, suggests or incites; or

b. predicts, prophesies or pronounces or otherwise expresses, in such manner as to incite, advice, suggest or prompt,

the killing or the destruction of any person bound by oath under the constitution to uphold the sovereignty and integrity of India or any public servant shall be deemed to be a disruptive activity within the meaning of this section.

(4) Whoever harbours or conceals, or attempts to harbour or conceal, any disruptiionist shall be punishable with imprisonment for a term which shall not be less than five years but which may be extend to imprisonment for life and shall also be liable to fine.

2. Habeas Corpus—In habeas corpus proceedings if the detention is legal at the time of the disposal of the petition the Court cannot order release of the person detained by issuing a writ of habeas corpus. Therefore, the legality or otherwise of the detention shall also be considered on the date of final disposal of the petition. *Bacha Bora v. State of Assam*, 1991 Cr LJ 2782 (Gau).

5. Possession of certain unauthorised arms, etc. in specified areas—Where any person is in possession of any arms and ammunition specified in Columns 2 and 3 of Category I or Category III (a) of Schedule I to the Arms Rules, 1962, or bombs, dynamite or other explosive substances unauthorisedly in a notified area, he shall, notwithstanding anything contained in any other law for the time being in force, be punishable with imprisonment for a term which shall not be less than five years but which may extend to imprisonment for life and shall also be liable to fine.

6. Enhanced penalties—

(1) If any person with intend to aid any terrorist or disruptionist, contravenes any provision of, or any rule made under the Arms Act, 1959, the Explosives Act, 1884, the Explosives Substances Act, 1908 or the Inflammable Substances Act, 1952, he shall, notwithstanding anything contained in any of the aforesaid Acts or the rules made thereunder, be punishable with imprisonment for a term which shall not be less than five years but which may extend to imprisonment for life and shall also be liable to fine.

(2) For the purposes of this section, any person who attempts to contravene or abets, or attempts to abet, or does any act preparatory to the contravention of any provision of any law, rule or order, shall be deemed to have contravened that provision, and the provision of sub-section (1) shall, in relation to such person, have effect subject to the modification that the reference to "imprisonment for life" shall be construed as a reference to "imprisonment for ten years".

7. Conferment of powers—

(1) Notwithstanding anything contained the Code or in any other provision of this Act, the Central Government may, if it considers it necessary or expedient so to do,—

a. for the prevention of, and for coping with, any offence under Section 3 or Seciton 4; or

b. for any case or class or group of cases under Section 3 or Section 4;

in any State or part thereof, confer, by notification in the official Gazette, on any officer of the Central Government, powers exercisable by a police officer under the Code in such State or part thereof or, as the case may be, for such case or class or group of cases and in particular, the powers of arrest, investigation and prosecution of persons before any Court.

(2) All officers of police and all officers of Government are hereby required and empowered to assist the officer of the Central Government referred to in sub-section (1), in the execution of the provisions of this Act or any rule or order made thereunder.

(3) The provisions of the Code shall, so far as may be and subject to such modifications made in this Act, apply to the exercise of the powers by an officer under sub-section (1).

[5][**7-A. Powers of investigating officers**—If an officer investigating an offence committed under this Act has reason to believe that any property in relation to which an investigation is being conducted is a property derived or obtained from the commission of any terrorist act and includes proceeds of terrorism he shall, with the approval of the Superintendent of Police, make an order seizing such property and where it is not practicable to seize such property, he may make an order of attachment directing that such property shall not be transferred or otherwise dealt with except with the prior permission of the officer making such order, or of the Designated Court and a copy of such order shall be served on the persons concerned:

Provided that the investigating officer shall duly inform the Designated Court within forty-eight hours of the attachment of such property and the said Court shall either confirm or revoke the order of attachment so issued.]

8. Forfeiture of property of certain persons—

(1) Where a person has been convicted to any offence punishable under this Act or any rule made thereunder, the Designated Court may, in addition to awarding any punishment, by order in writing, declare that any property, movable or immovable or both, belonging to the accused and specified in the order, shall stand forfeited to the Government free from all encumbrances.

(2) Where any person is accused of any offence under this Act or any rule made thereunder, it shall be open to the Designated Court trying him to pass an order that all or any properties, movable or immovable or both belonging to him, shall, during the period of such trial, be attached, and where such trial ends in conviction, the properties so attached shall stand forfeited to Government free from all encumbrances.

(3) (a) If upon a report in writing made by a police officer or an officer referred to in sub-section (1) of Section 7, any Designated Court has reason to believe that any person, who has committed an offence punishable under this Act or any rule made thereunder, has absconded or is concealing himself so that he may not be apprehended, such court may, notwithstanding anything contained in Section 82 of the Code, publish a written proclamation requiring him to appear at a specified place and at a specified time not less than fifteen days but not more than thirty days from the date of publication of such proclamation.

[5] Ins. by Act 43 of 1993, Section 5.

(b) The Designated Court issuing a proclamation under Clause (a) may, at any time, order the attachment of any property, movable or immovable or both, belonging to the proclaimed person, and thereupon the provisions of Sections 83 to 85 of the Code shall apply to such attachment as if such attachment were made under that Code.

(c) If, within six months from the date of the attachment, any person, whose property is, or has been, at the disposal of the Government under sub-section (2) of Section 85 of the code, appears voluntarily or is apprehended and brought before the Designated Court by whose order the property was attached, or the Court to which such Court is subordinate, and proves to the satisfaction of such Court that he did not abscond or conceal himself for the purpose of avoiding apprehension and that he had not received such notice of the proclamation as to enable him to attend within the time specified therein, such property or, if the same has been sold, the net proceeds of the sale and the residue of the property, shall, after satisfying therefrom all costs incurred in consequence of the attachment, be delivered to him.

(4) Where any shares in a company stand forfeited to the Government under this sub-section, then, the company shall, notwithstanding anything contained in the Companies Act, 1956, or the articles of association the company, forthwith register the Government as the transferee of such shares.

Part III
Designated Courts

9. Designated Courts—

(1) The Central Government or a State Government may, by notification in the official Gazette, constitute one or more Designated Courts for such area or areas, or for such case or class or group of cases as may be specified in the notification.

(2) Where a notification constituting a Designated Court for any area or areas or for any case or class or group of cases is issued by the Central Government under sub-section (1), and a notification constituting a Designated Court for the same area or areas or for the same case or class or group of cases has also been issued by a State Government under that sub-section, the Designated Court constituted by the Central Government, whether the notification constituting such Court is issued before or after the issue of the notification constituting the Designated Court by the State Government, shall have, and the Designated Court constituted by the State Government shall not have, jurisdiction to try any offence committed in that area or areas or, as the case may be, the case or class or group of cases,

and all cases pending before any Designated Court constituted by the State Government shall stand transferred to the Designated Court constituted by the Central Government.

(3) Where any question arises as to the jurisdiction of any Designated Court, it shall be referred to the Central Government whose decision thereon shall be final.

(4) A Designated Court shall be presided over by a Judge to be appointed by the Central Government or, as the case may be, the State Government, with the concurrence of the Chief Justice of the High Court.

(5) The Central Government or, as the case may be, the State Government may also appoint, with the concurrence of the Chief Justice of the High Court additional Judges to exercise jurisdiction in a Designated Court.

(6) A person shall not be qualified for appointment as a Judge or an additional Judge of a Designated Court unless he is, immediately before such appointment a Sessions Judge or an additional Sessions Judge in any State.

(7) For the removal of doubts, it is hereby provided that the attainment by a person appointed a judge or an Additional Judge of a Designated Court of the age of superannuation under the rules applicable to him in the service to which he belongs, shall not affect his continuance as such Judge or Additional Judge.

(8) Where any Additional Judge or Additional Judges is or are appointed in a Designated Court, the Judge of the Designated Court may, from time to time, by general or special order, in writing, provide for the distribution of business of the Designated Court among himself and the additional Judge or Additional Judges and also for the disposal of urgent business in the event of his absence or the absence of any Additional Judge.

10. Place of sitting—A Designated Court may, on its own motion or on an application made by the Public Prosecutor, and if it considers it expedient or desirable so to do, sit for any of its proceedings at any place, other than its ordinary place of sitting :

Provided that nothing in this section shall be construed to change the place of sitting of a Designated Court constituted by a State Government to any place outside that State.

11. Jurisdiction of Designated Courts.—

(1) Notwithstanding anything contained in the Code, every offence punishable under any provision of this Act or any rule made thereunder shall be triable only by the Designated Court within whose local jurisdiction

it was committed or, as the case may be, by the Designated Court constituted for trying such offence under sub-section (1) of Section 9.

(2) If, having regard to the exigencies of the situation prevailing in a State, the Central Government is of the opinion that,—

(a) the situation prevailing in such State is not conducive to a fair, impartial or speedy trial, or

(b) it is not likely to be feasible without occasioning the breach of peace or grave risk to the safety of the accused, the witnesses, the Public Prosecutor and the Judge of the Designated Court or any of them, or

(c) it is not otherwise in the interests of justice,

It may, with the concurrence of the Chief Justice of India (such occurrence to be obtained on a motion moved in that behalf by the Attorney-General), transfer any case pending before a Designated Court in that State to any other Designated Court within that State or in any other State.

(3) Where the whole or any part of the area within the local limits of the jurisdiction of a Designated Court has been declared to be, or forms part of, any area which has been declared to be a disturbed area under any enactment for the time being in force making provision for the suppression of disorder and restoration and maintenance of public order, and the Central Government is of opinion that the situation prevailing in the State is not conducive to fair, impartial or speedy trial within the State, of offences under this Act or the rules made thereunder which such Designated Court is competent to try, the Central Government may, with the concurrence of the Chief Justice of India, specify, by notification in the official Gazette, in relation to such Court (hereafter in this sub-section referred to as the local Court) a Designated Court outside the State (hereinafter in this section referred to as the specified court), and thereupon,—

a. it shall not be competent at any time during the period of operation of such notification, for such local court to exercise any jurisdiction in respect of, or try, any offence under this Act or the rules made thereunder;

b. the jurisdiction which would have been, but for the issue of such notification, exercisable by such local court in respect of such offences committed during the period of operation of such notification shall be exercisable by the specified court;

c. all cases relating to such offences pending immediately before the date of issue of such notification before such local court shall stand transferred on that date to the specified court;

d. all cases taken cognizance of by, or transferred to, the specified court under Clause *(b)* or Clause *(c)* shall be dealt with and tried in accordance with this Act (whether during the period of operation of such notification or thereafter) as if such offences had been committed within the local limits of the jurisdiction of the specified court or, as the case may be, transferred for trial to it under sub-section (2).

Explanation 1.—A notification under this sub-section in relation to any local court shall cease to operate on the date on which the whole or, as the case may be, the aforementioned part of the area within the local limits of its jurisdiction, ceases to be a disturbed area.

Explanation 2.—For the purposes of this section, "Attorney-General" means the Attorney-General of India or, in his absence, the Solicitor-General of India or, in the absence of both, one of the Additional Solicitors-General of India.

12. Power of Designated Courts with respect to other offences.—

(1) When trying any offence, a Designated Court may also try any other offence with which the accused may, under the Code, be charged at the same trial if the offence is connected with such other offence.

(2) If, in the course of any trial under this Act of any offence, it is found that the accused person has committed any other offence under this Act or any rule made thereunder or under any other law, a the Designated Court may convict such person of such other offence and pass any sentence authorised by this Act or such rule or, as the case may be, such other law, for the punishment thereof.

13. Public Prosecutors—

(1) For every Designated Court, the Central Government or, as the case may be, the State Government, shall appoint a person to be the Public Prosecutor and may appoint one or more persons to be the Additional Public Prosecutor or Additional Public Prosecutors;

provided that the Central Government or, as the case may be, the State Government, may also appoint for any case or class or group of cases a Special Public Prosecutor.

(2) A person shall not be qualified to be appointed as a Public Prosecutor or an Additional Public Prosecutor or a Special Public Prosecutor under this section unless he has been in practice as an Advocate for not less than seven years or has held any post, for a period of not less than seven years, under the Union or a State, requiring special knowledge of law.

(3) Every person appointed as a Public Prosecutor or an Additional Public Prosecutor or a Special Public Prosecutor under this section shall be deemed to be a Public Prosecutor within the meaning of clause *(u)* of Section 2 of the Code and the provisions of the Code shall have effect accordingly.

14. Procedure and powers of Designated Courts.—A Designated Court may take cognizance of any offence, without the accused being committed to it for trial, upon receiving a complaint of facts which constitute such offence or upon a police report of such facts.

(2) Where an offence triable by a Designated Court is punishable with imprisonment for a term not exceeding three years or with fine or with both, the Designated Court may, notwithstanding anything contained in sub-section (1) of Section 260 or Section 262 of the Code, try the offence in a summary way in accordance with the procedure prescribed in the Code and the provisions of Section 263 to 265 of the Code, shall, so far as may be, apply to such trial:

Provided that when, in the course of a summary trial under this sub-section, it appears to the Designated Court that the nature of the case is such that it is undesirable to try it in a summary way, the Designated Court shall recall any witnesses who may have been examined and proceed to re-hear the case in the manner provided by the provisions of the Code for the trial of such offence and the said provisions shall apply to and in relation to a Designated Court as they apply to and in relation to a Magistrate:

Provided further that in the case of any conviction in a summary trial under this section, it shall be lawful for a Designated Court to pass a sentence of imprisonment for a term not exceeding two years.

(3) Subject to the other provisions of this Act, a Designated Court shall, for the purpose of trial of any offence, have all the powers of a Court of Session and shall try such offence as if it were a Court of Session so far as may be in accordance with the procedure prescribed in the Code for the trial before a Court of Session.

(4) Subject to the other provisions of this Act, every case transferred to a Designated Court under sub-section (2) of Section 11 shall be dealt with as if such case had been transferred under Section 406 of the Code to such Designated Court.

(5) Nothwithstanding anything contained in the Code, a Designated Court may, if it thinks fit and for reasons to be recorded by it, proceed with the trial in the absence of the accused or his pleader and record the evidence of any witness, subject to the right of the accused to recall the witness for cross-examination.

15. Certain confessions made to police officers to be taken into consideration.—

(1) Nothwithstanding anything in the Code or in the Indian Evidence Act, 1872, but subject to the provisions of this section, a confession made by a person before a police officer not lower in rank than a Superintendent of

Police and recorded by such police officer either in writing or on any mechanical device like cassettes, tapes or sound tracks from out of which sounds or images can be reproduced, shall be admissible in the trial of such person [6][or co-accused, abettor or conspirator] for an offence under this Act or rules made thereunder:

[7][Provided that co-accused, abettor or conspirator is charged and tried in the same case together with the accused].

(2) The police officer shall, before recording any confession under sub-section (1), explain to the person making it that he is not bound to make a confession and that, if he does so, it may be used as evidence against him and such police officer shall not record any such confession unless upon questioning the person making it, he has reason to believe that it is being made voluntarily.

16. Protection of witnesses.—

[8][(1) Nothwithstanding anything contained in the Code, the proceedings under this Act may be held in *camera* if the Designated Court so desires.]

(2) A Designated Court may, on an application made by a witness in any proceedings before it or by the Public Prosecutor in relation to such witness or on its own motion, take such measures as it deems fit for keeping the identity and address of any witness secret.

(3) In particular, and without prejudice to the generality of the provisions of sub-section (2), the measures which a Designated Court may take under that sub-section may include,—

a. the holding of the proceedings at a place to be decided by the Designated Court;

b. the avoiding of the mention of the names and addresses of the witnesses in it orders or judgments or in any records of the case accessible to public;

c. the issuing of any directions for securing that the identity and addresses of the witnesses are not disclosed.

d. that it is in the public interest to order that all or any of the proceedings pending before such a court shall not be published in any manner.

---

[6] Ins. by Act 43 of 1993, Section 6(a).
[7] Ins. by Act 43 of 1993, Section 6(b).
[8] Ins. by Act 43 of 1993, Section 7.

(4) Any person who contravenes any direction issued under sub-section (3) shall be punishable with imprisonment for a term which may extend to one year and with fine which may extend to one thousand rupees.

17. Trial by Designated Courts to have precedence—The trial under this Act of any offence by a Designated Court shall have precedence over the trial of any other case against the accused in any other court (not being a Designated Court) and shall be concluded in preference to the trial of such other case and accordingly the trial of such other case shall remain in abeyance.

18. Power to transfer cases to regular courts—Where, after taking cognizance of any offence, a Designated Court is of opinion that the offence is not triable by it, it shall, notwithstanding that it has no jurisdiction to try such offence, transfer the case for the trial of such offence to any court having jurisdiction under the Code and the court to which the case is transferred may proceed with the trial of the offence as if it had taken cognizance of the offence.

19. Appeal—

(1) Nothwithstanding anything contained in the Code, an appeal shall lie as a matter of right from any judgment, sentence or order, not being an interlocutory order, of a Designated Court to the Supreme Court both on facts and on law.

(2) Except as aforesaid, no appeal or revision shall lie to any court from any judgment, sentence or order including an interlocutory order of a Designated Court.

(3) Every appeal under this section shall be preferred within a period of thirty days from the date of the judgment; sentence or order appealed from:

Provided that the Supreme Court may entertain an appeal after the expiry of the said period of thirty days if it is satisfied that the appellant had sufficient cause for not preferring the appeal within the period of thirty days.

Part IV
Miscellaneous

20. Modified application of certain provisions of the Code.—

(1) Nothwithstanding anything contained in the Code or any other law, every offence punishable under this Act or any rule made thereunder shall be deemed to be a cognizable offence within the meaning of clause (c) of Section 2 of the Code, and "cognizable case" as defined in that clause shall be construed accordingly.

(2) Section 21 of the Code shall apply in relation to a case involving an offence punishable under this Act or any rule made thereunder subject to the modification that the reference to "the State Government" therein shall be construed as a reference to "the Central Government or the State Government".

(3) Section 164 of the Code shall apply in relation to a case involving an offence punishable under this Act or any rule made thereunder, subject to the modification that the reference in subsection (1) thereof to "Metropolitan Magistrate or Judicial Magistrate" shall be construed as a reference to "Metropolitan Magistrate, Judicial Magistrate, Executive Magistrate or Special Executive Magistrate.

(4) Section 167 of the Code shall apply in relation to a case involving an offence punishable under this Act or any rule made thereunder subject to the modifications that,—

a. the reference in sub-section (1) thereof to "Judicial Magistrate" shall be construed as a reference to Judicial Magistrate or Executive Magistrate or Special Executive Magistrate;

b. the reference in sub-section (2) thereof to "fifteen days," "ninety days" and "sixty days," wherever they occur, shall be construed as references to "sixty days." [9][one hundred and eighty days] and [8][one hundred and eighty days], respectively; and

(bb)sub-section (2-A) thereof shall be deemed to have been omitted.

[10][(bbb) in sub-section (2), after the proviso, the following proviso shall be inserted, namely:—

"Provided further that, if it is not possible to complete the investigation within the said period of one hundred and eighty days, the Designated Court shall extend the said period up to one year, on the report of the Public Prosecutor indicating the progress of the investigation and the specific reasons for the detention of the accused beyond the said period of one hundred and eighty days.]

(5) Section 268 of the Code shall apply in relation to a case involving an offence punishable under this Act or any rule made thereunder subject to the modifications that—

a. the reference in sub-section (1) thereof—

i. to "the State Government" shall be construed as a reference to "the Central Government or the State Government";

ii. to "order of the State Government" shall be construed as a reference to "order of the Central Government or the State Government, as the case may be"; or

[9] Subs. by Act 43 of 1993, Section 8(a).

[10] Ins. by Act 43 of 1993, Section 8(b).

b. the reference in sub-section (2) thereof, to "State Government" shall be construed as a reference to "Central Government or the State Government, as the case may be".

(6) Sections 366 to 371 and Section 392 of the Code shall apply in relation to a case involving an offence triable by a Designated Court subject to the modifications that the references to "Court of Session" and "High Court", wherever occurring therein, shall be construed as references to "Designated Court" and "Supreme Court", respectively.

(7) Nothing in Section 438 of the Code shall apply in relation to any case involving the arrest of any person on an accusation of having committed an offence punishable under this act or any rule made thereunder.

(8) Notwithstanding anything contained in the Code, no person accused of an offence punishable under this Act or any rule made thereunder shall, if in custody, be released on bail or on his own bond unless,—

a. the Public Prosecutor has been given an opportunity to oppose the application for such release, and

b. where the Public Prosecutor opposes the application, the Court is satisfied that there are reasonable grounds for believing that he is not guilty of such offence and that he is not likely to commit any offence while on bail.

(9) The limitations on granting of bail specified in sub-section (8) are in addition to the limitations under the Code or any other law for the time being in force on granting of bail.

[11][20-A. Cognizance of offence—

(1) Notwithstanding, anything contained in the Code, no information about the commission of an offence under this Act shall be recorded by the police without the prior approval of the District Superintendent of Police.

(2) No court shall take cognizance of any offence under this Act without the previous sanction of the Inspector-General of Police, or as the case may be, the Commissioner of Police.]

21. Presumption as to offences under Section 3—

(1) In a prosecution for an offence under sub-section (1) of Section 3, if it is proved—

a. that the arms or explosives or any other substances specified in Section 3 were recovered from the possession of the accused and there is reason to believe that such arms or explosives or other substances of similar nature, were used in the commission of such offence; or

[11] Ins. by Act 43 of 1993, Section 9.

b. that by the evidence of an expert the fingerprints of the accused were found at the site of the offence or on anything including arms and vehicles used in connection with the commission of such offence.

c. [12][* * *]

d. [12][* * *]

(2) In a prosecution for an offence under sub-section 3 of Section 3, if it is proved that the accused rendered any financial assistance to a person accused of, or reasonably suspected of, an offence under that section, the Designated Court shall presume, unless the contrary is proved, that such person has committed the offence under that sub-section.

22. Identification of accused—Where a person has been declared a proclaimed offender in terrorist case, the evidence regarding his identification by witnesses on the basis of his photograph shall have the same value as the evidence of a test identification parade.

23. Saving—

(1) Nothing in this Act shall affect the jurisdiction exercisable by, or the procedure applicable to, any Court or other authority under any law relating to the naval, military or air forces or other armed forces of the Union.

(2) For the removal of doubts, it is hereby declared that for the purposes of any such law as is referred to in sub-section (1), a Designated Court shall be deemed to be a Court of ordinary criminal justice.

24. Saving as to orders—Where an order purports to have been made and signed by any authority in exercise of any power conferred by or under this Act, a Court shall, within the meaning of the Indian Evidence Act, 1872, presume that such order was so made by that authority.

25. Overriding effect—The provisions of this Act or any rule made thereunder or any order made under any such rule shall have effect notwithstanding anything inconsistent therewith contained in any enactment other than this Act or in any instrument having effect by virtue of any enactment other than this Act.

26. Protection of action taken under this Act—No suit, prosecution or other legal proceeding shall lie against the Central Government or State Government or any other authority on whom powers have been conferred under this Act or any rules made thereunder, for anything which is in good faith done or purported to be done in pursuance of this Act or any rules made thereunder or any order issued under any such rule.

[12] Clauses (c) and (d), ommitted by Act 43 of 1993, Section 10.

27. Power of the Supreme Court to make rules—The Supreme Court may, by notification in the Official Gazette, make such rules, if any, as it may deem necessary for carrying out the provisions of this Act relating to Designated Court.

28. Power to make rules—

(1) Without prejudice to the powers of the Supreme Court to make rules under Section 27, the Central Government may, by notification in the Official Gazette, make rules for carrying out the provisions of this Act.

(2) In particular, and without prejudice to the generality of the foregoing power, such rules may provide for all or any of the following matters namely:

(a) regulating the conduct of persons in respect of areas the control of which is considered necessary or expedient and the removal of such persons from areas.

(b) The entry into, and search of,—

(i) any vehicle, vessel or aircraft; or

(ii) any place, whatsoever,

reasonably suspected of being used for committing the offence referred to in Section 3 or Section 4 or for manufacturing or storing anything for the commission of any such offence.

(c) Conferring powers upon,—

(i) the Central Government;

(ii) a State Government;

(iii) an Administrator of a Union Territory under Article 239 of the Constitution;

(iv) an officer of the Central Government not lower in rank than of a Joint Secretary; or

(v) an officer of a State Government not lower in rank than that of a District Magistrate,

to make general or special orders to prevent or cope with terrorist acts or disruptive activities;

(d) the arrest and trial of persons contravening any of the rules or any order made thereunder;

(e) the punishment of any person who contravenes or attempts to contravene or abets or attempts to abet the contravention of any rule or order made thereunder with imprisonment for a term which may extend to seven years or for a term which may not be less than six months but which may extend to seven years or with fine or with imprisonment as aforesaid and fine;

(f) Providing for the seizure and detention of any property in respect of which such contravention, attempt or abetment as is referred to in Clause (e) has been committed and for the adjudication of such seizure and detention, whether by any court or by any other authority.

29. **Rules to be laid before Houses of Parliament**—Every rule made by the Central Government under this Act shall be laid, as soon as may be after it is made, before each House of Parliament, while it is in session, for a total period of thirty days which may be comprised in one session or in two or more successive sessions, and if, before the expiry of the session immediately following the session or the successive sessions aforesaid, both Houses agree in making any modification in the rule or both Houses agree that the rule should not be made, the rule shall thereafter have affect only in such modified form or be of no effect, as the case may be; so, however, that any such modification or annulment shall be without prejudice to the validity of anything previously done under that rule.

30. **Repeal and Saving**—

(1) The Terrorist and Disruptive Activities (Prevention) Ordinance, 1987 (2 of 1987) is hereby repealed.

(2) Notwithstanding such repeal, anything done or any action taken under the said Ordinance shall be deemed to have been done or taken under the corresponding provisions of this Act.

DOCUMENT NO. 12

THE SAARC CONVENTION (SUPPRESSION OF TERRORISM) ACT, 1993

No. 36 of 1993

April 26, 1993

An Act to give effect to the South Asian Association for Regional Cooperation Convention on Suppression of Terrorism and for matters connected therewith or incidental thereto.

WHEREAS a Convention on the Suppression of Terrorism was signed on behalf of the Government of India at Kathmandu on the 4th day of November, 1987;

AND WHEREAS India, having ratified the said Convention, should make provisions for giving effect thereto and for matters connected therewith or incidental thereto;

BE it enacted by Parliament in the Forty-fourth Year of the Republic of India as follows:—

1. **Short title, extent and application.** (1) This Act may be called the SAARC Convention (Suppression of Terrorism) Act, 1993.

(2) It extends to the whole of India and, subject to the provisions of section 6, it applies also to any offence under this Act committed outside India by any person.

2. **Definitions.** In this Act, unless the context otherwise requires,—

(a) "Convention" means the South Asian Association for Regional Cooperation Convention on Suppression of Terrorism signed at Kathmandu on the 4th day of November, 1987 as set out in the Schedule;

(b) "Convention country" means a country in which the Convention is for the time being in force.

3. Application of the Convention. Notwithstanding anything to the contrary contained in any other law, the provisions of Articles I to VIII of the Convention shall have the force of law in India.

4. Hostage-taking. (1) Whoever, by force or threat of force or by any other form of intimation, seizes or detains any person and threatens to kill or injure that person with intent to cause a Convention country to do or abstain from doing any act as the means of avoiding the execution of such threat, commits the offence of hostage-taking.

(2) Whoever commits the offence of hostage-taking shall be punished with imprisonment for a term which may extend to ten years, and shall also be liable to fine.

5. Provisions as to Extradition Act. For the purposes of the Extradition Act, 1962 (34 of 1962), in relation to a Convention country, an offence under sub-section (1) of section 4 or any other offence specified in Article I of the Convention, shall not be considered to be an offence of a political character.

6. Offences committed outside India. (1) When an offence under sub-section (1) of section 4 or any other offence specified in Article I of the Convention is committed outside India,—

(a) by a citizen of India, whether on the high seas or elsewhere;

(b) by a person, not being such citizen, on any ship or aircraft, registered in India; or

(c) by a person, not being such citizen, in a Convention country,

he may be dealt with in respect of such offence as if it had been committed at any place within India at which he may be found.

(2) Notwithstanding anything contained in sub-section (1), the Central Government may, by general or special order published in the Official Gazette, direct that the offence under sub-section (1) of section 4 or any other offence specified in Article I of the Convention may be inquired into or tried at any place within India.

7. Previous sanction necessary for prosecution. No prosecution for an offence under this Act shall be instituted except with the previous sanction of the Central Government and the sanction granted under this section shall be deemed to be a sanction granted under section 188 of the Code of Criminal Procedure, 1973 (2 of 1974).

8. Protection of action taken in good faith. (1) No suit, prosecution or other legal proceeding shall lie against any person for anything which is in good faith done or intended to be done in pursuance of the provisions of this Act.

(2) No suit or other legal proceeding shall lie against the Central Government for any damage caused or likely to be caused for anything which is in good faith done or intended to be done in pursuance of the provisions of this Act.

The Schedule
[See Section 2(a)]
SAARC Regional Convention on Suppression of Terrorism

THE MEMBER STATES OF THE SOUTH ASIAN ASSOCIATION FOR REGIONAL COOPERATION (SAARC)

MINDFUL of the principles of cooperation enshrined in the SAARC Charter;

RECALLING that at the Dhaka Summit on December 7–8, 1985, the Heads of State or Government of the member States of the SAARC recognised the seriousness of the problem of terrorism as it affects the security and stability of the region;

ALSO RECALLING the Bangalore Summit Declaration of 17th November, 1986, in which the Heads of State or Government of SAARC, agreed that cooperation among SAARC States was vital if terrorism was to be prevented and eliminated from the region; unequivocally condemned all acts, methods and practices of terrorism as criminal and deplored their impact on life and property, socioeconomic development, political stability, regional and international peace and cooperation; and recognised the importance of the principles laid down in UN Resolution 262 (XXV) which among others required that each State should refrain from organising, instigating, assisting or participating in acts of civil strife or terrorist acts in another State or acquiescing in organised activities within its territory directed towards the commission of such acts;

AWARE of the danger posed by the spread of terrorism and its harmful effect on peace, cooperation, friendship and good neighbourly relations and which could also jeopardise the sovereignty and territorial integrity of States;

HAVE RESOLVED to take effective measures to ensure that perpetrators of terroristic acts do not escape prosecution and punishment by providing for their extradition or prosecution, and to this end;

HAVE AGREED as follows:—

Article I

Subject to the overall requirements of the law of extradition, conduct constituting any of the following offences, according to the law of the Contracting State, shall be regarded as terroristic and for the purpose of extradition shall not be regarded as a political offence or as an offence connected With a political offence or as an offence inspired by political motives:—

(a) an offence within the scope of the Convention for the Suppression of Unlawful Seizure of Aircraft, signed at the Hauge, on December 16, 1970;

(b) an offence within the scope of the Convention for the Suppression of Unlawful Acts against the Safety of Civil Aviation, signed at Montreal, on September 23, 1971;

(c) an offence within the scope of the Convention on the Prevention and Punishment of Crimes against Internationally Protected Persons, including Diplomatic Agents, signed at New York, on December 14, 1973;

(d) an offence within the scope of any Convention to which the SAARC member States concerned are parties and which obliges the parties to prosecute or grant extradition;

(e) murder, manslaughter, assault causing bodily harm, kidnapping hostage-taking and offences. relating to firearms, weapons, explosives and dangerous substances when used as a means to perpetrate indiscriminate violence involving death or serious bodily injury to persons or serious damage to property;

(f) an attempt or conspiracy to commit an offence described in sub-paragraphs (a) to (e), aiding, abetting or counselling the commission of such an offence or participating as an accomplice in the offences so described.

Article II

For the purpose of extradition between SAARC member States, any two or more Contracting States may, by agreement, decide to include any other serious offence involving violence, which shall not be regarded as a political offence, or in offence connected with a political offence or an offence inspired by political motives.

Article III

1. The provisions of all extradition treaties and arrangements applicable between Contracting States are hereby amended as between Contracting States to the extent that they are incompatible with this Convention.

2. For the purpose of this Convention and to the extent that any offence referred to in Article I or agreed to in terms of Article II in not listed as an extraditable offence in any extradition treaty existing between Contracting States, it shall be deemed to be included as such therein.

3. Contracting States undertake to include these offences as extraditable offences in any future extradition treaty to be concluded between them.

4. If a Contracting State which makes extradition conditional on the existence of a treaty receives a request for extradition from another Contracting State with which it has no extradition treaty, the requested State may, at its option, consider this Convention as the basis for extradition in respect of the offences set forth in Article I or agreed to in terms of Article II. Extradition shall be subject to the law of the requested State.

5. Contracting States which do not make extradition conditional on the existence of a treaty, shall recognise the offences set forth in Article I or agreed to in terms of Article II as extraditable offences between themselves, subject to the law of the requested State.

Article IV

A Contracting State in whose territory a person suspected of having committed an offence referred to in Article I or agreed to in terms of Article II is found and which has received a request for extradition from another Contracting State, shall, if it does not extradite that person, submit the case without exception and without delay, to its competent authorities, so that prosecution may be considered. These authorities shall take their decisions in the same manner as in the case of any offence of a serious nature under the law of that State.

Article V

For the purpose of Article IV, each Contracting State may take such measures as it deems appropriate, consistent with its national laws, subject to reciprocity, to exercise its jurisdiction in the case of an offence under Article I or agreed to in terms of Article II.

Article VI

A Contracting State in whose territory an alleged offender is found, shall, upon receiving a request for extradition from another Contracting State, take appropriate measures, subject to its national laws, so as to ensure his presence for purposes of extradition or prosecution. Such measures shall immediately be notified to the requesting State.

Article VII

Contracting States shall not be obliged to extradite, if it appears to the requested State that by reason of the trivial nature of the case or by reason of the request for the surrender or return of a fugitive lender not being made in good faith or in the interests of justice or for any other reason it is unjust or inexpedient to surrender or return the fugitive offender.

Article VIII

1. Contracting States shall, subject to their national laws, afford one another the greatest measure of mutual assistance in connection with proceedings brought in respect of the offences referred to in Article I or agreed to in terms of Article II including the supply of all evidence at their disposal necessary for the proceedings.

2. Contracting States shall cooperate among themselves, to the extent permitted by their national laws, through consultations between appropriate agencies, exchange of information, intelligence and expertise and such other cooperative measures as may be appropriate, with a view to preventing terroristic activities through precautionary measures,

Article IX

1. The Convention shall be open for signature by the member States of SAARC at the SAARC Secretariat in Kathmandu.

2. It shall be subject to ratification. Instruments of ratification shall be deposited with the Secretary-General of SAARC.

Article X

This Convention shall enter into force on the fifteenth day following the date of the deposit of the seventh Instrument of Ratification with the Secretary-General of SAARC.

Article XI

The Secretary-General of SAARC shall be the depository of this Convention and shall notify member States of signatures to this Convention and all deposits of Instruments of Ratification. The Secretary General, shall transmit certified copies of such Instruments to each member State. The Secretary-General shall also inform member States of the date on which this Convention will have entered into force in accordance with Article X.

IN WITNESS WHEREOF the undersigned, being duly authorised thereto by their respective Governments, have signed this Convention.

DONE at Kathmandu on this fourth day of November one thousand nine hundred and eighty-seven, in eight originals, in the English language, all texts being equally authentic.

DOCUMENT NO. 13

PARLIAMENT RESOLUTION ON JAMMU AND KASHMIR

February 22, 1994

Following increasing terrorist violence and Pakistan's attempts to highlight the Kashmir dispute, both houses of the Indian Parliament unanimously adopted a resolution on February 22, 1994, emphasizing that Jammu and Kashmir was an integral part of India, and that Pakistan must vacate parts of the State under its occupation. The text of the resolution follows.

"This House note with deep concern Pakistan's role in imparting training to the terrorists in camps located in Pakistan and Pakistan Occupied Kashmir, the supply of weapons and funds, assistance in infiltration of trained militants, including foreign mercenaries into Jammu and Kashmir with the avowed purpose of creating disorder, disharmony and subversion:

reiterates that the militants trained in Pakistan are indulging in murder, loot and other heinous crimes against the people, taking them hostage and creating an atmosphere of terror;

Condemns strongly the continued support and encouragement Pakistan is extending to subversive and terrorist activities in the Indian state of Jammu & Kashmir;

Calls upon Pakistan to stop forthwith its support to terrorism, which is in violation of the Simla Agreement and the internationally accepted norms of inter-State conduct and is the root cause of tension between the two countries reiterates that the Indian political and democratic structures and the Constitution provide for firm guarantees for the promotion and protection of human rights of all its citizens;

regard Pakistan's anti-India campaign of calumny and falsehood as unacceptable and deplorable.

notes with deep concern the highly provocative statements emanating from Pakistan urges Pakistan to refrain from making statements which vitiate the atmosphere and incite public opinion;

expresses regret and concern at the pitiable conditions and violations of human rights and denial of democratic freedoms of the people in those areas of the Indian State of Jammu and Kashmir, which are under the illegal occupation of Pakistan;

On behalf of the People of India,

Firmly declares that—

(a) The State of Jammu & Kashmir has been, is and shall be an integral part of India and any attempts to separate it from the rest of the country will be resisted by all necessary means;

(b) India has the will and capacity to firmly counter all designs against its unity, sovereignty and territorial integrity;

and demands that—

(c) Pakistan must vacate the areas of the Indian State of Jammu and Kashmir, which they have occupied through aggression; and resolves that—

(d) all attempts to interfere in the internal affairs of India will be met resolutely."

The Resolution was unanimously adopted. Mr. Speaker: The Resolution is unanimously passed.

February 22, 1994

http://www.kashmir-information.com/LegalDocs/ParliamentRes.html

DOCUMENT NO. 14

THE PREVENTION OF TERRORISM ORDINANCE, 2001

No. 9 of 2001

October 24, 2001

*The **Prevention of Terrorism Act,** enacted on March 28, 2002, replaced the Prevention of Terrorism Ordinance (POTO) 2001. The Act has now come into force after the President of India gave his assent.*

MINISTRY OF LAW, JUSTICE AND COMPANY AFFAIRS
(Legislative Department)
New Delhi, The 24th October, 2001/Kartika 2, 1923 (Saka)

THE PREVENTION OF TERRORISM ORDINANCE, 2001
No. 9 OF 2001

Promulgated by the President in the Fifty-second Year of the Republic of India.

An Ordinance to make provisions for the prevention of, and for dealing with, terrorist activities and for matters connected therewith.

WHEREAS Parliament is not in session and the President is satisfied that circumstances exists which render it necessary for him to take immediate action;

NOW, THEREFOR, in exercise of the powers conferred by clause (1) of article 123 of the Constitution, the President is please to promulgate the following Ordinance;-

Chapter I
Preliminary

Short Title, Extent, Application, Commencement, Duration and Savings

1. (1) This Ordinance may be called the Prevention of Terrorism Ordinance, 2001.

(2) It extends to the whole of India.

(3) Every person shall be liable to punishment under this Ordinance for every act or omission contrary to the provisions thereof, of which he is held guilty in India.

(4) Any person who commits an offence beyond India which is punishable under this Ordinance shall be dealt with according to the provisions of this Ordinance in the same manner as if such act had been committed in India.

(5) The provisions of this Ordinance apply also to—

(a) citizens of India outside India,

(b) persons in the service of the Government, wherever they may be, and

(c) persons on ships and aircrafts, registered in India, wherever they may be

(6) It shall come into force at once and shall remain in force for a period of five years from the date of its commencement, but its expiry under the operation of this sub-section shall not affect—

(a) the previous operation of, or anything duly done or suffered under this Ordinance, or

(b) any right, privilege, obligation or liability acquired, accrued or incurred under this Ordinance, or

(c) any penalty, forfeiture or punishment incurred in respect of any offence under this Ordinance, or

(d) any investigation, legal proceeding or remedy in respect of any such right, privilege, obligation, liability, penalty, forfeiture or punishment as aforesaid,

and, any such investigation, legal proceeding or remedy may be instituted, continued or enforced and any such penalty, forfeiture or punishment may be imposed as if this Ordinance had not expired.

Definitions

2. (1) In this Ordinance, unless the context otherwise requires,—

(a) "Code" means the Code of Criminal Procedure, 1973,

(b) "Designated Authority" shall mean such officer of the Central Government not below the rank of Joint Secretary to the Government, or such officer of the State Government not below the rank of Secretary to the Government, as the case may be, as may be specified by the Central Government or as the case may be, the State Government, by a notification published in the Official Gazette;

(c) "proceeds of terrorism" shall mean all kinds of properties which have been derived or obtained from commission of any terrorist act or have been acquired through funds traceable to a terrorist act, and shall include cash, irrespective of person in whose name such proceeds are standing or in whose possession they are found;

(d) "property" means property and assets of every description, whether corporeal or incorporeal, movable or immovable, tangible or intangible and deeds and instruments evidencing title to, or interest in, such property or assets;

(e) "Public Prosecutor" means a Public Prosecutor or an Additional Public Prosecutor or a Special Public Prosecutor appointed under section 28 and includes any person acting under the directions of the Public Prosecutor.

(f) "Special Court" means a Special Court constituted under section 23;

(g) "terrorist act" has the meaning assigned to it in sub-section (1) of section 3, and the expression "terrorist" shall be construed accordingly;

(h) "State Government", in relation to a Union territory, means the Administrator thereof;

(i) words and expressions used but not defined in this Ordinance and defined in the Code shall have the meanings respectively assigned to them in the Code.

(2) Any reference in this Ordinance to any enactment or any provision thereof shall, in relation to an area in which such enactment or such provision is not in force, be construed as a reference to the corresponding law or the relevant provision of the corresponding law, if any, in force in that area.

Chapter II
Punishment for, and Measures for Dealing with, Terrorist Activities

Punishments for Terrorist Acts

3. (1) Whoever,—

(a) with intent to threaten the unity, integrity, security or sovereignty of India or to strike terror in the people or any section of the people does any act or thing by using bombs, dynamite or other explosive substances or inflammable substances or fire arms or other lethal weapons or poisons or noxious gases or other chemicals or by any other substances (whether biological or otherwise) of a hazardous nature or by any other means whatsoever, in such a mariner as to cause or likely to cause, death of; or injuries to any person or persons or loss of, or damage to, or destruction of, property or disruption of any supplies or services essential to the life of the community or causes damage or destruction of any property or equipment used or intended to be used for the defence of India or in connection with any other purposes of the Government of India, any State Government or any of their agencies, or detains any person and threatens to kill or injure such person in order to compel the Government or any other person to do or abstain from doing any act;

37 of 1967

(b) is or continues to be a member of an association declared unlawful under the Unlawful Activities (Prevention) Act, 1967. or voluntarily does an act aiding or promoting in any manner the objects of such association and in either case is in possession of any unlicensed firearms, ammunition, explosive or other instrument or substance capable of causing mass destruction and commits any act resulting in loss of human life or grievous injury to any person or causes significant damage to any property, commits a terrorist act.

Explanation—For the purposes of this sub-section, "a terrorist act" shall include the act of raising funds intended for the purpose of terrorism—

(2) Whoever commits a terrorist act, shall,—

(i) if such act has resulted in the death of any person, be punishable with death or imprisonment for life and shall also be liable to fine;

(ii) in any other case, be punishable with imprisonment for a term which shall not be less than five years but which may extend to imprisonment for life and shall also be liable to fine.

(3) Whoever conspires or attempts to commit, or advocates, abets, advises or incites or knowingly facilitates the commission of, a terrorist act or any act preparatory to a terrorist act, shall be punishable with imprisonment for a term which shall not be less than five years but which may extend to imprisonment for life and shall also be liable to fine.

(4) Whoever voluntarily harbours or conceals, or attempts to harbour or conceal any person knowing that such person is a terrorist shall be punishable with imprisonment for a term which shall not be less than three years but which may extend to imprisonment for life and shall also be liable to fine:

Provided that this sub-section shall not apply to any case in which the harbour or concealment is by the husband or wife of the offender.

(5) Any person who is a member of a terrorist gang or a terrorist organisation, which is involved in terrorist acts, shall be punishable with imprisonment

for a term which may extend to imprisonment for life or with fine which may extend to rupees ten lakh or with both.

Explanation—For the purposes of this sub-section, "terrorist organisation" means an organisation which is concerned with or involved in terrorism.

(6) Whoever knowingly holds any property derived or obtained from commission of any terrorist act or has been acquired through the terrorist funds shall be punishable with imprisonment for a term which may extend to imprisonment for life or with fine which may extend to rupees ten lakh or with both.

(7) Whoever threatens any person who is a witness or any other person in whom such witness may be interested, with violence, or wrongfully restrains or confines the witness, or any other person in whom the witness may be interested, or does any other unlawful act with the said intent, shall be punishable with imprisonment which may extend to three years and fine.

(8) A person receiving or in possession of information which he knows or believes to be of material assistance—

(i) in preventing the commission by any other person of a terrorist act, or

(ii) in securing the apprehension, prosecution or conviction of any other person for an offence involving the commission, preparation or instigation of such an act,

and fails, without reasonable cause, to disclose that information as soon as reasonably practicable to the police, shall be punishable with imprisonment for a term which may extend to one year or with fine or with both:

Provided that a legal practitioner of the accused shall not be bound to disclose such information which he might have received while defending the accused.

Possession of Unauthorized Arms, etc.

4. Where any person is in unauthorized possession of any,—

(a) arms or ammunition specified in columns (2) and (3) of Category I or Category III (a) of Schedule I to the Arms Rules, 1962, in a notified area,

(b) bombs, dynamite or hazardous explosive substances or other lethal weapons capable of mass destruction or biological or chemical substances of warfare in any area, whether notified or not,

he shall be guilty of terrorist act notwithstanding anything contained in any other law for the time being in force, and be punishable with imprisonment for a term which may extend to imprisonment for life or with fine which may extend to rupees ten lakh or with both.

Explanation—In this section "notified area" means such area as the State Government may, by notification in the Official Gazette, specify.

Enhanced Penalties

5. (1) If any person with intent to aid any terrorist contravenes any provision of, or any rule made under, the Arms Act, 1959, the Explosives Act, 1884, the Explosive Substances Act, 1908 or the Inflammable Substances Act, 1952, he shall, notwithstanding anything contained in any of the aforesaid Acts or the rules made thereunder, be punishable with imprisonment for a term which may extend to imprisonment for life and shall also be liable to fine.

(2) For the purposes of this section, any person who attempts to contravene or abets, or does any act preparatory to the contravention of any provision of any law, rule or order, shall be deemed to have contravened that provision, and the provisions of sub-section (I) shall, in relation to such person, have effect subject to the modification that the reference to "imprisonment for life" shall be construed as a reference to "imprisonment for ten years".

Holding of Proceeds of Terrorism Illegal

6. (1) No person shall hold or be in possession of any proceeds of terrorism.

(2) Proceeds of terrorism, whether held by a terrorist or by any other person and whether or not such person is prosecuted or convicted under this Ordinance, shall be liable to be forfeited to the Central Government or the State Government, as the case may be, in the manner provided under this Chapter.

Powers of Investigating Officers

7. (1) If an officer (not below the rank of Superintendent of Police) investigating an offence committed under this Ordinance, has reason to believe that any property in relation to which an investigation is being conducted, represents proceeds of terrorism, he shall, with the prior approval in writing of the Director General of the Police of the State in which such property is situated, make an order seizing such property and where it is not practicable to seize such property, make an order of attachment directing that such property shall not be transferred or otherwise dealt with except with the prior permission of the officer making such order, or of the Designated Authority, or the Special Court, as the case may be, before

whom the properties seized or attached are produced and a copy of such order shall be served on the person concerned.

(2) The investigating officer shall duly inform the Designated Authority or, as the case may be, the Special Court, within forty-eight hours of the seizure or attachment of such property.

(3) It shall be open to the Designed Authority or the Special Court before whom the seized or attached properties are produced either to confirm or revoke the order of attachment so issued:

Provided that an opportunity of making a representation by the person whose property is being attached shall be given.

(4) In the case of immovable property attached by the investigating officer, it shall be deemed to have been produced before the Designated Authority or the Special Court, as the case may be, when the investigating officer notifies his report and places it at the disposal of the Designated Authority or the Special Court, as the case may be.

(5) The investigating officer may seize and detain any cash to which this Chapter applies if he has reasonable grounds for suspecting that—

(a) it is intended to be used for the purposes of terrorism;

(b) it forms the whole or part of the resources of an organisation declared as terrorist organisation under this Ordinance:

Provided that the cash seized under this sub-section by the investigating officer shall be released not later than the period of forty-eight hours beginning with the time when it is seized unless the matter involving the cash is before the Designated Authority, or as the case may be, the Special Court and such authority or, as the case may be, the Court passes an order allowing its retention beyond forty-eight hours.

Explanation—For the purposes of this sub-section "cash" means—

(a) coins and notes in any currency;

(b) postal orders;

(c) traveller's cheques;

(d) banker's drafts, and

(e) such other monetary instruments as the Central Government, or as the case may be, the State Government may specify by an order made in writing.

Forfeiture of Proceeds of Terrorism

8. Where any property is seized or attached in the belief that it constitutes proceeds of terrorism and is produced before the Designated Authority,

it shall, on being satisfied that the said property consists of proceeds of terrorism, order forfeiture of such property, whether or not the person from whose possession it is seized or attached, is prosecuted in a Special Court for an offence under this Ordinance.

Issue of Show Cause Notice Before Forfeiture of Proceeds of

9. (1) No order forfeiting any proceeds of terrorism shall be made under section 8 unless the person holding or in possession of such proceeds is given a notice in writing informing him of the grounds on which it is proposed to forfeit the proceeds of terrorism and such person is given an opportunity of making a representation in writing within such reasonable time as may be specified in the notice against the grounds of forfeiture and is also given a reasonable opportunity of being heard in the matter.

(2) No order of forfeiture shall be made under sub-section (I), if such person establishes that 'he is a *bona fide* transferee, of such proceeds for value without knowing that they represent proceeds of terrorism,

(3) It shall be competent for the Designated Authority to make an order in respect of property seized or attached,—

(a) directing it to be sold if it is a perishable property and the provisions of section 459 of the Code shall, as nearly as may be practicable, apply to the net proceeds of such sale;

(b) nominating any officer of the Central or State Government, in the case of any other property, to, perform the function of the Administrator of such property subject to such conditions as may be specified by the Designated Authority.

Appeal

10. (1) Any person aggrieved by an order of forfeiture under section 8 may, within one month from the date of the receipt of such order, appeal to the High Court within whose jurisdiction, the Designated Authority, who passed the order appealed against, is situated.

(2) Where an order under section 8 is modified or annulled by the High Court or where in a prosecution instituted for the contravention of the provisions of this Ordinance, the person against whom an order of forfeiture has been made under section 8 is acquitted, such property shall be returned to him and in either case if it is not possible for any reason to return the forfeited property, such person shall be paid the price therefor as if the property had been sold to the Central Government with reasonable interest calculated from the day of seizure of the property and such price shall be determined in the manner prescribed.

Order of Forfeiture not to Interfere with Other Punishments

11. The order of forfeiture made under this Ordinance by the Designated Authority, shall not prevent the infliction of any other punishment to which the person affected thereby is liable under this Ordinance.

Claims by Third Party

12. (1) Where any claim is preferred, or any objection is made to the seizure of any property under section 7 on the ground that such property is not liable to seizure, the Designated Authority, or as the case may be, the Special Court, before whom such property is produced, shall proceed to investigate the claim or objection:

Provided that no such investigation Shall be made where the Designated Authority or the Special Court considers that the claim or objection was designed to cause unnecessary delay.

(2) In case claimant or objector establishes that the property specified in the notice issued under section 9 is not liable to be attached or forfeited under the Ordinance, the said notice shall be withdrawn or modified accordingly.

Powers of Designated Information

13. The Designated Authority, acting under the provisions of this Ordinance, shall have all the powers of a Civil Court required for making a full and fair enquiry into the matter before it.

Obligation to Furnish Information

14. (l) Notwithstanding anything contained in any other law, the officer investigating any offence under this Ordinance, with prior approval in writing of an officer not below the rank of a Superintendent of Police, may require any officer or authority of the Central Government or a State Government or a local authority or a Bank, company, or a firm or any other institution, establishment, organisation or any individual to furnish information in their possession in relation to such offence, on points or matters, where the investigating officer has reason to believe that such information will be useful for, or relevant to. the purposes of this Ordinance.

(2) Failure to furnish the information called for under sub-section (1), or deliberately furnishing false information shall be punishable with imprisonment for a term which may extend to three years or with fine or with both.

(3) Notwithstanding anything contained in the Code, the offence under sub-section (l) shall be tried as a summary case and the procedure prescribed in Chapter XXI of the said Code [except sub- section (2) of section 262] shall be applicable thereto.

Certain Transfers to be Null and Void

15. Where, after the issue of an order under section 7 or issue of a notice under section 9, any property referred to in the said order or notice is transferred by any mode whatsoever, such transfer shall, for the purpose of the proceedings under this Ordinance, be ignored and if such property is subsequently forfeited, the transfer of such property shall be deemed to be null and void.

Forfeiture of Property of Certain Persons

16. (1) Where any person is accused of any offence under this Ordinance, it shall be open to the Special Court trying him to pass an order that all or any of the properties, movable or immovable or both belonging to him, shall, during the period of such trial, be attached, if not already attached under this Ordinance.

(2) Where a person has been convicted of any offence punishable under this Ordinance, the Special Court may, in addition to awarding any punishment, by order in writing, declare that any property, movable or immovable or both, belonging to the accused and specified in the order, shall stand forfeited to the Central Government or the State Government, as the case may be, free from all encumbrances.

Company to Transfer Shares to Government

17. Where any shares in a company stand forfeited to the Central Government or the State Government, as the case may be, under this Ordinance, then, the company shall on receipt of the order of the Special Court, notwithstanding anything contained in the Companies Act, 1956, or the articles of association of the company, forthwith register the Central Government or the State Government, as the case may be, as the transferee of such shares.

Chapter III
Terrorist Organisations

Declaration of an Terrorist Organisation

18. (l) For the purposes of this Ordinance an organisation is a terrorist organisation if.—

(a) it is listed in the Schedule, or

(b) it operates under the same name as an organisation listed in that Schedule.

(2) The Central Government may by order, in the Official Gazette.—

(a) add an organisation to the Schedule;

(b) remove an organisation from that Schedule:

(c) amend that Schedule in some other way.

(3) The Central Government may exercise its power under clause (a) of sub-section (2) in respect of an organisation only if it believes that it is involved in terrorism.

(4) For the purposes of sub-section (3) an organisation shall be deemed to be involved in terrorism if it—

(a) commits or participates in acts of terrorism,

(b) prepares for terrorism,

(c) promotes or encourages terrorism, or

(d) is otherwise involved in terrorism.

Denotification of Terrorist Organisation

19. (1) An application may be made to the Central Government for the exercise of its power under clause (b) of sub-section (2) of section 18 to remove an organisation from the Schedule.

(2) An application may be made by—

a. The organisation, or

b. any person affected by inclusion of the organisation in the Schedule as a terrorist organisation.

(3) The Central Government may make rules to prescribe the procedure for admission and disposal of an application made under this section.

(4) Where an application under sub-section (I) has been refused, the applicant may apply for a review to the Review Committee constituted by the Central Government under sub-section (1) of section 59 within one month from the date of receipt of the order by the applicant.

(5) The Review Committee may allow an application for review against refusal to remove an organisation from the Schedule, if it considers that the decision to refuse was flawed when considered in the light of the principles applicable on an application for judicial review.

(6) Where the Review Committee allows review under sub-section (5) by or in respect of an organisation, it may make an order under this sub-section.

(7) Where an order is made under sub-section (6), the Central Government shall as soon as the certified copy of the order is received by it, make an order removing the organisation from the list in the Schedule.

Offence Relating to Membership of a Terrorist Organisation

20. (1) A person commits an offence if he belongs or professes to membership belong to a terrorist organisation:

Provided that this sub-section shall not apply where the person charged is able to prove—

(a) that the organisation was not declared as a terrorist organisation at the time when he became a member or began to profess to be a member; and

(b) that he has not taken part in the activities of the organisation at any time during its inclusion in the Schedule as a terrorist organisation.

(2) A person guilty of an offence under this section shall be liable, on conviction, to imprisonment for a term not exceeding ten years or with fine or with both.

Offence Relating to Support Given to a Terrorist Organisation

21. (1) A person commits an offence if—

(a) he invites support for a terrorist organisation, and

(b) the support is not, or is not restricted to, the provision of money or other property within the meaning of section 22.

(2) A person commits an offence if he arranges, manages or assists in arranging or managing a meeting which he knows is—

(a) to support a terrorist organisation,

(b) to further the activities of a terrorist organisation, or

(c) to be addressed by a person who belongs or professes to belong to a terrorist organisation.

(3) A person commits an offence if he addresses a meeting for the purpose of encouraging support for a terrorist organisation or to further its activities.

(4) A person guilty of an offence under this section shall be liable on conviction, to imprisonment for a term not exceeding ten years or with fine or with both.

Explanation:—For the purposes for this section, the expression "meeting" means a meeting of three or more persons whether or not the public are admitted.

Fund Raising for a Terrorist Organisation to be an Offence

22. (1) A person commits an offence if he—

(a) invites another to provide money or other property, and

(b) intends that it should be used, or has reasonable cause to suspect that it may be used, for the purposes of terrorism.

(2) A person commits an offence if he—

(a) receives money, or other property, and

(b) intends that it should be use or has reasonable cause to suspect that it may be used, for the purposes of terrorism.

(3) A person commits an offence if he—

(a) provides money or other property, and

(b) knows or has reasonable cause to suspect that it will or may be used for the purposes of terrorism.

(4) In this section, a reference to the provision of money or other property is a reference to its being given, lent or otherwise made available, whether or not for consideration.

(5) A person guilty of an offence under this section shall be liable on conviction, to imprisonment for a term not exceeding fourteen years, or with fine or with both.

Chapter IV
Special Courts

Special Courts

23. (1) The Central Government or a State Government, may, by notification in the Official Gazette, constitute one or more Special Courts for such area or areas, or for such case or class or group of cases, as may be specified in the notification.

(2) Where a notification constituting a Special Court for any area or areas or for any case or class or group of cases is issued by the Central Government under sub-section (1), and a notification constituting a Special Court for the same area or areas or for the same case or class or group of cases has also been issued by the State Government under that sub-section, the Special Court constituted by the Central Government, whether the notification constituting such Court is issued before or after the issue of the notification constituting the Special Court by the State Government, shall have, and the Special Court constituted by the State Government shall not have, jurisdiction to try any offence committed in that area or areas or, as the case

may be, the case or class or group of cases and all cases pending before any Special Court constituted by the State Government shall stand transferred to the Special Court constituted by the Central Government.

(3) Where any question arises as to the jurisdiction of any Special Court, it shall be referred to the Central Government whose decision in the matter shall be final.

(4) A Special Court shall be presided over by a judge to be appointed by the Central Government or, as the case may be, the State Government, with the concurrence of the Chief Justice of the High Court.

(5) The Central Government or, as the case may be, the State Government may also appoint, with the concurrence of the Chief' Justice of the High Court, additional judges to exercise jurisdiction of a Special Court.

(6) A person shall not be qualified for appointment as a judge or an additional judge of a Special Court unless he is. Immediately before such appointment, a sessions Judge or an additional sessions judge in any State.

(7) For the removal of doubts, it is hereby provided that the attainment, by a person appointed as a judge or an additional judge of a Special Court, of the age of superannuation under the rules applicable to him in the service to which he belongs, shall not affect his continuance as such judge or additional judge.

(8) Where any additional judge or additional judges is or are appointed in a Special Court, the judge of the Special Court may, from time to time, by general or special order, in writing, provide for the distribution of business of the Special Court among all judges including himself and the additional judge or additional judges and also for the disposal of urgent business in the event of his absence or the absence of any additional judge.

Place of Sitting

24. A Special Court may, on its own motion, or on an application made by the Public Prosecutor and if it considers it expedient or desirable so to do, sit for any of its proceedings at any place other than its ordinary place of sitting:

Provided that nothing in this section shall be construed to change the place of sitting of a Special Court constituted by a State Government to any place outside that State.

Jurisdiction of Special Courts

25. (1) Notwithstanding anything contained in the Code, every Jurisdiction of offence punishable under any provision of this Ordinance, shall be triable only by the Special Court within whose local jurisdiction it was

committed or, as the case may be, by the Special Court constituted for trying such offence under section 23.

(2) If, having regard to the exigencies of the situation prevailing in a State.—

(i) it is not possible to have a fair, impartial or speedy trial; or

(ii) it is not feasible to have the trial without occasioning the breach of peace or grave risk to the safety of the accused, the witnesses, the Public Prosecutor and a judge of the Special Court or any of them; or

(iii) it is not otherwise in the interests of justice,

the Supreme Court may transfer any case pending before a Special Court to any other Special Court within that State or in any other State and the High Court may transfer any case pending before a Special Court situated in that State to any other Special Court within the State.

(3) The Supreme Court or the High Court, as the case may be, may act under this section either on the application of the Central Government or a party interested and any such application shall be made by motion, which shall, except when the applicant is the Attorney-General of India, be supported by an affidavit or affirmation.

Power of Special Courts with Respect to Other Offences

26. (1) When trying any offence, a Special Court may also try any other offence with which the accused may, under the Code, be charged at the same trial if the offence is connected with such other offence.

(2) If, in the course of any trial under this Ordinance of any offence, it is found that the accused person has committed any other offence under this Ordinance or under any other law, the Special Court may convict such person of such other offence, and pass any sentence or award punishment authorized by this Ordinance or such rule or, as the case may be, under such other law.

Power to Direct or Samples, etc.

27. (1) When a police officer investigating a case requests the Court of a Chief Judicial Magistrate or the Court of a Chief Metropolitan Magistrate in writing for obtaining samples of hand writing, finger prints, foot prints, photographs, blood, saliva, semen, hair, voice of any accused person, reasonably suspected to be involved in the commission of an offence under this Ordinance, it shall be lawful for the Court of a Chief Judicial Magistrate or the Court of a Chief Metropolitan Magistrate to direct that such samples be given by the accused person to the police officer either through a medical practitioner or otherwise, as the case may be.

(2) If any accused person refuses to give samples as provided in sub-section (1), the court shall draw adverse inference against the accused.

Public Prosecutors

28. (1) For every Special Court, the Central Government or, as the case may be, the State Government, shall appoint a person to be the Public Prosecutor and may appoint one or more persons to be the Additional Public Prosecutor or Additional Public Prosecutors;

Provided that the Central Government or, as the case may be, the State Government, may also appoint for any case or class or group of cases, a Special Public Prosecutor.

(2) A person shall not be qualified to be appointed as a Public Prosecutor or an Additional Public Prosecutor or a Special Public Prosecutor under this section unless he has been in practice as an Advocate for not less than seven years or has held any post, for a period of not less than seven years, under the Union or a State, requiring special knowledge of law.

(3) Every person appointed as a Public Prosecutor or an Additional Public Prosecutor or a Special Public Prosecutor under this section shall be deemed to be a Public Prosecutor within the meaning of clause (u) of section 2 of the Code, and the provisions of the Code shall have effect accordingly.

Procedure and Powers of Special Courts

29. (1) Subject to the provisions of section 49, a Special Court may take cognizance of any offence, without the accused being committed to it for trial, upon receiving a complaint of facts that constitute such offence or upon a police report of such facts.

(2) Where an offence triable by a Special Court is punishable with imprisonment for a term not exceeding three years or with fine or with both, the Special Court may, notwithstanding anything contained in sub-section (1) of section 260 or section 262 of the Code, try the offence in a summary way in accordance with the procedure prescribed in the Code and the provisions of sections 263 to 265 of the Code, shall so far as may be, apply to such trial:

Provided that when, in the course of a summary trial under this sub-section, it appears to the Special Court that the nature of the case is such that it is undesirable to try it in a summary way, the Special Court shall recall any witnesses who may have been examined and proceed to re-hear the case in the manner provided by the provisions of the Code for the trial of such offence and the said provisions shall apply to and in relation to a Special Court as they apply to and in relation to a Magistrate:

Provided further that in the case of any conviction in a summary trial under this section, it shall be lawful for a Special Court to pass a sentence of imprisonment for a term not exceeding one year and with fine which may extend to rupees five lakh.

(3) Subject to the other provisions of this Ordinance, a Special Court shall, for the purpose of trial of any offence, have all the powers of a Court of Session and shall try such offence as if it were a Court of Session so far as may be in accordance with the procedure prescribed in the Code for the trial before a Court of Session.

(4) Subject to the other provisions of this Ordinance, every case transferred to a Special Court under section 25 shall be dealt with as if such case had been transferred under section 406 of the Code to such Special Court.

(5) Notwithstanding anything contained in the Code, but subject to the provisions of section 299 of the Code, a Special Court may, if it thinks fit and for reasons to be recorded by it, proceed with the trial in the absence of the accused or his pleader and record the evidence of any witness, subject to the right of the accused to recall the witness for cross-examination.

Protection of Witnesses

30. (1) Notwithstanding anything contained in the Code, the proceedings under this Ordinance may, for reasons to be recorded in writing, be held in camera if the Special Court so desires.

(2) A Special Court, if on an application made by a witness in any proceeding before it or by the Public Prosecutor in relation to such witness or on its own motion, is satisfied that the life of such witness is in danger, it may, for reasons to be recorded in writing, take such measures as it deems fit for keeping the identity and address of such witness secret.

(3) In particular, and without prejudice to the generality of the provisions of sub-section (2), the measures which a Special Court may take under that sub-section may include—

(a) the holding of the proceedings at a place to be decided by the Special Court;

(b) the avoiding of the mention of the names and addresses of the witnesses in its orders or judgments or in any records of the case accessible to public;

(c) the issuing of any directions for securing that the identity and address of the witnesses are not disclosed;

(d) a decision that it is in the public interest to order that all or any of the proceedings pending before such a court shall not be published in any manner.

(4) Any person who contravenes any decision or direction issued under sub-section (3) shall be punishable with imprisonment for a term which may extend to one year and with fine which may extend to one thousand rupees.

Trial by Special Courts to Have Precedence

31. The trial under this Ordinance of any offence by a Special Court shall have precedence over the trial of any other case against the accused in any other court (not being a Special Court) and shall be concluded in preference to the trial of such other case and accordingly the trial of such other case shall remain in abeyance.

Certain Confessions Made to Police Officers to be Taken into Consideration

32. (1) Notwithstanding anything in the Code or in the Indian Evidence Act, 1872, but subject to the provisions of this section, a confession made by a person before a police officer not lower in rank than a Superintendent of Police and recorded by such police officer either in writing or on any mechanical or electronic device like cassettes, tapes or sound tracks from out of which sound or images can be reproduced, shall be admissible in the trial of such person for an offence under this Ordinance or rules made thereunder.

(2) A police officer shall, before recording any confession made by a person under sub-section (1) explain to such person in writing that he is not bound to make a confession and that if he does so, it may be used against him;

Provided that where such person prefers to remain silent, the police officer shall not compel or induce him to make any confession.

(3) The confession shall be recorded in an atmosphere free from threat or inducement and shall be in the same language in which the person makes it.

(4) The person from whom a confession has been recorded under sub-section (1), shall be produced before the Court of a Chief Metropolitan Magistrate or the Court of a Chief Judicial Magistrate along with the original statement of confession, written or recorded on mechanical or electronic device within forty-eight hours.

(5) The Chief Metropolitan Magistrate or the Chief Judicial Magistrate, shall, record the statement, if any, made by the person so produced and get his signature or thumb impression and if there is any complaint of torture, such person shall be directed to be produced for medical examination before a Medical Officer not lower in rank than an Assistant Civil Surgeon and thereafter, he shall be sent to judicial custody.

Power to Transfer Cases to Regular Courts

33. Where, after taking cognizance of any offence, a Special Court is of the opinion that the offence is not triable by it, it shall, notwithstanding that it has no jurisdiction to try such offence, transfer the case for the trial of such offence to any court having jurisdiction under the Code and the court to which the case is transferred may proceed with the trial of the offence as if it had taken cognizance of the offence.

Appeal

34. (1) Notwithstanding anything contained in the Code, an appeal shall lie from any judgment, sentence or order, not being an interlocutory order, of a Special Court to the High Court both on facts and on law.

Explanation—For the purposes of this section, "High Court" means a High Court within whose jurisdiction, a Special Court which passed the judgment, sentence or order, is situated.

(2) Every appeal under sub-section (1) shall be heard by a bench of two Judges of the High Court.

(3) Except as aforesaid, no appeal or revision shall lie to any court from any judgment, sentence or order including an interlocutory order of a Special Court.

(4) Notwithstanding anything contained in sub-section (3) of section 378 of the Code, an appeal shall lie to the High Court against an order of the Special Court granting or refusing bail.

(5) Every appeal under this section shall be preferred within a period of thirty days from the date of the judgment, sentence or order appealed from:

Provided that the High Court may entertain an appeal after the expiry of the said period of thirty days if it is satisfied that the appellant had sufficient cause for not preferring the appeal within the period of thirty days.

Chapter V
Interception of Communication in Certain Cases

Definitions

35. In this Chapter, unless the context otherwise requires,—

(a) "electronic communication" means any transmission of signs, signals, writings, images, sounds, data or intelligence of any nature transmitted in whole or in part by a wire, radio, electromagnetic, photo electronic or photo optical system that affects inland or foreign commerce but does not include,—

(i) the radio portion of a cordless telephone communication that is transmitted between the wireless telephone hand-set and the base unit,

(ii) any wire or oral communication;

(iii) any communication made through a tone only paging device; or

(iv) any communication from a tracking device;

(b) "intercept" means the aural or other acquisition of the contents by wire, electronic or oral communication through the use of any electronic, mechanical or other device;

(c) "oral communication" means any oral communication uttered by a person exhibiting an expectation that such communication is not subject to interception under circumstances justifying such expectation but such term does not include any electronic communication;

(d) "wire communication" means any aural transmission made in whole or part through the use of facilities for the transmission of communications by the aid of wire, cable or other like connection between the point of origin and the point of connection, between the point of origin and the point of reception (including the use of such connection in switching station) and such term includes any electronic storage of such communication.

Appointment of Authority

36. The Central Government or the State Government, as the case may be, may appoint an officer not below the rank of Secretary to the Government in case of State Government and not below the rank of Joint Secretary to the Government in the case of Central Government, to be the Competent Authority for the purposes of this Chapter.

Application for Authorization of Interception of Wire, Electronic or Oral Communication

37. (1) A police officer not below the rank of Superintendent of Police supervising the investigation of any terrorist act under this Ordinance may submit an application in writing to the Competent Authority for an order authorizing or approving the interception of wire, electronic or oral communication by the investigating officer when he believes that such interception may provide, or has provided evidence of any offence involving a terrorist act.

(2) Each application shall include the following information:—

(a) the identity of the investigating officer making the application, and the head of the department authorizing the application;

(b) a statement of the facts and circumstances relied upon by the applicant to justify his belief that an order should be issued, including—

(i) details as to the offence of terrorist act that has been, is being, or is about to be committed;

(ii) a particular description of the nature and location of the facilities from which or the place where the communication is to be intercepted;

(iii) a particular description of the type of communications sought to be intercepted; and

(iv) the identity of the person, if known, committing the terrorist act whose communications are to be intercepted;

(c) a statement of the period of time for which the interception is required to be maintained, if the nature of the enquiry is such that the authorization of interception should not automatically terminate after the described type of communication has been first obtained;

(d) a particular description of facts establishing probable cause to believe that additional communications of the same type will occur thereafter; and

(e) where the application is for the extension of an order, a statement setting forth the results thus far obtained from the interception, or a reasonable explanation of the failure to obtain such results.

(3) The Competent Authority may require the applicant to furnish additional oral or documentary evidence in support of the application.

Decision by Competent Authority on Application for Interception

38. (l) Upon such application, the Competent Authority may reject the application, or issue an order, as requested or as modified, authorizing or approving interception of wire, electronic or oral communications, if the Competent Authority determines on the basis of the facts submitted by the applicant that—

(a) there is a probable cause for belief that an individual is committing, has committed, or is about to commit a particular offence described and made punishable under sections 3 and 6 of this Ordinance;

(b) there is a probable cause of belief that particular communications concerning that offence may be obtained through such interception;

(c) there is probable cause of belief that the facilities from which, or the place where, the wire, electronic or oral communications are to be intercepted are being used or are about to be used, in connection with the commission of such offence, leased to, or are listed in the name of or commonly used by such person.

(2) Each order by the Competent Authority authorizing or approving the interception of any wire, electronic or oral communication under this section shall specify—

(a) the identity of the person, if known, whose communications are to be intercepted;

(b) the nature and location of the communication facilities as to which, or the place where, authority to intercept is granted;

(c) a particular description of the type of communication sought to be intercepted, and a statement of the particular offence to which it relates;

(d) the identity of the agency authorized to intercept the communications, and the person authorizing the application; and

(e) the period of time during which such interception is authorized, including a statement as to whether or not the interception shall automatically terminate after the described communication has been first obtained.

Submission of Order of Inception to Review Committee

39. (1) The Competent Authority shall immediately after passing the order under sub-section (*l*) of section 38, but in any case not later than seven days from the passing of the order, submit a copy of the same to the Review Committee constituted under section 59 along with all the relevant underlying papers, record and his own findings, in respect of the said order, for consideration and approval of the order by the Review Committee.

(2) An order authorizing the interception of a wire, electronic or oral communication under this section shall, upon request of the applicant, direct that a provider of wire or electronic communication service, landlord, custodian or other person shall furnish to the applicant forthwith all information, facilities, and technical assistance necessary to accomplish the interception unobtrusively and with a minimum of interference with the services that such service provider, landlord, custodian, or person is providing to the person whose communications are to be intercepted.

Duration of an Order of Interception etc.

40. (1) No order issued under this section may authorize or approve the interception of any wire, electronic or oral communication for any period

longer than is necessary to achieve the objective of the authorization, nor in any event longer than sixty days and such sixty days period shall begin on the day immediately preceding the "day on which the investigation officer first begins to conduct an interception under the order or ten days after order is issued whichever is earlier.

(2) The extension of an order may be granted, but only upon an application for an extension made in accordance with sub-section (1) of section 37 and the Competent Authority making the findings required by sub-section (1) of section 38, and the period of such extension shall be no longer than the Competent Authority deems necessary to achieve the purposes for which it was granted and in no event for longer than sixty days at a time.

(3) Every order and extension thereof shall contain a provision that the authorization to intercept shall be executed as soon as practicable and shall be conducted in such manner as to minimize the interception of communications not otherwise subject to interception under this section and shall terminate upon attainment of the authorized objective, or in any event on the expiry of the period of said order or extension thereof.

Authority Competent to Carry Out Interception

41. (1) An interception under this Chapter may be conducted in whole or in part by a public servant, acting under the supervision of the investigating officer authorized to conduct the interception.

(2) Whenever an order authorizing an interception is issued pursuant to this section, the order may require reports to be made to the Competent Authority who issued the order showing that progress has been made towards achievement of the authorized objective and the need for continued interception and such report shall be made at such intervals as the Competent Authority may require.

Interception of Communication in Emergency

42. (1) Notwithstanding anything contained in any other provision of this section, an officer not below the rank of Additional Director General of Police or a police officer of equivalent rank who reasonably determines that—

(a) an emergency situation exists that involves—

(i) immediate danger of death or serious physical injury to any person;

(ii) conspiratorial activities threatening the security or interest of the State; or

(iii) conspiratorial activities, characteristic of a terrorist act, that requires a wire, electronic or oral communication to be intercepted before an order from the Competent Authority authorizing such interception can, with due diligence, be obtained, and

(b) there are grounds on which an order should be issued under this section to authorize such interception,

may authorize, in writing, the investigating officer to intercept such wire, electronic or oral communication, if an application for an order approving the interception is made in accordance with the provisions of sub-sections (1) and (2) of section 37 within forty-eight hours after the interception has occurred, or begins to occur.

(2) In the absence of an order approving the interception made under sub-section (1), such interception shall immediately terminate when the communication sought is obtained or when the application for the order is rejected, whichever is earlier; and in the event of an application for permitting interception being rejected under sub-section (1) of section 38 or an application under sub-section (1) of section 42 for approval being rejected, or in any other case where the interception is terminated without an order having been issued, the contents of any wire, electronic or oral communication intercepted shall be treated as having been obtained in violation of this section.

Protection of Information Collected

43. (a) The contents of any wire, electronic or oral communication intercepted by any means authorized by this section shall as far as possible, be recorded on tape or wire or other comparable device and shall be done in such manner as to protect the recording from editing or other alterations.

(b) Immediately upon the expiration of the period of order, or extension thereof, such recording shall be made available to the Competent Authority issuing such order and shall be sealed under his directions and kept in the custody of such person or authority as the Competent Authority orders, and such recordings shall not be destroyed except upon an order of the Competent Authority and in any event shall be kept for ten years.

(c) Applications made and orders issued under this section shall be sealed by the Competent Authority and custody of the applications and orders shall be kept in such manner as the Competent Authority directs, and shall not be destroyed except on an order of the Competent Authority, and in any event shall be kept for ten years.

Admissibility of Evidence Collected Through the Interception of Communications

44. Notwithstanding anything in the Code or in any other law for the time being in force, the evidence collected through the interception of wire,

electronic or oral communication under this Chapter shall be admissible as evidence against the accused in the Court during the trial of a case:

Provided that, the contents of any wire, electronic or oral communication intercepted pursuant to this Chapter or evidence derived therefrom shall not be received in evidence or otherwise disclosed in any trial, hearing or other proceeding in any court unless each accused has been furnished with a copy of the order of the Competent Authority, and accompanying application, under which the interception was authorized or approved not less than ten days before trial, hearing or proceeding:

Provided further that, the period of ten days may be waived by the judge trying the matter, if he comes to the conclusion that it was not possible to furnish the accused with the above information ten days before the trial, hearing or proceeding and that the accused will not be prejudiced by the delay in receiving such information.

Review of Authoritarian Order

45. (1) The Review Committee constituted by the Central Government or the State Government, as the case may be, shall review every order passed by the Competent Authority under section 38.

(2) Every order passed by the Competent Authority under section 38, or disapproved by the officer under section 42, shall be placed before the Review Committee, which shall be considered by the Review Committee within ten days after its receipt, to decide whether the order, was necessary, reasonable and justified.

(3) The Review Committee, after examining the entire record and holding such enquiry, if any, deemed necessary may, by order in writing, either approve the order passed By the Competent Authority or may issue order disapproving the same.

(4) On issue of an order of disapproval by the Review Committee, the interception, if any, already commenced shall be forthwith discontinued and the intercepted communication, if any, in the form of tape, wire or other device shall, thereupon, not be admissible as evidence in any case and shall be directed to be destroyed.

Interception and Disclosure of Wire, Electronic or Oral Communications Prohibited

46. Except as otherwise specifically provided in section 38, any police officer who—

(a) intentionally intercepts, endeavours to intercept, or procures any other person to intercept or endeavour to intercept any wire, electronic or oral communication;

(b) intentionally uses, endeavours to use, or procures any other person to use or endeavours to use any electronic, mechanical or other device to intercept any oral communication when—

(i) such device is affixed to or otherwise transmits a signal through a wire, cable, or other like connection used in wire communication; or

(ii) such device transmits communications by radio, or interferes with the transmission of such communication;

(c) intentionally discloses, or endeavours to disclose, to any other person, the contents of any wire, electronic or oral communication, knowing or having reason to know that the information was obtained through the interception of a wire, electronic or oral communication in violation of this Chapter,

(d) intentionally uses, or endeavours to use, the contents of any wire, electronic or oral communication, knowing or having reason to know that the information was obtained through the interception' of a wire, electronic or oral communication in violation of this Chapter; or

(e) intentionally discloses, or endeavours to disclose, to any other unauthorized person the contents of any wire, electronic or oral communication, intercepted by means authorized by section 38;

(f) intentionally continues the interception of wire, electronic or oral communication after the issue of an order of rejection by the Competent Authority under this Chapter.

(g) intentionally continues the interception of wire, electronic or oral communication after the issue of an order of disapproval by the Review Committee under sub-section (3) of section 45,

shall for such violation be punishable with imprisonment for a term which may extend to one year and with fine upto rupees fifty thousand.

Annual Report of Interceptions

47. (1) The Central Government and the State Government, as the case may be, shall cause an annual report to be prepared giving a full account of.—

(i) the number of applications for authorization of interceptions received by the Competent Authority from the Police Department in which prosecutions have been launched;

(ii) the number of such applications permitted or rejected;

(iii) the number of interceptions carried out in emergency situations and the number of approvals granted or rejected in such matters;

(iv) the number of prosecutions launched based on such interceptions and convictions resulting from such interceptions, along with an explanatory memorandum giving general assessment of the utility and importance of the interceptions authorized.

(2) An annual report shall be laid by the State Government before the State Legislature within three months of the completion of every calendar year:

Provided that, if the State Government is of the opinion that the inclusion of any matter in the annual report would be prejudicial to the security of the State or to the prevention or detection of any terrorist act, the State Government may exclude such matter from being included in such annual report.

(3) An annual report shall be laid by the Central Government before each House of Parliament within three months of the completion of every calendar year:

Provided that, if the Central Government is of the opinion that the inclusion of any matter in the annual report would be prejudicial to the security of the country or to the prevention or detection of any terrorist act, the Central Government may exclude such matter from being included in such annual report.

Chapter VI
Miscellaneous

Modified Application of Certain Provisions of the Code

48. (1) Notwithstanding anything contained in the Code or any other law, every offence punishable under this Ordinance shall be deemed to be a cognizable offence within the meaning of clause (c) of section 2 of the Code, and "cognizable case" as defined in that clause shall be construed accordingly.

(2) Section 167 of the Code shall apply in relation to a case involving an offence punishable under this Ordinance subject to the modification that in sub-section (2).—

(a) the references to "fifteen days", "ninety days" and "sixty days", wherever they occur, shall be construed as references to "thirty days", "ninety days" and "ninety days", respectively; and

(b) after the proviso, the following provisos shall be inserted, namely:—

"Provided further that if it is not possible to complete the investigation within the said period of ninety days, the Special Court shall extend the said period up to one hundred and eighty days, on the report of the Public Prosecutor indicating the progress of the investigation and the specific reasons for the detention of the accused beyond the said period of ninety days;

Provided also that if the police officer making the investigation under this Ordinance, requests, for the purposes of investigation, for police custody from judicial custody of any person from judicial custody, he shall file an affidavit stating the reasons for doing so and shall also explain the delay, if any, for requesting such police custody".

(3) Section 268 of the Code shall apply in relation to a case involving an offence punishable under this Ordinance subject to the modification that—

(a) the reference in sub-section (1) thereof—

(i) to "the State Government" shall be construed as a reference to "the Central Government or the State Government",

(ii) to "order of the State Government" shall be construed as a reference, to "order of the Central Government or the State Government, as the case may be" ; and

(b) the reference in sub-section (2) thereof, to "State Government" shall be construed as a reference to "Central Government or the State Government, as the case may be".

(4) Sections 366, 367 and 371 of the Code shall apply in relation to a case involving an offence triable by a Special Court subject to the modification that the reference to "Court of Session", wherever occurring therein, shall be construed as the reference to "Special Court".

(5) Nothing in section 438 of the Code shall apply in relation to any case involving the arrest of any person accused of having committed an offence punishable under this Ordinance.

(6) Notwithstanding anything contained in the Code, no person accused of an offence punishable under this Ordinance shall, if in custody, be released on bail or on his own bond unless the Court gives the Public Prosecutor an opportunity of being heard.

(7) Where the Public Prosecutor opposes the application of the accused to release on bail, no person accused of an offence punishable under this Ordinance or any rule made thereunder shall be released on bail until the court is satisfied that there are grounds for believing that he is not guilty of committing such offence:

Provided that after the expiry of a period of one year from the date of detention of the accused for an offence under this Ordinance, the provisions of sub-section (6) of this section shall apply.

(8) The restrictions on granting of bail specified in sub-sections (6) and (7) are in addition to the restrictions under the Code or any other law for the time being in force on granting of bail.

(9) Notwithstanding anything contained in sub-sections (6), (7) and (8), no bail shall be granted to a person accused of an offence punishable under this Ordinance, if he is not an Indian citizen and has entered the country unauthorisedly or illegally except in very exceptional circumstances and for reasons to be recorded in writing.

Cognizance of Offences

49. No Court shall take cognizance of any offence under this Ordinance without the previous sanction of the Central Government or as the case may be, the State Government.

Officers Competent to Investigate Offences Under this Ordinance

50. Notwithstanding anything contained in the Code, no police officer,—

(a) in the case of the Delhi Special Police Establishment, not below the rank of a Deputy Superintendent of Police or a police officer of equivalent rank;

(b) in the metropolitan areas of Mumbai, Kolkata, Chennai and Ahmedabad and any other metropolitan area notified as such under sub-section (1) of section 8 of the Code, not below the rank of an Assistant Commissioner of Police;

(c) in any other case not relatable to clause (a) or clause (b), not below the rank of a Deputy Superintendent of Police or a police officer of an equivalent rank, shall investigate any offence punishable under this Ordinance.

Arrest

51. (1) Where a police officer arrests a person, he shall prepare a custody memo of the person arrested.

(2) The person arrested shall be informed of his right to consult a legal practitioner as soon as he is brought to the police station.

(3) Whenever any person is arrested, information of his arrest shall be immediately communicated by the police officer to a family member or in his absence to a relative of such person by telegram, telephone or by any other means and this fact shall be recorded by the police officer under the signature of the person arrested.

(4) The person arrested shall be permitted to meet the legal practitioner representing him during the course of interrogation of the accused person:

Provided that nothing in this sub-section shall entitle the legal practitioner to remain present throughout the period of interrogation.

Presumption as to Offences Under Section 3

52. (1) In a prosecution for an offence under sub-section (1) of section 3, if it is proved—

(a) that the arms or explosives or any other substances specified in section 4 were recovered from the possession of the accused and there is reason to believe that such arms or explosives or other substances of a similar nature, were used in the commission of such offence; or

(b) that the finger-prints of the accused were found at the site of the offence or on anything including arms and vehicles used in connection with the commission of such offence,

the Special Court shall draw adverse inference against the accused.

(2) In a prosecution for an offence under sub-section (3) of section 3, if it is proved that the accused rendered any financial assistance to a person, having knowledge that such person is accused of, or reasonably suspected of, an offence under that section, the Special Court shall draw adverse inference against the accused.

Bar of Jurisdiction of Courts, etc.

53. No civil court or other authority shall have or, be entitled to, exercise any jurisdiction, powers or authority in relation to the matters referred to in section 19 and section 39 of the Ordinance.

Saving

54. (1) Nothing in this Ordinance shall affect the jurisdiction exercisable by, or the procedure applicable to, any court or other authority under any law relating to the naval, military or air forces or other armed forces of the Union.

(2) For the removal of doubts, it is hereby declared that for the purposes of any such law as is referred to in sub-section (1), a Special Court shall be deemed to be a court of ordinary criminal justice.

Overriding Effect

55. The provisions of this Ordinance shall have effect notwithstanding anything inconsistent therewith contained in any enactment other than this Ordinance or in any instrument having effect by virtue of any enactment other than this Ordinance.

Protection of Action Taken in Good Faith

56. No suit, prosecution or other legal proceeding shall lie against the Central Government or a State Government or any officer or authority of the Central Government or State Government or any other authority on whom powers

have been conferred under this Ordinance, for anything which is in good faith done or purported to be done in pursuance of this Ordinance:

Provided further that no suit, prosecution or other legal proceedings shall lie against any serving member or retired member of the armed forces or other para-military forces in respect, of any action taken or purported to be taken by him in good faith, in the course of any operation directed towards combating terrorism.

Punishment and Compensation for Malicious Action

57. (1) Any police officer who exercises powers corruptly or maliciously, knowing that there are no reasonable grounds for proceeding under this Ordinance, shall be punishable with imprisonment which may extend to two years, or with fine, or with both.

(2) If the Special Court is of opinion that any person has been corruptly or maliciously proceeded against under this Ordinance, the court may award such compensation as it deems fit to the person, so proceeded against and it shall be paid by the officer, person, authority or Government, as may be specified in the order.

Impounding of Passport and Arms Licence of Person Charge Sheeted Under this Ordinance

58. Notwithstanding anything contained in any other law for the time being in force, the passport and the arms licence of a person, who is charge sheeted for having committed any offence under this Ordinance, shall be deemed to have been impounded for such period as the Special Court may deem fit.

Review Committees

59, (1) The Central Government and each State Government shall, whenever necessary, constitute one or more Review Committees for the purposes of this Ordinance.

(2) Every such Committee shall consist of a Chairperson and such other members not exceeding three and possessing such qualifications as may be prescribed.

(3) A Chairperson of the Committee shall be a person who is, or who has been a Judge of a High Court, who shall be appointed by the Central Government, or as the case may be, the State Government, so however, that the concurrence of the Chief Justice of the High Court shall be obtained in the case of a sitting Judge:

Provided that in the case of a Union territory, the appointment of a person who is a Judge of the High Court of a State shall be made as a Chairperson with the concurrence of the Chief Justice of the concerned High Court.

Power of High Courts to Make Rules

60. The High Courts may, by notifications in the Official Gazette, make such rules, if any, as they may deem necessary for carrying out the provisions of this Ordinance relating to Special Courts within their territories.

Power to Make Rules

61. (1) Without prejudice to the powers of the High Courts to make rules under section 60, the Central Government may, by notification in the Official Gazette, make rules for carrying out the provisions of this Ordinance.

(2) In particular, and without prejudice to the generality of the foregoing power, such rules may provide for all or any of the following matters, namely:—

(a) regulating the conduct of persons in respect of areas the control of which is considered necessary or expedient and the removal of such persons from such areas;

(b) the entry into and search of,—

(i) any vehicle, vessel or aircraft; or

(ii) any place, whatsoever,

reasonably suspected of being used for committing the offences referred to in section 3 or section 4 or for manufacturing or storing anything for the commission of any such offence;

(c) conferring powers upon,—

(i) the Central Government;

(ii) a State Government:

(iii) an Administrator of a Union territory under article 239 of the Constitution;

(iv) an officer of the Central Government not lower in rank than that of a Joint Secretary; or

(v) an officer of a State Government not lower in rank than that of a District Magistrate,

to make general or special orders to prevent or deal with terrorist acts;

(d) the arrest and trial of persons contravening any of the rules or any order made thereunder;

(e) the punishment of any person who contravenes or attempts to contravene or abets or attempts to abet the contravention of any rule or order made thereunder with imprisonment for a term which may extend to one year or fine or both.

(f) providing for the seizure and detention of any property in respect of which such contravention, attempt or abetment as is referred to in clause (e) has been committed and for the adjudication of such seizure and detention, whether by any court or by any other authority.

(g) determination of the price of the forfeited property under sub-section (2) of section 10;

(h) the procedure of making application under sub-section (3) of section 19;

(i) the qualifications of the members of the Review Committee under sub-section (2) of section 59.

Schedule
(See Section 18)
Terrorist Organisations

1. Babbar Khalsa International.
2. Khalistan Commando Force.
3. Khalistan Zindabad Force.
4. International Sikh Youth Federation.
5. Lashkar-e-Taiba/Pasban-e-Ahle Hadis.
6. Jaish-e-Mohammed/Tahrik-e-Furqan.
7. Harkat-ul-Mujahideen/Harkar-ul-Ansar/Karkat-ul-Jehad-e-Islami.
8. Hizb-ul-Mujahideen/Hizb-Ulmujahideen Pir Panjal Regiment.
9. Al-Umar-Mujahideen.
10. Jammu and Kashmir Islamic Front.
11. United Leberation Front of Assam (ULFA).
12. National Democratic Front of Bodoland (NDFB).
13. People's Liberation Army (PLA).
14. United National Liberation Front (UNLF).
15. People's Revolutionary Party of Kangleipalk (PREPAK).
16. Kanleipak Communist Party (KCP)
17. Kanglei Yaol Kanba.Lup (KYKL).
18. Manipur People's Liberation Front (MPLF).
19. All Tripura Tiger Force.
20. National Liberation Front of Tripura.

21. Liberation Tigers of Tamil Eelam (LTTE).
22. Students Islamic Movement of India.
23. Deendar Anjuman.

K.R. NARAYANAN.
President

SUBHASH C. JAIN,
Secy. to the Govt. of India,

DOCUMENT NO. 15

THE PREVENTION OF TERRORISM ACT, 2002

Act No. 15 of 2002

March 28, 2002

The Prevention of Terrorism Act, enacted on March 28, 2002, replaced the ***Prevention of Terrorism Ordinance (POTO) 2001.*** *The Act has now come into force after the President of India gave his assent.*

The Prevention of Terrorism Act, 2002
Act No. 15 of 2002

An Act to make provisions for the prevention of, and for dealing with, terrorist activities and for matters connected therewith.

BE it enacted by Parliament in the Fifty-third Year of the Republic of India as follows:—

- **Preliminary**
- **Punishment for, and measures for dealing with terrorist activities**
- **Terrorist Organisations**
- **Special Courts**
- **Interception of communication in certain cases**
- **Miscellaneous**
- **The Schedule**

Chapter I
Preliminary

1. Short title, application, commencement, duration and savings.—

(1) This Act may be called the Prevention of Terrorism Act, 2002.

(2) It extends to the whole of India.

(3) Every person shall be liable to punishment under this Act for every act or omission contrary to the provisions thereof, of which he is held guilty in India.

(4) Any person who commits an offence beyond India which is punishable under this Act shall be dealt with according to the provisions of this Act in the same manner as if such act had been committed in India.

(5) The provisions of this Act apply also to—

(a) citizens of India outside India;

(b) persons in the service of the Government, wherever they may be; and

(c) persons on ships and aircrafts, registered in India, wherever they may be.

(6) Save as otherwise provided in respect of entries at serial numbers 24 and 25 of the Schedule to this Act, it shall be deemed to have come into force on the 24th day of October, 2001 and shall remain in force for a period of three years from the date of its commencement, but its expiry under the operation of this sub-section shall not affect—

(a) the previous operation of, or anything duly done or suffered under this Act, or

(b) any right, privilege, obligation or liability acquired, accrued or incurred under this Act, or

(c) any penalty, forfeiture or punishment incurred in respect of any offence under this Act, or

(d) any investigation, legal proceeding or remedy in respect of any such right, privilege, obligation, liability, penalty, forfeiture or punishment as aforesaid,

and, any such investigation, legal proceeding or remedy may be instituted, continued or enforced and any such penalty, forfeiture or punishment may be imposed as if this Act had not expired.

2. Definitions.—

(1) In this Act, unless the context otherwise requires,—

(a) "Code" means the Code of Criminal Procedure, 1973 (2 of 1974);

(b) "Designated Authority" shall mean such officer of the Central Government not below the rank of Joint Secretary to the Government, or such officer of the State Government not below the rank of Secretary to the Government, as the case may be, as may be specified by the Central Government or, as the case may be, the State Government, by a notification published in the Official Gazette;

(c) "proceeds of terrorism" shall mean all kinds of properties which have been derived or obtained from commission of any terrorist act or have been acquired through funds traceable to a terrorist act, and shall include cash irrespective of person in whose name such proceeds are standing or in whose possession they are found;

(d) "property" means property and assets of every description, whether corporeal or incorporeal, movable or immovable, tangible or intangible and deeds and instruments evidencing title to, or interest in, such property or assets and includes bank account;

(e) "Public Prosecutor" means a Public Prosecutor or an Additional Public Prosecutor or a Special Public Prosecutor appointed under section 28 and includes any person acting under the directions of the Public Prosecutor;

(f) "Special Court" means a Special Court constituted under section 23;

(g) "terrorist act" has the meaning assigned to it in sub-section (1) of section 3, and the expression "terrorist" shall be construed accordingly;

(h) "State Government", in relation to a Union territory, means the Administrator thereof;

(i) words and expressions used but not defined in this Act and defined in the Code shall have the meanings respectively assigned to them in the Code.

(2) Any reference in this Act to any enactment or any provision thereof shall, in relation to an area in which such enactment or such provision is not in force, be construed as a reference to the corresponding law or the relevant provision of the corresponding law, if any, in force in that area.

Chapter II
Punishment for, And Measures for Dealing With, Terrorist Activities

3. Punishment for terrorist acts.—

(1) Whoever,—

(a) with intent to threaten the unity, integrity, security or sovereignty of India or to strike terror in the people or any section of the people does any act or thing by using bombs, dynamite or other explosive substances or inflammable substances or firearms or other lethal weapons or poisons or noxious gases or other chemicals or by any other substances (whether biological or otherwise) of a hazardous nature or by any other means whatsoever, in such a manner as to cause, or likely to cause, death of, or injuries to any person or persons or loss of, or damage to, or destruction of, property or disruption of any supplies or services essential to the life of the community or causes damage or destruction of any property or equipment used or intended to be used for the defense of India or in connection with any other purposes of the Government of India, any State Government or any of their agencies, or detains any person and threatens to kill or injure such person in order to compel the Government or any other person to do or abstain from doing any act;

(b) is or continues to be a member of an association declared unlawful under the Unlawful Activities (Prevention) Act, 1967 (37 of 1967), or voluntarily does an act aiding or promoting in any manner the objects of such association and in either case is in possession of any unlicensed firearms, ammunition, explosive or other instrument or substance capable of causing mass destruction and commits any act resulting in loss of human life or grievous injury to any person or causes significant damage to any property, commits a terrorist act.

Explanation.—For the purposes of this sub-section, "a terrorist act" shall include the act of raising funds intended for the purpose of terrorism.

(2) Whoever commits a terrorist act, shall,—

(a) if such act has resulted in the death of any person, be punishable with death or imprisonment for life and shall also be liable to fine;

(b) in any other case, be punishable with imprisonment for a term which shall not be less than five years but which may extend to imprisonment for life and shall also be liable to fine.

(3) Whoever conspires or attempts to commit, or advocates, abets, advises or incites or knowingly facilitates the commission of, a terrorist act or any act preparatory to a terrorist act, shall be punishable with imprisonment for a term which shall not be less than five years but which may extend to imprisonment for life and shall also be liable to fine.

(4) Whoever voluntarily harbors or conceals, or attempts to harbour or conceal any person knowing that such person is a terrorist shall be punishable with imprisonment for a term which shall not be less than three years but which may extend to imprisonment for life and shall also be liable to fine:

Provided that this sub-section shall not apply to any case in which the harbour or concealment is by the husband or wife of the offender.

(5) Any person who is a member of a terrorist gang or a terrorist organisation, which is involved in terrorist acts, shall be punishable with imprisonment for a term which may extend to imprisonment for life or with fine which may extend to rupees ten lakh or with both.

Explanation.—For the purposes of this sub-section, "terrorist organisation" means an organisation which is concerned with or involved in terrorism.

(6) Whoever knowingly holds any property derived or obtained from commission of any terrorist act or has been acquired through the terrorist funds shall be punishable with imprisonment for a term which may extend to imprisonment for life or with fine which may extend to rupees ten lakh or with both.

(7) Whoever threatens any person who is a witness or any other person in whom such witness may be interested, with violence, or wrongfully restrains or confines the witness, or any other person in whom the witness may be interested, or does any other unlawful act with the said intent, shall be punishable with imprisonment which may extend to three years and fine.

4. Possession of certain unauthorized arms, etc.—

Where any person is in unauthorised possession of any—

(a) arms or ammunition specified in columns (2) and (3) of Category I or Category III (a) of Schedule I to the Arms Rules, 1962, in a notified area,

(b) bombs, dynamite or hazardous explosive substances or other lethal weapons capable of mass destruction or biological or chemical substances of warfare in any area, whether notified or not, he shall be guilty of terrorist act notwithstanding anything contained in any other law for the time being in force, and be punishable with imprisonment for a term which may extend to imprisonment for life or with fine which may extend to rupees ten lakh or with both.

Explanation.—In this section, "notified area" means such area as the State Government may, by notification in the Official Gazette, specify.

5. Enhanced penalties.—

(1) If any person with intent to aid any terrorist contravenes any provision of, or any rule made under the Explosives Act, 1884 (4 of 1884), the Explosive Substances Act, 1908 (6 of 1908), the Inflammable Substances Act, 1952 (20 of 1952) or the Arms Act, 1959 (54 of 1959), he shall, notwithstanding anything contained in any of the aforesaid Acts or the rules made thereunder, be punishable with imprisonment for a term which may extend to imprisonment for life and shall also be liable to fine.

(2) For the purposes of this section, any person who attempts to contravene or abets, or does any act preparatory to the contravention of any provision of any law, rule or order, shall be deemed to have contravened that provision, and the provisions of sub-section (1) shall, in relation to such person, have effect subject to the modification that the reference to "imprisonment for life" shall be construed as a reference to "imprisonment for ten years".

6. Holding of proceeds of terrorism illegal.—

(1) No person shall hold or be in possession of any proceeds of terrorism.

(2) Proceeds of terrorism, whether held by a terrorist or by any other person and whether or not such person is prosecuted or convicted under this Act, shall be liable to be forfeited to the Central Government or the State Government, as the case may be, in the manner provided under this Chapter.

7. Powers of investigating officers and appeal against order of Designated Authority.—

(1) If an officer (not below the rank of Superintendent of Police) investigating an offence committed under this Act, has reason to believe that any property in relation to which an investigation is being conducted, represents proceeds of terrorism, he shall, with the prior approval in writing of the Director General of the Police of the State in which such property is situated, make an order seizing such property and where it is not practicable to seize such property, make an order of attachment directing that such property shall not be transferred or otherwise dealt with except with the prior permission of the officer making such order, or of the Designated Authority before whom the properties seized or attached are produced and a copy of such order shall be served on the person concerned.

(2) For the removal of doubts, it is hereby provided that where an organisation is declared as a terrorist organisation under this Act and the investigating officer has reason to believe that any person has custody of any property which is being used or is intended to be used for the purpose of such terrorist organisation, he may, by an order in writing, seize or attach such property.

(3) The investigating officer shall duly inform the Designated Authority within forty-eight hours of the seizure or attachment of such property.

(4) It shall be open to the Designated Authority before whom the seized or attached properties are produced either to confirm or revoke the order of attachment so issued:

Provided that an opportunity of making a representation by the person whose property is being attached shall be given.

(5) In the case of immovable property attached by the investigating officer, it shall be deemed to have been produced before the Designated Authority, when the investigating officer notifies his report and places it at the disposal of the Designated Authority.

(6) The investigating officer may seize and detain any cash to which this Chapter applies if he has reasonable grounds for suspecting that—

(a) it is intended to be used for the purposes of terrorism;

(b) it forms the whole or part of the resources of an organisation declared as terrorist organisation under this Act:

Provided that the cash seized under this sub-section by the investigating officer shall be released not later than the period of forty-eight hours beginning with the time when it is seized unless the matter involving the cash is before the Designated Authority and such Authority passes an order allowing its retention beyond forty-eight hours.

Explanation.—For the purposes of this sub-section, "cash" means—

(a) coins and notes in any currency;

(b) postal orders;

(c) traveller's cheques;

(d) banker's drafts; and

(e) such other monetary instruments as the Central Government or, as the case may be, the State Government may specify by an order made in writing.

(7) Any person aggrieved by an order made by the Designated Authority may prefer an appeal to the Special Court and the Special Court may either confirm the order of attachment of property or seizure so made or revoke such order and release the property.

8. Forfeiture of proceeds of terrorism.—

Where any property is seized or attached on the ground that it constitutes proceeds of terrorism and the Special Court is satisfied in this regard under sub-section (7) of section 7, it may order forfeiture of such property, whether or not the person from whose possession it is seized or attached, is prosecuted in a Special Court for an offence under this Act.

9. Issue of show cause notice before forfeiture of proceeds of terrorism.—

(1) No order forfeiting any proceeds of terrorism shall be made under section 8 unless the person holding or in possession of such proceeds is given a notice in writing informing him of the grounds on which it is proposed to forfeit the proceeds of terrorism and such person is given an opportunity of making a representation in writing within such reasonable time as may be specified in the notice against the grounds of forfeiture and is also given a reasonable opportunity of being heard in the matter.

(2) No order of forfeiture shall be made under sub-section (1), if such person establishes that he is a bona fide transferee of such proceeds for value without knowing that they represent proceeds of terrorism.

(3) It shall be competent for the Special Court to make an order in respect of property seized or attached,—

(a) directing it to be sold if it is a perishable property and the provisions of section 459 of the Code shall, as nearly as may be practicable, apply to the net proceeds of such sale;

(b) nominating any officer of the Central or State Government, in the case of any other property, to perform the function of the Administrator of such property subject to such conditions as may be specified by the Special Court.

10. Appeal.—

(1) Any person aggrieved by an order of forfeiture under section 8 may, within one month from the date of the receipt of such order, appeal to the High Court within whose jurisdiction, the Special Court, who passed the order appealed against, is situated.

(2) Where an order under section 8 is modified or annulled by the High Court or where in a prosecution instituted for the contravention of the provisions of this Act, the person against whom an order of forfeiture has been made under section 8 is acquitted, such property shall be returned to him and in either case if it is not possible for any reason to return the forfeited property, such person shall be paid the price therefor as if the property had been sold to the Central Government with reasonable interest calculated from the day of seizure of the property and such price shall be determined in the manner prescribed.

11. Order of forfeiture not to interfere with other punishments.—

The order of forfeiture made under this Act by the Special Court, shall not prevent the infliction of any other punishment to which the person affected thereby is liable under this Act.

12. Claims by third party.—

(1) Where any claim is preferred, or any objection is made to the seizure of any property under section 7 on the ground that such property is not liable to seizure, the Designated Authority before whom such property is produced, shall proceed to investigate the claim or objection:

Provided that no such investigation shall be made where the Designated Authority considers that the claim or objection is designed to cause unnecessary delay.

(2) In case claimant or objector establishes that the property specified in the notice issued under section 9 is not liable to be forfeited under the Act, the said notice shall be withdrawn or modified accordingly.

13. Powers of Designated Authority.—

The Designated Authority, acting under the provisions of this Act, shall have all the powers of a civil court required for making a full and fair enquiry into the matter before it.

14. Obligation to furnish information.—

(1) Notwithstanding anything contained in any other law, the officer investigating any offence under this Act, with prior approval in writing of an officer not below the rank of a Superintendent of Police, may require any officer or authority of the Central Government or a State Government or a local authority or a bank, or a company, or a firm or any other institution, establishment, organisation or any individual to furnish information in their possession in relation to such offence, on points or matters, where the investigating officer has reason to believe that such information will be useful for, or relevant to, the purposes of this Act.

(2) Failure to furnish the information called for under sub-section (1), or deliberately furnishing false information shall be punishable with imprisonment for a term which may extend to three years or with fine or with both.

(3) Notwithstanding anything contained in the Code, the offence under sub-section (1) shall be tried as a summary case and the procedure prescribed in Chapter XXI of the said Code [except sub-section (2) of section 262] shall be applicable thereto.

15. Certain transfers to be null and void.—

Where, after the issue of an order under section 7 or issue of a notice under section 9, any property referred to in the said order or notice is transferred by any mode whatsoever, such transfer shall, for the purpose of the proceedings under this Act, be ignored and if such property is subsequently forfeited, the transfer of such property shall be deemed to be null and void.

16. Forfeiture of property of certain persons.—

(1) Where any person is accused of any offence under this Act, it shall be open to the Special Court trying him to pass an order that all or any of the properties, movable or immovable or both belonging to him, shall, during the period of such trial, be attached, if not already attached under this Act.

(2) Where a person has been convicted of any offence punishable under this Act, the Special Court may, in addition to awarding any punishment, by order in writing, declare that any property, movable or immovable or both, belonging to the accused and specified in the order, shall stand forfeited to the Central Government or the State Government, as the case may be, free from all encumbrances.

17. Company to transfer shares to Government.—

Where any shares in a company stand forfeited to the Central Government or the State Government, as the case may be, under this Act, then, the company shall, on receipt of the order of the Special Court, notwithstanding anything contained in the Companies Act, 1956 (1 of 1956), or the articles of association of the company, forthwith register the Central Government or the State Government, as the case may be, as the transferee of such shares.

Chapter III
Terrorist Organisations

18. Declaration of an organization as a terrorist organization.—

(1) For the purposes of this Act, an organisation is a terrorist organisation if—

(a) it is listed in the Schedule, or

(b) it operates under the same name as an organisation listed in that Schedule.

(2) The Central Government may by order, in the Official Gazette,—

(a) add an organisation to the Schedule;

(b) remove an organisation from that Schedule;

(c) amend that Schedule in some other way.

(3) The Central Government may exercise its power under clause (a) of sub-section (2) in respect of an organisation only if it believes that it is involved in terrorism.

(4) For the purposes of sub-section (3), an organisation shall be deemed to be involved in terrorism if it—

(a) commits or participates in acts of terrorism,

(b) prepares for terrorism,

(c) promotes or encourages terrorism, or

(d) is otherwise involved in terrorism.

19. Denotification of a terrorist organization.—

(1) An application may be made to the Central Government for the exercise of its power under clause (b) of sub-section (2) of section 18 to remove an organisation from the Schedule.

(2) An application may be made by—

(a) the organisation, or

(b) any person affected by inclusion of the organisation in the Schedule as a terrorist organisation.

(3) The Central Government may make rules to prescribe the procedure for admission and disposal of an application made under this section.

(4) Where an application under sub-section (1) has been refused, the applicant may apply for a review to the Review Committee constituted by the Central Government under sub-section (1) of section 60 within one month from the date of receipt of the order by the applicant.

(5) The Review Committee may allow an application for review against refusal to remove an organisation from the Schedule, if it considers that the decision to refuse was flawed when considered in the light of the principles applicable on an application for judicial review.

(6) Where the Review Committee allows review under sub-section (5) by or in respect of an organisation, it may make an order under this sub-section.

(7) Where an order is made under sub-section (6), the Central Government shall, as soon as the certified copy of the order is received by it, make an order removing the organisation from the list in the Schedule.

20. Offence relating to membership of a terrorist organization.—

(1) A person commits an offence if he belongs or professes to belong to a terrorist organisation:

Provided that this sub-section shall not apply where the person charged is able to prove—

(a) that the organisation was not declared as a terrorist organisation at the time when he became a member or began to profess to be a member; and

(b) that he has not taken part in the activities of the organisation at any time during its inclusion in the Schedule as a terrorist organisation.

(2) A person guilty of an offence under this section shall be liable, on conviction, to imprisonment for a term not exceeding ten years or with fine or with both.

21. Offence relating to support given to a terrorist organization.—

(1) A person commits an offence if—

(a) he invites support for a terrorist organisation, and

(b) the support is not, or is not restricted to, the provision of money or other property within the meaning of section 22.

(2) A person commits an offence if he arranges, manages or assists in arranging or managing a meeting which he knows is—

(a) to support a terrorist organisation, or

(b) to further the activities of a terrorist organisation, or

(c) to be addressed by a person who belongs or professes to belong to a terrorist organisation.

(3) A person commits an offence if he addresses a meeting for the purpose of encouraging support for a terrorist organisation or to further its activities.

(4) A person guilty of an offence under this section shall be liable on conviction, to imprisonment for a term not exceeding ten years or with fine or with both.

Explanation.—For the purposes of this section, the expression "meeting" means a meeting of three or more persons whether or not the public are admitted.

22. Fund raising for a terrorist organization to be an offence.—

(1) A person commits an offence if he—

(a) invites another to provide money or other property, and

(b) intends that it should be used, or has reasonable cause to suspect that it may be used, for the purposes of terrorism.

(2) A person commits an offence if he—

(a) receives money or other property, and

(b) intends that it should be used, or has reasonable cause to suspect that it may be used, for the purposes of terrorism.

(3) A person commits an offence if he—

(a) provides money or other property, and

(b) knows or has reasonable cause to suspect that it will or may be used for the purposes of terrorism.

(4) In this section, a reference to the provision of money or other property is a reference to its being given, lent or otherwise made available, whether or not for consideration.

(5) A person guilty of an offence under this section shall be liable on conviction, to imprisonment for a term not exceeding fourteen years or with fine or with both.

Chapter IV
Special Courts

23. Special Courts.—

(1) The Central Government or a State Government may, by notification in the Official Gazette, constitute one or more Special Courts for such area or areas, or for such case or class or group of cases, as may be specified in the notification.

(2) Where a notification constituting a Special Court for any area or areas or for any case or class or group of cases is issued by the Central Government under sub-section (1), and a notification constituting a Special Court for the same area or areas or for the same case or class or group of cases has also been issued by the State Government under that sub-section, the Special Court constituted by the Central Government, whether the notification constituting such Court is issued before or after the issue of the notification constituting the Special Court by the State Government, shall have, and the Special Court constituted by the State Government shall not have, jurisdiction to try any offence committed in that area or areas or, as the case may be, the case or class or group of cases and all cases pending before any Special Court constituted by the State Government shall stand transferred to the Special Court constituted by the Central Government.

(3) Where any question arises as to the jurisdiction of any Special Court, it shall be referred to the Central Government whose decision in the matter shall be final.

(4) A Special Court shall be presided over by a judge to be appointed by the Central Government or, as the case may be, the State Government, with the concurrence of the Chief Justice of the High Court.

(5) The Central Government or, as the case may be, the State Government may also appoint, with the concurrence of the Chief Justice of the High Court, additional judges to exercise jurisdiction of a Special Court.

(6) A person shall not be qualified for appointment as a judge or an additional judge of a Special Court unless he is, immediately before such appointment, a sessions judge or an additional sessions judge in any State.

(7) For the removal of doubts, it is hereby provided that the attainment, by a person appointed as a judge or an additional judge of a Special Court, of the age of superannuation under the rules applicable to him in the service to which he belongs, shall not affect his continuance as such judge or additional judge.

(8) Where any additional judge or additional judges is or are appointed in a Special Court, the judge of the Special Court may, from time to time, by general or special order, in writing, provide for the distribution of business of the Special Court among all judges including himself and the additional judge or additional judges and also for the disposal of urgent business in the event of his absence or the absence of any additional judge.

24. Place of sitting.—

A Special Court may, on its own motion, or on an application made by the Public Prosecutor and if it considers it expedient or desirable so to do, sit for any of its proceedings at any place other than its ordinary place of sitting:

Provided that nothing in this section shall be construed to change the place of sitting of a Special Court constituted by a State Government to any place outside that State.

25. Jurisdiction of Special Courts.—

(1) Notwithstanding anything contained in the Code, every offence punishable under any provision of this Act shall be triable only by the Special Court within whose local jurisdiction it was committed or, as the case may be, by the Special Court constituted for trying such offence under section 23.

(2) If, having regard to the exigencies of the situation prevailing in a State,—

(a) it is not possible to have a fair, impartial or speedy trial; or

(b) it is not feasible to have the trial without occasioning the breach of peace or grave risk to the safety of the accused, the witnesses, the Public Prosecutor and a judge of the Special Court or any of them; or

(c) it is not otherwise in the interests of justice,

the Supreme Court may transfer any case pending before a Special Court to any other Special Court within that State or in any other State and the High Court may transfer any case pending before a Special Court situated in that State to any other Special Court within the State.

(3) The Supreme Court or the High Court, as the case may be, may act under this section either on the application of the Central Government or a party interested and any such application shall be made by motion, which shall, except when the applicant is the Attorney-General of India, be supported by an affidavit or affirmation.

26. Power of Special Courts with respect to other offences.—

(1) When trying any offence, a Special Court may also try any other offence with which the accused may, under the Code, be charged at the same trial if the offence is connected with such other offence.

(2) If, in the course of any trial under this Act of any offence, it is found that the accused person has committed any other offence under this Act or under any other law, the Special Court may convict such person of such other offence and pass any sentence or award punishment authorised by this Act or such rule or, as the case may be, under such other law.

27. Power to direct for samples, etc.—

(1) When a police officer investigating a case requests the Court of a Chief Judicial Magistrate or the Court of a Chief Metropolitan Magistrate in writing for obtaining samples of handwriting, finger-prints, foot-prints, photographs, blood, saliva, semen, hair, voice of any accused person, reasonably suspected to be involved in the commission of an offence under this Act, it shall be lawful for the Court of a Chief Judicial Magistrate or the Court of a Chief Metropolitan Magistrate to direct that such samples be given by the accused person to the police officer either through a medical practitioner or otherwise, as the case may be.

(2) If any accused person refuses to give samples as provided in sub-section (1), the Court shall draw adverse inference against the accused.

28. Public Prosecutors.—

(1) For every Special Court, the Central Government or, as the case may be, the State Government, shall appoint a person to be the Public Prosecutor and may appoint one or more persons to be the Additional Public Prosecutor or Additional Public Prosecutors:

Provided that the Central Government or, as the case may be, the State Government, may also appoint for any case or class or group of cases, a Special Public Prosecutor.

(2) A person shall not be qualified to be appointed as a Public Prosecutor or an Additional Public Prosecutor or a Special Public Prosecutor under this section unless he has been in practice as an Advocate for not less than seven years or has held any post, for a period of not less than seven years, under the Union or a State, requiring special knowledge of law.

(3) Every person appointed as a Public Prosecutor or an Additional Public Prosecutor or a Special Public Prosecutor under this section shall be deemed to be a Public Prosecutor within the meaning of clause (u) of section 2 of the Code, and the provisions of the Code shall have effect accordingly.

29. Procedure and powers of Special Courts.—

(1) Subject to the provisions of section 50, a Special Court may take cognizance of any offence, without the accused being committed to it for trial, upon receiving a complaint of facts that constitute such offence or upon a police report of such facts.

(2) Where an offence triable by a Special Court is punishable with imprisonment for a term not exceeding three years or with fine or with both, the Special Court may, notwithstanding anything contained in sub-section (1) of section 260 or section 262 of the Code, try the offence in a summary way in accordance with the procedure prescribed in the Code and the provisions of sections 263 to 265 of the Code, shall so far as may be, apply to such trial:

Provided that when, in the course of a summary trial under this sub-section, it appears to the Special Court that the nature of the case is such that it is undesirable to try it in a summary way, the Special Court shall recall any witnesses who may have been examined and proceed to re-hear the case in the manner provided by the provisions of the Code for the trial of such offence and the said provisions shall apply to and in relation to a Special Court as they apply to and in relation to a Magistrate:

Provided further that in the case of any conviction in a summary trial under this section, it shall be lawful for a Special Court to pass a sentence of imprisonment for a term not exceeding one year and with fine which may extend to rupees five lakh.

(3) Subject to the other provisions of this Act, a Special Court shall, for the purpose of trial of any offence, have all the powers of a Court of Session and shall try such offence as if it were a Court of Session so far as may be in accordance with the procedure prescribed in the Code for the trial before a Court of Session.

(4) Subject to the other provisions of this Act, every case transferred to a Special Court under section 25 shall be dealt with as if such case had been transferred under section 406 of the Code to such Special Court.

(5) Notwithstanding anything contained in the Code, but subject to the provisions of section 299 of the Code, a Special Court may, if it thinks fit and for reasons to be recorded by it, proceed with the trial in the absence of the accused or his pleader and record the evidence of any witness, subject to the right of the accused to recall the witness for cross-examination.

30. Protection of witnesses.—

(1) Notwithstanding anything contained in the Code, the proceedings under this Act may, for reasons to be recorded in writing, be held in camera if the Special Court so desires.

(2) A Special Court, if on an application made by a witness in any proceeding before it or by the Public Prosecutor in relation to such witness or on its own motion, is satisfied that the life of such witness is in danger, it may, for reasons to be recorded in writing, take such measures as it deems fit for keeping the identity and address of such witness secret.

(3) In particular, and without prejudice to the generality of the provisions of sub-section (2), the measures which a Special Court may take under that sub-section may include—

(a) the holding of the proceedings at a place to be decided by the Special Court;

(b) the avoiding of the mention of the names and addresses of the witnesses in its orders or judgments or in any records of the case accessible to public;

(c) the issuing of any directions for securing that the identity and address of the witnesses are not disclosed;

(d) a decision that it is in the public interest to order that all or any of the proceedings pending before such a Court shall not be published in any manner.

(4) Any person who contravenes any decision or direction issued under sub-section (3) shall be punishable with imprisonment for a term which may extend to one year and with fine which may extend to one thousand rupees.

31. Trial by Special Courts to have precedence.—

The trial under this Act of any offence by a Special Court shall have precedence over the trial of any other case against the accused in any other court (not being a Special Court) and shall be concluded in preference to the trial of such other case and accordingly the trial of such other case shall remain in abeyance.

32. Certain confessions made to police officers to be taken into consideration.—

(1) Notwithstanding anything in the Code or in the Indian Evidence Act, 1872 (1 of 1872), but subject to the provisions of this section, a confession made by a person before a police officer not lower in rank than a Superintendent of Police and recorded by such police officer either in writing or on any mechanical or electronic device like cassettes, tapes or sound tracks from out of which sound or images can be reproduced, shall be admissible in the trial of such person for an offence under this Act or the rules made thereunder.

(2) A police officer shall, before recording any confession made by a person under sub-section (1), explain to such person in writing that he is not bound to make a confession and that if he does so, it may be used against him:

Provided that where such person prefers to remain silent, the police officer shall not compel or induce him to make any confession.

(3) The confession shall be recorded in an atmosphere free from threat or inducement and shall be in the same language in which the person makes it.

(4) The person from whom a confession has been recorded under sub-section (1), shall be produced before the Court of a Chief Metropolitan Magistrate or the Court of a Chief Judicial Magistrate along with the original statement of confession, written or recorded on mechanical or electronic device within forty-eight hours.

(5) The Chief Metropolitan Magistrate or the Chief Judicial Magistrate, shall, record the statement, if any, made by the person so produced and get his signature or thumb impression and if there is any complaint of torture, such person shall be directed to be produced for medical examination before a Medical Officer not lower in rank than an Assistant Civil Surgeon and thereafter, he shall be sent to judicial custody.

33. Power to transfer cases to regular courts.—

Where, after taking cognizance of any offence, a Special Court is of the opinion that the offence is not triable by it, it shall, notwithstanding that it has no jurisdiction to try such offence, transfer the case for the trial of such offence to any court having jurisdiction under the Code and the Court to which the case is transferred may proceed with the trial of the offence as if it had taken cognizance of the offence.

34. Appeal.—

(1) Notwithstanding anything contained in the Code, an appeal shall lie from any judgment, sentence or order, not being an interlocutory order, of a Special Court to the High Court both on facts and on law.

Explanation.—For the purposes of this section, "High Court" means a High Court within whose jurisdiction, a Special Court which passed the judgment, sentence or order, is situated.

(2) Every appeal under sub-section (1) shall be heard by a bench of two Judges of the High Court.

(3) Except as aforesaid, no appeal or revision shall lie to any court from any judgment, sentence or order including an interlocutory order of a Special Court.

(4) Notwithstanding anything contained in sub-section (3) of section 378 of the Code, an appeal shall lie to the High Court against an order of the Special Court granting or refusing bail.

(5) Every appeal under this section shall be preferred within a period of thirty days from the date of the judgment, sentence or order appealed from:

Provided that the High Court may entertain an appeal after the expiry of the said period of thirty days if it is satisfied that the appellant had sufficient cause for not preferring the appeal within the period of thirty days.

35. Transitional provisions and transfer of pending proceedings.—

(1) The jurisdiction conferred by this Act on a Special Court, shall, until a Special Court is constituted under section 23, in the case of any offence punishable under this Act, notwithstanding anything contained in the Code, be exercised by the Court of Session of the division in which such offence has been committed and it shall have all the powers and follow the procedure provided under this Chapter.

(2) On and from the date when the Special Court is constituted under section 23, every trial under the provisions of this Act, which would have been required to be held before the Special Court, shall stand transferred to that Court on the date on which it is constituted.

Chapter V
Interception of Communication in Certain Cases

36. Definitions.—

In this Chapter, unless the context otherwise requires,—

(a) "electronic communication" means any transmission of signs, signals, writings, images, sounds, data or intelligence of any nature transmitted in whole or in part by a wire, radio, electromagnetic, photo electronic or photo optical system that affects inland or foreign commerce but does not include—

(i) the radio portion of a cordless telephone communication that is transmitted between the wireless telephone hand-set and the base unit; or

(ii) any wire or oral communication; or

(iii) any communication made through a tone only paging device; or

(iv) any communication from a tracking device;

(b) "intercept" means the aural or other acquisition of the contents by wire, electronic or oral communication through the use of any electronic, mechanical or other device;

(c) "oral communication" means any oral communication uttered by a person exhibiting an expectation that such communication is not subject to interception under circumstances justifying such expectation but such term does not include any electronic communication;

(d) "wire communication" means any aural transmission made in whole or part through the use of facilities for the transmission of communications by the aid of wire, cable or other like connection between the point of origin and the point of connection, between the point of origin and the point of reception (including the use of such connection in switching station) and such term includes any electronic storage of such communication.

37. Appointment of Competent Authority.—

The Central Government or the State Government, as the case may be, may appoint an officer not below the rank of Secretary to the Government in the case of State Government and not below the rank of Joint Secretary to the Government in the case of Central Government, to be the Competent Authority for the purposes of this Chapter.

38. Application for authorization of interception of wire, electronic or oral communication.—

(1) A police officer not below the rank of Superintendent of Police supervising the investigation of any terrorist act under this Act may submit an application in writing to the Competent Authority for an order authorising or approving the interception of wire, electronic or oral communication by the investigating officer when he believes that such interception may provide, or has provided evidence of any offence involving a terrorist act.

(2) Each application shall include the following information:—

(a) the identity of the investigating officer making the application, and the head of the department authorising the application;

(b) a statement of the facts and circumstances relied upon by the applicant to justify his belief that an order should be issued, including—

(i) details as to the offence of terrorist act that has been, is being, or is about to be committed;

(ii) a particular description of the nature and location of the facilities from which or the place where the communication is to be intercepted;

(iii) a particular description of the type of communications sought to be intercepted; and

(iv) the identity of the person, if known, committing the terrorist act whose communications are to be intercepted;

(c) a statement of the period of time for which the interception is required to be maintained, if the nature of the enquiry is such that the authorisation of interception should not automatically terminate after the described type of communication has been first obtained;

(d) a particular description of facts establishing probable cause to believe that additional communications of the same type will occur thereafter; and

(e) where the application is for the extension of an order, a statement setting forth the results thus far obtained from the interception, or a reasonable explanation of the failure to obtain such results.

(3) The Competent Authority may require the applicant to furnish additional oral or documentary evidence in support of the application.

39. Decision by Competent Authority on application for interception

(1) Upon such application, the Competent Authority may reject the application, or issue an order, as requested or as modified, authorising or approving interception of wire, electronic or oral communications, if the Competent Authority determines on the basis of the facts submitted by the applicant that—

(a) there is a probable cause for belief that an individual is committing, has committed, or is about to commit, a particular offence described and made punishable under sections 3 and 4 of this Act;

(b) there is a probable cause of belief that particular communications concerning that offence may be obtained through such interception;

(c) there is probable cause of belief that the facilities from which, or the place where, the wire, electronic or oral communications are to be intercepted are being used or are about to be used, in connection with the commission of such offence, leased to, or are listed in, the name of or commonly used by such person.

(2) Each order by the Competent Authority authorising or approving the interception of any wire, electronic or oral communication under this section shall specify—

(a) the identity of the person, if known, whose communications are to be intercepted;

(b) the nature and location of the communication facilities as to which, or the place where, authority to intercept is granted;

(c) a particular description of the type of communication sought to be intercepted, and a statement of the particular offence to which it relates;

(d) the identity of the agency authorised to intercept the communications, and the person authorising the application; and

(e) the period of time during which such interception is authorised, including a statement as to whether or not the interception shall automatically terminate after the described communication has been first obtained.

40. Submission of order of interception to Review Committee.

(1) The Competent Authority shall, immediately after passing the order under sub-section (1) of section 39, but in any case not later than seven days from the passing of the order, submit a copy of the same to the Review Committee constituted under section 60 alongwith all the relevant underlying papers, record and his own findings, in respect of the said order, for consideration and approval of the order by the Review Committee.

(2) An order authorising the interception of a wire, electronic or oral communication under this section shall, upon request of the applicant, direct that a provider of wire or electronic communication service, landlord, custodian or other person shall furnish to the applicant forthwith all information, facilities and technical assistance necessary to accomplish the interception unobtrusively and with a minimum of interference with the services that such service provider, landlord, custodian or person is providing to the person whose communications are to be intercepted.

41. Duration of an order of inception, etc.

(1) No order issued under this section may authorise or approve the interception of any wire, electronic or oral communication for any period longer than is necessary to achieve the objective of the authorisation, nor in any event longer than sixty days and such sixty days period shall begin on the day immediately preceding the day on which the investigating officer first begins to conduct an interception under the order or ten days after order is issued whichever is earlier.

(2) The extension of an order may be granted, but only upon an application for an extension made in accordance with sub-section (1) of section 38 and the Competent Authority making the findings required by sub-section (1) of section 39, and the period of such extension shall be no longer than the Competent Authority deems necessary to achieve the purposes for which it was granted and in no event for longer than sixty days at a time.

(3) Every order and extension thereof shall contain a provision that the authorisation to intercept shall be executed as soon as practicable and shall be conducted in such manner as to minimise the interception of communications not otherwise subject to interception under this section and shall terminate upon attainment of the authorised objective, or in any event on the expiry of the period of said order or extension thereof.

42. Authority competent to carry out interception.

(1) An interception under this Chapter may be conducted in whole or in part by a public servant, acting under the supervision of the investigating officer authorised to conduct the interception.

(2) Whenever an order authorising an interception is issued pursuant to this section, the order may require reports to be made to the Competent Authority who issued the order showing that progress has been made towards achievement of the authorised objective and the need for continued interception and such report shall be made at such intervals as the Competent Authority may require.

43. Interception of communication in emergency.

(1) Notwithstanding anything contained in any other provision of this Chapter, an officer not below the rank of Additional Director General of Police or a police officer of equivalent rank who reasonably determines that—

(a) an emergency situation exists that involves—

(i) immediate danger of death or serious physical injury to any person; or

(ii) conspiratorial activities threatening the security or interest of the State; or

(iii) conspiratorial activities, characteristic of a terrorist act, that requires a wire, electronic or oral communication to be intercepted before an order from the Competent Authority authorising such interception can, with due diligence, be obtained; and

(b) there are grounds on which an order should be issued under this section to authorise such interception,

may authorise, in writing, the investigating officer to intercept such wire, electronic or oral communication, if an application for an order approving the interception is made in accordance with the provisions of sub-sections (1) and (2) of section 38 within forty-eight hours after the interception has occurred, or begins to occur.

(2) In the absence of an order approving the interception made under sub-section (1), such interception shall immediately terminate when the communication sought is obtained or when the application for the order is rejected, whichever is earlier; and in the event of an application for permitting interception being rejected under sub-section (1) of section 39 or an application under sub-section (1) of this section for approval being rejected, or in any other case where the interception is terminated without an order having been issued, the contents of any wire, electronic or oral communication intercepted shall be treated as having been obtained in violation of this section.

44. Protection of information collected.

(1) The contents of any wire, electronic or oral communication intercepted by any means authorised by this Chapter shall, as far as possible, be

recorded on tape or wire or other comparable device and shall be done in such manner as to protect the recording from editing or other alterations.

(2) Immediately upon the expiration of the period of order, or extension thereof, such recording shall be made available to the Competent Authority issuing such order and shall be sealed under his directions and kept in the custody of such person or authority as the Competent Authority orders, and such recordings shall not be destroyed except upon an order of the Competent Authority and in any event shall be kept for ten years.

(3) Applications made and orders issued under this Chapter shall be sealed by the Competent Authority and custody of the applications and orders shall be kept in such manner as the Competent Authority directs, and shall not be destroyed except on an order of the Competent Authority, and in any event shall be kept for ten years.

45. Admissibility of evidence collected through the interception of communications.

Notwithstanding anything in the Code or in any other law for the time being in force, the evidence collected through the interception of wire, electronic or oral communication under this Chapter shall be admissible as evidence against the accused in the Court during the trial of a case:

Provided that, the contents of any wire, electronic or oral communication intercepted pursuant to this Chapter or evidence derived therefrom shall not be received in evidence or otherwise disclosed in any trial, hearing or other proceeding in any court unless each accused has been furnished with a copy of the order of the Competent Authority, and accompanying application, under which the interception was authorised or approved not less than ten days before trial, hearing or proceeding:

Provided further that, the period of ten days may be waived by the judge trying the matter, if he comes to the conclusion that it was not possible to furnish the accused with the above information ten days before the trial, hearing or proceeding and that the accused will not be prejudiced by the delay in receiving such information.

46. Review of authorization order.

(1) The Review Committee constituted by the Central Government or the State Government, as the case may be, shall review every order passed by the Competent Authority under section 39.

(2) Every order passed by the Competent Authority under section 39, or disapproved by the officer under section 43, shall be placed before the Review Committee, which shall be considered by the Review Committee

within ten days after its receipt, to decide whether the order was necessary, reasonable and justified.

(3) The Review Committee, after examining the entire record and holding such enquiry, if any, deemed necessary may, by order in writing, either approve the order passed by the Competent Authority or may issue order disapproving the same.

(4) On issue of an order of disapproval by the Review Committee, the interception, if any, already commenced shall be forthwith discontinued and the intercepted communication, if any, in the form of tape, wire or other device shall, thereupon, not be admissible as evidence in any case and shall be directed to be destroyed.

47. Interception and disclosure of wire, electronic or oral communications prohibited.

Except as otherwise specifically provided in section 39, any police officer who—

(a) intentionally intercepts, endeavours to intercept, or procures any other person to intercept or endeavour to intercept any wire, electronic or oral communication;

(b) intentionally uses, endeavours to use, or procures any other person to use or endeavours to use any electronic, mechanical or other device to intercept any oral communication when—

(i) such device is affixed to, or otherwise transmits a signal through a wire, cable, or other like connection used in wire communication; or

(ii) such device transmits communications by radio, or interferes with the transmission of such communication;

(c) intentionally discloses, or endeavours to disclose, to any other person the contents of any wire, electronic or oral communication, knowing or having reason to know that the information was obtained through the interception of a wire, electronic or oral communication in violation of this Chapter;

(d) intentionally uses, or endeavours to use, the contents of any wire, electronic or oral communication, knowing or having reason to know that the information was obtained through the interception of a wire, electronic or oral communication in violation of this Chapter;

(e) intentionally discloses, or endeavours to disclose, to any other unauthorised person the contents of any wire, electronic or oral communication, intercepted by means authorised by section 39;

(f) intentionally continues the interception of wire, electronic or oral communication after the issue of an order of rejection by the Competent Authority under this Chapter;

(g) intentionally continues the interception of wire, electronic or oral communication after the issue of an order of disapproval by the Review Committee under sub-section (3) of section 46,

shall for such violation be punishable with imprisonment for a term which may extend to one year and with fine up to rupees fifty thousand.

48. Annual report of interceptions.

(1) The Central Government and the State Government, as the case may be, shall cause an annual report to be prepared giving a full account of—

(a) the number of applications for authorisation of interceptions received by the Competent Authority from the Police Department in which prosecutions have been launched;

(b) the number of such applications permitted or rejected;

(c) the number of interceptions carried out in emergency situations and the number of approvals granted or rejected in such matters;

(d) the number of prosecutions launched based on such interceptions and convictions resulting from such interceptions, along with an explanatory memorandum giving general assessment of the utility and importance of the interceptions authorised.

(2) An annual report shall be laid by the State Government before the State Legislature within three months of the completion of every calendar year:

Provided that, if the State Government is of the opinion that the inclusion of any matter in the annual report would be prejudicial to the security of the State or to the prevention or detection of any terrorist act, the State Government may exclude such matter from being included in such annual report.

(3) An annual report shall be laid by the Central Government before each House of Parliament within three months of the completion of every calendar year:

Provided that, if the Central Government is of the opinion that the inclusion of any matter in the annual report would be prejudicial to the security of the country or to the prevention or detection of any terrorist act, the Central Government may exclude such matter from being included in such annual report.

Chapter VI
Miscellaneous

49. Modified application of certain provisions of the Code.

(1) Notwithstanding anything contained in the Code or any other law, every offence punishable under this Act shall be deemed to be a cognizable offence within the meaning of clause (c) of section 2 of the Code, and "cognizable case" as defined in that clause shall be construed accordingly.

(2) Section 167 of the Code shall apply in relation to a case involving an offence punishable under this Act subject to the modification that in sub-section (2),—

(a) the references to "fifteen days", "ninety days" and "sixty days", wherever they occur, shall be construed as references to "thirty days", "ninety days" and "ninety days", respectively; and

(b) after the proviso, the following provisos shall be inserted, namely:—

"Provided further that if it is not possible to complete the investigation within the said period of ninety days, the Special Court shall extend the said period up to one hundred and eighty days, on the report of the Public Prosecutor indicating the progress of the investigation and the specific reasons for the detention of the accused beyond the said period of ninety days:

Provided also that if the police officer making the investigation under this Act, requests, for the purposes of investigation, for police custody from judicial custody of any person from judicial custody, he shall file an affidavit stating the reasons for doing so and shall also explain the delay, if any, for requesting such police custody.".

(3) Section 268 of the Code shall apply in relation to a case involving an offence punishable under this Act subject to the modification that—

(a) the reference in sub-section (1) thereof—

(i) to "the State Government" shall be construed as a reference to "the Central Government or the State Government",

(ii) to "order of the State Government" shall be construed as a reference to "order of the Central Government or the State Government, as the case may be"; and

(b) the reference in sub-section (2) thereof, to "the State Government" shall be construed as a reference to "the Central Government or the State Government, as the case may be".

(4) Sections 366, 367 and 371 of the Code shall apply in relation to a case involving an offence triable by a Special Court subject to the modification

that the reference to "Court of Session", wherever occurring therein, shall be construed as the reference to "Special Court".

(5) Nothing in section 438 of the Code shall apply in relation to any case involving the arrest of any person accused of having committed an offence punishable under this Act.

(6) Notwithstanding anything contained in the Code, no person accused of an offence punishable under this Act shall, if in custody, be released on bail or on his own bond unless the Court gives the Public Prosecutor an opportunity of being heard.

(7) Where the Public Prosecutor opposes the application of the accused to release on bail, no person accused of an offence punishable under this Act or any rule made thereunder shall be released on bail until the Court is satisfied that there are grounds for believing that he is not guilty of committing such offence:

Provided that after the expiry of a period of one year from the date of detention of the accused for an offence under this Act, the provisions of sub-section (6) of this section shall apply.

(8) The restrictions on granting of bail specified in sub-sections (6) and (7) are in addition to the restrictions under the Code or any other law for the time being in force on granting of bail.

(9) Notwithstanding anything contained in sub-sections (6), (7) and (8), no bail shall be granted to a person accused of an offence punishable under this Act, if he is not an Indian citizen and has entered the country unauthorisedly or illegally except in very exceptional circumstances and for reasons to be recorded in writing.

50. Cognizance of offences.

No court shall take cognizance of any offence under this Act without the previous sanction of the Central Government or, as the case may be, the State Government.

51. Officers competent to investigate offences under this Act.

Notwithstanding anything contained in the Code, no police officer,—

(a) in the case of the Delhi Special Police Establishment, below the rank of a Deputy Superintendent of Police or a police officer of equivalent rank;

(b) in the metropolitan areas of Mumbai, Kolkata, Chennai and Ahmedabad and any other metropolitan area notified as such under sub-section (1) of section 8 of the Code, below the rank of an Assistant Commissioner of Police;

(c) in any other case not relatable to clause (a) or clause (b), below the rank of a Deputy Superintendent of Police or a police officer of an equivalent rank,

shall investigate any offence punishable under this Act.

52. Arrest.

(1) Where a police officer arrests a person, he shall prepare a custody memo of the person arrested.

(2) The person arrested shall be informed of his right to consult a legal practitioner as soon as he is brought to the police station.

(3) Whenever any person is arrested, information of his arrest shall be immediately communicated by the police officer to a family member or in his absence to a relative of such person by telegram, telephone or by any other means and this fact shall be recorded by the police officer under the signature of the person arrested.

(4) The person arrested shall be permitted to meet the legal practitioner representing him during the course of interrogation of the accused person:

Provided that nothing in this sub-section shall entitle the legal practitioner to remain present throughout the period of interrogation.

53. Presumption as to offences under section 3.

(1) In a prosecution for an offence under sub-section (1) of section 3, if it is proved—

(a) that the arms or explosives or any other substances specified in section 4 were recovered from the possession of the accused and there is reason to believe that such arms or explosives or other substances of a similar nature, were used in the commission of such offence; or

(b) that the finger-prints of the accused were found at the site of the offence or on anything including arms and vehicles used in connection with the commission of such offence,

the Special Court shall draw adverse inference against the accused.

(2) In a prosecution for an offence under sub-section (3) of section 3, if it is proved that the accused rendered any financial assistance to a person, having knowledge that such person is accused of, or reasonably suspected of, an offence under that section, the Special Court shall draw adverse inference against the accused.

54. Bar of jurisdiction of courts, etc.

No civil court or other authority shall have or, be entitled to, exercise any jurisdiction, powers or authority in relation to the matters referred to in sections 19 and 40 of the Act.

55. Saving.

(1) Nothing in this Act shall affect the jurisdiction exercisable by, or the procedure applicable to, any court or other authority under any law relating to the naval, military or air forces or other armed forces of the Union.

(2) For the removal of doubts, it is hereby declared that for the purposes of any such law as is referred to in sub-section (1), a Special Court shall be deemed to be a court of ordinary criminal justice.

56. Overriding effect.

The provisions of this Act shall have effect notwithstanding anything inconsistent therewith contained in any enactment other than this Act or in any instrument having effect by virtue of any enactment other than this Act.

57. Protection of action taken in good faith.

No suit, prosecution or other legal proceeding shall lie against the Central Government or a State Government or any officer or authority of the Central Government or State Government or any other authority on whom powers have been conferred under this Act, for anything which is in good faith done or purported to be done in pursuance of this Act:

Provided that no suit, prosecution or other legal proceedings shall lie against any serving member or retired member of the armed forces or other para-military forces in respect of any action taken or purported to be taken by him in good faith, in the course of any operation directed towards combating terrorism.

58. Punishment and compensation for malicious action.

(1) Any police officer who exercises powers corruptly or maliciously, knowing that there are no reasonable grounds for proceeding under this Act, shall be punishable with imprisonment which may extend to two years, or with fine, or with both.

(2) If the Special Court is of the opinion that any person has been corruptly or maliciously proceeded against under this Act, the Court may award such compensation as it deems fit to the person, so proceeded against and it shall be paid by the officer, person, authority or Government, as may be specified in the order.

59. Impounding passport and arms licence of person chargesheeted under the Act.

Notwithstanding anything contained in any other law for the time being in force, the passport and the arms licence of a person, who is charge-sheeted for having committed any offence under this Act, shall be deemed to have been impounded for such period as the Special Court may deem fit.

60. Review Committees.

(1) The Central Government and each State Government shall, whenever necessary, constitute one or more Review Committees for the purposes of this Act.

(2) Every such Committee shall consist of a Chairperson and such other members not exceeding three and possessing such qualifications as may be prescribed.

(3) A Chairperson of the Committee shall be a person who is, or has been, a Judge of a High Court, who shall be appointed by the Central Government, or as the case may be, the State Government, so however, that the concurrence of the Chief Justice of the High Court shall be obtained in the case of a sitting Judge:

Provided that in the case of a Union territory, the appointment of a person who is a Judge of the High Court of a State shall be made as a Chairperson with the concurrence of the Chief Justice of the concerned High Court.

61. Power of High Courts to make rules.

The High Court may, by notification in the Official Gazette, make such rules, if any, as they may deem necessary for carrying out the provisions of this Act relating to Special Courts within their territories.

62. Power to make rules.

(1) Without prejudice to the powers of the High Courts to make rules under section 61, the Central Government may, by notification in the Official Gazette, make rules for carrying out the provisions of this Act.

(2) In particular, and without prejudice to the generality of the foregoing powers, such rules may provide for all or any of the following matters, namely:—

(a) regulating the conduct of persons in respect of areas the control of which is considered necessary or expedient and the removal of such persons from such areas;

(b) the entry into, and search of—

(i) any vehicle, vessel or aircraft; or

(ii) any place, whatsoever,

Reasonably suspected of being used for committing the offences referred to in section 3 or section 4 or for manufacturing or storing anything for the commission of any such offence;

(c) conferring powers upon—

(i) the Central Government;

(ii) a State Government;

(iii) an Administrator of a Union territory under article 239 of the Constitution;

(iv) an officer of the Central Government not lower in rank than that of a Joint Secretary; or

(v) an officer of a State Government not lower in rank than that of a District Magistrate,

to make general or special orders to prevent or deal with terrorist acts;

(d) the arrest and trial of persons contravening any of the rules or any order made thereunder;

(e) the punishment of any person who contravenes or attempts to contravene or abets or attempts to abet the contravention of any rule or order made thereunder with imprisonment for a term which may extend to one year or fine or both;

(f) providing for the seizure and detention of any property in respect of which such contravention, attempt or abetment as is referred to in clause (e) has been committed and for the adjudication of such seizure and detention, whether by any court or by any other authority;

(g) determination of the price of the forfeited property under sub-section (2) of section 10;

(h) the procedure of making application under sub-section (3) of section 19; and

(i) the qualifications of the members of the Review Committee under sub-section (2) of section 60.

63. Orders and rules to be laid before Houses of Parliament.

Every order and every rule made by the Central Government under this Act shall be laid, as soon as may be after it is made, before each House of Parliament, while it is in session, for a total period of thirty days which may be comprised in one session or in two or more successive sessions, and if, before the expiry of the session immediately following the session or the successive sessions aforesaid, both Houses agree in making any modification in the order or rule or both Houses agree that the order or rule should not be made, the order or rule shall thereafter have effect only in such modified form or be of no effect, as the case may be; so, however, that any such modification or annulment shall be without prejudice to the validity of anything previously done under that order or rule.

64. Repeal and saving.

(1) The Prevention of Terrorism (Second) Ordinance, 2001 is hereby repealed.

(2) Notwithstanding the repeal of the said Ordinance, anything done or any action taken under the said Ordinance shall be deemed to have been done or taken under the corresponding provisions of this Act.

The Schedule

(See section 18)

Terrorist Organisations

1. Babbar Khalsa International.
2. Khalistan Commando Force.
3. Khalistan Zindabad Force.
4. International Sikh Youth Federation.
5. Lashkar-e-Taiba/Pasban-e-Ahle Hadis
6. Jaish-e-Mohammed/Tahrik-e-Furqan
7. Harkat-ul-Mujahideen/Harkat-ul-Ansar/Harkat-ul-Jehad-e-Islami.
8. Hizb-ul-Mujahideen/Hizb-ul-Mujahideen Pir Panjal Regiment.
9. Al-Umar-Mujahideen.
10. Jammu and Kashmir Islamic Front.
11. United Liberation Front of Assam (ULFA).
12. National Democratic Front of Bodoland (NDFB).
13. People's Liberation Army (PLA).
14. United National Liberation Front (UNLF).
15. People's Revolutionary Party of Kangleipak (PREPAK).
16. Kangleipak Communist Party (KCP).
17. Kanglei Yaol Kanba Lup (KYKL).
18. Manipur People's Liberation Front (MPLF).
19. All Tripura Tiger Force.
20. National Liberation Front of Tripura.
21. Liberation Tigers of Tamil Eelam (LTTE).
22. Students Islamic Movement of India.

23. Deendar anjuman.
24. Communist Party of India (Marxist-Leninist)—People's War, all its formations and front organisations
25. Maoist Communist Centre (MCC), All its formations and front organisations.
26. Al Badr
27. Jamiat-ul-Mujahidden
28. Al-Qaida.
29. Dukhtaran-e-Millat (DEM)
30. Tamil Nadu Liberation Army (TNLA)
31. Tamil National Retrieval Troops (TNRT)
32. Akhil Bharat Nepali Ekta Samaj (ABNES)

Explanation.—For the purposes of this Schedule, serial numbers 24 and 25 shall be deemed to have been included with effect from the date of publication of S.O. No. 1194(E), dated the 5th December, 2001.

K.N. CHATURVEDI,
Addl. Secy. to the Govt. of India

DOCUMENT NO. 16

THE PREVENTION OF TERRORISM (REPEAL) ORDINANCE, 2004

September 21, 2004

The President of India, through an Ordinance promulgated on September 21, 2004, repealed the ***Prevention of Terrorism Act, 2002****. Presented below is the full text of the Ordinance:*

Promulgated by the President in the Fifty-fifth Year of the Republic of India.

An Ordinance to repeal the Prevention of Terrorism Act, 2002.

WHEREAS Parliament is not in session and the President is satisfied that circumstances exist which render it necessary for him to take immediate action;

NOW, THEREFORE, in exercise of the powers conferred by clause (1) of article 123 of the Constitution, the President is pleased to promulgate the following Ordinance:—

1. Short title and commencement.

(1) This Ordinance may be called the Prevention of Terrorism (Repeal) Ordinance, 2004.

(2) It shall come into force at once.

2. 15 of 2002.

(1) The Prevention of Terrorism Act, 2002 is hereby repealed.

(2) The repeal of the said Act shall not affect—

(a) the previous operation of, or anything duly done or suffered under, the said Act, or

(b) any right, privilege or obligation or liability acquired, accrued or incurred under the said Act, or

(c) any penalty, forfeiture or punishment incurred in respect of any offence under the said Act, or

(d) any investigation, legal proceeding or remedy in respect of any such right, privilege, obligation, liability, penalty, forfeiture or punishment as aforesaid,

and, any such investigation, legal proceeding or remedy may be instituted, continued or enforced and any such penalty, forfeiture or punishment may be imposed as if the said Act had not been repealed:

Provided that notwithstanding anything contained in this sub-section or in any other law for the time being in force, no court shall take cognizance of an offence under the repealed Act after the expiry of the period of one year from the commencement of this Ordinance.

(3) Notwithstanding the repeal of section 60 of the said Act, the Review Committee constituted by the Central Government under sub-section (*1*) of that section, whether or not an application under sub-section (*4*) of that section has been made, shall review all cases registered under that Act as to whether there is a *prime facie* case for proceeding against the accused thereunder and such review shall be completed within a period of one year from the commencement of this Ordinance and where the Review Committee is of the opinion that there is no *prima facie* case for proceeding against the accused, then,—

(a) in cases in which cognizance has been taken by the court, the cases shall be deemed to have been withdrawn; and

(b) in cases in which investigations are pending, the investigations shall be closed forthwith,

with effect from the date of issuance of the direction by such Review Committee in this regard.

(4) The Review Committee constituted by the Central Government under sub-section (*1*) of section 60 of the said Act shall, while reviewing cases, have powers of a civil court under the Code of Civil Procedure, 1908 in respect of the following matters, namely:—

(a) discovery and production of any document;

(b) requisitioning any public record or copy thereof from any court or office.

(5) The Central Government may constitute more Review Committees, as it may consider necessary, for completing the review within the period specified in sub-section (3).

President.

DOCUMENT NO. 17

THE UNLAWFUL ACTIVITIES (PREVENTION) AMENDMENT ACT, 2004

No. 29 of 2004

December 29, 2004

An Act further to amend the Unlawful Activities (Prevention) Act, 1967.

BE it enacted by Parliament in the Fifty-fifth Year of the Republic of India as follows:—

1. Short Title and Commencement

1. Short title and commencement.—

(1) This Act may be called the Unlawful Activities (Prevention) Amendment Act, 2004.

(2) It shall be deemed to have come into force on the 21st day of September, 2004.

2. Amendment of Long Title

2. Amendment of long title.—In the Unlawful Activities (Prevention) Act, 1967 (37 of 1967) (hereinafter referred to as the principal Act), in the long title, after the word "associations", the words ", and for dealing with terrorist activities," shall be inserted.

3. Substitution of Word "Code" for "Code of Criminal Procedure, 1898"

3. Substitution of word "Code" for "Code of Criminal Procedure, 1898".—In the principal Act, for the words and figures "Code of Criminal Procedure, 1898 (5 of 1898)", wherever they occur, the word "Code" shall be substituted.

4. Amendment of Chapter I

4. Amendment of Chapter I.—In Chapter I of the principal Act, for sections 1, 2 and 2A, the following sections shall be substituted, namely:—

'1. Short title, extent and application.—(1) This Act may be called the Unlawful Activities (Prevention) Act, 1967 (37 of 1967).

(2) It extends to the whole of India.

(3) Every person shall be liable to punishment under this Act for every act or omission contrary to the provisions thereof, of which he is held guilty in India.

(4) Any person, who commits an offence beyond India, which is punishable under this Act, shall be dealt with according to the provisions of this Act in the same manner as if such act had been committed in India.

(5) The provisions of this Act apply also to—

(a) citizens of India outside India;

(b) persons in the service of the Government, wherever they may be; and

(c) persons on ships and aircrafts, registered in India, wherever they may be.

2. Definitions.—

(1) In this Act, unless the context otherwise requires,—

(a) "association" means any combination or body of individuals;

(b) "cession of a part of the territory of India" includes admission of the claim of any foreign country to any such part;

(c) "Code" means the Code of Criminal Procedure, 1973 (2 of 1974);

(d) "court" means a criminal court having jurisdiction, under the Code, to try offences under this Act;

(e) "Designated Authority" means such officer of the Central Government not below the rank of Joint Secretary to that Government, or such officer of the State Government not below the rank of Secretary to that Government, as the case may be, as may be specified by the Central Government or the State Government, by notification published in the Official Gazette;

(f) "prescribed" means prescribed by rules made under this Act;

(g) "proceeds of terrorism" means all kinds of properties which have been derived or obtained from commission of any terrorist act or have been acquired through funds traceable to a terrorist act, irrespective of person in whose name such proceeds are standing or in whose possession they are found, and includes any property which is being used, or is intended to be used, for the purpose of a terrorist organisation;

(h) "property" means property and assets of every description, whether corporeal or incorporeal, movable or immovable, tangible or intangible and deeds and instruments evidencing title to, or interest in, such property or assets, and includes cash and bank account;

(i) "secession of a part of the territory of India from the Union" includes the assertion of any claim to determine whether such part will remain a part of the territory of India;

(j) "State Government", in relation to a Union territory, means the Administrator thereof;

(k) "terrorist act" has the meaning assigned to it in section 15, and the expressions "terrorism" and "terrorist" shall be construed accordingly;

(l) "terrorist gang" means any association, other than terrorist organisation, whether systematic or otherwise, which is concerned with, or involved in, terrorist act;

(m) "terrorist organisation" means an organisation listed in the Schedule or an organisation operating under the same name as an organisation so listed;

(n) "Tribunal" means the Tribunal constituted under section 5;

(o) "unlawful activity", in relation to an individual or association, means any action taken by such individual or association (whether by committing an act or by words, either spoken or written, or by signs or by visible representation or otherwise),—

> (i) which is intended, or supports any claim, to bring about, on any ground whatsoever, the cession of a part of the territory of India or the secession of a part of the territory of India from the Union, or which incites any individual or group of individuals to bring about such cession or secession; or
>
> (ii) which disclaims, questions, disrupts or is intended to disrupt the sovereignty and territorial integrity of India; or
>
> (iii) which causes or is intended to cause disaffection against India;

(p) "unlawful association" means any association,—

> (i) which has for its object any unlawful activity, or which encourages or aids persons to undertake any unlawful activity, or of which the members undertake such activity; or
>
> (ii) which has for its object any activity which is punishable under section 153A or section 153B of the Indian Penal Code (45 of 1860), or which encourages or aids persons to undertake any such activity, or of which the members undertake any such activity:
>
> Provided that nothing contained in sub-clause (ii) shall apply to the State of Jammu and Kashmir;

(q) words and expressions used but not defined in this Act and defined in the Code shall have the meanings respectively assigned to them in the Code.

(2) Any reference in this Act to any enactment or any provision thereof shall, in relation to an area in which such enactment or such provision is not in force, be construed as a reference to the corresponding law or the relevant provision of the corresponding law, if any, in force in that area.'.

5. Amendment of Section 5

5. Amendment of section 5.—In section 5 of the principal Act, in subsection (7), for the word and figures "Chapter XXXV", the word and figures "Chapter XXVI" shall be substituted.

6. Substitution of New Section for Section 10

6. Substitution of new section for section 10.—For section 10 of the principal Act, the following section shall be substituted, namely:—

"10. Penalty for being member of an unlawful association, etc.—Where an association is declared unlawful by a notification issued under section 3 which has become effective under sub-section (3) of that section,—

(a) a person, who-

(i) is and continues to be a member of such association; or

(ii) takes part in meetings of such association; or

(iii) contributes to, or receives or solicits any contribution for the purpose of, such association; or

(iv) in any way assists the operations of such association

shall be punishable with imprisonment for a term which may extend to two years, and shall also be liable to fine; and

(b) a person, who is or continues to be a member of such association, or voluntarily does an act aiding or promoting in any manner the objects of such association and in either case is in possession of any unlicensed firearms, ammunition, explosive or other instrument or substance capable of causing mass destruction and commits any act resulting in loss of human life or grievous injury to any person or causes significant damage to any property,—

(i) and if such act has resulted in the death of any person, shall be punishable with death or imprisonment for life, and shall also be liable to fine;

(ii) in any other case, shall be punishable with imprisonment for a term which shall not be less than five years but which may extend to imprisonment for life, and shall also be liable to fine.".

7. Substitution of New Chapters and Schedule for Chapter IV

7. Substitution of new Chapters and Schedule for Chapter IV.—For Chapter IV of the principal Act, the following Chapters and the Schedule shall be substituted, namely:—

'Chapter IV
Punishment for Terrorist Activities

15. Terrorist Act.—Whoever, with intent to threaten the unity, integrity, security or sovereignty of India or to strike terror in the people or any section of the people in India or in any foreign country, does any act by using bombs, dynamite or other explosive substances or inflammable substances or fire-arms or other lethal weapons or poisons or noxious gases or other chemicals or by any other substances (whether biological or otherwise) of a hazardous nature, in such a manner as to cause, or likely to cause, death of, or injuries to any person or persons or loss of, or damage to, or destruction of, property or disruption of any supplies or services essential to the life of the community in India or in any foreign country or causes damage or destruction of any property or equipment used or intended to be used for the defence of India or in connection with any other purposes of the Government of India, any State Government or any of their agencies, or detains any person and threatens to kill or injure such person in order to compel the Government in India or the Government of a foreign country or any other person to do or abstain from doing any act, commits a terrorist act.

16. Punishment for terrorist act.—

(1) Whoever commits a terrorist act shall,—

(a) if such act has resulted in the death of any person, be punishable with death or imprisonment for life, and shall also be liable to fine;

(b) in any other case, be punishable with imprisonment for a term which shall not be less than five years but which may extend to imprisonment for life, and shall also be liable to fine.

17. Punishment for raising fund for terrorist act.—Whoever raises fund for the purpose of committing a terrorist act shall be punishable with imprisonment for a term which shall not be less than five years but which may extend to imprisonment for life, and shall also be liable to fine.

18. Punishment for conspiracy, etc.—Whoever conspires or attempts to commit, or advocates, abets, advises or incites or knowingly facilitates the commission of, a terrorist act or any act preparatory to the commission of a terrorist act, shall be punishable with imprisonment for a term which shall not be less than five years but which may extend to imprisonment for life, and shall also be liable to fine.

19. Punishment for harbouring, etc.—Whoever voluntarily harbours or conceals, or attempts to harbour or conceal any person knowing that such person is a terrorist shall be punishable with imprisonment for a term which shall not be less than three years but which may extend to imprisonment for life, and shall also be liable to fine:

Provided that this section shall not apply to any case in which the harbour or concealment is by the spouse of the offender.

20. Punishment for being member of terrorist gang or organization.—Any person who is a member of a terrorist gang or a terrorist organisation, which is involved in terrorist act, shall be punishable with imprisonment for a term which may extend to imprisonment for life, and shall also be liable to fine.

21. Punishment for holding proceeds of terrorism.—Whoever knowingly holds any property derived or obtained from commission of any terrorist act or acquired through the terrorist fund shall be punishable with imprisonment for a term which may extend to imprisonment for life, and shall also be liable to fine.

22. Punishment for threatening witness.—Whoever threatens any person who is a witness or any other person in whom such witness may be interested, with violence, or wrongfully restrains or confines the witness, or any other person in whom the witness may be interested, or does any other unlawful act with intent to cause any of the said acts, shall be punishable with imprisonment which may extend to three years, and shall also be liable to fine.

23. Enhanced penalties.—

(1) If any person with intent to aid any terrorist contravenes any provision of, or any rule made under the Explosives Act, 1884 (4 of 1884) or the Explosive Substances Act, 1908 (6 of 1908) or the Inflammable Substances Act, 1952 (20 of 1952) or the Arms Act, 1959 (54 of 1959), or is in unauthorised possession of any bomb, dynamite or hazardous explosive substance or other lethal weapon or substance capable of mass destruction or biological or chemical substance of warfare, he shall, notwithstanding anything contained in any of the aforesaid Acts or the rules made thereunder, be punishable with imprisonment for a term which shall not be less than five years but which may extend to imprisonment for life, and shall also be liable to fine.

(2) Any person who, with intent to aid any terrorist, attempts to contravene or abets, or does any act preparatory to contravention of any provision of any law or rule specified in sub-section (1), shall be deemed to have contravened that provision under sub-section (1) and the provisions of that sub-section in relation to such person, have effect subject to the modification that the reference to "imprisonment for life" therein shall be construed as a reference to "imprisonment for ten years".

Chapter V
Forfeiture of Proceeds of Terrorism

24. Forfeiture of proceeds of terrorism.—

(1) No person shall hold or be in possession of any proceeds of terrorism.

(2) Proceeds of terrorism, whether held by a terrorist or by any other person and whether or not such terrorist or other person is prosecuted or convicted for any offence under Chapter IV or Chapter VI, shall be liable to be forfeited to the Central Government or the State Government, as the case may be, in the manner provided under this Chapter.

25. Powers of investigating officer and Designated Authority and appeal against order of Designated Authority.—

(1) If an officer investigating an offence committed under Chapter IV or Chapter VI, has reason to believe that any property in relation to which an investigation is being conducted, represents proceeds of terrorism, he shall, with the prior approval in writing of the Director General of the Police of the State in which such property is situated, make an order seizing such property and where it is not practicable to seize such property, make an order of attachment directing that such property shall not be transferred or otherwise dealt with except with the prior permission of the officer making such order, or of the Designated Authority before whom the property seized or attached is produced and a copy of such order shall be served on the person concerned.

(2) The investigating officer shall duly inform the Designated Authority within forty-eight hours of the seizure or attachment of such property.

(3) The Designated Authority before whom the seized or attached property is produced shall either confirm or revoke the order of seizure or attachment so issued within a period of sixty days from the date of such production:

Provided that an opportunity of making a representation by the person whose property is being seized or attached shall be given.

(4) In the case of immovable property attached by the investigating officer, it shall be deemed to have been produced before the Designated Authority, when the investigating officer notifies his report and places it at the disposal of the Designated Authority.

(5) The investigating officer may seize and detain any cash to which this Chapter applies if he has reasonable grounds for suspecting that—

(a) it is intended to be used for the purposes of terrorism; or

(b) it forms the whole or part of the resources of a terrorist organisation:

Provided that the cash seized under this sub-section by the investigating officer shall be released within a period of forty-eight hours beginning with the time when it is seized unless the matter involving the cash is before the Designated Authority and such Authority passes an order allowing its retention beyond forty-eight hours.

Explanation.—For the purposes of this sub-section, "cash" means—

(a) coins or notes in any currency;

(b) postal orders;

(c) traveller's cheques;

(d) banker's drafts; and

(e) such other monetary instruments as the Central Government or, as the case may be, the State Government may specify by an order made in writing.

(6) Any person aggrieved by an order made by the Designated Authority may prefer an appeal to the court within a period of thirty days from the date of receipt of the order, and the court may either confirm the order of attachment of property or seizure so made or revoke such order and release the property.

26. Court to order forfeiture of proceeds of terrorism.—Where any property is seized or attached on the ground that it constitutes proceeds of terrorism and the court confirms the order in this regard under sub-section (6) of section 25, it may order forfeiture of such property, whether or not the person from whose possession it is seized or attached, is prosecuted in a court for an offence under Chapter IV or Chapter VI.

27. Issue of show cause notice before forfeiture of proceeds of terrorism.—

(1) No order forfeiting any proceeds of terrorism shall be made under section 26 unless the person holding or in possession of such proceeds is given a notice in writing informing him of the grounds on which it is proposed to forfeit the proceeds of terrorism and such person is given an opportunity of making a representation in writing within such reasonable time as may be specified in the notice against the grounds of forfeiture and is also given a reasonable opportunity of being heard in the matter.

(2) No order of forfeiture shall be made under sub-section (1), if such person establishes that he is a bona fide transferee of such proceeds for value without knowing that they represent proceeds of terrorism.

(3) It shall be competent for the court to make an order in respect of property seized or attached,—

(a) directing it to be sold if it is a perishable property and the provisions of section 459 of the Code shall, as nearly as may be practicable, apply to the net proceeds of such sale;

(b) nominating any officer of the Central Government or the State Government, in the case of any other property, to perform the function of the Administrator of such property subject to such conditions as may be specified by the court.

28. Appeal.—

(1) Any person aggrieved by an order of forfeiture under section 26 may, within one month from the date of the receipt of such order, appeal to the High Court within whose jurisdiction, the court, which passed the order appealed against, is situated.

(2) Where an order under section 26 is modified or annulled by the High Court or where in a prosecution instituted for any offence under Chapter IV or Chapter VI, the person against whom an order of forfeiture has been made under section 26 is acquitted, such property shall be returned to him and in either case if it is not possible for any reason to return the forfeited property, such person shall be paid the price therefor as if the property had been sold to the Central Government with reasonable interest calculated from the day of seizure of the property and such price shall be determined in the manner prescribed.

29. Order for forfeiture not to interfere with other punishments.—The order of forfeiture made under this Chapter by the court, shall not prevent the infliction of any other punishment to which the person affected thereby is liable under Chapter IV or Chapter VI.

30. Claims by third party.—

(1) Where any claim is preferred or any objection is made to the seizure or attachment of any property under section 25 on the ground that such property is not liable to seizure or attachment, the Designated Authority before whom such property is produced, shall proceed to investigate the claim or objection:

Provided that no such investigation shall be made where the Designated Authority considers that the claim or objection is designed to cause unnecessary delay.

(2) Where an appeal has been preferred under sub-section (6) of section 25 and any claimant or objector establishes that the property specified in the notice issued under section 27 is not liable to be forfeited under this Chapter, the said notice shall be withdrawn or modified accordingly.

31. Powers of Designated Authority.—The Designated Authority, acting under the provisions of this Chapter, shall have all the powers of a civil court required for making a full and fair inquiry into the matter before it.

32. Certain transfers to eb null and void.—Where, after the issue of an order under section 25 or issue of a notice under section 27, any property referred to in the said order or notice is transferred by any mode whatsoever, such transfer shall, for the purpose of the proceedings under this Chapter, be ignored and if such property is subsequently forfeited, the transfer of such property shall be deemed to be null and void.

33. Forfeiture of property of certain persons.—

(1) Where any person is accused of an offence under Chapter IV or Chapter VI, it shall be open to the court to pass an order that all or any of

the properties, movable or immovable or both, belonging to him, shall, during the period of such trial, be attached, if not already attached under this Chapter.

(2) Where a person has been convicted of any offence punishable under Chapter IV or Chapter VI, the court may, in addition to awarding any punishment, by order in writing, declare that any property, movable or immovable or both, belonging to the accused and specified in the order, shall stand forfeited to the Central Government or the State Government, as the case may be, free from all encumbrances.

34. Company to transfer shares to Government.—Where any share in a company stand forfeited to the Central Government or the State Government, as the case may be, under this Chapter, then, the companyshall, on receipt of the order of the court, notwithstanding anything contained in the Companies Act, 1956 (1 of 1956), or the articles of association of the company, forthwith register the Central Government or the State Government, as the case may be, as the transferee of such share.

Chapter VI
Terrorist Organisations

35. Amendment of Schedule, etc.—

(1) The Central Government may, by order, in the Official Gazette,—

(a) add an organisation to the Schedule;

(b) add also an organisation to the Schedule, which is identified as a terrorist organisation in a resolution adopted by the Security Council under Chapter VII of the Charter of the United Nations, to combat international terrorism;

(c) remove an organisation from the Schedule;

(d) amend the Schedule in some other way.

(2) The Central Government shall exercise its power under clause (a) of sub-section (1) in respect of an organisation only if it believes that it is involved in terrorism.

(3) For the purposes of sub-section (2), an organisation shall be deemed to be involved in terrorism if it—

(a) commits or participates in acts of terrorism, or

(b) prepares for terrorism, or

(c) promotes or encourages terrorism, or

(d) is otherwise involved in terrorism.

36. Denotification of a terrorist organization.—

(1) An application may be made to the Central Government for the exercise of its power under clause (c) of sub-section (1) of section 35 to remove an organisation from the Schedule.

(2) An application under sub-section (1)may be made by—

(a) the organisation, or

(b) any person affected by inclusion of the organisation in the Schedule as a terrorist organisation.

(3) The Central Government may prescribe the procedure for admission and disposal of an application made under this section.

(4) Where an application under sub-section (1) has been rejected the applicant may apply for a review to the Review Committee constituted by the Central Government under sub-section (1) of section 37 within one month from the date of receipt of the order of such refusal by the applicant.

(5) The Review Committee may allow an application for review against rejection to remove an organisation from the Schedule, if it considers that the decision to reject was flawed when considered in the light of the principles applicable on an application for judicial review.

(6) Where the Review Committee allows review under sub-section (5) by or in respect of an organisation, it may make an order to such effect.

(7) Where an order is made under sub-section (6), the Central Government shall, as soon as the certified copy of the order is received by it, make an order removing the organisation from the Schedule.

37. Review Committees.—

(1) The Central Government shall constitute one or more Review Committees for the purposes of section 36.

(2) Every such Committee shall consist of a Chairperson and such other members not exceeding three and possessing such qualifications as may be prescribed.

(3) A Chairperson of the Committee shall be a person who is, or has been, a Judge of a High Court, who shall be appointed by the Central Government and in the case of appointment of a sitting Judge, the concurrence of the Chief Justice of the concerned High Court shall be obtained.

38. Offence relating to membership of a terrorist organization.—

(1) A person, who associates himself, or professes to be associated, with a terrorist organisation with intention to further its activities, commits an offence relating to membership of a terrorist organisation:

Provided that this sub-section shall not apply where the person charged is able to prove—

(a) that the organisation was not declared as a terrorist organisation at the time when he became a member or began to profess to be a member; and

(b) that he has not taken part in the activities of the organisation at any time during its inclusion in the Schedule as a terrorist organisation.

(2) A person, who commits the offence relating to membership of a terrorist organisation under sub-section (1), shall be punishable with imprisonment for a term not exceeding ten years, or with fine, or with both.

39. Offence relating to support given to a terrorist organization.—

(1) A person commits the offence relating to support given to a terrorist organisation,—

(a) who, with intention to further the activity of a terrorist organisation,—

(i) invites support for the terrorist organisation, and

(ii) the support is not or is not restricted to provide money or other property within the meaning of section 40; or

(b) who, with intention to further the activity of a terrorist organisation, arranges, manages or assists in arranging or managing a meeting which he knows is—

(i) to support the terrorist organisation, or

(ii) to further the activity of the terrorist organisation, or

(iii) to be addressed by a person who associates or professes to be associated with the terrorist organisation; or

(c) who, with intention to further the activity of a terrorist organisation, addresses a meeting for the purpose of encouraging support for the terrorist organisation or to further its activity.

(2) A person, who commits the offence relating to support given to a terrorist organisation under sub-section (1) shall be punishable with imprisonment for a term not exceeding ten years, or with fine, or with both.

40. Offence of raising fund for a terrorist organization.—

(1) A person commits the offence of raising fund for a terrorist organisation, who, with intention to further the activity of a terrorist organisation,—

(a) invites another person to provide money or other property, and intends that it should be used, or has reasonable cause to suspect that it might be used, for the purposes of terrorism; or

(b) receives money or other property, and intends that it should be used, or has reasonable cause to suspect that it might be used, for the purposes of terrorism; or

(c) provides money or other property, and knows, or has reasonable cause to suspect, that it would or might be used for the purposes of terrorism.

Explanation.—For the purposes of this sub-section, a reference to provide money or other property includes of its being given, lent or otherwise made available, whether or not for consideration.

(2) A person, who commits the offence of raising fund for a terrorist organisation under sub-section (1), shall be punishable with imprisonment for a term not exceeding fourteen years, or with fine, or with both.

Chapter VII
Miscellaneous

41. Continuance of association.—An association shall not be deemed to have ceased to exist by reason only of any formal act of its dissolution or change of name but shall be deemed to continue so long as any actual combination for the purposes of such association continues between any members thereof.

42. Power to delegate.—The Central Government may, by notification in the Official Gazette, direct that all or any of the powers which may be exercised by it under section 7, or section 8, or both, shall, in such circumstances and under such conditions, if any, as may be specified in the notification, be exercised also by any State Government and the State Government may, with the previous approval of the Central Government, by order in writing, direct that any power which has been directed to be exercised by it shall, in such circumstances and under such conditions, if any, as may be specified in the direction, be exercised by any person subordinate to the State Government as may be specified therein.

43. Officers competent to investigate offences under Chapter IV and VI.—Notwithstanding anything contained in the Code, no police officer,—

(a) in the case of the Delhi Special Police Establishment, constituted under sub-section (1) of section 2 of the Delhi Special Police Establishment Act, 1946 (25 of 1946), below the rank of a Deputy Superintendent of Police or a police officer of equivalent rank;

(b) in the metropolitan areas of Mumbai, Kolkata, Chennai and Ahmedabad and any other metropolitan area notified as such under sub-section (1) of section 8 of the Code, below the rank of an Assistant Commissioner of Police;

(c) in any case not relatable to clause (a) or clause (b), below the rank of a Deputy Superintendent of Police or a police officer of an equivalent rank,

shall investigate any offence punishable under Chapter IV or VI.

44. Protection of witnesses.—

(1) Notwithstanding anything contained in the Code, the proceedings under this Act may, for reasons to be recorded in writing, be held in camera if the court so desires.

(2) A court, if on an application made by a witness in any proceeding before it or by the Public Prosecutor in relation to such witness or on its own motion, is satisfied that the life of such witness is in danger, it may, for reasons to be recorded in writing, take such measures as it deems fit for keeping the identity and address of such witness secret.

(3) In particular, and without prejudice to the generality of the provisions of sub-section (2), the measures which a court may take under that sub-section may include—

(a) the holding of the proceedings at a place to be decided by the court;

(b) the avoiding of the mention of the name and address of the witness in its orders or judgments or in any records of the case accessible to public;

(c) the issuing of any directions for securing that the identity and address of the witness are not disclosed;

(d) a decision that it is in the public interest to order that all or any of the proceedings pending before such a court shall not be published in any manner.

(4) Any person who contravenes any decision or direction issued under sub-section (3) shall be punishable with imprisonment for a term which may extend to three years, and shall also be liable to fine.

45. Cognizance of offences.—No court shall take cognizance of any offence—

(i) under Chapter III without the previous sanction of the Central Government or any officer authorised by the Central Government in this behalf;

(ii) under Chapters IV and VI without the previous sanction of the Central Government or, as the case may be, the State Government, and where such offence is committed against the Government of a foreign country without the previous sanction of the Central Government.

46. Admissibility of evidence collected through the interception of communications.—Notwithstanding anything contained in the Indian Evidence Act, 1872 (1 of 1872) or any other law for the time being in force, the evidence collected through the inter-ception of wire, electronic or oral communication under the provisions of the Indian Telegraph Act, 1885 (13 of 1885) or the Information Technology Act, 2000 (21 of 2000) or any other law for the time being in force, shall be admissible as evidence against the accused in the court during the trial of a case:

Provided that the contents of any wire, electronic or oral communication intercepted or evidence derived therefrom shall not be received in evidence or otherwise disclosed in any trial, hearing or other proceeding in any court unless each accused has been furnished with a copy of the order of the competent authority under the aforesaid law, under which the interception was directed, not less than ten days before trial, hearing or proceeding:

Provided further that the period of ten days may be waived by the judge trying the matter, if he comes to the conclusion that it was not possible to furnish the accused with such order ten days before the trial, hearing or proceeding and that the accused shall not be prejudiced by the delay in receiving such order.

47. Bar of jurisdiction.—

(1) Save as otherwise expressly provided in this Act, no proceeding taken under this Act by the Central Government or the District Magistrate or any officer authorised in this behalf by the Central Government or the District Magistrate, shall be called in question in any civil court in any suit

or application or by way of appeal or revision, and no injunction shall be granted by any civil court or other authority in respect of any action taken or to be taken in pursuance of any power conferred by or under this Act.

(2) Notwithstanding anything contained in sub-section (1), no civil court or other authority shall have, or be entitled to exercise, any jurisdiction, powers or authority in relation to the matters referred to in section 36.

48. Effect of Act and rules, etc., inconsistent with other enactments.—The provisions of this Act or any rule or order made thereunder shall have effect notwithstanding anything inconsistent therewith contained in any enactment other than this Act or any instrument having effect by virtue of any enactment other than this Act.

49. Protection of action taken in good faith.—No suit, prosecution or other legal proceeding shall lie against—

(a) the Central Government or a State Government or any officer or authority of the Central Government or State Government or District Magistrate or any officer authorised in this behalf by the Government or the District Magistrate or any other authority on whom powers have been conferred under this Act, for anything which is in good faith done or purported to be done in pursuance of this Act or any rule or order made thereunder; and

(b) any serving or retired member of the armed forces or para-military forces in respect of any action taken or purported to be taken by him in good faith, in the course of any operation directed towards combating terrorism.

50. Saving.—Nothing in this Act shall affect the jurisdiction exercisable by, or the procedure applicable to, any court or other authority under any law relating to the navy, army or air force or other armed forces of the Union.

51. Impounding of passport and arms licence of person chargesheeted under the Act.—Notwithstanding anything contained in any other law for the time being in force, the passport and the arms licence of a person, who is charge-sheeted for having committed any offence under this Act, shall be deemed to have been impounded for such period as the court may deem fit.

52. Power to make rules.—

(1) The Central Government may, by notification in the Official Gazette, make rules for carrying out the provisions of this Act.

(2) In particular, and without prejudice to the generality of the foregoing powers, such rules may provide for all or any of the following matters, namely:—

(a) the service of notices or orders issued or made under this Act and the manner in which such notices or orders may be served, where the person to be served is a corporation, company, bank or other association;

(b) the procedure to be followed by the Tribunal or a District Judge in holding any inquiry or disposing of any application under this Act;

(c) determination of the price of the forfeited property under subsection (2) of section 28;

(d) the procedure for admission and disposal of an application under sub-section (3) of section 36;

(e) the qualifications of the members of the Review Committee under sub-section (2) of section 37; and

(f) any other matter which is required to be, or may be, prescribed.

53. Orders and rules to be laid before hoth Houses of Parliament.—Every order and every rule made by the Central Government under this Act shall be laid, as soon as may be after it is made, before each House of Parliament, while it is in session, for a total period of thirty days which may be comprised in one session or in two or more successive sessions, and if, before the expiry of the session immediately following the session or the successive sessions aforesaid, both Houses agree in making any modification in the order or rule or both Houses agree that the order or rule should not be made, the order or rule shall thereafter have effect only in such modified form or be of no effect, as the case may be; so, however, that any such modification or annulment shall be without prejudice to the validity of anything previously done under that order or rule.

The Schedule
[See Sections 2(1) (m) and 35]
Terrorist Organisations

1. Babbar Khalsa International.
2. Khalistan Commando Force.
3. Khalistan Zindabad Force.
4. International Sikh Youth Federation.
5. Lashkar-e-Taiba/Pasban-e-Ahle Hadis.
6. Jaish-e-Mohammed/Tahrik-e-Furqan.
7. Harkat-ul-Mujahideen/Harkat-ul-Ansar/Harkat-ul-Jehad-e-Islami.
8. Hizb-ul-Mujahideen/Hizb-ul-Mujahideen Pir Panjal Regiment.
9. Al-Umar-Mujahideen.
10. Jammu and Kashmir Islamic Front.
11. United Liberation Front of Assam (ULFA).
12. National Democratic Front of Bodoland (NDFB).
13. People's Liberation Army (PLA).
14. United National Liberation Front (UNLF).
15. People's Revolutionary Party of Kangleipak (PREPAK).

16. Kangleipak Communist Party (KCP).
17. Kanglei Yaol Kanba Lup (KYKL).
18. Manipur People's Liberation Front (MPLF).
19. All Tripura Tiger Force.
20. National Liberation Front of Tripura.
21. Liberation Tigers of Tamil Eelam (LTTE).
22. Students Islamic Movement of India.
23. Deendar Anjuman.
24. Communist Party of India (Marxist-Leninist)-People's War, All its Formations and Front Organisations.
25. Maoist Communist Centre (MCC), All its Formations and Front Organisations.
26. Al Badr.
27. Jamiat-ul-Mujahidden.
28. Al-Qaida.
29. Dukhtaran-e-Millat (DEM).
30. Tamil Nadu Liberation Army (TNLA).
31. Tamil National Retrieval Troops (TNRT).
32. Akhil Bharat Nepali Ekta Samaj (ABNES).'.

8. Repeal and Saving

8. Repeal and saving.—

(1) The Unlawful Activities (Prevention) Amendment Ordinance, 2004 (Ord. 2 of 2004) is hereby repealed.

(2) Notwithstanding such repeal, anything done or any action taken under the principal Act, as amended by the said Ordinance, shall be deemed to have been done or taken under the principal Act, as amended by this Act.

T. K. VISWANATHAN,
Secy. to the Govt. of India.

DOCUMENT NO. 18

THE WEAPONS OF MASS DESTRUCTION AND THEIR DELIVERY SYSTEMS (PROHIBITION OF UNLAWFUL ACTIVITIES) ACT, 2005

No. 21 of 2005

June 6, 2005

An Act to prohibit unlawful activities, in relation to weapons of mass destruction and their delivery systems and for matters connected therewith or incidental thereto.

WHEREAS India is determined to safeguard its national security as a Nuclear Weapon State;

AND WHEREAS India is committed not to transfer nuclear weapons or other nuclear explosive devices, or to transfer control over such weapons or explosive devices, and not in any way to assist, encourage, or induce any other country to manufacture nuclear weapons or other nuclear explosive devices;

AND WHEREAS India is committed to prevent a non-State actor and a terrorist from acquiring weapons of mass destruction and their delivery systems;

AND WHEREAS India is committed to the objective of global nuclear disarmament;

AND WHEREAS India is committed to its obligations as a State Party to the Convention on the Prohibition of the Development, Production, Stockpiling and Use of Chemical Weapons and on their Destruction and the Convention on the Prohibition of the Development, Production and Stockpiling of Bacteriological (Biological) and Toxin Weapons and on their Destruction;

AND WHEREAS India is exercising controls over the export of chemicals, organisms, materials, equipment and technologies in relation to weapons of mass destruction and their delivery systems under other relevant Acts;

AND WHEREAS it is considered necessary to provide for integrated legal measures to exercise controls over the export of materials, equipment and technologies and to prohibit unlawful activities in relation to weapons of mass destruction and their means of delivery.

BE it enacted by Parliament in the Fifty-sixth Year of the Republic of India as follows:-

1. Short title and commencement.—

(1) This Act may be called the Weapons of Mass Destruction and their Delivery Systems (Prohibition of Unlawful Activities) Act, 2005.

(2) It shall come into force on such date as the Central Government may, by notification in the Official Gazette, appoint.

2. Act in addition to other laws.—Save as otherwise expressly provided in this Act, the provisions of this Act shall be in addition to any other relevant Act for the time being in force in relation to any matter covered under this Act.

3. Extent and application.—

(1) It extends to the whole of India including its Exclusive Economic Zone.

(2) Every person shall be liable to punishment under this Act for every act or omission contrary to the provisions thereof, of which he is held guilty in India.

(3) Any person who commits an offence beyond India, which is punishable under this Act, shall be dealt with according to the provisions of this Act in the same manner as if such act had been committed in India.

(4) The provisions of this Act shall also apply to—

(a) citizens of India outside India;

(b) companies or bodies corporate, registered or incorporated in India or having their associates, branches or subsidiaries, outside India;

(c) any ship, aircraft or other means of transport registered in India or outside India, wherever it may be;

(d) foreigners while in India;

(e) persons in the service of the Government of India, within and beyond India.

(5) Notwithstanding the applicability of the provisions of any other Central Act relating to any activity provided herein, the provisions of this Act shall apply to export, transfer, re-transfer, transit and trans-shipment of material, equipment or technology of any description as are identified, designated, categorised or considered necessary by the Central Government, as pertinent or relevant to India as a Nuclear Weapon State, or to the national

security of India, or to the furtherance of its foreign policy or its international obligations under any bilateral, multilateral or international treaty, Covenant, Convention or arrangement relating to weapons of mass destruction or their means of delivery, to which India is a Party.

4. Definitions.—In this Act, unless the context otherwise requires,—

(a) "biological weapons" are—

(i) microbial or other biological agents, or toxins whatever their origin or method of production, of types and in quantities that have no justification for prophylactic, protective or other peaceful purposes; and

(ii) weapons, equipment or delivery systems specially designed to use such agents or toxins for hostile purposes or in armed conflict;

(b) "brought in transit" means to bring goods from any country into India by land, air, or amphibious means of transportation, where the goods are to be taken out from India on the same conveyance on which they are brought into India without any landing in India, but does not include a conveyance in innocent passage through Indian territory, Indian territorial waters or Indian airspace of a foreign conveyance carrying goods.

Explanation I.—A conveyance is a foreign conveyance if it is not registered in India.

Explanation II.—A conveyance is in "innocent passage" if it is not engaged in relevant activity and passes through or above Indian territorial waters or airspace without stopping or anchoring in India;

(c) "chemical weapons" means,—

(i) the toxic chemicals and their precursors, except where intended for—

(a) industrial, agricultural, research, medical, pharmaceutical or other peaceful purposes;

(b) protective purposes, namely those purposes directly related to protection against toxic chemicals and to protection against chemical weapons;

(c) military purposes not connected with the use of chemical weapons and not dependent on the use of the toxic properties of chemicals as a method of warfare; or

(d) law enforcement including domestic riot control purposes; as long as the types and quantities are consistent with such purposes;

(ii) the munitions and devices, specifically designed to cause death or other harm through the toxic properties of those toxic chemicals specified in sub-clause (i), which would be released as a result of the employment of such munitions and devices; and

(iii) any equipment specifically designed for use directly in connection with the employment of munitions and devices specified in sub-clause (ii), together or separately;

(d) "export" shall have the meaning assigned to this expression in the Foreign Trade (Development and Regulation) Act, 1992 (22 of 1992);

(e) "fissile material" and "radioactive material" shall have the meanings assigned to these expressions in the Atomic Energy Act, 1962 (33 of 1962);

(f) "item" means materials, equipment, and technology, of any description, notified under this Act or any other Act related to relevant activity;

(g) "non-State actor" is a person or entity not acting under the lawful authority of any country;

(h) "nuclear weapon or other nuclear explosive device" means any nuclear weapon or other nuclear explosive device as may be determined by the Central Government, whose determination in the matter shall be final;

(i) "public domain" means domain that has no restrictions upon dissemination of information within or from it; the existence of any legal rights to intellectual property in that information does not remove such information from being in public domain;

(j) "relevant activity" means,—

(i) the development, production, handling, operation, maintenance, storage or dissemination of a nuclear, chemical or biological weapon; or

(ii) the development, production, maintenance, storage or dissemination of missiles specially designed for delivering any such weapon;

(k) "re-transfer" means transfer of any item notified under this Act from any country or entity to which it has been exported from India, to yet another country or entity;

(l) "technology" means any information (including information embodied in software) other than information in the public domain, that is capable of being used in—

(i) the development, production or use of any goods or software;

(ii) the development of, or the carrying out of, an industrial or commercial activity or the provision of a service of any kind.

Explanation.—When technology is described wholly or partly by reference to the uses to which it (or the goods to which it relates) may be put, it shall include services which are provided or used, or which are capable of being used, in the development, production or use of such technology or goods;

(m) "terrorist" shall have the meaning assigned to this expression in the Unlawful Activities (Prevention) Act, 1967 (37 of 1967);

(n) "trans-shipment" means to remove goods from the conveyance on which they were brought into India and to place the goods on the same or another conveyance for the purpose of taking them out of India, where these acts are carried out on a "through bill of lading", "through airway bill" or "through manifest".

Explanation.—"through bill of lading", "through airway bill" and "through manifest" means respectively a bill of lading, airway bill and manifest, for the consignment of goods from a place outside India to a destination which is also outside India without a consignee in India;

(o) "unlawful" means without the authority of the Central Government and the expression "unlawfully" shall be construed accordingly;

(p) "weapons of mass destruction" means any biological, chemical or nuclear weapons.

5. Power to identify, designate, categorise or regulate certain activities.—

(1) The Central Government may identify, designate, categorise or regulate, the export, transfer, re-transfer, trans-shipment, or transit of any item related to relevant activity in such manner as may be prescribed.

(2) The Central Government may, by order published in the Official Gazette, designate or notify any item related to relevant activity for the purposes of this Act.

6. Power to appoint Advisory Committees.—For the purposes of this Act, the Central Government may appoint such Advisory Committees as it deems fit, and may appoint to them persons to exercise such powers and perform such duties as the Central Government may, by rules, prescribe.

7. Delegation of powers.—

(1) Subject to the provisions of this Act and any other law for the time being in force, related to relevant activity, the Central Government shall have the power to direct or assign to any authority, in such manner as it may deem appropriate, such powers as may be necessary to implement the provisions of this Act.

(2) The Central Government may appoint a Licensing Authority and an Appellate Authority and make provisions relating to such authority and

for licensing in such manner and in such form, as the Central Government may, by rules, prescribe.

(3) Without prejudice to the generality of the provisions contained in this Act, the authorities and mechanisms provided under other relevant Acts shall continue to deal with matters covered under those Acts:

Provided that in case of any doubt as to whether a matter falls within the scope of such relevant Acts or under this Act, the decision of the Central Government thereon shall be final.

8. Prohibition relating to weapons of mass destruction.—

(1) No person shall unlawfully manufacture, acquire, possess, develop or transport a nuclear weapon or other nuclear explosive device and their means of delivery.

(2) No person shall unlawfully transfer, directly or indirectly, to any one a nuclear weapon or other nuclear explosive device, or transfer control over such a weapon, knowing it to be a nuclear weapon or other nuclear explosive device.

(3) No person shall unlawfully manufacture, acquire, possess, develop or transport a biological or chemical weapon or their means of delivery.

(4) No person shall unlawfully transfer, directly or indirectly, to any one biological or chemical weapons.

(5) No person shall unlawfully transfer, directly or indirectly, to any one missiles specially designed for the delivery of weapons of mass destruction.

9. Prohibition relating to non-State actor or terrorist.—No person shall, directly or indirectly, transfer to a non-State actor or terrorist, any material, equipment and technology notified under this Act or any other Act related to relevant activity:

Provided that such transfer made to a non-State actor shall not include a transfer made as such to any person acting under lawful authority in India.

10. Prohibition as regards intimidating acts.—No person shall transfer, acquire, possess, or transport fissile or radioactive material, which is intended to be used to cause, or in a threat to cause, death or serious injury or damage to property for the purpose of intimidating people or a section of the people in India or in any foreign country, or compelling the Government of India or the Government of a foreign country or an international organisation or any other person to do so or abstain from doing any act.

11. Prohibition on export.—No person shall export any material, equipment or technology knowing that such material, equipment or technology is intended to be used in the design or manufacture of a biological weapon, chemical weapon, nuclear weapon or other nuclear explosive device, or in their missile delivery systems.

12. Prohibition on brokering.—No person who is a resident in India shall, for a consideration under the terms of an actual or implied contract, knowingly facilitate the execution of any transaction which is prohibited or regulated under this Act:

Provided that a mere carriage, without knowledge, of persons, goods or technology, or provision of services, including by a public or private carrier of goods, courier, tele-communication, postal service provider or financial service provider, shall not be an offence for the purposes of this section.

13. Regulation of export, transfer, retransfer, transit and transshipment.—

(1) No item notified under this Act shall be exported, transferred, re-transferred, brought in transit or transhipped except in accordance with the provisions of this Act or any other relevant Act.

(2) Any transfer of technology of an item whose export is prohibited under this Act or any other relevant Act relating to relevant activity shall be prohibited.

(3) When any technology is notified under this Act or any other relevant Act, as being subject to transfer controls, the transfer of such technology shall be restricted to the extent notified thereunder.

Explanation.—The transfer of technology may take place through either or both of the following modes of transfer, namely:—

(a) by a person or from a place within India to a person or place outside India;

(b) by a person or from a place outside India to a person, or a place, which is also outside India (but only where the transfer is by, or within the control of, person, who is a citizen of India, or any person who is a resident in India).

(4) The Central Government may notify any item as being subject to the provisions of this Act, whether or not it is covered under any other relevant Act; and when such item is exhibited, sold, supplied or transferred to any foreign entity or a foreigner who is resident, operating, visiting, studying, or conducting research or business within the territorial limits of India, or in its airspace or Exclusive Economic Zone, it shall constitute an offence.

14. Offences and penalties.—Any person who contravenes, or attempts to contravene or abets, the provisions of section 8 or section 10 of this Act, shall be punishable with imprisonment for a term which shall not be less than five years but which may extend to imprisonment for life, and shall also be liable to fine.

15. Punishment for aiding non-State actor or terrorist.—

(1) Any person who, with intent to aid any non-State actor or terrorist, contravenes the provisions of section 9 of this Act, shall be punishable with imprisonment for a term which shall not be less than five years but which may extend to imprisonment for life, and shall also be liable to fine.

(2) Any person who, with intent to aid any non-State actor or terrorist, attempts to contravene or abets, or does any act preparatory to contravention of sub-section (1), shall be deemed to have contravened that provision and the provision of sub-section (1) shall apply subject to the modification that the reference to "imprisonment for life" therein shall be construed as a reference to "imprisonment for ten years".

(3) While determining the punishment under this section, the court shall take into consideration whether the accused had the knowledge about the transferee being a non-State actor or not.

16. Punishment for unauthorized export.—

(1) Any person who knowingly contravenes, abets or attempts to contravene, the provisions of sub-section (4) of section 13 of this Act, shall be punishable with fine which shall not be less than three lakh rupees and which may extend to twenty lakh rupees.

(2) If any person is again convicted of the same offence under sub-section (1), then he shall be punishable for the second and every subsequent offence with imprisonment for a term which shall not be less than six months but which may extend to five years and shall also be liable to fine.

17. Punishment for violation of other provisions of the Act.—

(1) Where any person contravenes, or abets or attempts to contravene, any provision of this Act other than the provisions under sections 8, 9, 10 and sub-section (4) of section 13 of this Act, he shall be punishable with imprisonment for a term which shall not be less than six months but which may extend to five years and shall also be liable to fine.

(2) If any person is again convicted of the same offence under sub-section (1), then he shall be punishable for the second and every subsequent offence with imprisonment for a term which shall not be less than one year but which may extend to seven years and shall also be liable to fine.

18. Penalty for using false or making forged documents, etc.—

Where any person signs or uses, or causes to be signed or used, any declaration, statement or document submitted to the competent authority knowing or having reason to believe that such declaration, statement or document is forged or tampered with or is false in any material particular, and relates to items notified under this Act or any other relevant Act, including those related to relevant activity, he shall be punishable with fine which shall not be less than five lakh rupees or five times the value of the materials, equipment, technology or services, whichever is more.

19. Punishment for offences with respect to which no provision has been made.—Whoever contravenes any other provision of this Act or any rule or order made thereunder for which no specific punishment is provided, shall be punishable with imprisonment for a term which may extend to one year, or with fine, or with both.

20. Offences by companies.—

(1) Where an offence under this Act has been committed by a company, every person who at the time the offence was committed was in charge of, and was responsible to, the company for the conduct of the business of the company as well as the company, shall be deemed to be guilty of the offence and shall be liable to be proceeded against and punished accordingly:

Provided that nothing contained in this sub-section shall render any such person liable to any punishment, if he proves that the offence was committed without his knowledge or that he had exercised all due diligence to prevent the commission of such offence.

(2) Notwithstanding anything contained in sub-section (1), where any offence under this Act has been committed by a company and it is proved that the offence has been committed with the consent or connivance of, or is attributable to, any neglect on the part of, any director, manager, secretary or other officer of the company, such director, manager, secretary or other officer shall be deemed to be guilty of that offence and shall be liable to be proceeded against and punished accordingly.

Explanation.—For the purposes of this section—

(a) "company" means any body corporate and includes a firm and other association of individuals; and

(b) "director", in relation to a firm, means a partner in the firm.

21. Cognizance of offences.—No Court shall take cognizance of any offence under this Act without the previous sanction of the Central Government or any officer authorised by the Central Government in this behalf.

22. Bar of jurisdiction of civil courts.—No action or proceedings taken under section 5 and sub-sections (1) and (2) of section 7 of this Act by the Central Government or any officer authorised by it in this behalf shall be called in question in any civil court in any suit or application or by way of appeal or revision, and no injunction shall be granted by any civil court or other authority in respect of any action taken or to be taken in pursuance of any power conferred under those provisions.

23. Effect of other laws.—

(1) The provisions of this Act shall have effect notwithstanding anything inconsistent therewith contained in any enactment other than this Act or any other instrument having effect by virtue of any enactment other than this Act.

(2) Where any act or omission constitutes an offence punishable under this Act and also under any other relevant Act, then the offender found guilty of such offence shall be liable to be punished under that Act which imposes a greater punishment.

24. Protection of action taken in good faith.—No suit, prosecution or other legal proceeding shall lie against the Central Government or any officer or authority of the Central Government or any other authority on whom powers have been conferred pursuant to this Act, for anything which is in good faith done or purported to be done in pursuance of this Act or any rule or order made thereunder.

25. Special provisions as to Central Government.—Nothing in this Act shall affect the activities of the Central Government in the discharge of its functions relating to the security or the defence of India.

26. Power to make rules.—

(1) The Central Government may, by notification, make rules to carry out the provisions of this Act.

(2) In particular and without prejudice to the generality of the foregoing power, such rules may provide for all or any of the following matters, namely:—

(a) manner of regulating any item related to relevant activity under sub-section (1) of section 5;

(b) appointment of Advisory Committees, their powers and duties under section 6;

(c) appointment of Licensing and Appellate Authority and the manner of licensing under sub-section (2) of section 7; and

(d) any other matter which has to be, or may be, prescribed.

(3) Every rule made under this Act shall be laid, as soon as may be after it is made, before each House of Parliament, while it is in session for a total period of thirty days which may be comprised in one session or in two or more successive sessions, and if, before the expiry of the session immediately following the session or the successive sessions aforesaid, both Houses agree in making any modification in the rule or both Houses agree that the rule should not be made, the rule shall thereafter have effect only in such modified form or be of no effect, as the case may be; so, however, that any

such modification or annulment shall be without prejudice to the validity of anything previously done under that rule.

27. Power to remove difficulties.—

(1) If any difficulty arises in giving effect to the provisions of this Act, the Central Government may, by order published in the Official Gazette, make such provisions, not inconsistent with the provisions of this Act, as may appear to be necessary for removing the difficulty:

Provided that no order shall be made under this section after the expiry of the period of two years from the date of commencement of this Act.

(2) Every order made under this section shall be laid, as soon as may be after it is made, before each House of Parliament.

T.K. VISWANATHAN,
Secy. to the Govt. of India

C. INTERNATIONAL AGREEMENTS

DOCUMENT NO. 19

AGREEMENT BETWEEN INDIA AND PAKISTAN ON BILATERAL RELATIONS (SIMLA AGREEMENT)

July 2, 1972

1. The Government of India and the Government of Pakistan are resolved that the two countries put an end to the conflict and confrontation that have hitherto marred their relations and work for the promotion of a friendly and harmonious relationship and the establishment of durable peace in the sub-continent, so that both countries may henceforth devote their resources and energies to the pressing task of advancing the welare of their peoples.

In order to achieve this objective, the Government of India and the Government of Pakistan

HAVE AGREED AS FOLLOWS :

i. That the principles and purposes of the Charter of the United Nations shall govern the relations between the two countries;

ii. That the two countries are resolved to settle their differences by peaceful means through bilateral negotiations or by any other peaceful means mutually agreed upon between them. Pending the final settlement of any of the problems between the two countries, neither side shall unilaterally alter the situation and both shall prevent the organisation, assistance or encouragement of any acts detrimental to the maintenance of peaceful and harmonious relations;

iii. That the pre-requisites for reconciliation, good neighbourliness and durable peace between them is a commitment by both the countries to peaceful co-existence, respect for each other's territorial integrity and sovereignty and non-interference in each other's internal affairs, on the basis of equality and mutual benefit;

iv. That the basic issues and causes of conflict which have bedeviled the relations between the two countries for the last 25 years shall be resolved by peaceful means;

v. That they shall always respect each other's national unity, territorial integrity, political independence and sovereign equality;

vi. That in accordance with the Charter of the United Nations they will refrain from the threat or use of force against the territorial integrity or political independence of each other.

2. Both Governments will take all steps within their power to prevent hostile propaganda directed against each other. Both countries will encourage the dissemination of such information as would promote the development of friendly relations between them.

3. In order progressively to restore and normalise relations between the two countries step by step, it would agree that :

i. Steps shall be taken to resume communications, postal, telegraphic, sea, land including border posts, and air link including overflights;

ii. Appropriate steps shall be taken to promote travel facilities for the nationals of the other country;

iii. Exchange in the fields of science and culture will be promoted.

In this connection delegation from the two countries will meet from time to time to work out the necessary details.

4. In order to initiate the process of the establishment of durable peace, both the Governments agree that :

i. Indian and Pakistani forces shall be withdrawn to their side of the international border;

ii. In Jammu and Kashmir, the line of control resulting from the cease-fire of December 17, 1971 shall be respected by both sides without prejudice to the recognised position of either side. Neither side shall seek to alter it unilaterally, irrespective of mutual differences and legal interpretations. Both sides further undertake to refrain from the threat or the use of force in violation of this Line;

iii. The withdrawals shall commence upon entry into force of this Agreement and shall be completed within a period of 30 days thereof.

5. This Agreement will be subject to ratification by both countries, in accordance with their respective constitutional procedures, and will come into force with effect from the date on which the Instruments of Ratification are exchanged.

6. Both Governments agree that the respective Heads will meet again at a mutually convenient time in the future and that, in the meanwhile, the representatives of the two sides will meet to discuss further the modalities and arrangements for the establishment of durable peace and normalisation of relations, including the questions of repatriation of prisoners of war and civilians internees, a final settlement of Jammu and Kashmir and the resumption of diplomatic relations.

Sd/- **Indira Gandhi** Prime Minister Republic of India	Sd/- **Zulifkar Ali Bhutto** President Islamic Republic of Pakistan

Simla, the 2nd July 1972

DOCUMENT NO. 20

THE LAHORE DECLARATION

February 21, 1999

The Prime Ministers of the Republic of India and the Islamic Republic of Pakistan:

Sharing a vision of peace and stability between their countries, and of progress and prosperity for their peoples;

Convinced that durable peace and development of harmonious relations and friendly cooperation will serve the vital interests of the peoples of the two countries, enabling them to devote their energies for a better future;

Recognising that the nuclear dimension of the security environment of the two countries adds to their responsibility for avoidance of conflict between the two countries;

Committed to the principles and purposes of the Charter of the United Nations, and the universally accepted principles of peaceful co-existence;

Reiterating the determination of both countries to implementing the Simla Agreement in letter and spirit;

Committed to the objective of universal nuclear disarmament and non-proliferartion;

Convinced of the importance of mutually agreed confidence building measures for improving the security environment;

Recalling their agreement of 23 rd September, 1998, that an environment of peace and security is in the supreme national interest of both sides and that the resolution of all outstanding issues, including Jammu and Kashmir, is essential for this purpose;

Have agreed that their respective Governments:

- shall intensify their efforts to resolve all issues, including the issue of Jammu and Kashmir.

- shall refrain from intervention and interference in each other's internal affairs.
- shall intensify their composite and integrated dialogue process for an early and positive outcome of the agreed bilateral agenda.
- shall take immediate steps for reducing the risk of accidental or unauthorised use of nuclear weapons and discuss concepts and doctrines with a view to elaborating measures for confidence building in the nuclear and conventional fields, aimed at prevention of conflict.
- reaffirm their commitment to the goals and objectives of SAARC and to concert their efforts towards the realisation of the SAARC vision for the year 2000 and beyond with a view to promoting the welfare of the peoples of South Asia and to improve their quality of life through accelerated economic growth, social progress and cultural development.
- reaffirm their condemnation of terrorism in all its forms and manifestations and their determination to combat this menace.
- shall promote and protect all human rights and fundamental freedoms.

Signed at Lahore on the 21st day of February 1999.

Atal Behari Vajpayee	**Muhammad Nawaz Sharif**
Prime Minister of the Republic of India	Prime Minister of the Islamic Republic of Pakistan

DOCUMENT NO. 21

INDIA, EUROPEAN UNION JOINT DECLARATION AGAINST INTERNATIONAL TERRORISM

November 21, 2001

On November 23, 2001 India and the European Union (EU) signed a joint declaration against international terrorism. The resolution reaffirmed the central role of the United Nations in the efforts of the international community in the struggle against terrorism and called for an early adoption of the draft Comprehensive Convention on International terrorism and the Conventions for the Suppression of acts of Nuclear Terrorism. Full text of the declaration is reproduced below.

India and the European Union affirm that international terrorism is a threat to peace and security. It constitutes a challenge to all States and the entire humanity and a grave violation of human rights. Given their tolerant character, open, democratic and multicultural societies are specially vulnerable to terrorist attacks. The struggle against terrorism is not against any community or faith.

2. All States have a responsibility to refrain from providing moral, material or diplomatic support to acts of terrorism, and prevent the use of their territory for sponsoring terrorist acts against other States. India and the European Union support the adoption on the basis of international law of decisive measures against all States, individuals, and entities, which render support, harbour, finance, instigate or train terrorists or promote terrorism. There can be no religious ethnic, ideological or any other justification of terrorism. We support the fight against international terrorism, wherever it occurs and regardless of its motives.

3. It is necessary that all States cooperate through all lawful means to prevent and suppress the financing of acts of terrorism in their territories.

4. We welcome UNSCR 1373 which provides an important framework for international action against terrorism. We are committed to fully implement this resolution.

5. India and the European Union reaffirm the central role of the United Nations in the efforts of the international community in the struggle against terrorism. They agree that such a struggle must be conducted in observance of human rights and the rule of law, which it aims to safeguard and strengthen.

6. They call for an early adoption of the draft Comprehensive Convention on International Terrorism and the Convention for the Suppression of acts of Nuclear Terrorism. Adoption and implementation of these Conventions as well as all other UN conventions would assist in strengthening the international legal basis for effectively combating the global menace of terrorism.

Source: http://meadev.nic.in/ind-EU/decl-indo-eu-terr.htm

D. INDIA'S REPORTS TO THE UN

DOCUMENT NO. 22

INDIA'S 2001 COUNTER-TERRORISM REPORT TO THE UN

UN Security Council Resolution S/2001/1278

December 27, 2007

Distr.: General
27 Decmber 2001
English
Original: French

Letter dated 27 December 2001 from the Chairman of the Security Council Committee established pursuant to resolution 1373 (2001) concerning counter-terrorism addressed to the President of the Security Council

The Counter-Terrorism Committee has received the attached report from India, submitted pursuant to paragraph 6 of resolution 1373 (2001) (see annex).

I should be grateful if you would arrange for this letter and its annex to be circulated as a document of the Security Council.

(*Signed*) Jeremy **Greenstock**
Chairman
Counter-Terrorism Committee

Annex

[Original: English]

Letter dated 24 December 2001 from the Chargé d'affaires a.i. of the Permanent Mission of India to the United Nations addressed to the Chairman of the Security Council Committee established pursuant to resolution 1373 (2001) concerning counter-terrorism

I forward herewith India's report in response to Security Council resolution 1373 (2001) (see enclosure).

The report is in four parts. Of these, the first three, which are attached, are meant for general distribution, and may be circulated as documents of the Security Council.

The fourth section, which I am sending to you separately, is a confidential document, meant only for the information and use of the Counter-Terrorism Committee, and is not for wider distribution.

(*Signed*) Satyabrata **Pal**

Enclosure

Report by India to the Counter-Terrorism Committee Pursuant to Resolution 1373 (2001)

India's report concerning the implementation is organised under the following Sections:

Section I: Measures Against Terrorism: This Section addresses issues in Operative Para 2 of the Resolution which relates to aspects such as criminalisation of Terrorist Act, recruitment, training, supply of weapons and punitive measures against commission of terrorist acts.

Note: For orderly presentation, it is felt that it is useful to begin with Operative Para 2.

Section II: Financing of Terrorism: This Section addresses issues covered under Operative Para I of the Resolution on aspects such as financial flows, freezing of accounts and assets, contributions to funds for terrorist purpose, etc.

Section III: International Cooperation Against Terrorism: This Section deals with India's approach to international cooperation including bilateral and multilateral agreements, extradition arrangements, etc.

Section IV: External Support to Terrorism: This is a "confidential" Section wherein the extensive external support to Terrorism in India is documented. This Section is not for publication as it contains sensitive material.

Section I: Measures Against Terrorism

1. Resolution 1373 Operative Para-2 reads as follows:

Decides also that all States shall:

(a) Refrain from providing any form of support, active or passive, to entities or persons involved in terrorist acts, including by suppressing recruitment of members of terrorist groups and eliminating the supply of weapons to terrorists;

(b) Take the necessary steps to prevent the commission of terrorist acts, including by provision of early warning to other States by exchange of information;

(c) Deny safe heaven to those who finance, plan, support, or commit terrorist acts, or provide safe havens;

(d) Prevent those who finance, plan, facilitate or commit terrorist acts from using their respective territories for those purposes against other States or their citizens;

(e) Ensure that any person who participates in the financing, planning, preparation or perpetration of terrorist acts or in supporting terrorist acts is brought to justice and ensure that, in addition to any other measures against them, such terrorist acts are established as serious criminal offences in domestic laws and regulations and that the punishment duly reflects the seriousness of such terrorist acts;

(f) Afford one another the greatest measure of assistance in connection with criminal investigations or criminal proceedings relating to the financing or support of terrorist acts, including assistance in obtaining evidence in their possession necessary for the proceedings;

(g) Prevent the movement of terrorists or terrorist groups by effective border controls and controls on issuance of identity papers and travel documents, and through measures for preventing counterfeiting, forgery or fraudulent use of identity papers and travel documents.

2. Based on the above, the Committee under the Security Council has formulated the following questions:

Sub-paragraph (a): What legislation or other measures are in place to give effect to this sub-paragraph? In particular, what offences in your country prohibit (i) **recruitment to terrorist groups** and (ii) **the supply of weapons** to terrorists? What other measures help prevent such activities?

Sub-paragraph (b): What other steps are being taken **to prevent the commission of terrorist acts**, and in particular, what early warning mechanisms exist to allow exchange of information with other states?

Sub-paragraph (c): What legislation or procedures exist **for denying safe haven to terrorists**, such as laws for excluding or expelling the types of individuals referred to in this sub-paragraph? It would be helpful if States supplied examples of any relevant action taken.

Sub-paragraph (d): What legislation or procedures exist to prevent terrorists acting from your territory against other states or citizens? It would be helpful if States supplied examples of any relevant action taken.

Sub-paragraph (e): What steps have been taken **to establish terrorist acts as serious criminal offences** and to ensure that the punishment reflects the seriousness of such terrorist acts? Please supply examples of any convictions obtained and the sentence given.

Sub-paragraph (f): What procedures and mechanisms are in place to assist other states? Please provide any available details of how these have been used in practice.

Sub-paragraph (g): How **do border controls in your country prevent the movement of terrorists**? How do your procedures for issuance of **identity papers and travel documents** support this? What measures exist to prevent their forgery etc?

3. India has waged a sustained war against Terrorism for over two decades. As a victim of Terrorism mainly sponsored from across its border, the Indian State and its people are cognizant of the consequences of and to sensitive to the need to strengthen measures to combat Terrorism.

Prevention of Terrorism Ordinance (POTO):

4. The Prevention of Terrorism Ordinance (POTO) was promulgated by the President of India in exercise of his powers conferred by Article 123(1) of the Constitution of India on October 24, 2001 (at Annexure). The POTO specifically aims to deal with all aspects of prevention of Terrorism. An Ordinance, once promulgated, has the same effect and force as any other law for the time being in force in India. An Ordinance has to be approved by the Parliament and the intended legislation is currently under consideration and discussion. The POTO in its existing form, or the Act as adopted by the Indian Parliament after due consideration, will be the comprehensive piece of legislation specifically to tackle Terrorism.

5. Features in Prevention of Terrorism Ordinance: The full text is at Appendix I. The POTO has 61 Sections and is divided into six Chapters. It has a territorial as well as extra-territorial application. Some prominent features are:

Section 3(1) of the Ordinance defines **"terrorist acts"** as acts done with the intent to threaten the unity or integrity of India or to strike terror in any section of the people by using weapons and explosive substances or other methods (chemical, biological etc.) in a manner as to cause or likely to cause death or injuries to any person or persons or loss or damage to property or disruption of essential supplies and services etc.

Membership of an Association declared as "Unlawful" under "Unlawful Activities (Prevention) Act, 1967" would also be treated as **"terrorist act."**

The act of raising funds intended for the purpose of terrorism shall also be treated as **"terrorist act"**.

Section 18 of the Ordinance defines **"terrorist organizations"** and provides for their ban under a prescribed procedure as laid down. Any person who is a member or supports or invites support for a terrorist organization by way of raising finances, arranging or participating in meetings or encouraging support to such organizations in any other way commits an offence under the Ordinance.

Possession of explosives and weapons of mass destruction: Section 4 of the Ordinance relates to possession of unauthorized arms, explosive substances or other lethal weapons capable of mass destruction and/or used in biological and chemical warfare. Such acts will also be treated as **"terrorist acts"**;

Enhanced punishment has been prescribed for violation of Arms Act, 1959, The Explosives Act, 1884, The Explosive Substances Act, 1908 or the Inflammable Substances Act, 1952 with the intention to aid any terrorist;

Financing of terrorism: Proceeds of terrorism, whether held by terrorist or by any other person liable to be forfeited **(Section 6)**. Provisions of seizing properties, assets etc. of terrorist organization.

Under the Ordinance (Section 1(4) any person who commits an offence beyond India which is punishable under this Ordinance is to be dealt with according to the provisions of this Ordinance in the same manner as if such act had been committed in India. Activities of organizations/persons acting against India's interests while being based outside India are covered.

Special features/safeguards have been built in to prevent the possibility of misuse of the special power given to investigating authorities also keeping in view the observations of the Supreme Court of India.

6. The terrorist groups listed and banned under the Prevention of Terrorism Ordinance (POTO) are seen in the schedule under Section 18 of POTO. It is also provided under the Ordinance that this list could be modified, as necessary.

7. Apart from POTO, there are several other pieces of legislation under which unlawful acts or criminal acts which may amount to Terrorism can

be dealt with. Some of the acts available are listed below with short descriptions of the areas covered:

(i) The Indian Penal Code, 1860;

(ii) The Code of Criminal Procedure, 1973;

(iii) The Arms Act, 1959;

(iv) The Explosives Act, 1884;

(v) The Explosive Substances Act, 1908;

(vi) The Indian Telegraph Act, 1885;

(vii) The Armed Forces (Special) Powers Act, 1958;

(viii) The Unlawful Activities (Prevention) Act, 1967;

(ix) The Anti-Hijacking Act, 1982;

(x) The Merchant Shipping Act, 1948;

(xi) The United Nations Security Council Act, 1947.

Indian Penal Code, 1860:

Indian Penal Code, 1860 is the comprehensive criminal law of the country which deals with all the general offences. It deals with offences against human body, offences relating to religion, offences against property, offences relating to criminal breach of contracts of service, offences relating to marriage, offences against public tranquility, State, elections, public justice etc.

However, IPC does not provide for preventive action against terrorists. It only prescribes punishment for criminal acts after the commission of such acts. However, after the commission of the crime/terrorist act, the offenders are charged under relevant sections of IPC along with relevant sections of specific laws relating to that offence (if any).

The Code of Criminal Procedure 1973:

This is the uniform law of criminal procedure for the whole of India. The various sections of the Code provide for conduct of criminal proceedings in the courts of law.

The provisions for preventive action against terrorists/criminals are very mild in Cr.P.C. As per section 41, a Police Officer may arrest a person without warrant provided there is information that the person is likely to commit a cognizable offence (Section 109, 110 Cr.PC). However, the offender has to be produced before Executive Magistrate within 24 hours of detention.

Section 151 Cr.P.C. provides for arrests to prevent the commission of cognizable offence. A Police Officer knowing of a design to commit any cognizable offence may arrest without orders from the Magistrate and without a warrant the person so designing if it appears to such officer that the commission of the offence cannot be otherwise be prevented. However, no person arrested under this section shall be detained in custody for more than 24 hours.

The Arms Act 1959:

The Arms Act 1959 deals with acquisition, possession, manufacture, import and export of arms in India. The Act provides certain safeguards to prevent access to arms and weapons falling in hands of terrorists/anti social elements. The salient features of the Act are

No person can acquire small arms/weapons unless he holds in this behalf a license issued in accordance with Arms Act (Section 3).

Punishment of violation of this section is imprisonment for a term not less than one year but extendable up to three years. The offence also carries a fine in addition to imprisonment.

Certain categories of arms like automatic/semi-automatic weapons, artillery, anti-aircraft and anti-tank fire arms, weapons designed to discharge chemical agents, other specified weapons have been categorized as "prohibited arms" (Section 2).

Similarly, "prohibited ammunition" has been defined in the Act to include chemical agents, rockets, bombs, grenade, shells, missiles and such other articles as specified by Central Government. (Sec.2).

There is complete prohibition of acquisition or possession or of manufacture or sale of prohibited arms or prohibited ammunition. (Section 7)

Punishment for violation of this section is imprisonment for a term which shall not be less than five years but which may extend to ten years and shall also been liable to fine.

Central Government has powers to declare certain areas as "disturbed areas" whenever it is satisfied that there is extensive disturbance of public peace and tranquility or imminent danger of such disturbances in any area.

Punishment for offences under Arms Act in disturbed areas are higher than those prescribed in peaceful areas. Punishment for such offences under Section 3 in such areas is imprisonment for a term which shall not be less than three years but which may extend to seven years.

The Explosives Act 1884:

This Act was enacted to provide a comprehensive law regulating the manufacture, storage, sale, conveyance and importation of explosives throughout India.

As per Section 9(B) of the Act, whoever manufactures, imports or exports any explosives in contravention of rules or conditions of license is liable for imprisonment up to three years or with fine, or with both.

Whoever possesses, uses, sells or transports any explosive in violation of rules/license conditions shall be punishable with imprisonment up to two years or with fine or with both.

In case of specially dangerous explosives the punishment for offences mentioned above extend up to imprisonment for three years or fine or with both.

The Explosive Substances Act, 1908:

This Act was framed as the provisions of Indian Explosive Act, 1884 which was framed to prevent accidents. The Indian Penal Code also does not provide for any penalty for making or possessing explosive substances with unlawful intent and it does not in other cases always provide such severe penalties as were equisite to meet the increasing number of crimes.

As per this Act, punishment for causing explosion likely to endanger life or property is imprisonment for a term up to ten years (Section 3).

Punishment for attempt to cause explosion or for making or keeping explosive with intent to endanger life or property is imprisonment for a term up to seven years (Section 4).

The Indian Telegraph Act, 1885:

Section 5 of the Indian Telegraph Act, 1885 provides that on the occurrence of any public emergency or in the interest of public safety, the Central Government or a State Government or any officer specially authorized in this behalf by the Central Government or a State Government may if satisfied that it is necessary or expedient so to do in the interest of sovereignty and integrity of India, security of the State, friendly relations with Foreign States or public order or for preventing incitement to the commission of an offence, for reasons to be recorded in writing by order direct at any message or class of messages to or from any person or class of persons or relating to any particular subject brought for transmission by or transmitted or received by any Telegraph shall not be transmitted or shall be intercepted or detained, or shall be disclosed to the Government making the order or an officer thereof mentioned in the order.

This section authorizes Government to tap the phones/communication of terrorist organizations or organized crime syndicates.

The Armed Forces (Special) Powers Act, 1958:

Section 3 of the said Act empowers Central or State Government to declare the whole or any part of State as "disturbed area" when in its opinion the situation there is so disturbed that use of Armed Forces in aid of civil power is necessary.

Section 4 of the said Act confers special powers to any commissioned officer, warrant officer, noncommissioned officer or any other person of equivalent rank in Armed Forces in disturbed areas.

It allows the use of force against persons acting in contravention of any law or order for the time being in force in disturbed area.

To destroy any arms dump, shelter etc. from which armed attacks are made, any structure used for training camp, for armed volunteers or utilized as a hide out by armed gangs or absconders.

Arrest without warrant any person who has committed a cognizable offence or against a person who is likely to commit a cognizable offence.

Search and seizure of any premises without warrant.

The Unlawful Activities (Prevention) Act, 1967:

The object of this Act is to make powers available for dealing with activities directed against the integrity and sovereignty of India. "Unlawful activity" has been defined in relation to an individual or association as an action taken by such individual or association:

(i) which is intended, or supports any claim to bring about, on any ground whatsoever, the cession of a part of the territory of India or the secession of a part of the territory of India from the Union, or which incites any individual or group of individuals to bring about such cession or secession;

(ii) which disclaims, questions, disrupts or is intended to disrupt the sovereignty and territorial integrity of India;

"Unlawful association" has been defined as any association which has for its object any unlawful activity or encourages any unlawful activity or any activity punishable under section 153(A) or 153(B) of Indian Penal Code.

Section 7 of the said Act empowers the Central Government to prohibit the use of funds of an unlawful association. It effectively freezes the financial operations of an unlawful association.

Section 8 of the said Act empowers the Central Government to notify places used for the purpose of an unlawful association. It effectively restrains the use of moveable and immovable property by unlawful associations.

The punishment provided for unlawful activity is imprisonment up to seven years and fine. Any person assisting any unlawful activity is punishable for imprisonment up to five years or with fine or with both.

This was the first Act under which the assets of any terrorist organization could be frozen. The punishment provided for unlawful activity is also not commensurate with terrorist acts.

It provides for banning of organizations but it covers only those organizations who support cession or secession of a part of a territory of India from the Union or Acts which are intended to disrupt the sovereignty and territorial integrity of India.

The Anti-Hijacking Act, 1982:

A convention for suppression of unlawful seizure of aircraft was drawn up at the Diplomatic conference in The Hague in December, 1970. The Hague convention created a new international offence, the offence unlawful seizure of aircraft alias Hijacking. The convention covers offences committed by any person on board an aircraft in flight.

This Act was enacted to give effect to The Hague convention.

Section 4 of the said Act gives punishment for hijacking which shall be imprisonment for life and the person shall also be liable to fine.

Section 5 of the Act provides for punishment for acts of violence connected with hijacking. Any act of violence against any passenger or crew member is punishable with the same punishment with which the hijacker would have been punishable under any law for the time being in force in India if such act had been committed in India.

Section 7 provides that offences under section 4 and 5 shall be deemed to be extraditable offences.

The United Nations Security Council Act, 1947:

This act supplements other Acts, where necessary. Action can be taken against terrorist organisations, which are not banned under domestic legislation in India. As per the provisions of this Act, government can take necessary measures for implementation of the decisions of the UN Security Council.

8. It will be seen from the above that the specific questions raised in Operative Para-2 of UNSCR 1373 on issues inter-alia such as: steps being taken to prevent commission of terrorist acts; supply of weapons to terrorists; prohibition of recruitment to terrorist organisations; criminalisation of terrorist acts; are covered under these provisions.

9. Provisions relating to Passports, travel documents, visas are covered in the following paragraphs.

(a) Provisions in the Passport Manual to ensure that terrorists/suspected terrorist do not get passports:

Under Section 2 of the Passports Act, 1967, the passport authority is required to make such inquiry, as it may consider necessary before issuing a passport. The means of conducting such inquiry is through a police verification report, which is obtained through the State Police authorities. Most passports are issued after due police verification which inter-alia establishes the Indian nationality of the applicant. The police verification also establishes the antecedents of the applicant including any terrorist activity of the applicant or that of a suspected terrorist. In cases where a passport is issued without a Police Report for some reason, and a negative report is received later such passport applicants are contacted for clarification and where necessary, the passports are revoked or impounded. This system of issue of passports on Police Report overdue basis is not applicable in areas, which are sensitive from a security point of view. The list of States where passports are issued on police report overdue basis is periodically reviewed in consultation with the security agencies.

Under Clause 6(2) of the Passports Act, 1967, the Passport Authority has the power to refuse issue of passport to person in whose case issuing a passport is not in the interest of Security and Integrity of the Country or is not in Public Interest. The input regarding this is received from the concerned Security/Investigating Agencies.

(b) Passport (Entry into India) Act:

Foreigners Division, Ministry of Home Affairs (MHA) administers the Passport (Entry into India) Act, 1920. Powers under this act have been delegated to the State Governments. As per the provisions of this Act every person must be in possession of valid travel documents as defined in Passport (Entry into India) Rules, 1950. In case of foreigners, valid visa issued by the competent authority on the travel documents is also necessary. Violation of provisions of this Act attracts a penal provision of imprisonment up to a term of five years and with fine or with both.

(c) Provisions from the Visa Manual to ensure that suspected terrorists do not get visas to visit India:

Before issuing visas to foreigners, Indian Missions carry out several checks to ensure that visas are not granted to any persons in negative or suspect lists and thus to persons suspected of involvement in terrorist acts or are members of terrorist organisations.

The visa applicants are also interviewed, wherever necessary, to bring out facts which might have been purposefully suppressed or omitted to mention in their applications.

(d) The mechanism of blacklisting of terrorists:

Terrorists and other anti-social activists are blacklisted by Ministry of Home Affairs on the basis of inputs received from central intelligence agencies,

State Governments and Indian Missions/Posts abroad. The names and personal particulars of such personnel are circulated by MHA to all Indian Missions and Posts abroad and all immigration check posts in India. The names are removed from the black list only after receiving recommendation/consent to this effect from the originating agency and others.

(e) Prior Reference Category (PRC)/NEGATIVE LIST:

A negative list is maintained to prevent the entry of undesirable foreigners into the country. Missions/other agencies do not issue visas to persons whose name figure on the list without prior clearance. This list is periodically reviewed for deletion/addition of names, based on various inputs.

(f) HOW OUR PASSPORT AND VISA PROCEDURE SUPPLEMENTS THESE BORDER CHECKS:

As per the provisions of the passport (Entry into India) Act, 1920 and the rules framed under it, every person (except the nationals of Bhutan and Nepal) are required to be in possession of valid travel documents for entry into India. In case of a foreigner a valid visa issued by a competent authority is also required for entry into India. Entry into India is allowed only from the specified entry points (Immigration check-posts). Any person found entering into India without travel documents is arrested and handed over to the local police for taking further necessary action. Persons arrested for entering into India without travel documents or from unspecified points are liable to be awarded imprisonment up to a period of five years and with fine or with both. Persons who repeat the violation are liable to be awarded double the penalty prescribed for such violation. The stay and movement of foreigner inside the country is also governed by other acts viz., Foreigners Act, Registration of Foreigners Act etc. and rules made there under.

Every foreigner who enters into India on a visa for more than 180 days is required to get himself registered with the concerned Foreigners Registration office within 14 days of his arrival in India. Pakistani nationals are required to get themselves registered within 24 hours. Afghan nationals are required to get themselves registered within 7 days.

Section II: Financing of Terrorism

10. Security Council Resolution 1373 in Operative Paragraph 1 states:

1. Decides that all States shall:

   (a) Prevent and suppress the financing of terrorist acts;

   (b) Criminalize the wilful provision or collection, by any means, directly or indirectly, of funds by their nationals or in their territories with the intention that the funds should be used, or in the knowledge that they are to be used, in order to carry out terrorist acts;

(c) Freeze without delay funds and other financial assets or economic resources of persons who commit, or attempt to commit, terrorist acts or participate in or facilitate the commission of terrorist acts; of entities owned or controlled directly or indirectly by such persons; and of persons and entities acting on behalf of, or at the direction of such persons and entities, including funds derived or generated from property owned or controlled directly or indirectly by such persons and associated persons and entities;

(d) Prohibit their nationals or any persons and entities within their territories from making any funds, financial assets or economic resources or financial or other related services available, directly or indirectly, for the benefit of persons who commit or attempt to commit or facilitate or participate in the commission of terrorist acts, of entities owned or controlled, directly or indirectly, by such persons and of persons and entities acting on behalf of or at the direction of such persons;

11. The guidelines issued by the Committee has the following questions with regard to Operative Paragraph 1 of Financial Flows:

Sub-paragraph (a)—What measures if any have been taken to prevent and suppress the financing of terrorist acts in addition to those listed in your responses to questions on 1(b) to (d).

Sub-paragraph (b)—What are the offences and penalties in your country with respect to the activities listed in this sub-paragraph?

Sub-paragraph (c)—What legislation and procedures exist for freezing accounts and assets at banks and financial institutions? It would be helpful if States supplied examples of any relevant action taken.

Sub-paragraph (d)—What measures exist to prohibit the activities listed in this sub-paragraph?

12. **Introduction:** In describing the financial aspects related to Terrorism, some broad features of the Indian system need to be underlined; on the financial side traditionally there has been a highly regulated approach to foreign currency transactions and banking. Rules and regulations scattered over a number of Acts deal with several aspects (described below) and empower the Executive with wide powers to investigate; where necessary to prosecute; freeze and forfeit accounts or assets. At the same time, most transactions in the criminal world are unorganised, are informal, shadowy and as they are not through institutional mechanisms are extremely difficult to track, let alone offer evidence or proof for purposes of prosecution.

12(a). The criminal laws in general were used to prosecute and penalize terrorists. The need for special laws were felt when certain terrorists acts required to be prosecuted under a combination of legal provisions drawn from different legislations. The Indian Constitution provides for a Union List (subjects under the jurisdiction of the Central/Federal Government of India), States List (subjects under the jurisdiction of the State/Provincial Government), and Concurrent List (subjects under the jurisdiction of both). Subjects such as Arms, Explosive, Preventive Detention, National Security belong to the Union list; the Concurrent list deals with criminal laws and criminal procedure code.

Legal Provisions

13. As stated in the introduction, under the Indian Legislative framework, there are a number of laws, regulations and administrative arrangements to deal with illegal financial flows, and finances suspected with linkages to serious criminal activities. Depending on the nature of the criminal activity, one or more of these provisions could be used by the investigating and prosecuting authorities.

Broadly speaking the provisions work as follows:

A determination has to be made concerning criminal or terrorist activities of the individuals or entities. Based on such a determination, provisions as included in respective acts quoted below could be used for detention of persons, seizure, forfeiture of properties and prohibition on the use of funds.

(i) The Unlawful Activities (Prevention) Act, 1967(Act 37, 1967)
(Power to prohibit the use of funds of an unlawful association)

As per the provisions of Section 3 read with Section 7 of the Unlawful Activities (Prevention) Act, 1967, the Central Government may, by order in writing, prohibit any person (who has custody of any moneys, securities or credits which are being used or are intended to be used for the purpose of the unlawful association) from paying, delivering, transferring or otherwise dealing in any manner whatsoever with such moneys, securities or credits or with any other moneys, securities or credits which may come into his custody after the making of the order.

(ii) Conservation of Foreign Exchange & Prevention of Smuggling Activities Act, 1974 (52 of 1974)
(Power to make orders detaining certain persons)

The Act provides for preventive detention in certain cases for the purposes of conversion and augmentation of foreign exchange and prevention of smuggling activities and for matters connected therewith. Section 3 of the Conservation of Foreign Exchange & Prevention of Smuggling Activities Act, 1974, relates to power to make orders detaining any person with a view to preventing him from acting in any manner prejudicial to the conversion or augmentation of foreign exchange or with a view to prevent attempts at future smuggling or keeping of smuggled goods in future as referred to therein.

(iii) The Smugglers and Foreign Exchange Manipulators (Forfeiture of Property) Act, 1976 (Act 13 of 1976)
(Forfeiture of Property)

As per provisions of Section 7 read with provisions of Sections 2 and 6 of the Smugglers and Foreign Exchange Manipulators (Forfeiture of Property) Act, 1976 the Competent Authority, under the Act is empowered to pass orders for forfeiture of the properties of persons as referred to under Section 2 of the Act.

(iv) The Foreign Exchange Management Act, 1999
(Reserve Bank's powers to issue directions to authorized person)

For the purpose of securing compliance with the provisions of the Foreign Exchange Management Act, 1999 Rules/Regulations/Notifications/directions made or issued there under, Reserve Bank may in terms of Section 11 of the Act give directions to the authorized persons in regard to making of payment or doing or desist from doing any act relating to foreign exchange or foreign security.

(v) Code of Criminal Procedure, 1973
(Power of Police Officer to seize certain property)

As per provisions of Section 102, Police Officer is empowered to seize any property which may be alleged or suspected to have been stolen, or which may be found under circumstances, which create suspicion of the commission of any offence.

(vi) Banking Regulation Act, 1949
(Power of the Reserve Bank to give directions)

Section 35A of the Banking Regulation Act, 1949 empowers the Reserve Bank to issue directions to banking companies generally or to any banking company in particular. Amongst other criterion for exercise of such power, the public interest is also one of the criteria.

(vii) Forfeiture of Illegally Acquired Property under the NDPS Act.

Illicit drug trade generates large profits for the traffickers. As the money so generated is unaccounted, there are inherent difficulties in utilising the same. The traffickers therefore apply various techniques to launder the money to conceal its origin and there after use the same for legitimate transactions. To divest the drug traffickers of the profits generated by their illegal activities, is a significant approach to curtail their activities and great emphasis was laid on this aspect by the UN General Assembly Special Session on Narcotic Drugs & Psychotropic Substance.

Provisions have been made in Chapter V A of the NDPS Act, 1985 for tracing, identification, freezing and forfeiture of all properties attributable to drug trafficking.

The property derived out of drug trafficking of any person, his associates or relative, convicted of an offence punishable under the Narcotic Drugs and Psychotropic Substances Act with imprisonment for a term of 10 years or more or who has been convicted of a similar offence by the Competent Court of criminal jurisdiction outside India or a person in respect of whom an order of detention has been made under Prevention of Illicit Trafficking in Narcotic Drugs & Psychotropic Substances Act 1988 and such order of detention has not been revoked or set aside or who has been arrested or against whom a warrant of arrest has been issued can be frozen. Such properties on the conviction of the said person or completion of his detention period are liable to forfeiture.

By a recent amendment, the entire process of money laundering has also been made a punishable offence under the Narcotic Drugs & Psychotropic Substances Act.

14. Note on freezing, seizing and forfeiture of illegally acquired property.

The Smugglers and Foreign Exchange Manipulators (Forfeiture of Property) Act 1976 (SAFEM (FOP)A), provides for forfeiture of illegally acquired property of the persons convicted under the Sea Customs Act, 1978, the Customs Act, 1962 and the Foreign Exchange Regulation Act, 1973 and the persons detained under the Conservation of Foreign Exchange and Prevention of Smuggling Activities Act, 1974 and the Narcotic Drugs and Psychotropic Substances Act, 1985 (NDPS Act) provides for tracing, freezing, seizure and forfeiture of illegally acquired property of persons convicted under that Act or any corresponding law of any foreign country and those who are detained under the Prevention of Illicit Traffic in Narcotic Drugs and Psychotropic Substances Act, 1988 and Jammu & Kashmir Prevention of Illicit Traffic in Narcotic Drugs and Psychotropic Substances Act, 1988.

While the illegally acquired property covered under the respective Acts could be forfeited under both the above Acts, the NDPS Act also provides for tracing, freezing and seizing illegally acquired property. The Act also provides for forfeiture of the 'proceeds' of drug trafficking, including property acquired with such proceeds. Under the NDPS Act, officers who are in charge of police station and officers empowered under Section 53 of the Act can on receipt of information on holding of illegally acquired property take steps to trace and seize and if not possible to seize, freeze such illegally acquired property pending forfeiture. Orders of seizing or freezing have to be confirmed by the Competent Authority with in a period of 30 days. Once the property is due for forfeiture, the Competent Authority shall issue a notice for forfeiture to the affected persons. After giving them an opportunity to be heard, the Competent Authority may forfeit the illegally acquired property. Against the orders of the Competent Authority, the affected persons can go in appeal before the Appellate Tribunal for Forfeited Property.

Although participation in terrorism or other subversive activities are not grounds for forfeiture of the illegally acquired property under the above said Acts, since most of the terrorists commit offences like smuggling or drug trafficking, their property could be forfeited if they are either convicted under the relevant laws for smuggling or drug trafficking or against them orders for preventive detention are issued. As a matter of fact the main suspects of Mumbai serial blast case like Dawood Ibrahim, Tiger Memon, Iqbal Mirchi, Bhai Thakur and Mohd. Dossa were all involved in either smuggling or drug trafficking and at some point of time some orders of preventive detention were issued against them and on the basis of those orders their illegally acquired properties could be forfeited either under the SAFEM(FOP)A or under the NDPS Act.

Prevention of Terrorism Ordinance (POTO)

15. The Prevention of Terrorism Ordinance (POTO) was promulgated by the President of India in exercise of his powers conferred by Article 123(1) of the Constitution of India on October 24, 2001 (text at Annexure). (The Prevention of Organized Crime legislations in Karnataka, Maharashtra and Andhra Pradesh states are precursors of POTO; they deal with most the requirements of UNSCR. Other relevant legislations include Prevention of Unlawful Activities Act, Prevention of Disruptive Activities Act, Disturbed Areas Special Courts Act 1976, Terrorism Affected Areas (Special Courts) Act, 1984.) The POTO specifically aims to deal with all aspects of prevention of Terrorism. An Ordinance, once promulgated, has the same effect and force as any other law for the time being in force in India. An Ordinance has to be approved by the Parliament and the intended legislation is currently under consideration and discussion. The POTO in its existing form, or the Act as adopted by the Indian Parliament after due consideration, will be the comprehensive piece of legislation specifically to tackle Terrorism. (A description of the features of POTO is contained in Section I).

16. In POTO the term "Proceeds of Terrorism" has been defined in a broad manner to include all kinds of properties which:

(i) Have been derived or obtained from the commission of any terrorist act, or

(ii) Have been acquired through funds traceable to a terrorist act.

For this purpose the person in whose name such proceeds are standing or in whose possession they are recovered is immaterial.

Under POTO, a person also commits a terrorist act if he raises funds intended for purpose of terrorism.

Section III: UNSC 1373: Strengthening International Cooperation to Combat Terrorism

Operative Para-3 of 1373 reads as follows:

(a) Find ways of intensifying and accelerating the exchange of operational information, especially regarding actions or movements of terrorist persons or networks; forged or falsified travel documents; traffic in arms, explosives or sensitive materials; use of communications technologies by terrorist groups; and the threat posed by the possession of weapons of mass destruction by terrorist groups;

(b) Exchange information in accordance with international and domestic law and cooperate on administrative and judicial matters to prevent the commission of terrorist acts;

(c) Cooperate, particularly through bilateral and multilateral arrangements and agreements, to prevent and suppress terrorist attacks and take action against perpetrators of such acts;

(d) Become parties as soon as possible to the relevant international conventions and protocols relating to terrorism, including the International Convention for the Suppression of the Financing of Terrorism of 9 December 1999;

(e) Increase cooperation and fully implement the relevant international conventions and protocols relating to terrorism and Security Council resolutions 1269 (1999) and 1368 (2001);

(f) Take appropriate measures in conformity with the relevant provisions of national and international law, including international standards of human rights, before granting refugee status, for the purpose of ensuring that the asylum seeker has not planned, facilitated or participated in the commission of terrorist acts;

(g) Ensure, in conformity with international law, that refugee status is not abused by the perpetrators, organizers or facilitators of terrorist acts, and that claims of political motivation are not recognized as grounds for refusing requests for the extradition of alleged terrorists.

The Committee under Security Council in its guidelines has raised the following questions with regard to Operative Para 3:

Sub-paragraph (a): What steps have been taken to intensify and accelerate the exchange of operational information in the areas indicated in this subparagraph?

Sub-paragraph (b): What steps have been taken to exchange information and cooperate in the areas indicated in this sub-paragraph?

Sub-paragraph (c): What steps have been taken to cooperate in the areas indicated in this sub-paragraph?

Sub-paragraph (d): What are your government's intentions regarding signing and/or ratifying the conventions and protocols referred to in this sub-paragraph?

Sub-paragraph (e): Provide any relevant information on the implementation of the conventions, protocols and resolutions referred to in this sub-paragraph.

Sub-paragraph (f): What legislation, procedures and mechanisms are in place for ensuring asylum seekers have not been involved in terrorist activity before granting refugee status. Please supply examples of any relevant cases.

Sub-paragraph (g): What procedures are in place to prevent the abuse of refugee status by terrorists? Please provide details of legislation and/or administrative procedures which prevent claims of political motivation being recognised as grounds for refusing requests for the extradition of alleged terrorists. Please supply examples of any relevant cases.

17. India has consistently, over the decades, sought to intensify and strengthen international cooperation to combat the global phenomenon of terrorism through a variety of means.

Bilateral Mechanisms to Address Terrorism

18. **Joint Working Groups**

India has established Joint Working Groups with several key countries to exchange information and strengthen international cooperation to combat terrorism. In these Joint Working Groups there is an effort to explore ways of intensifying the exchange of information, especially regarding review of threat perceptions, early warnings, cooperation on administrative and judicial matters to prevent and suppress the commission of terrorist acts and to facilitate action against perpetrators of such acts. These Joint Working Groups meet periodically to review the status of cooperation in the fight against Terrorism. Apart from this, issues relating to the fight against terrorism are taken up in bilateral discussions.

19. **Bilateral Treaties to Combat International Terrorism**

India has entered into three types of bilateral treaties to combat international terrorism:

a. Agreements to Combat Terrorism and Organized Crime, Narcotic Drug offences, etc.

b. Extradition Treaties,

c. Treaties on Mutual Legal Assistance in Criminal Matters.

20. **Bilateral agreements to combat terrorism and organized crime, etc.**

These agreements are essentially framework agreements designed to facilitate exchange of operational information and development of joint programmes to combat organized crime and terrorism. Legally binding measures such as service of summons, search and seizure of persons, property or funds etc. are outside the scope of these agreements, as these subjects usually fall within the scope of treaties on mutual legal assistance in criminal matters. India has signed such agreements with Bulgaria, Croatia, China, Egypt, Oman, Italy, Romania and Russian Federation.

21. **Extradition treaties**

Extradition treaties are more focussed in operational scope and are designed to facilitate the transfer of fugitive offenders, suspected terrorists etc. so that they can stand trial in the State in which the offence is committed. Such treaties cover extradition in respect of almost all serious offences (i.e., offences punishable with a penalty of imprisonment of two years or more). The more recent treaties concluded by India provide for the 'no list' method for which extradition may be given. The recent treaties also deny the political exception plea as a defence against extradition.

India has concluded extradition treaties with Belgium, Bhutan, Canada, Hong Kong, Nepal Netherlands, Russia, Switzerland, UAE, UK, and USA. Such treaties have been signed, (but not yet exchanged), with Mongolia, Germany, Tunisia, Turkey and Uzbekistan. India has entered into extradition arrangements with Australia, Fiji, Papua New Guinea, Singapore, Sri Lanka, Sweden, Tanzania, and Thailand.

22. **Bilateral Treaties on Mutual Legal Assistance in Criminal Matters**

These treaties are designed to provide mutual legal assistance in criminal matters that are necessary for the prosecution of offences, searching persons and property in question, location of fugitives and property involved, transfer of witnesses and exhibits, freezing and confiscation of proceeds of crime, etc., and play a useful role in the punishment of crime and prosecution of offenders.

India has signed agreements on Mutual Legal Assistance in Criminal Matters with Canada, Switzerland, Turkey, Russian Federation, UAE, UK and Uzbekistan and signed, (but not yet exchanged), the agreements with France, Kazakhstan, Kyrgyzstan, Mongolia, Tajikistan and USA. The domestic legislation governing the procedural aspects of such cooperation is governed by the Code of Criminal Procedure, 1973 (sply ss. 105, 166A, 166B and Chapter VII-A of Cr. P.C. 1973).

Multilateral Arrangements and Agreements

23. International Conventions on Terrorism

Of the twelve International Sectoral Conventions on Terrorism which have been concluded under the aegis of the UN, India is a party to eleven of these conventions except the International Convention on the Physical Protection of Nuclear Material, 1979 and has taken steps to effectively implement its commitments under these Conventions. (List of Conventions to which India is a party is at Appendix II.)

There is proposed legislation, i.e., Prevention of Terrorism Ordinance to cover/address measures to suppress financing of Terrorism (which has been covered in Sections 1 and II in the report).

24. Regional Conventions on Terrorism

India is a party to the SAARC Regional Convention on Suppression of Terrorism, 1987. Pursuant to this convention, an enabling legislation titled "The SAARC Convention (Suppression of Terrorism) Act" was enacted in 1993.

25. Arrangements for Consideration of Status of Refugee/Asylum

There is no specific law in India to deal with refugees or asylum seekers and such cases are dealt with under existing laws pertaining to foreigners. "Foreigners" fleeing from neighboring countries into India due to ethnic violence, threat to their lives etc. are allowed to stay in India temporarily on humanitarian grounds. As and when the situation in their home country improves they are encouraged to return. Such foreigners who have been allowed to stay in India on humanitarian grounds may also be issued registration certificates and extensions are granted on their RCs for specified periods. Movements of all such refugees are monitored by specifically designated authorities who register foreigners. All efforts are made to ensure that suspected Terrorists do not misuse these arrangements to seek refuge in India.

Other Modalities of International Cooperation to Combat Terrorism

26. Cooperation with Interpol

India has been a member of Interpol since 1946 and there is an Indian member on secondment to the Interpol. There is considerable liaison with various Interpol member countries.

Within India, the Director CBI has been designated as the Head of National Central Bureau (NCB) India, Interpol, New Delhi. Under the supervision of the Director CBI there is an Interpol Wing in the Central Bureau of Investigation, whose day to day activities are supervised by an officer of the rank of Superintendent of Police who is designated as Assistant Director, Interpol.

Additionally, an informal arrangement has been made with all the States of the Union to have them designate one senior officer as an Interpol Liaison Officer (ILO) for helping the Indian Chapter of Interpol in carrying out its activities in India.

27. **The Mechanics of Red Corner Alerts**

Under Interpol there is a mechanism, i.e., issue of Red Corner Alerts, which is designed to facilitate international search for terrorists, fugitives from justice etc. A Red Corner Notice (RCN) is a Circular or a Notification issued by Interpol, upon a request from the member countries, calling for vigilance at border check posts etc so as to arrest and detain and possibly extradite them.

Whenever investigative agency draws a conclusion upon investigation that criminal or a suspected terrorist has fled national jurisdiction, a request is made to Interpol for issue of a Red Corner Alert. Interpol then assess whether the request is violative of any of the basic principles of coordination and cooperation of Interpol. Essentially, this scrutiny is restricted to seeing that the offences for which an RCN is sought to be issued are not political offences and they are not an affront to the sovereignty of any of member country. Another aspect which may be considered is whether the offences for which an RCN is sought to be issued is one for which extradition can be sought and granted as per the internationally acceptable norms. Interpol then issues a Red Corner Notice which clearly mentions that Extradition may be possible on the basis of bilateral agreements or Treaties, between the member countries.

This is a modality of cooperation that India has supported and used.

28. **Enhanced Cooperation and Full Implementation of Security Council Resolutions Relating to Terrorism**

As a victim of terrorism, India has, over the last two decades, consistently sought to priortise the need to combat terrorism in international fora, particularly in the UN. India has been supportive of all measures within the UN in the General Assembly, in the Sixth Committee and in the UN Security Council to address the complex global phenomenon of terrorism. It has supported the Security Council Resolutions 1269 and 1368 which note that terrorism poses a threat to international peace and security.

India has also supported and fully implemented resolutions 1267, 1333 and 1363 relating to terrorism by the Taliban regime in Afghanistan and had fully implemented the provisions of these resolutions.

Appendix I

The Prevention of Terrorism Bill, 2001

Arrangement of Clauses

Chapter I
Preliminary

Clauses

1. Short title, extent, application, commencement, duration and savings.
2. Definitions.

Chapter II
Punishment for, and Measures for Dealing with, Terrorist Activities

3. Punishment for terrorist acts.
4. Possession of certain unauthorized arms, etc.
5. Enhanced penalties.
6. Holding of proceeds of terrorism illegal.
7. Powers of investigating officers and appeal against order of Designated Authority.
8. Forfeiture of proceeds of terrorism.
9. Issue of show cause notice before forfeiture of proceeds of terrorism.
10. Appeal.
11. Order of forfeiture not to interfere with other punishments.
12. Claims by third party.
13. Powers of Designated Authority.
14. Obligation to furnish information.
15. Certain transfers to be null and void.
16. Forfeiture of property of certain persons.
17. Company to transfer shares to Government.

Chapter III
Terrorist Organisations

18. Declaration of an organisation as a terrorist organisation.
19. Denotifcation of a terrorist organisation.

20. Offence relating to membership of a terrorist organisation.
21. Offence relating to support given to a terrorist organisation.
22. Fund raising for a terrorist organisation to be an offence.

Chapter IV
Special Courts

23. Special Courts.
24. Place of sitting.
25. Jurisdiction of Special Courts.
26. Power of Special Courts with respect to other offences.

Clauses

27. Power to direct for samples, etc.
28. Public Prosecutors.
29. Procedure and powers of Special Courts.
30. Protection of witnesses.
31. Trial by Special Courts to have precedence.
32. Certain confessions made to police officers to be taken into consideration.
33. Power to transfer cases to regular courts.
34. Appeal.

Chapter V
Interception of Communication in Certain Cases

35. Definitions.
36. Appointment of Competent Authority.
37. Application for authorisation of interception of wire, electronic or oral communication.
38. Decision by Competent Authority on application for interception.
39. Submission of order of interception to Review Committee.
40. Duration of an order of interception, etc.
41. Authority competent to carry out interception.
42. Interception of communication in emergency.

43. Protection of information collected.

44. Admissibility of evidence collected through the interception of communications.

45. Review of authorisation order.

46. Interception and disclosure of wire, electronic or oral communications prohibited.

47. Annual report of interceptions.

Chapter VI
Miscellaneous

48. Modified application of certain provisions of the Code.

49. Cognizance of offences.

50. Officers competent to investigate offences under this Act.

51. Arrest.

52. Presumption as to offences under section 3.

53. Bar of jurisdiction of courts, etc.

54. Savings.

55. Overriding effect.

56. Protection of action taken in good faith.

57. Punishment and compensation for malicious action.

58. Impounding of passport and arms licence of person chargesheeted under the Act.

59. Review Committees.

60. Power of High Courts to make rules.

61. Power to make rules.

62. Orders and rules to be laid before Houses of Parliament.

63. Repeal and saving.

Schedule.

THE PREVENTION OF TERRORISM BILL, 2001
A
BILL

to make provisions for the prevention of, and for dealing with, terrorist activities and for matters connected therewith.

Be it enacted by Parliament in the Fifty-second Year of the Republic of India as follows:—

Chapter I
Preliminary

1. Short title, extent, application, commencement, duration and savings.

(*1*) This Act may be called the Prevention of Terrorism Act, 2001.

(2) It extends to the whole of India.

(*3*) Every person shall be liable to punishment under this Act for every act or omission contrary to the provisions thereof, of which he is held guilty in India.

(*4*) Any person who commits an offence beyond India which is punishable under this Act shall be dealt with according to the provisions of this Act in the same manner as if such act had been committed in India.

(*5*) The provisions of this Act apply also to—

(*a*) citizens of India outside India;

(*b*) persons in the service of the Government, wherever they may be; and

(*c*) persons on ships and aircrafts, registered in India, wherever they may be.

(*6*) It shall be deemed to have come into force on the 24th day of October. 2001 and shall remain in force for a period of three years from the date of its commencement, but its expiry under the operation of this sub-section shall not affect—

(*a*) the previous operation of, or anything duly done or suffered under this Act, or

(*b*) any right, privilege, obligation or liability acquired, accrued or incurred under this Act, or

(*c*) any penalty, forfeiture or punishment incurred in respect of any offence under this Act, or

(*d*) any investigation, legal proceeding or remedy in respect of any such right, privilege, obligation, liability, penalty, forfeiture or punishment as aforesaid, and, any such investigation, legal proceeding or remedy may be instituted, continued or enforced and any such penalty, forfeiture or punishment may be imposed as if this Act had not expired.

2. Definitions.

(*1*) In this Act, unless the context otherwise requires,—

(*a*) "Code" means the Code of Criminal Procedure. 1973;

(*b*) "Designated Authority" shall mean such officer of the Central Government not below the rank of Joint Secretary to the Government, or such officer of the State Government not below the rank of Secretary to the Government, as the case may be, as may be specified by the Central Government or as the case may be, the State Government, by a notification published in the Official Gazette;

(*c*) "proceeds of terrorism" shall mean all kinds of properties which have been derived or obtained from commission of any terrorist act or have been acquired .through funds traceable to a terrorist act, and shall include cash, irrespective of person in whose name such proceeds are standing or in whose possession they are found;

(*d*) "property" means property and assets of every description, whether corporeal or incorporeal, movable or immovable, tangible or intangible and deeds and instruments evidencing title to, or interest in, such property or assets;

(*e*) "Public Prosecutor" means a Public-Prosecutor or an Additional Public Prosecutor or a Special Public Prosecutor appointed under section 28 and includes any person acting under the directions of the Public Prosecutor;

(*f*) "Special Court" means a Special Court constituted under section 23;

(*g*) "terrorist act" has the meaning assigned to it in sub-section (*1*) of section 3, and the expression "terrorist" shall be construed accordingly;

(*h*) "State Government", in relation to a Union territory, means the Administrator thereof;

(*i*) words and expressions used but not defined in this Act and defined in the Code shall have the meanings respectively assigned to them in the Code.

(2) Any reference in this Act to any enactment or any provision thereof shall, in relation to an area in which such enactment or such provision is not in force, be construed as a reference to the corresponding law or the relevant provision of the corresponding law, if any, in force in that area.

Chapter II
Punishment for, and Measures for Dealing with, Terrorist Activities

3. Punishment for terrorist acts.

(1) Whoever,—

(*a*) with intent to threaten the unity, integrity, security or sovereignty of India or to strike terror in the people or any section of the people does any actor thing by using bombs, dynamite or other explosive substances or inflammable substances or fire arms or other lethal weapons or poisons or noxious gases or other chemicals or by any other substances (whether biological or otherwise) of a hazardous nature or by any other means whatsoever, in such a manner as to cause, or likely to cause, death of, or injuries to any person or persons or loss of, or damage to, or destruction of, property or disruption of any supplies or services essential to the life of the community or causes damage or destruction of any property or equipment used or intended to be used for the defence of India or in connection with any other purposes of the Government of India, any State Government or any of their Agencies, or detains any person and threatens to kill or injure such person in order to compel the Government or any other person to do or abstain from doing any act;

(*b*) is or continues to be a member of an association declared unlawful under the Unlawful Activities (Prevention) Act, 1967, or voluntarily does an act aiding or promoting in any manner the objects of such association and in either case is in possession of any unlicensed firearms, ammunition, explosive or other instrument or substance capable of causing mass destruction and commits any act resulting in loss of human life or grievous injury to any person or causes significant damage to any property.

commits a terrorist act.

Explanation.— For the purposes of this sub-section, "a terrorist act" shall include the act of raising funds intended for the purpose of terrorism.

(2) Whoever commits a terrorist act, shall,—

(*i*) if such act has resulted in the death of any person, be punishable with death or imprisonment for life and shall also be liable to fine;

(*ii*) in any other case, be punishable with imprisonment for a term which shall not be less than five years but which may extend to imprisonment for life and shall also be liable to fine.

(3) Whoever conspires or attempts to commit, or advocates, abets, advises or incites or knowingly facilitates the commission of, a terrorist act or any

act preparatory to a terrorist act, shall be punishable with imprisonment for a term which shall not be less than five years but which may extend to imprisonment for life and shall also be liable to fine.

(*4*) Whoever voluntarily harbours or conceals, or attempts to harbour or conceal any person knowing that such person is a terrorist shall be punishable with imprisonment for a term which shall not be less than three years but which may extend to imprisonment for life and shall also be liable to fine:

Provided that this sub-section shall not apply to any case in which the harbour or concealment is by the husband or wife of the offender.

(*5*) Any person who is a member of a terrorist gang or a terrorist organisation, which is involved in terrorist acts, shall be punishable with imprisonment for a term which may extend to imprisonment for life or with fine which may extend to rupees ten lakh or with both.

Explanation.— For the purposes of this sub-section, "terrorist organisation" means an organisation which is concerned with or involved in terrorism.

(*6*) Whoever knowingly holds any property derived or obtained from commission of any terrorist act or has been acquired through the terrorist funds shall be punishable with imprisonment for a term which may extend to imprisonment for life or with fine which may extend to rupees ten lakh or with both.

(*7*) Whoever threatens any person who is a witness or any other person in whom such witness may be interested, with violence, or wrongfully restrains or confines the witness, or any other person in whom the witness may be interested, or does any other unlawful act with the said intent, shall be punishable with imprisonment which may extend to three years and fine.

4. Possession of certain unauthorized arms, etc. Where any person is in unauthorised possession of any

> (*a*) arms or ammunition specified in columns (2) and (3) of Category I or Category III (a) of Schedule I to the Arms Rules, 1962, in a notified area,
>
> (*b*) bombs, dynamite or hazardous explosive substances or other lethal weapons capable of mass destruction or biological or chemical substances of warfare in any area, whether notified or not,

he shall be guilty of terrorist act notwithstanding anything contained in any other law for the time being in force, and be punishable with imprisonment for a term which may extend to imprisonment for life or with fine which may extend to rupees ten lakh or with both.

Explanation:— In this section "notified area" means such area as the State Government may, by notification in the Official Gazette, specify.

5. Enhanced penalties.

(1) If any person with intent to aid any terrorist contravenes any provision of, or any rule made under, the Arms Act, 1959, the Explosives Act, 1884, the Explosive Substances Act, 1908 or the Inflammable Substances Act, 1952, he shall, notwithstanding anything contained in any of the aforesaid Acts or the rules made thereunder, be punishable with imprisonment for a term which may extend to imprisonment for life and shall also be liable to fine.

(2) For the purposes of this section, any person who attempts to contravene or abets, or does any act preparatory to the contravention of any provision of any law, rule or order, shall be deemed to have contravened that provision, and the provisions of subsection (1) shall, in relation to such person, have effect subject to the modification that the reference to "imprisonment for life" shall be construed as a reference to "imprisonment for ten years".

6. Holding of proceeds of terrorism illegal.

(1) No person shall hold or be in possession of any proceeds of terrorism.

(2) Proceeds of terrorism, whether held by a terrorist or by any other person and whether or not such person is prosecuted or convicted under this Act, shall be liable to be forfeited-to the Central Government or the State Government, as the case may be, in the manner provided under this Chapter.

7. Powers of investigating officers and appeal against order of Designated Authority.

(1) If an officer (not below the rank of Superintendent of Police) investigating an offence committed under this Act, has reason to believe that any property in relation to which an investigation is being conducted, represents proceeds of terrorism, he shall, with the prior approval in writing of the Director General of the Police of the State in which such property is situated, make an order seizing such property and where it is not practicable to seize such property, make an order of attachment directing that such property shall not be transferred or otherwise dealt with except with the prior permission of the officer making such order, or of the Designated Authority, before whom the properties seized or attached are produced and a copy of such order shall be served on the person concerned.

(2) The investigating officer shall duly inform the Designated Authority within forty-eight hours of the seizure or attachment of such property.

(3) It shall be open to the Designated Authority before whom the seized attached properties are produced either to confirm or revoke the order of attachment so issued:

Provided that an opportunity of making a representation by the person whose property is being attached shall be given.

(*4*) In the case of immovable property attached by the investigating officer, it shall be deemed to have been produced before the Designated Authority when the investigating officer notifies his report and places it at the disposal of the Designated Authority.

(*5*) The investigating officer may seize and detain any cash to which this Chapter applies if he has reasonable grounds for suspecting that—

(*a*) it is intended to be used for the purposes of terrorism;

(*b*) it forms the whole or part of the resources of an organisation declared as terrorist organisation under this Act:

Provided that the cash seized under this sub-section by the investigating officer shall be released not later than the period of forty-eight hours beginning with the time when it is seized unless the matter involving the cash is before the Designated Authority and such authority passes an order allowing its retention beyond forty-eight hours.

Explanation:—For the purposes of this sub-section, "cash" means—

(*a*) coins and notes in any currency;

(*b*) postal orders;

(*c*) traveller's cheques;

(*d*) banker's drafts; and

(*e*) such other monetary instruments as the Central Government or, as the case may be, the State Government may specify by an order made in writing.

(*6*) Any person aggrieved by an order made by the Designated Authority may prefer an appeal to the Special Court and the Special Court may either confirm the order of attachement of property or seizure so made or revoke such order and release the property.

8. Forfeiture of proceeds of terrorism.

Where any property is seized or attached on the ground that it constitutes proceeds of terrorism and the Special Court is satisfied in this regard under sub-section (*6*) of section 7, it may order forfeiture of such property, whether or not the person from whose possession it is seized or attached, is prosecuted in a Special Court for an offence under this Act.

9. Issue of show cause notice before forfeiture of proceeds of terrorism.

(*1*) No order forfeiting any proceeds of terrorism shall be made under section 8 unless the person holding or in possession of such proceeds is given a notice in writing informing him of the grounds on which it is proposed to forfeit the proceeds of terrorism and such person is given an opportunity of making a representation in writing within such reasonable time as may be specified in the notice against the grounds of forfeiture and is also given a reasonable opportunity of being heard in the matter.

(2) No order of forfeiture shall be made under sub-section (*1*), if such person establishes that he is a *bona fide* transferee of such proceeds for value without knowing that they represent proceeds of terrorism.

(3) It shall be competent for the Special Court to make an order in respect of property seized or attached,—

(*a*) directing it to be sold if it is a perishable property and the provisions of section 459 of the Code shall, as nearly as may be practicable, apply to the net proceeds of such sale;

(*b*) nominating any officer of the Central or State Government, in the case of any other property, to perform the function of the Administrator of such property subject to such conditions as may be specified by the Special Court.

10. Appeal.

(*1*) Any person aggrieved by an order of forfeiture under section 8 may, within one month from the date of the receipt of such order, appeal to the High Court within whose jurisdiction, the Special Court, who passed the order appealed against, is situated.

(2) Where an order under section 8 is modified or annulled by the High Court or where in a prosecution instituted for the contravention of the provisions of this Act, the person against whom an order of forfeiture has been made under section 8 is acquitted, such property shall be returned to him and in either case if it is not possible for any reason to return the forfeited property, such person shall be paid the price therefor as if the property had been sold to the Central Government with reasonable interest calculated from the day of seizure of the property and such price shall be determined in the manner prescribed.

11. Order of forfeiture not to interfere with other punishments.

The order of forfeiture made under this Act by the Special Court, shall not prevent the infliction of any other punishment to which the person affected thereby is liable under this Act.

12. Claims by third party.

(*1*) Where any claim is preferred, or any objection is made to the seizure of any property under section 7 on the ground that such property is not liable to seizure, the Designated Authority before whom such property is produced, shall proceed to investigate the claim or objection:

Provided that no such investigation shall be made where the Designated Authority considers that the claim or objection was designed to cause unnecessary delay.

(*2*) In case claimant or objector establishes that the property specified in the notice issued under section 9 is not liable to be attached or forfeited under the Act, the said notice shall be withdrawn or modified accordingly.

13. Powers of Designated Authority.

The Designated Authority, acting under the provisions of this Act, shall have all the powers of a Civil Court required for making a full and fair enquiry into the matter before it.

14. Obligation to furnish information.

(*1*) Notwithstanding anything contained in any other law, the officer investigating any offence under this Act, with prior approval in writing of an officer not below the rank of a Superintendent of Police, may require any officer or authority of the Central Government or a State Government or a local authority or a Bank or a company, or a firm or any other institution, establishment, organisation or any individual to furnish information in their possession in relation to such offence, on points or matters, where the investigating officer has reason to believe that such information will be useful for, or relevant to, the purposes of this Act.

(*2*) Failure to furnish the information called for under sub-section (*1*), or deliberately furnishing false information shall be punishable with imprisonment for a term which may extend to three years or with fine or with both.

(*3*) Notwithstanding anything contained in the Code, the offence under sub-section (*1*) shall be tried as a summary case and the procedure prescribed in Chapter XXI of the said Code [except sub-section (*2*) of section 262] shall be applicable thereto.

15. Certain transfers to be null and void.

Where, after the issue of an order under section 7 or issue of a notice under section 9, any property referred to in the said order or notice is transferred by any mode whatsoever, such transfer shall, for the purpose of the proceedings under this Act, be ignored and if such property is subsequently forfeited, the transfer of such property shall be deemed to be null and void.

16. Forfeiture of property of certain persons.

(*1*) Where any person is accused of any offence under this Act, it shall be open to the Special Court trying him to pass an order that all or any of the properties, movable or immovable or both belonging to him, shall, during the period of such trial, be attached, if not already attached under this Act.

(*2*) Where a person has been convicted of any offence punishable under this Act, the Special Court may, in addition to awarding any punishment, by order in writing, declare that any property, movable or immovable or both, belonging to the accused and specified in the order, shall stand forfeited to the Central Government or the State Government, as the case may be, free from all encumbrances.

17. Company to transfer shares to Government.

Where any shares in a company stand forfeited to the Central Government or the State Government, as the case may be, under this Act, then, the company shall on receipt of the order of the Special Court, notwithstanding anything contained in the Companies Act, 1956, or the articles of association of the company, forthwith register the Central Government or the State Government as the case may be, as the transferee of such shares.

Chapter III
Terrorist Organisations

18. Declaration of an organisation as a terrorist organisation.

(*1*) For the purposes of this Act, an organisation is a terrorist organisation if—

(*a*) it is listed in the Schedule, or

(*b*) it operates under the same name as an organisation listed in that Schedule.

(2) The Central Government may by order, in the Official Gazette,—

(*a*) add an organisation to the Schedule;

(*b*) remove an organisation from that Schedule;

(*c*) amend that Schedule in some other way.

(3) The Central Government may exercise its power under clause (*a*) of sub-section (2) in respect of an organisation only if it believes that it is involved in terrorism.

(4) For the purposes of sub-section (3), an organisation shall be deemed to be involved in terrorism if it—

(*a*) commits or participates in acts of terrorism,

(*b*) prepares for terrorism,

(*c*) promotes or encourages terrorism, or

(*d*) is otherwise involved in terrorism.

19. Denotification of a terrorist organisation.

(*1*) An application may be made to the Central Government for the exercise of its power under clause (*b*) of sub-section (2) of section 18 to remove an organisation from the Schedule.

(2) An application may be made by—

(*a*) the organisation, or

(*b*) any person affected by inclusion of the organisation in the Schedule as a terrorist organisation.

(*3*) The Central Government may make rules to prescribe the procedure for admission and disposal of an application made under this section.

(*4*) Where an application under sub-section (*1*) has been refused, the applicant may apply for a review to the Review Committee constituted by the Central Government under sub-section (*1*) of section 59 within one month from the date of receipt of the order by the applicant.

(*5*) The Review Committee may allow an application for review against refusal to remove an organisation from the Schedule, if it considers that the decision to refuse was flawed when considered in the light of the principles applicable on an application for judicial review.

(*6*) Where the Review Committee allows review under sub-section (*5*) by or in respect of an organisation, it may make an order under this sub-section.

(*7*) Where an order is made under sub-section (*6*), the Central Government shall, as soon as the certified copy of the order is received by it, make an order removing the organisation from the list in the Schedule.

20. Offence relating to membership of a terrorist organisation.

(*1*) A person commits an offence if he belongs or professes to belong to a terrorist organisation:

Provided that this sub-section shall not apply where the person charged is able to prove—

(*a*) that the organisation was not declared as a terrorist organisation at the time when he became a member or began to profess to be a member, and

(*b*) that he has not taken part in the activities of the organisation at any time during its inclusion in the Schedule as a terrorist organisation.

(2) A person guilty of an offence under this section shall be liable, on conviction, to imprisonment for a term not exceeding ten years or with fine or with both.

21. Offence relating to support given to a terrorist organisation.

(*1*) A person commits an offence if—

(*a*) he invites support for a terrorist organisation, and

(*b*) the support is not, or is not restricted to, the provision of money or other property within the meaning of section 22.

(2) A person commits an offence if he arranges, manages or assists in arranging or managing a meeting which he knows is—

(*a*) to support a terrorist organisation,

(*b*) to further the activities of a terrorist organisation, or

(*c*) to be addressed by a person who belongs or professes to belong to a terrorist organisation.

(3) A person commits an offence if he addresses a meeting for the purpose of encouraging support for a terrorist organisation or to further its activities.

(4) A person guilty of an offence under this section shall be liable on conviction, to imprisonment for a term not exceeding ten years or with fine or with both.

Explanation.— For the purposes of this section, the expression "meeting" means a meeting of three or more persons whether or not the public are admitted.

22. Fund raising for a terrorist organisation to be an offence.

(1) A person commits an offence if he—

(*a*) invites another to provide money or other property, and

(*b*) intends that it should be used, or has reasonable cause to suspect that it may be used, for the purposes of terrorism.

(2) A person commits an offence if he—

(*a*) receives money or other property, and

(*b*) intends that it should be used, or has reasonable cause to suspect that it may be used, for the purposes of terrorism.

(3) A person commits an offence if he—

(*a*) provides money or other property, and

(*b*) knows or has reasonable cause to suspect that it will or may be used for the purposes of terrorism.

(4) In this section, a reference to the provision of money or other property is a reference to its being given, lent or otherwise made available, whether or not for consideration.

(5) A person guilty of an offence under this section shall be liable on conviction, to imprisonment for a term not exceeding fourteen years or with fine or with both.

Chapter IV
Special Courts

23. Special Courts.

(1) The Central Government or a State Government may, by notification in the Official Gazette, constitute one or more Special Courts for such area or

areas, or for such case or class or group of cases, as may be specified in the notification.

(*2*) Where a notification constituting a Special Court for any area or areas or for any case or class or group of cases is issued by the Central Government under sub-section (*1*), and a notification constituting a Special Court for the same area or areas or for the same case or class or group of cases has also been issued by the State Government under that subsection, the Special Court constituted by the Central Government, whether the notification constituting such Court is issued before or after the issue of the notification constituting the Special Court by the State Government, shall have, and the Special Court constituted by the State Government shall not have, jurisdiction to try any offence committed in that area or areas or, as the case may be, the case or class or group of cases and all cases pending before any Special Court constituted by the State Government shall stand transferred to the Special Court constituted by the Central Government.

(*3*) Where any question arises as to the jurisdiction of any Special Court, it shall be referred to the Central Government whose decision in the matter shall be final.

(*4*) A Special Court shall be presided over by a judge to be appointed by the Central Government or, as the case may be, the State Government, with the concurrence of the Chief Justice of the High Court.

(*5*) The Central Government or, as the case may be, the State Government may also appoint, with the concurrence of the Chief Justice of the High Court, additional judges to exercise jurisdiction of a Special Court.

(*6*) A person shall not be qualified for appointment as a judge or an additional judge of a Special Court unless he is, immediately before such appointment, a sessions judge or an additional sessions judge in any State.

(*7*) For the removal of doubts, it is hereby provided that the attainment, by a person appointed as a judge or an additional judge of a Special Court, or the age of superannuation under the rules applicable to him in the service to which he belongs, shall not affect his continuance as such judge or additional judge.

(*8*) Where any additional judge or additional judges is or are appointed in a Special Court, the judge of the Special Court may, from time to time, by general or special order, in writing, provide for the distribution of business of the Special Court among all judges including himself and the additional judge or additional judges and also for the disposal of urgent business in the event of his absence or the absence of any additional judge.

24. Place of sitting.

A Special Court may, on its own motion, or on an application made by the Public Prosecutor and if it considers it expedient or desirable so to do, sit for any of its proceedings at any place other than its ordinary place of sitting:

Provided that nothing in this section shall be construed to change the place of sitting of a Special Court constituted by a State Government to any place outside that State.

25. Jurisdiction of Special Courts.

(*1*) Notwithstanding anything contained in the Code, every offence punishable under any provision of this Act shall be triable only by the Special Court within whose local jurisdiction it was committed or, as the case may be, by the Special Court constituted for trying such offence under section 23.

(2) If, having regard to the exigencies of the situation prevailing in a State,—

(*i*) it is not possible to have a fair, impartial or speedy trial; or

(*ii*) it is not feasible to have the trial without occasioning the breach of peace or grave risk to the safety of the accused, the witnesses, the Public Prosecutor and a judge of the Special Court or any of them; or

(*iii*) it is not otherwise in the interests of justice,

the Supreme Court may transfer any case pending before a Special Court to any other Special Court within that State or in any other State and the High Court may transfer any case pending before a Special Court situated in that State to any other Special Court within the State.

(*3*) The Supreme Court or the High Court, as the case may be, may act under this section either on the application of the Central Government or a party interested and any such application shall be made by motion, which shall, except when the applicant is the Attorney-General of India, be supported by an affidavit or affirmation.

26. Power of Special Courts with respect to other offences.

(*1*) When trying any offence, a Special Court may also try any other offence with which the accused may, under the Code, be charged at the same trial if the offence is connected with such other offence.

(*2*) If, in the course of any trial under this Act of any offence, it is found that the accused person has committed any other offence under this Act or under any other law, the Special Court may convict such person of such other offence and pass any sentence or award punishment authorised by this Act or such rule or, as the case may be, under such other law.

27. Power to direct for samples, etc.

(*1*) When a police officer investigating a case requests the Court of a Chief Judicial Magistrate or the Court of a Chief Metropolitan Magistrate in writing for obtaining samples of hand writing, finger prints, foot prints, photographs, blood, saliva, semen, hair, voice of any accused person, reasonably suspected to be involved in the commission of an offence under this Act, it shall be lawful for the Court of a Chief Judicial Magistrate or the Court of a Chief Metropolitan Magistrate to direct that such samples be given by the accused person to the police officer either through a medical practitioner or otherwise, as the case may be.

(2) If any accused person refuses to give samples as provided in sub-section (*1*), the court shall draw adverse inference against the accused.

28. Public Prosecutors.

(*1*) For every Special Court, the Central Government or, as the case may be, the State Government, shall appoint a person to be the Public Prosecutor and may appoint one or more persons to be the Additional Public Prosecutor or Additional Public Prosecutors:

Provided that the Central Government or, as the case may be, the State Government, may also appoint for any case or class or group of cases, a Special Public Prosecutor.

(*2*) A person shall not be qualified to be appointed as a Public Prosecutor or an Additional Public Prosecutor or a Special Public Prosecutor under this section unless he has been in practice as an Advocate for not less than seven years or has held; any post, for a period of not less than seven years, under the Union or a State, requiring special knowledge of law.

(*3*) Every person appointed as a Public Prosecutor or an Additional Public Prosecutor or a Special Public Prosecutor under this section shall be deemed to be a Public Prosecutor within the meaning of clause (*u*) of section 2 of the Code, and the provisions of the Code shall have effect accordingly.

29. Procedure and powers of Special Courts.

(*1*) Subject to the provisions of section 49, a Special Court may take cognizance of any offence, without the accused being committed to it for trial, upon receiving a complaint of facts that constitute such offence or upon a police report of such facts.

(*2*) Where an offence triable by a Special Court is punishable with imprisonment for a term not exceeding three years or with fine or with both, the Special Court may, notwithstanding anything contained in sub-section (*1*) of section 260 or section 262 of the Code, try the offence in a summary way in accordance with the procedure prescribed in the Code and the provisions of sections 263 to 265 of the Code, shall so far as may be, apply to such trial:

Provided that when, in the course of a summary trial under this sub-section, it appears to the Special Court that the nature of the case is such that it is undesirable to try it in a summary way, the Special Court shall recall any witnesses who may have been examined and proceed to re-hear the case in the manner provided by the provisions of the Code for the trial of such offence and the said provisions shall apply to and in relation to a Special Court as they apply to and in relation to a Magistrate:

Provided further that in the case of any conviction in a summary trial under this section, it shall be lawful for a Special Court to pass a sentence of imprisonment for a term not exceeding one year and with fine which may extend to rupees five lakh.

(3) Subject to the other provisions of this Act, a Special Court shall, for the purpose of trial of any offence, have all the powers of a Court of Session and shall try such offence as if it were a Court of Session so far as may be in accordance with the procedure prescribed in the Code for the trial before a Court of Session.

(4) Subject to the other provisions of this Act, every case transferred to a Special Court under section 25 shall be dealt with as if such case had been transferred under section 406 of the Code to such Special Court.

(5) Notwithstanding anything contained in the Code, but subject to the provisions of section 299 of the Code, a Special Court may, if it thinks fit and for reasons to be recorded by it, proceed with the trial in the absence of the accused or his pleader and record the evidence of any witness, subject to the right of the accused to recall the witness for cross-examination.

30. Protection of witnesses.

(1) Notwithstanding anything contained in the Code, the proceedings under this Act may, for reasons to be recorded in writing, be held *in camera* if the Special Court so desires.

(2) A Special Court, if on an application made by a witness in any proceeding before it or by the Public Prosecutor in relation to such witness or on its own motion, is satisfied that the life of such witness is in danger, it may, for reasons to be recorded in writing, take such measures as it deems fit for keeping the identity and address of such witness secret.

(3) In particular, and without prejudice to the generality of the provisions of subsection (2), the measures which a Special Court may take under that sub-section may include—

(*a*) the holding of the proceedings at a place to be decided by the Special Court;

(*b*) the avoiding of the mention of the names and addresses of the witnesses in its orders or judgments or in any records of the case accessible to public;

(*c*) the issuing of any directions for securing that the identity and address of the witnesses are not disclosed;

(*d*) a decision that it is in the public interest to order that all or any of the proceedings pending before such a court shall not be published in any manner.

(*4*) Any person who contravenes any decision or direction issued under sub-section (*3*) shall be punishable with imprisonment for a term which may extend to one year and with fine which may extend to one thousand rupees.

31. Trial by Special Courts to have precedence.

The trial under this Act of any offence by a Special Court shall have precedence over the trial of any other case against the accused in any other court (not being a Special Court) and shall be concluded in preference to the trial of such other case and accordingly the trial of such other case shall remain in abeyance.

32. Certain confessions made to police officers to be taker, into consideration.

(*1*) Notwithstanding anything in the Code or in the Indian Evidence Act, 1872, but subject to the provisions of this section, a confession made by a person before a police officer not lower in rank than a Superintendent of Police and recorded by such police officer either in writing or on any mechanical or electronic device like cassettes, tapes or sound tracks from out of which sound or images can be reproduced, shall be admissible in the trial of such person for an offence under this Act or rules made thereunder.

(*2*) A police officer shall, before recording any confession made by a person under sub-section (*1*), explain to such person in writing that he is not bound to make a confession and that if he does so, it may be used against him:

Provided that where such person prefers to remain silent, the police officer shall not compel or induce him to make any confession.

(*3*) The confession shall be recorded in an atmosphere free from threat or inducement and shall be in the same language in which the person makes it.

(*4*) The person from whom a confession has been recorded under sub-section (*1*), shall be produced before the Court of a Chief Metropolitan Magistrate or the Court of a Chief Judicial Magistrate along with the original statement of confession, written or recorded on mechanical or electronic device within forty-eight hours.

(*5*) The Chief Metropolitan Magistrate or the Chief Judicial Magistrate, shall, record the statement, if any, made by the person so produced and get his signature or thumb impression and if there is any complaint of torture, such person shall be directed to be produced for medical examination before a Medical Officer not lower in rank than an Assistant Civil Surgeon and thereafter, he shall be sent to judicial custody.

33. Power to transfer cases to regular courts.

Where, after taking cognizance of any offence, a Special Court is of the opinion that the offence is not triable by it, it shall, notwithstanding that it has no jurisdiction to try such offence, transfer the case for the trial of such offence to any court having jurisdiction under the Code and the court to which the case is transferred may proceed with the trial of the offence as if it had taken cognizance of the offence.

34. Appeal.

(*1*) Notwithstanding anything contained in the Code, an appeal shall lie from any judgment, sentence or order, not being an interlocutory order, of a Special Court to the High Court both on facts and on law.

Explanation.— For the purposes of this section. "High Court" means a High Court within whose jurisdiction, a Special Court which passed the judgment, sentence or order, is situated.

(*2*) Every appeal under sub-section (*1*) shall be heard by a bench of two Judges of the High Court.

(*3*) Except as aforesaid, no appeal or revision shall lie to any court from any judgment, sentence or order including an interlocutory order of a Special Court.

(*4*) Notwithstanding anything contained in sub-section (*3*) of section 378 of the Code, an appeal shall lie to the High Court against an order of the Special Court granting or refusing bail.

(*5*) Every appeal under this section shall be preferred within a period of thirty days from the date of the judgment, sentence or order appealed from:

Provided that the High Court may entertain an appeal after the expiry of the said period of thirty days if it is satisfied, that the appellant had sufficient cause for not preferring the appeal within the period of thirty days.

Chapter V
Interception of Communication in Certain Cases

35. Definitions.

In this Chapter, unless the context otherwise requires,—

(*a*) "electronic communication" means any transmission of signs, signals, writings, images, sounds, data or intelligence of any nature transmitted in whole or in part by a wire, radio, electromagnetic, photo electronic or photo optical system that affects inland or foreign commerce but does not include,—

(*i*) the radio portion of a cordless telephone communication that is transmitted between the wireless telephone hand-set and the base unit;

(*ii*) any wire or oral communication;

(*iii*) any communication made through a tone only paging device; or

(*iv*) any communication from a tracking device;

(*b*) "intercept" means the aural or other acquisition of the contents by wire, electronic or oral communication through the use of any electronic, mechanical or other device;

(*c*) "oral communication" means any oral communication uttered by a person exhibiting an expectation that such communication is not subject to interception under circumstances justifying such expectation but such term does not include any electronic communication;

(*d*) "wire communication" means any aural transmission made in whole or part through the use of facilities for the transmission of communications by the aid of wire, cable or other like connection between the point of origin and the point of connection, between the point of origin and the point of reception (including the use of such connection in switching station) and such term includes any electronic storage of such communication.

36. Appointment of Competent Authority.

The Central Government or the State Government, as the case may be, may appoint an officer not below the rank of Secretary to the Government in the case of State Government and not below the rank of Joint Secretary to the Government in the case of Central Government, to be the Competent Authority for the purposes of this Chapter.

37. Application for authorisation of interception of wire, electronic or oral communication.

(*1*) A police officer not below the rank of Superintendent of Police supervising the investigation of any terrorist act under this Act may submit an application in writing to the Competent Authority for an order authorising or approving the interception of wire, electronic or oral communication by the investigating officer when he believes that such interception may provide, or has provided evidence of any offence involving a terrorist act.

(2) Each application shall include the following information,—

(*a*) the identity of the investigating officer making the application, and the head of the department authorising the application;

(*b*) a statement of the facts and circumstances relied upon by the applicant to justify his belief that an order should be issued, including—

(*i*) details as to the offence of terrorist act that has been, is being, or is about to be committed;

(*ii*) a particular description of the nature and location of the facilities from which or the place where the communication is to be intercepted;

(*iii*) a particular description of the type of communications sought to be intercepted; and

(*iv*) the identity of the person, if known, committing the terrorist act whose communications are to be intercepted;

(*c*) a statement of the period of time for which the interception is required to be maintained, if the nature of the enquiry is such that the authorisation of interception should not automatically terminate after the described type of communication has been first obtained;

(*d*) a particular description of facts establishing probable cause to believe that additional communications of the same type will occur thereafter; and

(*e*) where the application is for the extension of an order, a statement setting forth the results thus far obtained from the interception, or a reasonable explanation of the failure to obtain such results.

(3) The Competent Authority may require the applicant to furnish additional oral or documentary evidence in support of the application.

38. Decision by Competent Authority on application for interception.

(*1*) Upon such application, the Competent Authority may reject the application, or issue an order, as requested or as modified, authorising or approving interception of wire, electronic or oral communications, if the Competent Authority determines on the basis of the facts submitted by the applicant that—

(*a*) there is a probable cause for belief that an individual is committing, has committed, or is about to commit a particular offence described and made punishable under sections 3 and 6 of this Act;

(*b*) there is a probable cause of belie that particular communications concerning that offence may be obtained through such interception;

(*c*) there is probable cause of belief that the facilities from which, or the place where, the wire, electronic or oral communications are to be intercepted are being used or are about to be used, in connection with the commission of such offence, leased to, or are listed in the name of or commonly used by such person.

(2) Each order by the Competent Authority authorising or approving the interception of any wire, electronic or oral communication under this section shall specify—

(*a*) the identity of the person, if known, whose communications are to be intercepted;

(*b*) the nature and location of the communication facilities as to which, or the place where, authority to intercept is granted;

(*c*) a particular description of the type of communication sought to be intercepted, and a statement of the particular offence to which it relates;

(*d*) the identity of the agency authorised to intercept the communications, and the person authorising the application; and

(*e*) the period of time during which such interception is authorised, including a statement as to whether or not the interception shall automatically terminate after the described communication has been first obtained.

39. Submission of order of Interception to Review Committee.

(*1*) The Competent Authority shall immediately after passing the order under sub-section (*1*) of section 38, but in any case not later than seven days from the passing of the order, submit a copy of the same to the Review Committee constituted under section 59 along with all the relevant underlying papers, record and his own findings, in respect of the said order, for consideration and approval of the order by the Review Committee.

(2) An order authorising the interception of a wire, electronic or oral communication under this section shall, upon request of the applicant, direct that a provider of wire or electronic communication service, landlord, custodian or other person shall furnish to the applicant forthwith all information, facilities, and technical assistance necessary to accomplish the interception unobtrusively and with a minimum of interference with the services that such service provider, landlord, custodian, or person is providing to the person whose communications are to be intercepted.

40. Duration of an order of interception, etc.

(*1*) No order issued under this section may authorise or approve the interception of any wire, electronic or oral communication for any period longer than is necessary to achieve the objective of the authorisation, nor in any event longer than sixty days and such sixty day's period shall begin on the day immediately preceding the day on which the investigation officer first begins to conduct an interception under the order or ten days after order is issued whichever is earlier.

(2) The extension of an order may be granted, but only upon an application for an extension made in accordance with sub-section (*1*) of section 37 and the Competent Authority making the findings required by sub-section (*1*) of section 38, and the period of such extension shall be no longer than the Competent Authority deems necessary to achieve the purposes for which it was granted and in no event for longer man sixty days at a time.

(3) Every order and extension thereof shall contain a provision that the authorisation to intercept shall be executed as soon as practicable and shall be conducted in such manner as to minimise the interception of communications not otherwise subject to interception under this section and shall terminate upon attainment of the authorised objective, or in any event on the expiry of the period of said order or extension thereof.

41. Authority competent to carry out interception.

(*1*) An interception under this Chapter may be conducted in whole or in part by a public servant, acting under the supervision of the investigating officer authorised to conduct the interception.

(2) Whenever an order authorising an interception is issued pursuant to this section, the order may require reports to be made to the Competent Authority who issued the order showing that progress has been made towards achievement of the authorised objective and the need for continued interception and such report shall be made at such intervals as the Competent Authority may require.

42. Interception of communication in emergency.

(*1*) Notwithstanding anything contained in any other provision of this section, an officer not below the rank of Additional Director General of Police or a police officer of equivalent rank who reasonably determines that—

(*a*) an emergency situation exists that involves—

(*i*) immediate danger of death or serious physical injury to any person;

(*ii*) conspiratorial activities threatening the security or interest of the State;

or

(*iii*) conspiratorial activities, characteristic of a terrorist act, that requires a wire, electronic or oral communication, to be intercepted before an order from the Competent Authority authorising such interception can, with due diligence, be obtained, and

(*b*) there are grounds on which an order should be issued under this section to authorize such interception, may authorise, in writing, the investigating officer to intercept such wire, electronic or oral communication, if an application for an order approving the interception is made in accordance with the provisions of sub-sections (1) and (2) of section 37 within forty-eight hours after the interception has occurred, or begins to occur.

(2) In the absence of on order approving the interception made under sub-section(1), such interception shall immediately terminate when the communication sought is obtained or when the application for the order is rejected, whichever is earlier, and in the event of an application for permitting interception being rejected under sub-section (1) of section 38 or an application under sub-section (1) of section 42 for approval being rejected, or in any other case where the interception is terminated without an order having been issued, the contents of any wire, electronic, or oral communication intercepted shall be treated as having been obtained in violation of this section.

43. Protection of information collected.

(a) The contents of any wire, electronic or oral communication intercepted by any means authorised by this section shall as far as possible, be recorded on tape or wire or other comparable device and shall be done in such manner as to protect the recording from editing or other alterations.

(b) Immediately upon the expiration of the period of order, or extension thereof, such recording shall be made available to the Competent Authority issuing such order and shall be sealed under his directions and kept in the custody of such person or authority as the Competent Authority orders, and such recordings shall not be destroyed except upon on order of the Competent Authority and in any event shall be kept for ten years.

(c) Applications made and orders issued under this section shall be sealed by the Competent Authority and custody of the applications and orders shall be kept in such manner as the Competent Authority directs, and shall not be destroyed except on an order of the Competent Authority, and in any event shall be kept for ten years.

44. Admissibility of evidence collected through the interception of communications.

Notwithstanding anything in the Code or in say other law for the time being of in force, the evidence collected through the interception of wire, electronic or oral communication under this Chapter or evidence derived therefrom shall not be received in evidence or otherwise disclosed in any trial, hearing or other proceeding in any court unless each accused has been furnished with a copy of the order of the Competent Authority, and accompanying application, under which the interception was authorized or approved not less than ten days before trial, hearing or proceeding.

Provided further that, the period of ten days may be waived by the judge trying the matter, if he comes to the conclusion that it was not possible to furnish the accused with the above information ten days before the trial, hearing or proceeding and that the accused will not be prejudiced by the delay in receiving such information.

45. Review of authorisation order.

(*1*) The Review Committee constituted by the Central Government or the State Government, as the case may be, shall review every order passed by the Competent Authority under section 38.

(*2*) Every order passed by the Competent Authority under section 38, or disapproved by the officer under section 42, shall be placed before the Review Committee, which shall be considered by the Review Committee within ten days after its receipt, to decide whether the order, was necessary, reasonable and justified.

(*3*) The Review Committee, after examining the entire record and holding such enquiry, if any, deemed necessary may, by order in writing, either approve the order passed by the Competent Authority or may issue order disapproving the same.

(*4*) On issue of an order of disapproval by the Review Committee, the interception, if any, already commenced shall be forthwith discontinued and the intercepted communication, if any, in the form of tape, wire or other device shall, thereupon, not be admissible as evidence in any case and shall be directed to be destroyed.

46. Interception and disclosure of wire, electronic or oral communications prohibited.

Except as otherwise specifically provided in section 38, any police officer who—

(*a*) intentionally intercepts, endeavours to intercept, or procures any other person to intercept or endeavour to intercept any wire, electronic or oral communication;

(*b*) intentionally uses, endeavours to use, or procures any other person to use or endeavours to use any electronic, mechanical or other device to intercept any oral communication when—

(*i*) such device is affixed to, or otherwise transmits a signal through a wire, cable, or other like connection used in wire communication; or

(*ii*) such device transmits communications by radio, or interferes with the transmission of such communication;

(*c*) intentionally discloses, or endeavours to disclose; to any other person the contents of any wire, electronic or oral communication, knowing or having reason to know that the information was obtained through the interception of a wire, electronic or oral communication in violation of this Chapter;

(*d*) intentionally uses, or endeavours to use, the contents of any wire, electronic or oral communication, knowing or having reason to know that the information was obtained through the interception of a wire, electronic or oral communication in violation of this Chapter, or

(*e*) intentionally discloses, or endeavours to disclose, to any other unauthorised person the contents of any wire, electronic or oral communication, intercepted by means authorised by section 38;

(*f*) intentionally continues the interception of wire, electronic or oral communication after the issue of an order of rejection by the Competent Authority under this Chapter;

(*g*) intentionally continues the interception of wire, electronic or oral communication after the issue of an order of disapproval by the Review Committee under sub-section (*3*) of section 45,

shall for such violation be punishable with imprisonment for a term which may extend to one year and with fine up to rupees fifty thousand.

47. Annual report of interceptions.

(*1*) The Central Government and the State Government, as the case may be, shall cause an annual report to be prepared giving a full account of,—

(*i*) the number of applications for authorisation of interceptions received by the Competent Authority from the Police Department in which prosecutions have been launched;

(*ii*) the number of such applications permitted or rejected;

(*iii*) the number of interceptions carried out in emergency situations and the number of approvals granted or rejected in such matters;

(*iv*) the number of prosecutions launched based on such interceptions and convictions resulting from such interceptions, along with an explanatory memorandum giving general assessment of the utility and importance of the interceptions authorised.

(*2*) An annual report shall be laid by the State Government before the State Legislature within three months of the completion of every calendar year:

Provided that, if the State Government is of the opinion that the inclusion of any matter in the annual report would be prejudicial to the security of the State or to the prevention or detection of any terrorist act, the

State Government may exclude such matter from being included in such annual report.

(3) An annual report shall be laid by the Central Government before each House of Parliament within three months of the completion of every calendar year:

Provided that, if the Central Government is of the opinion that the inclusion of any matter in the annual report would be prejudicial to the security of the country or to the prevention or detection of any terrorist act, the Central Government may exclude such matter from being included in such annual report.

Chapter VI
Miscellaneous

48. Modified application of certain provisions of the Code.

(*1*) Notwithstanding anything contained in the Code or any other law, every offence punishable under this Act shall be deemed to be a cognizable offence within the meaning of clause (c) of section 2 of the Code, and "cognizable case" as defined in that clause shall be construed accordingly.

(2) Section 167 of the Code shall apply in relation to a case involving an offence punishable under this Act subject to the modification that in sub-section (2),—

(*a*) the references to "fifteen days", "ninety days" and "sixty days", wherever they occur, shall be construed as references to "thirty days", "ninety days" and "ninety days", respectively; and

(*b*) after the proviso, the following provisos shall be inserted, namely:—

"Provided further that if it is not possible to complete the investigation within the said period of ninety days, the Special Court shall extend the said period up to one hundred and eighty days, on the report of the Public Prosecutor indicating the progress of the investigation and the specific reasons for the detention of the accused beyond the said period of ninety days:

Provided also that if the police officer making the investigation under this Act, requests, for the purposes of investigation, for police custody from judicial custody of any person from judicial custody, he shall file an affidavit stating the reasons fordoing so and shall also explain the delay, if any, for requesting such police custody."

(*3*) Section 268 of the Code shall apply in relation to a case involving an offence punishable under this Act subject to the modification that—

(*a*) the reference in sub-section (*1*) thereof—

(*i*) to "the State Government" shall be construed as a reference to "the Central Government or the State Government",

(*ii*) to "order of the State Government" shall be construed as a reference to "order of the Central Government or the State Government, as the case may be"; and

(*b*) the reference in sub-section (2) thereof, to "State Government" shall be construed as a reference to "Central Government or the State Government, as the case may be".

(*4*) Sections 366,367 and 371 of the Code shall apply in relation to a case involving an offence triable by a Special Court subject to the modification that the reference to "Court of Session", wherever occurring therein, shall be construed as the reference to "Special Court".

(*5*) Nothing in section 438 of the Code shall apply in relation to any case involving the arrest of any person accused of having committed an offence punishable under this Act.

(*6*) Notwithstanding anything contained in the Code, no person accused of an offence punishable under this Act shall, if in custody, be released on bail or on his own bond unless the Court gives the Public Prosecutor an opportunity of being heard.

(*7*) Where the Public Prosecutor opposes the application of the accused to release on bail, no person accused of an offence punishable under this Act or any rule made thereunder shall be released on bail until the court is satisfied that there are grounds for believing that he is not guilty of committing such offence:

Provided that after the expiry of a period of one year from the date of detention of the accused for an offence under this Act, the provisions of sub-section (*6*) of this section shall apply.

(*8*) The restrictions on granting of bail specified in sub-sections (*6*) and (*7*) are in addition to the restrictions under the Code or any other law for the time being in force on granting of bail.

(*9*) Notwithstanding anything contained in sub-sections (*6*), (*7*) and (*8*), no bail shall be granted to a person accused of an offence punishable under this Act, if he is not an Indian citizen and has entered the country unauthorisedly or illegally except in very exceptional circumstances and for reasons to be recorded in writing.

49. Cognizance of offences.

No Court shall take cognizance of any offence under this Act without the previous sanction of the Central Government or, as the case may be, the State Government.

50. Officers competent to investigate offences under this Act

Notwithstanding anything contained in the Code, no police officer,—

(*a*) in the case of the Delhi Special Police Establishment, below the rank of a Deputy Superintendent of Police or a police officer of equivalent rank;

(*b*) in the metropolitan areas of Mumbai, Kolkata, Chennai and Ahmedabad and any other metropolitan area notified as such under sub-section (*1*) of section 8 of the Code, below the rank of an Assistant Commissioner of Police;

(*c*) in any other case not relatable to clause (*a*) or clause (*b*), below the rank of a Deputy Superintendent of Police or a police officer of an equivalent rank,

shall investigate any offence punishable under this Act.

51. Arrest.

(*1*) Where a police officer arrests a person, he shall prepare a custody memo of the person arrested.

(*2*) The person arrested shall be informed of his right to consult a legal practitioner as soon as he is brought to the police station.

(*3*) Whenever any person is arrested, information of his arrest shall be immediately communicated by the police officer to a family member or in his absence to a relative of such person by telegram, telephone or by any other means and this fact shall be recorded by the police officer under the signature of the person arrested.

(*4*) The person arrested shall be permitted to meet the legal practitioner representing him during the course of interrogation of the accused person:

Provided that nothing in this sub-section shall entitle the legal practitioner to remain present throughout the period of interrogation.

52. Presumption as to offences under section 3.

(*1*) in a prosecution for an offence under sub-section (*1*) of section 3, if it is proved—

(*a*) that the arms or explosives or any other substances specified in section 4 were recovered from the possession of the accused and there is reason to believe that such arms or explosives or other substances of a similar nature, were used in the commission of such offence; or (*b*) that the finger-prints of the accused were found at the site of the offence or on anything including arms and vehicles used in connection with the commission of such offence,

the Special Court shall draw adverse inference against the accused.

(*2*) In a prosecution for an offence under sub-section (*3*) of section 3, if it is proved that the accused rendered any financial assistance to a person, having knowledge that such person is accused of, or reasonably suspected of, an offence under that section, the Special Court shall draw adverse inference against the accused.

53. Bar of jurisdiction of courts, etc.

No civil court or other authority shall have or, be entitled to, exercise any jurisdiction, powers or authority in relation to the matters referred to in section 19 and section 39 of the Act.

54. Savings.

(*1*) Nothing in this Act shall affect the jurisdiction exercisable by, or the procedure applicable to, any court or other authority under any law relating to the naval, military or air forces or other armed forces of the Union.

(*2*) For the removal of doubts, it is hereby declared that for the purposes of any such law as is referred to in sub-section (*1*), a Special Court shall be deemed to be a court of ordinary criminal justice.

55. Overriding effect.

The provisions of this Act shall have effect notwithstanding anything inconsistent therewith contained in any enactment other than this Act or in any instrument having effect by virtue of any enactment other than this Act.

56. Protection of action taken in good faith.

No suit, prosecution or other legal proceeding shall lie against the Central Government or a State Government or any officer or authority of the Central Government or State Government or any other authority on whom powers have been conferred under this Act, for anything which is in good faith done or purported to be done in pursuance of this Act:

Provided that no suit, prosecution or other legal proceedings shall lie against any serving member or retired member of the armed forces or other para-military forces in respect of any action taken or purported to be taken by him in good faith, in the course of any operation directed towards combating terrorism.

57. Punishment and compensation for malicious action.

(*1*) Any police officer who exercises powers corruptly or maliciously, knowing that there are no reasonable grounds for proceeding under this

Act, shall be punishable with imprisonment which may extend to two years, or with fine, or with both.

(2) If the Special Court is of the opinion that any person has been corruptly or maliciously proceeded against under this Act, the court may award such compensation as it deems fit to the person, so proceeded against and it shall be paid by the officer, person, authority or Government, as may be specified in the order.

58. Impounding of passport and arms licence of person charge-sheeted under the Act.

Notwithstanding anything contained in any other law for the time being in force, the passport and the arms licence of a person, who is charge sheeted for having committed any offence under this Act, shall be deemed to have been impounded for such period as the Special Court may deem fit.

59. Review Committees.

(*1*) The Central Government and each State Government shall, whenever necessary, constitute one or more Review Committees for the purposes of this Act.

(2) Every such Committee shall consist of a Chairperson and such other members not exceeding three and possessing such qualifications as may be prescribed.

(3) A Chairperson of the Committee shall be a person who is, or who has been, a Judge of a High Court, who shall be appointed by the Central Government, or as the case may be, the State Government, so however, that the concurrence of the Chief Justice of the High Court shall be obtained in the case of a sitting Judge:

Provided that in the case of a Union territory, the appointment of a person who is a Judge of the High Court of a State shall be made as a Chairperson with the concurrence of the Chief Justice of the concerned High Court.

60. Power of High Courts to make rules.

The High Courts may, by notifications in the Official Gazette, make such rules, if any, as they may deem necessary for carrying out the provisions of this Act relating to Special Courts within their territories.

61. Power to make rules.

(*1*) Without prejudice to the powers of the High Courts to make rules under section 60, the Central Government may, by notification in the Official Gazette, make rules for carrying out the provisions of this Act.

(2) In particular, and without prejudice to the generality of the foregoing powers, such rules may provide for all or any of the following matters, namely:—

(*a*) regulating the conduct of persons in respect of areas the control of which is 3 considered necessary or expedient and the removal of such persons from such areas;

(*b*) the entry into, and search of.—

(*i*) any vehicle, vessel or aircraft; or

(*ii*) any place, whatsoever,

reasonably suspected of being used for committing the offences referred to in section 3 or section 4 or for manufacturing or storing anything zfor the commission of any such offence;

(*c*) conferring powers upon,—

(*i*) the Central Government;

(*ii*) a State Government;

(*iii*) an Administrator of a Union territory under article 239 of the Constitution;

(*iv*) an officer of the Central Government not lower in rank than that of a Joint Secretary; or

(*v*) an officer of a State Government not lower in rank than that of a District Magistrate,

to make general or special orders to prevent or deal with terrorist acts;

(*d*) the arrest and trial of persons contravening any of the rules or any order made thereunder;

(*e*) the punishment of any person who contravenes or attempts to contravene or abets or attempts to abet the contravention of any rule or order made thereunder with imprisonment for a term which may extend to one year or fine or both.

(*f*) providing for the seizure and detention of any property in respect of which such contravention, attempt or abetment as is referred to in clause (*e*) has been committed and for the adjudication of such seizure and detention, whether by any court or by any other authority;

(*g*) determination of the price of the forfeited property under sub-section (2) of section 10;

(*h*) the procedure of making application under sub-section (3) of section 19;

(*i*) the qualifications of the members of the Review Committee under sub-section (2) of section 59.

62. Orders and rules to be laid before Houses of Parliament.

Every order and every rule made by the Central Government under this Act shall be laid, as soon as may be after it is made, before each House of Parliament, while it is in session, for a total period of thirty days which may be comprised in one session or in two or more successive sessions, and if, before the expiry of the session immediately following the session or the successive sessions aforesaid, both Houses agree in making any modification in the order or rule or both Houses agree that the order or rule should not be made, the order or rule shall thereafter have effect only in such modified form or be of no effect, as the case may be; so, however, that any such modification or annulment shall be without prejudice to the validity of anything previously done under that order or rule.

63. Repeal and saving.

(*1*) The Prevention of Terrorism Ordinance, 2001, is hereby repealed.

(2) Notwithstanding such repeal, anything done or any action taken under the said Ordinance shall be deemed to have been done or taken under the corresponding provisions of this Act.

Schedule
(See section 18)
Terrorist Organisations

1. Babbar Khalsa International.
2. Khalistan Commando Force.
3. Khalistan Zindabad Force.
4. International Sikh Youth Federation.
5. Lashkar-E-Taiba/Pasban-E-Ahle Hadis.
6. Jaish-E-Mohammed/Tahrik-E-Furqan.
7. Harkat-Ul-Mujahideen/Harkat-Ul-Ansar/Harkat-Ul-Jehad-E-Islami.
8. Hizb-Ul-Mujahideen/Hizb-Ulmujahideen Pir Panjal Regiment.
9. Al-Umar-Mujahideen.
10. Jammu And Kashmir Islamic Front.
11. United Leberation Front of Assam (ULFA).
12. National Democratic Front of Bodoland (NDFB).
13. People's Liberation Army (PLA).

14. United National Liberation Front (UNLF).
15. People's Revolutlonary Party of Kangllipalk (PREPAK).
16. Kanleipak Communist Party (KCP).
17. Kanglei Yaol Kanba Lup (KYKL)
18. Manipur People's Libratiôn Front (MPLF).
19. All Tripura Tiger Force.
20. National Liberation Front of Tripura.
21. Liberation Tigers of Tamil Eelam (LITE).
22. Students Islamic Movement of India.
23. Deendar Anjuman.

Statement of Objects and Reasons

The country faces multifarious challenges in the management of its internal security. There is an upsurge of terrorist activities, intensification of cross border terrorist activities and insurgent groups in different parts of the country. Very often, organized crime and terrorist activities are closely interlinked. Terrorism has now acquired global dimensions and has become a challenge for the entire world. The reach and methods adopted by terrorist groups and organizations take advantage of modem means of communication and technology using high-tech facilities available in the form of communication systems, transport, sophisticated arms and various other means. This has enabled them to strike and create terror among people at will. The existing criminal justice system is not designed to deal with the types of heinous crimes with which the proposed law deals with.

2. In view of the situation, as stated above, it was felt necessary to enact a legislation for the prevention of, and for dealing with terrorists' activities. However, sufficient safeguards are sought to be provided in the proposed law to prevent the possibility of its misuse.

3. Circumstances existed which rendered it necessary for the President to promulgate the Prevention of Terrorism Ordinance, 2001 on 24th October, 2001.

4. The Prevention of Terrorism Bill, 2001 seeks to replace the aforesaid Ordinance.

L. K. Advani.

New Delhi;
The 4th December, 2001.

Notes on Clauses

Clause 1.—This clause makes provision for short-title, extent, application, commencement, duration and savings. Sub-clause (4) makes the provisions of the Bill applicable to any person even beyond India if he commits an offence punishable under this legislation.

Clause 2.—This clause makes provision for the definition of the terms used in the Bill. Sub-clause (1) (c) defines 'proceeds of terrorism' as all kinds of properties which have been derived or obtained from commission of any terrorist act or have been acquired through funds traceable to a terrorist act which will include cash irrespective of person in whose name such proceeds are standing or in whose possession they are found.

Clause 3.—Defines the acts of terrorism which are punishable under the Bill. This clause makes provisions for punishment for terrorist acts. It provides for—

(*i*) punishment of death or imprisonment for life to a person who has committed a terrorist act which has resulted in the death of any person [sub-clause (2)(i)]:

(*ii*) punishment to a person who conspires or attempts to commit, or advocates, abets, advises or incites or knowingly facilitates the commission of a terrorist act or any act preparatory to a terrorist act [sub-clause (3)];

(*iii*) punishment to a person who voluntarily harbours or conceals any person knowing that such a person is a terrorist. The proviso to sub-clause (4) exempts any case in which the harbour or concealment is by the husband or wife of the offender. [sub-clause (4)];

(*iv*) punishment to a member of a terrorist gang or terrorist organization which is involved in terrorist acts [sub-clause (5)];

(*v*) punishment to a person who knowingly holds any property derived or obtained from commission of any terrorist act or has been acquired through the terrorist funds [sub-clause (6)];

(*vi*) protection of the witness by providing for punishment to a person who threatens a witness with violence or wrongfully restrains or confines the witness or commits any unlawful act with the above intention [sub-clause (7)];

Clause 4.—This clause provides for punishment to a person who is in unauthorized possession of arms and ammunition specified in columns (2) and (3) of Category I or Category III (a) of Schedule I to the Arms Rules, 1962, in a notified area. The clause also provides for punishment of unauthorised possession of bombs, dynamite or hazardous explosive substances or other lethal weapons of mass destruction or biological or chemical substances of warfare in any area.

Clause 5.—This clause provides for enhanced penalties to a person who with intention to aid any terrorist contravenes any provision of or rule made under the Arms Act, 1959, the Explosives Act, 1884, the Explosive Substances Act, 1908 or the Inflammable Substances Act, 1952.

Clause 6.—This clause bars the holding or possession or any proceeds of terrorism by any person.

Clause 7.—This clause empowers an officer not below the rank of Superintendent of Police investigating an offence committed under this Bill to make an order with the prior approval of the Director General of Police of the State, seizing such property or an order of attachment where it is not practicable to seize that property which he has reason to believe in relation to which an investigation is bong conducted, represents proceeds of terrorism.

This clause empowers the investigating officer to seize and detain any cash if he has reasonable grounds for suspecting that (a) it is intended to be used for the purposes of terrorism; (b) it forms the whole or part of the resources of an organization declared as terrorist organization under this Bill.

The proviso to sub-clause (5) provides that the cash seized shall be released not later than the period of forty-eight hours beginning with the time when it is seized unless the matter involving the cash is before the designated authorities and such authority, the court passes an order allowing its retention beyond forty-eight hours.

Clause 8.—This clause provides for forfeiture of proceeds of terrorism by the Special Court.

Clause 9.—This clause provides that a show cause notice shall be given in writing before an order forfeiting any proceeds of terrorism is made under clause 8 of this Bill.

Clause 10.—This clause provides for appeal to the High Court against the order of the Special Court for forfeiture under clause 8, within one month.

Clause 11.—This clause provides that the order of forfeiture under clause 8 does not interfere with other punishments which the person affected is liable under this Bill.

Clause 12.—This clause provides for investigation by the Designated Authority or as into the claim or objection preferred to the seizure of any property under clause 7.

Clause 13.—This clause confers the powers of a Civil Court on the Designated Authority.

Clause 14.—This clause provides that an officer investigating any offence under the Bill, with prior approval in writing of an officer not below the rank of Superintendent of Police may require any officer or authority of the Central Government, or a State Government or a local authority or a Bank or a Company, or a firm or any other institution, establishment, organisation or any individual to furnish information in their possession in relation to such offence, on points or matters, where the investigating officer has reason to believe that such information would be useful or relevant to the purposes of this Bill.

Sub-clause (2) of this clause provides for punishment for failure to furnish information called for under sub-clause (*1*).

Clause 15.—This clause provides that after issue of an order under clause 7 or issue of a show cause notice under clause 9, transfer of a property referred to in the said order or notice shall be deemed to be null and void.

Clause 16.—This clause provides that it shall be open to the Special Court trying any person accused of an offence under the Bill to pass an order attaching all or any of the properties, movable or immovable or both belonging to him during the period of the trial.

Clause 17.—This clause provides that where any shares in a company stand forfeited to the Central Government or the State Government, as the case may be, the company shall forthwith register the Central Government or the State Government, as the case may be, as the transferee of such shares notwithstanding the provisions in the Companies Act, 1956 or the Articles of Association of the company.

Clause 18.—This clause provides for declaration of an organisation as a terrorist organisation.

Clause 19.—This clause provides for application for de-notification of a terrorist organisation.

Clauses 20,21 and 22.—These clauses provide for offences relating to membership of a terrorist organisation, support and fund raising for terrorist organisations.

Clauses 23, 24, 25, 26 and 27.—These clauses provide for constitution of Special Courts to try offences committed under the Bill, their jurisdiction, and their powers with respect to other offences.

Clause 28.—This clause provides for appointment of Public Prosecutor for every Special Courts.

Clause 29.—This clause provides for procedure and powers of the Special Courts.

Clause 30.—This clause makes provision for protection of witnesses.

Clause 31.—This clause provides that trial of an offence under this Bill by any Special Court against accused gets precedence over trial of any other offence in any other Courts (not being Special Courts).

Clause 32.—This clause provides for admissibility of confessions made to a police officer under certain conditions that such confessions have to be made before a police officer not lower in rank than that of a Superintendent of Police and unlike as in the Terrorist and Disruptive Activities (Prevention) Act. 1987 have to be further recorded with a Chief Judicial Magistrate within forty-eight hours.

Clause 33.—This clause provides that a Special Court may transfer the trial of the case to a regular court if the Special Court is of the opinion that the offence is not triable by it.

Clause 34.—This clause provides for appeal against any judgment, sentence or order not being an interlocutory in nature.

Clause 35.—This clause provides for definition of a 'electronic communication', 'intercept', 'oral communication' and 'wire communication' for the purpose of the clauses in Chapter V dealing with interception of communication in certain cases.

Clause 36.—This clause provides for appointment of the Competent Authority for the purposes of Chapter V.

Clauses 37 and 38.—These clauses provide for the procedure and decision for interception of the wire, electronic and oral communications.

Clause 39.—This clause provides that the Competent authority which has passed an order under clause 38(1), may submit a copy of the order within the stipulated time to the Review Committee constituted under clause 59.

Clause 40.—This clause provides for the duration of an order of interception of electronic, wire and oral communication.

Clause 41.—This clause provides that an interception under Chapter V may be conducted by a public servant, acting under the supervision of the investigating officer authorised to conduct the interception.

Clause 42.—This clause provides that an officer not below the rank of Additional Director General of Police or a police officer of equivalent rank may authorise interception under Chapter V without the prior permission of the Competent Authority under certain circumstances and conditions.

Clause 43.—This clause provides for protection of information collected through interception under Chapter V.

Clause 44.—This clause provides that the evidence collected through interception of communications under Chapter V is admissible as evidence against the accused in the Court during the trial of a case.

Clause 45.—This clause provides that the Review Committee constituted by the Central Government or the State Governments, as the case may be, review every order passed by the Competent Authority under clause 38.

Clause 46.—This clause prohibits unauthorised interception of communication and also disclosure of intercepted communications to unauthorised persons. The clause also provides for punishment for violation of the clause.

Clause 47.—This clause provides that the Central Government and the State Government, as the case may be, shall prepare annual reports of the full account of the applications for interception, the number of such applications permitted or rejected, number of interceptions carried out in emergency situation and the number of prosecutions and convictions resulting from such interceptions. Such annual reports are to be laid before the House of Parliament or State Legislature, as the case may be within the stipulated time.

Clause 48.—This clause provides for modified applications of sections 2. 167, 268, 366, 367, 371 and 438 of the Code of Criminal Procedure. 1973 in case of a proceeding under the Bill.

Clause 49.—This clause provides that no Court shall take cognizance of any offence under this Bill without the previous sanction of the Central Government or the State Governments, as the case may be.

Clause 50.—This clause provides that no police officer below the rank of the Deputy Superintendent of Police or equivalent rank is competent to investigate an offence under this Bill.

Clause 51.—This clause provides for the procedure of a arrest of a person under this Bill

Clause 52.—This clause provides that the Special Court may draw adverse inference against the accused if arms or explosives or any other substances specified in clause 4 are recovered from the possession of the accused or the finger prints of the accused are found at the place of the offence.

Clause 53.—This clause bars jurisdiction of civil court or any other authority in relation to matters related to clause 19 and clause 39 of this Bill.

Clause 54.—This clause provides that the jurisdiction exercisable by and the procedure applicable to, any court or other authority under any law relating to the naval, military and air force or other armed forces of the Union will not be affected by this Bill.

Clause 55.—This clause provides that the provision of the Bill shall have overriding effect over the provisions of other enactments.

Clause 56.—This clause provides for protection against prosecution or other legal proceedings for action taken in good faith by the Central Government or a State Government or any officer or authority of that Government under the Bill.

Clause 57.—This clause provides for punishment in cases where any police officer exercises powers under the Bill corruptly or maliciously.

Clause 58.—This clause provides for impounding of passport and arms licence of a person chargesheeted for having committed an offence under the Bill.

Clause 59.—This clause provides for constitution of Review Committee by the Central Government or the State Governments, as the case may be, for the purpose of this Bill.

Clause 60.—This clause confers upon the High Courts the power to make rules relating to Special Courts.

Clause 61.—This clause confers powers upon the Central Government to make rules for carrying out the provisions of the Bill.

Clause 62.—This clause provides that the orders and rules made by the Central Government under the Bill shall be laid before each House of Parliament within the stipulated time.

Clause 63.—This clause seeks to repeal the Prevention of Terrorism Ordinance, 2001.

Financial Memorandum

Clause 23 of the Prevention of Terrorism Bill. 2001 provides for constitution of Special Courts by the Central Government or the State Government and also for appointment of Judges and Additional Judges of those Courts. Clause 28 of the said Bill provides for appointment of Public Prosecutor, Additional Public Prosecutor and Special Public Prosecutor by the Central Government or the State Government, as the case may be.

2. The expenditure towards the setting up of Special Courts by the State Governments and towards salary and allowances of the Judges, Additional Judges, Public Prosecutors, Additional Public Prosecutors and Special Public Prosecutors and the staff of such courts will be defrayed out of the Consolidated Fund of the States concerned. The expenditure towards setting up of Special Courts by the Central Government in any State or Union territory will be met out of the Consolidated Fund of India. The likely expenditure on each Special Court and on the salary and allowances of the Judges, Additional Judges, Public Prosecutors, Additional Public Prosecutors and Special Public Prosecutors and staff of such courts for five months is expected to be Rs. 20 lakhs out of which Rs. 10 lakhs would be of a recurring nature and Rs. 10 lakhs of a non-recurring nature. As it is not

possible at this stage to visualize the number of such courts that may have to be established, it is, therefore, not possible to give an estimate of actual expenditure that may have to be incurred on this behalf.

3. Sub-clause (1) of clause 59 of the Bill, provides, *inter alia*, for constitution of one or more Review Committees by the Central Government. Some expenditure of a recurring nature will have to be incurred in connection with the Review Committees and it is not possible at this stage to make an accurate estimate of the expenditure which may be involved.

4. The provisions of the Bill do not involve any other expenditure of a recurring or nonrecurring nature.

Memorandum Regarding Delegated Legislation

Sub-clause (*3*) of clause 19 of the Bill empowers the Central Government to make rules to prescribe the procedure for admission and disposal of an application made under subclause (*1*) of clause 19.

2. Clause 60 of the Bill empowers the High Courts to make such rules, if any, as they may deem necessary for carrying out the provisions of the Bill relating to Special Courts within their territories.

3. Clause 61 of the Bill empowers the Central Government to make rules for carrying out the provisions of the Bill to provide for all or any of the following manors, namely:—

(*a*) regulating the conduct of persons in respect of areas the control of which is considered necessary or expedient and the removal of such persons from such areas;

(*b*) the entry into, and search of any vehicle, vessel, or air craft; or any place, whatsoever;

(*c*) conferring powers upon the Central Government, State Government, Administrator of a Union territory under article 239 of the Constitution, an officer of the Central Government not lower in rank than that of a Joint Secretary, or an officer of a State Government not lower in rank than that of a District Magistrate to make general or special orders to prevent or deal with terrorist acts;

(*d*) the arrest and trial of persons contravening any of the rules or any order made thereunder;

(*e*) punishment of any person who contravenes or attempts to contravene or abets or attempts to abet the contravention of any rule or order made thereunder with imprisonment for a term which may extend to one year or fine or both;

(*f*) providing for the seizure and detention of any property in respect of which such contravention, attempt or abetment as is referred to in clause (e) has been committed and for the adjudication of such seizure and detention, whether by any court or by any other authority;

(*g*) determination of the price of the forfeited property under sub-section (2) of section 10;

(*h*) the procedure for admission or disposal of an application under sub-section (3) of section 19;

(*i*) the qualifications of the members of the Review Committee under sub-section (2) of section 59.

4. The Matters in respect of which the rules may be made under the foregoing provisions relate to matters of detail or procedure. The delegation of legislative power is, therefore, of a normal character.

Memorandum Explaining the Modifications Contained in the Bill to Replace the Prevention of Terrorism Ordinance 2001

The Prevention of Terrorism Bill, 2001, which seeks to repeal the Prevention of Terrorism Ordinance, 200) proposes to make the following modifications, in addition to modifications of consequential or drafting nature, which arc as under:—

(i) It is being provided that the legislation shall remain in force for a period of three years instead of five years from the date of its commencement.

(ii) Sub-clause (8) of clause 3 which makes provision for punishment of person who is in possession of an information which he knows or believes to be of material assistance in preventing the commission of terrorist act and fails to disclose that information to the police, is being omitted.

(iii) Clause 7 is being modified to delete reference to the Special Courts, thus doing away with concurrent jurisdiction of the Designated Authority and the Special Courts and to provide for an appeal against the order made by the Designated Authority to the Special Court.

(iv) Clause 8 is being modified to vest power of forfeiture of the proceeds of terrorism in the Special Court instead of the Designated Authority.

(v) Sub-clause (3) of clause 47 of the Bill makes provision for laying of an anual interception report by the Central Government before each House of Parliament. In clause 62 of the Bill, similar provision has been made for the orders and rules also.

Lok Sabha
A
Bill

to make provisions for the prevention of, and for dealing with, terrorist activities and for matters connected therewith.

(*Shri L. K. Advani, Minister of Home Affairs*)

Appendix II

I. India is a Party to the following international anti-terrorism conventions:

1. The Convention on Offences and Certain Acts Committed on Board Aircraft, signed at Tokyo on 14th September 1963;
(Implemented by the Tokyo Convention Act, 1975).

2. The Convention for the Suppression of Unlawful Seizure of Aircraft, signed at the Hague on 16 December 1970;
(Implemented by the Anti Hijacking Act, 1982).

3. The Convention for the Suppression of Unlawful Acts against the Safety of Civil Aviation, signed at Montreal on 23rd September 1971;
(Implemented by the Suppression of Unlawful Acts Against Safety of Civil Aviation Act, 1982).

4. The Convention on the Prevention and Punishment of Crimes against Internationally Protected Persons, including Diplomatic Agents, adopted by the General Assembly of the UN on 14th December, 1973;
(No implementing legislation is required as the offenses covered are punishable under the Indian Penal Code).

5. The International Convention against the Taking of Hostages, adopted by the General Assembly of the UN on 17th December, 1979;
(Implemented by Section 364 A of Indian Penal Code, 1860, inserted by Criminal Law Amendment Act, 1993, s.2).

6. The Protocol for the Suppression of Unlawful Acts of Violence at Airports Serving international Civil Aviation, Supplementary to the Convention for the Suppression of Unlawful Acts against the Safety of Civil Aviation, signed at Montreal on 24th February 1988;

7. The Convention for the Suppression of Unlawful Acts against the Safety of Maritime Navigation, done at Rome on 10th March, 1988;
(Implementation by Amending Merchant Shipping Act, 1948).

8. The Protocol for the Suppression of Unlawful Acts against the Safety of Fixed Platforms located on the Continental shelf, done at Rome on 10th March, 1988;
(Implementation by Amending Merchant Shipping Act, 1948).

9. The Convention on the Marking of Plastic Explosives for the purpose of Detection, signed at Montreal on 1st March 1991;

10. The International Convention for the Suppression of Terrorist Bombings adopted by the General Assembly of the UN on 15th December, 1997;

11. In addition, India has signed the International Convention for the Suppression of Financing of Terrorism, adopted by the General Assembly of the UN on 9th December 1999.
(Many aspects of financing of Terrorism are addressed in recent legislation, i.e., the Prevention of Terrorism Ordinance.)

Appendix III

The Gazette of India

Extraordinary

Part II-Section 3-Sub-Section (II)
Published by Authority

New Delhi, Wednesday, December 5, 2001/Agrahayana 14, 1923

Ministry of Home Affairs
Order

New Delhi, the 5th December, 2001

S. O.1194(E).—In exercise of the powers conferred by clause (a) of Sub-section (2) of Section 18 of the Prevention of Terrorism Ordinance, 2001 (9 of 2001), and on being satisfied that (1) the Communist Party of India (Marxist—-Leninist)—People's War, all its formations and front organisations; and (2) the Maoist Communist Centre (MCC), all its formations and front organisations are involved in terrorism, the Central Government hereby adds the organisations aforesaid to the Schedule to the said Ordinance with effect from the date of publication of this Order, and the said Schedule shall stand amended as under:

Schedule
(See Section 18)

"24. Communist Party of India (Marxist—Leninist)—People's War, all its formations and front organisations.

25. Maoist Communist Centre (MCC), all its formations and front organisations".

[F.No. II-13014/10/2001-Legal Cell]
A. K. JAIN, Jt. Secy.

DOCUMENT NO. 23

INDIA'S 2002 COUNTER-TERRORISM REPORT TO THE UN

UN Security Council Resolution
S/2002/883

August 7, 2002

Distr.: General
7 August 2002
Original: English

Letter dated 31 July 2002 from the Chairman of the Security Council Committee established pursuant to resolution 1373 (2001) concerning counter-terrorism addressed to the President of the Security Council

I write with reference to my letter of 12 April 2002 (S/2002/457).

The Counter-Terrorism Committee has received the attached supplementary report from India, submitted pursuant to paragraph 6 of resolution 1373 (2001) (see annex).

I would be grateful if you could arrange for this letter and its annex to be circulated as a document of the Security Council.

(*Signed*) Jeremy **Greenstock**
Chairman
Security Council Committee established pursuant to resolution 1373 (2001) concerning counter-terrorism

Annex

Letter dated 12 July 2002 from the Permanent Representative of India to the United Nations addressed to the Chairman of the Security Council Committee established pursuant to resolution 1373 (2001) concerning counter-terrorism

In response to your letter of 22 March 2002, on behalf of my Government, I have the honour to submit herewith to the Counter-Terrorism Committee additional information to the report transmitted to the Committee on 24 December 2001, on the measures taken by the Republic of India to implement the provisions of Security Council resolution 1373 (2001) of 28 September 2001 (see enclosure).

The report is in three parts. Section I covers developments since the submission of India's initial report to the Committee. Section II provides details of the organizational and administrative machinery/mechanisms to tackle terrorism, both from the law and order angle and to monitor and regulate the illicit financial transactions that finance terrorism. Section III provides answers to the specific queries raised by the Committee. I should be grateful if you would have the present letter and the enclosed report (all three parts) circulated as a document of the Security Council.

My Government stands ready to provide the Committee with further information as necessary, or if requested to do so by the Committee, and to assist it in the assessment of the implementation of the resolution.

(*Signed*) V. K. **Nambiar**

Enclosure
Security Council Resolution 1373 (2001): Supplementary Report Submitted by India*

India's Approach to Counter Terrorism

For two decades India has waged a struggle against terrorism, particularly cross border terrorism. During this period a large number of civilians and security personnel have lost their lives apart from rendering hundreds of thousands homeless. The terrorist attacks in USA on 11 September and other attacks such as on Legislative Assembly of Jammu and Kashmir and the terrorist attack on the Indian Parliament on December 13 underscored the fact that terrorism is a global phenomenon that transcends borders and regions. Linkages with illicit trafficking and small arms, narcotics and money laundering have enhanced the lethal reach and destructive potential of terrorism. A matter of further concern is the growing nexus

* The annexes are on file with the Secretariat and are available for consultation.

between extremism of various types, including religious fundamentalism and terrorism. India has consistently pointed out to the international community that the fight against terrorism must be given the highest priority. India also believes that to be effective, the fight against terrorism has to be long term, comprehensive and sustained. It cannot be ad-hoc, selective or compartmentalized in terms of regions, religions or organisations. There can be no justification for terrorism on any grounds: religious, political, ideological or any other. It is also important to ensure that terrorists are denied support and that the international community acts to ensure that no country supports or provide safe havens for terrorists to act with impunity. To combat terrorism effectively, strong domestic measures need to be complemented by strengthened international cooperation to ensure that the fight against terrorism is not restricted only to the perpetrators but also encompasses the States who sponsor them.

India has been supportive of all international efforts, particularly in the UN, to combat terrorism. It is in this framework that India supports UN Security Council Resolution 1373 and is fully committed to implementing it. India is also a signatory to all the 12 UN Sectoral Conventions on Terrorism.

India has submitted its National Report on Measures Taken to Implement UN Security Council Resolution 1373. This has provided information on the measures already in place to tackle terrorism, encompassing both the criminalization and penalization of terrorist acts etc., and to suppress the financing of terrorism. It had also provided information on measures to strengthen international cooperation to combat terrorism.

The Supplementary Report

Further to India's National Report, this Supplementary Report seeks to respond to the questions and clarifications raised by the CTC. The Supplementary Report is structured in three parts:—

(a) Section I covers developments since submission of India's initial report to the CTC. This section inter alia deals with Prevention of Terrorism Act (POTA)—a comprehensive piece of Counter Terrorism legislation that had been adopted by the Indian Parliament since the submission of our initial report to the CTC.

(b) Section II has some details of the organisational and administrative machinery/mechanisms to tackle terrorism, both from the law and order angle and to monitor and regulate the illicit financial transactions that finance terrorism. These agencies have been functional even before POTA and were instruments for combating Terrorism under the existing legislation. With POTA, the legislative authority is now strengthened.

(c) Answers to the specific queries raised by the CTC are covered in Section III.

Section I
Developments Since Submission of Initial Report

Prevention of Terrorism Act, 2002

Since the submission of India's initial report to the CTC, a comprehensive piece of counter terrorism legislation—the Prevention of Terrorism Act—was adopted by Parliament on 26.3.2002.

Salient Features of Prevention of Terrorism Act, 2002

(i) It shall **extend to the whole of India**. It shall remain in force for a period of 3 years.

(ii) Section 3 of the Act defines **'Terrorist Act'** as any act or thing done by using bomb, dynamite or other explosive substances or fire arms or lethal weapons or poisons or noxious gases or other chemicals or by any other substances (whether biological or otherwise) of hazardous nature or by other means in such a manner as to cause or likely to cause death or injuries to any person or persons or loss or damage to or destruction of property or disruption of any supplies or services essential to the life of the community or causes damage or destruction to any property or equipment used or intended to be used in the defence of India in order to compel the Government or any other person to do or abstain from doing any act.

Membership of a terrorists gang or a terrorists organisation involved in terrorist acts shall also constitute a terrorist act. It is provided to proscribe terrorist outfits under the procedure prescribed for making additions or deletions in the list of such terrorist organisations. A person commits an offence if he invites support for a terrorist organisation. A person also commits an offence if he arranges, manages or assists in arranging or managing a meeting which he knows is:

(a) to support a terrorist organisation,

(b) to further the activities of a terrorist organisation, or

(c) to be addressed by a person who belongs or professes to belong to a terrorist organisation.

A person commits an offence if he addresses a meeting and the purpose of his address is to encourage support for a terrorist organisation or to further its activities.

A person also commits an offence under the Act if he wears an item of clothing, or wears, carries or displays an article in a public place in such a way or in such circumstances as to arouse reasonable suspicion that he is a member or supporter of a terrorist organisation. The provisions are similar to the ones obtaining in the UK Terrorism Act, 2000.

Further, whoever is or continues to be a member of an association declared unlawful under the Unlawful Activities (Prevention) Act, 1967, or voluntarily does an act aiding or promoting in any manner the objects of such association and in either case is in possession of any unlicensed firearms, ammunition, explosive or other instrument or substance capable of causing mass destruction and commits any act resulting in loss of human life or grievous injury to any person or causes significant damage to any property, commits a terrorist act.

Possession of certain unauthorised arms or other explosive substances or other lethal weapons capable of mass destruction and/or use in biological or chemical warfare unauthorisedly in a notified area constitutes an offence under this Act. However possession of hazardous explosives or such lethal weapons in any area whether notified or not shall also constitute an offence under this Act.

Terrorist acts also includes acts of fund raising by persons/organizations if such funds are intended for the purposes of terrorism. There are also provisions of seizing properties, assets etc. of terrorist organisations.

(iii) Provision under Section 3(6) seeks to punish those persons who may knowingly come in possession of property derived or obtained from commission of any terrorist act or has been acquired through the terrorist funds.

(iv) In Section 3(7) a new provision has been made for punishment of whoever threatens any person who is a witness or any other person in whom such witness may be interested. This is a salutary provision for protection of witnesses.

(v) Section 14 provides a new provision which makes it obligatory to furnish information in respect of a terrorist offence. Failure to furnish the information called for or deliberately furnishing false information to investigating officer shall be punishable with imprisonment for a term which may extend to three years or fine or both. The investigating officer can call for such information only with prior approval in writing of an officer not below the rank of Superintendent of Police.

(vi) Section 27 provides a new provision wherein a Police Officer investigating a case under the Act can request the Court in writing for obtaining samples of handwriting, finger-prints, foot-prints, photographs, blood, saliva, semen, hair of any accused person who is reasonably suspected to be involved in the commission of an offence under this Act. If any accused person refuses to give such samples, the Court shall draw adverse inference against the accused. This is a salutary provision keeping in view the technological advances in Forensic Sciences and the desirability of promoting scientific investigation of cases.

(vii) Section 29(2) provides that a Special Court may try an offence which is punishable with imprisonment for a term not exceeding three years or fine or both in a summary way. In such cases the punishment prescribed on conviction would be one year imprisonment with fine upto Rs 5 lakhs.

(viii) Section 30 makes special provisions for protection of witnesses including holding of the Court proceedings in camera.

(i) Section 32 provides for admissibility of confessions made to a Police Officer.

(ii) Bail Provision:

Section 49(6) of the Act provides that no person accused of an offence punishable under this Act shall, if in custody, be released on bail or on his own bond unless the Court gives the public prosecutor an opportunity of being heard. Section 49(7) of the Act requires the magistrate to satisfy himself only regarding the innocence of the accused before granting bail to him.

Section 49(9) also provides that bail shall not be granted to a person accused of an offence punishable under this Act if he is not an Indian citizen and has entered the country (India) unauthorizedly/illegally except in exceptional circumstances and for reasons to be recorded therefor.

(ix) *Protection for action taken in good faith and punishment for corrupt and malicious prosecution of any person under this Act*

Section 57 of the Act provides for protection to public servants for their actions under the Act in good faith while at the same time providing for punishment which extends to two years or fine or both against any Police Officer who knowingly or maliciously proceeds against any person for an offence under this Act when there are no reasonable grounds for proceedings against him. Further, Section 58 also provides for compensation to a person who has been corruptly and maliciously proceeded against under the Act. These are salutary provisions which will go a long way in curbing misuse of the Act.

(x) *Trial by Special Courts*

The Act retains the provisions regarding trial by Special Courts as in the TADA (P) Act, 1987 and Criminal Law (Amendment) Bill, 1995 and also provides that trial by Special Courts will have precedence over the trial by any other courts and shall be concluded in preference to trial in any other case. Section 28 and 29 provide for appointment of a Public Prosecutor and procedures and powers of Special Courts respectively.

(xi) Provisions have been made under Part V to provide for special powers of interception of wire, electronic or oral communication and the admissibility of such evidence with a view to make the provisions more effective while dealing with organised crime/terrorist activity. These are on the lines of provisions existing in Maharashtra Control of Organised Crime Act, 1999.

(xii) Provisions have been made under Section 60 of the Act for constitution of Review Committees by the Central Government as well as by the State Govts. The Chairperson of the Committee shall be a person who is, or who has been, a judge of a High Court.

Specific safeguards have been provided for in the Act with a view to prevent the possibility of the misuse of the special powers given to the investigating authorities and address the concern of violation of human rights raised in different quarters while also seeking to ensure that the provisions of the Act are not so diluted as to render them ineffective in combating terrorism.

Sectoral Conventions

Since submission of the National Report to the CTC India has become a signatory to the Convention on the Physical Protection of Nuclear Material. India is now signatory to all 12 sectoral conventions on terrorism. Measures are being taken for early ratification of Convention on Suppression of Financing of Terrorism.

Section II

(A) Organisational and Administrative Machinery to Deal with Criminalization and Penalization of Terrorism from the Law and Order Perspective

There is an elaborate machinery to deal with the criminalization and penalization of Terrorism from the law and order perspective both at the Centre and the State. The administrative setup at the federal Centre indicating the various agencies, security, police and paramilitary forces etc. is indicated in Chart I. In Chart II the structure of the police has been explained. In Chart III the administrative and organisational set up at the State level is indicated. Chart IV shows the administrative set up to track and deal in the immigration control, tracking etc. of foreigners, including those linked to terrorism.

Chart-I

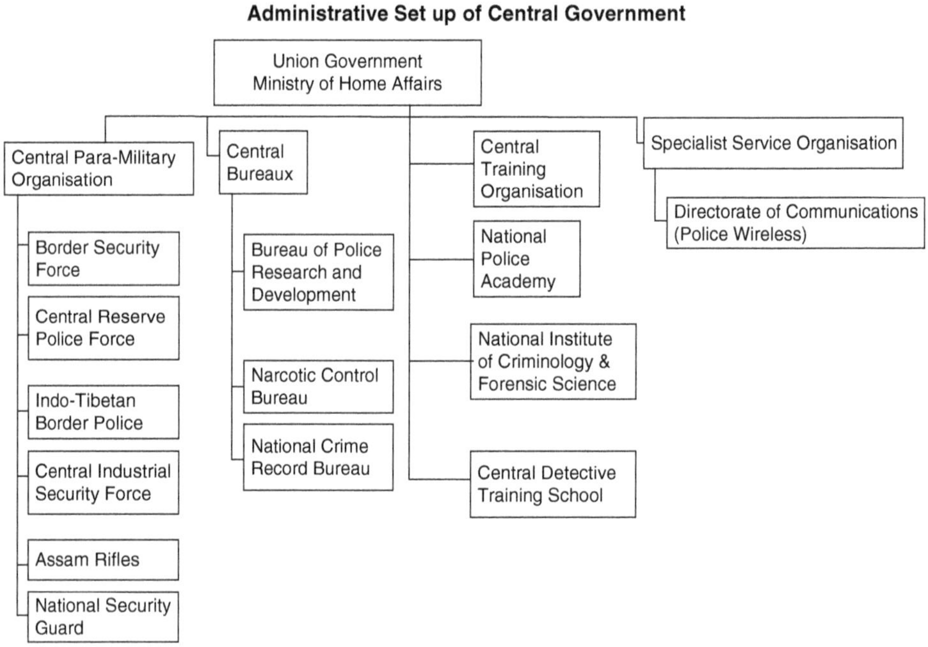

Chart-II: Structure of Police in India

India is a country having federal polity. State governments have been made responsible for law and order and normal police functions under the Constitution. Central Government plays a supportive role in the functioning of State Police Forces by providing—

Additional police forces for law and order duties;
Specialist services;
Training in the specialised areas;
Help in natural calamities.

Central Government maintains a number of police organisations for specific duties like border policing, augmenting the State Forces etc. It also provides specialised services for computerisation, research and development and communication. Training is imparted to various levels of police officials at Central Training Institutions like National Police Academy, Central Detective Training School, National Institute of Criminology and Forensic Sciences and Central Forensic Science Laboratories. The training infrastructure available with Central Para Military Forces is also shared with State Police. The role of Central Government is shown in the organisational chart annexed herewith.

At the State level, police is responsible for maintenance of law and order crime control, security, traffic control etc. Director General of Police who is assisted by one or more Additional DGPs responsible for various functional aspects, heads Police Force in the State. Each State is divided into zones and these zones are further divided into ranges, which are headed by Inspector General of Police and Deputy Inspector General of Police respectively. Each range includes about four districts, which are headed by Superintendent of Police. The districts are further divided into various police stations which are the basic units of policing in India. Registration of crime, investigation, law and order and maintenance of security is the responsibility of the concerned police stations. Sub-Inspectors or Inspector-level officials head Police Stations. Superintendent of Police functions under general control and supervision of the District Magistrate. Organisational structure of police at the State level is annexed herewith.

Chart-III Administrative Set up of State Government

Foreigners Regional Registration Officers (FRROs) are performing the work of immigration as well as registration of foreigners in five cities under Bureau of Immigration.

Administrative Set up of State Government

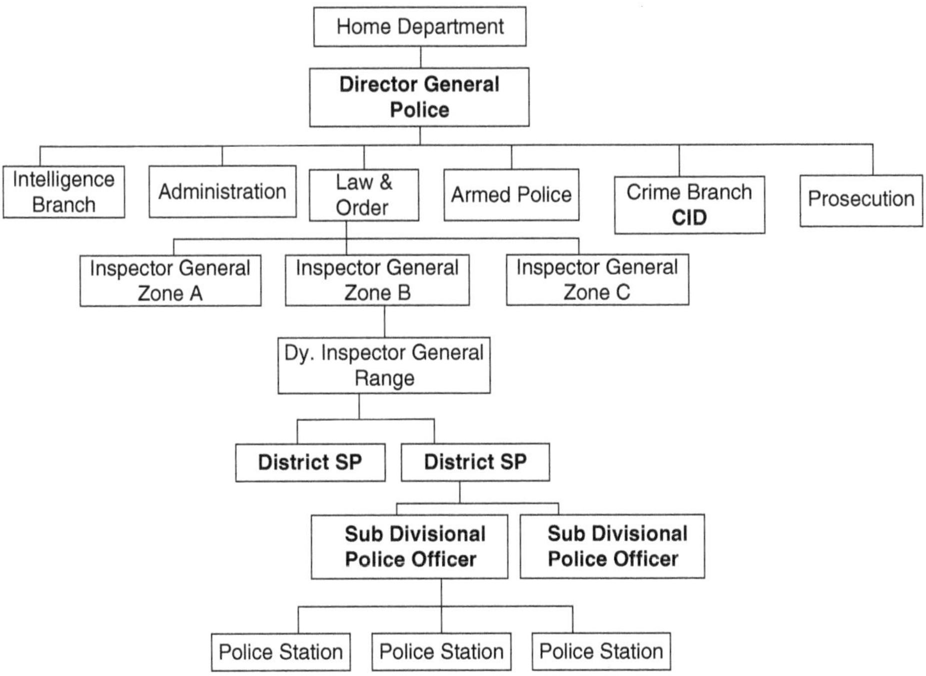

ORGANISATIONAL CHART WITH BRIEF DESCRIPTIVE INDICATION OF FUNCTIONS OF THE ADMINISTRATIVE MACHINERY FOR IMMIGRATION CONTROL

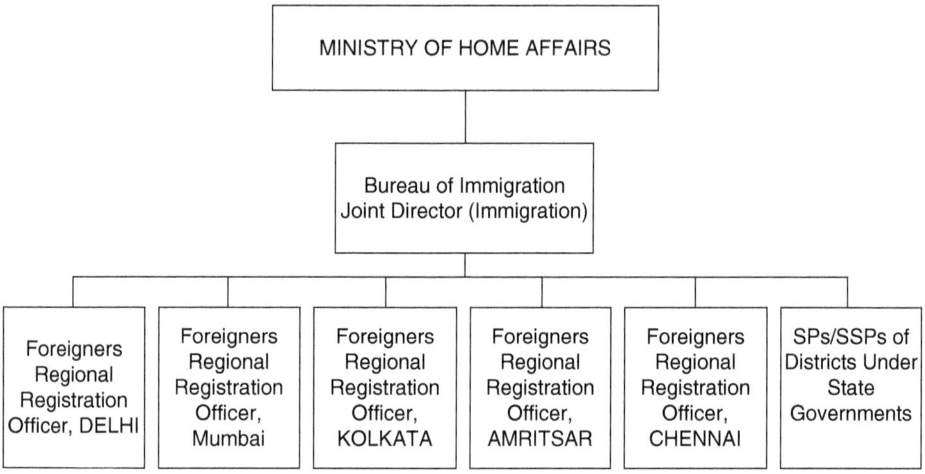

In rest of the places, State Governments have appointed SPs/SSPs of every district who have been delegated powers by the Central Government to perform immigration as well as registration duties on behalf of the Central Government.

***

A number of agencies also operate with the mandate to collect intelligence regarding terrorist groups, acts etc. Such agencies include the Intelligence Bureau which is headed by a Director and has offices all over India. Where intelligence gathered on criminal activity reveals involvement of terrorists, this information is passed on to police authorities by the IB, who then register a case and then process it according to normal legal processes.

(B) Organisational and Administrative Mechanisms to Address Illicit Financial Transactions which can be Linked to Terrorist Activity

There are a range of mechanisms that monitor and track illicit financial transactions which are often the channel used by terrorists in India to finance terrorism. Such mechanisms include the **Directorate of Enforcement** which monitors the Foreign Exchange Management Act, the **Central Board of Direct Taxes** which investigates evasion of income tax and the **Directorate of Revenue Intelligence** which essentially monitors violation of Customs Laws and proceeds driving from smuggling activities. Where in the process of collecting information on possible violations of income tax, customs laws, these bodies find evidence of linkages to terrorism, this information is processed and then passed on to Police authorities to register a case and initiate proceedings within the framework of Indian domestic legal framework. Detailed description of each of these bodies is indicated below:

(i) Enforcement Directorate

The Directorate of Enforcement functions under the Ministry of Finance, Department of Revenue, Government of India, and is entrusted with the task of enforcing the provisions of Foreign Exchange Regulation Act, 1973 (FERA) (since repealed with effect from 1.6.2000 with a saving clause to finalise the pending investigations till 31.5.2002) and Foreign Exchange Management Act, 1999 (FEMA). The Directorate is headed by Director of Enforcement. The Directorate has its Head Office at New Delhi with 7 Zonal Offices at Ahmedabad, Bangalore, Chennai, Calcutta, Delhi, Jalandhar and Mumbai. Each Zonal Office is headed by an officer of the rank of Deputy Director of Enforcement. There are Sub-Zonal Offices under Zonal Offices.

Action against Terrorists

So far as involvement of terrorists in various FERA/FEMA violations is concerned, the Directorate primarily initiates action on receipt of information to this effect from CBI and/or Police authorities who are entrusted with the job of nabbing terrorists activities. The involvement of the persons involved in terrorist activities, vis-à-vis, provisions of FERA/FEMA are restricted to their indulgence in hawala money transactions. Broadly speaking, hawala transactions are those transactions where money (in Indian or foreign currencies) is received or paid in compensation of certain acts/goods, etc. The relevant provisions of FERA/FEMA prohibit receipt and distribution of payments in India without the permission of the RBI as per instructions of persons residing outside India. As and when such cases are referred to the Directorate by Police and other agencies, necessary action is taken.

(ii) Central Board of Direct Taxes

The Investigation Wing under the Income Tax Department is engaged in investigations into the cases of evasion of Income Tax and generation of black money. The Investigation Wing functions under the overall supervision of the Director Generals of Income Tax (Inv) stationed all over the India.

Investigations regarding evasion of Income tax are conducted on the basis of intelligence gathered by the Department from various source such as informants, general public, other Government agencies, etc. In certain cases intelligence is also gathered in house. In suitable cases search and seizure operations under the provisions of Income Tax Act are carried out to unearth undisclosed income. In other cases, suitable action under the Income Tax Laws is taken to bring undisclosed income to tax.

Whenever information relating to any other Government agency such as Police, Enforcement Directorate, Customs & Central Excise, Department of Company Affairs, SEBI etc. is collected by the Income Tax Department, the same is passed on to the concerned Agency/Department for further necessary action.

(iii) Directorate of Revenue Intelligence

Directorate of Revenue Intelligence functions under the Central Board of Excise & Customs in the Ministry of Finance, Department of Revenue. Headed by Director General in New Delhi, it is divided into four zones, each under the charge of an Additional Director General and further sub-divided into Regional Units, Sub-Regional Units and Intelligence Cells with a complement of Additional Directors, Joint Directors, Deputy Directors, Assistant Directors, Senior Intelligence Officers and Intelligence Officers.

Directorate of Revenue Intelligence is charged essentially with collection of intelligence, its analysis, collation, interpretation and dissemination on matters relating to violations of customs laws. DRI also substantially enforces the anti-narcotic laws. In order to ensure effective discharge of its responsibilities, DRI maintains close liaison with all the important enforcement agencies in India like the Central Economic Intelligence Bureau, Income Tax Department, Enforcement Directorate, Narcotics Control Bureau, Directorate General of Foreign Trade, Border Security Force, Central Bureau of Investigation, Coast Guard, the State Police authorities and also with all the Customs and Central Excise Commissionerates. It also maintains close liaison with the World Customs Organisation, Brussels, the Regional Intelligence Liaison Office at Tokyo, INTERPOL and foreign Customs Administrations. Thus if in the course of such investigations any matter concerning illegal or criminal activities, including terrorism comes to notice, it will be passed on to relevant law enforcement agencies.

Officers of Directorate of Revenue Intelligence are basically trained to detect fraud/activities connected with smuggling having revenue implications and those related to trafficking in Narcotics & Psychotropic Substances. However, as indicated in para above, while performing these basic tasks whenever any possible involvement/complicity of terrorism is detected, the information is shared/passed on to the appropriate authority.

The Charter of DRI

- Collection of intelligence about smuggling of contraband goods, narcotics, under-invoicing etc. through sources of India and abroad, including secret sources.
- Analysis and dissemination of such intelligence to the field formation for action.

- Working out of intelligence by the Directorate officers themselves to a successful conclusion, where necessary.
- Keeping watch over important seizures and investigation cases.
- Associating or taking over the investigations which warrant specialised handling by the Directorate.
- Guiding important investigation/prosecution cases.
- Functioning as the liaison authority for exchange of information among ESCAP countries for combating international smuggling and customs frauds in terms of the recommendation of the ESCAP conference.
- Keeping liaison with foreign countries, Indian Missions and enforcement agencies abroad on anti-smuggling matters.
- To keep liaison with CBI and through them with the INTERPOL.
- To coordinate, direct and control anti-smuggling operations on the Indo-Nepal border.
- To refer cases registered under the Customs Act to the Income Tax Department for action under the Income Tax Act.
- To keep statistics of seizures and prices/rates etc. for watching trends of smuggling and supply required material to the Ministry of Finance and other Ministries.
- To study and suggest remedies for loopholes in law and procedures to combat smuggling.

(iv) Intelligence Bureau

The Intelligence Bureau also plays an important role in suppression of financing of terrorism. As regards the financial transactions which impinge upon national security the organisation collects intelligence inputs, analyses them. These are then shared with the various agencies like the DRI, Income Tax and State Police. Donations and other financial flows from abroad are also tracked where there is a possible link with terrorism.

Financing of terrorist related activities is mainly done through the clandestine channel of hawala. IB gathers intelligence of such activity and once there is sufficient evidence of involvement with terrorism and the mechanisms by which the money is coming to the terrorists, the information is further developed and passed on to the police authorities who then register a case and proceed according to the law.

Comments on UN Counter-Terrorism Committee (CTC) Questionnaire

Sub-Paragraph		Comments of CTC	Comments of the Government of India
1(a)	(i)	Is the Prevention of Terrorism Ordinance (POTO) still in force or when will the Prevention of Terrorism Ordinance enter into force?	Parliament has enacted a comprehensive Anti Terrorism Legislation, viz., Prevention of Terrorism Act, 2002 (POTA). The Act was notified on 28th March, 2002 but as per the provisions of the Act itself, it comes into force from 24th October 2001, the day from which the Prevention of Terrorism Ordinance, 2001 (POTO) was promulgated. It replaces the Prevention of Terrorism Ordinance, 2001 (POTO).
1(a)	(ii)	It is stated in paragraph 12 of the report that "most transactions in the criminal world are unorganised, are informal, shadowy and as they are not through institutional mechanisms are extremely difficult to tract, let alone offer evidence or proof for purposes of prosecution". As a member of the G-20, India has nevertheless pledged to stop abuse of informal banking networks, particularly Hawalah. Please comment on how this is or will be reflected by Indian legislation.	India is committed to preventing abuse of informal banking networks such as *hawala*, since terrorist organisations misuse hawala to finance their activities. This is certainly a difficult task given the informal, amorphous nature of such transactions, apart from the difficulties of gathering hard evidence or proof for the purposes of prosecution. Efforts are underway to strengthen the Foreign Exchange Management Act to prevent informal banking activities like Hawala. In any case, these are illegal under the existing Banking Laws and the Regulations of the Reserve Bank of India concerning dealing in foreign exchange. As and when these operators and organisations are detected they are prosecuted under the relevant laws like Conservation of Foreign Exchange and Prevention of Smuggling Act, Customs Act, Income Tax Act and also proceededagainst under the provisions of the Foreign Exchange Management Act as the case may be.
	(iii)	Does India put natural or legal persons other than banks (e.g. attorneys, notaries) under a legal obligation to report suspici ous transactions that might be linked to terrorist activities?	Section 14 (1) of the POTA casts obligation upon any officer, authority of Central Government or a State Government or a local authority or a Bank, or a Company, or a firm or any other institution, establishment, organisation or any individual to furnish information in their possession in relation to such offence, on points or matters where such information will be useful for, or relevant to, the purposes of this Act, namely preventing Terrorism.

			Failure to furnish information as called for is punishable with imprisonment up to 3 years or with fine or with both.
1(a)	(iv)	Has India enacted an anti money laundering legislation?	The Money-laundering bill (legislation) is under consideration by the Indian Parliament.
1(b)	(i)	Could you please clarify how the acts listed in this sub-paragraph are criminalized in India?	Section 3 (1) (b) of POTA defines act of raising funds intended for the purpose of terrorism to be a "Terrorist act." Section 3(2)(b) of POTA prescribes the punishment for such act of raising funds. The punishment prescribed is imprisonment for a term which shall not be less than 5 years but which may extend to imprisonment for life and shall also be liable to fine. Section 22 of the POTA makes fund raising for a terrorist organisation to be an offence. A person guilty of an offence under this section is liable on conviction, to imprisonment for a term not exceeding 14 years or with fine or with both.
1(b)	(ii)	What measures are there to prevent or punish acts committed by terrorist organisations operating from India by fund raising for example, but for a cause not likely to affect Indian interests?	To deal with terrorist entities operating in India but for a cause unlikely to affect Indian interests, the UN Security Council Act, 1947, has provisions which enables Government of India to give domestic effect to the decisions of the UN Security Council. In the orders passed under this legislation, necessary action is being taken, particularly with regard to such terrorist entities notified by the UN. The provisions of POTA criminalize all fund raising by terrorist organisations.
1(c)	(i)	According to the report (Paragraph 13), a determination has to be made before persons can be detained, property seized or forfeited or the use of funds prohibited; could you please clarify who is entitled to make this determination in the context of sub-paragraph 1(c) of the Resolution.	Section 6–17 of the POTA deal with the seizure and forfeiture of property. "Proceeds of Terrorism" is defined to mean "all kinds of properties which have been derived or obtained from commission of any terrorist act or have been acquired through funds traceable to terrorist act." The act of raising funds has also been defined as terrorist act.

Sub-Paragraph		Comments of CTC	Comments of the Government of India
			Section 7 of the POTA provides that if an Officer (not below the rank of Superintendent of Police) investigating an offence committed under this Act, has reasons to believe that any property in relation to which an investigation is being conducted, represents proceeds of terrorism, he shall seize such property with the prior approval in writing of the Director General of Police of the State in which such property is situated. This section is also applicable to properties of an organisation declared as Terrorist Organisation under the Act. Investigating officer shall duly inform the designated authority within 48 hours of the seizure or attachment of such property. It shall be open to the designated authority to either confirm or revoke the order of seizure/attachment after an opportunity has been given to person whose property is being attached. Under Section 8 of the POTA, the authority to order forfeiture of proceeds of terrorism is the Special Court. Under Section 10 of POTA, appeal against the order of the Special Court lies to High Court within whose jurisdiction the Special Court is situated.
1(c)	(ii)	According to paragraph 14 of the report, the Narcotic Drugs and Psychotropic Substances Act, 1985 (NDPS Act) provides for tracing, freezing and seizing of illegally acquired property; do the Unlawful Activities (Prevention) Act, 1967 (Act 37, 1967) or other legal provisions serve the same purposes, including g tracing, in respect of funds and other financial assets or economic resources, be they of legal or illegal origin, of the persons and entities described in sub-paragraph 1 (c) of the Resolution?	Section 7 of POTA contains provisions for an investigating officer not below the rank of Superintendent of Police to seize or attach property in relation to terrorism when investigation is being conducted after obtaining the approval of Director General of Police. Therefore, under POTA, there is sufficient provision to seize all property, including cash which is intended for the purpose of terrorism.

1(c)	(iii)	What are the legal provisions governing the forfeiture or seizure of proceeds of terrorist activities, especially if they are not related to offences like smuggling or drug trafficking?	Already described in detail in para 1 c(i) above.
1(d)	(i)	Please identify the legal provisions, which implement this sub-paragraph in India.	Section 22 of POTA makes the act of providing any money or other property to organisations involved in terrorist activities an offence punishable with imprisonment for a term not exceeding fourteen years or with fine or with both. Under Section 3(3) of the Act, whoever abets a terrorist act (act of raising funds) by providing money or other property, shall be punishable with imprisonment for a term which shall not be less than 5 years but which may extend to imprisonment for life and shall also be liable to fine.
1(d)	(ii)	How does the financial tracking system see that funds received by associations are not diverted from their stated purposes to terrorist activities?	The receipt of funds by Associations from external sources is governed by **Foreign Contribution (Regulation) Act, 1976 read with Foreign Contribution (Regulation) Rules, 1976**. The act requires the permission of the Central Government for the acceptance and utilisation of foreign contribution by Associations. Under Section 5 of the Act, organisations of the political nature, not being a political party, notified as such by the Central Government can receive foreign contributions only with the prior permission of the Central Government. Under Section 6(1) and 1(a) of the Act, associations having a definite cultural, economic, educational, religious or social programme can receive foreign contribution after getting themselves registered with the Central Government or after obtaining its prior permission. Section 4 of the Act provides for the prohibited category of the persons who cannot receive any foreign contribution.

Sub-Paragraph		Comments of CTC	Comments of the Government of India
			Under Section 10 of the Act, Central Government is empowered to place a registered association in the prior permission category. Under the same section, any individual association or organisation can also be prohibited by the Central Government from accepting any foreign contribution. Applications for grant of registration or prior permission to accept foreign contribution are to be made to the Ministry of Home Affairs in the prescribed form. The said application is examined on the basis of a set of administrative guidelines framed by the Ministry. These guidelines covers parameters such as security and public interest, financial standing of the applicant in its chosen field of activity, nationality of its office bearers, past violations of the provisions of the Act etc. **Monitoring:** Every association registered under the Act or granted prior permission to receive foreign contributions, is to file an annual return duly certified by a chartered accountant with this ministry, intimating the receipt of foreign contribution during the year and manner of its utilisation within four months of the close of the financial year. A 'Nil' report is also mandatory. Central Government can also order the inspection of the accounts/records of an association or the audit of its books and accounts. **Penal Provisions:** The penal provisions in the Act for dealing with cases of contravention of its provisions include punishment with imprisonment for a term, which may extend to five years, or with fine or with both. The Central Government can also prohibit payment of currency received in contravention of the Act or seize and confiscate any article or currency it believes has been acquired by a person in contravention of the provisions of the Act.

			Indian Income Tax Act and Societies Registration Act: The provisions of the Indian Income Tax Act and Societies Registration Act also enable the authorities to monitor and track use of funds by charitable organisations, and registered societies to ensure that diversion of funds from stated purposes are detected.
2 (a)		Could you kindly indicate the manner in which India is able to prevent entities and individuals to, clandestinely or under any other pretext, recruit, collect funds or to provide any other form of support to terrorist activities to be carried out inside or outside India? Please outline the measures, both legislative and practical, preventing entities and individuals from recruiting, collecting funds or soliciting other forms of support for terrorist activities to be carried out inside or outside India, including in particular: • the carrying out, within or from India, of recruiting, collecting of funds and soliciting of other forms of support from other countries; and • deceptive activities such as recruitment based on a representation to the recruit that the purpose of the recruitment is one (e.g. teaching) different from the true purpose and collection of funds through front organisations.	The police and the intelligence agencies are sensitised to prevent recruitment to such entities or organisations. In addition, all States maintain an updated data/information base with regard to the activities of terrorist groups.

Sub-Paragraph		Comments of CTC	Comments of the Government of India
2(b)		Please describe the mechanism for inter-agency co-operation, also between the Federal States of India, as regards an early warning mechanism for the exchange of information with other states as well as for a unified approach in implementing the resolution, in particular as regards the interaction between the authorities responsible for narcotics control, financial tracking and security (including as regards border controls—sub-paragraph 2 (g).	Ministry of Home Affairs (MHA) at the federal level is the nodal ministry for co-ordination between the federal agencies and the state level intelligence agencies regarding terrorism matters. The intelligence agencies under MHA and other federal ministries are in regular touch with the intelligence agencies of the States. Any information received by any of the intelligence agencies is shared with sister agencies at federal level and State level to prevent terrorist acts. India, which has faced terrorist violence as a part of cross border terrorism during the last 20 years, has developed a system for inter-agency cooperation both at national and State levels. Realising the need for early warning in real time and adequate follow up action to counter terrorist activities, an institutionalised mechanism has been established where different agencies pool their resources/information on aspects related to counter terrorism to ensure synergy in collection and analysis. At a centralised place, necessary data is maintained and is shared with all the concerned agencies. Similar institutionalised mechanisms have also been established in States, which are witnessing terrorist activities.
2(c)		How does India implement sub-para 2(c) of the resolution?	India's policy is to deny safe haven and any support to terrorists. The extensive domestic legislation dealing with all dimensions of terrorism, the elaborate administrative machinery both on the law and order side as also to ensure that illicit financial transactions are not misused to finance terrorism as also the State and Centre police forces, intelligence agencies etc. all ensure that no safe haven is available to those who are terrorists or in any way support, finance, train etc. terrorists.

2(d)		Could you please elaborate on the statement in paragraph 7 of the report according to which the "provisions for preventive action against terrorist/criminals are very mild" in the Code of Criminal Procedure 1973?	Under Section 151 Code of Criminal Procedure (Cr.P.C), a Police Officer knowing of a design to commit any cognizable offence may arrest without warrant any person, if it appears that the commission of the offence cannot be otherwise prevented. The provision has been described as mild because, no person detained under this section can be detained for more than 24 hours. If no evidence can be gathered against the person within 24 hours under any other law then he would have to be released. It may not be possible to gather evidence against a suspected terrorist within 24 hours. However, in those cases involving terrorists it is not uncommon to obtain a Court order for police custody for a longer period for further investigation. The earlier comment had been made in the context of how the existing provisions of C.P.C. facilitate, beside preventing terrorist acts, proper investigation and prosecution of terrorist offences. Both POTA and the Indian Penal Code (IPC) have provisions to prevent those who finance, plan, facilitate or commit acts of terror from using Indian territories for such acts.
2(e)	(i)	Are terrorist acts in the sense of subparagraph 2(e) established as serious criminal offences in India, if these acts have neither been committed in India nor against Indian interests?	The UN Security Council Act, 1947 empowers the Union Government to take any measure short of use of armed forces to implement the UN Security Council Resolution under Article 41 of the UN Charter. The Act can be invoked against terrorist organisations, which have been listed by UN Security Council.
2(e)	(ii)	Has India implemented sub-paragraph 2(e) of the Resolution in regard to terrorist organisations, which do not fall under section 18(1) of the Prevention of Terrorism Ordinance?	Under the provisions of the above Act, India is issuing notifications freezing the assets of terrorist organisations listed by UN Sanctions Committee under UNSCR 1267, 1333 and 1390. The Act also has extraterritorial jurisdiction and is being invoked against organisations not listed under Section 18(1) of POTA.

Sub-Paragraph		Comments of CTC	Comments of the Government of India
2(e)	(iii)	Are the relevant provisions of the Indian Penal Code applicable to acts committed abroad by an Indian citizen or by a person who has his or her habitual residence in India?	Indian Penal Code is applicable to acts committed abroad by Indian citizens (Section 4—extra territorial offences). Section 4 of the Indian Penal Code deals with the extension of Code to extra-territorial offences and provides as follows: "The provisions of this code shall apply also to any offence committed by: (1) any citizen of India in any place without and beyond India; (2) any person on any ship or aircraft registered in India wherever it may be. *Explanation*—In this section the word "offence" includes every act committed outside (India) which, if committed in (India) would be punishable under this Code.
	(iv)	Are the relevant provisions of the Indian Penal Code also applicable when the acts have been committed abroad by a foreign national who happens to be in India?	Indian Penal Code is applicable to the acts committed beyond India by a person who happens to be in India (Section 3 – punishment of offences committed beyond India but which by law may be tried within India). By virtue of Section 4(1), the extra-territorial effect of IPC is limited to Indian citizens. However, by virtue of Section 4(2) of the IPC it extends to any person if an offence is committed by that person on a ship or aircraft registered in India. Further, in the context of extradition, Section 34 of the Extradition Act has extensive extra-territorial jurisdiction. By virtue of this provision a foreign national who has committed an extradition offence abroad but who happens to be in India, can be prosecuted in India for such offence. Section 34 of the Extradition Act, 1962, provides as follows: "34. An extradition offence committed by any person in a foreign State shall be deemed to have been committed in India and such person shall be liable to be prosecuted in India for such offence."

2(f)	(i)	Does India have any legal provisions or regulations governing the implementation of sub-paragraph 2(f) apart from the agreements and arrangements described in Section III of the report such as a law on mutual legal assistance in criminal matters?	India has a well developed law on mutual assistance in criminal matters which enables India to seek from and extend cooperation to foreign States in respect of mutual legal assistance in criminal matters. This law is contained in the Code of Criminal Procedure, 1973. (Cr. P.C.). The relevant sections of the Cr. P.C. are Ss. 105, 105A to 105L, and 166A and 166B. It includes execution of judicial processes; assistance in relation to orders of attachment or forfeiture of property, identifying unlawfully acquired; management of property so seized or forfeited; procedure to be followed in case of letter of request; letter of request to competent authority for investigation in a country or place outside India; and the execution of a letter of request from a country or place outside India to a Court or authority for investigation in India.
2(f)	(ii)	Is the existence of a bilateral agreement or agreement or arrangement a prerequisite for India before it can afford legal assistance to other countries as requested by this sub-paragraph?	Under Section 105 of the Cr. P.C., 1973, for the service or execution of summons or warrants in relation to criminal matters, reciprocal arrangements would be necessary. Similarly for other purposes dealt with in Sections 105A to 105L, reciprocal arrangements would be necessary. In reciprocal agreements or arrangements both countries agree to extend mutual legal assistance in criminal matters subject to their national laws. Thus, this requirement is less formal arid is strictly based on reciprocity. It is different from the move formal bilateral agreements on mutual judicial assistance in criminal matters, which are applicable strictly in accordance with their terms and conditions.
2(f)	(iii)	How long does it take on the average to implement a request for judicial assistance in criminal investigations or criminal proceedings relating to the financing or support of terrorist acts?	It depends on the nature of the case, but every effort is made to extend expeditious assistance.

Sub-Paragraph		Comments of CTC	Comments of the Government of India
2(g)		Please explain how the procedures for the issuance of identity papers and travel documents support the prevention of the counterfeiting, forgery or fraudulent use of those documents and what measures exist to prevent their forgery etc.	To prevent counterfeiting, forgery and fraudulent use of passport, India has introduced Machine Readable Passports which will have the photograph and signature of the applicant scanned on to the booklet. This and other security features built into the newly designed passports will check the instances of tempering of passports including substitution of photographs, counterfeiting and forgery. These cannot be elaborated upon for security reasons.
3(a)		With which countries has India build Joint Working Groups to exchange information to combat terrorism and has it the intention to build such working groups with other countries, too?	India has Joint Working Groups with a number of countries, including USA, UK, EU, France, China, Kazakhstan and welcomes all efforts to strengthen international cooperation to combat terrorism, including through such mechanisms with other countries.
3(b)		Apart from being a member of INTERPOL, Has India entered into bilateral or multilateral agreements for the cooperation in administrative matters?	India has a range of agreements, e.g., double taxation avoidance agreements etc. with a large number of countries designed to enhance cooperation in administrative matters. We are active members of the World Customs Organisation and Indian Customs share information with counterpart organisations whenever they are approached for assistance.
3(c)	(i)	Could India provide the CTC with the model of a bilateral agreement to combat terrorism?	Agreement establishing a Joint Working Group with Kazakhstan is enclosed.
3(c)	(ii)	Is there a difference between the extradition treaties and the extradition arrangements, which are mentioned under paragraph 21 of the report?	There is difference between an extradition treaty and an extradition arrangement. While an extradition treaty is a more formal agreement providing modalities for the extradition of fugitive offenders in accordance with the terms and conditions of the treaty, under the extradition arrangement, the two countries agree to reciprocally extend their national extradition laws with respect to each other. This understanding is usually reached after mutual consultations/ exchange of letters. At the national level a gazette notification, indicating such reciprocity, is issued.

3(d)		It is understood from paragraph 23 and appendix II of the report that India is not yet a party to the Convention on the Physical Protection of Nuclear Material signed at Vienna on 3 March 1980, of the International Convention for the Suppression of the Financing of Terrorism adopted by the General Assembly of the United Nations on 9 December 1999; the CTC is therefore looking forward to receiving a progress report on the ratification of these two international legal instruments.	Since submission of the National Report to the CTC India has acceded to the Convention on the Physical Protection of Nuclear Material. Measures are being taken for early ratification of Convention on Suppression of Financing of Terrorism. The **Prevention of Terrorism Act, 2002** also provides for criminalizing the financing of terrorism with adequate penalties.
3(e)	(i)	What is the intention of the Indian government regarding the introduction of an implementing legislation for the three international conventions listed in Appendix II of the report under points 6, 9 and 10?	After the adoption of POTA, a comprehensive piece of counter terrorism legislation, additional implementing legislation with regard to these three conventions may not be necessary.
3(e)	(ii)	Have the crimes set forth in the relevant UN conventions been included as extraditable offences into the bilateral treaties, which India has concluded with other countries as provided for in several UN Conventions against terrorism?	In extradition treaties that India has concluded with foreign States, no-list method is adopted and an extradition offence under most of the treaties, means an offence punishable with an imprisonment of more than one year. Thus all the offences falling within the scope of relevant UN Conventions are automatically get covered within the scope of the bilateral extradition treaties. Even in cases where there is no extradition treaty made by India with any foreign State, the Central Government may, by notified order, treat any convention to which India and a foreign State are Parties, as an extradition treaty made by India with that foreign State providing for extradition in respect of the offences specified in the Convention {Section 3(4) of the Extradition Act, 1962}.
3(f) and (g)	(i)	Please elaborate on the efforts, which are made in order to implement these sub-paragraphs.	The police and the intelligence agencies ensure that no foreigner with suspicious links related to terrorism can find residence in India. Adequate checks are carried out in this regard before regularizing the stay in India.

Sub-Paragraph		Comments of CTC	Comments of the Government of India
3(f) and (g)	(ii)	Could India please make clear whether requests for extradition of alleged terrorists could be refused on political grounds?	No. Extradition of alleged terrorists cannot be refused on political grounds. Section 31(2) of the Extradition Act makes clear that the terrorist offences such as: (i) Offences under the Anti-Hijacking Act, 1982. (ii) Offences under the Suppression of Unlawful Acts Against Safety of Civil Aviation Act, 1982. (iii) An offence within the scope of the International Convention on the Punishment of Crimes against Internationally Protected Persons including Diplomatic Agents, opened for signature at New York on 14th December, 1973. (iv) An offence within the scope of the International Convention against the Taking of Hostages, opened for signature at New York on 18th December, 1979. v) Culpable homicide, murder (Sections 299–304 IPC). (vi) Voluntarily causing hurt or grievous hurt by a dangerous weapon or means (Sections 321–333 of IPC). (vii) Offences under the Explosive Substances Act, 1908. (viii) Possession of a firearm or ammunition with intention to endanger life (Section 27 of the Arms Act, 1959). (ix) The use of a firearm with intention to resist or prevent the arrest or detention (Section 28 of Arms Act, 1959). (x) Causing of loss or damage to property used for public utilities or otherwise with intention to endanger life (Section 425 read with Section 44 of IPC).

			(xi) Wrongful restraint and wrongful confinement (Sections 339 to 348 of IPC). (xii) Kidnapping and abduction including taking of hostages (Sections 359 to 369 of IPC). (xiii) Offences related to terrorism and terrorist acts. (xiv) Abetting, conspiring or attempting to commit, including participating as an accomplice in the commission of the offences listed above. shall not be regarded as offences of a political character.
		The CTC could be grateful to know whether your Government has addressed any of the concerns expressed in paragraph 4 of the Resolution.	India is signatory to the Biological Weapons Convention as also the Chemical Weapons Convention and is committed to ensure that terrorists do not have access to weapons of mass destruction. Efforts to address linkages between terrorism and illicit trafficking in drugs etc. have been described extensively both in the National Report and elsewhere in the Supplementary Report. Apart from domestic legislation such as NDPS Act (described earlier in the National Report) etc. to tackle illicit trafficking in drugs, India has several bilateral agreements for exchange of information and mutual assistance on drug related matters.
		Other Matters: It would also be useful to the CTC to have an organisational chart of the administrative machinery, such as police, immigration control, customs, taxation and financial supervision authorities, to give practical effect to the laws, regulations and other documents that are seen by your government as contributing to compliance with the Resolution.	Included in Part II of the Report.

DOCUMENT NO. 24

INDIA'S 2003 COUNTER-TERRORISM REPORT TO THE UN

UN Security Council Resolution
S/2003/452

April 21, 2003

Distr.: General
21 April 2003

Original: English

Letter dated 21 April 2003 from the Chairman of the Security Council Committee established pursuant to resolution 1373 (2001) concerning counter-terrorism addressed to the President of the Security Council

I write with reference to my letter of 13 November 2002 (S/2002/1248).

The Counter-Terrorism Committee has received the attached third report from India submitted pursuant to paragraph 6 of resolution 1373 (2001) (see annex).

I would be grateful if you could arrange for the present letter and its annex to be circulated as a document of the Security Council.

(*Signed*) Inocencio F. **Arias**

Chairman

Security Council Committee established pursuant to resolution 1373 (2001) concerning counter-terrorism

Annex

Letter dated 28 March 2003 from the Permanent Representative of India to the United Nations addressed to the Chairman of the Security Council Committee established pursuant to resolution 1373 (2001) concerning counter-terrorism

In response to your letter dated 30 October 2002, I have the honour to transmit herewith, to the Counter-Terrorism Committee, the Government of India's third report (see enclosure).

While we note that the Committee had requested a response to the questions and comments raised in your letter under reference by 30 January 2003, our response was delayed owing to the effort to present as comprehensively as possible the required information. While apologizing for this delay, we do hope the Committee would understand the importance the Government of India attaches to the work of the Counter-Terrorism Committee.

(*Signed*) V. K. **Nambiar**

Enclosure
Responses to CTC Questions*

Que. 1.3 According to Section III of the supplementary report, efforts "are underway to strengthen the Foreign Exchange Management Act to prevent informal banking activities like Hawala". According to Section II of the same report, this Act (FEMA) as well as the Foreign Exchange Regulation Act (FERA) "prohibit receipt and distribution of payments in India without the permission of the RBI 'Reserve Bank of India' as per instructions of persons residing outside India". In the context of paragraph 1 of the Resolution, please elaborate on how India prevents or proposes to prevent the abuse of the hawala system by persons residing in India, both regarding informal banking activities that are undertaken upon instruction by persons residing in India and resulting in the transfer of money or financial means to persons residing either within or outside India.

Ans:

Hawala transactions are illegal because permission from the Reserve Bank of India (the Central Monetary Authority of the country) is required for most types of foreign exchange transactions. There are some exceptions permitted under the law, but the transfer of money to and from the country through Hawala [i.e. non-banking channels] is in contravention of the Foreign Exchange Management Act (FEMA).

* The annexes are on file with the Secretariat and are available for consultation.

Hawala is a criminal offence under Sections 8(i) and 9(i)(b)and (d) of the Foreign Exchange Regulation Act (FERA) 1973. Penalties of up to five times the amount in contravention can be imposed for breach of these legal provisions. In addition, the offender can be prosecuted under Sec.56 of FERA in which the punishment prescribed is imprisonment of up to seven years with fine in cases where the amount involved exceeds Rupees 100,000. The Foreign Exchange Management Act [FEMA] enacted recently to replace FERA imposes civil liability for the offender for the contravention of its sections 3, 4, 5, 6 and 8. FEMA applies to all branches, offices and agencies outside India owned or controlled by a person resident in India and to any contravention committed outside India by any person to whom FEMA is applicable. Article 13 (2) of FEMA confers on the competent authority the power to direct the confiscation of any currency, security or any other money or property in respect of which any contravention has occurred.

Several authorities in India such as the Enforcement Directorate, the Police, the Customs, the Income Tax, and the state police organisations monitor activities relating to Hawala transactions. The Enforcement Directorate which is responsible for revenue intelligence, the Customs and the Police have adequate powers to initiate action against anybody indulging in illegal foreign exchange transactions, including Hawala. Several hundreds of cases of this nature have been caught and dealt with by the relevant Indian authorities.

In addition to the above, the Conservation of Foreign Exchange and Protection of Smuggling Activities Act, 1974 (COFEPOSA) contains stringent provisions enabling authorities to detain offenders for a period extending up to one year for indulging in illegal foreign exchange activities, including Hawala. A copy of the Act is enclosed for the information of the CTC. This covers all types of informal activities not under the purview of the Reserve Bank of India's regulations.

Que. 1.4 According to Section III of the supplementary report, India can implement orders of attachment or forfeiture of property upon request of foreign State on the basis of Sections 105, 105A to 105L, and 166A and 166B of the Code of Criminal Procedure. In the answer given in sub-paragraph 2(f) of Section III, it seems that India can only extend assistance on the basis of a bilateral treaty or at least a bilateral arrangement. Is this also the case in relation to the freezing of funds? If so, could such arrangements be made ad hoc?

Ans:

As far as freezing of funds of terrorist entities is concerned, India will be in a position to take action on a request of a foreign State on the basis of mutuality of assistance and where adequate proof is furnished that such freezing is required given the nature of an offence or an intended terrorist offence.

We do not have any *ad hoc* arrangements to deal with matters relating to freezing of funds as such cases could be subject to challenge in the courts of law in India.

Que. 1.5 Effective implementation of paragraph 1 of the Resolution also requires the existence of legal provisions or administrative measures that ensure that funds and other economic resources collected by non-profit organizations (e.g. religious, charitable or cultural organizations) are not diverted for other than the stated purposes, particularly for financing of terrorism. Please elaborate on how India (proposes to) ensures this, in particular regarding contributions received by non-profit organizations in India, from domestic sources and in Indian currency. Please clarify whether and how the Indian Income Tax Act and the Societies Registration Act, are applicable in that regard.

Ans:

For monitoring the collection and use of funds and other economic resources by non-profit organisations (for example, religious, charitable, cultural and other non-profit organisations) and for ensuring that these are not diverted for use other than the stated purposes, India had enacted as far back as 1860 the Societies Registration Act. Several states of the Union of India have, since, enacted their own Societies Registration Acts to replace the 1860 Act that contain detailed provisions relating to the registration, maintenance of accounts, collection and use of resources, audit of accounts, etc. These Acts also provide for the establishment of a separate agency for administering the law.

The above-mentioned legislation imposes certain mandatory obligations on non-profit organizations such as the filing of annual reports, intimation of change in membership and change of location, and filing of audit reports. The funds of the relevant association or society may be utilised only for the objects set forth in the Memorandum of Association. Furthermore, the funds of the society cannot be shared among members. If these requirements are not fulfilled, registration of the society is liable to be cancelled or the name of the society liable to be removed from the Register of Societies. If a registered society is determined to be not functioning according to the provisions of the Act, the Government have the right to dissolve the entity and to appoint a special officer to administer the society.

Under the Prevention of Terrorism Act 2002 (POTA), terrorist acts include acts of fund-raising by persons or organisations if such funds are intended for the purposes of terrorism. When a non-profit organisation is found diverting funds for purposes of terrorism, that organisation's name may be removed from the Register of Societies and the organisation itself may be prosecuted under POTA and its properties and assets seized under that Act.

In addition, the Foreign Contribution (Regulation) Act, 1976 (FCRA) enables the competent authorities in the Government of India to monitor closely the receipt of foreign resources by organisations in India and their use. The Government of India and the state governments maintain databases in respect of these organisations. In discharging their responsibilities, close and continuous interaction exists between the concerned authorities of the Government of India and state governments, including intelligence agencies and the police, to track and monitor any suspicious charitable organisations which might *inter alia* divert funds, etc. for terrorist purposes. Such information is then processed by the police in cooperation with other agencies where such suspicions are confirmed.

The Income-Tax Act prohibits the expenditure of funds by non-profit organisations for objects other than those set forth in the memorandum of association; their funds may be invested only in scheduled banks, public deposits, bonds and government securities. Auditors of such organisations are required to certify the nature of the grant as well as donations and that the grants and donations are spent for the purpose for which they were received. The Income-Tax structure of the country includes a separate Directorate General that deals with institutions that are given exemptions from income tax (religious, charitable, cultural and other non profit organisations). Such organisations are required to file regular statements with the authorities concerned. The field-level officers of the Directorate General monitor the accounts of these organisations. Therefore, an appropriate legislative framework exists, as well as adequate enforcement mechanisms, at the level of both in the Government of India and the state governments, to monitor and check the collection and use of funds and other economic resources by non-profit organisations. [Annexures—The Smugglers and Foreign Exchange Manipulators (Forfeiture of Property) Act, 1976 and, COFEPOSA Act, 1974].

Que. 1.6 Does a national-level body have responsibility for freezing funds and other financial assets or economic resources of persons and entities described in sub-paragraph 1(c) of the Resolution?

Ans:

General provisions concerning assistance in relation to orders of attachment or forfeiture of property are dealt with under section 105C of the Criminal Procedure Code (Cr.P.C,), 1973. Under section 105C(3) where a letter of request is received by the Government of India from a court or authority in a contracting State requesting attachment or forfeiture of property in India, derived or obtained, directly or indirectly, by any person from the commission of an offence committed in that contracting State, the Government may forward such letter of request to the Court, as it thinks fit, for execution in accordance with the provisions of sections 105D to 105J (both inclusive) or, as the case may be, with any other law in force. A copy of Section 105C is enclosed for ready reference. In addition, with respect to terrorist offences, property may also be forfeited under the provisions of the Prevention of Terrorism Act, 2002 (POTA).

Que. 1.7 What legislation or procedures exist for denying safe haven to terrorists, such as laws for excluding or expelling the types of individuals referred to in sub-paragraph 2(c) of the Resolution? It would be helpful if India supplied examples of any relevant action taken.

Ans:

As far as the legislation and procedures of denial of entry to terrorists is concerned, section 3, sub section (4) of the Prevention of Terrorism Act, 2002 (POTA) provides for punishment for anybody who voluntarily harbours or conceals any person while knowing that such person is a terrorist.

The system of immigration control instituted and implemented by the Government of India is very stringent and utilises the necessary data-bases to check for terrorists/criminals. In addition, immigration authorities, customs authorities and intelligence agencies are fully equipped to ensure that no undesirable individuals/persons can enter India or seek safe haven in the country. We have extensive border controls on our land borders as well as a very strong coast guard agency to patrol the extensive Indian coast-line.

The relevant pieces of legislation—the Foreigners Act 1946; Foreigners Orders issued by the Ministry of Home Affairs from time to time;: and the Passport Act 1967 provide the appropriate and sufficient legal framework to implement sub-paragraph 2(c) of Resolution 1373. According to the Foreigners Act 1946 a person who is not a citizen of India is a foreigner and is governed by provisions of the Foreigners Act. Under the provisions of this Act, the Government of India have the power to issue orders either generally or with respect to all foreigners or any prescribed class or description of foreigners. Such orders may prohibit, regulate or restrict the entry of foreigners into India, departure therefrom or presence or continued presence therein. Under Section 7, the Act imposes an obligation on hotel-keepers and others to furnish information in respect of foreigners accommodated in such places. The Foreigners [Report to Police] Order of 1971 obligates every householder or other person to report to the nearest police station the arrival or presence in his/her premises of a foreigner. Any person contravening the provisions of the Foreigners Act is liable for punishment with imprisonment for a term which may extend to five years.

From the above, it will be clear that there are adequate laws, procedures and enforcement agencies in India to prevent terrorists from seeking safe haven in the country.

Que. 1.8 Section 3 of the Prevention of Terrorism Act, 2002, criminalizes terrorist acts perpetrated against Indian interests, mostly in India itself. Effective implementation of sub-paragraphs 2(d) and (e) of the Resolution requires that the use of Indian territory for the purpose of financing, planning, facilitating or committing terrorist acts against other States and their citizens be criminalized. Please outline the provisions which India proposes to introduce into its domestic legislation in order to comply with this requirement.

Ans:

As far as the implementation of sub-paragraphs (2) and (3) of Resolution 1373 is concerned, the Indian Penal Code (IPC) (45 of 1860) contains adequate provisions to deal with persons, who plan, organise or take any other action anywhere that could constitute an offence. Copies of the relevant extracts of IPC sections 2. 3, 4, 121, 121A, 122 and 123 are enclosed. In addition, under section 3(1) and 3 (3) of POTA, the definition of terrorist acts includes acts calculated "to strike terror in any section of the people". (The term 'people' is widely interpreted to mean people anywhere. That the Al-Qaeda, which has not yet been found to be operating in India, has been banned in India under POTA is indicative of this). In addition, the Arms Act, 1959; the Explosives Act, 1884 and the Explosive Substances Act, 1908 contain very stringent punishments in regard to such acts.

The Security Council Act, 1947 empowers the Government of India to implement the decisions of the United Nations Security Council adopted under Chapter VII of the UN Charter. Furthermore, a proposal to notify an order in respect of Resolution 1373 under the Act is at an advanced stage of consideration of the authorities. Similarly, a proposal to give effect to the provisions of the International Convention for the Suppression of the Financing of Terrorism, 1999 either under the existing laws or, if necessary, by way of an enabling legislation is currently under consideration. Once these exercises are completed, the obligations contained in sub-paragraphs 2(d) and 2(e) of Resolution 1373 would be implemented.

It would thus be clear that, at present, we have adequate laws and enforcement machinery for purposes of taking action against persons who finance, plan, facilitate or commit terrorist act against other States and their citizens.

Que. 1.9 Is the existence of a bilateral agreement or arrangement a pre-requisite for India before it can offer legal assistance or extradite criminals to other countries?

Ans:

Yes, the existence of a bilateral agreement or arrangement is a pre-requisite before India can extradite a criminal to another country. As far as the offer of legal assistance is concerned, under section 166B of the Criminal

Procedure Code (Cr.PC), 1973 (copy enclosed), upon receipt of a letter of request from a court or an authority of another country for examination of any person, etc., the Government of India would forward it to the relevant court to proceed appropriately. In addition, India has a number of mutual legal assistance agreements/treaties with other countries. India continues to be willing to enter into such agreements with other countries.

Que. 1.10 Effective implementation of sub-paragraph 2(e) of the Resolution requires that States ensure that persons who participate in the financing, planning, preparation or preparation of terrorist acts or support such acts are brought to justice either by submitting the case without undue delay to their respective competent authorities for the purpose of prosecution or by extraditing these persons. In that context, please clarify whether, according to Section 34 of the Extradition Act, a person can be prosecuted in India if he or she has committed an offence abroad to which no bilateral extradition treaty is applicable or if India decides not to extradite this person.

Ans:

Section 34 of the Extradition Act 1962 provides that an extradition offence committed by any person in a foreign state shall be deemed to have been committed in India and such persons shall be liable to be prosecuted in India for such an offence. Extradition offences have been defined under section 2 to mean:-

(i) in relation to a foreign state being a treaty state, an offence provided for in the extradition treaty with that state:

(ii) in relation to a foreign state other than a treaty state an offence punishable with imprisonment for a term, which shall not be less than one year under the laws of India or of a foreign state and includes a composite offence. By composite offence is meant "an act or conduct of a person which occurred, whole or in part in a foreign state or in India but its effect or extended effects, taken as a whole would constitute an extradition offence in India or in a foreign state as the case may be".

Under section 34 of the Extradition Act, a person can be prosecuted in India if India decides not to extradite such a person. In the absence of a bilateral treaty, an arrangement can be worked out or, if applicable, an international Convention containing a provision for the obligation to extradite or prosecute can be invoked.

Que. 1.11 According to the supplementary report, even in cases where there are no extradition treaty concluded by India with another country, the Central Government may, by notified order, treat any convention, to which India and the foreign state are parties, as an extradition treaty concluded by both states and providing for extradition in respect of the

offences specified in the relevant international conventions and protocols against terrorism. Has the Central Government ordered to treat these conventions and protocols between India and all respective parties to the international legal instruments as such extradition treaties?

Ans:

Steps are being taken to notify all anti-terrorism Conventions under sector 3 of the Extradition Act so that in the absence of a bilateral Extradition Treaty or arrangement, such Conventions/Protocols may be treated as a basis for extradition between India and a Party to such Convention/Protocol.

The attention of the Committee is drawn to a recent instance of such an order. A notification has been issued in regard to Portugal. A copy of the text of the notification is enclosed.

Que. 1.12 Sub-paragraph 3(d) of the Resolution requires all States to become parties as soon as possible to all the relevant international conventions and protocols relating to terrorism. The CTC would appreciate receiving information on the progress made regarding the ratification by India of the International Convention for the Suppression of the Financing of Terrorism.

Ans:

The Government of India has decided very recently to ratify the International Convention for Suppression of the Financing of Terrorism.

Que. 1.13 Please explain how you have implemented the Protocol on the Suppression of Unlawful Acts of Violence at Airports Serving International Civil Aviation, supplementary to the Convention for the Suppression of Unlawful Acts against the Safety of Civil Aviation, the Convention on the Marking of Plastic Explosives for the Purpose of Detection and Convention on the Physical Protection of Nuclear Material into your domestic legislation.

Ans:

Implementing legislation for the Protocol on the Suppression of Unlawful Acts of Violence at Airports serving International Civil Aviation supplementary for the Convention for the Suppression of Unlawful Acts against the Safety of Civil Aviation is reflected in The Suppression of Unlawful Acts against the Safety of Civil Aviation (Amendment Act), 1994. Legislation to implement the Convention of Marking of Plastic Explosives is under process.

DOCUMENT NO. 25

INDIA'S 2004 COUNTER-TERRORISM REPORT TO THE UN

UN Security Council Resolution
S/2003/452

June 3, 2004

Distr.: General
3 June 2004

Original: English

Letter dated 1 June 2004 from the Chairman of the Security Council Committee established pursuant to resolution 1373 (2001) concerning counter-terrorism addressed to the President of the Security Council

I write with reference to my predecessor's letter of 2 December 2003 (S/2003/1152). The Counter-Terrorism Committee has received the attached fourth report from India submitted pursuant to paragraph 6 of resolution 1373 (2001) (see annex). I would be grateful if you could arrange for the present letter and its annex to be circulated as a document of the Security Council.

(*Signed*) Alexander V. **Konuzin**
Chairman
Security Council Committee established pursuant
to resolution 1373 (2001) concerning counter-terrorism

Annex

Letter dated 28 May 2004 from the Permanent Representative of India to the United Nations addressed to the Chairman of the Counter-Terrorism Committee

On behalf of the Government of India, I have the honour to refer to the letter dated 21 November 2003 from the Chairman of the Counter-Terrorism Committee and to submit herewith India's response to the Committee's questionnaire (see enclosure). The report also contains some introductory paragraphs explaining India's overall perspective on the compilation of national reports and the future work of the Committee.

The Government of India stands ready to provide the Committee with any further information that may be required.

(*Signed*) V. K. **Nambiar**

Enclosure*
Government of India Fourth Report to the Counter Terrorism Committee

Introduction

India has firmly and consistently supported U.N. Security Council Resolutions 1373 and the work of the Counter Terrorism Committee (CTC). The three National Reports submitted by India to the CTC have attempted to give a comprehensive picture of steps taken by India to counter terrorism. Based on its own long experience of tackling terrorism the following points are being brought to the attention of the CTC with regard to India's perspective on the future work of the CTC and the compilation of National Reports. The Counter Terrorism Committee could look into some of these aspects in its future work.

- The emphasis in the CTC questionnaire and in its reporting requirement is on the legislative aspect. The operational, procedural and administrative aspects are also vital in devising an appropriate counter terrorism strategy. With the many complexities arising out of geography, large population, porous borders, lack of development in some sectors etc., anti-terrorism strategies in India are built on a combination of 'on the ground experience' and 'administrative practices'. Local intelligence and policing are key to efforts to prevent, where possible, and combat, where necessary, acts of terrorism. Our reports try to capture the efforts made in this regard but often it is not possible to give an exhaustive description of mechanisms available.

* Annexes are on file with the Secretariat and are available for consultation.

- Looking at the future, counter terrorism measures will require a multi-track approach in many fields. The skills and technologies involved may vary from country to country and within a country from region to region. In tackling issues relating to border controls, money transfers, control of small arms, forged documents, etc., law enforcement officials will have to devise strategies depending on the needs of the situation. The experiences of countries in different regions and at different stages of development are likely to yield different approaches. Counter terrorism measures, therefore, have to cater to regional, national as well as context and functional specificities.
- The linkages between organized crime and terrorism need to be addressed. India welcomes the steps taken by the UN in this direction, and the latest effort by the UN Office on Drugs and Crime in Vienna to compile reports by member-States.
- A number of UN Security Council Resolutions mandate taking action against individuals/entities listed in the relevant lists. However, the information supplied by the Counter Terrorism Committee/UN Security Council is often inadequate, as neither the details regarding the identity of individuals nor the requisite information on the facts concerning offences committed by them is supplied to states to enable them to take effective action. In the absence of such information, the probability of attempts to trace, detect, identify or deter such persons yielding fruitful results is low. Adherence to the due process of law requires relevant information, including that of the alleged offences committed by persons/entities listed in these resolutions to enable effective measures to be taken against them.

The compilation of the measures employed in Counter Terrorism efforts, described in the reports submitted to the CTC, is undertaken after extensive inter-agency and inter-ministerial consultations involving administrative, technical and procedural matters. This exercise to revise and update the information being provided to the CTC is ongoing and will continue in an appropriate manner in the future.

1. Implementation Measures

Effectiveness in the Protection of the Financial System

1.1 Effective implementation of sub-paragraph 1 (a) requires States to have in place effective executive machinery for preventing and suppressing the financing of terrorist acts. In this context, does India provide its administrative, investigative, prosecutorial and judicial authorities with specific training aimed at enforcing its laws in relation to:

- **typologies and trends aimed at countering terrorist financing methods and techniques;**

— **techniques for tracing property, which represents the proceeds of crime or which is to be used to finance terrorism, with a view to ensuring that such property is frozen, seized or confiscated?**

Please outline relevant programs and/or courses. What mechanisms/programs has India put in place to train its different economic sectors in the detection of unusual and suspicious financial transactions related to terrorist activities and in the prevention of the movement of illicit money?

India's administrative, investigative, and prosecutorial authorities are provided specific training in enforcing laws relating to countering terrorist financing and money laundering. Administrative, investigative and prosecutorial officers are deputed to reputed national institutes to upgrade their skills, methods, techniques, etc. in investigation of cases. Some of these institutes are:

(i) National Police Academy, Hyderabad;

(ii) Military Intelligence Training School and Depot, Pune;

(iii) Central Bureau of Investigation (CBI) Academy, Ghaziabad;

(iv) Intelligence Bureau Central Training School, New Delhi; and

(v) National Judicial Academy, Bhopal.

The Central Bureau of Investigation Academy, Ghaziabad, for example, provides training, inter alia, on (i) scientific aids to investigation, (ii) scientific interrogation techniques, and (iii) investigation of cyber crime.

The Military Intelligence Training School and Depot, Pune addresses intelligence dissemination and investigation of cases relating to terrorist activities including financing of terrorist activities.

Courses on money laundering including detection of unusual and suspicious financial transactions are also offered at the National Academy of Customs, Excise and Narcotics, Faridabad; the Reserve Bank of India Training College, Mumbai; and the Staff College of the State Bank of India (SBI), Hyderabad.

1.2 The CTC would appreciate receiving the main provisions of the Money Laundering Act (2003), together with an outline as to how the said provisions address the requirements of the Resolution.

The Prevention of Money Laundering Act (**PMLA**) has made the act of money laundering a criminal offence.

Under Section 3 of the **PMLA**:

> "Whosoever directly or indirectly attempts to indulge or knowingly assist or knowingly is a party or is actually involved in any process or activity connected with the proceeds of crime and projecting it as untainted property shall be guilty of the offence of money laundering."

The Act also provides a schedule which lists out offences under various acts.

Section 4 of the **PMLA** provides for punishment for the offence of money laundering with rigorous imprisonment for a period ranging from 3 to 7 years and fine, which may extend to Rupees 500,000 (approximately US$ 10,000).

Section 5 to 11 of the **PMLA** provide for attachment of property involved in money laundering, adjudication of such offences, confirmation of attachment of such properties and their ultimate confiscation on conclusion of a trial for any scheduled offence.

Sections 12 to 15 of the **PMLA** impose obligations on Banking Companies, Financial Institutions and Intermediaries to maintain proper records of all transactions, the nature and value of which may be prescribed and to furnish information of such transactions to the authority designated under the **PMLA** within a prescribed time and verification and maintenance of the records of the identity of all clients in such manner as may be prescribed.

Section 16 to 19 of the **PMLA** provides for the power of survey, search and seizure, search of persons, arrests etc.

Section 24 of the Act provides that the burden of proving that the proceeds of crime are untainted property shall be on the accused.

The Act also provides for establishment of the Appellate Tribunal and Special Courts for speedy disposal of cases under the **PMLA**.

Section 56 provides for agreements with foreign countries for enforcing the provisions of **PMLA** and exchange of information for the prevention of any attempts under **PMLA** or under corresponding law of the country with whom the agreement has been made or for the investigation of cases relating to any offence under **PMLA**.

A copy of the **PMLA** is enclosed at **Annexure-I**.

1.3 In regard to implementation of sub-paragraph 1 (a), could India please identify which Indian agency is in charge of receiving and analyzing reports on suspicious transactions, including transactions allegedly linked with the financing of terrorism? What powers have been entrusted to the agency with a view to dealing with those reports?

The Central Economic Intelligence Bureau (CEIB) is the apex organization for receiving and analyzing information pertaining to economic intelligence. The CEIB was set up in 1985 for coordinating/strengthening intelligence gathering activities, investigation and enforcement of economic offences and laws by various agencies. The CEIB liaises with the concerned departments at the Central and State levels. The CEIB analyses all reports pertaining to economic intelligence received from different agencies, such as the Central Board of Direct Taxes, the Central Board of Excise and Customs etc., that are in charge of receipt/analyses of suspicious transaction reports (STRs). In the banking system, under the direction of the Reserve Bank of India (India's Central Bank), various banks (regional headquarters and headquarters) receive and analyze these reports.

1.4 Sub-paragraph 1 (a) of the Resolution, as well as Article 18 of the International Convention for the Suppression of the Financing of Terrorism, require financial institutions and other intermediaries to identify their clients and to report suspicious financial transactions to the relevant authorities. In this regard, could India provide the CTC with an outline of the legal provisions which enable it to meet those requirements in full? The CTC would welcome an outline of the legal provisions which oblige financial intermediaries (such as lawyers, accountants, notaries and other professionals, when engaged in financial transactions) to report suspicious transactions to the relevant authorities. The CTC would also appreciate receiving an outline of the relevant legal provisions as regards Offshore Banking Units and bureaux de change. In the absence of such provisions, the CTC would ask India to indicate the steps, which it intends taking in order to comply in full with this aspect of the Resolution. The CTC would also appreciate receiving an outline of the criteria used to determine what constitute suspicious transactions under India law.

Chapter IV of the Prevention of Money Laundering Act (**PMLA**) deals with the obligations of banking companies, financial institutions and intermediaries. Section 12 of the **PMLA** requires every banking company or financial institution and intermediary to maintain a record of all transactions, the nature and value of which may be prescribed whether it is a single transaction or series of transactions integrally connected to each other and where such series of transactions take place within one month, furnish such information to the Director (appointed under the **PMLA**) within the time prescribed. These records shall be maintained for five years from the date of cessation of the transaction. Further, when the principal officer of the banking company, financial institution and intermediaries has reason to believe that such transaction is valued below the prescribed value, he shall furnish such information to the Director within the prescribed time. If the Director finds during the enquiry that the provisions of Section 12 of the Act have been contravened then, without prejudice to any other action that may be taken under the Act, he may, by order, levy a fine which shall not be less than Rupees 10,000 (approximately US$ 200) — but may extend to Rupees 100,000 (approx. US$ 2000) for each failure. Thus it is mandatory for the banking company, financial institutions and intermediaries including insurance companies to comply with the provisions of the Act.

Bureaux de Change are also covered under the Prevention of Money Laundering Act.

Section 14 of **PMLA** provides for protection of banking companies, financial institutional, intermediaries and their officers from any civil proceedings for the act of furnishing information under the **PMLA**.

Individual cash transactions over Rupees 10 million (approx. US$ 200,000) each and all suspicious transactions have to be reported by Banks.

1.5 The CTC notes from India's supplementary report that the Foreign Exchange Regulation Act and the Foreign Exchange Management Act prohibit receiving and distributing payments throughout India without the permission of the Reserve Bank of India. In this regard, has India introduced legal provisions to regulate money remittance/transfer services, including informal money or value transfer systems (such as Hawala)? Is there a requirement to license or register those services? Must they identify their customers and report any suspicious transactions to the competent authorities? In the absence of such provisions, could India indicate the steps which it intends taking in order fully to comply with this aspect of the Resolution?

Hawala transactions (Informal Money Transfer Systems) are not permitted under the Foreign Exchange Management Act (**FEMA**) and are illegal. India has consistently taken the stand that "registration" of Hawala is an oxymoron as Hawala transactions, especially those relating to terrorist activities are, by their very nature, clandestine. The system is so largely based on trust that licencing or registration cannot succeed. The solution for eliminating/reducing Hawala is to extend regular money transfer services, making them more customer-friendly and accessible. Our response to the suggestions for regulating the 'informal' money transfer (Hawala) has been presented before various international fora on several occasions. In fact, we have consistently maintained that 'informal' cross border money transfers violate the provisions of **FEMA** and are therefore, illegal. Our position regarding informal value transfer/Hawala has been that since it is an illegal activity it can only be curbed and cannot be regulated.

Wire Transfer Services are allowed in India only after the concerned banking/non-banking entity registers with the Reserve Bank of India, and regular reports are received for this. The Suspicious Transactions Reporting system has still not been fully introduced in this sector but should become operational once the Financial Intelligence Unit (FIU), (being set up under the Department of Revenue, Ministry of Finance), becomes fully functional.

For other forms of remittances such as use of banking channels for money remittances, under the 'Money Transfer Service Scheme' (MTSS), a licence is required from the Reserve Bank of India, before a banking/non-banking entity can receive instructions from an overseas money transfer service provider to transfer amounts up to a certain limit to the beneficiaries. Any money transfer service carried out in India by any other agency without proper licence is illegal.

A copy of the Reserve Bank of India's guidelines on the registration of wire transfer services is enclosed at **Annexure-II**.

1.6 In relation to money laundering and the financing of terrorism, could India provide an outline of any special strategy which it may have developed with a view to enabling its investigative agencies effectively to prevent resources from being transferred to terrorists (for example, through the under-invoicing of exports and the over-invoicing of imports, through the manipulation of real estate transactions and that of high value commodities such as gold, diamond and etc.)

Apart from **PMLA** and Prevention of Terrorism Act (POTA), the Government of India has enacted Foreign Exchange Management Act (**FEMA**), 1999 as a successor to the Foreign Exchange Regulation Act, 1973. The provisions of **FEMA** aim at preventing resources, either by way of under-invoicing of exports and over-invoicing of imports, from being transferred to undesirable elements including terrorists. Section 3 of **FEMA** prohibits dealings in foreign exchange etc. It lays down that:

> "3. Save as otherwise provided in this Act, rules or regulations made thereunder, or with the general or special permission of the Reserve Bank, no person shall —
>
> (a) deal in or transfer any foreign exchange or foreign security to any person not being an authorized person;
>
> (b) make any payment to or for the credit of any person resident outside India in may manner;
>
> (c) receive otherwise through an authorized person, any payment by order or on behalf of any person resident outside Indian in any manner;
>
> **Explanation** — For the purpose of this clause, where any person in, or resident in, India receives any payment by order or on behalf of any person resident outside India through any other person (including an authorized person) without a corresponding inward remittance from any place outside India, then, such person shall be deemed to have received such payment otherwise than through an authorized person;
>
> (d) enter into any financial transaction in India as consideration for or in association with acquisition or creation or transfer of a right to acquire, any asset outside India by any person.
>
> **Explanation** — For the purpose of this clause, "financial transaction" means making any payment to, or for the credit of any person, or receiving any payment for, by order or on behalf of any person, or drawing,

issuing or negotiating any bill of exchange or promissory note, or transferring any security of acknowledging any debt."

Section 4 of FEMA 1999 restrains any person resident in India from acquiring, holding, owning, possessing or transferring any foreign exchange, foreign security or any immovable property situated outside India except as specifically provided in the Act; while Section 7 deals with exports of goods and services. The Enforcement Directorate mandate includes acquisition of foreign currency illegally by person in India, non-repatriation of the proceeds of the exported goods, siphoning off of foreign exchange against fictitious and bogus imports, illegal acquisition of foreign exchange through Hawala etc.

1.7 In the context of the effective implementation of sub-paragraph 1 (a) of the Resolution, please explain the rules for identifying persons or entities which maintain bank accounts; or on whose behalf a bank account is maintained (i.e. the beneficial owners); or who are the beneficiaries of transactions conducted by professional intermediaries; as well as any other person or entity connected with a financial transaction. Are there any identification obligations imposed on customers who operate trusts with a view to obtaining information about the trustees, settlers/ grantors and beneficiaries? Please outline any procedures which enable foreign law enforcement agencies or other counter-terrorist entities to obtain such information in cases where terrorist links are suspected.

The Reserve Bank of India (RBI) has issued 'Know Your Customer' (KYC) guidelines to banks in August, 2002 requiring all banks, inter alia, to verify the identity of the customer on the basis of reliable documents or through introduction by an existing account holder or a person known to the bank. In November, 2003, the RBI instructed all banks to ensure that customer identification for all existing accounts is also carried out on the basis of reliable documents within a fixed time frame. The issue relating to the identity of the beneficial owners is being examined. Under the Indian Trusts Act, 1882, it is mandatory for the trustees to give their name and addresses that are to be verified by a witness. Similarly under the Societies Registration Act, 1860, it is mandatory to disclose the names and addresses of the members and office bearers of the society.

The draft Rules under the Prevention of Money Laundering Act (**PMLA**), 2002 are in the process of being finalized by the Department of Revenue, Government of India and some of these issues including the arrangement for sharing the information with external agencies are expected to be addressed in the Rules. Sections 56, 57, 58 and 59 of the **PMLA**, 2002 are relevant in this regard.

So far as the issue of assistance to foreign law enforcement agencies in respect of individuals having terrorist links is concerned, such assistance including mutual legal assistance may be extended through the existing bilateral mutual legal assistance treaties or under general provisions of the Criminal Procedure Code, 1973.

1.8 As regards the implementation of sub-paragraphs 1 (a) and (c) of the Resolution, as well as Article 8 of the International Convention for the Suppression of the Financing of Terrorism, the CTC would be grateful if India could indicate the magnitude of the financial assets frozen, seized and confiscated in relation to the prevention of financing of terrorism.

Various assets suspected to be linked to terrorist financing have been seized under the Income Tax Act and Prevention of Terrorism Act (**POTA**) and are under disposal. While three bank accounts were frozen under **POTA**, no money was found in these accounts. It has been found that terrorist financing in India is mostly conducted through informal channels such as Hawala, Fake Indian Currency Notes (FICN), drug smuggling, etc.

As to the magnitude of financial assets frozen/confiscated in relation to the International Convention for the Suppression of the Financing of Terrorism, so far we have not detected any accounts relating to the terrorist entities included in the relevant UN Security Council resolutions. Prior to September 2001, two accounts of the Ariana Airlines were frozen, pursuant to the decision of the UN Security Council.

In addition a small number of bank accounts were also frozen under Indian domestic laws. However, no significant amount of money was found in these accounts and it is the assessment of Indian authorities that terrorists do not maintain accounts in their own names and their preferred source of financing is through informal channels. (This aspect has also been highlighted elsewhere in this report).

1.9 With regard to the effective implementation of paragraph 1 (d) of the Resolution, please indicate the number of cases in which India has taken judicial action against non-profit organizations on account of their suspected involvement in the financing of terrorism? Has India frozen the assets of any non-profit organization because of their links with terrorist groups or terrorist activities? The CTC would also welcome receiving examples of cases in which sanctions were imposed on those terrorist organizations. In regard to the auditing and monitoring of the collection and use of funds by charities, how does India coordinate the work of the various bodies entrusted with this work?

Financing of terrorism is an offence under the Prevention of Terrorism Act (POTA) which is implemented by the Ministry of Home Affairs and its subsidiary agencies. Government of India has recently issued an enabling notification to facilitate implementation of Security Council resolutions under India's United Nations Security Council Act. This is expected to further strengthen action against organizations in the future.

Over 30 organizations have been banned under the POTA. The procedure for proscribing organizations is laid down in Section 18 of POTA.

As far as overseas donations to charities are concerned, applications received by the Ministry of Home Affairs (MHA), are duly scrutinized and field enquiries conducted by the concerned agencies for establishing the genuineness of both the organization and the professed aims/objectives. If claims are found to be genuine, permission is accorded for making donations under the Foreign Contributions Regulatory Act (FCRA). The coordination of the work of various bodies is undertaken by a nodal unit in the Ministry of Home Affairs.

1.10 As regards the implementation of sub-paragraph 1 (a) and (d), could India please provide the CTC with statistics on the number of cases where sanctions for providing support to terrorists or terrorist organizations were imposed on:

— financial and non-financial institutions;
— financial intermediaries.

Action on specific cases of providing support to terrorists or terrorist organizations is taken under relevant laws, including Prevention of Terrorism Act (POTA), and the Indian Penal Code (IPC). In January 2004, the Government of India issued an Order, under the UN Security Council Act 1947, empowering the Central Government to take measures to give effect to Resolutions 1267, 1333, 1390 and 1455 adopted by the United Nations Security Council requiring all States to take measures to combat international terrorism to:

(a) prevent and suppress the financing of any terrorist act;

(b) prohibit any willful provision or collection, directly or indirectly, of funds by any individual or entity whether in or outside India, with the intention of using such funds or having the knowledge that they shall be used to carry out any terrorist act;

(c) freeze, seize or attach funds and other financial assets or economic resources, held by or on behalf of the individuals or entities listed in the Schedule;*

(d) prohibit any individual or entity from making any funds, financial assets or economic resources or financial or other related services available directly, or indirectly, for the benefit of individuals or entities listed in the Schedule;

(e) prevent the entry into or the transit through India of individuals listed in the Schedule;

(f) prevent any direct or indirect supply, sale and transfer, in or outside India, of arms and ammunition and other related materials to the individuals or entities listed in the Schedule.

* (Taliban/Al Qaeda Sanctions list of the 1267 Committee.)

No information is available with regard to cases where sanctions had to be applied on institutions for supporting terrorist actions.

Effectiveness of Counter-Terrorism Machinery

1.11 Effective implementation of 1373-related legislation covering all aspects of the Resolution requires States to have in place effective and coordinated executive machinery as well as to create and utilize adequate national and international anti-terrorist strategies. In this context, does India's counter-terrorism strategy and/or policy targeting (at national and/or sub-national level) deal with the following forms or aspects of counter terrorist activity:

— Criminal investigation and prosecution;

— Counter-terrorist intelligence (human and technical);

— Special forces operations;

— Physical protection of potential terrorist targets;

— Strategic analysis and forecasting of emerging threats;

— Analysis of efficiency of anti-terrorist legislation and relevant amendments;

— Border and immigration control, control preventing the trafficking in drugs, arms, biological and chemical weapons, their precursors and the illicit use of radioactive materials;

— Coordination of provincial agencies in alt those areas.

If possible, could India please outline the legal provisions and other administrative procedures as well as the best practices in this regard?

Under the Constitution of India, public order and police, (Entries 1 and 2 of List II of the Seventh Schedule of the Constitution of India), are responsibilities of states (provinces). At the same time, the Constitution confers on the Union the responsibility to protect every state (province) against external aggression and internal disturbances, and to ensure that the government of every state is carried on in accordance with the provisions of the Constitution. In pursuance of these obligations, the Union Ministry of Home Affairs extends manpower and financial support, guidance and expertise to state governments for the maintenance of security, peace and harmony without infringing upon the constitutional rights of states.

In India investigation and prosecution of all types of crimes including terrorist cases are, therefore, dealt with by the state police & state prosecution machinery. Most states have formed Anti-Terrorist Cells/Special Operational Groups/Special Task force to deal with terrorist activity within their jurisdiction.

A Multi Agency Centre (MAC) has been set up in the Ministry of Home Affairs for coordinating counter-terrorism efforts. The Centre pools, processes and disseminates actionable intelligence and converts raw intelligence into actionable intelligence on terrorist activities in the country.

States have formed Special Operational Groups/Special Task Force/Special Intelligence Cell to conduct operations against terrorists. There are also specialized well-trained security forces at Central Government level for dealing with grave & difficult situations. The intelligence agencies at state & national level and the Multi Agency Centre analyze and forecast the emerging threats. Central Government & State Governments review the efficiency of counter terrorism measures from time to time to strengthen and streamline their efforts.

To check illegal migration, infiltration of terrorists, and trafficking in drugs, arms and other contraband across India's international borders, the Government of India has a system of border control in place. India has implemented stringent immigration controls which utilize necessary data bases to check for terrorists/criminals and to prevent trafficking of drugs. India has comprehensive legislation in place, namely the Narcotics Drugs & Psychotropic Substance Act, 1985 to regulate and control drugs and psychotropic substances as well as their precursors. This law covers both domestic as well as international trafficking in these substances. The Act also empowers custom authorities to interdict and seize narcotic drugs and psychotropic substances and their precursors and prosecute offenders. The Border Security Force also has powers to seize narcotic drugs and psychotropic substances and precursor chemicals being trafficked across India's international borders. A number of state agencies including state police have been empowered to enforce the provisions of the Act. A special agency, namely, Narcotic Control Bureau has also been created both to enforce the provisions of the Act as well as to coordinate among the various central and state agencies which are empowered under the Act.

Under Indian Arms Act, 1959, the illegal possession, transit, sale of arms/ammunition is punishable. Prevention of Terrorism Act, 2002 contains provisions penalizing the unauthorized possession of arms/ammunitions, bombs, dynamites or hazardous explosive substances or other lethal weapons capable of mass destruction or biological/chemical substances of warfare. Criminal intelligence departments & officers of the level of Director

General of Police coordinate the function of various investigation agencies in the State.

Counter-terrorism intelligence is collected by the Special Branches of State Police as well as Intelligence & Security Agencies at central level. These organizations use both human intelligence & technical intelligence to gather actionable intelligence against terrorists.

The Atomic Energy Act, 1962 contains provisions which prevent the illicit acquisitions, possession, disposal, export, import of radioactive substances and whoever contravenes any provisions of the Act can be punished with imprisonment and fine. India is also party to the Convention on Physical Protection of Nuclear Material (CPPNM). India also co-sponsored the Resolution on the 'Code of Conduct on the Safety and Security of Radioactive Sources' adopted at the last IAEA General Conference.

For streamlining intelligence efforts, the Intelligence Bureau (IB) has been designated as the nodal agency for counter terrorism. In order to optimize intelligence flows and coordination between multifarious agencies in the field of counter terrorism, a Multi Agency Center (MAC) has been created in the Intelligence Bureau at New Delhi supported by subsidiary Multi Agency Centers at state levels. The Joint Task Force on Intelligence (JTFI) in the IB has been created for coordinating and synergizing the efforts of the intelligence wings of the central police organizations and special branches of the state police forces. The JTFI is supported by inter-state Intelligence support teams (ISISTs) meant for dealing with internal security threats concerning more than one state. The states have been requested to streamline and strengthen the special branches to be able to make full use of this mechanism.

In order to sensitize the state governments to the emerging threats in the internal security scenario and to ensure a coordinated approach for tackling the problems pertaining to internal security, two conferences, one of the Chief Secretaries and Director Generals of Police of States and the other of the Chief Ministers of states are now held every year.

The proper and effective management of borders is vitally important for national security, particularly cross border terrorism. The steps taken by the Government in this regard include additional raising of Border Guard Forces, deployment of hi-tech electronic surveillance equipments on the borders to act as force multiplier for effective border management, a pilot project for issue of multi purpose national identity cards in some states and Union Territories on an experimental basis, detection and deportation of illegal immigrants, a perspective plan for integrated infrastructure development of border areas and action plan to strengthen the coastal security.

Mutual Legal Assistance Treaty (MLAT) in Criminal Matters facilitate the widest measures of mutual assistance in the service of summons, execution of warrant and other judicial documents and improve the effectiveness of both countries in the suppression of crime, investigation, prosecution of crime related to terrorism and tracing, restraint, forfeiture or confiscation of proceeds and instruments of crime through cooperation. India has signed agreements on MLAT with a number of countries.

India has established Joint Working Groups on Counter Terrorism with a number of countries to exchange information and strengthen international cooperation to combat terrorism.

1.12 The CTC would be grateful if India could please provide it with information concerning its counter terrorist efforts including, inter alia, an outline of targeted programs, the agencies involved as well as a description of the coordination mechanisms utilized by the agencies charged with implementing the provisions of Paragraph 2 and 3 of the Resolution. The CTC is particularly interested in the following areas:

- **— the recruitment to terrorist groups:**
- **— the tracing of links between criminal activities (in particular, drug trafficking) and terrorism;**
- **— the prevention of the establishment of terrorist safe havens and other forms of passive or active support for terrorists or terrorist groups, including inter alia, logistic support of terrorists (e.g. using of global information infrastructure).**

The Multi-Agency Center (MAC) and Subsidiary Multi-Agency Centers led by the Intelligence Bureau have been established for sharing information among various agencies including linkages between criminal activities such as drug trafficking and terrorism. In the event of any information gathered during drug investigations pointing to the financing of terrorist through drug trafficking, institutional arrangements exist for sharing of such information and for acting upon it. Similarly, information on cases involving joint seizures of arms, ammunition, explosives and drugs is also shared with concerned agencies.

Coordination mechanism has also been described at 1.11 above.

The details of targeted programs cannot be provided for reasons of confidentiality.

1.13 In the context of the effective implementation of sub-paragraph 2 (e), the CTC notes that the Prevention of Terrorism Act (2002), contains legal provisions concerning the interception of communications. Please indicate whether special investigative techniques can be used in India in cases of terrorism (e.g. observation; undercover operations; controlled delivery; "pseudo-purchases" or other "pseudo-offences", etc.). Please explain what these techniques consist of as well as the legal conditions

which govern their use (especially, whether they may only be applied to suspects, whether they may only be applied if approved by a court, the period for which they may be used, etc.). Could India indicate whether those techniques can be used in cooperation with another State?

Special investigative techniques such as surveillance, undercover operations, etc. are used in India in cases of terrorism as well as other serious offences. Techniques such as "pseudo-purchases" or "pseudo-offences" are not backed by any legal provision. "Controlled delivery" has been legalized under the Narcotics Drugs & Psychotropic Substance Act, 1985. The provision under the Act is as follows:

> "Controlled delivery" means the techniques of allowing illicit or suspect consignments of narcotic drugs, psychotropic substances, out of, or through or into the territory of India with the knowledge and under the supervision of an officer empowered in this behalf or duly authorized under section 50-A with a view to identifying the persons involved in the commission of an offence under the Act."

Cooperation with another State in investigative techniques is a matter of bilateral understanding. The details cannot be gone into because of confidentiality.

1.14 The CTC noted from sub-paragraph 30 (1) of the Prevention of Terrorism Act (2002) that it has procedures in place aimed at protecting witnesses. In this regard, please indicate whether India has taken measures to protect persons who are vulnerable in the prosecution of terrorist cases (e.g. protection of the victims, of collaborators of justice, of judges and prosecutors)? Please describe the legal and administrative provisions in place to ensure this protection. Could India please indicate whether these measures can be utilized in cooperation with or at the request of another State?

The Constitution of India enjoins upon the State to protect the life & liberty of its citizens. The protection of witnesses as per provisions of Prevention of Terrorist Act (**POTA**), 2002 includes in-camera trials, keeping the identity & address of witnesses' secret, not mentioning the names and addresses of the witnesses in orders or judgments or in any records of the case accessible to public. In case of danger to the life of witnesses, judges, prosecutors, the State Police provide adequate police protection.

As per Section 3(7) of **POTA** 2002, whoever threatens any person who is a witness or any other person in whom such witness may be interested, with violence, or wrongfully restrains or confines the witness, or any other person in whom the witness may be interested, or does any other unlawful act with the said intent, shall be punishable with imprisonment which may extend to three years and fine.

State police organizations after assessing the threat perception makes adequate arrangements to protect individuals. These measures can also be utilized in co-operation with or at the request of another State to the extent it is specifically provided under mutual legal assistance agreement.

1.15 In regard to the effective implementation of sub-paragraphs 1 (d) and 2 (e) of the Resolution, as well as of Article 5 of the International Convention for the Suppression of the Financing of Terrorism, please indicate whether India has introduced measures to establish the civil, criminal or administrative liability of legal persons for criminal offences, in particular offences related to terrorist activities? Please specify and provide an outline of the relevant legal provisions. Is it possible to assign liability to the legal person when no natural person has been convicted or identified?

The answer below should be read along with answer to question 1.2. As per the Prevention of Money Laundering Act (PMLA), 2002 and the Foreign Exchange Management Act (FEMA), person has been defined as "persons including an individual, a Hindu undivided family, a company, a firm, an association or persons or a body of individuals, whether incorporated or not, every artificial juridical person, not falling within any of the preceding sub-clauses, and any agency, office or branch owned or controlled by any of the above persons mentioned in the preceding sub-clauses".

Similarly, the term 'person' in the Indian Penal Code (IPC) includes any company, or an association, or a body of person, whether incorporated or not. This definition is applicable wherever the term 'person' is used in Criminal Procedure Code, Prevention of Terrorism Act (POTA), 2002 and Narcotics Drugs and Psychotropic Substance Act, 1985.

1.16 The CTC noted from the third report of India (page 7) that legislation to implement the Convention on the Marking of Plastic Explosives is in process. In this regard, the CTC would be content to receive a progress report on the enactment of the relevant legislation, as welt as on the steps taken by India to implement the International Convention for the Suppression of the Financing of Terrorism to which India has recently become a party.

In India, plastic explosives are not manufactured in the civilian sector. They are manufactured only in Defence Organizations which are exempted under Section 14 of the Explosives Act. Separately the Explosive Rules, 1983 are being revised to incorporate the provisions on the marking of plastic explosives. The manufacture, possession, sale, import, transport etc. of explosives is controlled and regulated.

The legislation to implement the Convention on the Marking of Plastic Explosives is under process.

Sections 6–17 of the Prevention of Terrorism Act (POTA) cover the entire gamut of financing of terrorism activities. The activities and channels relating to money laundering and informal movement of funds are regulated under the Prevention of Money Laundering Act (PMLA), the structure for implementation of which is under process. Other specific laws have also been used, description of which have been provided in our earlier reports to the CTC. As far as detection of cases and disruption of financing channels are concerned, those based on intelligence driven investigations and prosecution is undertaken under the relevant laws.

1.17 Effective implementation of sub-paragraph 2 (a) of the Resolution requires each Member State, inter alia, to criminalize the recruitment to terrorist groups within its territory, whether the terrorist groups are operating within its territory or abroad. From previous report, it is not clear whether India taw contains special provisions in this regard. In particular, it is not clear whether any of the provisions in India law address the following situation i.e.: the recruitment of persons in India with a view to undertaking terrorist activities in other countries. It is worth noting, in this respect, that this form of recruitment is sometimes based on a falsehood or deception. For example, persons may be recruited to work as teachers, although the real purpose of their recruitment may be very different. The CTC would be grateful for an outline of the legal provisions which will enable India to meet the requirements of this aspect of the Resolution. In their absence, the CTC would appreciate receiving an indication from India as to the steps which it intends taking in order to comply with this aspect of the Resolution.

The answer to this question is partly covered in the answer provided to question 1.11.

Under Section 1.4 of the Prevention of Terrorism Act (POTA), "any person who commits an offence beyond India which is punishable under this Act shall be dealt with according to the provisions of this Act in the same manner as if such act had been committed in India".

Under Section 18 (4) of the Prevention of Terrorism Act, an organization shall be deemed to be involved in terrorism if it —

(a) commits or participates in acts of terrorism,

(b) prepares for terrorism,

(c) promotes or encourages terrorism, or

(d) is otherwise involved in terrorism.

Section 4 of Indian Penal Code also provides for applications of Indian Penal Code in cases where any citizen of India commits offences in any place without and beyond India. The Indian Penal Code also deals with the cases of waging war against other Governments at peace with the Government of India. (Sections 125–127).

As far as criminalizing recruitment to terrorist groups Section 3 (3) of the Prevention of Terrorism Act provides that "Whoever conspires or attempts to commit, or advocates, abets, advises or incites or knowingly facilitates the commission of, a terrorist act or any act preparatory to a terrorist act, shall be punishable with imprisonment for a term which shall not be less than five years but which may extend to imprisonment for life and shall also be liable to fine."

1.18 With regard to the implementation of sub-paragraphs 2 (a) and (d), India in its third report refers (at page 6) to sections 2, 3, 4, 121, 121A, 122 and 123 of the Indian Penal Code. The CTC notes that those legal provisions do not appear adequately to meet the requirements of the above mentioned sub-paragraphs. In particular, the provisions would appear inadequate to prevent the activities of those who use the territory of India to finance, plan, facilitate or commit terrorist acts against other States or their citizens. The CTC would appreciate receiving an outline of the legal provisions, if any, which enable India to meet these requirements. In their absence, could India indicate the steps which it intends taking to remedy the situation?

The existing provisions in Indian Penal Code and other legislations are found adequate to deal with the cases of financing, planning, facilitating or committing terrorist acts against other state or their citizens. It may also be noted that any case of intended hostile activity against a foreign Government will be dealt with by the Indian intelligence, administrative and police machinery effectively.

1.19 In the context of the effective implementation of sub-paragraph 2 (e), could India provide the CTC with information relating to the number of persons prosecuted in India for:

- **— terrorist activities;**
- **— the financing of terrorist activities;**
- **— recruiting to terrorist organizations;**
- **— providing support to terrorists or terrorist organizations.**

How many of these persons have been prosecuted for inviting support (including recruitment) for:

- **— proscribed organizations; and**
- **— other terrorist groups or organizations?**

Please outline the procedure used to proscribe foreign terrorist organizations (other those listed by the Security Council), as well as data as regards

the number of organizations involved and/or corresponding examples. How long does it take to proscribe a terrorist organization at the request of another State or based on information supplied by another State?

As far as the spectrum of terrorist activities is concerned, they include covert activities, open activities, charitable activities, etc. As and when information is received about such activities, proper investigation and action is undertaken. Given the diversity of different types of such activities, a wide range of laws are applied including the Indian Penal Code, Indian Arms Act, Indian Explosives Act, Public Security Act, Public Safety Act, Prevention of Terrorism Act, Prevention of Money Laundering Act etc. Since these also cover general criminal activities involving use of firearms, explosives, and other violent means, it is difficult to segregate which cases are specifically terrorist activities from those which are directly related to such crimes. Also given the wide dispersal of cases over different parts of the country, it is difficult to collate figures.

If the Government of India believes that an organization is involved in terrorism, it can list such an organization in the Schedule of the Act, proscribing it as a terrorist organization in accordance with Section 18(3) of the Prevention of Terrorism Act (POTA).

Effectiveness of Customs, Immigration and Border Controls

1.20 Effective implementation of sub-paragraphs 2 (c) and (g) of the Resolution requires the enforcement of effective customs, immigration and border controls so as to prevent the movement of terrorists and the establishment of safe havens. In this regard, please outline the legal and administrative procedures developed by India in order to protect its port facilities and ships, persons working in those port facilities and ships, cargo, cargo transport units as well as ships' stores from the risks of a terrorist attack. Have the competent Indian authorities put procedures in place to review and up-date transport security plans periodically? If yes, please outline.

The legal provisions contained in the Indian Ports Act, 1908 are applicable for protecting port facilities and ships, persons working in those port facilities and ships, cargo, cargo transport units as well as ships' stores from the risks of a terrorist attack. An internal security apparatus is maintained at Indian Ports by the concerned Port Authorities as well as by the State Police. Some of the major ports are provided additional security by the Central Industrial Security Force. Government of India has designated the Indian Register of Shipping (**IRS**) as the nodal agency to implement the International Ship and Port Facility Security (ISPS) Code. Accordingly, **IRS** inspects all ports and sends its reports to the Ministry of Shipping on a regular basis for taking necessary action. Transport security is periodically reviewed in accordance with the prescribed procedures.

As the provisions of the Passport (Entry into India) Act, 1920 and the rules framed under it, every person, (except for nationals of Bhutan and Nepal), are required to be in possession of valid travel documents for entry into India. In case of a foreigner, a valid visa issued by a competent authority is required for entry into India. Entry into India is allowed only from specified entry points (immigration check-posts). Any person found entering into India without travel documents is arrested and handed over to the local police for taking further necessary action. Persons arrested for entering into India without travel documents or from unspecified points are liable to be awarded imprisonment up to a period of five years or with fine or with both. Persons who repeat the violation are liable to be awarded double the penalty prescribed for such violation. The stay and movement of foreigners inside the country is also governed by other Acts viz. Foreigners Act, Registration of Foreigner Act etc. and rules made there under.

Every foreigner who enters India with validity of their visa exceeding more than 180 days is required to register himself/herself with the concerned Foreigners' Registration Office within 14 days of his/her arrival in India.

1.21 In the context of the implementation of sub-paragraphs 2(b) and (j), has India implemented the standards and recommendations of the International Civil Aviation Organization (Annex 17)? Please inform the CTC as to whether ICAO has conducted a safety audit of India's international airports.

All standards of Annexure-17 to the Chicago Convention on International Civil Aviation are implemented at all civilian airports in India through clearly laid out rules and regulations, standard practices and procedures. Matters pertaining to safety and security of airports in India are within the purview of the Directorate General of Civil Aviation (**DGCA**). The Bureau of Civil Aviation Security (BCAS), an attached office of the Ministry of Civil Aviation headquartered in New Delhi, is responsible for laying down the standards of pre-embarkation security and anti-sabotage measures in respect of civil flights in India. Actual enforcement on the ground is entrusted to the respective local Police. The Bureau is headed by an Officer of the rank of Director General of Police designated as Commissioner of Security, Civil Aviation (COSCA). It has 4 (Four) Regional Offices in Delhi, Calcutta, Mumbai and Chennai. Officers of the Bureau visit airports from time to time to monitor the enforcement.

The International Civil Aviation Organization (**ICAO**) has not yet conducted safety audit of India's international airports. However, aerodrome license audit inspection of Kolkata and Chennai airports have been carried out by DGCA officials under the auspices of European Association of Aerospace Industries (EU/AECMA)—India Civil Aviation Project. Further, safety audits of Delhi and Mumbai airports have been carried out in association with the Cooperative Development of Operational Safety and Continued Airworthiness Project (COSCAP) experts and action is in progress in respect of airports at Ahmedabad and Hyderabad. **ICAO** audit is likely to follow sometime in August/September 2004.

Effectiveness of Controls Preventing Access to Weapons by Terrorists

1.22 Effective implementation of sub-paragraph 2 (a) of the Resolution requires each Member State, inter alia, to have in place an appropriate mechanism to deny access to weapons to terrorists. With regard to this requirement of the Resolution as well as to the provisions of the Convention on the Marking of Plastic Explosives for the purpose of Detection and the International Convention for the Suppression of Terrorist Bombings please provide the CTC with information relevant to the following questions:

— What national laws, regulations and administrative procedures exist to exercise effective control over firearms, ammunitions, explosives in following areas:

- **production;**
- **acquisition;**
- **transit;**
- **retransfer?**

— What national measures exist to prevent the manufacture, stockpiling, transfer and possession of unmarked or inadequately marked:

- **Small and light weapons;**
- **Other firearms, their part and components and ammunition;**
- **Plastic explosives;**
- **Other explosives and their precursors**

— Please specify procedures of export control and existing mechanism of exchange of information of sources, routs and methods of traders in arms.

— Has India's Custom Service implemented intelligence-based risk management on borders to identify high-risk goods? Please outline data elements required by Customs Administrations to identify high risk consignment prior to shipment.

— Has India implemented, using risk assessment principles, any special security measures on the import, export and transit movement of firearms, such as conducting security checks on the temporary storage, warehouses and means of transport carrying firearms, and requiring persons involved in these operations to undergo security vetting? If yes, please give details.

India has comprehensive legislation to exercise effective control over firearms, ammunitions, explosives etc, in the form of the Arms Act, 1959 and rules made there under.

The Government of India took a policy decision regarding manufacturing activity in this area wherein it was decided that only those manufacturers would be allowed to continue their work whose units existed before independence of the country in 1947.

As per the existing provisions of the Arms Act, 1959, no person can acquire, possess, or carry firearms or ammunition without holding a licence issued under the Act. Also with a view to put stringent control over transfer/re-transfer of the firearms/ammunition, the Act provides that no person shall provide, obliterate, remove, alter, forge any name, number or any other identification mark or stamp or otherwise, shown on the firearms. No one is permitted to sell/transfer any firearm which does not bear the name of the maker, manufacturer's number or other identification mark or stamp, in the approved manner. Every firearms dealer has to maintain registers in the prescribed manner, indicating receipt, disposal, and balance of stock in hand and daily sales of arms/ammunition of different categories etc.

The Arms Act, 1959 along with the Arms Rules 1962 & The Arms Amendment Rules 1998 contains provisions to deal with illegal production, acquisition, transit, transfer, re-transfer etc. of arms of all kinds. Sections 3 to 12 & Section 25 to 33 are relevant in this context.

The manufacture, possession, sale import, transport etc. of explosives is controlled and regulated as per the provisions of Explosives Rules, 1983 framed under the Explosives Act, 1884. As per the provisions of Explosives Rules, 1983, no person can manufacture, possess, sell, transport, import, or export explosives without having proper licence/approval from the Department of Explosives. The Department of Explosives is the statutory authority under the Explosives Act to issue licence for manufacture, possession, and sale etc. of explosives after due clearances from security agencies and local authorities as per the procedures laid down in the statute.

As per the Arms Act, 1959, no person can deposit any arms/ammunition in any warehouse without the approval of the Government. Where any arms or ammunition is found in any premises or vehicle or other place, the concerned person is liable to be punished for that offence as per the provisions of the Arms Act, 1959. Further, adequate powers have been delegated to officials for the purpose of ascertaining whether any contravention of the Act or the Rules made there under are being committed. In these circumstances, the competent authority is authorized to stop and inspect any vessel or vehicle or other means of conveyance and seize them.

The Directorate General of Customs and Central Excise is committed to install a Risk Management Module based on all identifiable risk parameters, including intelligence, in respect of imported cargo, at 23 Indian Customs Electronic Data Interchange System (ICES) locations by June, 2004. A similar Risk Management Module for export goods has been developed and will be commissioned at all 23 ICES locations in the current year. The risk parameters in the Risk Management System have the provision to flash alert and generate specific direction regarding suspect goods, importers or exporters, and also cover security parameters. The risk management system is also designed to target invoice manipulation apart from other relevant factors.

India's domestic policy on Small Arms and Light Weapons is statutorily regulated under The Arms Act, 1959 and The Arms Rules, 1962, as amended from time to time, which cover all aspects of lawful possession, manufacture, sale, transfer, transport, export, import of arms and ammunition and provide penal provisions for their violation. In addition to The Arms Act, 1959 and The Arms Rules, 1962, the Government of India has enacted other laws providing for penal provisions related to illegal possession, manufacture, etc. of small arms and light weapons which include Prevention of Terrorism Act (2002), Armed Forces (special powers) Act, Indian Penal Code, The Army Act and analogous laws.

All small arms manufactured in India have to be invariably proof-tested and bear identification mark stamping before their sale, as per the statutory provisions under the Arms Act, 1959. The Arms Act, 1959 provides that arms which do not bear specified identification marks may not be sold or transferred. Further, any person found in possession of a weapon without identification marks would be presumed to have removed/obliterated the marks unless proven otherwise and is liable to prosecution under the Arms Act, 1959.

The Central and State Police forces take action according to the provisions of the Arms Act, 1959 and the Arms Rules, 1962, and inter alia conduct routine checks to detect the cases of possession/manufacture/sale of small arms and light weapons. In case of any incident involving illicit arms, necessary action is taken by the concerned authorities under the provisions of the Arms Act and rules thereunder.

The Indian Customs Electronic Data Interchange System (ICES) has a self-contained mechanism to enforce existing regulatory instructions. In the event of import of such items by mis-declaration, the risk management system has been developed to alert Customs authorities against all such suspect consignments enabling detection, even if no prior intelligence is available with Custom authorities.

1.23 With regard to the effective implementation of sub-paragraph 2 (a), could India outline its mechanism and procedures as regards the implementation of the legal provisions or controls imposed on the export of goods; the transfer of technologies; the provision of technical assistance overseas; activities connected with the trade in controlled goods; with particular regard to denying terrorists access to weapons or hazardous materials. The CTC would appreciate it if India could provide it with statistics on the use of legal provisions to prevent terrorists from gaining access to weapons.

Through appropriate legislative, procedural and administrative measures, India has instituted an effective and comprehensive system to regulate strategic exports from India to ensure that these do not fall into wrong hands—whether state or non-state actors. Laws such as The Explosive Substances Act, 1908; The Narcotic Drugs and Psychotropic Substances Act, 1985; The Environment Protection Act, 1986; The Atomic Energy Act, 1962; The Foreign Trade (Development and Regulation) Act, 1992; The Customs Act, 1962 form the legal basis of India's system of export controls. Various agencies of the Government are empowered to enforce the provisions of these laws.

With the objective of exercising control over the export of goods and technology of direct and indirect application to Weapons of Mass Destruction and the means of their delivery, the Government of India has specified a list of dual-use Special Chemicals, Organisms, Materials, Equipment and Technologies (SCOMET), the export of which is either prohibited or permitted only under license and the conditions included therein. This list is notified in Appendix 3 to Schedule II of the ITC (HS) Classifications of Export and Import Items, 2002–2007.

All munitions are manufactured or traded in by entities that are wholly owned, controlled by or are on contract to the Government of India. Legal and administrative measures are in place for regulating exports of military stores which are permitted only under written permission of the relevant agencies of the Government unless specified otherwise in the Government's Export Import Policy. This permission inter alia rests upon end-use and end-user certification on a government to government basis and is in conformity with the Government of India's foreign policy objectives, which includes a ban on exports to countries under UN embargo.

1.24 The CTC is aware that India may have covered some or all of the points in the preceding paragraphs in reports or questionnaires submitted to other organizations involved in monitoring international standards. The CTC would be content to receive a copy of any such report or questionnaire as part of India's response to these matters as well as details of any efforts to implement international best practices, codes and standards which are relevant to the implementation of resolution 1373.

DOCUMENT NO. 26

INDIA'S 2007 COUNTER-TERRORISM REPORT TO THE UN

UN Security Council Resolution
S/2007/196

April 11, 2007

Distr.: General
11 April 2007

Original: English

Letter dated 10 April 2007 from the Chairman of the Security Council Committee established pursuant to resolution 1373 (2001) concerning counter-terrorism addressed to the President of the Security Council

The Counter-Terrorism Committee has received the attached report from India submitted pursuant to paragraph 6 of resolution 1373 (2001), as well as the response of India to resolution 1624 (2005) (see annex).

I would be grateful if you could arrange for the present letter and its annex to be circulated as a document of the Security Council.

(*Signed*) Ricardo Alberto **Arias**
Chairman
Security Council Committee established pursuant
to resolution 1373 (2001) concerning counter-terrorism

Annex

Letter dated 20 March 2007 from the Permanent Representative of India to the United Nations addressed to the Chairman of the Counter-Terrorism Committee

In pursuance of the obligation of all Member States emanating from Security Council resolution 1624 (2005) to implement and report additional measures to combat terrorism, I have the honour to forward the fifth report of India in this regard (see enclosure). The report may also be read in continuation of the fourth report of India (S/2004/451) forwarded under cover of our letter of 28 May 2004, as mandated by resolution 1373 (2001).

(*Signed*) Nirupam **Sen**

Enclosure*
Fifth Report of the Government of India to the Counter-Terrorism Committee

Introduction

India has always strongly condemned terrorism in all its forms and manifestations. We believe that there can be no justification whatsoever for any act of terrorism. The fight against terrorism has to be long term, sustained and comprehensive. As the threat of terrorism transcends national boundaries, it needs to be countered cooperatively by member states.

As a country which has unfortunately been at the receiving end of terrorism, India has both a strong national resolve as well as a well developed and specialized apparatus to fight this scourge. India has played a proactive and constructive role in further strengthening counter-terrorism cooperation at various levels—bilateral, regional and international. India had presented a draft Comprehensive Convention on International Terrorism at the United Nations as far back as in 1996 and continues its engagement with other member states for an expeditious adoption of this Convention. India also made a positive contribution to the discussions leading to the adoption of a Global Counter-Terrorism Strategy by the UN General Assembly in September, 2006.

Government of India attaches utmost importance to the fulfillment of its obligations under the relevant counter-terrorism resolutions of the United Nations. India has been a firm and consistent supporter of the UN Security Council Resolution 1373 and the work of the Counter-Terrorism Committee(CTC). Since 2001, Government of India has submitted four National Reports to the CTC, which have attempted to give a comprehensive picture of steps taken by India to counter terrorism.

* Annexes are on file with the Secretariat and are available for consultation.

As in earlier reports, the compilation of Government of India's responses to the specific issues/questions raised by the CTC, in its 5th report, is based on extensive inter-ministerial and inter-agency consultations. A unique dimension to India's 5th report is the fact that it is being filed after the visit of a 14-member composite delegation of UN counter-terrorism experts, led by the Executive Director of the Counter-Terrorism Executive Directorate (CTED) and including representatives of CTED, Monitoring Team of UNSC's 1267 Committee, INTERPOL, UNODC and WCO, in November, 2006.

Besides having a first hand assessment of Government of India's fulfillment of its obligations under UNSC resolutions on counter-terrorism, especially 1373(2001) and 1267(1999), the visiting delegation got a detailed picture of the legal and policy framework as well as the elaborate and specialized machinery for counter-terrorism in India. The visit was also utilized by both sides for an extensive and mutually fruitful exchange of views on a wide range of issues related to counter-terrorism. The indepth discussions during the visit included practically all specific issues on which Government of India has given its responses in its 5th report to the CTC.

Specific Issues/Questions Raised by CTC and GoI's Responses

Implementation Measures

1. Protection of the Economic and Financial System

1.1 In its 4th report, India states that its Financial Intelligence Unit (FIU) is in the process of being set up. The Committee would appreciate an update on this process. If the FIU has been established, is it independent, autonomous, adequately structured, funded, staffed and provided with sufficient technical and other resources to fully perform its authorized functions?

Response:

The Financial Intelligence Unit-India (FIU-IND) has been set up as the central national agency under the Department of Revenue, Ministry of Finance, Government of India, w.e.f. 18.11.2005, with a view to coordinate and strengthen collection and sharing of financial intelligence through an effective national, regional and global network to combat money laundering and related crimes. The FIU-IND is an independent body reporting directly to Economic Intelligence Council (EIC) headed by the Finance Minister.

FIU-IND is headed by Director FIU-IND, an officer of the rank of Joint Secretary to the Government of India and is assisted by a highly trained technical group of financial experts, analysts and IT specialists. FIU-IND enjoys functional independence, autonomy and the necessary budgetary support to fully perform its authorized functions.

1.2 The Committee notes that wire transfer services must register with the Reserve Bank of India. How many currency remittance/wire transfer services are registered and/or licensed in your country? What are the penalties for failure to register or to obtain a license?

Response:

As per the Money Service Transfer scheme of the Government, all the wire transfer service agencies are to be registered with the Reserve Bank of India.

A list of agency arrangements entered into by banks and financial institutions with overseas principals to undertake Inward Money Transfer Service is enclosed **(Annexure I).** RBI has granted permission to 10 overseas entities for tie-ups with 27 Indian Agencies under the Money Transfer Service Scheme (MTSS). Permission for MTSS is granted under Section 3 (c) of the Foreign Exchange Management Act 1999. Failure to register is liable to penalties applicable for violation of the provisions of the Act, which are covered in Chapter IV thereof.

1.3 How many formal and informal currency and asset remittance services do you believe exist, in addition to those that have registered or obtained licences? What measures are you taking to close down such operations?

Response:

The so called informal services relate to illegal transfer of money through unofficial channels, commonly known as "hawala" transactions. Due to the very nature of such transactions which are all clandestine, it is not possible to indicate any number. The number of cases registered against them, however, can give an indication of the scale of their operations. In 2004, 224 such cases were registered by issuance of show cause notices by the concerned authorities, involving a sum of US$ 725 million.

These operations are illegal and are covered under Section 3 of Foreign Exchange Management Act(FEMA), 1999. The Directorate of Enforcement, which is the nodal agency to deal with these cases, has made some fresh proposals to Ministry of Finance for further strengthening the legal framework to deal with such cases.

1.4 The Committee is aware that draft rules under the PMLA are in the process of being finalised. It would be pleased to receive a progress report and, if possible, a copy of draft rules.

Response:

The rules under the Prevention of Money Laundering Act have since been notified with effect from 1 July 2005. These rules are available at the website: http//finmin.nic.in/law/moneylaunderingrule.pdf. A copy of these rules is enclosed **(Annexure II).**

1.5 The Committee takes note of the fact that India has recently issued an enabling notification to facilitate implementation of Security Council Resolutions under its United Nations Security Act which is expected to further strengthen action against non-profit organizations operating under false pretences and thereby to help prevent the financing of terrorism. The Committee would appreciate further information on that and an explanation of how it will function.

Response:

The United Nations (Security Council) Act, 1947 (43 of 1947) was enacted to enable the Central Government to implement the Security Council Resolutions adopted under Chapter VII of the Charter of the United Nations. Section 2 of the Act authorises the Central Government to adopt such measures as it may consider necessary to implement such resolutions. In order to implement the Security Council Resolution 1373 and other relevant resolutions adopted by the Security Council under Chapter VII of the Charter to combat international terrorism, the Central Government issued an Order entitled the "prevention and Suppression of terrorism (Implementation of Security Council Resolutions) Order 2004". This Order was further strengthened and was published in the Official Gazette on 23 March, 2006. A copy of the 2006 Order is enclosed at **Annexure III**. In pursuance of this order, the concerned agencies are notified to take necessary action against the listed entities and individuals as per the relevant domestic laws.

Non Governmental Organisations (NGOs) in India can be registered under the Societies Registration Act, Indian Trusts Act or the Charitable and Religious Endowments Act. Acceptance and utilization of foreign contributions by these organisations is governed by the Foreign Contribution (Regulation) Act, 1976. Associations working in cultural, economic, educational, religious or social fields can accept foreign contribution only after obtaining registration or prior permission under the Act. The Act contains, *inter alia*, provisions for monitoring the utilization of foreign contribution received by an association, inspection of its accounts and penal provisions for violation of the Act. The Foreign Contribution (Regulation) Rules, 1976 prescribe the documentation such as the application forms, annual returns and the manner of maintenance of accounts etc.

Monitoring of Utilization of Foreign Contribution Received by an Association

Donations received by charitable organizations can be spent only for the stated purpose for which the donation was made or for any general purpose falling under the scope of the activities carried out by the organization. Every association registered under the Act or, granted prior permission to receive foreign contribution, is required to file an annual return, duly certified by a chartered accountant, with the Ministry of Home Affairs, intimating the receipt of foreign contribution during the year and the manner of its utilization. A "nil" return is also mandatory. This return forms the basis of the Annual Report on the Receipt of Foreign contribution by Voluntary Associations prepared by the Ministry of Home Affairs. This report is shared with state governments and intelligence agencies. In case of any violation or on receipt of a complaint against the association, the Central Government can order

(i) inspection of the accounts/records of an association; or

(ii) audit of its books and accounts.

Based on the inspection report, penal action, if required, is taken against the association as per the penal provisions of the Act. These include:

Penal Provisions

The Act contains a number of provisions under which the Central Government can initiate action against an association, receiving foreign contribution, that is found indulging in activities that are likely to affect prejudicially,

i) the sovereignty and the integrity of India;

ii) public interest;

iii) freedom or fairness of election by Legislature;

iv) friendly relations with any foreign state; or

v) harmony between religious, racial, linguistic or regional groups, castes or communities.

The penal provisions include:

i) prohibiting the association from accepting foreign contribution

ii) placing the association in the prior permission category for accepting foreign contribution

iii) seizure and confiscation of any article or currency that is believed to have been acquired by the association in contravention of the provisions of the Act

iv) sanction of prosecution of an association for contravening the provisions of the Act

v) Imposition of a sentence of imprisonment with terms ranging from one year to five years, or with fine or with both.

The Income Tax Act prohibits the expenditure of funds by NGOs any where except for the stated purposes or may be invested in schedule banks, public deposits and bonds and government securities. The management of the organisation and as well as the auditors of such organisations are required to certify the nature of the grant or donations. The auditors are also required to certify that donations/grants are spent for the purpose for which they were received. The Income tax department after a thorough scrutiny of the accounts and balance sheet of the organisation, issues the income tax exemption certificate, which is required to be obtained by the organisation concerned every year.

Effectiveness of CT Measures

1.6 Without compromising sensitive information, or ongoing investigations, the Committee would welcome information on India's use of the following:

- ***Investigation Techniques;***
- ***Tracking the funds of Criminal Groups; and***
- ***Intercepting Communications.***

Response:

Agencies concerned with interdiction and investigation utilize all sources including HUMINT, TECHINT, OSINT etc. laid down in the existing laws and procedures within the framework of the rule of law. Further details are confidential in nature and cannot be shared.

Customs Controls

1.7 How does India implement the common standards for electronic reporting and for the promotion of supply chain security, established by the World Customs organizations (WCO) and the international standards established in the revised international convention on the simplification and harmonization of customs procedures (Kyoto Convention)?

Inputs:

Electronic information forwarded by the Trade and Transport Departments is in line with the standards specified by the World Customs Organisation (WCO). Indian customs data elements have been mapped with reference to the WCO model. Data requirements are based on international specifications like International Civil Aviation Organisation, IMO-FAL etc. India has signed the International Convention on Mutual Administrative Assistance in Customs Matters (Johannesburg Convention), a WCO convention aimed at enhancing cooperation among Customs Administration of various countries to ensure supply chain security. As regards the implementation of the Standards of the revised International Convention on the Simplification and Harmonization of Customs Procedures (the Kyoto Convention), India is a contracting party t the Convention and has accepted the General Annex and has in place legislation and procedures to cover these Standards.

1.8 Does India utilize advance Passenger Manifest Programme to verify the names of inbound passengers on international flights against CT databases before landing?

Response:

India is in the process of implementing the Advance Passengers Information System (APIS). Under this system, airlines are required to provide information about the passengers on board to the Immigration Authorities in India. This information is to be furnished in prescribed format by electronic means within fifteen minutes of taking off of the aircraft from the destination. The APIS was implemented from July 1, 2006 on a pilot basis at the Indira Gandhi International (IGI) Airport, Delhi with data from Air India. Modalities are being worked out to implement it for all airlines from IGI Airport, Delhi. Subsequently, it will be extended to 22 major Immigration Check Points.

APIS is expected to enhance passenger profiling and utilise the resources in a focused manner on suspected passengers instead of concentrating on all passengers.

1.9 Does India have any immigration database systems or an integrated electronic Customs network?

Response:

India has an Immigration data base system. Further details cannot be shared as the information is sensitive in nature. A Customs network consisting of high speed leased lines connecting 34 Customs locations has been set up. There is also a plan for creating a countrywide connectivity linking all Customs, Central Excise and Service tax locations.

1.10 Is India's system for the granting of Motor vehicle, business and other licenses integrated into its terrorism watch system?

Response:

Under the existing system for grant of a motor vehicle license, applicants are required to furnish only a proof of residence. The GoI is contemplating an amendment to the Central Motor Vehicles Rules, 1989 which will enable it to seek details pertaining to nationality, along with a proof of legal presence in the country in respect of foreigners while granting a motor vehicle license.

The Companies Act, 1956, governs the incorporation of both limited and private companies. The Registrar of Companies has 20 offices in different parts of the country. For incorporation of companies, information that needs to be furnished includes name, Memorandum of Association, Articles of Association, List of Promoters and Proof of Identity of Promoters. Each Registrar of Companies allots CIN Number (Certificate of Incorporation Number) to a company incorporated in his jurisdiction. The Registrar of Companies conducts verification on the basis of the information furnished.

GoI is in the process of rendering the entire process simpler and more secure with online incorporation of Companies. The applicant would be required to file necessary information on-line to the Registrar of Companies which will also issue the Certificate of Incorporation Number (CIN). The CIN in this case, however, would be allotted by the system only. The system will also allocate a Director Identification Number (DIN), a number unique to an individual even if he/she is a director in more than one company.

1.11 The Committee is aware that India is developing a perspective plan for integrated infrastructure development of border areas and an action plan to strengthen coastal security. The Committee would welcome an update on the development of these plans.

Response:

An Inter-Ministerial Task Force has been set up by the Government of India to further streamline the Border Area Development Programme (BADP). The Task Force has been entrusted with the responsibility of assessing/analyzing the design, planning and implementation of the BADP. It has held extensive discussions with the State and District authorities on issues related to border areas.

A plan to strengthen the security of the coastal areas by strengthening the infrastructure for patrolling and surveillance of the coastline has been formulated for implementation over a period of five years. The plan aims at enhancing the capabilities of the State Governments to police the coast including the coastal waters. It envisages setting up coastal police stations, outposts and check-posts in the coastal areas. The coastal police stations will be equipped with vehicles, vessels and equipment for mobility on coast and in waters close to the coast. The coastal police stations will have a marine police component with personnel trained by the Coast Guard in maritime functioning.

1.12 The Committee notes that India is committed to installing a risk management module based on all identifiable risk parameters at 23 of the Indian Customs Electronic Data Interchange System (ICES) locations by June 2004 and would appreciate a progress report.

Response:

A Risk Management System was initially implemented in two major customs locations and its expansion to other major Customs centers has been taking place with a view to cover all major locations. As on September 22, 2006, Risk Management Systems (RMS) in Imports has been implemented at all ports/air cargo complexes/ICDs in Mumbai, Chennai, Delhi, Bangalore and Kolkata. The RMS now covers 13 major Customs locations. 10 more locations are proposed to be covered by the RMS by March 2007.

Immigration Control

1.13 Does India maintain computerized immigration records and, if so, do they include data on asylum seekers? What measures have been taken to prevent such data from being shared accidentally with asylum seekers' countries of origin?

Response:

India maintains computerized Immigration records, viz entry and exit of foreigners is recorded and stored in computerized form. India does not have a refugee law and is not a signatory to 1951 Geneva Convention and 1967 Protocol. Thus, there is no system of seeking or granting asylum to anybody in India following a legal procedure and therefore, the question of maintaining data on 'asylum seekers' does not arise. Data of a large number of registered Afghans, Tibetans, Myanmarese, Sudanis, Sri Lankans, Vietnamese and Stateless Refugees, etc., who are staying in India as refugees with Government permission is maintained separately. Several of these refugees carry on their efforts for settlement/asylum in a third country through UNHCR.

1.14 Are the locations of asylum seekers in India monitored? If so, is the compilation of information conducted at a local or national level? Is the information shared with the office of UNHCR pursuant to the GA resolution 428 (V)?

Response:

As regards monitoring the locations and activities of asylum seekers in India, the activities of foreigners referred to in the previous para are monitored as per requirement. However, such information is not shared with UNHCR.

1.15 India has indicated that it has made every effort to ensure that suspected terrorists do not misuse the authorization of temporary stay on humanitarian grounds as a means to seek refuge in India. The Committee would be grateful to receive details of the measures taken in that regard.

Response:

As far as immigration is concerned, India maintains a negative list of the suspected terrorists on the basis of inputs received from various agencies including the Interpol. The purpose is to prevent entry into/exit from the country and to monitor their movements.

1.16 India is in the process of issuing new identity documents. The Committee would be grateful to know what your country has done to improve the quality of its identification, travel and similar document in order to meet minimum international security standards aimed at making them impossible to duplicate, falsify or obtain fraudulently.

Response:

India is a member of the Technical Advisory Group on Machine Readable Travel Documents (TAG-MRTD) of the International Civil Aviation Organisation (ICAO). India participated in the last meeting of TAG-MRTD of ICAO held at Montreal on 26–30 September 2005. Presently all travel documents are machine-readable and the security and data features conform to ICAO standards. All Passport Authorities in India started issuing Machine-readable Passports (MRPs) since 2001. The issuance of MRPs from Indian Missions abroad has already commenced and is likely to be achieved by March 2007. The photograph and signature of the applicant are scanned and printed on the passport booklet. The personal particulars and the Machine Readable Zone (MRZ) are also computer-printed which makes substitution of photograph and signature and tampering with the data extremely difficult; thereby considerably reducing instances of forgery and impersonation. Several security features have been incorporated in the travel documents:-(i) the Indian emblem has been incorporated on the cover material of the passport booklets in the form of Ultra Violet feature; (ii) the ink used on the visa pages is bi-fluorescent which glows in red colour under U.V. shortwave and blue colour under U.V. longwave; and, (iii) the thread used in passport booklets also has U.V. features.

1.17 Does India permit legal name changes without residency? If so, some form of positive identification such as fingerprinting or photographing, used to verify the applicant's identity prior to the name change?

Response:

While applying for issue of any identification papers, a residency proof is required. The applicant has to provide his/her photograph and necessary documents for obtaining his/her identification papers. However, no fingerprinting system is maintained for verification of identity prior to name change.

1.18 Does India have technology and trained personnel at border locations to examine and detect forged, falsified or stolen documents? If not, is there a plan to provide this capability?

Response:

India initiated a Comprehensive Modernisation Programme of Immigration Check Posts (ICPs) in 2004–5. The programme is likely to be completed shortly.

Major components of this programme, including the status as of December 2006 are given below:

(i) **Upgradation of Computer Systems:** Computer systems upgraded at 19 Immigration Check Posts (ICPs). Action under progress at 12 ICPs.

(ii) **Installation of New Immigration Control System (ICS) software:** ICS software installed at 16 ICPs. Action under progress at 14 ICPs.

(iii) **Installation of Passport Reading Machines (PRMs):** PRMs installed at 15 ICPs. Action under progress at 11 ICPs.

(iv) Upgradation and networking of Central Foreigners Bureau (CFB) of Bureau of Immigration (BoI) with major ICPs is underway.

(v) A **Questionable Document Examiner (QDX)** machine to detect fraudulent/forged travel documents has been installed at Mumbai International airport. Action under progress at 28 ICPs.

The immigration personnel are imparted suitable induction training by the Bureau of Immigration. Long term refresher and sensitization courses are also held on various aspects of immigration including detection of forged, falsified and stolen documents.

2. Implementation of Resolution 1624 (2005)

Paragraph 1

2.1 What measures does India have in place to prohibit by law and to prevent incitement to commit a terrorist act or acts? What further steps, if any, are under consideration?

Response:

The Indian Parliament amended the Unlawful Activates (Prevention) Act, 1967 in 2004 (UAPA), by incorporating provisions to deal with all facets of terrorism including incitement to commit a terrorist act. Section 18 of the UAPA provides for imprisonment for a term not less than 5 years but which may extend to imprisonment for life and also liable to fine against any person who conspires or attempt to commit or advocates, abets, advises or incites or knowingly facilitates the commission of a terrorist act, or any act preparatory to the commission of a terrorist act. Further, the act also criminalizes raising of funds, holding proceeds of terrorism, harbouring of a terrorist etc. and provides for enhanced penalties to any person who, with the intent to aid any terrorist, attempts to contravene or abets or does any act preparatory to contravention of any provision of the Explosives Act, 1884 or the Explosive Substances Act, 1905 or the Inflammable Substances Act, 1952 or the Arms Act, or is in unauthorized possession of any bomb, dynamite or hazardous explosive substance or other lethal weapon or substance capable of mass destruction or biological or chemical substance of warfare.

2.2 *What measures does India have to deny safe haven to any person with respect to whom there is credible and relevant information giving serious reasons for considering that they have been guilty of incitement to commit a terrorist act or acts?*

Response:

India is a member of the Interpol. It has put in place extradition mechanisms with several countries and is signatory to all UN Conventions on anti-terrorism. India has entered into Mutual Legal Assistance Treaties (MLATs) in criminal matters to facilitate mutual assistance in investigation, prosecution, prevention of crime, serving summons and other judicial documents, execution of warrants and other judicial commissions and tracing, restraint, forfeiture or confiscation of proceeds and instruments of crime.

India has also established Joint Working Groups (JWGs) with a number of countries on counter-terrorism and agreements on co-operation in combating illicit trafficking or abuse of narcotic drugs and psychotropic drugs and substances.

As mentioned above, UAPA is a comprehensive law to deal with all facets of terrorism. Section 19 of UAPA provides punishment with imprisonment for a term which shall not be less than three years but which may extend to imprisonment for life and also liable to fine if any person voluntarily harbours or conceals or attempts to harbour or conceal any person knowing that such person is terrorist. Further, this provision also applies in relation to a terrorist who has committed an act of terror in a foreign country in view of the fact that the definition of an act of terror in Section 15 of the UAPA is country central. Hence, India has an adequate legal framework to deny safe heaven to terrorists.

Paragraph 2

2.3 *How does India cooperate with other States in strengthening the security of its international borders with a view to preventing those guilty of incitement to commit a terrorist act or acts from entering their territory, including by combating fraudulent travel documents and, to the extent attainable, by enhancing terrorist screening and passenger security procedures?*

Response:

India has entered into several bilateral and multilateral mechanisms to cooperate with other States in curbing the scourge of terrorism. These include:

a) Joint Working Group on Counter Terrorism with BIMSTEC (includes Bangladesh, Bhutan, Myanmar, Nepal and Sri Lanka);

b) MoU with China;

c) Joint Working Group on Border issues with Bangladesh;

d) Indo-Bhutan Group on Border Management and Security issues; and

e) Bilateral Agreement with Myanmar for maintenance of peace and tranquility in border areas.

Paragraph 3

2.4 What International efforts is India participating or considering participating in/initiating in order to enhance dialogue and broaden understanding among civilizations in an effort to prevent the indiscriminate targeting of different religious and cultures?

Response:

India is a nation inhabited by diverse cultural, religious and linguistic groups and has a long history of peaceful and harmonious existence in a multi-ethnic, multi-religious, multi-lingual and multi-cultural milieu. This has been possible only through a long heritage of dialogue and assimilation among people and myriad influences through the centuries. India believes that the process of encouraging the dialogue should also involve formulation of common approaches towards targeting eradication of poverty, working towards environmental sustainability, fostering national and international co-operation to reduce economic and social inequalities. The Government of India through its National Common Minimum Programme addresses issues such as elimination of disparities in access, empowerment of women and securing a rightful place for the disadvantaged and the minorities. Several measures have been taken to boost the confidence of these sections and special efforts in a spirit of positive discrimination are being made to bring up the socio-economic and educational levels of these categories.

An International Conference on "**Dialogue Among Civilization—Quest for New Perspectives**" was held in New Delhi on 9–10 July 2003. It was attended by representatives from more than 80 countries.

Ms. Shobana Bhartia, Hon'ble Member of Parliament and Managing Director of the Hindustan Times, is member of the High-level Group of eminent persons established under the "Alliance of Civilizations" initiative (launched in July 2005) of the UN Secretary General.

The activities of Indian Council for Cultural Relations (ICCR) in the field of cultural exchange by the way of performing/non-performing art/exchange of distinguished personalities, exhibitions, seminars/symposia, provision of scholarship to foreign students, running of Cultural Centres abroad, publication etc. contribute to India's efforts to enhance dialogue and broaden understanding amongst civilizations. This is obviously a short illustrative list. The impeccable credentials of a country like India with a well known pluralistic ethos hardly needs to be overemphasised.

2.5 What steps is India taking to counter incitement of terrorist acts motivated by extremism and intolerance and to prevent subversion of educational, cultural and religious institutions by terrorists and their supporters?

Response:

Since time immemorial, India has preserved a rich tradition of peaceful coexistence firmly established in tolerance and abhorrence of any kind of extremism and violence. Our founding fathers left no stone unturned to get these age old principles enshrined in our Constitution. Subsequently, adequate provisions were incorporated in the Constitution of India for protection of the rights and well being of the minorities and their institutions in the country. Apart from the right to equality before law, Articles 25 to 30 (Part III on Fundamental Rights) explicitly spell out various rights for its citizens including Minorities as enshrined in the Constitution and Part VI A on Fundamental Duties enjoin upon all its citizens to religiously adhere in letter and spirit to the provisions of the Constitution.

In order to effectively implement the various Constitutional and Legal provisions, the Government has put in place an institutional mechanism which encompasses an independent judiciary, a free media, separate independent bodies like the National Commission for Minorities and the National Human Rights Commission apart from Ministries at the Central level, like the Ministry of Home Affairs and the Ministry of Social Justice and Empowerment and likewise at the State level. Some of the other steps undertaken include upgradation and modernization of police infrastructure and training and also of intelligence gathering techniques, closely monitoring the activities of fundamentalist organizations and their leaders, setting up of peace and integration committees with fair representation of women, and evolving norms for harmonious celebration of festivals of different communities.

In addition to the above, the Government extends financial grants to voluntary organizations to promote national integration and communal harmony through their programmes and confers Communal Harmony Awards through National Foundation of Communal Harmony. The Ministry of Home Affairs has also instituted another award, known as "Kabir Puraskar", to honour those citizens who display exemplary acts of physical and moral courage in saving the lives and properties of members of another community during communal riots. "Quami Ekta week" is also observed every year during the month of November.

Paragraph 4

2.6 What is India doing to ensure that any measures taken to implement paragraph 1, 2 and 3 of resolution 1624 (2005) comply with all of its obligations under international law, in particular international human rights law, refugee law and humanitarian law?

Response:

The Indian legal system provides for sufficient checks and balances to ensure that measures taken to implement the steps laid down in the UN Security Council Resolution 1624 are in accordance with the relevant laws in force, the principles of natural justice and the process of law, principle of non-refoulement, presumption of innocence until proven guilty and other principles of international human rights law and international humanitarian law.

3. Assistance and Guidance

3.1 The Committee wishes to emphasize once more the importance that it attaches to the provision of assistance and advice in connection with the implementation of the resolutions. The Committee's Directory of Assistance (www.un.org/sc/ctc) is frequently updated to include new relevant information on available assistance.

3.2 The Committee notes with appreciation India's meeting with CTED, held on 1 November 2005 at India's initiative, and the detailed presentation on its counter-terrorism strategy that India made to the Committee on 2 November 2005. In particular, the Committee welcomes India's offer, during the presentation, to provide technical assistance in the field of counter-terrorism. As a follow-up to this offer, the Committee would like to receive information on areas in which India might be in a position to provide assistance to other States in relation to implementation of the resolutions.

Response:

India has an elaborate, professional and experienced counter-terrorism machinery. In the framework of its Joint Working Groups (JWGs) with several countries, India is providing technical assistance in some cases and in general looks at proposals for capacity building positively. During the visit of a composite delegation of counter-terrorism experts at the UN led by Executive Director of CTED in November 2006, Government of India had made detailed presentations on a wide range of issues including the areas in which it can provide technical assistance to other Member States for implementation of the relevant UN Security Council resolutions. For example,

India can offer assistance to other countries under the auspices of CTC in the following areas:

a) Training of immigration personnel in detection of forged, falsified or stolen documents

b) Technical assistance in computerization of immigration systems

c) Assistance in providing training of personnel involved in the implementation and enforcement of Anti Money Laundering and Terrorist Financing law in the following areas:

(i) Establishment of Financial Intelligence Units;

(ii) Analysis of intelligence related to Money Laundering and Terrorist Financing;

(iii) In the development of information and communication technology for building a comprehensive tool for analysis of Financial Information and other data relating to the above; and

(iv) Cooperation in any other mutually identified areas.

3.3 Furthermore, in light of the specific areas related to India's implementation of resolution 1373(2001) outlined in Section 1 of this letter, and based on India's reports to the Committee and on other relevant information available, the Committee, with assistance from the CTED experts, has conducted a preliminary analysis of the India's technical assistance needs in order to identify priority areas in which the Committee believes India may benefit from receiving technical assistance. With the agreement of and in cooperation with the Government of India, the aim is to identify the best possible way for India to benefit from technical assistance in order to strengthen its implementation of the provisions of this resolution.

3.4 The analysis identified, on a preliminary basis, the following potential areas of assistance needs, with the understanding that further assessments may be necessary. The points below represent selected areas, amongst the areas referred to in the resolution, where assistance might be particularly useful:

- *Training in terrorist financing investigation techniques;*
- *Training in money laundering investigation techniques;*
- *Training in border patrol and security investigation techniques;*
- *Regulation of alternative currency transfer systems to ensure that they are not used for terrorist purposes; and*
- *Regulation of charitable and non-profit organizations to ensure that they, and funds provided to them, are not used for terrorist purposes.*

Response:

India has considerable expertise in the above mentioned areas at strategic, tactical and operational levels. While exchange of experience, workshops etc. are essential for keeping abreast of developments, India's requirements are peculiar to its own circumstances. As such, training areas can best be decided bilaterally and through agency-to-agency contacts, rather than through multilateral agencies to ensure focus on specific aspects rather than generic sensitization where our expertise is already of international standards.

India has considerable expertise in the areas of terrorist financing & money laundering and as such does not require training for its officers in the Terrorist Financing Investigation Techniques. India also has bilateral arrangements with 25 countries, which provide inter-alia for capacity building particularly by sharing of experiences and exchange of information to bring the investigation capabilities on a common platform. The Border Guarding Forces such as BSF, ITBP, SSB and Coast Guards have their own captive training institutions and run specific courses for upgrading the capacity of their personnel.

As a further illustration, it may be stated that FIU-IND does not require any technical assistance for training and regulation. It has the inherent capacity to deal with various money laundering related issues including investigation techniques. It has been ensured that officers possessing substantial experience in financial transactions analyses and investigation of financial crimes form part of FIU-IND, who possess the desired capacity to give effect to the provisions of the Act.

In view of the foregoing, Government of India does not consider it necessary that the above list of areas identified by CTED is circulated amongst Member States.

3.5 The Committee would like to receive your country's approval to share the above-mentioned points with providers of technical assistance that may be in a position to provide assistance in these selected areas (other parts of this letter will not be shared). This would enable the Committee to facilitate the provision of technical assistance. The Committee would appreciate receiving your country's response no later than 30 days from the date of this letter. If your country's response is not received within that period, the Committee will assume that the points could be shared with the donor states and organizations. The actual provision of assistance will naturally be subject to the India's request and consent. The Committee would also welcome any comments India may have regarding this section(Section 3 on 'assistance and guidance')

Response:

As already conveyed, Government of India does not consider it necessary to share the above-mentioned points with providers of technical assistance.

4. Further Guidance and Submission of Future Reports

4.1 The Committee wishes to maintain the constructive dialogue it has established with India concerning measures taken in implementation of the resolutions, particularly with regard to the areas identified in this letter as priorities. The Committee and its Executive Director stand ready to provide further clarification on any of the matters raised in this letter. The Executive Director can be contacted through Ms. Elena Rigacci Hay (telephone: +1 212 457 1733; fax: +1 212 457 4041; email: cted@ un.org). The Committee, through its Executive Directorate, may also contact the competent authorities of your country in order to discuss any other matters related to the implementation of the resolutions.

4.2 The Committee would like to receive from India further information on the questions raised and comments made in Section 1 and 2 of this letter by 20 March 2006. It would also be grateful if India would provide an update on assistance received thus far, including whether such assistance has met or is expected to meet its needs in areas related to the resolutions. As with previous reports, it is the Committee's intention to circulate this further report as a document of the Security Council. It is open to India, if it so desires, to submit a confidential annex to the report for the attention of the Committee and its Executive Directorate alone.

4.3 At a future stage of its work, the Committee may have further comments or questions for India arising from other aspects of the resolutions. It would be grateful to be kept informed of any new developments regarding your country's implementation of the resolutions.

Response:

CTC's observations under Section 4 have been overtaken by developments. Government of India accepted the visit of composite delegation of counter-terrorism experts in the UN in November 2006. which was led by the Executive Director of CTED and comprised, besides CTED officials, representatives of the Monitoring Team of UNSC's 1267 Committee, INTERPOL, UNODC and WCO.

The visit provided a very useful opportunity to the UN counter-terrorism experts to obtain indepth information about India's legal and policy framework as well as its well developed machinery for counter-terrorism. Besides making a first hand assessment of Government of India's fulfillment of its obligations under the relevant Security Council resolutions on counter-terrorism, the visit was utilized by both sides to have a comprehensive and mutually beneficial exchange of views on a gamut of issues related to counter-terrorism.

DOCUMENT NO. 27

REPORT OF INDIA'S MISSION TO THE UN ON SMALL ARMS AND LIGHT WEAPONS

June 11, 2007

Introduction

The Government of India believes that combating and eradicating illicit trade in Small Arms and Light Weapons (SALW) in all its aspects is a key element in global, regional and national security. It is also necessary for the social and economic development of many countries. India has supported international co-operation to achieve this goal multilaterally, regionally and bilaterally. The following is a report on Government of India's policy and efforts to implement the UN Programme of Action to Prevent, Combat and Eradicate the Illicit Trade in Small Arms and Light Weapons in All Its Aspects (UN PoA).

National Level

National Point of Contact and Coordination Agency (II.4, II.5)

The office of Joint Secretary, Disarmament and International Security Affairs Division, Ministry of External Affairs, Government of India, New Delhi is the national point of contact for international liaison on matters related to implementation of the UN PoA.

Government of India has set up an Inter-Ministerial Task Force in 2002 whose members include representatives from the Ministries of External Affairs, Defence and Home Affairs and National Security Council Secretariat. The Task Force meets regularly to provide inputs related to policy guidance, research and monitoring of efforts to prevent, combat and eradicate the illicit trade in SALW.

Provision of Laws, Regulations and Administrative Procedures/Law Enforcement (II.2, II.3, II.6)

India's domestic policy on SALW is regulated statutorily under the **Arms Act (1959)** and **Arms Rules (1962)**, amended from time to time. These legislations and various executive instructions from Central and State governments have evolved a good mechanism for effective control and regulation of SALW in India. The .Arms Act (1959) and Arms Rules (1962) cover all aspects of lawful possession of manufacture, sale, transfer, transport, export, import of arms and ammunition, and provide penal provisions for violation of these acts. The Arms Act (1959) and Arms Rules (1962) are Central Government legislations and State Governments have a specified role in their implementation. The provisions of the Arms Act and Arms Rules seek to classify fire arms and other prohibitive weapons so as to ensure that (i) dangerous weapons of Military patterns are not available to civilians, particularly the anti-social elements and that (ii) weapons for self defence can be possessed by citizens in special cases only under duly issued licences.

As per entry 5 of List 1 of the Seventh Schedule to the Constitution of India, the Central Government has the exclusive jurisdiction on matters relating to arms, firearms, ammunition and explosives. The Ministry of Home Affairs of the Indian Government administers the Arms Act and has taken all possible measures to arrest the proliferation and trafficking in small arms and light weapons. The violators of the provisions of the Arms Act are meted out punitive punishments as provided in the Arms Act which range from imprisonment with fine to death sentence.

The Government of India thus has a comprehensive and effective mechanism to control all aspects of small arms and light weapons in India.

In addition to these, Government of India has also enacted several other laws which have penal provisions related to illegal possession, manufacture etc of SALW. These include **Unlawful Activities (Prevention) Act 1967 as amended in September, 2004, Armed Forces (Special Powers) Act, Indian Penal Code, the Army Act** and the analogous laws.

A specific distinction in terms of caliber (prohibited and non-prohibited bore) exists as far as possession and trading in firearms by civilians is concerned. Prohibited bore weapons are those in use by security forces/police and license for these are, as a rule, not issued to civilians.

Problem of Illicit SALW in India

India continues to face the problem of proliferation of illicit SALW which are smuggled into the country by various anti-national groups. The seizures of illicit SALW, by security forces, from terrorists provide an indicative assessment of the problem they pose. In Jammu and Kashmir and the north eastern areas alone, the security forces have, since 1990, seized approximately 44,000 weapons of all types, whose markings clearly indicated that these were brought into India through illicit channels from outside the country. This continues to pose a significant challenge to the Government. In the last two years alone (2005–06), the number of illicit SALW seized or confiscated by security forces in Jammu and Kashmir and in the north eastern areas was approximately 5,400. The Government of India remains committed to taking all necessary measures to put an end to such illicit flows. At the same time, the government has also taken effective measures to ensure that the weapons confiscated/seized by security/police forces do not find their way back into illicit trade channels or fall into the hands of unscrupulous elements. A small amount of crude "country-made" weapons are also found to be produced clandestinely in India. Updated tables listing the arms seized/confiscated by security/police forces in the last two years (2005 & 2006) are at **Annexure I** and **II** respectively.

Since almost all terrorist activities involve the use of illegal weapons, including small arms, organisations indulging in such activities are declared as "unlawful" under the provisions of relevant acts. A list of 32 organisations which have been banned by the Government under the Unlawful Activities (Prevention) Act 1967 as amended in 2004. for their activities is at **Annexure III**.

Manufacture, Marking, Record Keeping and Tracing of the Small Arms & Light Weapons (II.7, II.8, II.9)

The manufacture and production of SALW in India is fully controlled by Government of India. The manufacture of SALW is regulated under a licensing system established by the Arms Acts (1959) and Arms Rules (1962). Sections 5 and 7 of the Arms Act (1959) and Article 20 of Arms Rules (1962) prohibit the manufacture, transfer and repair of any SALW without a license. Through the licensing mechanism,

Government of India is able to regulate the categories and types of weapons which may be manufactured and the transactions which may be carried out in their respect.

SALW for armed forces/police as well as for civilian use are primarily manufactured by Indian Ordnance Factories controlled by the Ministry of Defence. These factories are engaged in the manufacture of all categories of small arms. The policy of the Government of India for manufacture of arms and ammunition in the private sector is based on the Industry Policy Resolution, 1956. The private sector is primarily engaged in the manufacture of single and double-barrel and air rifles/pistols. Even after liberalisation of the Indian economy and removal of licensing regime for major industries, the manufacture of arms like revolvers, pistols and rifled weapons—and ammunition thereof—has not been allowed in the private sector by the Government of India.

Marking

All small arms produced/manufactured in India are uniquely marked. This applies to arms that are produced for private/personal use and those which are used by armed forces, police or para-military forces. The Arms Act (1959) provides (Section 8) that arms which do not bear specified identification marks may not be sold or transferred. Further, under Arms Act (1959), any person found in possession of a weapon without identifications marks would be presumed to have removed/obliterated the marks unless proven otherwise.

The SALW produced by Indian ordnance factories are marked by stamping/engraving or laser marking to indicate the type/nomenclature of the weapon, **country of origin**, registration number, manufacturer/factory of origin and the year of manufacture on one or more of the vital and critical components of a small arm—the body, the chamber, the cylinder, the breech block and the barrel—during the final stages of production. A record of each and every weapon manufactured by the factory is kept along with the information on the concerned dealer/indenter to show receipts, disposal, balance of stock in hand and daily sales of Arms and Ammunition of different categories and provide such other information as may be required. Allotment of these registration numbers for the armed forces/police and para-military forces is done centrally and a record is maintained of these registration numbers along with the indent. This provided for a double check on the records.

Private sector manufacturers of firearms are required by law to get every firearm stamped to show: the maker's name and registered trademark; the serial number of the weapons as entered in his register and the year of stamping; and proof-mark (Arms Rules (1959) Section 25). The parts of the weapons to be marked are also specified under these provisions. In order to implement the international instrument on marking and tracing of SALW, suitable instructions have now been given by the Government of India to the States to ensure that the country of origin ie word 'IN' is suitably marked on all arms manufactured by the private sector arms manufacturers.

Further if an imported firearm kept for sale by a dealer does not bear the manufacturer's name, the concerned importer is required to engrave appropriate Identification marks (identifying me importer), as allotted by the Government under these provisions (Section 25, Arms Rules (1962).

The Magistrates and designated police officers are empowered under the Arms Rules to inspect the premises of arm manufacturing units, arms dealers, examine the stock and account of receipts and disposal of arms and ammunition or any other register or document.

The Government of India has issued necessary instructions to all procurement agencies of the three Services not to import any small arms which do not have markings indicating country of origin.

Record Keeping

All ordnance factories maintain detailed records of small arms manufactured by them. Private firms and persons authorised to manufacture firearms against license issued under the Arms Rules of 1962 are required to maintain a Gun Manufacturing Register which records information including Serial Numbers and Date, Month and Year of manufacture. They are also required to maintain a Register of Rectification in which the Serial Numbers stamped on guns which are not passed by the Proof House on first submission are to be entered with a cross reference to the Gun Manufacturing Register. A designated Inspecting Officer inspects these registers regularly.

According to existing laws (Arms Act of 1959, Section 3), a proper license is a prerequisite for possession of any SALW. District authorities may issue license after duly making police enquiries. Due to the gravity of the problem of proliferation of illicit SALW—and the onslaught of terrorism, Government of India has, since 1987, withdrawn substantially, the license issuing powers of State/District authorities—who may not now, issue license for prohibited bore weapons. Since 1987, their powers have been limited to issuing licenses for non-prohibited bore weapons and these licenses are valid for a limited geographical area. Under the existing law, all civilians are required to get their weapons/inspected once a year by a competent authority—this is also recorded in the license.

A record of arms sold in the civilian market (non-prohibited bore) is also required to be kept by each arms dealer under Section 26 of the Arms Rules (1962) in a Sale and Transfer Register. These records are regularly checked by the concerned state/district authorities.

License for possession of prohibited bore weapons may only be issued, under special conditions, by the Ministry of Home Affairs, Government of India, who also maintains a record of all such weapons in possession of civilian population. Licences for prohibitive bore weapons are issued by the Central Govt. in the case of a person having threat from terrorists/anti social elements and to certain defence personnel who were allotted weapons during their tenure by Defence establishment.

Armed forces/police and para-military forces maintain a permanent record of all weapons in their possession.

State Stockpile Management and Security (II.10, II.17, II.18)

The SALW held by the armed forces, police and other para-military forces are managed under a comprehensive system of regulations issued by Central and State Governments. The concerned government agency issues arms and ammunitions to armed forces, para-military forces and police as per the authorised scale and requirements. Under Chapter XX of the Defence Service Regulations (Regulations for the Army), specific and exhaustive provisions have been laid down for management and security of SALW held by the Army. These stocks are checked every quarter.

Police arms and ammunition which have been classified as obsolete or unserviceable are earmarked for destruction before they are destroyed by the concerned State Police Forces at a central location under proper supervision.

Disposal of Seized and Confiscated Weapons (II.16)

In the course of law enforcement activities—and operations against terrorists, Government authorities regularly seize/confiscate weapons belonging to both "prohibited" and "non-prohibited" bore categories. Detailed instructions have been issued by the Government of India for disposal of such arms and ammunition. The main aim of the Government is to ensure that these weapons do not find their way back into the illicit trade channels or fall into the hands of unscrupulous elements.

Destruction of Country-Made Weapons:

Country-made weapons seized during the special drives or in the course of implementation of the law, after they are no longer required for any judicial purposes, are mutilated/defaced and are destroyed by the concerned State Police forces at a central location under proper supervision.

Disposal of Prohibited Bore Small Arms:

Details of SALW which are seized/confiscated by the police or paramilitary forces are sent to Ministry of Home Affairs after duly taking care of all the legal requirements. If required, in cases where the same type of weapons are already in use by the security forces—and for which spares would be available, the seized/confiscated weapons are re-allocated to units of security forces for counter-terrorist operations. Other prohibited bore weapons seized by security forces are destroyed at the Central Ordinance Depot.

Disposal of Non-Prohibited Bore Small Arms:

Serviceable weapons of non-prohibited bore which are seized and confiscated by police or other law enforcement agencies may be disposed by allotment to eligible persons holding a valid license for such weapons. Such weapons are required to meet all the requirements laid out in the Arms Act (1959) in terms of having proper markings. The allotment is based on the realization of the price which is fixed by the Government. A monthly statement of all such seized stock is required to be sent to the Ministry of Home Affairs by the concerned State Police Department. All obsolete/unserviceable weapons and firearms and their components are destroyed.

To ensure the security—and prevent misuse—of seized/confiscated weapons, a detailed inventory of these weapons in maintained in "seizure memos". Such details include, *inter-alia*, the make and type of weapon. Their storage in local police stations is normally not allowed. These weapons are usually stored in a central location, such as in State Police Headquarters, so as to ensure their safety and proper supervision. Pending their disposal, a monthly statement of stocks of such weapons held by State Governments is sent to the Central Government (Ministry of Home Affairs).

Export Controls (II.11, II.12, II.15)

Export of all lethal items as well as other equipment and stores manufactured by Defence Public Sector Undertakings (DPSUs) and Indian Ordnance Factories (which includes SALWs) is governed by a regime administered by the Ministry of Defence in consultation with the Ministry of External Affairs. DPSUs and ordnance factories may export their items only on receipt of a 'No-Objection Certificate' (NOC) from the Department of Defence Production and Supplies, Ministry of Defence. The grant of an NOC is subject, *inter alia*, to an end-user certificate-on a government-to-government basis-and to conformity with foreign policy objectives-which includes a ban on exports to countries under UN embargo.

In addition, provisions of the Arms Act (1959) and Arms Rules (1962) have very stringent provisions governing the export and import of small arms. Section 10 of the Arms Act (1959) requires that any one intending to engage in export/import of arms should first acquire the requisite license. Furthermore, license for export is not granted for automatic weapons and weapons which are in use by the police or armed forces of the country, weapons of "current and popular bore" (Section 33, Arms Rules (1962)) for which ammunition is available domestically, and certain antique weapons.

Similarly import of arms by individuals or commercial entities is permitted only against a license. Such imports are, as a rule, allowed only to renowned shooters/rifle clubs for their own use on the recommendation of the concerned Government Department. Furthermore, under the "Exim Policy 2002–2007", transfer of the imported firearm/s is not permitted during the lifetime of the importer/licensee.

Global and Regional Level

India recognizes that close international co-operation is required to prevent, combat and eradicate the illicit trade in SALW. To this end, India has supported the efforts of international organisations and the initiatives taken under UN auspices. India has already supplied copies of its domestic legislation to UN DDA **(II.23)**

International Instrument Against Terrorism and Trans-National Organised Crime (II.38)

India has been a victim of cross-border terrorism for over two decades. India unequivocally condemns terrorism in all its forms and manifestations and strongly believes that there can be no justification, whatsoever, for any act of terrorism. The international community must have a policy of zero tolerance on terrorism and make further concerted efforts to fight this scourge. "We must ensure that the issue is not obfuscated by efforts of some to veer the discussion towards so called "root causes of terrorism".

India is a party to all the thirteen sectoral UN Conventions on terrorism. India is fully committed to fulfilling its obligations under the various Security Council resolutions on counter terrorism, including UNSCR 1373. Government of India (GoI) has submitted five national reports to UNSC's Counter Terrorism Committee in compliance with UNSCR 1373. GoI had accepted a proposal by the UN authorities for a visit by a 14-member delegation of UN Counter-Terrorism experts, led by Executive Director of UNSC's Counter Terrorism Executive Directorate (CTED) and included representatives of CTED, Monitoring Team of UNSC's 1267 Committee related to Al Qaeda/Taliban, INTERPOL, United Nations' Office on Drugs and Crime (UNDOC) and World Customs Organisation (WCO). Besides giving first hand information to the delegation on GoI's compliance of Security Council resolutions on counter terrorism, the visit provided a very useful opportunity to both sides for comprehensive discussions in this area.

India had introduced a draft Comprehensive Convention on International Terrorism (CCIT) at the United Nations as far back as 1996. India remains constructively engaged with other member states with the objective of an expeditious finalization of CCIT. India has also supported the UN Global CTS and the Plan of Action, adopted by member states on 8 September, 2006. India is firmly of the view that an early conclusion of the CCIT is imperative to any consolidation of counter terrorism efforts within the UN.

As mentioned earlier, India has a very strict export policy for SALW to ensure effective implementation of UN arms embargoes **(II.32)**

International Cooperation to Combat Illicit Trade in SALW

Considering that the illicit trade in SALW is closely linked with terrorism, illicit drug trafficking, money laundering and other trans-national organised crimes, India has taken bilateral initiatives with a number of countries to put in place arrangements which would help combat the illicit trade in SALW (**II.27**). The agreements aim at enhancing cooperation in combating organized crime and international terrorism. They provide for exchange of documentation, information and experience on the activities of persons involved in organized crime and terrorism, including, inter-alia, illicit trade in arms, and funding of international terrorism. Most recently India signed a **MoU with Italy on Combating International Terrorism and Transnational Crime (February 2007)**. India has so far entered into agreement with 25 countries to set-up Joint Working Groups on combating terrorism and transnational crime.

At the regional level, India along with other member states of BIMSTEC (Bay of Bengal Initiative for Multi-Sectoral Technical and Economic Cooperation) have established a Joint Working Group to coordinate efforts in areas such as intelligence sharing and capacity building as well as to strengthen joint efforts on counter terrorism and trans-national crime. The Joint Working Group has had three meetings so far with the last meeting having been held in Nay Pyi Taw, Myanmar in January 2007. Similarly, India has a Joint Working Group arrangement with European Union (EU).

India has been actively associated with various workshops and seminars that have been organized either under UN auspices or by other interested parties to further effective international cooperation on this important subject. Most recently India attended a workshop on SALW held in Tokyo on 12–13 March 2007.

E. US PERSPECTIVES

DOCUMENT NO. 28

INTERNATIONAL TERRORISM IN SOUTH ASIA

CRS Report RS21658

November 3, 2003

K. Alan Kronstadt
Analyst in Asian Affairs
Foreign Affairs, Defense, and Trade Division

Summary

This report reviews the international terrorist environment in South Asia, concentrating on Afghanistan, Pakistan, and India.[1] With U.S.-led counterterrorism efforts focused especially on Southwest Asia, the existence of international terrorist groups and their supporters in South Asia is identified as a threat to both regional stability and to the attainment of key U.S. policy goals. Al Qaeda forces that fled from Afghanistan with their Taliban supporters remain active on Pakistani territory, and Al Qaeda is believed to have links with indigenous Pakistani terrorist groups that have conducted anti-Western attacks and that support separatist militancy in Indian Kashmir. A significant portion of Pakistan's ethnic Pashtun population is reported to sympathize with the Taliban and even Al Qaeda. This report will be updated periodically.

In the wake of the September 2001 terrorist attacks on the United States, President Bush launched major military operations in South and Southwest Asia as part of the global U.S.-led anti-terrorism effort. Operation Enduring Freedom in Afghanistan has seen substantive success with the vital assistance of neighboring Pakistan. Yet the United States increasingly is concerned

[1] The report excludes discussion of Sri Lanka and Nepal, where the activities of groups identified by the United States as engaging in terrorism have only minor international dimensions. See also CRS Report RL31624, *Pakistan-U.S. Anti-Terrorism Cooperation*, by K. Alan Kronstadt, and CRS Report RL30588, *Afghanistan: Current Issues and U.S. Policy*, by Kenneth Katzman.

that members of Al Qaeda and its Taliban supporters have found haven and been able to at least partially regroup in Pakistani cities and in the rugged Pakistan-Afghanistan border region inhabited by ethnic Pashtuns who express solidarity with anti-U.S. forces. Al Qaeda also reportedly has made alliances with indigenous Pakistani terrorist groups that have been implicated in both anti-Western attacks in Pakistan and terrorism in Indian Kashmir, while also seeking to oust the government of President Gen. Pervez Musharraf. Along with these concerns, the United States expresses an interest in the cessation of "cross-border infiltration" by separatist militants based in Pakistani-controlled areas who cross the Kashmiri Line of Control (LOC) to engage in terrorist activities in Indian Kashmir and in Indian cities.

Al Qaeda, the Taliban, and Pakistani Terrorist Groups

The Al Qaeda-Taliban Nexus. Among the central goals of Operation Enduring Freedom were the destruction of terrorist training camps and infrastructure within Afghanistan, the capture of Al Qaeda and Taliban leaders, and the cessation of terrorist activities in Afghanistan.[2] Most, but not all, of these goals have been achieved. However, since the Taliban's ouster from power in Kabul and subsequent retreat to the rugged mountain region near the Afghanistan-Pakistan border, what the U.S. military calls its "remnant forces" have been able to regroup and to conduct "hit-and-run" attacks against U.S.-led coalition forces, possibly in tandem with suspected Al Qaeda fugitives. These forces are then able to find haven on the Pakistani side of the border.[3] Al Qaeda founder Osama bin Laden may himself be in a remote area of Pakistan near Afghanistan. The frequency of these attacks has increased throughout 2003 and, in October, U.S. Special Envoy to Afghanistan Zalmay Khalilzad reportedly warned that resurgent Taliban and Al Qaeda forces are presenting a serious threat to Afghani reconstruction efforts.[4]

Indigenous Pakistani Terrorist Groups. In January 2002, Pakistan banned five extremist organizations, including Lashkar-e-Taiba (LET), Jaish-e-Mohammed (JEM), and Sipah-e-Sahaba Pakistan (SSP). The United States designates LET and JEM as Foreign Terrorist Organizations (FTOs); SSP appears on the State Departments's terrorism "watch list." Following Al Qaeda's 2001–2002 expulsion from Afghanistan and ensuing relocation

---

[2] Al Qaeda members are most readily identified as being Arabs or other non-Afghanis who are fighting an international jihad, while Taliban members are ethnic Pashtun Afghanis who are fighting for Islamic rule in Kabul.

[3] Pakistan's western regions are populated by conservative ethnic Pashtuns who share intimate religious and tribal linkages with their counterparts in Afghanistan and who are seen to sympathize with Taliban and sometimes Al Qaeda forces while holding vehement anti-Western and anti-American sentiments (see, for example, Eliza Griswold, "Where the Taliban Roam," *Harper's*, September 2003; Owais Tohid, "Tribes Inflamed By Qaeda Hunt," *Christian Science Monitor*, October 20, 2003).

[4] Carlotta Gall, "Taliban May Be Planning Larger Attacks, U.S. Envoy Says," *New York Times*, October 7, 2003.

of some core elements to Pakistani cities such as Karachi and Peshawar, some Al Qaeda activists are believed to have joined forces with indigenous Pakistani Sunni militant groups, including LET, JEM, SSP, and Lashkar-i-Jhangvi, an FTO-designated offshoot of the SSP.[5] Al Qaeda reportedly was linked to anti-U.S. and anti-Western terrorist attacks in Pakistan during 2002, although the primary suspects in such attacks have been from indigenous Pakistani groups.[6] During 2003, Pakistan's domestic terrorism mostly has involved Sunni-Shia conflict.[7] Some analysts believe that, by redirecting Pakistan's internal security resources, this increase in sectarian violence may ease pressure on Al Qaeda and so allow that group to operate more freely.[8]

In a landmark January 2002 speech, President Musharraf vowed to end Pakistan's use as a base for terrorism, and he criticized religious extremism and intolerance in the country. In the wake of the speech, about 3,300 extremists were arrested and detained, though perhaps half of these have since been released. These releases included the founders of both Lashkar-e-Taiba and Jaish-e-Muhammad. Though officially banned, these groups continue to operate under new names: LET is now Jamaat al-Dawat; JEM is now Khudam-ul Islam; and Harakat-ul Mujahideen is now Jamiat-ul Ansar.[9]

Pakistan-U.S. Anti-Terrorism Cooperation

According to the U.S. Departments of State and Defense, Pakistan has afforded the United States unprecedented levels of cooperation by allowing the U.S. military to use bases within the country, helping to identify and detain extremists, and deploying tens of thousands of its own security forces to secure the Pakistan-Afghanistan border. Top U.S. officials regularly praise Pakistani anti-terrorism efforts. In the spring of 2002, U.S. military and law enforcement personnel reportedly began engaging in direct, low-profile efforts to assist Pakistani security forces in tracking and apprehending

---

[5] U.S. Department of State, *Patterns of Global Terrorism- 2002*, April 30, 2003; Hasan Mansoor, "Karachi Killings Reveal Sectarian-Jihadi Nexus," *Friday Times* (Lahore), October 10, 2003.

[6] The most notable of these attacks were the January 2002 kidnaping and ensuing murder of *Wall Street Journal* reporter Daniel Pearl; a March grenade attack on a Protestant church in Islamabad that killed five, including a U.S. Embassy employee and her daughter; a May car bombing that killed 14 outside a Karachi hotel, including 11 French defense technicians; and a June car bombing outside the U.S. consulate in Karachi that killed 12 Pakistani nationals. Arrests and some convictions have resulted in each of these cases.

[7] About three-quarters of Pakistan's Muslims are Sunnis. Major sectarian violence in 2003 included a July strike on a Quetta mosque that killed more than 50 Shiite worshipers (blamed on the SSP), and the October assassination of Maulana Azam Tariq, leader of the militant Sunni SSP and member of the Pakistani parliament, who was gunned down with four others in Islamabad.

[8] "Pakistan: A New Wave of Sunni-Shiite Violence?," Stratfor.com, October 7, 2003.

[9] Paul Watson, "Revolving Doors for Pakistan's Militants," *Los Angeles Times*, November 17, 2002; "Musharraf Says Heads of Two Extremist Groups Did Nothing Illegal," Agence France-Presse, March 2, 2003; "Militant Suspects Freed in Pakistan," BBC News, January 31, 2003. On FTO issues, see CRS Report RL32120, *The 'FTO List' and Congress*, by Audrey Kurth Cronin.

fugitive Al Qaeda and Taliban fighters on Pakistani territory. The State Department reports that Islamabad has facilitated the transfer of more than 400 captured alleged terrorists to U.S. custody, including several top suspected Al Qaeda leaders.[10] Pakistan also ranks fourth in the world in seizing terrorist assets.[11]

Despite Pakistan's "crucial" cooperation, there remain doubts about Islamabad's commitment to core U.S. concerns in the vast "lawless zones" of the Afghani-Pakistani border region where Islamic extremists find shelter.[12] Especially worrisome are indications that the Taliban receive significant logistical and other support inside Pakistan. Senator Richard Lugar and Senator Joseph Biden reportedly have voiced such worries, including concern that elements of Pakistan's Inter-Services Intelligence agency (ISI) might be helping members of the Taliban and perhaps even Al Qaeda.[13] In August 2003, at least three Pakistani army officers, including a lieutenant colonel, were arrested on suspicion of having ties to Islamic extremists. In late September, Deputy Secretary of State Armitage was quoted as saying he does "not think that affection for working with us extends up and down the rank and file of the Pakistani security community." In October testimony before the Senate Foreign Relations Committee, Assistant Secretary of Defense for International Security Affairs Peter Rodman said, "There are elements in the Pakistani government who we suspect are sympathetic to the old policy of before 9/11," adding that there still exists in northwestern Pakistan a radical Islamic infrastructure that "spews out fighters that go into Kashmir as well as into Afghanistan."[14]

Military Operations. In an effort to block infiltration along the Pakistan-Afghanistan border, Islamabad had by the end of 2002 deployed some 70,000 troops to the region. In June 2003, in what may have been a response to increased U.S. pressure, Islamabad for the first time sent its armed forces into the traditionally autonomous western Federally Administered Tribal Areas in search of renegade Al Qaeda and Taliban fighters who have eluded the U.S.-led campaign in Afghanistan. By September, Islamabad had up to 25,000 troops in the tribal areas, and a major border operation reportedly

[10] Among those captured are Abu Zubaydah (March 2002), believed to be Al Qaeda's field commander; Ramzi bin al-Shibh (September 2002), said to be a key figure in the planning of the September 2001 terrorist attacks on the United States; and Khalid Mohammed (March 2003), alleged mastermind of the September 2001 attacks and close associate of Osama bin Laden.

[11] U.S. Department of State, *Patterns of Global Terrorism—2002*, April 30, 2003.

[12] Statement of George Tenet Before the Senate Select Committee on Intelligence, "Worldwide Threats to National Security," February 6, 2002.

[13] James Dao, "Terror Aid From Pakistan Concerns Senators," *New York Times*, February 13, 2003. See also, Testimony of Timothy Hoyt Before the Joint Hearing of the Subcommittees on Asia and the Pacific and International Terrorism, Nonproliferation, and Human Rights, October 29, 2003.

[14] Zaffar Abbas, "Pakistan Arrests Army Officers," BBC News, August 31, 2003; "Armitage—Some Pakistanis Reluctant to Work With US," Reuters News, September 30, 2003; "Transcript: Senate Foreign Relations Committee Holds Hearing on Security and Democracy in Afghanistan," Federal Documents Clearing House, October 16, 2003.

took place in coordination with U.S.-led forces on the Afghani side of the border. In early October, Pakistani security forces engaged suspected Al Qaeda fugitives in the South Waziristan district, killing 8 and capturing 18 others.[15] Pakistan has lost at least 12 of its own security personnel in gun battles with Al Qaeda fighters. The October operations have encouraged U.S. officials, who see in them a positive trend in Islamabad's commitment to tracking and capturing wanted extremists on Pakistani territory. Still, these officials admit that the Pakistani government finds it more difficult politically to pursue Taliban members who enjoy ethnic and familial ties with Pakistani Pashtuns.[16]

Madrassas and Pakistan Islamists. A notable development in September 2003 was the arrest by Pakistani security forces of 19 Indonesian and Malaysian nationals at a Karachi madrassa (Islamic school). The men are suspected of running a sleeper cell of the Jemaah Islamiyah (JI) terrorist network in what would be the first indication that JI, a group linked to Al Qaeda, is operating in Pakistan.[17] Among the approximately 10,000 madrassas in Pakistan are some that have been implicated in teaching militant anti-Western, anti-American, and anti-Hindu values. Many of these madrassas are financed and operated by Pakistani Islamist political parties such as Jamaat-e-Ulema Islam (JUI, closely linked to the Taliban), as well as by multiple unknown foreign entities. While President Musharraf has in the past pledged to crack down on the more extremist madrassas in his country, there is little concrete evidence that he has done so.[18]

The Muttahida Majlis-e-Amal (MMA)—a coalition of six Islamist opposition parties—holds about 20% of Pakistan's National Assembly seats, while also controlling the provincial assembly in the North West Frontier Province (NWFP) and leading a coalition in the provincial assembly of Baluchistan. Pakistan's Islamists, including the leadership of some of their legal political parties, are notable for their virulent expressions of anti-American sentiment; they have at times called for "jihad" against what they view as the existential threat to Pakistani sovereignty that alliance with Washington entails. In addition to decrying President Musharraf's cooperation with the United States, many also are viewed as opposing the U.S.-supported Kabul government. In September 2003, Afghani President Karzai called on

[15] John Lancaster, "Pakistan Touts Control of Border," *Washington Post*, September 2, 2003; "Pakistan Army Launches Border Operation," BBC News, September 4, 2003; "Pakistan's Army Kills 12 in Attacks Against Qaeda," *New York Times*, October 2, 2003.

[16] See the testimony of both William Taylor and Brig. Gen. Gary North in "Transcript: Senate Foreign Relations Committee Holds Hearing on Security and Democracy in Afghanistan," Federal Documents Clearing House, October 16, 2003.

[17] O. Tohid, "Pakistan Widens Terror Dragnet," *Christian Science Monitor*, September 26, 2003.

[18] Ahmed Rashid, "Afghanistan and Pakistan—Safe Haven for the Taliban," *Far Eastern Economic Review*, October 16, 2003; "Pakistan: The Mullahs and the Military," International Crisis Group Report 49, March 20, 2003. See also CRS Report RS21654, *Islamic Religious Schools, Madrasas*, by Febe Armanios.

Pakistani clerics to stop supporting Taliban members who seek to destabilize Afghanistan.[19]

Terrorism in Kashmir and India

Separatist violence in the Indian Jammu and Kashmir state has surged in recent months. New Delhi consistently blames Pakistan-based militant groups for lethal attacks on Indian civilians, as well as on government security forces, in both Kashmir and in major Indian cities. India holds Pakistan responsible for providing material support and training facilities to Kashmiri militants. Most often blamed for terrorism in India are FTO-designates Lashkar-e-Taiba, Jaish-e-Mohammed, and Harakat ul-Mujahideen, and Hizbul Mujahideen, the latter identified on the State Department's terrorism watch list. According to the U.S. government, several anti-India militant groups fighting in Kashmir are based in Pakistan and are closely linked to Islamist groups there:

- Harakat ul-Mujahideen, based mainly in Muzaffarabad (Azad Kashmir) and Rawalpindi, is aligned with the Jamiat-i Ulema-i Islam Fazlur Rehman party (JUI-F), itself a constituent of the MMA Islamist coalition in Pakistan's National Assembly;
- Hizbul Mujahideen, believed to have bases in Pakistan, is the militant wing of Pakistan's largest Islamic political party and MMA member, the Jamaat-i-Islami;
- Jaish-e-Mohammed, based in both Peshawar and Muzaffarabad, also is aligned with JUI-F; and
- Lashkar-i-Taiba, based in Muzaffarabad and near Lahore, is the armed wing of a Pakistan-based, anti-U.S. Sunni religious organization formed in 1989.[20]

Pakistan's powerful and largely autonomous ISI is widely believed to have provided significant support for militant Kashmiri separatists over the past decade in what is perceived as a proxy war against India.[21] In March 2003, the chief of India's Defense Intelligence Agency reported providing the United States with "solid documentary proof" that 70 Islamic militant camps are operating in Pakistani Kashmir. In May, the Indian Defense Minister

[19] See "MMA Calls for Change in Foreign Policy," *Dawn* (Karachi), September 10, 2003. JUI leader Maulana Fazlur Rehman reportedly said he considers Americans to be "criminals" and the Taliban "innocent" ("MMA Opposes Pak-US Military Drive," *News* (Karachi), June 24, 2003). "Karzai Tells Pakistan Clerics—Don't Back Taliban," Reuters News, September 12, 2003.

[20] See U.S. Department of State, *Patterns of Global Terrorism—2002*, April 30, 2003.

[21] "Although Pakistan did not begin the [1989] uprising in Kashmir, the temptation to fan the flames was too great for Islamabad to resist. Using guerrilla-warfare expertise gained during the Afghan war, Pakistan's ISI began to provide active backing for Kashmiri Muslim insurgents" Dennis Kux, *The United States and Pakistan 1947–2000: Disenchanted Allies* (Washington: Woodrow Wilson Center Press), 2001, p. 305.

claimed that about 3,000 "terrorists" were being trained in camps on the Pakistani side of the LOC. Some Indian officials have suggested that Al Qaeda may be active in Kashmir.[22] Deputy Secretary of State Armitage reportedly received a June 2002 pledge from Pakistani President Musharraf that all "cross-border terrorism" would cease, followed by a May 2003 pledge that any terrorist training camps in Pakistani-controlled areas would be closed. Yet, in September, Indian PM Vajpayee reportedly told President Bush that continued cross-border terrorism from Pakistan was making it difficult for India to maintain its peace initiative, and current infiltration rates are widely believed to be on the rise.[23] Musharraf adamantly insists that his government is doing all it can to stem infiltration at the LOC and calls for a joint Pakistan-India monitoring effort there.

In signs that the United States may be increasing its pressure on Islamabad to further stem terrorist activities, the Treasury Department in October 2003 designated the Pakistan-based Al Akhtar Trust as a terrorist support organization under Executive Order 13224. Al Akhtar is said to be carrying on support for Al Qaeda and Taliban terrorist activities funded by the previously-designated Al Rashid Trust. The United States also in October identified Indian crime figure Dawood Ibrahim as a "global terrorist" with links to both Al Qaeda and Lashkar-e-Taiba. Ibrahim, wanted by the Indian government for 1993 Bombay bombings that killed some 300 and injured thousands more, is believed to be in Pakistan.[24] These moves by the U.S. government were welcomed in New Delhi, where officials continuously are urging greater U.S. attention to anti-India terrorism emanating from Pakistan.

[22] "India Says It Has Given Proof of 70 Islamic Militant Camps in Pakistan-Controlled Kashmir," Associated Press Newswires, March 14, 2003; "3,000 'Terrorists' Being Trained in Pakistani Kashmir: India," Agence France-Presse, July 30, 2003. In October, the Indian Chief of Army Staff raised the possibility of an Al Qaeda presence, as "most of the terrorists killed in [Jammu and Kashmir] are foreign nationals these days" ("Al Qaeda Presence Not Ruled Out in J&K," *Hindu* (Madras), October 12, 2003).

[23] Chidanand Rajghatta, "Cross-Border Terror Continues, Vajpayee Tells Bush," *Times of India* (Delhi), September 25, 2003; Scott Baldauf, "Insurgents Push Into Kashmir," *Christian Science Monitor*, October 7, 2003.

[24] "U.S. Designates Al Akhtar," U.S. Treasury Department Press Release, October 14, 2003; "U.S. Designates Dawood Ibrahim," U.S. Treasury Department Press Release, October 16, 2003.

DOCUMENT NO. 29

INDIA: CHRONOLOGY OF EVENTS

CRS Report
RS21589

December 3, 2003

K. Alan Kronstadt
Analyst in Asian Affairs
Foreign Affairs, Defense, and Trade Division

Summary

This report provides a reverse chronology of major events involving India and India-U.S. relations from September 2001.[1] For a substantive review, see CRS Issue Brief IB93097, *India-U.S. Relations*. This report will be updated regularly.

Acronyms

BJP:	Bharatiya Janata Party
LOC:	Line of Control (Kashmir)
SAARC:	South Asian Association for Regional Cooperation

12/02/03—Mr. Shashank, a career foreign service officer, replaced Kanwal Sibal as **India's new foreign secretary**. Shashank promised to seek normalization of India-Pakistan relations. On the same day, India and Brazil signed a defense cooperation agreement. Also, India's navy chief said that New Delhi had agreed to pay Moscow $652 million for the 29-year-old Russian aircraft carrier Admiral Gorshkov.

[1] Entries are on a day-to-day basis going back 60–90 days, then include periodic high-profile events. Sources include U.S. Department of State Washington File, *New York Times*, *Washington Post*, Associated Press, BBC News, Reuters News, Agence France-Presse, *Hindu* (Madras); *Hindustan Times* (Delhi); *Indian Express* (Mumbai); *Dawn* (Karachi), and *Daily Times* (Lahore).

12/01/03—Voters in the Indian states of Rajasthan, Madhya Pradesh, Chattisgarh, and New Delhi went to the **polls to choose new state legislatures** in what is viewed to be an important test of BJP and Congress Party strength ahead of national elections in 2004. Exit polling suggests that the BJP fared better than expected. Election-related violence left at least five people dead. On the same day, **Pakistan and India agreed to restore airline overflight and landing rights** by January 1, 2004. Also, President Musharraf offered to withdraw all of Pakistan's 50,000 troops from Kashmir if New Delhi agreed to pull back its estimated 700,000 soldiers from the disputed region. India had no immediate response to the offer.

11/29/03—During a joint press conference with the European Union president, PM Vajpayee said that India was already in the "second phase" of economic reforms and was concentrating on infrastructure development.

11/26/03—At midnight, **Pakistan and India began a formal cease-fire** at their shared international border, as well as along the LOC and Actual Ground Position Line on the Siachen glacier. The United States hailed the move as "steps toward peace [that] offer hope for real progress in the region."

11/24/03—An Indian government spokesman announced New Delhi's intention to match Pakistan's cease-fire order at the LOC while extending it to the Siachen glacier area to the north. He also warned that the cease-fire would fail unless Pakistan halts its material support for Kashmiri insurgents.

11/23/03—In a major address, **Pakistani PM Jamali announced a unilateral cease-fire** by Pakistani forces at the LOC to begin on the final night of Ramadan (11/26). On the same day, Indian External Affairs Minister Sinha strongly rejected the notion that warming India-U.S. or India-ASEAN ties are aimed at "containing" China. He did, however, add that the Islamabad-Beijing nuclear and missile proliferation "nexus" caused serious concerns in new Delhi. Also, India test-fired for a fifth time the BrahMos cruise missile it developed jointly with Russia.

11/21/03—Representatives of the Kashmiri separatist Hurriyat Conference said they had drafted a "road map" to resolve the dispute over Kashmir. On the same day, India's Supreme Court halted ten high-profile trials related to communal violence in Gujarat in early 2002. The action may pave the way for an indictment of the state's Hindu nationalist BJP government, which has been accused of complicity in the rioting.

11/20/03—During a visit to New Delhi, Under Secretary of Commerce Juster reiterated President Bush's desire to further strengthen relations with India on a broad front, while noting that, from the U.S. perspective, India could do much to make the country more attractive for U.S. trade and investment. On the same day, a 48-hour house-to-house battle between Indian soldiers and two suspected separatist militants in Srinagar, Kashmir ended with the rebels, three soldiers, and a civilian dead. New Delhi held an offshoot of the Pakistan-based Lashkar-e-Taiba terrorist group responsible for the attack.

11/19/03—Violence between Assamese- and Hindi-speaking people in India's northeastern Assam state left 25 dead and more than 100 homes destroyed by fire. Rioting spurred by a controversial railway job recruitment program brought army troops to the region and led the separatist militant United Liberation Front of Assam to demand that all Hindi speakers leave the state.

11/14/03—David Mulford, chairman of Credit Suisse First Boston, former Treasury Department official (1984–1992), and personal friend of President Bush, was nominated to be the **next U.S. Ambassador to India**. On the same day, a notable **sign of improved India-China relations** came when the two nations' navies held their first-ever joint exercises off the coast of Shanghai. Also, PM Vajpayee arrived in Syria, where the New Delhi and Damascus governments signed nine agreements meant to boost trade in such areas as agriculture and information technology.

11/12/03—A press report quoted an Indian Defense Ministry spokesman as saying that India is actively upgrading Tajikistan's Anyi air base and has plans to station troops and warplanes there to support its energy security interests in Central Asia.

11/10/03—India's Supreme Court issued a stay on the arrest of six journalists imprisoned on the orders of the Tamil Nadu state assembly in what was described by many as an egregious attack on press freedoms.

11/09/03—Press reports indicated that Air India plans to buy a total of 28 new aircraft from both Airbus Industrie and Boeing over the next five years in deals worth $2.1 billion.

11/07/03—Pakistani President Musharraf vowed to rectify "through all means possible" the "imbalance" being created by India's "massive acquisition of arms." On the same day, authorities in Indian Kashmir said that suspected militants had shot and killed a prominent member of the state's governing People's Democratic Party.

11/03/03—A spokesman for Pakistan's Foreign office claimed that Indian "repression and state terrorism" in Kashmir had intensified in recent months.

11/02/03—PM Vajpayee told a meeting of top Indian military commanders that their strategic planning should extend to horizons beyond South Asia, from the Persian Gulf in the west to the Straits of Malacca in the east to Afghanistan, Central Asia, and China in the north.

11/01/03—PM Vajpayee said that "a meaningful dialogue with Pakistan is only possible when we see sincerity in their efforts to stop cross-border infiltration and to dismantle the infrastructure of terrorism." On the same day, Defense Minister Fernandes reportedly said that "India is serious about taking back its portion [of Kashmir] illegally held by Pakistan." Also, the head of India's air force said that, contrary to previous reports, India will use its satellites for communications purposes only, and not for weapons delivery.

10/29/03—In its first detailed response to New Delhi's 10/22 initiative, **Islamabad welcomed India's proposals** and accepted several of them—including a restoration of sporting ties, the establishment of a joint coast guard hotline, and the resumption of travel negotiations—while also expressing disappointment that India continues to shun direct bilateral dialogue with Pakistan. Islamabad's response came in the form of a 13-point list of measures, some of which New Delhi said were attached with "impractical, extraneous, or delaying conditions."

10/27/03—PM Vajpayee began a visit to the northeastern state of Nagaland, the first such visit by an Indian Prime Minister in six years. He discussed with Naga officials further devolvement of power and announced a $76 million development package for the state, which has been wracked by separatist violence for more than 50 years.

10/25/03—Deputy PM Advani said that his talks with Kashmiri separatists will involve "no compromise on the country's unity and sovereignty," but that New Delhi is willing to consider a "decentralization" of power.

10/23/03—Indian national Security Advisor Mishra met with a top Chinese official in New Delhi to discuss a long-standing border dispute. On the same day, a press report indicated that a retired top Indian nuclear scientist is believed to have assisted in the construction of Iran's nuclear power plant.

10/22/03—**The Indian government unveiled a set of 12 proposals** meant to improve its relations with Pakistan. Many of the steps involve increasing people-to-people contacts between Pakistan and India. The United States warmly welcomed the Indian initiative. New Delhi also announced that Deputy PM Advani would represent India's central government in its **first-ever proposed negotiations with Kashmiri separatists.**

10/21/03—In the first official visit of its kind in many years, a group of three Pakistani civil servants traveled to Indian-held Kashmir to inspect hydroelectric projects on the Chenab River there.

10/17/03—**Up to 60,000 Hindu activists were arrested** across the state of Uttar Pradesh as they tried to reach a banned rally in the town of Ayodhya, site of a controversial temple that is claimed by both Hindus and Muslims. On the same day, apparent Islamic militants launched an attack on the home of the Chief Minister of Jammu and Kashmir, killing two Indian soldiers. Indian Deputy PM Advani blamed the attack on the Pakistan-based Lashkar-e-Taiba terrorist group.

10/16/03—**The U.S. Treasury Department identified Indian crime figure Dawood Ibrahim as a "global terrorist"** with links to both Al Qaeda and Lashkar-e-Taiba. Ibrahim, wanted by the Indian government for 1993 Bombay bombings that killed and injured thousands, is believed to be in Pakistan. On the same day, India's External Affairs Minister said Pakistan has done "nothing at all to stop cross-border terrorism."

10/14/03—Defence Minister Fernandes reportedly indicated that India and Israel have agreed in principal to hold joint military exercises in the future.

10/13/03—A press report indicated that U.S. officials are reviewing an Indian request to purchase 12 PAC-3 tactical missile defense systems from the United States, a purchase that some analysts claim will upset the balance of power in South Asia. On the same day, India and Singapore signed a defense cooperation agreement establishing a bilateral Defense Policy Dialogue.

10/10/03—India signed an estimated $1 billion deal to purchase Il-76 transport planes from Russia that will be outfitted with sophisticated **Phalcon airborne early warning systems** in Israel. The Pakistani government and some independent analysts claim that the purchase will upset the balance of power in South Asia.

10/08/03—**India and the Association of Southeast Asian Nations(ASEAN) signed their first accords**, agreeing to expand trade relations and cooperate in combating international terrorism. India also joined ASEAN's 1976 Treaty of Amity and Cooperation. On the same day, India-China relations were improved when it emerged that Beijing was conceding New Delhi's sovereignty over the previously contested Himalayan state of Sikkim.

10/06/03—India's Chief of Air Staff announced that a new aerospace command had begun work to develop weapons platforms for space.

10/05/03—U.S. and Indian naval forces began their largest-ever joint exercises off India's southern coast.

10/03/03—Secretary of State Powell said that progress is being made on the "glide path" toward agreement on the "Trinity" issues of high-technology trade, and space and civilian nuclear cooperation.

10/01/03—Apparent leftist rebels attempted to assassinate the chief minister of India's southern Andhra Pradesh state in a landmine attack.

09/28/03—Secretary of State Powell stated that for "a variety of reasons," including domestic politics, **India would not be in a position to provide troops for service in Iraq**. On the same day, the newly-elected head of the Hurriyat Conference of Kashmiri separatist groups, hardliner Syed Ali Shah Geelani, reportedly claimed that the Lashkar-e-Taiba and Jaish-e-Mohammed terrorist groups are "friends" and "benefactors" of his organization.

09/25/03—While speaking to the U.N. General Assembly, Indian PM Vajpayee contended that Pakistan had "let terrorism become a tool of blackmail." He also told President Bush that continued cross-border terrorism from Pakistan was making it difficult for India to maintain its peace initiative.

09/24/03—While speaking to the U.N. General Assembly, Pakistani President Musharraf criticized the "brutal suppression of the Kashmiris" under "Indian occupation."

09/23/03—Indian Defense Minister Fernandes said that a U.S.-Israel-India axis against terrorism "does not seem feasible" because of continued links with Pakistan.

09/15/03—**The Hurriyat Conference of Kashmiri separatists formally split** after a dispute between hardliners and moderates.

09/14/03—**Surging separatist violence in Kashmir** reportedly killed as many as 437 civilians, Islamic militants, and Indian security men during the first two weeks of September.

09/09/03—A high-level U.S. Navy delegation arrived in New Delhi for negotiations on the sale to India of 8 P3 Orion maritime patrol aircraft.

09/08/03—**Israeli PM Sharon arrived in India** to discuss the strengthening of political and military ties between Israel and India. Indian Muslim groups and leftist political parties denounced the diplomacy.

09/05/03—US and Indian special forces soldiers began a two-week joint exercise in Ladakh near the India-China border.

09/03/03—British company BAE Systems was awarded a $1.7 billion contract to supply India with 66 Hawk fighter jets, the majority of which are to be built under license in Bangalore.

09/01/03—The **first-ever session of Indian's Nuclear Command Authority** met to "consolidate India's nuclear deterrent."

08/03—**Two car bombs exploded in Mumbai, India**, killing 52 and spurring New Delhi to suggest a role of Pakistan-based terrorist groups in the attack. Also, apparent Independence Day-related separatist violence left 34 civilians and 6 rebels dead in India's northeastern Tripura state.

07/03—Full diplomatic relations between New Delhi and Islamabad were restored after an 18-month hiatus when the new Indian ambassador arrived in Pakistan. Also, India rejected an American request to send peacekeeping troops to Iraq, saying it would only consider doing so under an "explicit" U.N. mandate. Finally, Indian Foreign Secretary Sibal led a delegation to Washington for the first meeting of the U.S.-India High-Technology Cooperation Group.

06/03—A major improvement in relations between the world's two most populous countries came when **Indian PM Vajpayee traveled to China**, the first visit by an Indian leader in more than a decade.

04/03—**A significant thaw in India-Pakistan relations** came with the first direct contact between national leaders since the July 2001 summit in Agra, India. The two agreed to restore full diplomatic relations, reopen key transportation links, and pursue further confidence-building measures.

03/03—The Indian government called the U.S.-led war in Iraq "unjustified" and "avoidable." Also, apparent Muslim extremists shot and killed 24 Hindu villagers in Indian Kashmir.

02/03—The incumbent BJP suffered an upset loss to the Congress Party in state elections in the Hindu-majority northern state of Himachal Pradesh.

01/03—**India and Iran launched a "strategic partnership"** with the signing of the New Delhi Declaration and seven other substantive agreements. India also signed a "landmark" defense cooperation protocol with Russia. Also, India announced that it has set up a Nuclear Command Authority.

12/02—Elections in the state of Gujarat, the site of communal violence earlier in 2002, resulted in an unexpectedly decisive victory for the incumbent Hindu-nationalist BJP party, which ran a divisive communal campaign.

10/02—**State elections in India's Jammu and Kashmir**, widely recognized as being free and fair, resulted in the ousting of the long-ruling National Conference and the seating of a new coalition government that vowed to "soften" policy toward separatist militants. Also, India announced a major redeployment of troops away from border areas, signaling **an end to a tense 10-month-long military face-off** with Pakistan.

09/02—Gunmen stormed a Hindu temple in Gujarat and killed 23 worshipers. The attackers were suspected to be Islamic militants seeking revenge for February 2002 anti-Muslim rioting in the state.

06/02—Intense international diplomatic pressure—including multiple visits to the region by senior U.S. government officials—apparently was sufficient to persuade New Delhi to refrain from taking military action against Pakistan. Key to the effort were explicit promises by Pakistani President Musharraf to U.S. Deputy Secretary of State Armitage that all infiltration of militants across the Line of Control and into Indian-held Kashmir would be halted.

05/02—**A terrorist attack on an Indian army base in Jammu and Kashmir killed 34**, mostly women and children. New Delhi blamed the attack on the "cross-border terrorism" of Pakistan-sponsored Islamic militants and vowed to fight a "decisive war."

02/02—After Muslims reportedly set fire to a train carrying Hindu activists, killing 58, **India's worst communal rioting in more than a decade** spread across the Gujarat state and resulted in the deaths of up to 2,000, mostly Muslims, at the hands of vengeful Hindu mobs. Human rights groups accused top state governmental leaders of abetting the violence.

12/01—**A terrorist attack on the Indian Parliament complex in New Delhi killed 14**. India blamed the attack on Pakistan-backed Kashmiri militants and began a massive military mobilization along the Pakistan-India frontier. Also in December, the United States designated two Pakistan-based militant groups—Lashkar-e-Taiba and Jaish-e-Mohammed—as Foreign Terrorist Organizations under U.S. law.

10/01—**A terrorist attack on the assembly building in India's Jammu and Kashmir state killed 34**. New Delhi blamed the attack on Pakistan-backed separatist militants.

09/01—After major terrorist attacks on the United States, **India offered its full support for U.S. counterterrorism efforts** in the region.

DOCUMENT NO. 30

TYPOLOGIES AND OPEN SOURCE REPORTING ON TERRORIST ABUSE OF CHARITABLE OPERATIONS IN POST-EARTHQUAKE PAKISTAN AND INDIA

U.S. Treasury

March 9, 2007

I. Statement of Purpose

Following the tragic October 2005 earthquake that affected Pakistan and India, international relief organizations, including U.S.-based charities, initiated a vigorous campaign to deliver relief to the victims in the region. With the onset of winter, these groups have accelerated their efforts to deliver emergency assistance to millions of people in urgent need. However, due to the remoteness of the areas most affected by the earthquake, weak to nonexistent government regulation or oversight of the charitable sector, and the ongoing presence of militant groups in the region, many U.S.-based charities and donors have expressed concern about the risk of terrorist abuse and diversion of charitable funds, assets, and services. These aid groups have also cited a need for information regarding the types of terrorist abuse that may occur and the terrorist groups that may be operating in the region so that they may better protect themselves from this ongoing threat. This paper addresses this need by: (i) identifying general typologies and examples of terrorist abuse and exploitation of charitable organizations, and (ii) describing the recent activities of militant groups and terrorist organizations in the region affected by the earthquake, as reported in open source channels.

Charities are encouraged to use this information in developing and applying reasonable measures to: (i) protect against terrorist abuse of earthquake relief efforts in Pakistan and India, and (ii) prevent directly or indirectly supporting terrorist organizations and their designated supporters that may be operating in areas where post-earthquake relief operations are underway. Although the percentage of charities directly affected by terrorist abuse may be small, terrorists continue to rely on the charitable sector as a primary source and conduit of terrorist support. This abuse threatens the integrity of the sector as a whole. This risk of terrorist abuse is especially high in the earthquake zone, making it crucial for charities funding or administering post-earthquake relief to take reasonable protective measures to ensure that their funds and services go to their intended beneficiaries.

The information contained in this paper is not exhaustive, nor is the specific reporting cited in this paper verified or endorsed by the U.S. Government. However, the U.S. Government believes this information is important in promoting the charitable sector's awareness and encouraging the sector to take reasonable responsive measures to protect against terrorist organizations and their supporters that may be active in the region. In addition to the information provided in this paper, the U.S. Government encourages charities to review the U.S. Department of the Treasury's *Anti-Terrorist Financing Guidelines: Voluntary Best Practices for U.S.-Based Charities* (Guidelines)[1] and adopt a risk-based approach that includes all reasonable protective measures against terrorist abuse as described in greater detail in the Guidelines.

II. Typologies of Terrorist Abuse of Charities

The charitable sector is one that has consistently faced a high risk of abuse from terrorists and terrorist organizations. Charities operating overseas in areas of high risk are especially vulnerable to this abuse. Since the terrorist attacks of September 11, 2001, the United States has designated forty-one charities worldwide for supporting terrorist activity.[2] In addition, the United States has designated several Foreign Terrorist Organizations (FTOs)[3] that have operated under various names that appear as potential fundraising front organizations for terrorist activity. Terrorist abuse of the charitable sector can take many forms, including:

(i) establishing front organizations or using charities to *raise funds* in support of terrorist organizations;

(ii) establishing or using charities to *transfer funds, other resources, and operatives* across geographical boundaries;

---

1 The U.S. Department of the Treasury recently revised the Guidelines and released them in December 2005. The Guidelines are available online at http://www.treas.gov/offices/enforcement/key-issues/protecting/docs/guidelines_charities.pdf.

2 *See* U.S. Department of the Treasury: Protecting Charitable Organizations, *at* http://www.treas.gov/offices/enforcement/key-issues/protecting/charities_exec-orders.shtml; *see also* U.S. Department of the Treasury Office of Foreign Assets Control, *at* http://www.treas.gov/offices/enforcement/ofac/actions/2003.shtml.

3 Section 302 of the Antiterrorism and Effective Death Penalty Act of 1996 (AEDPA) amended the Immigration and Nationality Act to authorize the Secretary of State, in consultation with the Attorney General and the Secretary of the Treasury, to designate organizations as "Foreign Terrorist Organizations" (FTOs). All designated FTOs have also been designated pursuant to Executive Order 13224 and are included on the U.S. Department of the Treasury's list of Specially Designated Nationals and Blocked Persons, which is maintained by the Office of Foreign Asset Controls, at http://www.treas.gov/offices/enforcement/ofac/sdn/.

(iii) defrauding charities through branch offices or aid workers to *divert funds* to support terrorist organizations; and

(iv) leveraging charitable funds, resources, and services to *recruit members and foster support* for terrorist organizations and their ideology;

The following typologies describe these instances of abuse in more detail.

1) Establishing Front Organizations or Using Charities to Raise Funds in Support of Terrorist Organizations

Terrorists or terrorist organizations may establish or use charities to raise funds directly for their operations. Many of the charities that have been designated as front organizations applied for and received tax-exempt status.[4] This cover of legitimacy often extends to the organization's operations, in which the asserted charitable activities are used to disguise funds that are raised for or transferred to terrorist support. Reports indicate that many of these charities engaged in aggressive fund raising, often targeted toward ethnic or religious communities.[5] Typically, fund-raising appeals describe the organization's purported charitable work in broad charitable terms, but provide sparse details of how funds are actually spent.

Example: The Holy Land Foundation for Relief and Development (HLF), originally known as the Occupied Land Fund, was established in California in 1989 as a tax-exempt charity and relocated to Texas in 1992. It had offices in California, New Jersey, and Illinois, and individual representatives spread throughout the United States, the West Bank, and Gaza. HLF provided millions of dollars of material and logistical support to HAMAS offices in the West Bank and Gaza and other charitable organizations that are part of HAMAS or controlled by HAMAS members. HLF and several of its directors were indicted on criminal charges in July 2004 and are awaiting trial in February 2006.[6]

Example: Jamal Muhammad Farah al-Tawil, Al-Islah Charitable Society's founder and chairman, was a high-ranking Hamas activist in the West Bank who was deported to south Lebanon in December 1992 and currently is in custody in Israel. He was formerly in contact with the Hamas leadership in Syria and Lebanon and regularly received payments from them through an Arab Bank account opened specifically for that purpose. He has stated in interrogations that he opened the Al-Islah Charitable Society branch in Ramallah to provide legal cover for transferring funds to Hamas. The Society provided financial aid to Hamas detainees and

[4] *See* Financial Action Task Force on Money Laundering, *Report on Money Laundering Typologies 2003–2004*, 8 [hereinafter FATF Report 2003-2004].

[5] *Id.*

[6] *See* U.S. Department of the Treasury, Additional Background Information on Charities Designated under Executive Order 13224, *at* http://www.treas.gov/offices/enforcement/key-issues/protecting/charities_execorder_13224-e.shtml#hlf.

their families and transferred funds to the heads of the terrorist infrastructure in Ramallah.[7] In June 2004, Israeli authorities closed down Al-Islah Charitable Society. The organization is no longer in operation.[8]

Example: A registered charity involved in child welfare used videotapes depicting religious "freedom fighters" in action in various countries, along with graphic images of atrocities perpetrated against members of that religion. The tapes appealed to viewers to send donations to a post office box number to help in the struggle. The charity distributed these tapes through religious establishments in the region. The same post office box number was associated with a further appeal in magazines that published articles by well known extremists.[9]

Example: A nonprofit organization solicited donations from local charities in a donor region in conjunction with fund raising efforts conducted at its headquarters in a beneficiary region. The nonprofit organization falsely asserted that it was collecting funds for orphans and widows. In fact, the finance chief of the organization served as the head of organized fund-raising for Usama bin Laden. The funds that the nonprofit organization collected were actually turned over to Al Qaeda operatives.[10]

2) Using Charities to Transfer Funds, Other Resources, and Operatives Across Geographical Boundaries

In addition to raising funds for terrorists, terrorist organizations may also exploit international charitable activity to transfer funds, resources, and operatives from one geographic location to another. Since the constant transfer of resources is part of normal business operations for many charities, they are highly vulnerable to this type of terrorist abuse.

Example: The group leader of the terrorist group Jaish-e-Mohammed, Mastoid Zahra, set up two organizations registered in Pakistan as humanitarian aid agencies: Al Akhtar Trust and Elkhart Trust. Jaish-e-Mohammed hoped to give the impression that the two new organizations were separate entities and sought to use them to deliver arms and ammunition to their members under the guise of providing humanitarian aid to refugees and other needy groups. These efforts included providing financial and logistical support as well as arranging travel for Islamic extremists. During a custodial interview in early 2003, a senior Al Qaeda detainee related that Al Akhtar Trust was one of the primary

[7] *See* http://www.intelligence.org.il/eng/sib/12_04/interpal_app_b.htm.

[8] See Israeli Army Shuts Down PLFP Offices in Nablus, Confiscates Contents, BBC MONITORING (June 11, 2004).

[9] *See* FATF Report 2003–2004, *supra* note 4, at 8–9.

[10] *See* Financial Action Task Force on Money Laundering, *Combating the Abuse of Non-Profit Organizations: International Best Practices*, 7 (Oct. 11, 2002) [hereinafter FATF Best Practices].

relief agencies that Al Qaeda used to move supplies into Qandahar, Afghanistan.[11]

3) Defrauding of Charities by Branch Offices or Aid Workers

Branch offices of charities may intentionally defraud headquarters or certain employees may use their positions at charities as cover for illicit terrorist activity.

Example: The office director for a branch office of a charity in a beneficiary region defrauded donors from a donor region for the purpose of funding terrorism. The branch office padded the number of orphans it claimed to care for by providing names of orphans that either did not exist or had died. The additional funds sent from headquarters to the branch office to care for these nonexistent orphans were diverted to Al Qaeda terrorists.[12]

Example: A branch office located in a beneficiary region provided a means of funneling money to known local terrorist organizations. It directed funds received from headquarters that were intended for orphanage projects and diverted those funds directly to local terrorists.[13]

Example: An employee working for an aid organization in a war-ravaged region used his employment to support the ongoing activities of a known terrorist organization from another region. While working for the aid organization as a monitor, the employee secretly made contact with weapons smugglers and used his employment as a cover while brokering and exporting weapons to the terrorist organization.[14]

4) Leveraging Charitable Funds, Other Resources, and Services to Recruit Members and Foster Support for Terrorist Organizations and Ideologies

Terrorist organizations will often engage in charitable activity. Usually, however, such charitable activity will be conducted in a manner that primarily furthers terrorist, rather than charitable purposes, in that it will be made available only to those sympathetic to the terrorist organization's cause, or will be coordinated with the terrorist organization's efforts to generate propaganda, increase recruitment and support, strengthen terrorist infrastructures, conduct training, enhance operational capacity, and execute attacks. Supporting charitable activity associated with terrorist organizations therefore foments continued violence and undermines peace initiatives and responsible leadership.

---

11 *See* Press Release, U.S. Department of the Treasury (Oct. 14, 2003), *available at* http://www.treas.gov/press/releases/js899.htm.
12 *See* FATF Best Practices, *supra* note 10, at 8.
13 *Id.*
14 *Id.*

Example: The designated terrorist entity Elehssan Society serves as the fundraising and distribution arm of Palestinian Islamic Jihad (PIJ), which the United States has designated a FTO. The organization continues to receive funding directly from PIJ. In February 2005, PIJ claimed responsibility for the February terrorist attack in Tel-Aviv, Israel, that killed five and wounded more than fifty people. In recent years, Elehssan has cooperated with PIJ to distribute funds to the families of PIJ prisoners and deceased members, and was informed by PIJ when entitlements were sent. Elehssan also maintains lists of PIJ-associated families who are to receive compensation, including the families of PIJ suicide bombers.[15]

Example: An Israeli military court charged Ahmed Salatna, a Hamas activist and director of a local charity in the West Bank town of Jenin, with directing nine million Euros over the last nine years to the families of Palestinian suicide bombers in the West Bank and Gaza. A portion of these funds was diverted from donations sent to Ahmed Salatna from the U.S.-designated Hamas front charity Interpal, which is based in the United Kingdom.[16]

Example: The senior leadership of Hezbollah continues to openly raise funds for its movement via charities and political advocacy organizations that are associated with or controlled by the group while simultaneously carrying out their mission of indoctrinating and recruiting jihadist sympathizers and supporters.[17] For instance, the leader of Hezbollah, Sheikh Hassan Nasrallah, frequently attends fundraisers and delivers speeches at charitable organizations, even as he issues statements advocating militancy, as he told a viewing audience on *Al Manar* television: "The intifada in Palestine today is our front line, so that our support is not only an obligation but also a necessity, and we have, therefore, taken it upon ourselves to aid the intifada, not only in words but in deeds."[18]

III. Open Source Reports of Recent Terrorist Activity in Pakistan and India

The following compilation of open source reports details the extent to which activity by militant groups and designated terrorist organizations occurs in the Pakistani and Indian earthquake zones. Such activity primarily involves leveraging charitable aid and resources to recruit support and membership for terrorist organizations and their ideology among victims of the earthquake.

[15] See U.S. Designates Charity as Front for Palestinian Terrorists: Treasury says Elehssan Society finances Palestinian Islamic Jihad, STATE NEWS SERVICE (May 4, 2005).
[16] See Silver, Eric, Charity Cash for Palestinian Poor Was Siphoned to Suicide Bombers, FINANCIAL TIMES (Nov. 28, 2005).
[17] See Hezbollah Stuck in 'Wooden-Speak' Rut: Hezbollah's Dilemma, TORONTO STAR (Nov. 9, 2003).
[18] *See* Al Manar Television (Feb. 1, 2002).

- Philp, Catherine, *Militant-linked Groups Fill Aid Gap*, The Australian (Oct. 18, 2005).

For many Kashmiri villagers who suffered from injuries and the destruction of their homes after the October 8 earthquake, help came in a strange form. Rescuers and aid workers were from Jamaat-ul-Dawa, one of the country's most prominent Islamic extremist groups and the parent organization of a U.S.-designated armed group, Lashkar-e-Taiba. Jamiat-i-Islami, an Islamic political party with ideological links to Hamas, is also running relief efforts, as is Al-Rasheed Trust, which the United States designated as a terrorist supporter in 2003. The relief efforts have done much to increase the groups' standing in the community. Those who have benefited from the groups' rescue efforts seem unconcerned by any suggestion they may be involved in violence. "If Dawa people hadn't helped us, we would have died," Mrs Wahid said. "Nobody came to help us. We are grateful to them and we offer them our support back."

- Laila Bokhari, *Political Struggle Over Earthquake Victims*, Norwegian Defense Research Establishment (Nov. 23, 2005).

In the months since the earthquake struck South Asia, militant groups like Lashkar-e-Taiba and Jaish-e-Mohammed, both of which have been banned by the Pakistani government, have actively provided humanitarian aid to the affected areas. Jaish-e-Mohammed members have trekked across harsh terrain on donkeys to reach isolated areas and provide water, food, and medicine. Both groups also offer housing and are planning for reconstruction of mosques and schools. Other groups, such as Hizb-ul-Mujahideen, have been running large soup kitchens and collecting money in several major Pakistani cities to benefit earthquake victims. Moreover, Islami Inquilabi Mahaz, which took responsibility for the October 30 New Delhi attacks and is currently aiding the relief efforts, has stated that they intend to demonstrate that they are still an active group, despite suffering major losses from the earthquake.

Jamaat-ul-Dawa, one of the largest jihadist groups operating in Pakistan and one that is also providing humanitarian assistance to the impacted areas, has offered orphaned children "an escape from misery through a religious education." Local aid organizations operating in the earthquake zone have observed members of Jamaat-ul-Dawa take away young children to care for them. The article notes that these groups have actively recruited children in the past.

Pakistani President Musharraf has admitted that these militant groups have exploited the fact that authorities have failed to respond adequately to humanitarian needs and that Pakistani authorities would be cautious about stopping anyone from providing assistance.

- *Terror Groups Train PoK Orphans for Militancy in J-K*, The Sunday Times (Nov. 13, 2005).

Pakistan's leading human rights organization, Ansar Burney Welfare Trust, has claimed that Pakistan-based militant groups that are active in Jammu and Kashmir are taking orphans of the October 8 earthquake off the streets and putting them in training camps. The organization also claims it has evidence that sympathetic government officials have been giving children to the militant groups. Jamaat-ud-Dawa, one of the largest militant groups in Pakistan, has called for orphans to be handed over for an Islamic education. Although the popularity of Islamic militants has risen sharply due to their relief activities after the earthquake struck, human rights campaigners allege that the militants are using this newfound popularity to smuggle weapons and increase recruitment efforts. http://www.timesonline.co.uk/article/0,,2089-1869841,00.html

- Kremmer, Christopher, *Charities Linked to Extremists Lead Quake Relief*, Age (Nov. 21, 2005).

In addition to relief efforts in which many militant groups are engaging, the militants are reportedly taking orphaned children under their wing for indoctrination in their extensive network of orphanages. Offering work to some of the million people estimated by the International Labour Organization to have lost their livelihoods due to the quake will likely be another route to recruitment.

http://www.theage.com.au/news/world/charities-linked-to-extremists-lead-quake-relief/2005/11/20/1132421545811.html#

- *Monitorial Observation on Appearance of Quake Relief Ads by Militant Groups in Mainstream Urdu Press*, FBIS Report (Oct. 25, 2005).

Following the October earthquake that affected South Asia, mainstream Pakistani media has been publishing the same advertisements as the jihadi publications. These ads generally seek funds to support the relief efforts launched by militant organizations: (i) On October 14, the conservative Islamic daily, Rawalpindi Nawa-e Waqt, published a front page ad by Jamaat ul-Dawa (JD), a group banned by the Pakistani government in January 2002, which included contact information and details on how to contribute; (ii) on October 15, the same daily, Nawa-e Waqt, published a front page appeal for donations by Al Rashid Trust, which the United States has designated as a terrorist supporter but which currently functions openly in Pakistan; (iii) on October 19, Nawa e-Waqt carried a picture of a convoy of trucks used by Al Rashid Trust to move relief supplies; and (iv) on October 19, a widely circulated daily, Rawalpindi Jang carried a front page advertisement by Al Rashid Trust stating that the group had established an initial relief fund of 5 million rupees (approximately $84,000) and wanted further donations to support additional relief work.

- Yasin, Asim, *Rehabilitation of Quake-affected Kashmir*, The News (Dec. 4, 2005).

The federal government of Pakistan has sought cooperation from all political parties of Azad Jammu and Kashmir for the rehabilitation and reconstruction of the people and villages devastated by the October earthquake. The Minister for Kashmir Affairs and Northern Areas, Makhdoom Syed Faisal Salah Hayat, has praised religious groups, including Jamaat ul-Dawa and Al-Rasheed Trust, for their relief efforts and has stated that in the future these organizations would be included as part of official reconstruction efforts.

- *Banned Outfits and Welfare Organizations Remain Active in Relief Activities*, Islamabad Ausaf (Oct. 21, 2005).

Banned jihadi groups and welfare organizations have played a very active role in the relief and rescue activities in quake-affected areas. They have been transporting relief goods to remote areas since the earthquake struck. The groups that are working in the area include Jamaat ul-Dawa, Al Rasheed Trust, Al Akhtar Trust, Al Furqan Trust, Amina Welfare Trust, Islamic Relief Council, Jamaat-e Islami, Al Khidmat, students from Lal Mosque of Islamabad, and Jamiat Afridia.

- Walsh, Declan, *Pakistani Extremists Take Lead on Earthquake Disaster Aid: International Relief Agencies Are Only Beginning To Arrive*, Chronicle Foreign Service (Oct. 17, 2005).

Jamaat ul-Dawa (JD), the parent organization of Lashkar-e-Taiba, has moved to the forefront of a growing relief operation for survivors of the October 8 earthquake in Pakistan and Kashmir. A spokesman for JD, Salman Shahid, gave a tour of the field hospital the group has set up. The group has diesel generators that power X-ray equipment, a dental department, ambulances, and rows of tents. Shahid stated, "Everything is funded by private donations. We even have surplus supplies of food and medicine." Armed men wearing camouflage guard the trucks that bring supplies, because in the initial days after the earthquake, JD's aid supplies were looted.

JD has positioned itself as a countrywide Islamic development group. JD runs madrassas (schools), provides free medical care to the poor, and dispatches preachers to mosques across the country. Some diplomats and security officials claim that JD uses its charitable operations to recruit young men willing to fight an anti-Indian jihad in Kashmir. Despite this claim, people who are currently receiving relief assistance from the group praise the charitable work that JD performs, saying that its good work puts Musharraf's government to shame. "There is only government in name," said quake victim Abdul Majid. "They hold press conferences in Islamabad but do nothing on the ground." http://sfgate.com/cgi-bin/article.cgi?file=/c/a/2005/10/17/MNGJEF9G 0M1.DTL

- Yusufzai, Ashfaq, *Pakistan: Militants Gain Legitimacy Through Quake Relief*, IPS (Nov. 28, 2005).

Pakistan President General Pervez Musharraf has admitted publicly that "an administrative vacuum created by the civil administration (immediately after the earthquake) has thus been filled by militant organizations." Soon after the earthquake, Pakistanis, including thousands of volunteers, had begun collecting donations and rushing to the troubled areas to see how they could help. However, voluntary activities soon lost steam because of a lack of funds and coordination, and it was only the militant organizations that could maintain the momentum of relief activity.

The militant groups have set up mobile hospitals, established tented villages, and built an orphanage on land acquired close to Rawalpindi, Pakistan's military hub. Jamaat ul-Dawa, one of the primary militant groups providing relief aid, has also been distributing essentials, ranging from crutches for the crippled, tents, and hard cash. There is a fear by some that the militant groups will use the opportunity of helping to care for orphans to increase their recruitment. http://www.ipsnews.net/news.asp?idnews=31203

- Narayanswamy, Anupama, *Charity Tied to Terrorist Group Offers Quake Aid*, The Washington Times (Oct. 13, 2005).

A Muslim charity linked to Kashmiri terrorists sent truckloads of relief goods yesterday to northern Pakistan's earthquake-hit region, in what it described as a new "jihad" or holy war to help victims of the devastating earthquake. There is concern that the militants' relief assistance might provide an opportunity to win broad support for their cause. "If the government is slow in helping, and the militants are helping them, the sympathy levels for the militants' cause could become higher," said Miriam Rajkumar, South Asia specialist at the Carnegie Endowment for International Peace.

- *Al Qaeda's Zawahri Urges Muslim Aid to Quake Victims*, Reuters (Oct. 23, 2005).

Al Qaeda's second in command, Ayman al-Zawahri, urged Muslims in a video broadcast to help Pakistan's earthquake victims even though Pakistan's government was an "agent" of the United States: "I call on all Muslims and Islamic charity organizations in particular to go to Pakistan and give a helping hand to the victims there." http://www.alertnet.org/thenews/newsdesk/L23357407.htm

- *Jihadis Become Aid Workers in Kashmir Quake Zone*, Agence France Presse (Oct. 18, 2005).

Members of militant groups Hizb ul-Mujahideen and Jamaat-ul-Dawa, an offshoot of Lashkar-e-Taiba, which the United States has designated as a terrorist organization, are playing a vital role in the ongoing earthquake relief efforts around Muzaffarabad, Kashmir. Within hours after the earthquake struck, the militants headed for the mountains and brought aid to heavily damaged villages.

- Wilkinson, Isambard, *Islamist Groups Win Support for Pakistan Quake Aid*, THE DAILY TELEGRAPH (NOV. 2, 2005).

Islamic groups are widely regarded as having provided the most efficient aid operations in some areas after the Pakistan earthquake struck in Kashmir and the North West Frontier Province (NWFP). The best organized aid relief came from groups such as Pakistan's main radical Islamic party, Jamaat i-Islami, Lashkar-e-Taiba, and Hizb ul-Mujahideen. Several Islamist groups have been praised by normally hostile sectors of the Pakistani media for providing aid relief. In addition, British and American soldiers are now providing aid for earthquake victims in the same areas as Islamic groups such as the al-Rasheed Trust, which the Bush administration has designated for channeling funds to Al Qaeda.

- Lancaster, John & Kamran Khan, *Extremists Fill Aid Chasm after Quake*, WASHINGTON POST (Oct. 16, 2005).

Militant groups have maintained a visible presence in Muzaffarabad and the surrounding Kashmiri region since the October 8 earthquake struck. Groups that have ongoing relief operations include Jamaat ul-Dawa, the charitable wing of Jamiat-i-Islami, and Al Rasheed Trust. These groups' visible relief work is effective and has bolstered their prestige in the community, possibly at the expense of Gen. Pervez Musharraf, Pakistan's president, and the army, whose initial response was widely criticized as slow and disorganized. One victim who was receiving aid from a mobile hospital set up by Jamaat ul-Dawa stated that he did not know or care if the group was involved in violence, and further said, "Every 10 minutes a doctor or medical attendant comes in to check on me. I have a very high opinion about this organization." http://www.washingtonpost.com/wp-dyn/content/article/2005/10/15/AR2005101501392.html

- Baid, Samuel, *Terrorists Wear a Human Mask in PoK*, DAILY EXCELSIOR (NOV. 10, 2005).

Banned terrorist and charity organizations are taking advantage of inefficient government relief operations to help villagers and rehabilitate their image. The terrorist groups providing relief aid include Jaish-e-Mohammad and Lashkar-e-Taiba, while banned Islamic charities include Al Rashid Trust, Al Akhtar Trust, and Ummah Tamir-e-Nau. The article questions where these banned organizations are getting their funds and relief goods, and it notes that there have been many complaints from unidentified people of looting of relief goods. One report alleged looting of relief goods by the Pakistan Army, which the article contends is the main supporter of the terrorist groups now providing relief aid in the affected areas.

DOCUMENT NO. 31

INDIA AND PAKISTAN ENGAGEMENT: PROSPECTS FOR BREAKTHROUGH OR BREAKDOWN?

United States Institute of Peace (USIP)
Special Report 129

January 2005

About the Report

While much depends upon the nascent peace process between India and Pakistan, there are many reasons to believe that the prospects for a breakdown are greater than those for a breakthrough. To assess such prospects, the United States Institute of Peace convened a roundtable of South Asia experts. This Special Report, written by program officer Christine Fair of the Institute's Research and Studies Program, draws upon the roundtable discussions, as well as interviews with other regional analysts—particularly Shahid Javed Burki, Stephen Cohen, Husain Haqqani, Dennis Kux, Polly Nayak, Terasita Schaffer, Ashley Tellis, and Marvin Weinbaum.

This Special Report considers means by which the India-Pakistan peace process can be sustained in at least a minimally positive way. In particular, the report explores the utility of the United States in ensuring the momentum of this opening; it also considers the role for other key players in the area, such as Russia and China.

The views expressed in this report do not necessarily reflect those of the United States Institute of Peace, which does not advocate specific policy positions.

About the Institute

The United States Institute of Peace is an independent, nonpartisan federal institution created by Congress to promote the prevention, management, and peaceful resolution of international conflicts. Established in 1984, the Institute meets its congressional mandate through an array of programs, including research grants, fellow-ships, professional training, education programs from high school through graduate school, conferences and workshops, library services, and publications. The Institute's Board of Directors is appointed by the President of the United States and confirmed by the Senate.

Summary

- Over the past year, India and Pakistan have been taking tentative steps toward improving their bilateral relations. The foreign ministers of both countries met in early September to review the progress made on the Indo-Pakistani "roadmap to peace," which the two sides agreed on in mid-February. While still deeply divided over the issue of Kashmir and in agreement that the tangible outcomes have been minimal to date, both reaffirmed their commitment to the ongoing process. Despite changes in India's leadership, this process is still lumbering forward.
- This emerging détente is worthy of attention for several reasons. First, South Asia is the only region in the world where two nuclear-armed neighbors are in active conflict; the most recent crisis came during 2001–2002, when close to a million troops faced off for nearly a year along the Indo-Pakistani border. Second, Pakistan is a critical—if imperfect—partner

in the global War on Terror. The United States wants to ensure Pakistan's active support in counterterrorism activities along the Pakistan-Afghanistan border and within Pakistan. Third, one of the few means that Pakistan has developed to coerce concessions from India has been the use of militants—generations of which Islamabad has nurtured to secure Pakistan's interests in Kashmir and Afghanistan. These so-called mujahideen threaten the security of South Asia and beyond.

- Given the complexities and challenges facing both states, what motivated both to undertake this process? Observers generally agree that both India and Pakistan were confronting several internal political changes during this initial period of rapprochement, and that the commencement of this process reflected both countries' internal political dynamics. For India's part, the past two years of sustained dissonance with Islamabad has strained its ability to continue an internal dialogue with the various groups in Kashmir. Further, the ongoing discord with Islamabad has frustrated India's efforts to improve its economic growth and expand its political influence beyond South Asia. India understands that the resolution of this conflict will be necessary to achieve its ultimate goal of becoming an important global power.

- Regarding Pakistan's motives, some analysts suggested that this initiative would give both Pakistan's armed forces and the militants a much-needed respite from the last two years of persistent confrontation. Although Pakistan has endured its standoff with India, it has also confronted numerous threats along its border with Afghanistan, and its own internal security environment continues to deteriorate. Sectarian violence and organized criminal activity have racked Pakistan's commercial and financial hub, Karachi, for decades with no relief in sight. Domestically, May 2004 was Pakistan's bloodiest month since Pervez Musharraf came to power in 1999.

- Both India and Pakistan were also believed to have undertaken this peace offensive with the United States and other international actors as the main intended audience. The 2001–02 crisis rattled nerves in Washington and beyond as the two nuclear-armed enemies wavered on the brink of war. Following the 1998 nuclear tests and the 1999 Kargil crisis, the confrontation of 2001–02 left the United States and others weary of playing referee in these recurrent conflicts. In addition to both states' incentives for normalization of relations, there is an increasing tendency within U.S. and international circles to press for a *resolution* of the conflict rather than just its *management*. More active mediation or facilitation by the United States would be welcomed in Pakistan, which has long sought international intervention in this dispute. India would likely resist such overtures, maintaining that this is a strictly bilateral issue, as enshrined in the 1972 Shimla Accord.

- Although the grounds for optimism are tangible, there are equally compelling reasons to be doubtful about a settlement of the Indo-Pakistani dispute in the near future, the most fundamental of which is the inherent asymmetry of desired objectives with respect to the disposition of Kashmir: India seeks to engage Pakistan to legitimize the territorial status quo by finding some means to formalize the Line of Control (LOC) in Kashmir as the legal international border. Pakistan seeks to engage India to find some means of altering, in various ways, the status quo and publicly rejects the possibility of transforming the LOC into the international border as a viable means of dispute resolution.
- Both countries' internal constraints also do not bode well for a fundamentally new approach to resolving their conflict. On balance, the political and security dynamic in Pakistan is not comforting, suggesting that even if India is able to accommodate Pakistan's demand on *process*, it is far from obvious that Islamabad would be capable of packaging this and marketing it to its citizens and other stakeholders (the army, for example) as a form of "progress" on Pakistan's core concerns. This factor is a central element in keeping Pakistan engaged in the process and creating a public demand for a just peace. In addition, a *resolution* of the Kashmir issue means that Pakistan's extensive and formidable militant infrastructure would have to be dismantled.
- India also has a number of domestic compulsions of its own: it is a rich and vibrant—if imperfect—democracy, and reaching consensus on contentious issues such as relations with Pakistan can be perhaps even more of a challenge in its diverse and active polity. Since the Kargil crisis and the ongoing attacks within Indian-administered Kashmir and within India proper, many Indians have grown weary of Pakistan's tactics. Hard-liners feel that they should not have to reward Pakistan for ceasing activities that Islamabad should not have started in the first place. The results of India's April–May 2004 general elections have also added an additional layer of uncertainty to this analysis: the electorate dismissed the Bharitya Janata Party (BJP)—the party that spearheaded the recent peace overture. Although the new Congress Party government affirmed its commitment to the peace process, it is far from certain that it has the domestic clout to continue the engagement.
- If history is any guide, the likelihood that this process will break down is high, and the probability of a meaningful breakthrough is quite slim. USIP roundtable participants agreed that the outcome of this round of engagement ultimately will turn on the understanding held by New Delhi and by Islamabad on the core issues of the engagement and the concomitant progress made on each. Many participants felt that while breakthrough is certainly not likely, neither is a breakdown of the kind

witnessed after the 1999 Lahore Declaration, whose resulting engagement suffered many onslaughts, the ultimate of which was the Kargil offensive in the spring of 1999. In light of these considerations, the roundtable participants generally concurred that stalemate is the most likely outcome of the current engagement process.

Introduction

Over the past year, India and Pakistan have been taking tentative steps toward improving their bilateral relations. The foreign ministers of both countries met in early September 2004 to review the progress that has been made thus far. While still deeply divided over the issue of Kashmir and in agreement that the tangible outcomes have been minimal to date, both reaffirmed their commitment to the ongoing process. This opening began when India's then–prime minister Atal Vajpayee met with Pakistan's president Pervez Musharraf on the sidelines of a January 2004 regional summit. Later, in mid-February, India and Pakistan agreed on a six-month "roadmap to peace," which ostensibly would address all outstanding bilateral concerns. Despite changes in India's leadership, this process is still lumbering forward.

This emerging détente is worthy of attention for several reasons. First, South Asia is the only region in the world where two nuclear armed-neighbors are in active conflict. Their most recent crisis was in 2001–2002, when the two wavered on the brink of war for nearly a year, with more than one million troops lined up across the Indo-Pakistan border. Finding some means to resolve—rather than manage—their bilateral dispute is crucial to minimizing the likelihood of conventional conflict between the two and the possibility of either country's resorting to "the nuclear option."

Second, Pakistan is a critical—if imperfect—partner in the global War on Terror. The United States wants to ensure Pakistan's active support in counterterrorism activities along the Pakistan-Afghanistan border and within Pakistan. Consequently, the United States was disconcerted by the strategic distraction posed by the near war of 2001–02 as Islamabad swung some of its forces from the Pakistan-Afghanistan border to defensive positions along the border with India.

Third, one of the few means that Pakistan has developed to coerce concessions from India has been the use of militants—generations of which Islamabad has nurtured to fight Pakistan's proxy wars in Kashmir and Afghanistan. Consequently, Pakistan has established an expansive infrastructure to recruit, train, and deploy militants organized under various Islamist rubrics. These so-called mujahideen threaten the security of South Asia and beyond. Once trained, these militants ostensibly could operate anywhere in the world given adequate logistical support. Therefore, Pakistan's militants are not simply a regional problem, but potentially a threat with global reach—members of one of Kashmir's main militant groups, Lashkar-e-Taiba, were recently arrested in Basra, Iraq.

Background: A Bitter Past of Failure

Since their overt nuclearization in 1998, India and Pakistan attempted to make peace three times—including this most recent effort. In 1998 and 1999, optimism soared as the two adversaries embarked upon a much-lauded "bus diplomacy" campaign, culminating in the historic visit of Indian prime minister Vajpayee to Pakistan and the penning of an important agreement with his Pakistani counterpart Nawaz Sharif. Speaking beneath the Minar-e-Pakistan, a monument in Lahore commemorating the founding of Pakistan, Vajpayee signaled to many Pakistanis that India finally recognizes the legitimacy of the Pakistani state. The statement was doubly important because Vajpayee's base of support was among Hindu nationalists, who historically espoused the goal of "Akand Bharat," or a "greater India" that includes Pakistan. Such rhetoric naturally has fueled Pakistan's persistent belief that India desires the collapse of the state.

A Brief History of Kashmir

As British India was partitioned into Muslim Pakistan and Hindu India in 1947 as part of the independence process, Britain allowed the nominal rulers of the subcontinent's "princely states" (essentially tax collectors for the British Crown) to decide their allegiance to either of the new, independent countries. The Hindu ruler of Kashmir did not decide until the following year, when he acceded to India's rule in exchange for an Indian force that halted an invasion by Pakistani "tribesmen" and established a de facto partition, known as the Line of Control, dividing the geostrategically important region into Pakistani-controlled and Indian-controlled portions.

India then took the Kashmir issue to the UN Security Council, which passed a resolution in 1948 requesting Pakistan to withdraw its "tribesmen" from the area and that a plebiscite be conducted to determine Kashmiris' desires for rule. Neither action has been taken to date.

In the 1962 Indo-Chinese border war, the People's Republic of China occupied the northwestern Ladakh region of Kashmir. Three years later, India and Pakistan fought another border war, which stretched to the Line of Control. A UN-brokered cease-fire agreement was affirmed by India and Pakistan at a 1966 summit.

Following the Indo-Pakistani conflict of 1971, India's Indira Gandhi and Pakistan's Zulfikar Ali Bhutto signed the 1972 Shimla Accord, agreeing "to settle their differences by peaceful means through bilateral negotiations or by any other peaceful means mutually agreed upon between them." They affirmed that neither will try to unilaterally alter the Line of Control.

In the late 1980s, militancy increased in Kashmir, as the Soviet Union withdrew from Afghanistan and many mujahideen relocated to Kashmir with support from the Pakistani government. The territorial conflict was increasingly infused with religious ideology, as mujahideen in Kashmir viewed the conflict as a "jihad." At the same time, Hindu nationalism continued to gain strength in the Indian heartland.

Violence rose in Kashmir during the 1990s, as Pakistani-supported Islamic militants launched sporadic assaults on non-Muslims, who fled mainly to the southern Jammu region. India responded with repression. Both sides were accused of mass human rights abuses. In 1998, the Hindu fundamentalist Bharitya Janata Party came to power; both India and Pakistan declared themselves nuclear powers after conducting overt weapons tests. The following year, Indian prime minister Atal Behari Vajpayee met with his Pakistani counterpart, Nawaz Sharif, in Lahore; three months later, Pakistan-based militants invaded Kargil in the Indian-controlled portion of Kashmir. President Clinton convinced Sharif to withdraw Pakistani forces from Kargil; Sharif was overthrown by General Pervez Musharraf, the chief advocate of the Kargil offensive, shortly thereafter.

On October 1, 2001, a terrorist attack on the Kashmir legislature in Srinagar left 38 dead. Two months later, 14 were killed in a terrorist attack on the Indian parliament on December 13; India responded by massing hundreds of thousands of troops on the Pakistani border, including along the Line of Control.

More than 30 people were killed in another terrorist attack on the families of Indian troops in Kashmir on May 14, 2002. In response to India's announcement of retaliation, Pakistan hinted at the use of nuclear weapons. U.S. diplomats managed to defuse the crisis, and Pakistan pledged to stop cross-border infiltration.

Despite the promise of progress signaled by the Lahore engagement, all hopes were dashed upon the Himalayan peaks of Kargil in the spring of 1999: Pakistan launched a limited territorial war in the Kargil-Dras sectors of Kashmir under the military leadership of Chief of Army Staff Pervez Musharraf. Many believe that the planning for this operation was concurrent with the Lahore Peace Process, confirming many Indians' conviction that Pakistan is inherently duplicitous and an unworthy negotiation partner. This belief in Pakistani perfidy was exacerbated when the chief advocate of the Kargil offensive, General Musharraf, executed a bloodless coup and deposed Prime Minister Sharif.

Despite tremendous Indian misgivings and mistrust, both sides again tried to make peace in July 2001 in the Indian city of Agra. Few were optimistic

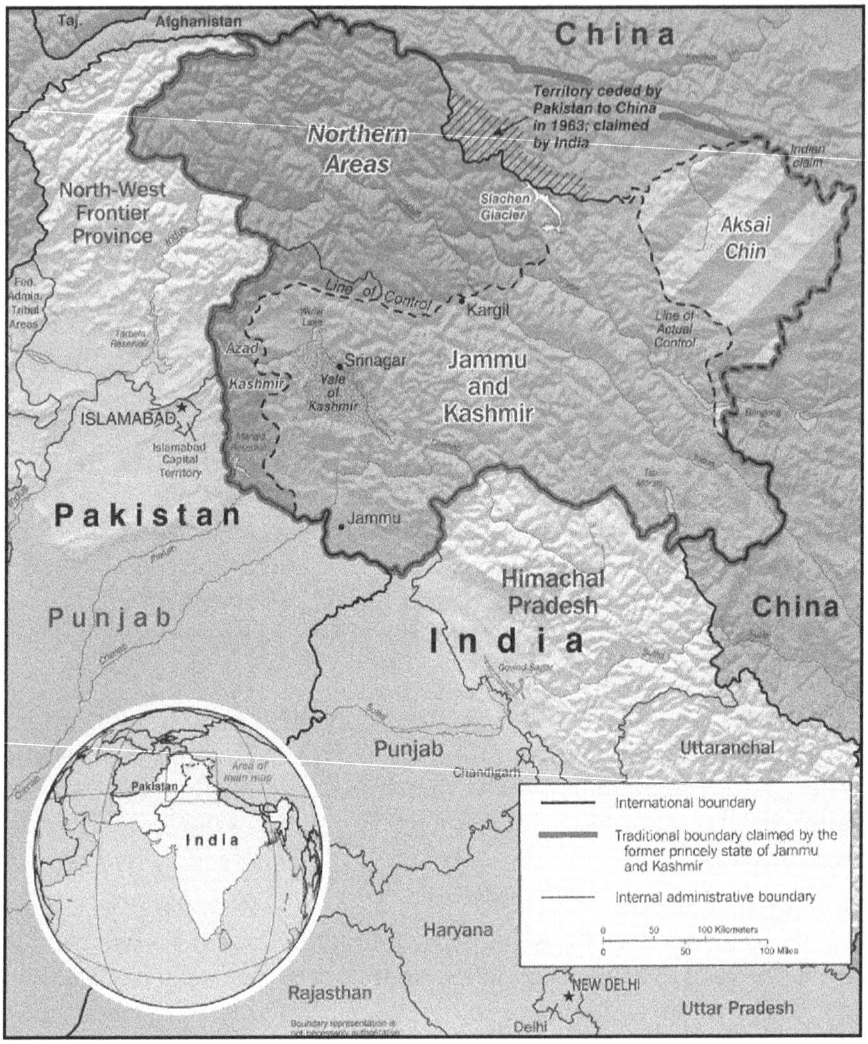

The Kashmir Region

about the prospects for that effort as neither side could even agree on how to describe the central issues of their dispute. In the run-up to the summit, the Indian government expressed concern about how Indian protocol would handle a visit by a Pakistani chief executive, which was unprecedented. Musharraf rendered this concern moot by declaring himself president. The Agra summit broke down amid mutual recriminations and disappointment without so much as a joint statement or a commitment to reconvene discussions at a later time.

With two recent disappointing failures under their belts, both states again are attempting to forge peace. This current round began in early January 2004, when Vajpayee traveled to Pakistan to participate in a summit convened by the South Asian Association for Regional Cooperation (SAARC).

While speculation was rife that Vajpayee would meet with Musharraf on the sidelines, neither confirmed or denied the rumors until a meeting was imminent. On January 5, the two heads of state met in what the Indian Foreign Office deemed a "courtesy call." This was the first formal encounter between the two leaders since the failed Agra Summit of 2001.

The event was significant because it signaled a formal end of a ten-month crisis that unfolded following the December 2001 terrorist attack on the Indian parliament and another terrorist attack on family members of Indian troops in Kashmir's Kaluchak in May 2002. New Delhi alleged that the perpetrators were militant groups backed by Islamabad and responded with a massive mobilization of forces along India's border with Pakistan. In turn, Pakistani troops were amassed to check the Indian deployments. With more than a million soldiers confronting each other along their shared border, India and Pakistan were in a near state of war that persisted through October 2002.

Given the level of bitterness and distrust that permeated Indo-Pakistani relations, this meeting between Vajpayee and Musharraf has generated considerable optimism among international observers. Yet many questions loom about the durability of this nascent process and its prospects for even limited degrees of success.

Many South Asia analysts are doubtful that substantive progress is likely in large part because the desired outcomes of India and Pakistan are fundamentally at odds: Pakistan seeks a means to engage India to *alter* the status quo with regard to the disputed disposition of Kashmir. In other words, Pakistan does not accept the current de facto border (the Line of Control, or LOC) that divides the disputed territory of Kashmir into distinct portions administered by Pakistan and India. India, conversely, seeks a negotiation process that will eventually *ratify* the status quo in Kashmir, principally through transforming the LOC into the international border. In the absence of significant change in these tightly held positions, it is difficult to envision meaningful progress being made toward sustainable settlement. These conflicting objectives are discussed in greater length below.

Motives for Moving Toward Peace Now

Given the complexities and challenges facing both states, what motivated both to undertake this process? Several prominent analysts believe India had the initiative throughout: Prime Minister Vajpayee consented to participate in the SAARC summit in Islamabad, but he provided no assurances that either discussions with Musharraf or renewed bilateral talks with Pakistan were on the table. Brajesh Mishra, Vajpayee's trusted national security adviser, laid the groundwork for a potential meeting between

Musharraf and Vajpayee. The SAARC summit was well underway before the Indian side announced its consent to a bilateral meeting. Many believe that the Indians were responding to the noticeably different tone used by Pakistani prime minister Mir Zafarullah Jamali at the summit, where he refrained from criticizing India. This likely reflected a conscious decision on behalf of Islamabad to signal to New Delhi its willingness to engage India constructively.

Observers generally agree that both India and Pakistan were confronting several internal political changes during this initial period of rapprochement, and that the commencement of this process reflected both countries' internal political dynamics. For India's part, the past two years of sustained dissonance with Islamabad has strained its ability to continue an internal dialogue with the various groups in Kashmir. Such normalizing of relations between Srinagar (the political epicenter of Kashmir) and New Delhi is fundamental to bringing about some degree of peace to the embattled valley. Further, the ongoing discord with Islamabad has frustrated India's efforts to improve its economic growth and expand its political influence beyond South Asia. India understands that the resolution of this conflict will be necessary to achieve its ultimate goal of becoming an important global power.

Some observers were cynical about India's opening to Islamabad and dismissed it as a mere tactical move to woo the country's Muslim electorate and ensure a victory for Vajpayee's Bharitya Janata Party (BJP) in spring 2004. Others, more optimistically, believed that Prime Minister Vajpayee was truly a man of peace who genuinely sought to end his career with a major breakthrough with India's long-standing nemesis.

Pakistan's motives are even more shrouded in uncertainty. Some analysts suggested that this initiative would give both Pakistan's armed forces and the militants a much-needed respite from the past two years of persistent confrontation. Although Pakistan has endured its standoff with India, it has also confronted numerous threats along its border with Afghanistan, and its own internal security environment continues to deteriorate. Sectarian violence and organized criminal activity have racked Pakistan's commercial and financial hub, Karachi, for decades with no relief in sight. Domestically, May 2004 was Pakistan's bloodiest month since Pervez Musharraf came to power in 1999.

Both India and Pakistan were also believed to have undertaken this peace offensive with the United States and other international actors as the main intended audience. The 2001–02 crisis rattled nerves in Washington and beyond as the two nuclear-armed enemies wavered on the brink of war. Following the 1998 nuclear tests and the 1999 Kargil crisis, the confrontation of 2001–02 left the United States and others weary of playing referee in these recurrent conflicts.

Reasons to Be Hopeful?

The confluence of motives for Indo-Pakistan détente suggests there is room for guarded optimism. Both countries have a stake in normalization. Commentators within Pakistan maintain that since coming to power in 1999, Musharraf has come to appreciate the toll Pakistan's policies have taken on its social, political, and economic development. They argue moreover that Pakistan's reliance on Islamist militant proxies poses greater risks to the integrity of the Pakistani state than it does to the Indian state; this argument has become more salient in the post–9/11 world. Many observers recognize that without a workable settlement with India, Pakistan will be unlikely to abandon its strategic reliance on proxy elements. Finding ways of dismantling militancy in Pakistan is beginning to gain traction among some circles, creating constituencies for conflict resolution.

India also would prefer to redirect the energy and resources it invests in the confrontation with Pakistan and use them to pursue its long-sought-after quest for great-power status. Because achieving these objectives requires resolution of Kashmir and all other significant outstanding concerns with Pakistan, India is motivated to find some means of putting these issues in the past as a prerequisite for a more promising future.

In addition to both states' incentives for normalization of relations, there is an increasing tendency within U.S. and international circles to press for a *resolution* of the conflict rather than just its *management*. Many policymakers and analysts openly question how long the United States and the international community are willing and able to play "crisis manager," suggesting a requirement for resolution rather than management.

More active mediation or facilitation by the United States would be welcomed in Pakistan, which has long sought international intervention in this dispute. India would likely resist such overtures, maintaining that this is a strictly bilateral issue, as enshrined in the 1972 Shimla Accord. Yet India's position has not prevented it from using the United States to coerce desired behavior from Islamabad. Many note that this use is tantamount to a form of intervention and exposes the contradiction between what India says and what it does. Further, this reliance may represent some degree of willingness to permit some form of "facilitation"—a term that India prefers to mediation.

Despite Indian opposition, advocates of the conflict's resolution rightly point out that even if the *nature* of the dispute is bilateral, the *consequences* of any major conflict between the two states undoubtedly will be far reaching. In the event of a nuclear exchange (whether by accident or by design) the region will be severely affected and the international community will have to mobilize and deploy vast resources to address the humanitarian crisis following what would be the postwar era's first nuclear war. Thus a resolution of the conflict is of concern to the international community at large and merits third-party facilitation (or some other substitute form of mediation).

Even More Reasons to Be Doubtful

Although the grounds for optimism are tangible, there are equally compelling reasons to be doubtful about a settlement of the Indo-Pakistani dispute in the near future, the most fundamental of which is the inherent asymmetry of desired objectives with respect to the disposition of Kashmir. In addition to this basic barrier to a breakthrough, both states have their own internal constraints and problems that may well frustrate the prospects for a fundamentally new approach to resolving their conflict. Each of these concerns will be discussed below.

Objectives of Engagement Are Structurally in Conflict

India and Pakistan disagree over the centrality of the Kashmir dispute in their historically bitter relations. For Pakistan, Kashmir is a pivotal dispute that precludes normalization with India. New Delhi is loath to concede that there is even a valid dispute over Kashmir, claiming that the 1947 accession of the Princely State of Kashmir to India during Partition is as an indisputable fact; thus it prefers to place the Kashmir-related tensions within a basket of several other issues—the so-called "composite dialogue." Indeed, one of the central problems that has undermined past Indo-Pakistani détente efforts has been the simple fact that both states approach the issue for reasons that are in fundamental conflict:

- India seeks to engage Pakistan to legitimize the territorial status quo by finding some means to formalize the LOC as the legal international border. Thus for India, the status quo is a basis for a solution to the ongoing dispute over the disposition of Kashmir.
- Pakistan seeks to engage India to find some means of altering, in various ways, the status quo and publicly rejects the possibility of transforming the LOC into the international border as a viable means of dispute resolution. For Pakistan the status quo is the problem, not the solution to the problem.

These diametrically opposed objectives are typically reflected in the ways in which both states engage each other. For example, Pakistan historically has sought to place the Kashmir issue at the top of the bilateral agenda. As the weaker state, Pakistan cannot surrender the primacy of the Kashmir issue because it fears that it may never be resolved. Or, worse yet, Pakistan fears that the dispute over Kashmir may be permanently deferred while India seeks a separate peace with the Kashmiris; such an accord between New Delhi and Srinagar could be presented to Islamabad as a fait accompli, with the expectation that Islamabad simply acquiesces. Both of these options disconcert Pakistan because they disregard any acknowledgment of Pakistan's interests in the final disposition of Kashmir.

Pakistan has been supporting militant elements operating within Indian-administered Kashmir and, in recent years, in the Indian hinterland to compel India to acquiesce on the disputed territory. Consequently, Pakistan has resisted (and in all likelihood will continue to resist) Indian demands that it end its support for militants in Kashmir as a prerequisite for engagement. From Islamabad's perspective, there are few benefits to be had from shutting down the militancy, as Pakistan believes that this is the *only* card it can play against its much larger adversary. Yet if Pakistan remains unwilling or unable to seriously address its own internal security concerns and permanently abandon militancy as a tool of foreign policy, it may well find itself diplomatically and politically isolated.

Conversely, India has moved substantially from its Cold War preference for economic isolationism and political nonalignment. Since the mid-1990s, India has pursued a sophisticated foreign policy that includes comprehensive "Look East" and "Look West" initiatives. Currently, New Delhi enjoys better relations with Pakistan's immediate neighbors and regional allies (for example, Iran, Afghanistan, the Central Asian states, and Israel) than does Islamabad. Ominously, Pakistan's sense of insecurity will only deepen as India continues to develop into a global—rather than just a regional—power.

India for its part has no compunction about walking away from a process that prefigures Kashmir as the primary focus of negotiation; in the near and long term, it principally seeks an end to Pakistan-supported militancy. Although India has paid a high price for fighting the insurgency there, it is confident that it can sustain the status quo indefinitely. It also believes that Pakistan may not be able to continue in the same manner ad infinitum; in a war of attrition, New Delhi is confident that it will prevail over its reckless adversary.

With these conflicting objectives and strategies, it is easy to understand why previous efforts at rapprochement between the two countries have failed and why the current initiative merits a great deal of skepticism. Pessimists point out that the objectives held by India and Pakistan have not changed substantially, and that this elemental asymmetry is likely to persist as a structural barrier to substantive engagement even if procedural engagement continues. In other words, although New Delhi will episodically engage in "talks" with Islamabad on a variety of issues (perhaps including Kashmir), it will continue to seek internal solutions to the Kashmir problem.

Pakistan's Internal Constraints and Challenges

Pakistan faces several immediate challenges that jeopardize the viability of this emerging peace process. Musharraf has survived numerous attempts on his life, and future attempts cannot be dismissed. He rebuffed the various pressures to step down as Army chief of staff in December 2004 and has announced that he would remain both president and Army chief. Furthermore, Musharraf's moves to oust Pakistani premier Jamali exposed the fiction that power lies anywhere but within Army headquarters in Rawalpindi. This revelation raises a few questions. First, to what extent is the peace process dependent upon the interests of President Musharraf and his ability to keep control of the levers of power? Second, what are Musharraf's interests in pursuing peace with India? Third, what would compel him to abandon the peace process?

Since the December 2001 and May 2002 attacks, the United States has tried periodically to persuade Islamabad to cease and desist from its reliance on proxy elements to prosecute its foreign policy objectives toward Kashmir and to refrain from trying to redraw maps with force. However, Islamabad has consistently maintained that it can go only so far in dissociating itself from the militant elements based in Pakistan. The recent attempts on Musharraf's life have legitimized claims that additional concessions will further jeopardize him. Instead, Pakistan has chosen to calibrate the activities of the insurgents under its control with the fluctuating intensity of U.S. pressure. This carefully balanced strategy has allowed Pakistan to retain U.S. support while preserving the use of militants as an instrument of state power.

Because of the attempts on his life, Musharraf has been motivated to take *aspects* of Pakistan's internal security much more seriously while remaining unwilling to systematically and permanently dismantle the militant infrastructure in the country. Instead, Musharraf's regime has attempted to disaggregate Pakistan's militants into two groups: the good *jihadis* (freedom fighters in Kashmir) and the bad (for example, sectarian groups, al Qaeda, and Taliban remnants). While the latter have become targets of state elimination campaigns, the former have been given considerable leeway. The fact that Pakistan's militant groups are still operating, recruiting, and publishing—despite various bans—suggests that there is more bark than bite to some of Pakistan's policies.

The Pakistani Army is also a serious impediment to movement away from militancy in Kashmir. For all intents and purposes, the army dictates Pakistan's foreign policy and is the single most important institution domestically. The centrality of the army in the Pakistani state casts doubt on the sincerity of Islamabad's intent to abandon its strategic use of proxy warfare in the near or distant future. The Pakistani Army gains legitimacy to interfere in the country's domestic affairs in part from the ongoing security competition with India over Kashmir, so the army has little incentive to resolve outstanding concerns with its principal adversary to the east.

Clearly, Islamabad's approach contains several contradictory elements. First, its tenacious support of militancy in Kashmir stands in opposition to Musharraf's own recognition that militancy is a diminishing asset in the post–9/11 world. Few countries now are willing to distinguish between "freedom fighters" and "terrorists" and between "terrorist movements" and "insurgencies." Second, given the ongoing morphing of groups that operate in Kashmir and the sectarian groups that target Shi'a individuals and organizations in Pakistan, pretending that such distinctions really exist continues to pose innumerable internal security challenges. Third, in light of the various attempts on Musharraf's life, there can be little doubt that he appreciates the reality that continued support of this militancy poses a greater danger to himself than to India. Fourth, Pakistan is experiencing an Islamicization of criminal activity and a criminalization of some Islamist activities. All of this bodes ill for Pakistan's ability to make the transition into a robust state with a stable civil society for its citizens.

One recurrent theme in Pakistan's various offers to temper its militant elements is the insistence that India "create space" for Musharraf to do more to counter them. The term "create space" sometimes implies specific action to be undertaken by New Delhi, such as a partial troop demobilization. More often it suggests that India take a hiatus from publicly criticizing Pakistan or placing demands on it as criterion for engagement. Islamabad argues that it has gone about as far as it can go with respect to containing jihadist groups, and that it needs such space—however defined—in order to contain them further. Cynics suggest that this is just another tactic with which Musharraf justifies keeping the militancy option open.

While Islamabad's *intentions* with respect to the jihadists are uncertain, so is its ability to meaningfully contend with them. Even if Islamabad were wholeheartedly devoted to tackling these internal security challenges, it is doubtful it has the resources to do so: Pakistan's police are corrupt, ill equipped, poorly paid, infiltrated by a variety of nefarious elements, and incapable of performing the most elementary aspects of criminal investigation and evidence gathering. In addition, Pakistan's judicial system has suffered because of the swift reprisals of militant groups targeting judges who convict their cadres or leaders. As a result, Pakistan's entire internal security apparatus remains largely ineffectual.

Pakistan's domestic political environment provides further sources of pessimism for the likely outcome of Indo-Pakistani engagement. Musharraf's credibility has suffered in recent years. Musharraf has weathered all pressures to step down as Army chief and has announced that he will remain in that position. Further, Pakistan recently has had a change in the patina of its domestic leadership. In the waning days of June 2004, Prime Minster Jamali "resigned," amid all-too-adamant assertions that he had not been pressured to do so by the Musharraf regime. Prime Minister Chaudhry Shujaat Hussain became the interim premier to warm the bench for Shaukat Aziz to take the helm of the soon-to-be reconstituted civilian institutions.

Pakistan's internal dynamics could have significant implications for its foreign policy initiatives toward India. In the event that Pakistan's domestic security situation continues to degrade, Musharraf may find himself in even greater peril. His ability to exert influence on Islamist elements may wane, putting himself and his corps commanders at risk. In the event of future attacks on his life, Musharraf may choose to let rapprochement with India slide. Should he not survive such an attack, his successor would also likely desist from pursuing an opening with India. The attempted assassination of Corps Commander Lieutenant General Ahsan Azeem in June 2004, suggests that Musharraf is not the only target in the sites of the militants. Such attempts to target Musharraf's principal bastion of support may soften the resolve of the army to support Musharraf's policies writ large—particularly those toward New Delhi and Kashmir.

On balance, the political and security dynamic in Pakistan is not comforting, suggesting that even if India is able to accommodate Pakistan's demand on *process*, it is far from obvious that Islamabad would be capable of packaging this and marketing it to its citizens and other stakeholders (the army, for example) as a form of "progress" on Pakistan's core concerns. This factor is a central element in keeping Pakistan engaged in the process and creating a public demand for a just peace.

India's Internal Sources of Resistance to Engaging Islamabad

Ironically, although Islamabad demands understanding of its deeply complex and convoluted domestic situation and its fundamental constraints on policy innovation, India also has a number of domestic compulsions of its own: it is a rich and vibrant—if imperfect—democracy, and reaching consensus on contentious issues such as relations with Pakistan can be perhaps even more of a challenge in its diverse and active polity. Since the Kargil crisis and the ongoing attacks within Indian-administered Kashmir and within India proper, many Indians have grown weary of Pakistan's tactics. Hard-liners feel that they should not have to reward Pakistan for ceasing activities that Islamabad should not have started in the first place. Such hardened positions likely will dictate how far New Delhi can go in creating the kind of "space" Islamabad demands.

The results of India's April–May 2004 general elections have also added an additional layer of uncertainty to this analysis: the electorate dismissed the

BJP—the party that spearheaded this peace overture. To the astonishment of most onlookers, the Indian voters returned the Congress Party to power (along with several allies) after a long hiatus in opposition to the BJP. Although the new Congress government affirmed its commitment to the process, it is far from certain that it has the domestic clout to continue the engagement.

In the several days following the May 2004 Congress Party victory, many observers on the subcontinent and beyond wondered about the fate of the nascent engagement process. Some of these apprehensions, however, may have been misplaced: the Congress government is perhaps even more eager to explore the possibilities of détente with Pakistan. Despite its best intentions, concerns persist that the Congress Party has no "hard-line" constituencies, which may render it vulnerable to domestic critics. Will the Congress Party have the heft and credentials to carry the complex and fissiparous Indian populace along the process of engagement? With such burdens of credibility, will India be able to provide Pakistan's minimal expectations to keep the process alive under a Congress government?

Making the Most out of a Stalemate

If history is any guide, the likelihood that this process will break down is high, and the probability of a meaningful breakthrough is quite slim. USIP roundtable participants agreed that the outcome of this round of engagement ultimately will turn on the understanding held by New Delhi and by Islamabad on the core issues of the engagement and the concomitant progress made on each. Many participants felt that while breakthrough is certainly not likely, neither is a breakdown of the kind witnessed after the 1999 Lahore Declaration, whose resulting engagement suffered many onslaughts, the ultimate of which was the Kargil offensive in the spring of 1999. In light of these considerations, participants generally concurred that stalemate is the most likely outcome of the current engagement process.

India's domestic compulsions regarding Pakistan and the intractable Kashmir problem will preclude it from satisfying Islamabad's basic requirements for "progress" in order to permit the engagement to continue. Absent such progress, Pakistan has very little reason for strategically abandoning militancy. For its part, Islamabad's fixations on its own domestic constraints without a realistic appraisal of India's will encourage it to have unrealistic demands of New Delhi. Few of the USIP roundtable participants saw any prospects for breaking out of this pernicious—if predictable—circle.

More than his Indian counterpart, Musharraf faces incentives that predispose him to prefer stalemate to any other outcome. Certainly, he has every reason to want to avoid another damaging episode on his watch: not only will such an episode aggravate tensions with India, it will also distract Pakistan from its problems with Afghanistan and its efforts to sustain its relationship with the United States. Yet Musharraf has no reason to truly solve the Kashmir issue, even if it were his to solve. Such an overture would be perilous for him personally and disastrous for the institution of the army, which is thoroughly vested in conflict with India. It is important to appreciate that it is the *institution* of the army, perhaps more than any of its senior leaders, that many army officers seek to protect: the army is seen as one of the only functioning and competent institutions in Pakistan, a status that the military will act to cultivate and protect over the long term. On balance, Musharraf likely seeks a series of small steps towards normalization, each with its own opportunity for reneging.

Several roundtable participants believed that if New Delhi could reach some sort of resolution with the Kashmiris, Islamabad could be presented with a fait accompli; many other participants rejected this scenario out of hand: any solution without Pakistan's fingerprints would not be palatable to Islamabad and would have no takers among Pakistan's elites. Rather, New Delhi needs to work out a package that would give Islamabad something to sell to its general public, which has been fed a steady diet of propaganda about attaining Kashmir for the past fifty years. If meaningful steps could be made on addressing Kashmiris' welfare and full enfranchisement, Islamabad could claim movement on these issues as victories of sorts. In other words, Islamabad could claim, with varying degrees of legitimacy, that these various improvements for the lives of the Kashmiris would not have happened without Pakistan's insistence.

Keeping the Momentum Going

If stalemate is the best likely outcome of the current Indo-Pakistani engagement process, what can be done to make the best of this less-than-optimal situation? What can be done to prevent any backsliding while simultaneously creating a climate that could enable forward movement in the future? To achieve these modest objectives, all relevant parties must creatively devise several tactical means by which both India and Pakistan can be persuaded to stay at the bargaining table, even if meaningful progress is not being made on their respective core strategic issues. As one prominent South Asia analyst explained, for this to succeed, essentially two minimal conditions must be met simultaneously:

- Pakistan must suspend its conclusion that no meaningful progress is happening on Kashmir and that the only resort at Pakistan's disposal is the continued calibration of the intensity of the insurgency.
- India must also suspend its conclusion that it is not seeing a meaningful decrease in terrorism, that there is little positive utility from engaging

Pakistan, and that it should kill militants while seeking to deal with the Kashmiris independently.

Clearly, success in keeping this engagement alive will require both sides to be much more invested in the peace process than they are at present. Both states need to begin an internal dialogue process whereby their respective peoples can begin to appreciate the benefits of peace. In Pakistan, this process may mean authoring and promulgating new national narratives that do not singularly rely on the acquisition of Kashmir as a prerequisite to completing the Pakistani state. India must seriously engage the dilemma of how it treats Kashmiris: How can the state deny them basic rights while simultaneously claiming them as citizens? Both countries must do more to create constituencies for peace.

Roundtable participants offered more concrete means by which the process may be encouraged, even if movement is not being made on core issues. Many of these means could constitute a tactical form of engagement that could, in principle, satisfy the two above-noted constraints. Key proposals are discussed below.

- *Expanding the contacts of Kashmiris on both sides of the Line of Control.* One of the ways of doing this is establishing bus service linking Muzaffarabad in Pakistan-administered Kashmir to Srinagar in Indian-administered Kashmir; another "bus option" would link Suchetgar in Pakistan-administered Kashmir and Jammu in Indian-administered Kashmir. Many families on both sides of the LOC have been separated for decades. Provision of such a service may make movement within the disputed territory more feasible, facilitate the reunion of families, and even encourage marital and other family alliances across the LOC. Kashmiri proponents also maintain that this service would permit Kashmiri political leaders to forge contacts across the divided territory. While USIP roundtable participants acknowledged that there are technical challenges in this proposal (for example, required paperwork, security issues, and so forth), all agreed that these concerns could be resolved if the political leaders made this proposal a priority.
- *Expand population contacts within India and Pakistan.* Although the Muzaffarabad-Srinagar bus idea has captured the attention of many, some participants cautioned that this is not the only area worthy of attention. Rather, population contacts should be expanded and reunions of families scattered across India and Pakistan should be encouraged. To increase the ease of obtaining visas and facilitate travel between the two states, consulates could be established in Karachi and in Bombay. Another means of expanding people-to-people contacts is the development of educational exchanges. Currently, many Pakistanis must go abroad to receive quality higher-education opportunities. India's excellent postsecondary

institutions may be a cost-effective alternative for Pakistanis seeking high-quality education while encouraging interpersonal contacts among Pakistani and Indian citizens.

- *Pipelines for peace.* Several roundtable participants were hopeful about the benefits of a natural gas pipeline through Iran, Pakistan, and India in fostering confidence between the two states. Some believed that cooperation could be worked out through the auspices of the World Bank, whose role in negotiating the Indus Water Treaty was raised as a potential template. However, the involvement of Iran in the project would likely complicate such an initiative, given the antipathy that exists between Tehran and Washington.
- *Expanding markets to build confidence.* Despite the gravity and importance of the pipeline scheme, the option poses many significant conundrums. For this reason, the pipeline proposal should not singularly focus the attention of policymakers. Arguably, bilateral efforts could be more profitably spent legalizing and regularizing the trade that already exists between the two countries. Currently much of the movement of products between India and Pakistan is facilitated through the black market and includes food products, engineering equipment, tires, entertainment media, and so forth. Legalizing this trade would do much for both states' coffers.
- *Integrating Kashmir into extant South Asia trade agreements.* Former World Bank vice president Shahid Javed Burki has proposed that Kashmir be thoroughly integrated into the South Asia Free Trade Agreement, bringing economic benefits to all three parties, while leaving the status quo intact. Such economic integration would require massive infrastructure projects (for example, roads, lines of communication, fuel transport), integration of electrical grids, and possibly even a reworking of the Indus Water Treaty, which governs bilateral water sharing from the waters of the Indus River Basin. Burki believes that this project could create constituencies for normalization while deferring the nettlesome question of Kashmir's ultimate disposition.

What Role for the United States and the International Community?

Roundtable participants discussed the manifold costs and benefits of various forms of U.S. involvement in the Indo-Pakistani engagement process. Some contended that a fundamental long-term component of peace in South Asia will be determined substantially by the character that Pakistan assumes over the next several years, and the United States, they noted, has a highly debated, but nonetheless important role in shaping the country's future. To this end, many suggested that efforts must be directed toward encouraging Pakistan to democratize and develop functioning and accountable civilian institutions.

However, participants contested the role of the United States in facilitating a bilateral rapprochement. A small but vocal minority countered that the United States has no positive role to play. Opponents of such a role contended that the status of the United States has diminished in India because of flagging attention to the Indo-U.S. security relationship and because of the renaissance in U.S.-Pakistan relations. Despite robust intergovernmental relations between the United States and Pakistan, anti-U.S. sentiment is rife among Pakistan's general public, with no visible signs of waning in any policy-relevant future. This dual trend of antagonizing both Islamabad and New Delhi has compromised the utility of the United States in facilitating any movement toward normalization, opponents contend.

Pressler Amendment Sanctions Against Pakistan

The 1985 Pressler Amendment (after former U.S. senator Larry Pressler, R-SD) to the Foreign Assistance Act of 1961, bans most economic and military assistance to Pakistan unless annual U.S. presidential certification finds that the country does not possess a nuclear device and that U.S. aid would reduce the risk of Pakistan possessing such a device. During the 1980s, ample evidence suggested that Pakistan was enriching uranium for a nuclear device and that the country could assemble a weapon; however, Pressler Amendment sanctions were not invoked until 1990.

The Pressler Amendment joined the earlier Symington Amendment and Glenn Amendment to the 1961 Foreign Assistance Act, which invoked sanctions against countries that elude International Atomic Energy Agency safeguards on nuclear materials and technology, or against non-nuclear countries that conduct nuclear tests. Although India conducted a "peaceful" nuclear explosion in 1974, and Pakistan was accelerating its nuclear program, the Symington and Glenn amendments did not apply retroactively to India or Pakistan.

Since the mid-1990s the Pressler Amendment sanctions have found many exemptions and waivers—most notably under the Brown Amendment and especially the two Brownback Amendments, the latter of which give the U.S. president permanent authority to waive the sanctions under the Symington and Pressler Amendments that banned all military and economic assistance to Pakistan since 1990.

Shortly after the 9/11 terrorist attacks against the United States, President Bush signed an executive order that lifted economic and military sanctions against India and Pakistan for their nuclear tests, in advance of enlisting Pakistan's assistance for Operation Enduring Freedom and the routing of the Taliban and al Qaeda redoubts in Afghanistan.

Proponents of a positive U.S. role countered with alternative views, pointing out that the United States now enjoys better relations with both governments than it has in decades. As a consequence of the U.S. position on the 1999 Kargil crisis that came down in favor of the status quo, India no longer reflexively rejects any role for the United States. Moreover, since December 2001, India has implicitly relied upon the United States to exert its influence over Pakistan in order to gain concessions from Islamabad. Pakistan, for its part, is enjoying renewed relations with the United States, which it has not enjoyed since 1990, when Pressler Amendment sanctions were invoked.

If a primary role for the United States is questionable, is there any space for key states in the international community to keep India and Pakistan productively engaged? China, Russia, and the United States have all played significant roles of crisis manager throughout the past five decades of security competition between India and Pakistan, and all three states, for their own various reasons and with varying intensity, have an interest in South Asian deterrence stability. Perhaps the time has come for these and other states to seriously ponder how they may help ensure that this process moves, even if only procedurally. Rather than undertake action unilaterally, perhaps the key crisis managers in the past can act in concert, devising collective security guarantees that will permit both India and Pakistan to continue talking at the tactical level, even if strategic issues are deferred.

As the foregoing discussion suggests, without creativity and commitment to dispute resolution, it is difficult to imagine normalization of Indo-Pakistani relations in the policy-relevant future. However, the stakes have never been higher. Not only do the peoples of India and Pakistan deserve a livable peace with minimized risk of conventional or nuclear exchanges, the South Asian region—indeed, the international community as a whole—also deserves some respite from this ongoing conflict.

An online edition of this report can be found at our website (www.usip.org), together with additional information on the subject.

United States
Institute of Peace
1200 17th Street NW
Washington, DC 20036
www.usip.org

DOCUMENT NO. 32

QUICKSTEP OR KADAM TAAL?: THE ELUSIVE SEARCH FOR PEACE IN JAMMU AND KASHMIR

United States Institute of Peace (USIP)
Special Report 133

March 2005

By Praveen Swami

About the Report

At first glance, India and Pakistan today seem closer to peace than at any point in the past several decades. The cease-fire that went into place along the Line of Control in December 2003 has held; terrorist violence in Jammu and Kashmir has been in steady decline since the two nuclear-armed states almost went to war in 2002; and both countries have succeeded in sustaining a wide-ranging and high-level dialogue process. All this appears to suggest that conditions exist for resolution of one of the world's most intractable and bloody conflicts, the India-Pakistan war over Jammu and Kashmir.

Yet the current détente process between India and Pakistan suffers from the same structural infirmities that led past peace initiatives to collapse. Instead of looking for a resolution of the grand historical conflict in Jammu and Kashmir, peacemakers might do well to focus on the problems of the state's peoples—thus building a base from which creative democratic solutions might eventually emerge.

Praveen Swami is a Randolph Jennings Senior Fellow at the United States Institute of Peace. A journalist with *Frontline*, a major Indian magazine, Swami has covered the conflict in Jammu and Kashmir for more than a decade.

The views expressed in this report do not necessarily reflect those of the United States Institute of Peace, which does not advocate specific policy positions.

About the Institute

The United States Institute of Peace is an independent, nonpartisan federal institution created by Congress to promote the prevention, management, and peaceful resolution of international conflicts. Established in 1984, the Institute meets its congressional mandate through an array of programs, including research grants, fellowships, professional training, education programs from high school through graduate school, conferences and workshops, library services, and publications. The Institute's Board of Directors is appointed by the President of the United States and confirmed by the Senate.

Board of Directors

Members Ex Officio

Summary

- Since December 2003, India and Pakistan have maintained a successful cease-fire along the militarily volatile Line of Control as part of a dialogue process that is addressing a wide range of disputes between the two nuclear-armed neighbors.
- A key component of the dialogue centers on the disputed region of Jammu and Kashmir, of which both India and Pakistan control a part. (China holds a third part.) Both states claim sovereignty over the entire region.

- The current round of India-Pakistan détente has led to some optimism that the dispute over Jammu and Kashmir, one of the bloodiest conflicts in the world, could be ripe for resolution.
- Pakistan has recently advocated plans for what it believes is a workable final territorial solution to the problem—essentially, a partition of Jammu and Kashmir along ethnic-religious lines. India, however, has rejected these proposals, arguing that such a partition is repugnant to its secular values and could lead to a worsening of tensions elsewhere in South Asia.
- This dissonance in perceptions points to a larger set of problems in the dialogue process, all of which could take several years, if not decades, to work through.
- A second dialogue track, between India and secessionist politicians in Jammu and Kashmir, also appears to have reached stalemate.
- Although Pakistan has helped bring about a significant reduction in terrorist violence within Jammu and Kashmir, much of the infrastructure of terrorism is still intact—and the possibility of crisis-inducing terrorist strikes remains.
- Stalemate between the main actors has meant that the peoples of Jammu and Kashmir have yet to see any gains from the dialogue process and the India-Pakistan détente.
- Rather than wait for a grand resolution of these complex issues, we need to find ways to deliver concrete gains to the peoples of Jammu and Kashmir—principally, though not exclusively, through a cessation of violence. Peacemaking may thus be better served by turning attention away from the "Kashmir problem" to the "problems of Kashmiris."

Introduction

"Spring will return to the beautiful Valley soon," India's former prime minister Atal Behari Vajpayee promised a Srinagar audience in April 2002, quoting a passage from the Kashmiri poet Ghulam Ahmed Mehjoor, "the flowers will bloom again and the nightingales will return, chirping." More than two years later, it is beginning to look like the end might indeed be in sight for one of the most bitterly fought conflicts in the world. Both India and Pakistan are engaged in negotiations, their borders are quiet, and some counterterrorist military formations are being withdrawn from Jammu and Kashmir. Is peace, then, somewhere around the corner—or at least not too many blocks away?

One metaphor, favored by optimists, for what is now under way is the proverbial step forward; another, which might meet with the approval of pessimists, is the parade-ground technique of marching vigorously on one spot, known to both Indian and Pakistani soldiers as the *kadam taal*. This report examines the status of two related ongoing processes, the India-Pakistan détente and the efforts by India to engage political secessionists within the Indian state of Jammu and Kashmir. It looks at the prospects these twin processes have for ending one of the world's most murderous conflicts—one that has claimed almost forth thousand lives since 1988, one-third of them civilian. Although the current process of dialogue holds some reasons for hope, it suffers from the same structural infirmities that have led past initiatives to collapse. Thus, a wholly new paradigm of peace-making may be needed to secure abiding gains.

A View of the Landscape

Although it is easy to be pessimistic about the prospects of peace in Jammu and Kashmir—cynics have had an alarming record of success in their prognosis—several features of the current situation are in fact heartening.

India-Pakistan dialogue has survived the coming to power of the United Progressive Alliance government in New Delhi in 2004. Both countries have agreed to open a bus route from Srinagar, in Indian-administered Kashmir, to Muzaffarabad, on the Pakistan-administered side. Even though the service will initially be limited, the symbolic bridging of the Line of Control has generated great public enthusiasm. Dialogue is also under way on issues ranging from watershed management to the activation of a railway line that would speed access between southern Punjab and the industrial hubs of western India. Meanwhile, the national security advisers for both India and Pakistan have maintained regular contact, a process of covert diplomacy that has mirrored the public engagement between the two countries.

Second, violence within Jammu and Kashmir has been in steady decline since the India-Pakistan near war of 2002. Data from India's Union Ministry of Home Affairs show that the numbers of fatalities of both civilians and combatants, as well as the overall numbers of violent acts carried out by jihadi groups, have fallen to levels similar to those seen before the Kargil War of 1999, which started an escalatory cycle (see figures 1 and 2). More important, the number of foreign terrorists, mainly Pakistani nationals, killed by Indian forces has dropped to low levels. It is hard to reliably quantify the level of infiltration by jihadi cadres across the Line of Control, but the empirically demonstrated fact that fewer people, whether foreign or Indian nationals, are being killed suggests that General Musharraf has at least partially delivered on his 2002 promise to end cross-border terrorism.

It would be simplistic to give General Musharraf sole credit for the declining levels of violence. The near war of 2002, provoked by a terrorist attack on India's parliament by the Jaish-e-Mohammad, a jihadi group, may have

Figure 1. Fatalities from violence in Jammu and Kashmir, 1988–2004.

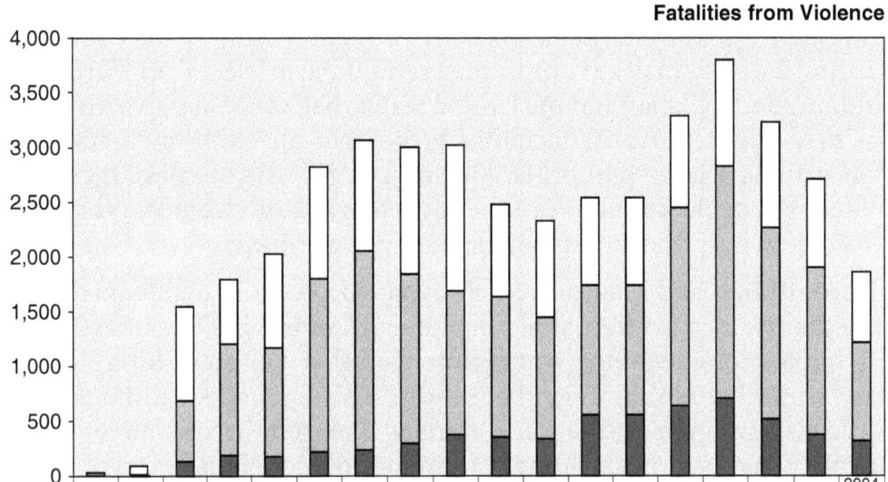

	1988	1989	1990	1991	1992	1993	1994	1995	1996	1997	1998	1999	1999	2000	2001	2002	2003	2004 (to Nov. 18)
Civilians	29	79	862	594	859	1,023	1,012	1,161	1,333	840	877	799	799	842	971	966	807	645
Terrorists	1	0	552	1,016	991	1,584	1,818	1,545	1,313	1,282	1,111	1,184	1,184	1,808	2,119	1,747	1,526	895
Indian Forces	1	13	132	185	177	216	236	297	376	355	339	555	555	638	706	518	377	320

Source: Data compiled by author from public and private sources.

Figure 2. Incidents of violence in Jammu and Kashmir, 1989–2004.

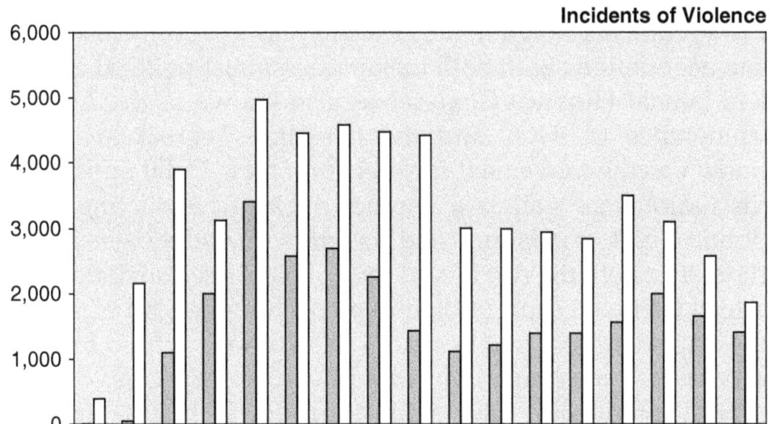

	1989	1990	1991	1992	1993	1994	1995	1996	1997	1998	1999	1999	2000	2001	2002	2003	2004 (to Nov. 18)
Attacks on Indian Forces	6	49	1,098	1,999	3,413	2,573	2,693	2,253	1,432	1,116	1,211	1,390	1,390	1,560	1,994	1,654	1,407
Total Incidents of Terrorist Violence	390	2,154	3,905	3,122	4,971	4,457	4,584	4,479	4,424	3,004	2,993	2,938	2,836	3,505	3,101	2,575	1,866

Source: Data compiled by author from public and private sources.

awakened Pakistan's military establishment to the perils of maintaining its subconventional offensive against India at the levels witnessed after 1999. Alternatively, the enormous pressure brought to bear by the United States during the crisis may have prompted rethinking in Islamabad. Furthermore, India, aided by Israel and the United States, has made massive investments in new counterterrorist technology, notably an electronic and physical fence along a large part of the Line of Control. Any or all of these factors combined could account for the reduced levels of violence. Whatever the truth, however, the fact is that violence has declined.

Third, Indian and Pakistani forces have successfully maintained a cease-fire that went into effect along the Line of Control in December 2003. One of India's long-standing complaints was that Pakistani forces provided covering fire to infiltrating jihadi cadre. This has ended. Although Indian officials say some infiltration continues, Pakistani troops no longer seem actively involved in shielding it from interdiction. India's recent efforts to build public confidence in peacemaking have been helped by the reduction of hostilities along the Line of Control, which has paved the way for the withdrawal of some troops engaged in counterterrorist operations in Jammu and Kashmir. No figures are available regarding how many troops India eventually intends to remove, but several thousand soldiers are reported to have been moved out since November 2004.

Fourth, but by no means least important, India has set parameters for dialogue with political entities within Jammu and Kashmir on the state's future relationship with India. During his November 2004 visit to Srinagar, Prime Minister Singh made clear that his government was willing to pursue negotiations with both major secessionist political groups: the centrist Kul Jamaat Hurriyat Conference, also known as the All Parties Freedom Conference (APHC), and the hard-line Tehreek-i-Hurriyat (TH), also known as the Movement for Freedom. New Delhi appears to center these discussions, as well as a parallel track of negotiating with mainstream political parties in Jammu and Kashmir, on widening federal autonomy for the states. Both the APHC and the TH have rejected dialogue on autonomy, which falls well short of their demand for secession from India. However, the important fact here is that N. N. Vohra, a retired bureaucrat who has served the government of India in various capacities and now acts as its official interlocutor with political groups in Jumma and Kashmi, finally has a clear mandate that can be brought to the table.

Together, these four conditions suggest that the environment is favorable for peacemaking. Rarely in recent years has there been a conjunction of regimes with a stated commitment to dialogue, the willingness to scale back border tensions, the ability to reduce violence, and a vision of what political concessions can be made. Although the necessary conditions for a dialogue have been met, however, the question of whether these are *sufficient* to yield a meaningful outcome remains.

The India-Pakistan Dialogue Axis

As India-Pakistan dialogue proceeds, what are the prospects for both sides arriving at a mutually acceptable vision of Jammu and Kashmir? Speaking at a dinner in Islamabad on October 25, 2004, General Musharraf outlined the contours of new ideas for an eventual resolution of the conflict over Jammu and Kashmir. Based on a partition of the state's territory, the ideas were greeted with considerable enthusiasm by some observers, who saw it as a potentially decisive step forward.

In essence, General Musharraf advocated the division of the territory of the entire pre-independence monarchical state of Jammu and Kashmir. A part of this territory is now administered by India (Jammu and Kashmir), and another part is administered by Pakistan (Azad Kashmir and the Northern Areas of Gilgit, Hunza, and Baltistan; a part of the territory administered by Pakistan was unilaterally ceded by it to China). In Musharraf's vision, the seven major constituent geographical units of the region would be offered independence or joint control by India and Pakistan, or, alternatively, be administered by the United Nations. Five of these units are in India—the Kashmir valley and the Muslim-majority areas of Jammu, both of which lie north of the Chenab River; the Shia-dominated Kargil area; the Hindu-majority areas of Jammu south of the Chenab River; and Buddhist-majority Ladakh. The two other areas, Azad Kashmir and the Northern Areas, both of which have a Muslim majority, are in Pakistan.

Musharraf's ideas were summarily dismissed by India, despite the fact that they marked a considerable departure from the traditional Pakistani claim to all the territory of Jammu and Kashmir. Understanding India's reaction to Musharraf's plan is key to a coherent appraisal of the future of détente between the two countries. The idea of partitioning Jammu and Kashmir along ethnic-religious lines was first advocated in September 1950 by UN special representative for India and Pakistan Sir Owen Dixon, who suggested that this could be brought about either through agreement between the two countries or by plebiscite. Sensitive to the consequences of ethnic-religious partitions in South Asia—the division of British India into the states of India and Pakistan had cost more than five hundred thousand lives—the Dixon Plan, as it came to be known, was rejected out of hand by India. Pakistan at first rejected the Dixon Plan, but the idea had gathered some momentum in that country by the early 1960s. Partition is believed to have been discussed in 1963 by the eminent Kashmir leader Sheikh Mohammad Abdullah and the foreign minister who served the Pakistani military ruler Field Marshall Ayub Khan, Zulfikar Ali Bhutto, who went on to become president of Pakistan.

Pakistan seems to have persuaded itself in recent years that India would, sooner or later, come to accept the partition plan in some form or other. In 1999, Pakistan's foreign minister, Sartaj Aziz, called for a districtwide referendum on the future of Jammu and Kashmir, a repackaging of the Dixon Plan that marked a sharp departure from the official position. Aziz's ideas were anticipated in a report by a New York–based organization, the Kashmir Study Group, which argued for the creation of one or two new states from the Muslim-majority areas of Jammu and Kashmir. Together, the Kashmir Study Group said, these would constitute a "sovereign entity but one without an international personality." The new state would have its own legislature, flag, and gendarmerie, but its security would be jointly guaranteed by India and Pakistan.

From the point of view of Pakistan, an ethnic-religious partition seems an eminently reasonable solution to the conflict over Jammu and Kashmir. Pakistan came into existence on the basis of the religious affiliation of the majority of its citizens, and advocates of partition-based solutions believe that the same principle should apply to Jammu and Kashmir as well. Advocates of partition-based solutions, by some accounts, have found a sympathetic hearing from at least some elements within the U.S. State Department, perhaps because the idea appears to offer a way out of a stalemate. Critics have noted the impracticability of the idea, however. Nowhere in the world have two nuclear-armed adversaries jointly guaranteed the security of a third state. Among other things, it is unclear how disputes between the new entity and the two states bordering it, both of which would have compelling security interests there, would be mediated.

India's concerns, however, transcend the purely pragmatic—just as, for Pakistan, Jammu and Kashmir is not simply a territorial issue, but a national project. For India, ideologically committed to a secular nation-state, the idea of an ethnic-religious partition is repugnant. State-level leaders in Jammu and Kashmir, as well as senior figures in India's central government, have flatly rejected any movement in this direction, and no change in the Indian position seems likely in the near future. Although General Musharraf was at pains to package his proposal as one founded on geography rather than ethnic-religious identity, the fact is that the two coincide so closely as to render the distinction trivial. India is also concerned about the long-term consequences any ethnic-religious partition might have for the rest of the union. Should its sole Muslim-majority province secede on the basis of its religious identity, the position of Hindu fundamentalist groups seeking to replace India's secular order with a state founded on theocratic principles would be strengthened.

The point here is simple: despite the illusion of forward momentum generated by Musharraf's new ideas (or not-so-new ideas), both India and

Pakistan fundamentally stand where they have for decades. The two states are far from having a shared vision of the future for Jammu and Kashmir, something that could strain the sustainability of the détente as it proceeds. Second, and perhaps more important, cross-border terrorism has decreased, not ended. As such, it remains a part of Pakistan's negotiating strategy, a disturbing fact with potentially grave long-term consequences for the peace process itself. It is also worth remembering that agreements, *in themselves*, are worth little. India and Pakistan reached negotiated settlements in 1966 and 1973, after all; neither prevented further bloodshed.

The India-Kashmir Dialogue Axis

If India and Pakistan still have some distance to travel to agreement on Jammu and Kashmir, what about the second component of the peace process—the negotiations between India and secessionists in its part of Jammu and Kashmir?

As things stand, the status of talks between India and secessionists in Jammu and Kashmir induces less optimism than does the détente with Pakistan. Centrist APHC elements held a single round of direct talks with the National Democratic Alliance regime of Prime Minister Atal Behari Vajpayee but have since refused to continue the process. There are several reasons. The most important APHC leader, Maulvi Umar Farooq, and his immediate family came under terrorist attack for defying jihadi injunctions not to negotiate with New Delhi. Because Maulvi Farooq as yet has no male heir, a factor of enormous import to the clerical dynasty he represents, the threat of assassination is all the more grave. Centrist leaders such as Maulvi Farooq are conscious of the potential costs of peacemaking: both his father, Maulvi Mohammad Farooq, and another prominent moderate, Abdul Gani Lone, were executed by jihadi groups opposed to their decision to engage India in dialogue.

To persuade jihadi groups to withdraw their opposition, APHC leaders placed several preconditions for talks with New Delhi, notably permission to visit Pakistan. New Delhi has been reluctant to make such concessions for two major reasons. First, its principal interest in the dialogue process within Jammu and Kashmir is to establish a track of negotiation independent of Pakistan. To involve Pakistan, even symbolically, at the outset of the dialogue would subvert the process itself. New Delhi is also reluctant to give the impression of recognizing the APHC, which is just one of several pro-India secessionist political organizations active in Jammu and Kashmir, as the sole spokesperson for all the people in the state. Opponents of the APHC's demands within the Indian establishment argue that allowing the APHC to visit Pakistan would concede to the organization the de facto status of the representative of a nation.

Pakistan has good reason to be less than delighted at the prospect of the political process within Jammu and Kashmir actually succeeding. A negotiated settlement between India and secessionists in Jammu and Kashmir would marginalize Pakistan, a fact that has provoked a predictable response from pro-Pakistan parties to the conflict. The United Jihad Council, an Islamabad-based apex body made up of several organizations designated by the United States of America as terrorist, has condemned centrists for even considering negotiations with New Delhi. So has Islamist leader Syed Ali Shah Geelani, who heads the TH. Previously a member of the APHC, Geelani formed the TH to protest, among other things, the decision of some moderate secessionists to contest the 2002 elections in Jammu and Kashmir through proxy candidates. Even if the APHC or other centrist secessionist groups engage New Delhi in dialogue and arrive at a settlement, therefore, the opposition of terrorist groups and the TH make it unclear if this would achieve the aim of peacemaking—an end to violence. Indeed, the Jamaat-ud-Dawa, the parent religious-political organization of the Lashkar-e-Taiba, one of the largest terrorist groups in Jammu and Kashmir, has opposed even General Musharraf's partition idea, arguing in a recent issue of its journal *Voice of Islam* that the proposal is a sign of "cowardice under pressure."

Jihadi threat is not the only factor at work. History suggests that political accommodation, while perhaps desirable, does not in itself secure an end to violence. In November 2004, when Prime Minister Singh visited Srinagar for the first time, two terrorists attempted to attack his rally with rocket-propelled grenade launchers. The officer responsible for the police operation that prevented the attack, Javed Makhdoomi, was cited as a suspect in a 1966 counterterrorism investigation conducted by the force he now commands. So was one of his contemporaries, the current Jammu and Kashmir law minister, Muzzafar Beigh—and some figures who have occupied prominent positions in earlier governments, like National Conference leader Bashir Ahmad Kitchloo. Since the 1950s, India has succeeded in co-opting pro-independence and pro-Pakistan elements; author Manoj Joshi records that the 1966 suspects were brought on board through a well-planned, if covert, process. The recruitment of dissidents to the ranks of the Indian establishment did not stop the emergence of other terrorist groups in the 1970s and 1980s, however. In fact, one can argue that co-optation may have provided the promise of impunity to those considering violence.

The closer the APHC and New Delhi come to reaching a deal, then, the more interest jihadi groups will have in sharpening their knives to slaughter the doves. Evidence that momentum toward peace can, paradoxically, lead to an escalation in killing is not hard to come by. Prime Minister Atal Behari Vajpayee declared a unilateral cease-fire in 2000–2001 in an effort to strengthen the hands of moderate elements in the Hizb-ul-Mujaheddin, the largest terrorist group operating in Jammu and Kashmir. Its Pakistan-based leader, Mohammad Yusuf Shah (better known by his nom de guerre, Syed Salahuddin), responded by sharply escalating attacks on both Indian forces and civilians and, in the end, succeeded in forcing India to resume offensive military operations. A similar upsurge in violence and political assassinations was recorded prior to the several elections held in Jammu and Kashmir after 1995. Optimists saw these elections to the state's legislature and India's parliament as elements of a normalization process that would lead to the displacement of armed groups by political forces.

So far, neither APHC moderates nor the Indian establishment have found means to break the impasse created by pressure from jihadi groups, and it is hard to see exactly what might be done unless Pakistan acts to decisively strip terrorist groups of the infrastructure that facilitates their violent operations. India, as it has often done in the past, has responded to the stalemate by pumping in significant amounts of central development aid in an effort to build a mass constituency for peace. The available empirical evidence, however, does not affirm conventional wisdom that there is a causal relationship between jihadi violence and economic deprivation. Contrary to popular perception, the roots of the problem in Jammu and Kashmir do not appear to lie in economic conditions. Jammu and Kashmir are among the most food-secure regions in India and have the lowest percentage of population living below the poverty line of any state in the union. Per capita central development aid since the mid-1990s, not including reimbursements to the state government for security expenditure, is higher than for any other state in India. Although economic development is indisputably a good thing, there is no reason to believe that progress will in itself end violence—particularly because the problem itself is not the consequence of deprivation. Indeed, scholar Sumit Ganguly has pointed out that the rise of terrorism in the early 1980s may paradoxically have been the consequence of growing *affluence:* the result of the frustrations of a new social class that had both education and economic opportunity but that was denied political power. It is worth noting, in this context, that although a decade and a half of violence have retarded economic progress in Jammu and Kashmir, it has not generated the kinds of economic devastation other conflicts of this kind have caused elsewhere in the world. Interestingly, the state's economic backbone, the agricultural sector, has grown steadily through the years of carnage. The emphasis placed by Indian policymakers on economic development as a conflict-resolution measure may risk being a means of avoiding addressing difficult questions of politics and ideology.

Part of the problem seems to be a failure by Indian policymakers to understand the limitations of their peacemaking paradigm. Writing in 1966, the home minister of Jammu and Kashmir, D. P. Dhar, noted that

> Pakistan's attempt to build up a movement of espionage and subversion inside the State of Jammu and Kashmir continues to be an unabated and

> undeterred menace. . . . While the administrative machinery in general and the law and order machinery in particular have to continue to be vigilant and alert, we also have to take an urgent political view of the situation. In Kashmir, we have to seek and strive for the emotional enlistment of the people with the rest of the country.

Prime Minister Vajpayee or Prime Minister Singh could have authored much the same text. "Emotional enlistment" has, variously, meant the co-optation of dissident formations and the large-scale dissemination of economic aid. What is not clear is whether the current dialogue with secessionists has any greater structural purpose than merely winning over a section of dissidents and throwing money at the state's people—something that has done precious little to halt the bloodshed in Jammu and Kashmir over the years.

The point here is not that dialogue, economic aid, or political accommodation are *bad* things. It is, instead, to suggest that although these instruments are means to achieve certain ends, policymakers must also be acutely conscious of what they *cannot* achieve.

Moving Peacemaking Forward

Where, then, does the peace process stand?

Making peace is at best a protracted process. Whether Pakistan will be willing to wait the course or to accept a solution that falls short of its expectations is still unclear—and is likely to remain so for some time to come. Given the pressures that have been brought to bear on General Musharraf by Islamist groups, he may see a resumption of full-scale jihad in Jammu and Kashmir as a means of deflecting the attention of those opposed to his pro–United States stance and of rebuilding his religious legitimacy. Although he has cut back on cross-border infiltration, General Musharraf has so far shown a disturbing unwillingness to actually dismantle the infrastructure of terror. Media reports from Pakistan suggest that organizations such as the Lashkar-e-Taiba—designated as terrorist by the United States and charged with some of the worst atrocities against civilians in Jammu and Kashmir—remain free to recruit personnel and raise funds; evidence has even surfaced that some of its cadres have begun to operate in Iraq.

With its eyes focused firmly on Afghanistan and the Middle East, the United States has so far shown little enthusiasm to push General Musharraf to end the activities of such groups—a policy that could end up undermining another key policy goal, a stable South Asia. No great imagination is needed to envision the consequences of a large-scale act of terrorism; the military crisis of 2002 made these clear to even the most obtuse observer. In the short term, the United States needs to ensure that Pakistan moves toward shutting down terrorist organizations, rather than merely containing their activities. The U.S. record on this count is far from heartening. Pakistan is reported to have promised U.S. envoy Richard Gates as early as 1990 that it would shut down terrorist training camps. It did not. Similar commitments made by General Musharraf in 2002 have yet to be met. As Pakistan's principal source of aid, the United States could impress upon Pakistan that violence can no longer be used as a negotiating tool—and that the principal beneficiary of efforts to end violence would not be the Indian state, which has demonstrated its ability to wage an endless war of attrition. Those who would gain most from an end to violence would be ordinary residents of Jammu and Kashmir, the principal victims of a war waged in their name.

Over the longer run, U.S. policymakers need to consider seriously whether their traditional modes of intervention in South Asia have yielded desirable outcomes. It may be oversimplifying it to say that these interventions have consisted of providing economic and military incentives to Pakistan to alleviate its anxieties about the threat it believes its powerful eastern neighbor poses to its existence as a nation-state. Yet the core idea seems to be that alleviating Pakistan's security concerns will lead it to a more accommodative position. Decades of such incentives have done little to take the edge off Pakistan's anxieties about India. Indeed, the existence of what looks like a blank check from the United States could encourage irresponsible behavior and perpetuate the existence of militarist elements in Pakistan that have a vested interest in continued hostilities with India. In a larger sense, the assumption widespread in Washington that third-party intervention, albeit one conducted behind the scenes, will help break the India-Pakistan deadlock could also use some careful examination. This assumption is founded on the experience of the 2002 crisis, but one could argue that conventional military deterrence, or the threat of nuclear escalation, had a more important role in preventing war than international diplomacy did. The jury is still out on these questions, but history gives no reason for comfort in the usefulness of diplomacy: UN intervention failed to break the India-Pakistan deadlock in 1947–48; the Soviet Union could not bring about a breakthrough during the talks that took place after the 1965 war; years of quiet U.S. intervention since the late 1980s have failed to stave off a succession of near-calamitous crises.

I have no alternate prescription for the things the United States *should* be doing. Instead, I would make the somewhat heretical proposal that this might be a good time *not* to be searching for grand solutions, a good time to *stop* looking for one-shot cures. A decade and a half of seemingly uninterrupted crisis have generated a policymaking climate in which activity and meaningful activity are often conflated. Part of the reason why the problem has proved so resistant to resolution is the search for a deus ex machina, a device that will lead a centuries-long history of violence to an instant happy conclusion. It may be useful for policymakers to stop talking about one single Kashmir problem that can be resolved through some free-floating exercise of pure reason. What we call the Kashmir problem is in fact several problems, for which Jammu and Kashmir is only a stage. Among other things, the problem involves irreconcilable ideas about the basis of nationhood, a crisis of religious and ethnic identity, and the still far-from-spent forces that led to the partition of India. For jihadi groups and their supporters in Pakistan's establishment, the war in Jammu and Kashmir is merely part of an ever-larger war, one between Islam and unbelief. And, thanks to the involvement of both public and covert organizations with deep purses, the Kashmir problem is also an *enterprise:* a tawdry business in which there is substantial profit for several actors.

What, then, might an alternate road map look like? The sad truth is that an abiding resolution to the conflict over Jammu and Kashmir may have to wait until India and Pakistan are able to reinvent their relationship, to re-imagine it free of the trauma of partition—a process that could take generations. In the meantime, peacemakers might do well to focus their energies on the problems of Kashmiris—or the many heterogeneous peoples of Jammu and Kashmir—rather than the problem of Kashmir. In some sense, the grand geopolitical narrative called the conflict in Kashmir, on which the world has for decades lavished its diplomatic energies, has displaced the lived experiences of those who form its core. For parents who must shop on Srinagar's streets or send their children to school in Sopore, what the world calls the Kashmir problem is the lived experience of grenades and gunfire. For the people of Jammu and Kashmir, who have had to live with incessant violence and the hardship it brings for fifteen years, sustaining the reduction of violence seen since 2001 may be more important than anything else. Ensuring that the everyday lives of ordinary people become more secure must be a cardinal objective of peacemaking.

For this to occur, however, all parties must understand that dialogue is merely a process—one that does not guarantee any particular outcome. If the contours of a final resolution do not appear clear today, however, there are things that could be done to improve the everyday lives of the peoples of Jammu and Kashmir on both sides of the Line of Control. For one, the United States needs to persuade Pakistan to deepen the process of military de-escalation by making clear that the use of violence as a medium of political dialogue is unacceptable. Both India and Pakistan need to allow space for a genuine dialogue on greater political autonomy for the regions of Jammu and Kashmir under their control, rather than seeing dialogue as an instrument through which their eventual territorial goals can be realized or obstructed. A wide-ranging dialogue on autonomy would give meaning and content to democracy on both sides of the Line of Control. Collaboration on economic issues is also possible between the two states. In the wake of the December 2003 cease-fire, small-scale barter-based commerce spontaneously erupted along some parts of the Line of Control. Authorities brought this short-lived border enterprise to a quick end, but it served to illustrate the potential that exists. At a larger level, fruit and nuts from Jammu and Kashmir have a market in Pakistan, while grain, cloth, and meat products can flow the other way. In several areas, collaborative use of watersheds would benefit villagers on both sides of the Line of Control. Such interaction would not jeopardize the final territorial claims of either country, but would help develop a grassroots interest in peace. I am not proposing that trade or political dialogue would constitute a resolution of the problem in Jammu and Kashmir; rather, that they might help create conditions from which a resolution could emerge.

One could argue that all these ideas—and others similar to them—are palliatives. In the absence of a cure, though, it seems unreasonable to refuse symptomatic relief. It is also true that even small steps forward involve difficult issues. India and Pakistan both seem to wish to allow greater freedom of movement across the Line of Control, yet negotiations to enable such movement are stalled because of concerns in both countries about the sovereignty implications of the travel documents that will be used to make the journey. Pessimism must be tempered by the very fact that there is *some* sign of movement, however small. General Musharraf's new plans may have been intended to prepare his audience at home for less than what official propaganda has promised for generations. The distance that has been traversed is evident from the fact that in 1950 the governor general of Pakistan, Khwaja Nizamuddin, thundered that "Pakistan would remain incomplete until the whole of Kashmir is liberated." The prime minister of the Pakistan-administered province of Azad Kashmir in turn asserted that the dispute "will be decided only on the battlefield."

No politician can, with any seriousness, suggest that war is any longer an option. Yet, prisoners of their own paradigms, both sides seem unable to move forward. Responses in both countries to an ongoing dispute over a hydroelectric project on the Chenab River are instructive. In early 2005, Pakistan moved the World Band for the appointment of an arbitrator, claiming India was being intransigent on the question. In India, the Pakistani decision was widely seen as a sinister ruse to force third-party intervention in Jammu and Kashmir. Some commentators in Pakistan, conversely, claimed the dam threatened Pakistan's irrigation networks, and threw out dark hints of the threat of nuclear war. Little public discourse took place in either country on the details of what is, after all, a technical dispute over river-water usage. Both sides were reluctant to give ground, believing it would compromise their positions on India-Pakistan relations in general and Jammu and Kasmir in particular. Both countries urgently need to find ways to break down their dispute into discrete, bite-sized chunks—or risk adding another chapter of failed peacemaking to their tragic history.

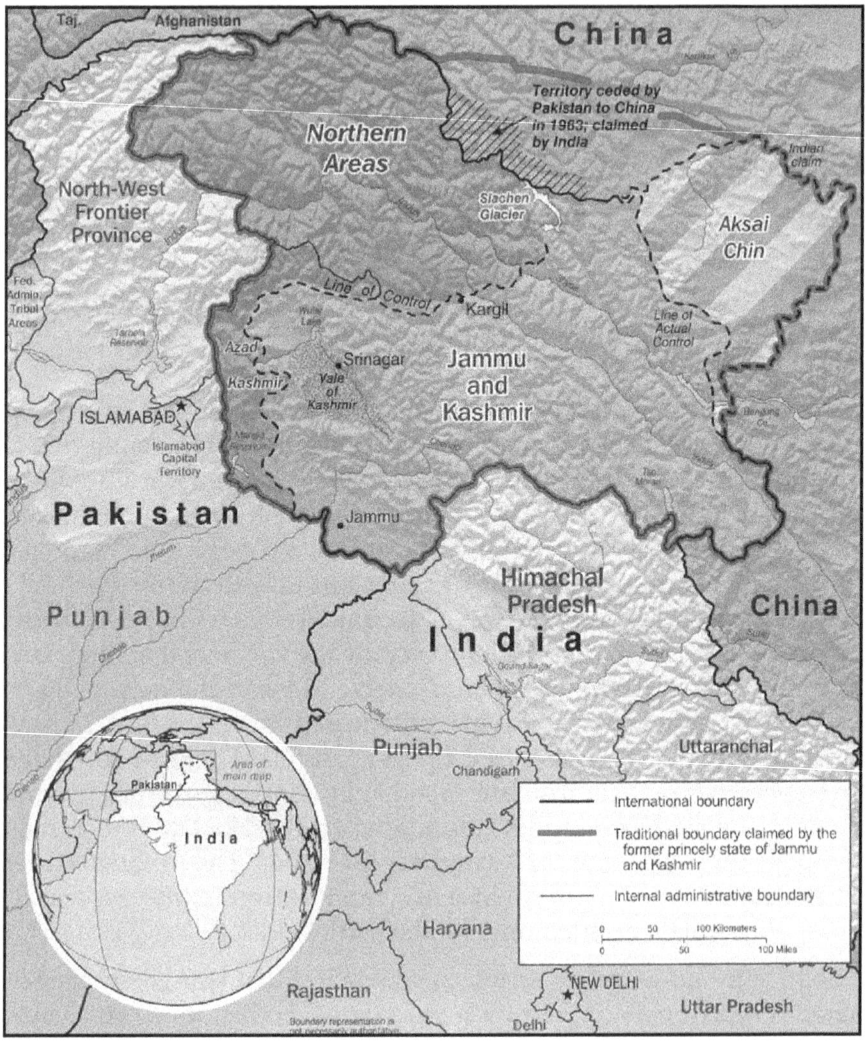

The Kashmir Region

For more information on this topic, see our website (www.usip.org), which has an online edition of this report containing links to related websites, as well as additional information on the subject.

United States Institute of Peace
1200 17th Street NW
Washington, DC 20036

F. OTHER NON-INDIAN PERSPECTIVES

DOCUMENT NO. 33

INTERNATIONAL COMMISSION OF JURISTS' REPORT, 1995

Human Rights in Kashmir: Report of a Mission by Sir William Goodhart (United Kingdom) Dr. Dalmo de Abreu Dallari (Brazil Ms Florence Butegwa (Uganda) Professor Vitit Muntarbhorn(Thailand) Geneva, Switzerland

The members of the ICJ Mission were the first representatives of any international human rights organisation to be authorised by the Indian Government to visit Kashmir in 1995, since the start of the popular upring in occupied Kashmir in 1989.

After visiting Delhi, the ICJ mission spent two days in Srinagar and two days in Jammu. Regrettably, the Indian authorities severely restricted its movements in Srinagar. The ICJ mission had been assured in Delhi that it would be allowed to hold meetings in a hotel in central Srinagar, to which anyone who wished to meet the mission would have access. However, this assurance was overruled by Lt. Gen. Zaki, the Governor's security adviser in Srinagar, who also refused to allow the members to accept an invitation to visit the Bar Association's offices in the Court precinct. As a result, the ICJ mission had to hold its meetings in a State guesthouse in a military cantonment outside Srinagar.

Recent years have been a tragedy for Kashmir. One aspect of the tragedy manifested itself to us on a fine summer evening in Kashmir, looking out from an empty Pari Mahal over an empty Dal Lake, once swarming with activity. Another aspect manifested itself in the refugee camps of Jammu and Azad Kashmir, where victims of the tragedy demonise each other and maimed men and assaulted women are presented to tell their well-rehearsed stories.

International standards of human rights pertain to Jammu and Kashmir as elsewhere. Significantly, the 1948 Universal Declaration of Human Rights establishes universal benchmarks in relation to civil, political, economic, social and cultural rights for measuring the practices of States against international norms.

In regard to India, it is all the more significant that the country is also a party to the 1966 ICCPR which reinforces universal standards in the civil and political field, closely linked with the Rule of Law. The human rights propounded in this instrument include the right to self-determination, the right against arbitrary arrest, security of the person, freedom from torture, and equality before the law. India is also a party to the 1966 ICESCR and the 1965 International Convention on the Elimination of All Forms of Racial Discrimination. Regrettably, Pakistan has not become a party to either the ICCPR or the ICESCR.

At the time of accession to the ICCPR, India showed her reluctance to accept the totality of human rights standards by entering reservations to articles 9 (right against arbitrary arrest and detention), 19 (freedom of expression), 21 (right of peaceful assembly) and 22 (freedom of association). Articles 19, 21 and 22 were made subject to reasonable restrictions referred to in article 19 of the Constitution of India.

Of particular concern has been the failure of India to abide by the standards set by the ICCPR because of a variety of legislative discrepancies dealt with below. These have been aggravated by numerous malpractices on the part of governmental personnel operating in Jammu and Kashmir, documented extensively but both national and international sources.

India has treated the situation of Jammu and Kashmir as a state of emergency but has avoided classifying it as such in international terms, thereby obstructing the call for accountability and transparency inherent in the comments of the Human Rights Committee.

India has been reluctant to classify the conflict in Jammu and Kashmir as a non-international armed conflict under the Geneva Conventions for fear of internationalising the Kashmir issue. At the time of the ICJ mission's visit to India, it had not allowed the International Committee of the Red Cross (ICRC), a key international organisation, offering protection and assistance in such situations, to operate in Jammu and Kashmir. This has regrettably prevented access to affected parties and has impeded the quest for assistance and protection of innocent persons.

The special status of Jammu and Kashmir has been eroded in recent times by legislative and executive encroachment form India; article 370 has been diluted by India so as to confer greater powers upon it to administer Jammu and Kashmir.

Jammu and Kashmir Public Safety Act 1978

By this Act, the Government may detain a person "with a view to preventing him from acting in any manner prejudicial . . . to the security of the State and the maintenance of public order.

Terrorist and Disruptive Activities (Prevention) Act (TADA) 1987

The Act established special courts or "designated courts" to try those arrested for terrorist acts and disruptive activities. It confers broad discretion upon the authorities to arrest persons and to try them.

Armed Forces Special Powers Act 1990

This Act gives the Governor or the Central Government power to declare the whole or part of the State to be a disturbed area and to authorize the use of the armed forces in aid of the civil power.

Other Laws

Other laws have been promulgated or revived recently with negative impact on human rights. In February 1992, an ordinance was issued under Article 370 of the Indian Constitution extending presidential rule in relation to Jammu and Kashmir from the previous period of three years to four years; this prolonged the use of presidential rule as opposed to reversion to an elected system. In July 1992 the Indian Parliament passed the Jammu and Kashmir Legislature (Delegation of Power) Bill which transferred parliamentary powers to deal with that state to the President of India. In 1992, the Jammu and Kashmir Government also recommended that the central government should revive a variety of old laws so as to be able to administer the region more closely. These included the Jammu and Kashmir Criminal Law Amendment Act, which permitted the confiscation of property of unlawful bodies without the need to seek approval from a designated tribunal.

There have been grave breaches of human rights by the Indian security forces in Kashmir.

Extra-Judicial Executions

The deliberate killing of people in police or military custody is simple murder and is the most serious of all the allegations against the security forces. The ICJ mission has no doubt that such killings have occurred on a significant scale. What is far more difficult is to estimate the numbers, particularly as the security forces often claim that the victim has been killed in "crossfire".

Torture

Numerous incidents of torture committed by government personnel have been documented by a variety of sources.

Torture is virtually a matter of routine use in interrogation. The forms of torture range from electric shocks to beatings, other forms of violence and sexual abuse. To prevent hospitals from documenting torture evidenced by patients' symptoms, since 1990 medical records have been removed from hospitals.

Disappearances

These practices occur sporadically. Most of the disappearances do not involve killing but arise because a detainee has been held incommunicado or been moved out of the State without notice. This is compounded by the fact that the applications for habeas corpus are not responded to effectively by the courts.

Rape

The most serious allegation relates to the village of Kunan Poshpora, where it is alleged that at least 23 women were raped by soldiers of the 4th Rajputana Rifles on the night of 23/24 February 1991.

The Indian Government was initially slow to take action against members of the security forces accused of rape, apart from one case where a Canadian tourist was raped. In recent months, it appears that more action has been taken. Many rapes took place in the course of crackdowns, where men and women in the districts being searched were separated. Changes in crackdown procedure—including the presence of women members of the security forces with the units conducting the crackdowns—appear to have had some effect in reducing the number of rapes. There is no evidence that the government has encouraged rape or used it as a deliberate policy. It would indeed have been insane to do so, as nothing would be more calculated to strengthen support for the militants.

Assaults

Innumerable assaults have been witnessed in Jammu and Kashmir. Many are in relation to the cordon-and-search operations, which often end in violence. Particularly vulnerable groups included women and children.

Doctors and other medical personnel have also been assaulted and harassed by security forces while trying to help the injured. The patients themselves have been assaulted while undergoing treatment and have at times been prevented from receiving medical care. These assaults have taken place when security forces raid hospitals.

Destruction of Property and Theft

There are many incidents of arson by the security forces. These have led to hundreds of houses and shops being burnt, along with other property such as barns and haystacks. There have also been many cases of looting and theft.

Constraints Upon Personal and Family Life

In substance, there is a state of emergency in Kashmir and this undermines much of daily personal and family life. The curfews and instances of violence already noted prevent children from attending school. The abuses committed by government forces against men and women disrupt personal and family life continually. Health services have also been affected by raids and curfews, resulting in depletion of health personnel, particularly in rural areas. The situation is now aggravated by the fact that militants are increasingly violent towards innocent civilians.

Conclusions

Regarding the right of self-determination:

The peoples of the State of Jammu and Kashmir acquired a right of self-determination at the time of the partition of India.

The right has neither been exercised nor abandoned and therefore remains capable of exercise.

Full or limited independence for Kashmir is a possible option.

The parties should be encouraged to seek a negotiated solution to be put to the peoples of the state for ratification in a referendum.

Both India and Pakistan should recognize and respond to the call for self-determination for the people of Jammu and Kashmir within its 1947 boundaries, inherent in the relevant United Nations resolutions. The United Nations should re-activate its role as a catalyst in this process.

DOCUMENT NO. 34

MUSLIMS, TERRORISM AND RISE OF THE HINDU RIGHT IN INDIA

Working Paper No. 389
The Australian National University:
Strategic and Defence Studies Centre

May 2004

Sandy Gordon

Strategic And Defence Studies Centre

The aim of the Strategic and Defence Studies Centre, which is located in the Research School of Pacific and Asian Studies in The Australian National University, is to advance the study of strategic problems, especially those relating to the general region of Asia and the Pacific. The centre gives particular attention to Australia's strategic neighbourhood of Southeast Asia and the Southwest Pacific. Participation in the centre's activities is not limited to members of the university, but includes other interested professional, diplomatic and parliamentary groups. Research includes military, political, economic, scientific and technological aspects of strategic developments. Strategy, for the purpose of the centre, is defined in the broadest sense of embracing not only the control and application of military force, but also the peaceful settlement of disputes that could cause violence.

This is the leading academic body in Australia specialising in these studies. Centre members give frequent lectures and seminars for other departments within The Australian National University and other universities and Australian service training institutions are heavily dependent upon SDSC assistance with the strategic studies sections of their courses. Members of the centre provide advice and training courses in strategic affairs to the Australian Department of Defence and Department of Foreign Affairs and Trade. Regular seminars and conferences on topics of current importance to the centre's research are held.

Since its inception in 1966, the centre has supported a number of visiting and research fellows, who have undertaken a wide variety of investigations. Recently the emphasis of the centre's work has been on problems of security and confidence-building in Australia's neighbourhood; the defence of Australia; arms proliferation and arms control; policy advice to the higher levels of the Australian Defence Department; and the strategic implications of developments in Southeast Asia, the Indian Ocean and the Southwest Pacific.

Publications Program

The centre maintains a comprehensive collection of reference materials on strategic issues. Its publications program, which includes the Canberra Papers on Strategy and Defence and SDSC Working Papers, produces up to two dozen publications a year on strategic and defence issues. An abridged list of SDSC publications appears at the end of this volume.

Editorial Board

SDSC Working Papers

Series Editor: Meredith Thatcher

Published and distributed by:

Strategic and Defence Studies Centre

The Australian National University

Canberra ACT 0200

Australia

Tel: 026125 9921

Fax: 0262480816

About the Author

Sandy Gordon was awarded his BA from the University of Sydney in 1965 and his PhD from Cambridge University in 1976, where he specialised in the political economy of India. He joined the Australian Public Service in 1977, subsequently working in the Office of National Assessments, AusAID (where he was in charge of the China Program), and as Executive Director of the Asian Studies Council and Australian Literacy Council. He was promoted to the senior executive service in 1987.

In 1990 he became a Fellow at the Strategic and Defence Studies Centre, Australian National University, where he published extensively on South Asia and the Indian Ocean. He is the author of India's Rise to Power, published by the Macmillan Press. In 1996 he was appointed Special Adviser, Intelligence, in the Australian Federal Police and in 1997 he became Coordinator of Intelligence at the AFP, a position he held until 1990. In that year he became Co-Chair of the Council for Security Cooperation in the Asia-Pacific Transnational Crime Working Group and a member of the National Expert Advisory Committee on Illicit Drugs.

He currently lectures on terrorism, intelligence and South Asia at the Australian Defence Force Academy, University of New South Wales.

This paper represents the author's views alone. It has been drawn entirely from open sources, and has no official status or endorsement.

Abstract

India is located in the heart of a region in which more puritanical forms of Islam have been gaining ground for several decades. This radicalisation of Islam in South Asia has been furthered by the 'war on terror', and particularly the 2003 invasion of Iraq. Against this background, elements within India's predominantly Hindu population have been seeking to 'Hinduise' India's secular polity, sometimes directing violence against India's 130 million Muslims in the process.

In response to these regional and domestic developments, a small minority of Indian Muslims outside Kashmir has chosen to take up the bomb and the Kalashnikov. This movement is closely tied to violent jihadi movements in neighbouring countries, especially the Gulf and Pakistan.

The recently ousted Hindu-led coalition government that has governed in New Delhi for the last seven years has at times responded harshly to this terrorism. Were it to continue, such a response could precipitate a classic downward spiral into terrorism and counter-terrorism. Any such development would have profound implications for India and the region.

This paper examines the prospects for such a development in the context of the recent election of a more secular, Congress-led coalition in New Delhi. It argues that while the new government will seek to return India to its secular roots, now that the Bharatiya Janata Party is out of office at the centre, elements within the Hindu Right are likely to foment unrest between Hindus and Muslims, particularly at the periphery of Indian politics, in order to 'claw back' political power at the centre. Any such tactics may well cancel out the secular strategies of the new government.

Introduction

Hinduism in its traditional form is diverse and syncretic. The 'Hindu Right'[1] has in recent decades, however, been seeking to recreate Hinduism as a more defined religion that commands a dominant political hold over India. This experiment with India's secular settlement is being undertaken against a background in which Wahhabi and Salafist interpretations of Islam have spread from Saudi Arabia, diminishing the Sufi and other more liberal traditions of Islam of India and its neighbours. The so-called 'war on terror', the attack by the US and its allies on Afghanistan and especially the 2003 war in Iraq have also intensified the radicalisation of Islam in South Asia. The rise of Hindu politics and radical Islam are now interwoven into a tight fabric that will prove difficult to unravel.

One little recognised outcome of the rise of the Hindu Right has been the advent of 'home-grown terrorism'[2] perpetrated by disaffected Indian Muslims in response.[3] Such terrorism is still confined to a very small percentage of Indian Muslims and is by no means the most prevalent form of terrorism in India. The Maoist and separatist campaigns in central, eastern and northeastern India are probably more serious in terms of loss of life and property. However, given the spread of India's 130 million Muslims throughout the country and the potential linkages with radical Islamic organisations in the region, especially Pakistan, the potential of the terrorism

[1] The term 'Hindu Right' is in some ways unsatisfactory. As we shall see in this paper, it covers a wide spectrum of views about the role of Hinduism in politics. However, it is a better term than 'Hindu chauvinism', 'Hindu extremism' or 'Hindu fundamentalism'.

[2] By 'home-grown' I mean terrorism perpetrated by Indian Muslims who are neither originally from Kashmir nor Pakistan. This terminology is in no way intended to imply that Kashmiris from Indian Kashmir are not Indian. The term 'terrorism' is notoriously difficult to define. By terrorism I mean planned or actual acts of violence by sub-national groups against persons or property that are indiscriminate, directed at non-combatant members of the disciplined services or civilians and intended to cause general fear in order achieve political, religious or ideological outcomes separate from the actual physical damage planned or occasioned. I do not include acts of advocacy or legitimate industrial advocacy or unrest. Although states can act in a terrorist-like fashion against their own or another people, I do not include them because the types of remedial action needed are quite different.

[3] However, for a persistent voice drawing attention to the advent of home-grown terroristic behaviour on the part of India's Muslims, and the alleged Pakistani involvement in it, see B. Raman's writings on the web site of the South Asia Analysis Group, http://saag.org.

perpetrated by disaffected Muslims to destabilise the country is far greater. As this paper will argue, moreover, the potential for terrorism by disaffected Muslims to enter a downward spiral remains strong, despite the victory of secular forces in the just-completed national elections.

The Hindu-leaning Bharatiya Janata Party (BJP) and its coalition partners fought those elections initially on a platform of a 'shining' India that called for all religions to 'rise on the same tide'. Once this strategy appeared to be failing, the BJP attempted openly to woo the Muslim vote, a strategy that also failed given the party's basic negative view of Muslims. In assessing the future of communal relations in India, it remains to be seen how the BJP will assess this electoral failure and what kind of leadership it will establish to replace the defeated one. In this context, it is noteworthy that under the BJP-led government, the needs of governance and presence in the central government of 'statesman-like' figures such as former Prime Minister Vajpayee meant that the party's position on communal issues was far more moderate at the centre than in the states and at the grass-roots. Moreover, there is evidence that the attempt to woo Muslim voters at the last election was tactical rather than indicative of a change of heart on the part of the Hindu politicians. Finally, the relatively narrow loss of the Hindu-oriented parties suggests they may seek to stir up further communal unrest as they struggle to regain their political hold.

Such unrest in the past resulted in the destruction of the Babri mosque at Ayodhya (henceforth the Ayodhya mosque) in 1992 and the vicious Gujarat riots of early 2002. With hindsight, these events may come to be seen as a 'defining events', just as we now regard the 1983 riots in Sri Lanka as the defining event that triggered the long civil war between Tamils and Sinhalese. But were Ayodhya and Gujarat defining events? And can India—a country in which Muslims are in a majority in only one state (Kashmir) and 4 per cent of electorates—be likened to Sri Lanka, where Tamils are in a clear majority in the north and north east, and in which they can therefore subscribe to policies of autonomy and even independence? And if India were to enter into a downward spiral of terrorism and counter-terrorism, what would such a development portend for the future of India and the region?

Given the size of the Muslim community in India, the consequences of any such development would be profound. Gujarat, which has been at the epicentre of anti-Muslim violence in recent years, is just across a long and porous border from Pakistan. Should the current attempt to improve relations between India and Pakistan fail (a possibility further discussed below), problems over the border would provide an excellent opportunity for Pakistan to 'fish in troubled waters', just as it has in Kashmir.

An aggressive and sustained program of terrorism would also slow the economic growth spurt India has experienced in the last decade of economic liberalisation and could lead to decades of economic stagnation. Much of the terrorism to date has occurred in the commercial and industrial heartland areas of Mumbai (formerly Bombay), Maharashtra and Gujarat. Maharashtra is the most industrialised state in India. Its economy constitutes about 20 per cent of India's GDP. It commands approximately 30 per cent of India's exports and its ports handle 50 per cent of India's trade.[4] The value of cheque transactions in Mumbai is 10 times that of its nearest Indian competitor city.[5] We should also note that recent communal unrest in Hyderabad triggered a frisson of fear on the part of foreign investors that the burgeoning call centre industry would collapse as a result of instability.[6] Such episodes illustrate the vulnerability of high technology investment to any perceived instability.

Any downward spiral into violence would also seriously circumscribe India's emergence as a key Indian Ocean power. It would cause India's military to focus even more than it now does on domestic developments. It would cut the financial roots that sustain India's program of military modernisation. It would provide an almost endless cadre upon which international *jihad* could draw. Finally, it would feed into the powerful sense of grievance already evident amongst Muslims from Europe to Southeast Asia.

A downward spiral into terrorism is by no means certain, however. India's constitution and some of its major institutions are still predominantly secular in both declaratory and operational manifestations. A secular government is now in power in New Delhi. Above all, India is so large and diverse that any unrest in one place is quickly dissipated into the polity as a whole. Nevertheless, as we shall further explore, the destruction of the Ayodhya mosque and riots in Gujarat have already contributed to a steady rise in terrorist incidents perpetrated by disaffected Muslims.

This paper examines the historical legacy bequeathed at Independence, which was one of apparent secularism. It then identifies those economic and political forces that are acting to undermine these conditions within India. It assesses the role of external conditions such as Islamic militancy in surrounding countries, and especially Pakistan. And finally, it seeks to assess whether we are witnessing the commencement into a downward spiral of violence and counter-violence in India, or whether India's size,

---

[4] 'The economic powerhouse', *The Hindu*, Vol. 20, Issue 23 (http://flonnet.com/fl2023/stories/20031121004510600.htm).

[5] 'The economic powerhouse', *The Hindu*, Vol. 20, Issue 23 (http://flonnet.com/fl2023/stories/20031121004510600.htm).

[6] 'Riots give call centres the jitters', *Times of India*, 9 December 2003 (http://timesofindia.indiatimes.com/cms.dll/articleshow/347268.cms).

diversity and vibrant liberal-democratic traditions will be sufficient to minimise any such development.

India's Secular Traditions and Their Erosion

The freedom struggle led by Mahatma Gandhi and Jawaharlal Nehru left a powerful legacy of secularism and inclusion that should have provided for the national integration of Muslims. Article 25 of the Indian Constitution enshrines the right of all citizens to profess, practise and propagate their religion. Individual Muslims have been able to achieve prominence in national life. The first President, Maulana Azad, was a Muslim and there is even a Muslim president today (Abdul Kalam) appointed under the just-defeated Hindu-led coalition. Indian cultural, economic and political life has been replete with Muslim film stars, musicians, cricketers, judges, politicians and industrialists. There are numerous institutions supporting inter-communal national life and a wealth of non-government organisations maintaining a vigorous civil society. In short—or so the argument runs—Muslims are fully integrated into the life of the nation and have no need to resort to large-scale violence.[7]

Indeed, as Ashutosh Varshney's study of communal violence shows, in most of India civic institutions still act to mitigate and defuse any violence by providing a means within which inter-communal communication can occur. Consequently, such violence is manifest mainly in a few, large urban locations subject to rapid social change, rather than in the vast extent of the country.[8]

Juxtaposed to this view of an India in which secularism has taken deep root, however, is a picture of an India in which '. . . secularism is a thin new crust beneath which Hinduism roils'.[9] In its most base form, Hindu politics seeks to harness this visceral attitude to obtain electoral traction and further its agenda. According to Paul Brass, for example, communal rioting constitutes 'learned' and manipulated behaviour supported by networks of 'specialists', some of whom are Hindu nationalist politicians. This process involves not only manipulation of riots themselves, but also of the subsequent interpretation of the causes of the riot in order to support the political purposes of the dominant community. Brass argues, moreover, that communal unrest is 'endemic' in India, not just confined to the cities

---

[7] This view of course relates to Indian Muslims outside Kashmir. The 'traditional' view is probably best captured by the classic text on government in India: W Morris-Jones' *The Government and Politics of India*, (London: Hutchinson University Library, 1971), p. 252.

[8] Ashutosh Varshney, *Ethnic Conflict and Civic Life: Hindus and Muslims in India* (New Haven: Yale University Press, 2002), *passim*. Varshney examines a series of 'matched' cities and discovers that rioting can only be said to be endemic in about 24 places in the entirety of India.

[9] Robert W. Stern, *Changing India: Bourgeois revolution on the subcontinent*, Cambridge University Press, (New Delhi: Cambridge University Press [Foundation Books in India], 1993), p. 26.

identified by Varshney.[10] Brass's work is hotly contested by Varshney and in turn strongly defended by Brass himself.[11]

Varshney's work was published just before the 2002 Gujarat riots. Although those riots do not overturn his findings, they seem to illustrate the fact that social change has become so rapid and the attendant breakdown in institutions so pronounced that cities hitherto considered inured to communal violence are no longer so. For example, Varshney compares Surat favourably to Ahmedabad as being resistant to communalism.[12] However, Surat was an important location of the 2002 Gujarat riots, which did not touch the old city in which Varshney's social structures remained intact, but swept through the new slums built up at the urban fringe.

More importantly, Varshney's findings relate to incidents of communal violence rather than terrorism. Although the two are related, since one act (communal violence) can trigger the other (terrorism), the distinction in terms of the present paper is important.

Communal violence is usually a spontaneous affair that is quickly over, after which life usually returns to normal. As Varshney shows throughout his work, it is usually amenable to the effective functioning of the civil society. It has been a feature of Indian life, particularly urban life, for a considerable period. Terrorism, in contrast, is secret, planned and constant. It almost always has a political purpose, whereas communal violence can have such a purpose but often does not. Terrorism can be conducted well away from the locations in which it is spawned. It can be assisted from outside the country and can therefore constitute an important strategic tool in international competition. Crucially, its secret, on-going nature allows for 'rational players' to engage in it for long-term goals even though it may initially damage their community.

Given the structural differences between terrorism and communalism and the quickening pace of social and economic change in India, arguments concerning institutionalised secularism as a buffer preventing a downward spiral into chronic terrorism may not apply, or may no longer be as relevant as they once were. However, Muslims are a minority in all areas of India except Kashmir (where they are a majority in revolt against Indian rule) and the Laccadive Islands. This fact seems to support another argument to the effect that, as a minority, Muslims can only lose from violent

[10] Paul R. Brass, *The Production of Hindu-Muslims Violence in Contemporary India*, (Seattle: University of Washington Press, 2003), pp. 6–15.

[11] For Brass's reply to Varshney's review of Brass's book, see 'Response to Ashutosh Varshney by Paul Brass', *The Mail Archive*, 5 December 2003 (http://www.mail-archive.com/sapac@www.resident-lounge.com/msg00137.html).

[12] Varshney, Ethnic Conflict and Civic Life, pp. 282–3.

confrontation with the *status quo* powers. As the veteran Indian journalist Khuswant Singh points out, in all communal violence in India since Independence, over 75 per cent of the causalities—in terms of lives lost and property destroyed—were Muslim.[13] Singh's view is generally reinforced by official findings of a Minorities Commission study into communal riots between 1985–87.[14]

Equally, it could be argued, there is no incentive for Muslims to challenge the *status quo* through peaceful political means, since they are in a majority in only four per cent of electorates. Given India's 'first past the post' voting system, it would be most unlikely Muslims could ever gain a significant voting bloc in the parliament, far less exercise a balance of power. Muslims themselves often argue that it makes more sense to align with the secular party that has best prospects rather than to form an independent electoral bloc. For example, in the context of the aftermath of the Gujarat riots of 2002, some Muslims flirted with forming a separate political party. Important Muslim leaders, however, strongly opposed such a move on the grounds that it would further divide the Muslim vote, thus working in favour of the 'Hindu groups'—sound advice as it transpired in the context of the election.[15]

The political restraints within which the Muslim community in India is required to operate, and the fact that Muslims tend to be the losers in terms of direct recourse to communal violence (as distinct from terrorism), could be important indicators of a future recourse to terrorism, should governments in India fail to deal sensitively with the issue of communal relations. However, as argued below, neither in political nor economic life is the position of Muslims in India all it should be, and it may even be deteriorating.

The Changing Economic Situation of Muslims in India

As a minority, Muslims were considered by the British to be less threatening than the Hindu majority and therefore to be cultivated.[16] Like Sikhs, they were considered a 'martial race' and were present in significant

---

[13] *SoundVision.com*, 'Profile of Muslims in India', (http://www.soundvision.com/info/india/profile.asp).

[14] The Minorities Commission found that, in this period, 60% of deaths were of Muslims and 73% of losses were incurred by Muslims. See Steven Wilkinson, 'Putting Gujarat in Perspective', *Economic and Political Weekly*, 27 April 2004, p. 2, (http://www.epw.org.in/showarticles.php?root=2002&leaf=04&filename=4387&filetype=html).

[15] Yoginder Sikand, 'No separate Muslim political party: JUH', *The Milli Gazette*, 1–15 February 2004 (http://www.milligazette.com/archives/2004/01-15Feb04-print-edition/011502200486).

[16] Asghar Ali Engineer subscribes to both the 'divide and rule' interpretation and to the élite determination theory:

> Communalism . . . is not the product of religion; it is, in fact the product of politics of the élite of a religious community . . . And when a third party in the form of a colonial authority is present it [communalism] assumes grave proportions. Though the British colonial rulers cannot be solely held responsible for the genesis of communalism, they did play a vital role in promoting it as well as in its genesis. Right from the day the British rulers sensed the damage Hindu-Muslim unity could cause to their empire, they began dividing the two communities . . .

numbers in the army, paramilitary and police. Many of the large landlords, particularly in the north, were Muslim, having emerged as revenue collectors and landowners under the Mughals. Muslims were also prominent in the handicrafts, especially weaving and brass work.

Since Independence, however, their position has significantly declined. The handicraft industry has been largely destroyed by economic modernisation and they have not maintained the position they enjoyed under the British in public sector employment.

The Indian Army comprised 30–36 per cent Muslims at the time of Partition. Many of these, of course, opted to transfer to Pakistan. But since then, Muslim representation has reduced to two per cent, well below their overall representation in the community. In independent India only two Muslims rose to the rank of Lieutenant General and only six attained Major General.[17] In 1985, George Fernandes, who became Defence Minister under the BJP-led coalition government, admitted: 'The Muslim is not wanted in the Armed Forces because he is always suspect—whether we want to admit it or not. Most Indians consider Muslims a fifth column for Pakistan'.[18] The Army is crucial in quelling communal riots and its intercession is still welcomed by Muslims as relatively neutral and professional. However, some reports claim that the Army balked at being brought in to quell the original Ayodhya incident in 1992 because a Hindu confrontation with the Army could have affected the loyalty of the largely Hindu troops.[19] If true, this would represent a worrying departure.

Prior to independence, Muslims constituted 40 per cent of the Indian police, meaning that they were over-represented. They constitute only 7 per cent today, thus being under-represented.[20] However, Wilkinson has convincingly argued that there is no correlation between Muslim police representation by state and the performance of the states in dealing with communal unrest.[21] This being the case, the lack of representation amongst

---

'Gujarat Riots in the Light of the History of Communal Violence', Economic and Political Weekly, 14 December 2002, p. 2 (http://www.epw.org.in/showArticles.php?root=2002&leaf=12&filename=5265&filetype=html).

[17] The following is from A.G. Noorani's review of *Khaki and Ethnic Violence in India: Army, Police and Paramilitary Forces During Communal Riots* by Omar Khalidi (New Delhi: Three Essays Collective, 2003). The review appeared in *Frontline*, 'Book Reviews', 13 October 2003 as in 'Muslims in the Forces', CounterCurrents. org, 15 October 2003 (http://countercurrents.org/comm-noorani131003.htm).

[18] Noorani's review of Khaki and Ethnic Violence in India: Army, Police and Paramilitary Forces During Communal Riots by Khalidi, p. 3.

[19] Noorani's review of Khaki and Ethnic Violence in India: Army, Police and Paramilitary Forces During Communal Riots by Khalidi, p. 4.

[20] Noorani's review of Khaki and Ethnic Violence in India: Army, Police and Paramilitary Forces During Communal Riots by Khalidi, p. 5.

[21] Steven Wilkinson, 'Putting Gujarat in Perspective', *Economic and Political Weekly*, 27 April 2002 *passim* and Table 1, p. 4, (http://www.epw.org.in/showarticles.php?root=2002&leaf=04&filename=4387&filetype=html).

police may be important not so much in terms of the capacity of police to quell communal unrest, but rather in terms of perception. Such under-representation could also be symptomatic of a wider lack of Muslim representation in government institutions that would have important economic implications, given the economic importance of government employment in developing countries. To add to the economic woes of Muslims, they constitute only three per cent of the élite of the civil service, the Indian Administrative Service (IAS) and only 4.4 per cent of employees in the central bureaucracy as a whole.[22]

In addition to these problems of representation, Muslims have suffered disproportionately because they were strongly represented in important crafts like brass working, formerly a major industry in cities such as Moradabad in Uttar Pradesh (which has subsequently suffered from severe communal unrest) and handloom weaving, which was an important craft in the southern state of Tamil Nadu. The decline of these industries has induced severe poverty amongst some former practitioners.

Recent work by India's National Sample Survey Organisation (NSSO) indicates that Muslims are economically disadvantaged in relation to Hindus. Generally, Muslims in the towns fare worse than those in the country. In rural areas, 48 per cent of Muslims above age seven are illiterate compared to 44 per cent of Hindus. In cities, the figures are 30 per cent of Muslims and 19 per cent of Hindus. India's 43 million Urdu speakers are being further pushed into 'functional illiteracy' as a result of the decline of Urdu script. Muslims also consume less. In towns, 40 per cent of Muslims belong to the bottom 20 per cent in terms of consumption, whereas the figure for Hindus is only half that, at 22 per cent. In the country, the gap is narrower, at 29 and 26 per cent respectively. A higher percentage of Muslims is landless or only marginal in terms of landholding. Only 27 per cent of Muslim families in towns had a working member whereas the figure for Hindus is 43 per cent. The NSSO data also show that the situation of Muslims *vis à vis* Hindus in relation to all these indicators actually worsened during the 1990s.[23]

But the economic position of Muslims, while distressing, is not their major problem. That comes from a profound change in the Indian political framework in favour of a more robustly Hindu outlook.

[22] 'Common questions, uncommon answers', *The Milli Gazette*, 1 November 2002 (http://www.milligazette.com/Archives/01112002/0111200254.htm); Omar Khalidi, *Indian Muslims Since Independence*, Vikas Publishing House Private Ltd, p. 77.

[23] C. Rammanohar Reddy, 'Deprivation Affects Muslims More', Countercurrents.org (http://countercurrents.org/comm-reddy070803.htm).

Muslims and the Rise of Hindu Politics

Hindu politics in India speaks with many voices. Moderates, such as the former Prime Minister, A.B. Vajpayee, avow that they support India's secular institutions. His former deputy, L.K. Adwani, is less supportive. However, below that, the range of Hindu advocacy extends to the vicious and violent, often manifest at the grass-roots. The problem for the BJP hierarchy is, however, that the party is dependent upon the grass-roots electoral cadre for much of its political success. As such, the leadership often finds itself 'riding the tiger' of strident communalism.

The oldest and most extensive of these Hindu-oriented, cadre organisations is the Rashtriya Swayamsevak Sangh (RSS—National Volunteer Corps). The RSS is ostensibly a social organisation with no political aspirations. But it is much more than that. It is shadowy, with no membership lists or public accounts, and does not pay taxes. It contains within it a cadre of Hindu young men (no women) dressed in brown shirts and shorts reminiscent of the Hitler Youth. These cadre cells now number 25,000. Although no actual membership numbers are kept, we can assume from the number of cells that the membership would be from 250,000 to several million.[24] Collectively, the Hindu political interests are known as the 'Sangh Parivar' (Sangh Family). This grouping consists of the RSS; the political manifestation of the Sangh Parivar, the Bharatiya Janata Party (BJP—Indian People's Party); the cultural and religious mobilisation wing, the Vishwa Hindu Parishad (VHP—World Hindu Council); the paramilitary wing, the Bajrang Dal; and the service wing, the Seva Vibhag.[25] The Bajrang Dal practises the type of violence reminiscent of Hitler's 'Brown Shirt' street thugs.

The agenda of the Sangh Parivar is to unite a hitherto highly disparate Hindu grouping into a unified, dominant community. According to the Sangh Parivar, Indian government and institutions—far from being secular as laid down in the Constitution—should reflect the innate 'Hindu-ness' (known as *Hindutva*) of Indian society. Minorities (especially Christians and Muslims, who, unlike Sikhs, Jains and Parsis, are not considered 'people of the soil') should keep a low profile and reflect their overall *Hindutva* qualities in terms of culture. Muslim family law, which still exists within the secular Constitution, should be abolished. Kashmir's separate rights under Article 370 of the Constitution should also be abolished. Hindus should throw off the perception that they are accommodating and 'weak'

---

[24] For the number of RSS cells (chakas) see the RSS website at http://www.rss.org/New_RSS/History/Evolution.jsp.

[25] 'The Foreign Exchange of Hate: IDRF and the American Funding of Hindutva', Sabrang Communications Mumbai and The South Asia Citizens Web, France (http://www.stopfundinghate.org/sacw/part2.html).

and India should take its place in the world as a strong nation. For, in the words of an earlier RSS leader: 'It is significant that all Hindu gods are armed'.[26]

In practice, this agenda has involved violence against Christians and Muslims and manipulation of the state apparatus—especially in relation to education and policing—in those states in which the BJP has been in power. Tribal people, who have in the past gravitated away from Hinduism to Christianity because of their low status, have been coerced (including by beatings and 'tonsuring' of women) back into the fold. Tribals were, for the first time, a significant factor in the anti-Muslim rioting that took place in Gujarat in 2002.

According to A.A. Engineer, the Sangh Parivar depends on riots, nexus with the police, 'ethnic cleansing' (although he doesn't use the term) and violence as stepping-stones to political power. They first tried such methods in the vicious Ahmedabad riots of 1969 and, finding them successful there, applied them to the whole of India. The destruction of the Ayodhya mosque in 1992 was only one such stepping stone, if the most important.[27]

The mosque, located near the northern city of Ayodhya, was allegedly built on the birth-place of the Hindu God Ram (Ram *janmbhoomi*). Ram is an important God for the Sangh Parivar because he is widely popular (especially in the north) and seen as a unifying force of the diverse Hindus. Significantly, the forces that led to the destruction of the mosque were led by the former Deputy Prime Minister, L.K. Adwani. Although Adwani's leadership role in the destruction of the mosque was patent, in a highly controversial decision the Central Bureau of Investigation (CBI) decided to lay no charges against him.[28]

The Sangh Parivar continues to extract mileage out of the Ayodhya mosque issue by seeking to build a temple to Ram on the site of the destroyed mosque, still owned by the Muslim authorities that controlled it. The Archaeological Survey of India has reported that there are remains of a preexisting temple on the site. However, a number of leading academic archaeologists have been critical of the standard of work that led to this conclusion.[29]

Partly as a result of these activities, and partly due to the collapse of the Congress party, a weak, Hindu-led coalition first emerged in Indian politics in 1996, to be further consolidated (although still in coalition) in 1998.

---

[26] Golwaker, the second head of the RSS, quoted in K.R. Mulkani, *The RSS Story* (New Delhi: Impex, 1980, p. 42).

[27] Asghar Ali Engineer, 'Gujarat Riots in the Light of the History of Communal violence', *Economic and Political Weekly*, 14 December 2002 (http://www.epw.org.in/showArticles.php?root=2002&leaf=12&filename=5265&file type=html), pp. 11–12.

[28] A. G. Noorani, 'How Advani went scot-free', *The Hindu*, Vol. 21/2, 17–30 January 2004.

[29] For one such critique see a report of an interview with Professor Suraj Bhan, 'It was not a temple', *Frontline*, Volume 20, No. 19, September 13–26, 2003.

However, well before that, the political climate for Muslims had been vitiated by the use of the 'communal card', both by the Congress party and the BJP, in order to garner votes.[30]

Once in power at the centre, both the coalition nature of the BJP's dependence on power and the needs of governance dictated a more moderate approach by the party on Hindu issues. However, as a party, their political power was heavily dependent on the other components of the Sangh Parivar, and especially those activists working near or at the grass-roots. This meant that power was always likely to be exercised with less constraint close to the grass-roots. Often these grass-roots activities are generated by local concerns, but are also part of a wider strategic aim to garner electoral success for the BJP.

Although Hindu power was exercised with restraint at the centre, the advent of a Hindu-oriented central government provided scope for more radical agendas at the state and grass-roots levels. For example, in education (a state-level function under the Constitution), the Sangh seeks to emulate the Muslim system of *madrassas* (parochial schools). The Vidya Bharati Akhil Bharatiya Shiksha Sansthan network, created by the RSS in 1978, focuses on moral, extracurricular and physical education for 'mind, body and spirit'. The Vidya Bharati system supervises over 18,000 schools across India, with 1.8 million students and 80,000 teachers. A shared curriculum is used across the country. The system also operates 60 graduate institutions. About 5,000 Vidya Bharatis are endorsed by Education Boards, primarily in states where the BJP is in power or influential. According to Chatterji, 'As the Sangh infiltrates into regulatory bodies and actively leads the rewriting of textbooks and reorganisation of the curriculum, the classroom transforms it into an agent of Hindutva'.[31]

At the grass-roots political level, the program of the Sangh has been even more troubling. For example, in Chickmagulkur, Karnataka, local-level Hindu chauvinists are reported to be attempting to 'Hinduise' a famous Sufi shrine, the Baba Budan Dargah, noted for its syncretic form of worship. This agitation is touted as the 'Ayodhya' of southern India and is linked to the 2005 state-level elections in Karnataka. While the BJP benefits politically, the actual campaign is in the hands of the more extremist organisations such as the Bajrang Dal and VHP. The High Court of Karnataka has ruled against the Hindu claims, but the Karnataka state government

[30] One of the most effective charges levelled against the Congress party by the Hindu parties was that it attempted to 'appease' Muslims to garner their vote. Mrs Gandhi, however, also had a propensity to emphasise Hindu values in her political rhetoric. In her political comeback in the South following the Emergency, she even attempted to portray herself as a goddess by arriving in a jeep in villages late at night illuminated from below. (Recounted to the author by one of her entourage).

[31] Angana Chatterji, *Asian Age*, 12 November, 2003 as in Countercurrents.org, 24 November 2003 (http://www.countercurrents.org/comm-angana1121103.htm).

has been reluctant to intercede for fear of alienating the Hindu vote, so the agitation continues unchecked.[32]

Even in the southern state of Kerala, noted for its tolerance and high levels of education, the Sangh Parivar has reportedly been active in fomenting communalism and practising a form of 'ethnic cleansing'. According to one account, on 2 May 2003, in Marad, Kozhikode District, nine Hindus were killed by Muslims. The source claims that the local RSS/BJP had used this event to push all Muslims from Marad. However, the killings by Muslims were, in fact, revenge for the killing of Muslims by Hindus the year before—those Hindus killed being the alleged perpetrators of the earlier killing.[33]

Problems of Hindu extremism at the grass-roots are likely to be exacerbated as a result of further BJP victories at state-level elections in 2003. In Madhya Pradesh, for example, the Chief Minister, Uma Bharti, a noted Hindu holy woman or 'nun', is seeking to implement policies of cow protection reminiscent of the campaign of the 1960s that was used to mobilise Hindus against the beef-eating Muslims.[34]

Often extremism amongst the Hindu community is explained or justified by the existence of Muslim extremism, especially as allegedly exported by Pakistan. For example, retired Lieutenant Colonel Jayant Chitale reportedly started a group near Abarmath, Thane (near Mumbai), which raised alleged 'suicide squads' against the 'enemy country' [Pakistan]. In the Thane camp 45 young Hindus aged between 16 and 29 allegedly underwent training. Following this training in 'suicide attacks', they were to wait a year to see if Muslim terrorism abated before launching attacks.[35]

This last case is an example of a strange symbiosis between extremist actors on both sides of the India-Pakistan border. In an odd way they each need the other. This is further illustrated by an interview conducted by Jessica Stern with the public-affairs director of the Lashkar-e-Toiba (LeT), a Pakistan-based extremist organisation about which we will hear more. According to Stern:

> The Lashkar-e-Toiba public-affairs director told me he was 'happy' about the growth of the Hindu extremist group Bajrang Dal, the arch-nemesis of the Pakistani militant groups. It provides a *raison d'être* for Islamic

[32] Parvathi Menon, 'A communal campaign', *The Hindu*, 8 December 2003 (http://www.hinduonnet.com/the hindu/thscrip/print.pl?file=20031219002604100. htm&date. . .).

[33] Mukundan C. Menon, 'Marad: Untold Story of an RSS "Liberated Area" ', Countercurrents.Org, 26 May 2003 (http://countercurrents.org/comm-menon260503.html).

[34] See Ram Puniyani, 'Uma Bharti's Cow Agenda', Countercurrents.org, 3 March 2004 (http://countercurrents.org/comm-puniyani250204.htm).

[35] *The Milli Gazette*, Sunday 13 July 2003. The group was reportedly an offshoot of the Pune-based Maharashtra Military Force (MMF). Although this reference is from a Muslim source, the MMF is itself well documented. (http://www.milligazette.com'Archives/01122002/0112200286.htm).

fundamentalism in Pakistan, he said. 'What is the logic for stopping the *jihadi* groups' activities if the Indian government supports groups like Bajrang Dal?'[36]

The use of communal riots and attacks on Muslims to garner political power reached its apotheosis in the state of Gujarat in 2002. Gujarat has an important history for the Sangh Parivar. As noted, the Sangh was able to capitalise on the dreadful 1969 riots in Ahmedabad to consolidate its hold. When the police eliminated a leading Muslim Gangster called Latif, this further weakened the position of Muslims, who had nobody to protect them from the Hindu gangs who were mobilised by the Sanghis. After the BJP captured power in the state in 1993, the situation began further to worsen.[37]

The riots of April–May 2002 were thus a culmination of a long process of deliberate erosion by the Sangh Parivar of secular institutions in Gujarat and of use of communal violence for political ends. In fact, the BJP government, led by Narendra Modi, faced scheduled elections in March 2003—elections some felt it was likely to lose, but subsequently won, probably assisted by the government's role in the riots.[38]

The riots themselves were triggered by an attack on a train containing Hindu activists. The attack, allegedly undertaken by local Muslims at the town of Godhra, involved the torching of the train and the killing of 58 Hindus. The resulting pogrom against Muslims killed 900 according to official figures of the state government, but some accounts put the figure nearer 2000.[39] Allegedly, the police stood by and refused to assist Muslim victims. Rioters apparently came prepared with lists of Muslim properties, presumably provided by municipal authorities.[40] The Home Minister, charged with maintaining order, was himself allegedly involved in encouraging the rioters.[41] In addition, tens of thousands of Muslims were kept in camps in appalling conditions following the riots. Prior to Gujarat's state elections, they were turned out of these camps with nowhere to go.

---

[36] Jessica Stern, Terror in the Name of God: Why Religious Militants Kill (New York: Ecco, 2003) p. 263.

[37] Asghar Ali Engineer, 'Gujarat Riots in the Light of the History of Communal violence', *Economic and Political Weekly*, 14 December 2002, pp. 11–12 (http://www.epw.org.in/showArticles.php?root=2002&leaf=12&filename=5265&file type=html).

[38] Engineer, 'Gujarat Riots in the Light of the History of Communal violence', *Economic and Political Weekly*, p. 14.

[39] 'Guilty verdict in Gujarat case', BBC News, 24 November 2003 (http://news.bbc.co.uk/go/pr/fr/-/2/hi/south_asia/3234604.stm).

[40] '. . .though we have witnessed government inaction or indifference . . . we have never seen governmental machinery involved in executing the riots and the chief minister justifying it instead of controlling it'. (Engineer, 'Gujarat Riots in the Light of the History of Communal violence', *Economic and Political Weekly*, p.16.)

[41] Manus Dasgupta, 'Pandya instigated the mob, alleges witness', *The Hindu*, 18 July 2003 (http://www.hinduonnet.com/stories/2003071804280100.htm).

The Muslim Reaction

As already mentioned, the Muslim reaction to the problems the community has suffered has been restrained by factors associated with its minority status and the way it is distributed throughout India. However, in view of the depth of the problems suffered, an element within the community has increasingly tended to react in terms of violent, secret, politically inspired action that meets all the definitional hallmarks of terrorism. This terrorism, moreover, is increasingly generated within those states of India outside the Muslim majority state of Kashmir.

Following the destruction of the mosque at Ayodhya in 1992, there was a spate of rioting around India, in which as many as 2000 Muslims may have died. This rioting was especially bad in Mumbai, fuelled by the activities of the Hindu chauvinist Shiv Sena party.[42]

In the aftermath of this rioting, there occurred in Mumbai in March 1993 what was at the time one of the worst terrorist events anywhere in the world in terms of lives lost, and the worst ever in India.[43] This was a series of synchronised bombings around the city in which 257 people died in a single day and about 1,000 were injured.

Indian authorities allege that these outrages were committed by the Mumbai gang leader, Dawood Ibrahim, and two other leading gangsters, 'Tiger' Memon and Chhota Shakeel. They further allege that Ibrahim and his cohorts were assisted by Pakistan's Inter Services Intelligence Directorate (ISI), which provided explosives, landed by 'country craft' north of Mumbai. They point out that the explosive used was RDX, normally available only to military forces. The Indians also allege that Ibrahim was subsequently given safe haven in Karachi. He is on the list of 20 alleged terrorists that India sought to extradite from Pakistan following the bombing of the Indian parliament in December 2001. Significantly, he was also recently placed on the United States' list of wanted terrorists, indicating that US authorities believe that the Indian allegation has some truth.[44]

Ibrahim has never been brought to trial for the alleged offence and so his role, and the alleged role of the ISI, must remain somewhat conjectural. However, the central point is that the bombings were almost certainly conducted by Indian Muslims in revenge for the destruction of the Ayodhya

[42] The term 'chauvinist' is used advisedly in the case of the Shiv Sena.

[43] The bombing of the US marine barracks and French troops in Beirut in 1983, allegedly by Hezbollah, resulted in a higher number of deaths. Depending on one's definition of terrorism, the attack on unarmed civilians in Punjab at Jallianwala Bagh in 1919 was a far worse event. In that attack, the official death toll was 379, but the number who died was probably greater. However, some definitions of terrorism do not include 'state terrorism'.

[44] For a good account of the bombings and the above list of accusations, see Praveen Swami, 'The spreading tentacles of terror', *The Hindu*, 31 August 2003 (http://www.hindu.com/2003/08/31/stories/2003083100251400.htm).

mosque and subsequent rioting against Muslims. They also marked the start of a steady pattern of domestically inspired terrorist attacks by Muslims. These actions included bombing of trains and attacks on political headquarters of the Hindu right. Most significantly, many of the attacks were not perpetrated by Kashmiris as part of the on-going separatist movement in that state, but were seemingly perpetrated by non-Kashmiri Indian Muslims in revenge for Ayodhya and other perceived acts against Muslims. While they were a new phenomenon, they were containable and did not attract widespread international attention.

One commentator who has consistently pointed to the rise of homegrown terrorism since the destruction of the Ayodhya mosque, however, is B. Raman, a former additional secretary in the Cabinet Secretariat and senior member of the Indian external intelligence service, the Research and Analysis Wing (of Cabinet) (RAW). According to Raman:

> This *jihadi* iceberg has been forming for years since the Babri *masjid* demolition of December 1992—not only in Mumbai, but also in Andhra Pradesh, Tamil Nadu, Kerala, New Delhi and other parts of India. While India focused on *jihadi* terrorism in J&K [Jammu and Kashmir], it did not pay the same attention to this iceberg threatening the rest of India.[45]

Raman's voice has now been joined by others pointing to the effects of the Ayodhya mosque demolition and the 2002 riots in Gujarat in radicalising a section of India's Muslim population. For example, Praveen Swami wrote in the respected, Left-leaning journal, *Frontline,* that memories of the destruction of the mosque had started to fade amongst Muslims prior to the Gujarat riots of 2002, and not even the plight of Muslims in Kashmir raised much interest. However,

> [Then] . . . in 2002, came the communal massacres in Gujarat . . .[LeT] cells based in Kuwait and Dubai have emerged as central to several major terrorist actions in India over the last two years. Many of those involved are not stereotypical seminary-educated fanatics, but people with jobs and families—with lives they seem willing to sacrifice to avenge one of India's worst communal pogroms.[46]

Examples of terrorism since 1992 are given in **Appendix A.**[47] It should be stressed that this chronicle is by no means exhaustive of terrorism in India. It has been selected from a long list of available examples in order to illustrate points for this paper about Islamic terrorism. Furthermore, because of

---

[45] B. Raman 'Mumbai: Tip of the jihadi iceberg', *Asia Times,* 1 September 2003 (http://www.atimes.com/atimes/printN.html), p. 2.

[46] *Terrorism: Lethal Remittance,* by Praveen Swami, Vol. 21, Issue 1, 3–16 January 2004 (http://www.hinduonnet.com/fline/fl2101/stories/20040116003 202600.htm).

[47] This compilation has relied heavily on the South Asia Terrorism Portal (SATP) website, which gives timelines for 2000–4 at http://www.satp.org/satporgtp/countries/india/timeline/2000 (01–03).htm. Press extracts are also used but not acknowledged. They are mainly drawn from the Internet versions of *The Hindu* and *The Times of India.*

the concern of the paper with terrorism outside Kashmir, the list obviously does not deal with the violence there. A number of interesting trends emerge from these accounts of Muslim terrorism.

–Terrorism in India and the death and destruction wrought by terrorism is a serious problem by international standards. Terrorism perpetrated by disaffected Muslims is increasingly pronounced. These acts are fuelled by extensive availability of weapons and high explosives.

–Although some Pakistani and Indian Kashmiri Muslims have certainly been involved in attacks in Indian states other than Kashmir during the period under review, importantly, there is a significant *home-grown* element consisting of non-Kashmiri Indian Muslims involved in these activities. Moreover, in the many incidents in which Pakistanis and Kashmiris were involved outside Kashmir, they were often assisted by non-Kashmiri Indian Muslims.

–The involvement of home-grown terrorists increased sharply in the aftermath of the Gujarat riots. Within Mumbai, the suburb of Ghatkopar has suffered in particular in the aftermath of the 2002 rioting in Gujarat. Ghatkopar is home to many Gujaratis, suggesting that these are revenge attacks for the 2002 rioting against Muslims in Gujarat. The role of the Gujarat riots in radicalising Muslims is further reinforced by the statements of those arrested. The increase in home-grown terrorism post 2001 could also in part reflect the broader radicalisation of the Muslim community associated with the 'war on terrorism', attack on Afghanistan and especially the Iraq war.

–Outside Kashmir, the rising body of activism has focused on Mumbai, Gujarat and western India. Other terrorism 'hot spots' include western Uttar Pradesh and Hyderabad and Chennai (formerly Madras) in the South.

–The Muslim reaction has in part been fuelled by modern communications technology such as videos detailing the atrocities on Muslims perpetrated during the Gujarat riots and web sites devoted to the Gujarat atrocities.

–The organisers of the attacks are often members of the educated middle class rather than the poor and uneducated. As with terrorism more generally, however, the actual 'foot soldiers' undertaking the attacks are often less well educated and less well placed.

–In a number of instances, expatriate Indian workers in the Gulf have been involved. The Gulf countries most concerned have been Dubai (UAE), Kuwait and Saudi Arabia.

–Three organisations—which are further discussed below—appear to have been prominently involved in many of the attacks. These are the Lashkar-e-Toiba (LeT), the Student's Islamic Movement of India (SIMI) and Ahl-e-Hadith (also known as Ahle Hadees in the Urdu rendition). A further two organisations, al Ummah and Deendar Anjuman, have also been involved. Jaish-e-Mohammed has also been prominent, but has not been as closely identified with recruiting of Indians as LeT.

–The type of explosive most commonly used has been the classic 'home brew' used in many of the Mumbai bombings—the mix of ammonium nitrate, potassium chlorate and sulphuric acid. There has also been considerable use of gelignite (sometimes described as 'gelatine' or 'gelatin' by the Indian police and press) and the military explosive RDX. The significance of the types of explosive used is further discussed in the section on the role of Pakistan, below.

–Another interesting feature of the rise of terrorism in India has been the role of India's so-called 'mafia dons'—that is, major organised crime figures. Not only have they had a role in protecting the Muslim community from Hindu inspired attacks (as in the case of the gangster Latif in Gujarat), but they have also apparently perpetrated such attacks themselves, as in the case of the alleged role of Dawood Ibrahim and his fellow gangsters in the 1993 Mumbai bombings. Additionally, the dons are likely to be heavily involved in channeling arms and explosives into India via smuggling routes from Pakistan, or indirect routes via Nepal and Bangladesh.[48] They are also extensively involved in terrorism financing through the operations of the informal money market, the *hawala* system.

Some commentators dispute the role of the Gujarat riots in causing a quickening pace of terrorism. Swapan Dasgupta, for example, argues that it is the growing number of 'Muslim ghettos' rather than 'riot affected areas' that are the main recruiting grounds. These include Assam, from which, he says, 300 Muslim youths were sent for training in Pakistan, Hyderabad and western Uttar Pradesh. He further argues that it is not rich, middle class professionals who are conducting terrorism but poor people motivated by 'small-time maulvis [preachers] running obscure madrassas' as is the case in the 25 August, 2003 Mumbai bombings. He also points to *madrassas* funded by Pakistan and Arab money. He says that a 'jihadi' force within India was motivated by Harkat-al-Mujahideen as early as 1993 and

[48] See for example, *The Times of India*, 12 March 2003, which claims extensive smuggling of arms takes place across the border and that Ibrahim is in collusion with the ISI to destabilise the border area. (http://times ofindia.com/cms.dll/xml/uncomp/articleshow?msid=243342).

that up to 5,000 (non-Kashmiri) Indians have been trained in Pakistani camps.[49]

The causes of terrorism are complex and cannot be sheeted home to any one factor. Nevertheless, there seems little doubt that both Ayodhya in 1992 and Gujarat in 2002 were important factors in alienating some Muslims, whatever the role played by Pakistan or the existence of 'ghettos'. Moreover, nobody is claiming that Gujarat riot victims are themselves the only ones turning to terrorism. Rather, Gujarat has been a motivating factor within the Muslim community as a whole, especially given the graphic way the stories of the atrocities have been spread by modern technology.

It is true, on the other hand, that as a means of defending themselves against attacks by Hindus, Muslims have increasingly chosen to live in Muslim ghettos rather than mixed suburbs. This phenomenon goes back at least as far as the post-Ayodhya Mumbai riots of 1992–93 instigated by the Shiv Sena. But it has gathered pace and become something of a Muslim mantra following the Gujarat riots of 2002. These latter riots witnessed the brutal killing of a prominent Muslim parliamentarian, Ahsan Jafri, and his family. Jafri had gone out of his way to live and work inter-communally and the murder of he and his family was a particular shock to the Muslim community.

Following the Gujarat riots, Kaleem Kawaja, writing in the leading Muslim on-line journal, *The Milli Gazette*, argued that those who were in areas in which Muslims constituted over 20 per cent of the population fared much better in the riots than those in which they constituted only 10 per cent, in that they were better able to defend themselves through strength in numbers. The author concluded that the lesson to be drawn is that Muslims should establish their own Muslim-dominated areas.[50] As a result of such arguments and the deteriorating communal circumstances, walls are now being built between Muslim and non-Muslim suburbs. Even middle class Muslims are being forced out of mixed suburbs into ghettoised suburbs.[51]

If Varshney's argument that secular, inter-communal activities and institutions play an important role in defusing communal tensions is correct, then the separation of communities into suburbs and districts—some of them gated—can only be to the detriment of long-term communal harmony in India.

---

[49] Swapan Dasgupta, 'Gujarat is not the main recruiting ground for jihad', Rediff.com, 8 September 2003 (http://www.rediff.com/news/2003sep/08guest.htm).

[50] Kaleem Kawaja, 'Muslims in India: live together to survive, *The Milli Gazette*, Vol. 3, No. 23 (http://www.milligazette.com/Archives/01122002/0112200266.htm).

[51] See 'Ahmedabad's ghettos', by Dionne Bunsha, *Frontline*, Vol. 20, Issue 20, net version (http://www.flonnet.com/fl2020/stories/20031010003303900.htm), pp. 1–5.

Finally, the intensive and on-going involvement of the Pakistan-based LeT and the large number of Pakistanis who have allegedly crossed into Indian states outside Kashmir to undertake terrorism[52] raises the issue of the nature of any on-going, official support from Pakistan for terrorism in India proper.

Lashkar-e-Toiba and the Role of Pakistan

Many Indian commentators and officials believe that the rise of domestic terrorism in India proper has been inspired and assisted by the Pakistani authorities, especially the ISI. Such views are not confined to the present day BJP and Hindu-oriented parties, but are more widely held and have a relatively long history. For example, Indira Gandhi frequently alluded to the role of the 'foreign hand' of Pakistan in many of India's ills.

Today, the phenomenon of finding the hand of Pakistan in India's domestic terrorism problem has in no way diminished. B. Raman, for example, argues that the rise of home-grown terrorism in India was masterminded by the ISI using the four principal *jihadi* organisations operating in Kashmir. According to Raman, the ISI was keen to use the camps of the organisations in Pakistani Kashmir rather than camps in Pakistan proper, presumably to disguise the official Pakistani involvement. Raman further argues that the ISI decided to strike initially in Maharashtra, Tamil Nadu and Kerala 'because of their strategic significance in the eyes of Pakistan's military-intelligence establishment'. Mumbai is the economic and financial capital of India and all three states are important in India's nuclear and space establishments. Raman adds that, of the four *jihadi* organisations, only the LeT was able to take root in India.[53]

The parent organisation and political arm of LeT is Markaz-Dawa-al-Irshad (now known as Jamaat-ud-Dawaa Wahhabi educational institution). LeT changed its name after the September 11 and Lok Sabha attacks of 2001 to Paspen-e-Ahle Hadith. However, it is still widely known as LeT. Hafez Sayeed is the 'Emir' of the group.[54] LeT and Markaz advocate the creation of two independent homelands for the Muslims of South and North India,

---

[52] See **Appendix A**. However, the Appendix was not framed with a view to demonstrating the extent of Pakistani border crossings. A better indication of that is provided by the SATP site at footnote 47, above.

[53] B. Raman 'Mumbai: Tip of the jihadi iceberg', *Asia Times*, 1 September 2003 (http://www.atimes.com/atimes/printN.html), pp. 2–3. See also 26 August 1998, B. Raman 'Markaz Dawa al Irshad: Talibanisation of Nuclear Pakistan', SAAG Papers, http://www.saag.org/papers/papers6.html. The four jihadi organisation are: Harkat–ul-Mujahideen (HuL); Harkat-ul-Jihad-ul-Islami (HUJI); Lashkar-e-Toiba (LeT); Jaish-e-Mohammed (JEM).

[54] 'Lashkar-e-Toiba: its past, present and future', B. Raman, Paper 175, South Asia Analysis Group (http://www.saag.org/papers2/paper175.htm); Jessica Stern, *Terror in the Name of God: Why Religious Militants Kill* (New York: Ecco, 2003) p. 108.

as well as one embracing the whole of Kashmir and Pakistan. Despite its focus on Kashmir, LeT is as much a Pakistani as a Kashmiri organisation. It is also a member of Osama bin Laden's International Islamic Front for Jihad Against the US and Israel.[55] Of all the Pakistani *jihad* groups, LeT has developed the strongest international profile. It is active in the Gulf states, particularly Dubai, Kuwait and Saudi Arabia and even allegedly has adherents in far-off Australia.[56]

LeT also apparently has links with Indian groups such as the SIMI. Again, as evidenced from the chronicle of events at **Appendix A**, SIMI has been the most important of the home-grown elements in domestic Indian terrorism.

SIMI was originally an offshoot of Jamaat-i-Islami Hind (JIH). Until 1987, all presidents of SIMI had been senior members of JIH.[57] It was founded in 1977 by Dr Mohammad Ahmadullah Siddiqui, now an American academic. However, Siddiqui maintains the organisation has completely changed and doesn't agree with its militant direction.[58] It should also be stressed that JIH does not support violence. Raman maintains that SIMI became violent when a hard core of its membership (who came from Indian states other than Kashmir) was fighting the Soviets in Afghanistan. According to him, 'The ISI motivated them [the students] against India, gave them *jehadi* inculcation in Afghanistan and sent them back to India for starting a *jehad*'.[59]

However, Upadhaya contends that SIMI was always a revolutionary Islamic organisation seeking establishment of an Islamic state in India and the return of the Caliphate along the lines advocated by the founder of the Jamaat-i-Islami (the parent body of the JIH), Sayyid Maududi. He maintains it is in touch with a wide range of like-minded organisations around the world. According to him, SIMI's hold on Muslim students was greatly strengthened by the destruction of the mosque at Ayodhya in 1992.[60]

SIMI was banned by the Government of India in September 2001 following the September 11 attacks on the United States. In implementing the ban, Home Minister Pande claimed SIMI was associated with al Qaeda, had links with the ISI, was regularly visited by the head of Hamas, was in close

---

[55] 'Lashkar-e-Toiba: its past, present and future', B. Raman, Paper 175, South Asia Analysis Group (http://www.saag.org/papers2/paper175.htm).

[56] The presence of the LeT in the Gulf is alluded to throughout this paper and is evident from **Appendix A**. In a recent Australian case, a medical student and the alleged terrorist Willie Brigitte were both alleged to have trained with LeT in Pakistan.

[57] R. Upadhaya, 'Students [sic] Islamic Movement of India', South Asia Analysis Group, paper No. 825, 30 October 2003, p. 2 (http://www.saag.org/papers9/papers825.html).

[58] Interview with Siddiqui (who is now an academic in the US) by Rediff.com on 2 September 2003 (http://www.rediff.com/news/2003/sep/02inter.html).

[59] B. Raman (a retired public servant) 'Islamic Terrorism in India: The Hydra-Headed Monster', South Asia Analysis Group paper 526, 3 October 2002, p. 1 (http://saag.org/papers6/papers526.html).

[60] Upadhaya, 'Students [sic] Islamic Movement of India', pp. 2–5.

touch with the Hizbul Mujahideen of Kashmir, disseminated 'anti-national' literature and allegedly instigated violence in Uttar Pradesh, Maharashtra and Madhya Pradesh. With the ban, the head of SIMI, Shahid Badra Falahi, was jailed.[61] In July 2003, SIMI activists Mohammed Yasin Patel and Mohammed Afsal Jaffrey were also sentenced to five years under the Prevention of Terrorism Act (POTA) for being members of a banned organisation (SIMI) and seven years for sedition.[62]

Another important organisation of which some of the members are allegedly associated with terrorism in India is Ahl-e-Hadith. Both Markaz and LeT are closely affiliated with this Wahhabi, 'fundamentalist' organisation. Ahl-e-Hadith has in recent years spread throughout India, even the South, where it has been popular with returned guest workers from the Gulf. It is also active in the Gulf States. As such, it provides an important recruiting base in India and the Gulf for LeT. At least some of those accused of terrorism in India were allegedly recruited through Ahl-e-Hadith.

If LeT, Ahl-e-Hadith and SIMI have been the important players in terms of terrorist activity in India, what, if anything, does this say about the role of Pakistan?

Despite the persistent accusations of Indian officials that ISI is directly involved in fostering terrorism in India, and despite the fact that at least some of the activists in India received training in Pakistan, there is little hard evidence of Pakistani *official* and *direct* involvement in terrorism in India, as distinct from Kashmir. That said, there are a number of pointers suggesting some kind of possible indirect involvement.[63]

On many occasions the explosive RDX has been used in terrorist attacks in India or seized from terrorists in India (see **Appendix A**). These reportedly include the infamous 1993 Mumbai attacks. The *Times of India* reported on 16 September 2003 that as many as 10,000 police, coast guard vessels and naval helicopters were patrolling the 100 km long Thane–Raigad coast to interdict a 'huge consignment' of explosives (believed to be RDX) that 'Intelligence' said was being shipped from Pakistan. Police maintained the recent interrogation of Jaish-e-Mohammed terrorist Atiq Ahmed by Delhi police revealed a small consignment of RDX had already found its way in by sea.[64]

---

[61] Onkar Singh, 'Ban result of SIMI's anti-national activities: Swami', Rediff.com, 27 September 2001 (http://www.rediff.com/news/2001/sep/27simi1.htm).

[62] *The Hindu*, 22 July 2003, 'SIMI activists sentenced' (http://wwwhinduonnet.com/stories/200307 2207640102.html).

[63] By direct assistance I mean a terrorist activity in India actually planned and supported by Pakistani officials. Indirect assistance might include official assistance to a Pakistani or Kashmiri group that is known to be carrying out terrorism in India outside Kashmir.

[64] Somit Sen, 'Police launch massive operation on west coast', *Times of India*, 16 March 2004 (http://timesofindia.indiatimes.com/cms.dll/articleshow?msid=183368).

RDX (cyclotrimethylenetrinitramine) is principally a military explosive produced in government factories for military purposes. Its main non-military use is for blasting caps. However, in that capacity it would be practically impossible to obtain sufficient quantities for terrorism. While RDX could have 'leaked' from a military environment—perhaps from the Indian Army—this is a less likely source than Pakistan, and especially the Pakistani military in the form of the ISI. It is also interesting to note that the South Asia Terrorism Portal website's chronicle of events mentions several seizures of RDX in the possession of 'ISI agents' operating near the border with Pakistan, but well away from Kashmir.[65] It is possible, however, that these so-called 'agents' are LeT and other *jihadi* group operatives bringing arms and RDX originally supplied by the ISI *for purposes in Kashmir* into India for attacks outside Kashmir. Such a view is consonant with the clear intention of LeT to target India more generally.

However, the most common explosive used in India is not RDX but the classic 'home brew' used in many of the Mumbai bombings, the mix of ammonium nitrate, potassium chlorate and sulphuric acid. All these chemicals are easily obtainable within India. This formula has at times been available on the Internet and is broadly similar to the mix used for the Oklahoma and Bali bombings. Use of this explosive mix suggests that to a significant degree India's terrorism problem is home-grown or, less likely, the result of training by Pakistan to disguise any involvement on its part.

The August 2003 Mumbai bombings, along with a number of other seizures and bombings, involved gelignite.[66] Gelignite is a form of dynamite and is a common explosive for mining and excavation. It would be readily available on the Indian black market. (It is also interesting to note as an aside that it appears to have been the explosive used in the bombings in Madrid of 11 March 2004.) The material used in the August 2003 Mumbai bombings was allegedly shipped over the border from Nepal. Nepal has previously been used by the ISI to smuggle goods and people into India in the context of activities in Kashmir. It is also a favoured smuggling route for Indian organised crime.[67] Use of the Nepalese route is not, of course, proof of Pakistani official involvement, but it could well be an indication of the on-going involvement of Muslim criminals in supporting terrorism in India.

---

[65] http://www.satp.org/satporgtp/countries/india/timeline/2000-04.htm.

[66] Interestingly, the Indian government laboratory analysing the explosive reported it to be RDX. The police, however, insisted it was 'gelatine'.

[67] *The Times of India* claims that a leaked intelligence report said:

> Dawood's [Ibrahim] D company colluded with the ISI to create political instability and lawlessness and was concentrating on districts along the Indo-Nepal border, the report said.

The report further concerned smuggling drugs and arms from Kathmandu to India, Times of India, 12 March 2004 (http://timesofindia.com/cms.dll/xml/uncomp/articlessgow?msid=243342).

In terms of the possible involvement of Pakistan, more telling than the type of explosives used is the intensive role of LeT in fostering terrorism in India and in training Indian terrorists in Pakistan. LeT, along with the other *jihadi* groups in Pakistan active in Kashmir, has had a very close relationship with the Pakistani authorities, especially the ISI. This relationship developed in the context of the Afghan anti-Soviet war and continued 'full-throttle' throughout Pakistan's campaign of proxy war in Indian Kashmir. It is difficult to envisage that a group like LeT could be involved in terrorism in India outside Kashmir—including training of terrorist cadre in Pakistan and provision of explosives across the border—without the knowledge and presumably tacit approval of Pakistani authorities. However, it should be noted that this type of tacit approval, or 'turning a blind eye', is not the same thing as direct involvement. It should also be noted that, following the Indian mobilisation after the attack on the Lok Sabha of December 2001, which brought the two nations close to war, Pakistan would probably be wary of any deliberate involvement in a group like LeT in terms of its Indian operations beyond Kashmir.

Indeed, a safer strategy for Islamabad—because less obviously associated with Pakistan—would be to proffer arms by way of support to Indian insurgents in the northeast of the country. The recent enormous haul of arms in Chittagong Port, Bangladesh, has all the hallmarks of some kind of official involvement, given the size and cost of the shipment.[68] But again, the origin, funding and destination of this shipment, while intriguing, must remain conjectural.

What does the targeting of terrorist attacks in India tell us about the possible role of Pakistan? It appears at first glance that the targeting does have a 'strategic hand' guiding it. This would explain attacks focused on important financial centres like Mumbai and IT locations like Bangalore, Hyderabad and Chennai. It is also possible, however, that those seeking to initiate terrorism in India—home-grown or sponsored from Pakistan—have targeted important economic targets like Mumbai according to their own strategic calculations or for other than strategic reasons. It is quite possible that the educated cadre of SIMI, for example, is capable of planning terrorism strategically.

Moreover, Mumbai is in many respects a logical choice for home-grown attacks mounted in revenge for Gujarat. As already observed, there are many Gujaratis living there and it is an important location of Gujarati business interests. It is noted for its high degree of communal unrest, partly

[68] Haroon Habib, 'A deadly cargo', *Frontline*, Vol. 21, Issue 10, 8–21 May 2004, http://www.flonnet.com/fl2110/stories/20040521000206100.htm. One possibility is that the shipment does not involve another state sponsor, but is for insurgent groups such as the ULFA that has acquired funds by illicit drug dealing.

because of the activities of the local Shiv Sena party. It is freewheeling and an important location of money laundering and gangster activity. It is the location of vast slums and a high degree of social dissonance. In short, there are many other explanations for the high incidence of terrorism in Mumbai and western India than any role of Pakistan.

Whatever the truth of any involvement by Pakistani authorities in terrorism in India, the central analytical point for this paper is that there has been a rise in *home-grown* terrorism by non-Kashmiri Indian Muslims since the 1992 destruction of the mosque at Ayodhya and especially since the Gujarat riots of 2002. While it was convenient for India's former Hindu-leaning government to attribute these attacks to the machinations of Pakistan, and while there may certainly be some help from Pakistan for such activities, to a significant degree they are a direct response by dissatisfied Muslims to events triggered by the Hindu Right elements themselves.[69] Any involvement of Pakistan is likely to consist of facilitation of an existing trend rather than the creation of that trend. But, at the very least, it can be noted that Pakistan has been tardy in cracking down on groups like LeT in whatever guise such groups are currently travelling.

In view of the apparent home-grown nature of recent terrorism, the crucial issue therefore remains: how has Indian government policy in response to these developments acted either to reinforce the terrorism tendency or to mitigate the circumstances that have given rise to it?

Government Strategies and Repression

The issue of the role of government in either mitigating terrorism in India or exacerbating the problem is complicated by India's federal structure. As already noted, at the state level, BJP governments, and in some cases even BJP-leaning governments, have acted to 'appease' what they see as the Hindu vote.[70]

At the federal level, however, the policy direction has been more complex. After an initial delay in dispatching the Army to Gujarat to quell the 2002 riots, the policy framework set by then Prime Minister Vajpayee was more statesman-like. At the highest strategic level, the Vajpayee government was well aware of the economic consequences of any downward spiral into

[69] See 'Pandya murder trial begins today', Praveen Swami, *The Hindu*, 1 October 2003 (http://www.hindu.com/2003/10/01/stories/2003100109891200.htm). This provides a picture of a local Muslim cleric who actively sought out financial assistance from a Pakistani group, Lashkar-e-Toiba, while he was in the Gulf, to start a terrorist cell. Financial support was subsequently allegedly provided.

[70] Even the AIADMK government of Jayalithaa in Tamil Nadu, which was in alliance with the BJP-led government at the centre, has acted in ways likely to alienate minorities in order to shore up its position. See S. Viswanathan, 'The Spread in the South: Tamil Nadu', *Frontline*, Vol. 21, Issue 6, 13–26 March 2004.

domestic violence in India and sought to moderate its policies accordingly. For example, even the Deputy Prime Minister, L.K. Adwani, who is noted for his close links to the RSS, reaffirmed faith in secularism in the context of his keynote address to inaugurate the Modi government's 'Vibrant Gujarat' campaign to attract international investment. In doing so, he said he would like to see Ahmedabad develop into a more '*cosmopolitan* city' (emphasis added).[71]

The BJP government even went so far in the context of the 2004 election campaign as to attempt to woo the Muslim vote, especially once it became apparent that it was losing support halfway through the extended election period. This strategy not only included the moderate Vajpayee, but also L.K. Adwani. Prior to the election, the latter set out on a *yatra* (journey) reminiscent of his 1990 *Rath Yatra* that was in turn a prelude to the destruction of the Ayodhya mosque. On the latter occasion, however, the *yatra* was not so much directed towards Hindu interests as the selling of a 'shining', predominantly secular image of India in which all religions and interests would 'rise on the same tide'. Ironically, this *yatra* attracted criticism from both the Left, which argued it was intended to replicate the 1990 *yatra* as a form of political 'dog whistling', and the Hindu Right, which saw Adwani's criticism of the Gujarat riots as a betrayal.[72] However, as pointed out above, at the regional and local levels the Sangh Parivar has been anything but reflective of this moderate position.

Moreover, India's reaction to its terrorism problem has been similar to that of many Western countries—to tighten the legal framework in order to 'crack down' on terrorism. An early expression of the Indian legislation was the Terrorist and Disruptive Activities (Prevention) Act (TADA). According to Human Rights Watch, TADA is notorious for facilitating tens of thousands of politically motivated detentions, torture, and other human rights violations against political opponents in the late 1980s and early 1990s. TADA was replaced by POTA in 2002. This act sets forth a broad definition of terrorism that includes acts of violence or disruption of essential services carried out with 'intent to threaten the unity and integrity of India or to strike terror in any part of the people'. POTA also makes it a crime not to provide authorities with 'information relating to any terrorist activity'. The Act allows for up to three months' preventive detention without charge.[73] It was under POTA, for example, that the Muslim college teacher, S.A.R. Geelani, was sentenced to death for involvement in the Lok Sabha attack of December 2001. However, the Delhi High Court

[71] 'Advani reaffirms faith in secularism', *The Hindu*, 29 September 2003 (http://www.thehindu.com/2003/09/20/stories/2003092906150100.htm).

[72] 'Advani's riot talk draws ire', *The Times of India*, 9 March 2004 (http://timesofindia.indiatimes.com/articleshow/msid-548063,prtpage-1.cms).

[73] Human Rights Watch, World Report 2002: India, p. 5 (http://www.hrw.org/wr2k2/asia6.html).

released him on appeal saying there was no admissible evidence against him at all.[74]

In recognition of the widespread abuse of POTA, in October 2003 the Act was amended to make the findings of the Union and State Committees that oversight its implementation mandatory and to ensure that where the same person was considered by POTA by state and federal authorities, the federal jurisdiction would prevail.[75]

The converse of the draconian prosecution of some Muslims in India through TADA and POTA is the near failure of the authorities to obtain prosecution outcomes against Hindus in the context of the Gujarat riots. According to Harsh Mander, of the 240 people held by the Gujarat state authorities under POTA, 239 are Muslim, one is a Sikh and not one is Hindu. The four major petitions pending before the Gujarat High Court filed by respected writers, artists and activists have been deliberately delayed by the state authorities and the only one to have gone forward is the *Best Bakery* case. That case became notorious when the witness withdrew her evidence, allegedly as a result of intimidation from Hindu Right elements. However, recently the Indian Supreme Court has ruled that the *Best Bakery* case should be removed from Gujarat and heard elsewhere in India, since there is no guarantee of a fair hearing in Gujarat. To date, only one set of convictions of Hindus has been obtained as a result of the Gujarat riots—for a massacre of 14 Muslims at Ghodasar on 3 March 2003.[76]

Despite the adjustment to POTA and the intervention of the Supreme Court in the *Best Bakery* case, the overall climate for human rights in India has been in decline in recent years. Legislation like POTA, poor resourcing, political interference and corruption have caused India's hard-pressed security services to act in a heavy-handed fashion towards Muslims and other minorities. Any further decline in behaviour on the part of the agencies could quickly produce that fatal violence-counter violence cycle so typical of terrorist insurgency. And once the gears of this cycle lock in, experience the world over shows that they are especially difficult to disengage.

Outlook

The destruction of the mosque at Ayodhya occurred twelve years ago. Over two years have passed since the terrible riots in Gujarat. Those two

[74] Siddharth Narrain, 'Reversing a verdict', *Frontline*, Vol. 20, Issue 23 (http://flonnet.com/fl2023/stories/20031121005002000.htm).

[75] *The Hindu*, J. Venkatesan, 'Ordinance to amend POTA promulgated' (http://www.hindu.com/2003/10/28/sories/2003102808990100.html).

[76] *The Times of India Online*, 24 November 2003 (http://timesofindia.indiatimes.com/articleshow/msid-301359,prtpage-1cms).

events have produced a worrying increase in terrorism perpetrated by non-Kashmiri Indian Muslims. Such people are apparently driven by a combination of factors, including continuing economic stagnation of the community, the repercussions of the so-called 'war on terrorism', the growing role of Wahhabi and Salafist forms of Islam in South Asia and frustration and despair at the growing power of the Sangh Parivar in Indian political life and the way the Hindu Right has used communalism to garner that power. Terrorism has become a constant of Indian life. While most acts of terrorism have been relatively minor, several have constituted major terrorism attacks by any standards.

India is so large and diverse that the level of violence has been somewhat obscured from the public gaze. Such violence has not yet jeopardised foreign investment and the economic renaissance that has attracted so much international attention. Even Mumbai and western India, which have been a focus of much of the unrest, continue to prosper. Present levels of terrorism are containable within the Indian polity.

Another positive factor is the election of the Congress-led central government. Congress will rely on the votes of 62 Marxists and 55 socialists, all of whom will have strong secular credentials. Congress itself has striven in recent years to reassert its secular credentials. There will be pressure on the new government by those elements on the Left to repeal or modify the hated POTA legislation. Congress is likely to meet these demands on POTA and also intervene in education departments to ensure that a secular position is reasserted.

Congress has also pledged to continue former Prime Minister Vajpayee's resolute efforts towards a settlement with Pakistan of the Kashmir issue. Although such a settlement would not entirely solve communal problems between Hindus and Muslims in India, it would certainly help to remove the sense in India that Muslims are a 'fifth column' for Pakistan.

However, these positive elements suggesting an improvement in the lot of Muslims and a diminution in the threat of home-grown terrorism may not be as effective as could be hoped.

With or without Vajpayee, the *jihadi* groups in Pakistan will do their best to derail the peace initiative through a significant terrorist attack. But what is even more troubling is that the Hindu Right out of office may well seek to act as a spoiler of any attempt at rapprochement with Pakistan. Indeed, former Deputy Prime Minister L.K. Adwani hinted as much in an interview prior to the election.[77] The presence of the Hindu Right as spoiler would make it more difficult for a Congress-led government to give any

[77] See Siddharth Varadarajan, 'BJP may play spoiler in foreign affairs', *The Times of India Online*, 15 May 2004 (http://timesfindia.indiatimes.com/articleshow/msid-676324,prtpage-1.cms).

ground on Kashmir. It would also make it more difficult for the government not to blame Pakistan for any substantial terrorist event perpetrated by *jihadi* groups as they attempt to derail the peace process.

And, despite the secular victory, there are many other uncertainties that cloud the future. Each of these is potentially interconnected in a mutually reinforcing 'witch's brew' of possibility. These include the great difficulty of ensuring that India's vast security framework continues to uphold basic human rights norms, the propensity of the Sangh Parivar to act out its communal role forthrightly at the grass-roots level, where it is still in government in a number of important states, the prospect of further political instability in Pakistan with possibly a greater role for Islamic interests and the prospect for a 'change of guard' from the Vajpayee leadership of the BJP to that of L.K. Adwani, or some other figure who would likely be more chauvinist, particularly with the party now out of office.

In this latter respect, the recent loss of the national election by the BJP does not auger well. The more strident elements within the Sangh Parivar already have knives out for the moderate leadership, arguing that their policy of seeking Muslim votes and peace on Kashmir 'betrayed' Hindus and caused the electoral loss.[78] This presages a shift to more militant political methods reminiscent of the original Ayodhya campaign. For example, out of office, the Hindu Right is likely to push much harder for the construction of a temple to Ram on the mosque site than they could while exercising the responsibilities of office. In this respect, it is ironic that a victory for the secular forces in the national election may well have a worse outcome for peace with Pakistan and better communal relations in India than a solid BJP victory would have.

[78] See Sultan Shahin, 'BJP: You can cry if you want', *Asia Times Online*, 15 May 2004 (http://www.atimes.com/atimes/South_Asia/FE15Df04.html).

Appendix A
Some Major Incidents of Terrorism from 1993 to the Present

1993	
March 1993	serial blasts in Mumbai—257 killed. The bombings were allegedly masterminded by the gangsters Dawood Ibrahim, Chhota Shakeel and 'Tiger' Memon in response to the destruction of the Babri mosque at Ayodhya and the subsequent anti-Muslim riots. The RDX explosives allegedly came from Pakistan and Dawood Ibrahim was allegedly subsequently given safe haven in Pakistan.
8 August 1993	bombing of the RSS office in Chennai (then Madras), 11 killed. This attack was the alleged work of a South Indian extremist Muslim organization, the Al Ummah (or Al Umah). Imam Ali, of Al Ummah, was trained in camps in Pakistani Kashmir. Al Ummah was allegedly started with the connivance of the LeT.
December 1993	bombings of five trains—two die, 22 injured. A group of Muslims were convicted. They were allegedly seeking to revenge the Ayodhya mosque destruction.
1998	
February 1998 1998	bombing at Virar, Mumbai—9 killed serial bombing in Coimbatore—kills 58, injures 250, also blamed on Al Ummah.
2000	
2000	*passim*—Andhra and Karnataka serial bombings of churches. These activities are allegedly linked to Deendar Anjuman, an orthodox Islamic organisation believing Christians are also Muslims.
17 January 2000	police arrest three persons, including a Pakistani, in Delhi, and recover 860g of RDX, two ABCD timers and four electronic detonators from them. The Pakistani national was arrested earlier in 1998 for circulating counterfeit currency.
3 August 2000	police raid the residence of a top leader of the Deendar Anjuman in Nuzvid, Krishna district of Andhra Pradesh, and recover 200 timer devices.
11 August 2000	one person is killed and 45 injured in a powerful explosion in Ahemedabad, Gujarat.

August 2000	bombing of the Sabarmati Express near Faizabad, Uttar Pradesh. Student's Islamic Movement of India (SIMI) activists allegedly involved.
3 September 2000	SIMI activists—Mohammed Maroof and Abdul Mobin—confess to their role in a series of bomb blasts in Uttar Pradesh on the eve of Independence Day. They also reveal that a new terrorist outfit called Qaafila-e-Saaqt Jaan (QSJ) has been founded in Uttar Pradesh.
10 October 2000	Delhi police arrest a medical student who is a supporter of the Tehriq-ul-Mujahideen (TuM) and seize some explosives and one million rupees.
24 November 2000	Maharashtra Police says an estimated 150 LeT terrorists are suspected to have infiltrated into India to kill important leaders.
6 December 2000	Delhi Police arrest an ISI agent, a resident of Lahore, Pakistan and seize 10 kg of RDX, some arms, ammunition and documents.
22 December 2000	attack on an army barracks at the Red Fort, three killed. This was attributed to Kashmiri members of the LeT.

2001

17 January 2001	Delhi Police arrest a Pakistani terrorist of the Al Badr with one kg of RDX and a detonator. Police arrest two suspected 'ISI agents' in Bihar's Maharajgang district, while attempting to cross over into India from Nepal.
17 February 2001	Intelligence Bureau (IB) alerts district police chiefs in Bihar on the activities of Islamist terrorist outfits—linked to Osama Bin Laden—along the Nepal border. The IB says they might try to recruit youth for *jihad* in Kashmir.
18 April 2001	three Pakistani terrorists are killed in an encounter in Gomtinagar area, Lucknow. Nearly two kg of high quality chemical explosives, two AK rifles, and other arms and ammunition are recovered.
19 April 2001	police arrest three suspected supporters of the JeM in Allahabad for helping the terrorists killed in Lucknow a day earlier.

14 May 2001	the Uttar Pradesh government admits a rise in ISI activities in the state and says seven organisations, including the HM, LeT and HuA, are primarily responsible for cross-border terrorism along the Nepal border.
21 May 2001	an 18-inch IED containing about 750 grams of 'gelatin' and having a time mechanism and electronic detonator is found near the Vishwa Hindu Parishad (VHP), a Hindu religious organisation, office in Nagpur.
24 May 2001	police detect and defuse a time bomb near the headquarters of the Rashtriya Swayamsevak Sangh (RSS) in Nagpur.
15 June 2001	Delhi Police Special Cell foil an alleged plot by Osama bin Laden, to be executed through his aides, to blast the United States Embassy in New Delhi, by apprehending two suspected terrorists. Six kg of RDX, detonators and timers are recovered from one of the accused, a Sudanese national. His Indian accomplice is identified as Shameem of Bihar.
31 August 2001	a Delhi Court sentences a Kashmir terrorist to 14 years rigorous imprisonment for smuggling 1.4 kg of RDX, five detonators, and Pakistani currency to deliver to terrorists in Delhi.
27 September 2001	a report says ISI recruitment in Andhra Pradesh, in Hyderabad; Nalgonda, Warangal, Nizamabad and Karimnagar districts might have commenced in 1991. Recruits were sent to Pakistan for arms training, the report claims.
27 October 2001	14kg of RDX, two AK-47 rifles, two pistols, 296 pistol cartridges, an assortment of electronic detonators and timing devices and other explosives are seized near the India-Pakistan border at Santalpur, Patan district, Gujarat.
13 December 2001	attack on the Indian Parliament, 16 killed, including terrorists. Allegedly perpetrated by LeT and Jaish-e-Mohammed. The attack involved use of firearms and RDX.

26 December 2001	the annual year-end report of the Ministry of Home Affairs, for the year 2001, says 101 'ISI modules' were unearthed countrywide. The report holds that heightened challenges posed by foreign sponsored terrorist attacks characterised the internal security situation.

2002

5 January 2002	Delhi Police arrest a *hawala* (illegal money transaction) operator from Lal Kuan area of North Delhi for alleged involvement in financing ISI agents.
22 January 2002	attack on the American Centre, Kolkata. Four killed, allegedly by ARCF/HuJI.
23 January 2002	Farhan Malik, a Dubai-based criminal with links to the ISI and several terrorist outfits of Pakistan claims responsibility for the January 22 terrorist attack on the American Centre, Kolkata. He also threatens to execute more such attacks at other places. CBI informs the FBI that the ransom money taken by Aftab Ansari, the perpetrator of the American Center attack, to release a Kolkata businessman was used to finance Mohammed Atta, leader of the September 11 terrorist strikes in the US.
12 February 2002	reports say Aftab Ansari admitted meeting senior officials of the ISI in Dubai and Rawalpindi (Pakistan) at least five times since 1999. Five gangsters of the Dawood Ibrahim group are arrested and a huge cache of foreign-made firearms are recovered from their possession at the Mulund-Thane check-post near Mumbai. CBI say e-mail messages revealed Aftab Ansari's links with the Al Qaeda.
2 March 2002	two Hizb-ul-Mujahideen terrorists, including a founder member of the SIMI, are arrested in Kolkata, and large quantities of explosives are seized.
8 March 2002	Union Minister of State for Finance, Gingee N. Ramchandran, says in the Lok Sabha that preliminary investigations into recent cases of *hawala* transactions *prima facie* indicate linkages with terrorist activities. Forty-five *hawala* dealers have been arrested in Delhi and other parts of the country during the last three years, he adds.

19 March 2002	Minister of State for Home, Vidyasagar Rao, says the government is considering enacting new legislation to check the receipt and utilisation of foreign funds by *madrassas* and other organisations. He adds that there are 31850 *madrassas* in the country—1453 in border areas—and that the ISI is trying to manipulate and mislead scholars there.
3 July 2002	media reports say the Coast Guard has intercepted an abandoned Lebanese ship in the high seas 84 nautical miles off-Ratnagiri in Maharashtra. Two AK-47 rifles, with the inscriptions 'Allah' and 'Yusuf' are seized from the ship.
9 July 2002	five terrorists of the HM are arrested in Moradabad and a huge quantity of arms and ammunition, including three AK assault rifles, ammunition and RDX, are recovered from them.
11 July 2002	MDMK general secretary and Member of Parliament Vaiko is arrested by Madurai police in Chennai under POTA for making pro-LTTE speeches and statements. He is immediately taken to the Central Prison in Madurai.
14 August 2002	police arrest an alleged Al Ummah Mujahideen terrorist reportedly trained in Pakistan, while trying to set up a base in Delhi.
28 August 2002	Delhi Police arrest two LeT terrorists from Nizamuddin area and seize 4 kg RDX, a Chinese pistol, two detonators and bullets.
31 August 2002	LeT terrorists held in Ahmedabad for plotting to assassinate Gujarat Chief Minister Narendra Modi and some senior Rashtriya Swayamsevak Sangh (RSS) members.
4 September 2002	Andhra Inspector General of Police (Intelligence), A. Siva Shankar, says the ransom of 30 million rupees paid for the release of Kolkata industrialist Partha Roy Burman ultimately reached the perpetrators of the September 11 terrorist attacks in the US.
18 September 2002	Abu Salem, underworld don and a key accused in the 1993-Mumbai serial bomb blasts, is arrested in Lisbon, Portugal.
24 September 2002	around 35 persons are killed and nearly 100 injured when heavily armed, suspected LeT terrorists storm the Akshardham temple of the Swaminarayan sect in Gandhinagar, Gujarat. Allegedly perpetrated by LeT and Tehhreek-e-Qisas.

21 November 2002	suspected LeT terrorists set off blast near a temple in Hyderabad, Andhra Pradesh.
29 November 2002	Defence Minister George Fernandes says India has intelligence information and "human evidence" to support the charges that the ISI and the Al-Qaeda are using Bangladeshi territory for anti-India activities.
1 December 2002	police in Chennai, Tamil Nadu, arrest two extremists of the hitherto unknown Muslim Defence Force (MDF), an Islamist terrorist group, from a city suburb, and some detonators, gelatin sticks and other bomb-making material are seized.
2 December 2002	police begin to investigate the financial operations of the MDF. Chennai Police Commissioner K. Vijay Kumar says the MDF has links with the LeT and that it planned to set off blasts across the State. Reports say its chief, Abu Hamsa, resides in Saudi Arabia.
6 December 2002	Bombay Central Railway Station blast injures 25. Attributed by police to SIMI and LeT. Use of a 'crude' bomb.
22 December 2002	Ghatkopar (Mumbai) bus blast, 3 killed. Six people are arrested. The police allege they are LeT, Ahl-e-Hadith and SIMI associated. The explosive was ammonium nitrate, potassium chlorate and sulphuric acid. The network appears to have originated with expatriate Indians in Dubai, recruited through LeT. The alleged principal, Imran Rahman Khan, was of a poorly educated background and was allegedly activated to commit *jihad* by the Gujarat riots of 2002. He was allegedly influenced by Lashkar commander Abdul Bari, a one-time Hyderabad (India) resident, who had spent the last 12 years shuttling between his base in Saudi Arabia and Dubai and other Gulf states on organisational work. Bari's collection of video-tapes on riot carnage convinced Khan to join an assault team being sent to Mumbai. Members of SIMI also seem to have cooperated with the Lashkar in setting up several Gulf-based cells. Mohammad Altaf, a long-time SIMI activist from Parbhani, Maharashtra, was a trained chemical engineer working in Dubai when the Gujarat pogrom began. He made contact with Bari soon after and, through him, he came to know Khan.

22 December 2002	nine more Muslim Defence Force (MDF) activists are arrested in Sivaganga, Tirunelveli and Tuticorin districts, in Tamil Nadu.

2003

9 January 2003	Mumbai Police arrest the main accused in the December 2002 blasts in a bus in Ghatkopar, Mumbai, Imran Rehman Khan, under POTA immediately after his deportation from Dubai.
13 January 2003	Ghatkopar bus blast main accused Imran Rehman Khan discloses that he was summoned by the LeT to Dubai to formulate a plan "to avenge Gujarat killings".
16 January 2003	Tamil Nadu Chief Minister J Jayalalitaa declares the entire state as a "notified area" under section 4 (possession of certain unauthorized arms) of POTA.
18 January 2003	a report says the LeT is establishing branches in Kuwait, Saudi Arabia and some European countries.
26 January 2003	Mohammed Altaf, a SIMI activists and accused in the 2 December 2002 bomb blast in Ghatkopar, Mumbai, is deported from Dubai. He had allegedly supplied explosives and funds used in the incident.
27 January 2003	Vile Parle, Mumbai train blast, 1 killed, 30 injured.
29 January 2003	Mumbai Police suspect the LeT and SIMI were involved in the blasts near Vile Parle railway station, Mumbai. United Arab Emirates (UAE) based LeT terrorist Abu Hamza is suspected to have organised the blasts. The government is asked to seek his deportation.
31 January 2003	India and Thailand agree to convene a Joint Working Group on Security and cooperate in four areas: extradition, mutual legal assistance on criminal matters, work on security issues with or without international strategic content, and drive against narcotics.
22 February 2003	Deputy Prime Minister Advani reiterates in Himachal Pradesh the government's resolve to combat terrorism and divisive forces. He adds 171 'ISI centers' at 151 locations were unearthed.
1 March 2003	Delhi Court sentences to 10 years rigorous imprisonment two associates of the Babbar Khalsa, arrested on 14 October 2000, with 29kg RDX.

5 March 2003	POTA Court frames charges against nine persons, including six Pakistani nationals, for allegedly plotting to kill President APJ Abdul Kalam and attack the Bhabha Atomic Research Center, Mumbai, as well as other vital installations in Delhi.
13 March 2003	Mulund Station, Mumbai, train blast, 12 killed, 71 injured. This bombing took place one day after the 10 year memorial of the 1993 serial blasts. SIMI and Ahl-e-Hadith personnel were allegedly involved. One of the alleged accused in this blast, Ahmed, is a former aide of alleged terrorist, Dr Jalees Ansari, alleged mastermind of 60 bomb blasts in India. The blasts were detonated in the first class ladies carriage. Explosive used was a mix of ammonium nitrate, potassium chlorate and sulphuric acid.
16 March 2003	Deputy PM Advani says SIMI and JeM were responsible for the Mulund blast of 13 March, in Mumbai.
26 March 2003	assassination of former Home Minister of Gujarat, Haren Pandya. Pandya, the most bitter political opponent of Chief Minister Narendra Modi, was killed allegedly for his involvement in instigating mobs to conduct attacks during the Gujarat riots.[79] Pandya's father blamed the BJP—with L.K. Adwani in turn blaming Pakistan's ISI.[80] Two groups were arrested for this event, one of four Gujaratis by the Gujarat police, including the imam of a mosque, and another of 14 Kashmiris by the Delhi CBI. Each police force alleged they had the correct culprits. The explanation might have been that, whilst the event was staged by Kashmiris, support was provided by Gujaratis. An article also refers to 10 of the accused having been sent to Pakistan for training.[81]
27 March 2003	Deputy PM L. K. Advani says in Ahemedabad, Gujarat, the killing of former Home Minister Haren Pandya was a 'brutal act of terrorism' and accuses 'the terrorist-underworld nexus' for the killing.
4 April 2003	speaking in Indore, Madhya Pradesh, Deputy PM L. K. Advani says that the LeT is behind the killing of former Gujarat Home Minister Haren Pandya, Nadimarg massacre in J&K and Mulund train blast in Mumbai.

[79] Manas Dasgupta, 'Pandya instigated the mob, alleges witness', *The Hindu*, 18 July 2003 (http://www.hinduonnet.com/stories/2003071804420100.htm).
[80] Dionne Bunsha, 'Probe or Prosecution?', Frontline, 18 May 2003, as in Countercurrents.org (http://countercurrents.org/commbunsha180503.htm).
[81] B. G. Rajeswar, 'Police mole knew of Mumbai plot', Times of India, 4 September 2003.

19 April 2003	while speaking in New Delhi, Central Reserve Police Force (CRPF) Director General S. C. Chaube says that Pakistan is using Bangladesh and Nepal to support subversive activities in the northeastern region.
21 April 2003	Under POTA, Mumbai Police arrest Ghulam Akbar Khotal, an alleged SIMI activist from Ratnagiri, Maharashtra, in connection with 13 March Mulund railway station blast-case.
13 May 2003	an arms dump, including RDX and AK-46 rifles, allegedly belonging to the SIMI and LeT is recovered at Padgah in the Thane District of Maharashtra.
29 July 2003	Ghatkopar, Mumbai, bombing of a bus—three killed, 34 wounded. Allegedly SIMI, Ahl-e-Hadith and LeT were involved. This event was similar to five previous explosions since December 2002, in the use of the mix of ammonium nitrate, potassium chlorate and sulphuric acid.
30 July 2003	Mumbai Police says that two suspected LeT terrorists and a member of the Ahle-Hadees, an Islamist extremist group affiliated to the Saudi Arabia-based Wahabi sect, are responsible for the 29 July bomb blast.
17 August 2003	an unnamed security official says that Pakistan-based terrorist outfits LeT and HuJI are luring youths from different places of Gujarat and sending them to terrorist training camps in Pakistan occupied Kashmir (PoK) through Poonch district in Jammu and Kashmir.
25 August 2003	Mumbai blasts. 52 killed in two separate, timed explosions, one at the Gateway to India and one at the Jhaveri (jewelry) bazaar. Police arrest four—Syed Mohammed Hanif, his wife Fehmida Hanif, their daughter Farheen Hanif and Arshad Shafiq Mohammed—whom the police refer to as 'mere couriers'. All are India born. Police are also seeking a suspect, Nissar Ahmed Ansari (aka 'Nassir'), whom they believe is in charge of the 'terror nodule' operating since the December 2002 bombings. Police believe Nissar provided the team with explosives. The explosive was in each case allegedly 25 kg of 'gelatin'. It is noteworthy that 235 'gelatin' sticks, 13 alarm clocks and 22 detonators were subsequently recovered from Hanif's house in a slum in suburban Andheri. Similar recoveries were

made from Delhi Railway Station around the same time.[82] On 2 October, Zahid Patne, alias Patni, was arrested, allegedly for involvement in the August 25 twin blasts and Ghatkopar blast of July 2003. He is said to have been named by Arshad Ansari—who accused him of 'brain-washing' Ansari and Haneef. He is allegedly closely linked to Nissar, the alleged controller of the module. Police said the blast accused revealed links with conspirators in Hyderabad, Ernakulam and Chennai. They claimed the conspiracy was hatched in the Dubai office of LeT. Nissar was killed along with another man when police sought to stop them in a car. Documents, detonators and explosives were subsequently located in Nissar's house. Documents suggest that Nissar was planning another bombing on 11 September. As more arrests were made, the Mumbai police became progressively more confident of the important role of the LeT in orchestrating and planning the terrorist campaign—including many, if not most, of the blasts in Mumbai since December 2002. The police also referred to an ISI 'mole' called Asgar Ali, recruited by ISI agents in Andhra Pradesh.

19 September 2003 — a prime accused, Toufiq alias Chittu alias Rafique alias Yasar, in the 2 December 2002 bomb blast in Ghatkopar reveals that the decision to trigger the blast was taken in the Gulf by LeT operative Abu Hamza and was funded by the ISI.

10 November 2003 — Mumbai Police seize 750 grams of RDX from the shop of Hasan Batterywala, an accused in August 25 twin bomb blasts in Mumbai, at Kurla.

3 December 2003 — police at Chaderghat, near Hyderabad in Andhra Pradesh, arrest a Pakistan-trained 'Inter Service Intelligence' (ISI) agent, a resident of Yakutpura.

2004

10 January 2004 — six youths, suspected to be agents of the Inter Service Intelligence (ISI), Pakistan's external intelligence agency, are arrested from Hyderabad, Andhra Pradesh, and Siddipet in Medak district.

[82] Lyla Bavadam and Mahesh Vijapurker, 'Inter-state hunt for Mumbai terror controller', *The Hindu* (http://www.hinduonnet.com/thehindu/thscrip/print.pl?file=2003090307760100.htm&date=2).

DOCUMENT NO. 35

LASHKAR-E-TAYYIBA

AUSTRALIAN ATTORNEY-GENERAL

September 11, 2007

07/11689

The Hon David Jull MP
Chair
Parliamentary Joint Committee on Intelligence and Security
Parliament House
CANBERRA ACT 2600

Dear Mr Jull

I am writing to advise you that I have decided to re-list the Palestinian Islamic Jihad (PIJ), Lashkar-e-Tayibba (LeT) and the Hamas' Izz al-Din al-Qassam Brigades (Hamas Brigades) as terrorist organisations for the purposes of section 102.1 of the *Criminal Code Act 1995* (the Criminal Code).

The PIJ, LeT and the Hamas Brigades were last re-listed as terrorist organisations by the *Criminal Code Amendment Regulations 2005 (No. 13)*, with effect from 7 October 2005. Under subsection 102.1(3) of the Criminal Code these regulations will cease to have effect on 7 October 2007.

I am satisfied on reasonable grounds that the PIJ, LeT and the Hamas Brigades are organisations that are directly or indirectly engaged in, preparing, planning, assisting in or fostering the doing of a terrorist act (whether or not a terrorist act has occurred or will occur).

The re-listing of the PIJ, LeT and the Hamas Brigades will ensure that the offence provisions under Division 102 of the Criminal Code will apply.

My decision to re-list the PIJ, LeT and the Hamas Brigades was made following careful consideration of unclassified intelligence information provided by the Australian Security Intelligence Organisation (ASIO) in consultation with the Department of Foreign Affairs and Trade, in relation to these organisations, as well as legal advice provided to me by the Australian Government Solicitor.

Section 102.1A of the Criminal Code provides that the Parliamentary Joint Committee on Intelligence and Security may review the regulations as soon as possible after it has been made, and report the Committee's comments and recommendations to each House of the Parliament before the end of the applicable disallowance period for that House.

To assist the Committee, should it decide to review the regulations, I enclose a copy of the Statement of Reasons provided by ASIO, in relation to the PIJ, LeT and the Hamas Brigades upon which my decision to re-list these organisations was based. Additional information detailing the procedure followed for the purposes of re-listing the PIJ, LeT and the Hamas Brigades will be provided to you upon the registration of the regulations.

The action officer for this matter in my Department is Annabel Knott who can be contacted on (02) 6250 5423 or via email Annabel.Knott@ag.gov.au

Yours sincerely

Philip Ruddock

Editor's Note:
Profiles of Palestinian Islamic Jihad and the Hamas Brigades are omitted here.

Lashkar-e-Tayyiba (LeT/LT)

Also known as: Lashkar-e-Taiba, Lashkar-e-Toiba, Lashkar-i-Toiba, Lashkar-Tayyiba, Lashkar-i-Tayyaba, Lashkar-e-Tayyaba, the Army of the Righteous, Army of the Pure, Army of the Pure and Righteous, Soldiers of the Pure, Army of Medina, Jama'at ul-Da'awa, JuD, Jamaat-ud-Dawa, JUD, Jama'at al-Dawa, Jamaat ud-Daawa, Jamaat ul-Dawah, Jamaat-ul-Dawa, Jama'at-i-Dawat, Jamaiat-ud-Dawa, Jama'at-ud- Da'awah, Jama'at-ud-Da'awa, Jamaati-ud-Dawa, and Idara Khidmat-e-Khalq, the Party of Preachers, Party of the Calling, al Mansoorian, al Mansooreen, Paasban-e-Kashmir, Paasban-i-Ahle- Hadith, Pasban-e-Kashmir, Pasban-e-Ahle-Hadith, Paasban-e-Ahle-Hadis.

The following information is based on publicly available details about Lashkar-e-Tayyiba (LeT). These details have been corroborated by material from intelligence investigations into the activities of the LeT. ASIO assesses that the details set out below are accurate and reliable.

LeT is listed in the United Nations 1267 Committee's consolidated list and as a proscribed terrorist organisation by the governments of Canada, the United Kingdom, the United States, Pakistan and India.

Current Status of Lashkar-e-Tayyiba

LeT is a Sunni Islamic extremist organisation based in Pakistan. LeT was formed circa 1989 as the military wing of the Pakistan-based Islamic fundamentalist movement Markaz al-Dawa wal Irshad (MDI—Centre for Religious Learning and Propagation; also known as the Jamaat al-Daawa). Originally formed to wage militant jihad against the Soviet occupation of Afghanistan, LeT shifted its focus to the insurgency in Indian administered Kashmir (IAK) when Soviet troops withdrew from Afghanistan in the early 1990s. LeT is one of the largest and most brutal of the Pakistan-based militant groups active in Kashmir. LeT has conducted numerous attacks, including bombings, assassinations and kidnappings against Indian security forces (military and police), government, transport and civilians in IAK, as well as in India. The group is also credited with introducing the use of suicide squads to the conflict in IAK. In 2002, LeT was banned by the Pakistan government but the group continues to operate in Pakistan under the alias Jamaat ud-Dawa (JuD). Ostensibly created as a charitable organisation by LeT founder Hafiz Muhammad Saeed immediately prior to LeT being banned, JuD is an LeT front organisation, masking its activities and soliciting its funds.

LeT subscribes to a Salafist interpretation of Islam which has similarities to the Wahhabi form of Islam associated with al-Qa'ida and the Taliban. LeT receives funding from donors in the Middle-East (mainly Saudi Arabia), and through charitable donations collected from sympathisers in Pakistan, Kashmir, the United Kingdom and Persian Gulf states. LeT maintains links to the Taliban and al-Qa'ida, and to several domestic Islamic extremist groups, including the Kashmir focused terrorist group, Jaish-e-Mohammed (JeM), and the sectarian group Lashkar-e Jhangvi (LeJ). LeT is reported to have been involved with mujahideen in other places where Islamist conflicts have arisen including Bosnia, Chechnya and Kosovo. LeT has also participated in the post-Taliban insurgency in Afghanistan. In 2004, several LeT operatives were captured by British forces in Iraq. Indian and Pakistani initiatives to resolve the conflict in Kashmir have led to an overall reduction in the level of LeT infiltration and insurgent activity since 2002. However, LeT continues its attacks against Indian civilians and security forces. While LeT does not claim responsibility for its attacks on civilians, several recent attacks in IAK have been attributed to the group by Indian authorities, including the massacre of over thirty Hindus in two separate attacks in the Doda and Udhampur districts on 1 May 2006. The attacks occurred two days prior to peace talks between the Indian government and Kashmiri separatist groups, and were condemned by India as an attempt by LeT to sabotage the Kashmir peace process. LeT is also widely held to have been responsible for a number of significant attacks in India in recent years, including the 29 October 2005 serial explosions at marketplaces in New Delhi, and the 11 July 2006 serial bombings on trains in Mumbai, which killed more than 240 people in total. While two little known groups claimed responsibility for each of the Mumbai and New Delhi attacks, subsequent investigations have led Indian authorities to conclude that LeT was behind both attacks.

While IAK and Indian interests remain LeT's primary focus, some elements within LeT want to re-focus their activities and bring them more into line with Usama bin Laden's 'global jihad' against the US and Israel, and their allies. As members of a previously unknown group "Jundallah," LeT trained members were among a number of militants drawn from several Pakistani extremist groups responsible for the twin car-bomb attack near the US Consulate in Karachi on 26 May 2004. On 9 June 2004, the same terrorist cell was involved in a terrorist attack against a heavily-armed military convoy carrying Karachi's military commander resulting in seven deaths. In October 2006, LeT issued its own fatwa asking the Muslim community to kill Pope Benedict XVI, in response to a speech delivered by the Pope on 12 September 2006.

LeT operates a number of camps in Pakistan which provide both religious instruction and military style guerrilla training and support. Since being proscribed as a terrorist organisation by the Pakistan government in 2002, some LeT training facilities are now smaller in scale, some of which are mobile, and focused on preparing jihadists for either low intensity, hit and run type operations or suicide attacks.

Reporting indicates LeT may also be helping to facilitate training of foreigners who are possibly intending to conduct terrorism related activities in their countries of origin. Investigations indicate one of the British-born suicide bombers responsible for the 7 July 2005 attacks in London, Shehzad Tanweer, may have received training at a LeT camp in Pakistan. LeT is also suspected of providing some funding and logistical support to the disrupted British trans-Atlantic plane bombing plot in August 2006 using JuD as a cover. Several individuals with links to LeT have been arrested in Australia, the US, and Canada since 2003 for allegedly planning terrorist activities. In March 2007, a French court convicted French national, Willie Brigitte, of planning terrorist attacks in Australia in 2003 in conjunction with suspected LeT Chief for overseas operations, Sajid Mir. In June 2006, Brigitte's associate in Sydney, Faheem Khalid Lodhi, was convicted by a New South Wales Supreme Court jury of planning acts of terrorism (Mr Lodhi has appealed against his conviction). Aside from facilitating training, it is not clear whether the terrorist activities of any of these foreign born individuals have been sanctioned by LeT or are self-directed.

Objectives

LeT is a group that uses violence in pursuit of its stated objective to unite IAK with Pakistan under a radical interpretation of Islamic law. LeT's broader objectives include the establishment of an Islamic Caliphate across the Indian subcontinent. To this end, LeT intends to pursue the 'liberation,' not only of the Muslim-majority in Kashmir, but of all of India's Muslim population, even in areas where they do not form a majority. LeT has declared democracy to be antithetical to Islamic law and that LeT's jihad requires it to work toward turning Pakistan into a purely Islamic state.

Leadership and Membership

The leader of LeT is Hafiz Muhammad Saeed (sometimes rendered Hafiz Mohd Saeed). Saeed has been detained and subsequently released, by Pakistani authorities on several occasions. He was arrested in February 2006, for leading violent protests in response to the Danish cartoon controversy and again in August 2006, in the wake of the disrupted British airliner bombing plot.

LeT's estimated strength is reported to include several hundred trained militants. The majority of LeT's membership consists of jihadists from Pakistan and Afghanistan.

Lashkar-e-Tayyiba Engagement in Terrorist Activities

LeT conducts attacks in IAK on a monthly basis, primarily targeting Indian security forces but also non-Muslim civilians. Other significant attacks for which responsibility has been claimed by, or reliably attributed to, the LeT include:

- November 2005: Car bomb attack near the main entrance of the J&K Bank Corporate Headquarters in Srinigar which killed four civilians and injured 72;
- October 2005: Coordinated bomb attacks at marketplaces and on a bus in New Delhi, killing over 60 persons;
- May 2006: Massacre of Hindu civilians in Doda and Udhampur districts, Jammu & Kashmir, killing 34 civilians;
- May 2006: Attack on a Youth Congress rally at Sher-e-Kashmir Park in Srinigar, killing three political activists and two police officers;
- June 2006: Joint responsibility with Hizb-ul-Mujahideen (HM) for the kidnap and killing of seven Nepalese civilians and one Indian civilian in Kulgam, Jammu & Kashmir;
- July 2006: Serial bombings on trains in Mumbai, killing more than 200 persons; and
- February 2007: Attack on a Central Reserve Police Forces (CRPF) patrol party, killing two CRPF officers.

Conclusion

The Criminal Code provides that for an organisation to be listed as a terrorist organisation, the Attorney-General must be satisfied that:

(i) the organisation is directly or indirectly engaged in, preparing, planning, assisting in or fostering the doing of a terrorist act (whether or not a terrorist act has occurred or will occur); or

(ii) the organisation advocates the doing of a terrorist act (whether or not a terrorist act has occurred or will occur).

On the basis of the above information, ASIO assesses that LeT is directly preparing, planning, assisting in or fostering the doing of terrorist acts. It is submitted that the acts attributable to LeT are terrorist acts as they:

(i) are done with the intention of advancing a political cause, namely, 'liberating' Muslims in Indian-administered Kashmir and the establishment of an Islamic Caliphate across the Indian subcontinent.

(ii) are intended to coerce or influence by intimidation the government of a foreign country, namely India, and/or intimidate a section of the Indian public; and

(iii) constitute acts which cause serious physical harm to persons, including death, as well as serious damage to property.

This assessment is corroborated by information provided by reliable and credible intelligence sources.

DOCUMENT NO. 36

THE KASHMIR CONFLICT AND ITS GLOBAL REACH[1]

Intelligence and Terrorism Information Center at the Center for Special Studies (C.S.S)

June 21, 2006

Bluma Zuckerbrot-Finkelstein

There are currently numerous Islamic extremist organizations employing terror and violence to force the secession of Indian-held Kashmir from India. Some of these groups are Pakistani-based and some are Kashmiri. Some advocate the political independence of Kashmir, while others seek to unite Indian-held Kashmir with Pakistani-held Kashmir. Some are composed of Kashmiris, some of Pakistanis, and some have recruited Arabs, Afghans, and other foreigners into their ranks.

The decades-long conflict over Kashmir has critical regional and international implications for the United States and the international community. First, escalation of the conflict between India and Pakistan could trigger the destabilization of India and/or Pakistan and launch a domino effect on regional and international security. Secondly, escalation could lead to a nuclear confrontation between the two powers. Finally, the conflict has already spilled over into the realm of international terrorism, and its escalation could further endanger Westerners and Western interests.

This analysis will focus on several of the Pakistani-based groups whose goals extend beyond Kashmir. These groups are embedded in the South Asian and global jihad movements and pose serious threats to American and Western interests around the world.

Background to the Conflict

After the creation of the independent states of India and Pakistan in 1947, war broke out over territorial claims to the Muslim-dominated but then

[1] http://www.ajc.org/counterterrorismwatch

Hindu-ruled Kashmir region. India and Pakistan fought two wars over Kashmir, in 1947 and 1965. In 1972, the two nations signed an accord agreeing to respect the ceasefire line known as the Line of Control (LoC), a 750-km. border that divides villages and separates families.

Indian Kashmir, which includes the Kashmir Valley, Jammu, and Ladakh, comprises about ten million people and is generally referred to as Jammu and Kashmir (J&K). The Kashmir Valley is 80 percent Muslim while Jammu is 66 percent Hindu. Ladakh is almost evenly divided among Muslims and Buddhists. Pakistani Kashmir comprises about three million people and is 99 percent Muslim. A small portion of the Kashmir region is under Chinese sovereignty.

New Delhi claims J&K as an integral part of India. Islamabad maintains India has no legal right to the territory and demands that Kashmiris be allowed to vote in a referendum on their future.

Since 1989, Islamic militants allegedly supported by Pakistan have been waging a violent separatist rebellion against Indian rule in Kashmir. These militants are based in Pakistan, Pakistani-held Kashmir, and Indian Kashmir. Their targets include the Indian government, Indian troops and civilians in Indian Kashmir, and military and civilian targets in other parts of India.

Some separatist groups, like the Jammu-Kashmir Liberation Front (JKLF), are fighting for Kashmir to become an independent state. Both India and Pakistan reject this option. An estimated 90,000 people have been killed as a result of the separatist violence.

In 1999, Pakistani soldiers crossed the Line of Control (LoC) into Indian-held Kashmir and heavy fighting ensued for six weeks. Throughout 2000 and 2001, cross-border firing and shelling led to many civilian and military deaths. Pakistan-based terrorist groups are believed responsible for the October 2001 bombing at the Jammu and Kashmir state assembly building that killed thirty-eight people and the December 2001 assault on the Indian Parliament in New Delhi that killed fourteen people. India and Pakistan were on the verge of another full-scale war following the May 2002 Pakistani attack on the residential quarters of an Indian army base at Kaluchak, in J&K, that killed thirty-four people, mostly women and children. The U.S. played a key role in diffusing those tensions.

A November 2003 cease-fire reduced, but did not eliminate, cross-border infiltrations. In January 2004, India and Pakistan issued a joint "Islamabad Declaration" calling for renewed dialogue to bring about a "peaceful settlement of all bilateral issues, including Jammu and Kashmir, to the satisfaction of both sides." Bus service between Muzaffarabad in Pakistani Kashmir and Srinagar in Indian Kashmir was inaugurated in April 2005, and in the wake of the devastating October 2005 South Asian earthquake, five border crossings along the Line of Control were opened to help facilitate aid efforts.

Nevertheless, despite ongoing Pakistani-Indian dialogue and on the ground confidence-building developments, Pakistan and Kashmir-based terrorist groups continue to wage their campaign of separatist violence. Due to the deteriorating security situation in Kashmir following the earthquake, Islamic militant activity has reportedly increased in the region.

India charges the Pakistani government with actively assisting the violent Muslim separatists by providing them with training bases, materiel, funds, safe passage, and ideological support. According to the Rand Corporation, at least ninety-one insurgent training camps exist in Pakistani-held Kashmir. It is widely believed that the violent insurgency is directly controlled and managed by Pakistani intelligence? the Pakistani Inter-Services Intelligence Agency (ISI). Islamabad responds that it provides only moral and diplomatic support to what it calls Kashmiri "freedom fighters."

Leading Islamic Militant Groups with Links to Global Terrorism

Several of the groups waging the Kashmiri separatist war aim for pan-Islamic rule in Central Asia and worldwide jihad. Some are linked to Al-Qa`ida and have been involved in terrorist attacks against Americans and other Western targets.

Three of the major Islamic extremist groups currently operating in Kashmir are: Lashkar-e-Taiba (LET), Harkat ul-Mujahideen (HUM), and Jaish-e-Mohammed (JEM). All three are listed by the U.S. State Department as designated foreign terrorist organizations. LET and HUM are members of Osama bin Ladin's International Islamic Front For Jihad Against Jews and Crusaders and signed the organization's February 1998 fatwa urging attacks on Americans and Western interests. HUM and JEM have both been implicated in the 2002 kidnapping and murder of American journalist Daniel Pearl.

Lashkar-e-Taiba (LET)

LET, a.k.a. Army of the Righteous, Al-Mansoorian, was founded in 1990 as the military wing of the Markaz-ud-Dawa-wal-Irshad (MDI), Center for Religious Learning and Social Welfare, a Pakistani Wahhabi religious organization based in Muridke, near Lahore. MDI runs a vast network of Islamic schools, and healthcare services. Founded by Hafiz Muhammad Saeed, who remains its spiritual mentor, LET was initially created to participate in the Afghanistan Jihad. The group is currently led by Maulana Abdul Wahid Kashmiri and is one of the largest, best-trained, and most active groups fighting in Kashmir. Saeed now heads Jamaat ud-Dawa, Party for Preaching, a recasting of MDI.

Beyond challenging India's sovereignty over J&K, MDI/LET seeks the restoration of Islamic rule over all of India and the union of all Muslim majority regions in countries that surround Pakistan. In a 1997 interview Saeed said: "We feel that Kashmir should be liberated at the earliest. Thereafter, Indian Muslims should be aroused to rise in revolt against the Indian Union so that India gets disintegrated."

LET maintains terror training camps along the LoC and in Muzaffarabad, the capital of Pakistani-held Kashmir. It is believed to have offices and supporters throughout Pakistan. Hafiz Mohammad Saeed is on India's list of most-wanted terrorists.

LET began attacks against Indian troops and civilians in J&K in 1993. It is infamous for suicide attacks and cold-blooded massacres of non-Muslim civilians, including women and children. Two notorious massacres were the June 1998 murder of twenty-five Hindu villagers in Doda as they were returning from a wedding and the July 2002 massacre of twenty-seven Hindus in a slum area of Jammu. LET claimed responsibility for several attacks in 2001, including the January attack on the Srinagar airport that killed five Indians and the February attack on a Srinagar police station that killed eight police officers. LET is suspected of involvement in the December 2001 Indian Parliament attack and the May 2002 Kaluchak army base attack.

Three days before the Hindu festival of Dilawi, in October 2005, terrorists bombed two crowded marketplaces and a bus in New Delhi, killing fifty-nine people and wounding over 200 others. It is suspected that the little-known group Islamic Inqilabi Mahaz (IIM), Islamic Revolutionary Movement, which claimed responsibility for the bombings, is a front group for LET. In a telephone call to a media outlet, an IIM spokesman said, attacks will continue "until India pulls out all its troops from the state of Kashmir." IIM was one of two groups that claimed responsibility for the November 1997 killing of four American employees of Union Texas Petroleum in Karachi.

The Delhi bombings had followed the conviction of LET militant Mohammad Arif, a.k.a. Ashfaq, and six others for the December 2000 attack on the historic Red Fort monument in Delhi, which killed two guards and a civilian. LET had claimed responsibility for that attack.

In early November 2005, LET spokesman Abu Huzaifa denied LET involvement in the attacks claiming, "Lashkar does not believe in carrying out attacks against civilians, especially women and children. We reiterate that Lashkar had no hand in the Delhi attacks."

Also in October 2005, Islamic militants shot to death Ghulam Nabi Lone, 62, the J&K state education minister, at his home in Srinagar. Al-Mansoorian, another alleged front for LET, claimed responsibility.

LET's tentacles reach worldwide. LET members have reportedly participated in Islamic militant activities in Afghanistan, Chechnya, Bosnia, Kosovo, the Philippines, and Iraq. In July 2003, Saeed made clear his intentions toward the U.S.: "We do not fear America. We can defeat it through jihad very easily, but General Musharraf is holding us up. He has become the biggest enemy of jihad, and if we can get him out of the picture, we can take care of the infidels."

A 2004 editorial in the LET publication Ghazwa called for LET mujahideen (holy warriors) to fight in Iraq: "The Americans are dishonoring our mothers and sisters. Therefore, jihad against America has now become mandatory. We [LET] should send our mujahideen to Iraq to fight with the Iraqi mujahideen. Remember that the mujahideen are the last hope for Islam. If the mujahideen are not supported today, Islam will be erased from the map tomorrow."

Osama bin Ladin reportedly financed LET's parent organization and political wing, MDI, and is said to have paid for the construction of a guesthouse on MDI's huge campus headquarters near Lahore. This house was reportedly used as a hideout for 1993 World Trade Center bombing mastermind Ramzi Ahmed Yusef and Mir Aimal Kansi, convicted of killing two Central Intelligence Agency officers outside CIA headquarters in Virginia in January 1993. In March 2002, senior Al-Qa`ida lieutenant Abu Zubaydah was captured at a LET safe house in Faisalabad.

In September 2003, Pakistani authorities arrested fifteen Malaysian and Indonesian students studying in LET-run Islamic schools in Karachi, including Gun Gun Rusman Gunawan, convicted in Indonesia in October 2004 for facilitating and/or aiding terrorism in connection with the August 2003 bombing of the Marriott Hotel in Jakarta. The bombing was carried out by Jemaah Islamiyah (JI), an Al-Qa`ida affiliate. Gunawan is the brother of JI and Al-Qa'ida leader Hambali.

In what has become known as the "Virginia jihad" case, American authorities broke up a terrorist cell in Virginia in 2003 with links to LET. Several of the ten men convicted for various terrorism-related offenses admitted to training at an LET camp in Pakistan and were convicted of providing material support to the foreign terrorist organization. In April 2005, cleric Ali al-Timimi, was convicted of being the cell's mastermind and of inciting his followers to attend LET training camps in Pakistan.

In June 2005, a Paris court found a Pakistani man, Ghulam Rama, 67, and two French men of Pakistani origin, Hassan el-Cheguer, 31 and Hakim Mokhfi, 31, guilty of having links to LET. Rama, sentenced to five years in prison, served as a link in France to LET, helping the other two defendants attend LET terror training camps in Jammu and Kashmir.

In Australia, the trial of Pakistani-born Sydney architect Faheem Khalid Lodhi, 35, opened in February 2006. Accused of planning terrorist attacks against key infrastructure and defense targets in Sydney, Lodhi also stands accused of receiving terror training at a LET camp in Pakistan. Some of the bombing suspects linked to the July 7 train and bus bombings in London and the failed bombing attempt two weeks later are also alleged to have trained at an LET camp.

Harkat ul-Mujahideen (HUM)/Jamiat ul-Ansar (JUA)

Like LET, Harkat ul-Mujahideen (HUM), Movement of Holy Warriors, is a Sunni Pakistani-based Islamic extremist group originally created to participate in the Afghanistan jihad. Founded in 1985 as a splinter faction of the Harkat ul-Jihad-i-Islami, it merged with its parent organization in 1993 to become Harkat ul-Ansar (HUA). Following HUA's 1997 designation as a U.S. foreign terrorist organization, the group reorganized as HUM. In 2000, HUM leader Fazlur Rehman Khalil stepped down as HUM emir and became secretary-general. Replacing Khalil as emir was Farooqi Kashmiri. In 2003, HUM began using the name Jamiat ul-Ansar (JUA), "Group of Helpers."

HUM/JUA operates primarily in Kashmir against Indian troops and civilian targets. It operates terrorist training camps in Pakistan and maintained terror camps in eastern Afghanistan until they were destroyed by Coalition airstrikes following September 11, 2001.

HUM is believed to be linked to the Kashmiri militant group Al-Faran that kidnapped and later killed five Western tourists, including one American, in Kashmir in 1995.

In December 1999 HUM militants hijacked an Indian airliner en route from Nepal to India, stabbed one passenger to death, and demanded the release of several Islamic militants in Indian jails as a condition of releasing its Indian hostages. The Indian government subsequently released HUM militants Masood Azhar, who went on to found the Islamic extremist organization Jaish-e-Mohammed, and Ahmed Omar Sheikh, who was later convicted of the 2002 abduction and murder of U.S. journalist Daniel Pearl. HUM has also been linked to a planned attack on foreign diplomats and Pakistani government officials in September 2002 and foiled attacks against McDonald's and KFC restaurants in Karachi the same month.

HUM/JUA sees itself as engaged in a battle against America. The group's monthly magazine Al Hilal reportedly issues regular calls for volunteers to fight U.S. forces in Iraq and Afghanistan. The November 2003 issue of the magazine said:

[M]ujahideen attacks in Iraq and Afghanistan have bankrupted America politically, economically. . . . Due to the blessings of jihad, America's countdown has begun. It will declare defeat soon. . . .

Eagles of Jamiat ul Ansar: Our motto is to impose Khilafat-I-Rashida [the righteous Caliphate] on the whole world to get rid of the cruel and powerful. We have to retire the debt of our martyrs. We should promise to sacrifice our life, property and heart for the mission of the people who have sacrificed their lives. This is your moral and religious obligation-to help financially those few people who are sacrificing their lives so that they can concentrate on their battlefront and ultimately defeat non-Muslims.

American John Walker Lindh, currently serving a twenty-year prison sentence for aiding the Taliban in Afghanistan, allegedly trained at a HUM terror camp in the summer of 2001 before linking up with the Taliban.

A HUM offshoot, Harkat ul-Mujahideen Al-Alami, is believed responsible for the May 2002 suicide bombing outside Karachi's Sheraton Hotel that killed eleven French engineers and three Pakistanis and the June 2002 suicide bombing at the U.S. consulate in Karachi that killed twelve people. In August 2004, nine members of the offshoot group were convicted of the December 2002 attack on the Macedonian consulate in Karachi that killed three people. Jaish-e-Mohammed (JEM).

Jaish-e-Mohammed (JEM), Army of Mohammed, a.k.a. Tehrik ul-Furqaan, Khuddam-ul-Islam, is a Pakistani-based Islamic extremist group formed in 2000 by Maulana Masood Azhar, after his 1999 release from prison in India in the wake of the Indian Airlines hijacking. With armed supporters in Pakistan and in Indian Kashmir, the group aims to unite Kashmir with Pakistan.

Most JEM attacks have been suicide attacks against Indian targets in Kashmir. JEM claimed responsibility for the October 2001 suicide attack on the J&K legislative building in Srinagar that killed thirty-eight people but later denied the claim. The Indian government implicated JEM, along with LET, in the December 2001 Indian Parliament attack and in December 2002, a Delhi court convicted JEM militants Mohammad Afzal and Shaukat Hussain Guru for their roles in the Parliament attack. Afzal's death sentence was upheld by the Indian Supreme Court in August 2005.

Pakistani authorities suspect JEM militants of anti-Christian attacks in several Pakistani cities in 2002 and of assassination attempts against President Pervez Musharraf in December 2003. JEM militant Amjad Hussain Farooqui, implicated in the Musharraf assassination plots and of having sheltered Al-Qa`ida leader Khalid Sheikh Muhammad before his capture in March 2003, was reportedly killed by Pakistani forces in October 2004.

JEM maintains a women's wing, Banati Ayesha (Daughter of Ayesha) and in October 2005, a JEM woman blew herself up on a key highway in Indian Kashmir. She is believed to be the first female suicide bomber in the Kashmir conflict. Most recently, JEM claimed responsibility for the November 2, 2005, suicide car bombing in Srinagar at the site of the swearing in ceremony of the Chief Minister of J&K. Ten people were killed in the attack, including a woman and a child, which took place several hours before the ceremony.

It is believed that JEM leader Azhar has a longstanding alliance with Osama bin Ladin that dates back to 1993 when they allegedly cooperated in organizing attacks against U.S.—led forces in Somalia.

Pakistan and Counterterrorism

After the September 11 attacks, Pakistani President Musharraf increased his country's anti-terrorist activities. In a major speech in January 2002, the Pakistani leader vowed to end Pakistan's use as a base for terrorism and banned numerous terrorist groups, including LET and JEM. Pakistan has also lent the U.S. invaluable assistance in tracking and apprehending leading Al-Qa'ida and Taliban figures.

Nevertheless, while Islamabad has contributed greatly to combating Al-Qa`ida and Taliban activities on its soil, it has been slower to uproot its domestic and Kashmiri-based terrorist infrastructure. Pakistan pledges to crack down on Kashmiri terrorist infiltration across the Pakistani-Indian border and to shut down terrorist training camps in Pakistan-controlled territory have yielded little concrete actions and have been deemed cosmetic at best. Leaders and members of various Islamic extremist groups remain free to preach, raise funds, and engage in violent activities, including representatives of banned groups. Khalil of HUM/JUA and Azhar of JEM, for example, were both detained by Pakistani authorities and then released shortly thereafter.

SUBJECT INDEX

Doc/Pg

Arms Proliferation

Report of India's Mission to the UN on Small Arms and Light Weapons 27/367

Asia, South

International Commission of Jurists' Report, International Commission of Jurists, November 30, 1994. .... 33/443

International Terrorism in South Asia, Congressional Research Service Report, RS21658

Kronstadt, K. Alan, Specialist, Foreign Affairs, Defense and Trade Division, Congressional Research Service 28/377

Lashkar-e-Tayyiba

Ruddock, Philip, Australian Attorney General. 35/491

South Asian Association for Regional Cooperation Convention (Suppression of Terrorism) Act, The, Act No. 36 of 1993 .... 12/99

Congressional Research Service (CRS) Reports

India: Chronology of Events, Congressional Research Service Report, RS21589

Kronstadt, K. Alan, Specialist, Foreign Affairs, Defense and Trade Division, Congressional Research Service 29/385

International Terrorism in South Asia, Congressional Research Service Report, RS21658

Kronstadt, K. Alan, Specialist, Foreign Affairs, Defense and Trade Division, Congressional Research Service 28/377

Counterterrorism

An Overview on India-Pakistan Relations, Indian Ministry of External Affairs (PAI Division). 3/23

Armed Forces (Special Powers) Act, The, Act 28 of 1958 .... 9/63

Doc/Pg

India's 2001 Counter-Terrorism Report to the UN, UN Security Council Resolution S/2001/1278

Greenstock, Jeremy; Pal, Satyabrata, Chairman, Counter-Terrorism Committee; Chargé d'affaires a.i. of the Permanent Mission of India to the United Nations 22/215

India's 2002 Counter-Terrorism Report to the UN, UN Security Council Resolution S/2002/883

Greenstock, Jeremy; Nambiar, V. K., Chairman, Security Council Committee; Permanent Representative of India to the United Nations 23/283

India's 2003 Counter-Terrorism Report to the UN, UN Security Council Resolution S/2003/452

Arias, Inocencio F.; Nambiar, V. K., Chairman, Security Council Committee; Permanent Representative of India to the United Nations 24/311

India's 2004 Counter-Terrorism Report to the UN, UN Security Council Resolution S/2003/452

Konuzin, Alexander V.; Nambiar, V. K., Chairman, Security Council Committee; Permanent Representative of India to the United Nations 25/321

India's 2007 Counter-Terrorism Report to the UN, UN Security Council Resolution S/2007/196

Arias, Inocencio F.; Sen, Nirupam, Chairman, Security Council Committee; Permanent Representative of India to the United Nations 26/347

India's Country Report, November 30, 2004

Pathak, D.K. 1/1

Kashmir Conflict and its Global Reach, The, Intelligence and Terrorism Information Center at the Center for Special Studies (C.S.S) Report

Zuckerbrot-Finkelstein, Bluma 36/497

Prevention of Terrorism (Repeal) Ordinance, The, President of India 16/175

Prevention of Terrorism Act, The, Act No. 15 of 2002 .... 15/141

Prevention of Terrorism Ordinance, The, No. 9 of 2001

Narayanan, K.R.; Jain, Subhash C., President; Secretary to the Government of India 14/107

Prime Minister's Address to the Nation on the Mumbai Attacks

Singh, Dr. Manmohan, Prime Minister of India 8/61

Quickstep or Kadam Taal?: The Elusive Search for Peace in Jammu and Kashmir, United States Institute of Peace (USIP) Special Report 133

Swami, Praveen, Randolph Jennings Senior Fellow at the United States Institute of Peace 32/427

Doc/Pg

Report of India's Mission to the UN on Small Arms and Light Weapons 27/367

South Asian Association for Regional Cooperation Convention (Suppression of Terrorism) Act, The, Act No. 36 of 1993 . . . . 12/99

Speech of Prime Minister Dr. Manmohan Singh, Speech of the Prime Minister at Conference of Directors General of Police and Inspectors General of Police at New Delhi

  Singh, Dr. Manmohan, Prime Minister of India. 7/55

Speech of Union Home Minister Shivraj Patil, Speech of the Union Home Minister at Conference of Directors General of Police and Inspectors General of Police at New Delhi

  Patil, Shivraj, Union Home Minister 6/45

Terrorist and Disruptive Activities (Prevention) Act, Act No. 28 of 1987 (Amended by Act 43 of 1993). 11/79

Unlawful Activities (Prevention) Act, The, Act No. 37 of 1967 . . . . 10/67

Unlawful Activities (Prevention) Amendment, The, No. 29 of 2004. . . . . 17/177

Weapons of Mass Destruction and Their Delivery Systems (Prohibition of Unlawful Activities) Act, Act No. 21 of 2005

  Viswanathan, T.K., Secretary to the Government of India 18/195

European Union

India, European Union Joint Declaration against International Terrorism 21/213

First Responders

Speech of Prime Minister Dr. Manmohan Singh, Speech of the Prime Minister at Conference of Directors General of Police and Inspectors General of Police at New Delhi

  Singh, Dr. Manmohan, Prime Minister of India. 7/55

Speech of Union Home Minister Shivraj Patil, Speech of the Union Home Minister at Conference of Directors General of Police and Inspectors General of Police at New Delhi

  Patil, Shivraj, Union Home Minister 6/45

Human Rights

International Commission of Jurists' Report, International Commission of Jurists, November 30, 1994. . . . . 33/443

Terrorist and Disruptive Activities (Prevention) Act, Act No. 28 of 1987 (Amended by Act 43 of 1993). 11/79

Doc/Pg

India

Agreement Between India and Pakistan on Bilateral Relations (Simla Agreement)
Gandhi, Indira; Bhutto, Zulifkar Ali, Prime Minister Republic of India; President Islamic Republic of Pakistan 19/207

An Overview on India-Pakistan Relations, Indian Ministry of External Affairs (PAI Division).. 3/23

Armed Forces (Special Powers) Act, The, Act 28 of 1958 .... 9/63

Brief on India-Sri Lanka Relations, Indian Ministry of External Affairs (BSM Division: Sri Lanka)............................ 5/41

India and Pakistan Engagement: Prospects for Breakthrough or Breakdown?, United States Institute of Peace (USIP) Special Report 129.. 31/405

India, European Union Joint Declaration against International Terrorism 21/213

India: Chronology of Events, Congressional Research Service Report, RS21589
Kronstadt, K. Alan, Specialist, Foreign Affairs, Defense and Trade Division, Congressional Research Service 29/385

India's 2001 Counter-Terrorism Report to the UN, UN Security Council Resolution S/2001/1278
Greenstock, Jeremy; Pal, Satyabrata, Chairman, Counter-Terrorism Committee; Chargé d'affaires a.i. of the Permanent Mission of India to the United Nations............................ 22/215

India's 2002 Counter-Terrorism Report to the UN, UN Security Council Resolution S/2002/883
Greenstock, Jeremy; Nambiar, V. K., Chairman, Security Council Committee; Permanent Representative of India to the United Nations.. 23/283

India's 2003 Counter-Terrorism Report to the UN, UN Security Council Resolution S/2003/452
Arias, Inocencio F.; Nambiar, V. K., Chairman, Security Council Committee; Permanent Representative of India to the United Nations 24/311

India's 2004 Counter-Terrorism Report to the UN, UN Security Council Resolution S/2003/452
Konuzin, Alexander V.; Nambiar, V. K., Chairman, Security Council Committee; Permanent Representative of India to the United Nations 25/321

India's 2007 Counter-Terrorism Report to the UN, UN Security Council Resolution S/2007/196
Arias, Inocencio F.; Sen, Nirupam, Chairman, Security Council Committee; Permanent Representative of India to the United Nations 26/347

Doc/Pg

India's Country Report, November 30, 2004
Pathak, D.K. 1/1
International Commission of Jurists' Report, International Commission of Jurists, November 30, 1994. .... 33/443
Kashmir Conflict and its Global Reach, The, Intelligence and Terrorism Information Center at the Center for Special Studies (C.S.S) Report
Zuckerbrot-Finkelstein, Bluma 36/497
Kashmir: The True Story, Indian Ministry of External Affairs. 4/29
Lahore Declaration, The
Vajpayee, Atal Behari; Sharif, Muhammad Nawaz, Prime Minister of the Republic of India; Prime Minister of the Islamic Republic of Pakistan 20/211
Muslims, Terrorism and Rise of The Hindu Right in India, The Australian National University: Strategic and Defence Studies Centre, Working Paper No. 389
Gordon, Sandy 34/449
Parliament Resolution on Jammu and Kashmir, Indian Parliament Resolution 13/105
Prevention of Terrorism (Repeal) Ordinance, The, President of India 16/175
Prevention of Terrorism Act, The, Act No. 15 of 2002. .... 15/141
Prevention of Terrorism Ordinance, The, No. 9 of 2001
Narayanan, K.R.; Jain, Subhash C., President; Secretary to the Government of India 14/107
Prime Minister's Address to the Nation on the Mumbai Attacks
Singh, Dr. Manmohan, Prime Minister of India. 8/61
Quickstep or Kadam Taal?: The Elusive Search for Peace in Jammu and Kashmir, United States Institute of Peace (USIP) Special Report 133
Swami, Praveen, Randolph Jennings Senior Fellow at the United States Institute of Peace 32/427
Report of India's Mission to the UN on Small Arms and Light Weapons 27/367
Social Network Analysis of Terrorist Organizations in India, Institute for Defence Studies and Analysis, India, IDSA Report, 2004, November 30, 2003
Basu, Aparna, Fellow, GN Ramachandran Genome Informatics Knowledge Centre Institute of Genomics and Integrative Biology (at TCGA) 2/13
South Asian Association for Regional Cooperation Convention (Suppression of Terrorism) Act, The, Act No. 36 of 1993 .... 12/99

Doc/Pg

Speech of Prime Minister Dr. Manmohan Singh, Speech of the Prime Minister at Conference of Directors General of Police and Inspectors General of Police at New Delhi
Singh, Dr. Manmohan, Prime Minister of India. 7/55

Speech of Union Home Minister Shivraj Patil, Speech of the Union Home Minister at Conference of Directors General of Police and Inspectors General of Police at New Delhi
Patil, Shivraj, Union Home Minister 6/45

Terrorist and Disruptive Activities (Prevention) Act, Act No. 28 of 1987 (Amended by Act 43 of 1993). 11/79

Typologies and Open Source Reporting on Terrorist Abuse of Charitable Operations in Post-Earthquake Pakistan and India, U.S. Treasury 30/393

Unlawful Activities (Prevention) Act, The, Act No. 37 of 1967 . . . . 10/67

Unlawful Activities (Prevention) Amendment, The, No. 29 of 2004 . . . . . 17/177

Weapons of Mass Destruction and Their Delivery Systems (Prohibition of Unlawful Activities) Act, Act No. 21 of 2005
Viswanathan, T.K., Secretary to the Government of India 18/195

Intelligence

Social Network Analysis of Terrorist Organizations in India, Institute for Defence Studies and Analysis, India, IDSA Report, 2004, November 30, 2003
Basu, Aparna, Fellow, GN Ramachandran Genome Informatics Knowledge Centre Institute of Genomics and Integrative Biology (at TCGA) 2/13

International Cooperation

Agreement Between India and Pakistan on Bilateral Relations (Simla Agreement)
Gandhi, Indira; Bhutto, Zulifkar Ali, Prime Minister Republic of India; President Islamic Republic of Pakistan 19/207

An Overview on India-Pakistan Relations, Indian Ministry of External Affairs (PAI Division). 3/23

Brief on India-Sri Lanka Relations, Indian Ministry of External Affairs (BSM Division: Sri Lanka) 5/41

India and Pakistan Engagement: Prospects for Breakthrough or Breakdown?, United States Institute of Peace (USIP) Special Report 129. . . . . 31/405

India, European Union Joint Declaration against International Terrorism. 21/213

Doc/Pg

India: Chronology of Events, Congressional Research Service Report, RS21589

Kronstadt, K. Alan, Specialist, Foreign Affairs, Defense and Trade Division, Congressional Research Service 29/385

India's 2001 Counter-Terrorism Report to the UN, UN Security Council Resolution S/2001/1278

Greenstock, Jeremy; Pal, Satyabrata, Chairman, Counter-Terrorism Committee; Chargé d'affaires a.i. of the Permanent Mission of India to the United Nations 22/215

India's 2003 Counter-Terrorism Report to the UN, UN Security Council Resolution S/2003/452

Arias, Inocencio F.; Nambiar, V. K., Chairman, Security Council Committee; Permanent Representative of India to the United Nations 24/311

India's 2004 Counter-Terrorism Report to the UN, UN Security Council Resolution S/2003/452

Konuzin, Alexander V.; Nambiar, V. K., Chairman, Security Council Committee; Permanent Representative of India to the United Nations 25/321

India's 2007 Counter-Terrorism Report to the UN, UN Security Council Resolution S/2007/196

Arias, Inocencio F.; Sen, Nirupam, Chairman, Security Council Committee; Permanent Representative of India to the United Nations 26/347

India's Country Report, November 30, 2004

Pathak, D.K. 1/1

Lahore Declaration, The

Vajpayee, Atal Behari; Sharif, Muhammad Nawaz, Prime Minister of the Republic of India; Prime Minister of the Islamic Republic of Pakistan 20/211

Quickstep or Kadam Taal?: The Elusive Search for Peace in Jammu and Kashmir, United States Institute of Peace (USIP) Special Report 133

Swami, Praveen, Randolph Jennings Senior Fellow at the United States Institute of Peace 32/427

Report of India's Mission to the UN on Small Arms and Light Weapons 27/367

South Asian Association for Regional Cooperation Convention (Suppression of Terrorism) Act, The, Act No. 36 of 1993 .... 12/99

Doc/Pg

Islam

Muslims, Terrorism and Rise of The Hindu Right in India, The Australian National University: Strategic and Defence Studies Centre, Working Paper No. 389
Gordon, Sandy 34/449

Military – Role of

Armed Forces (Special Powers) Act, The, Act 28 of 1958 9/63

Nuclear Terrorism

India and Pakistan Engagement: Prospects for Breakthrough or Breakdown?, United States Institute of Peace (USIP) Special Report 129 . . . . . 31/405

Lahore Declaration, The
Vajpayee, Atal Behari; Sharif, Muhammad Nawaz, Prime Minister of the Republic of India; Prime Minister of the Islamic Republic of Pakistan 20/211

Weapons of Mass Destruction and Their Delivery Systems (Prohibition of Unlawful Activities) Act, Act No. 21 of 2005
Viswanathan, T.K., Secretary to the Government of India 18/195

Pakistan

Agreement Between India and Pakistan on Bilateral Relations (Simla Agreement)
Gandhi, Indira; Bhutto, Zulifkar Ali, Prime Minister Republic of India; President Islamic Republic of Pakistan 19/207

An Overview on India-Pakistan Relations, Indian Ministry of External Affairs (PAI Division) 3/23

India and Pakistan Engagement: Prospects for Breakthrough or Breakdown?, United States Institute of Peace (USIP) Special Report 129 . . . . . 31/405

India: Chronology of Events, Congressional Research Service Report, RS21589
Kronstadt, K. Alan, Specialist, Foreign Affairs, Defense and Trade Division, Congressional Research Service 29/385

International Commission of Jurists' Report, International Commission of Jurists, November 30, 1994 . . . . . 33/443

Kashmir Conflict and its Global Reach, The, Intelligence and Terrorism Information Center at the Center for Special Studies (C.S.S) Report
Zuckerbrot-Finkelstein, Bluma 36/497

Kashmir: The True Story, Indian Ministry of External Affairs 4/29

Doc/Pg

Lahore Declaration, The
Vajpayee, Atal Behari; Sharif, Muhammad Nawaz, Prime Minister of the Republic of India; Prime Minister of the Islamic Republic of Pakistan 20/211

Lashkar-e-Tayyiba
Ruddock, Philip, Australian Attorney General 35/491

Muslims, Terrorism and Rise of The Hindu Right in India, The Australian National University: Strategic and Defence Studies Centre, Working Paper No. 389
Gordon, Sandy 34/449

Parliament Resolution on Jammu and Kashmir, Indian Parliament Resolution 13/105

Quickstep or Kadam Taal?: The Elusive Search for Peace in Jammu and Kashmir, United States Institute of Peace (USIP) Special Report 133
Swami, Praveen, Randolph Jennings Senior Fellow at the United States Institute of Peace 32/427

Social Network Analysis of Terrorist Organizations in India, Institute for Defence Studies and Analysis, India, IDSA Report, 2004, November 30, 2003
Basu, Aparna, Fellow, GN Ramachandran Genome Informatics Knowledge Centre Institute of Genomics and Integrative Biology (at TCGA) 2/13

Typologies and Open Source Reporting on Terrorist Abuse of Charitable Operations in Post-Earthquake Pakistan and India, U.S. Treasury 30/393

State Sponsors of Terrorism

Kashmir: The True Story, Indian Ministry of External Affairs 4/29

Parliament Resolution on Jammu and Kashmir, Indian Parliament Resolution 13/105

Taliban

International Terrorism in South Asia, Congressional Research Service Report, RS21658
Kronstadt, K. Alan, Specialist, Foreign Affairs, Defense and Trade Division, Congressional Research Service 28/377

Terrorism – Criminal Prosecution

India's 2002 Counter-Terrorism Report to the UN, UN Security Council Resolution S/2002/883
Greenstock, Jeremy; Nambiar, V. K., Chairman, Security Council Committee; Permanent Representative of India to the United Nations 23/283

Doc/Pg

Terrorist and Disruptive Activities (Prevention) Act, Act No. 28 of 1987 (Amended by Act 43 of 1993)........................ 11/79

Terrorism – Financing of

India's 2001 Counter-Terrorism Report to the UN, UN Security Council Resolution S/2001/1278
 Greenstock, Jeremy; Pal, Satyabrata, Chairman, Counter-Terrorism Committee; Chargé d'affaires a.i. of the Permanent Mission of India to the United Nations 22/215

India's 2002 Counter-Terrorism Report to the UN, UN Security Council Resolution S/2002/883
 Greenstock, Jeremy; Nambiar, V. K., Chairman, Security Council Committee; Permanent Representative of India to the United Nations..23/283

India's 2003 Counter-Terrorism Report to the UN, UN Security Council Resolution S/2003/452
 Arias, Inocencio F.; Nambiar, V. K., Chairman, Security Council Committee; Permanent Representative of India to the United Nations 24/311

India's 2004 Counter-Terrorism Report to the UN, UN Security Council Resolution S/2003/452
 Konuzin, Alexander V.; Nambiar, V. K., Chairman, Security Council Committee; Permanent Representative of India to the United Nations 25/321

India's 2007 Counter-Terrorism Report to the UN, UN Security Council Resolution S/2007/196
 Arias, Inocencio F.; Sen, Nirupam, Chairman, Security Council Committee; Permanent Representative of India to the United Nations..26/347

Lashkar-e-Tayyiba
 Ruddock, Philip, Australian Attorney General 35/491

Prevention of Terrorism Act, The, Act No. 15 of 2002................. 15/141

Prevention of Terrorism Ordinance, The, No. 9 of 2001
 Narayanan, K.R.; Jain, Subhash C., President; Secretary to the Government of India 14/107

Typologies and Open Source Reporting on Terrorist Abuse of Charitable Operations in Post-Earthquake Pakistan and India, U.S. Treasury 30/393

Unlawful Activities (Prevention) Amendment, The, No. 29 of 2004 ..... 17/177

Terrorism – International

India and Pakistan Engagement: Prospects for Breakthrough or Breakdown?, United States Institute of Peace (USIP) Special Report 129 .... 31/405

Doc/Pg

India, European Union Joint Declaration against International Terrorism 21/213

India: Chronology of Events, Congressional Research Service Report, RS21589

Kronstadt, K. Alan, Specialist, Foreign Affairs, Defense and Trade Division, Congressional Research Service 29/385

International Commission of Jurists' Report, International Commission of Jurists, November 30, 1994 .... 33/443

International Terrorism in South Asia, Congressional Research Service Report, RS21658

Kronstadt, K. Alan, Specialist, Foreign Affairs, Defense and Trade Division, Congressional Research Service 28/377

Kashmir Conflict and its Global Reach, The, Intelligence and Terrorism Information Center at the Center for Special Studies (C.S.S) Report

Zuckerbrot-Finkelstein, Bluma 36/497

Kashmir: The True Story, Indian Ministry of External Affairs 4/29

Lashkar-e-Tayyiba

Ruddock, Philip, Australian Attorney General 35/491

Muslims, Terrorism and Rise of The Hindu Right in India, The Australian National University: Strategic and Defence Studies Centre, Working Paper No. 389

Gordon, Sandy 34/449

Parliament Resolution on Jammu and Kashmir, Indian Parliament Resolution 13/105

Prime Minister's Address to the Nation on the Mumbai Attacks

Singh, Dr. Manmohan, Prime Minister of India 8/61

Quickstep or Kadam Taal?: The Elusive Search for Peace in Jammu and Kashmir, United States Institute of Peace (USIP) Special Report 133

Swami, Praveen, Randolph Jennings Senior Fellow at the United States Institute of Peace 32/427

Social Network Analysis of Terrorist Organizations in India, Institute for Defence Studies and Analysis, India, IDSA Report, 2004, November 30, 2003

Basu, Aparna, Fellow, GN Ramachandran Genome Informatics Knowledge Centre Institute of Genomics and Integrative Biology (at TCGA) 2/13

Speech of Prime Minister Dr. Manmohan Singh, Speech of the Prime Minister at Conference of Directors General of Police and Inspectors General of Police at New Delhi

Singh, Dr. Manmohan, Prime Minister of India 7/55

Doc/Pg

Speech of Union Home Minister Shivraj Patil, Speech of the Union Home Minister at Conference of Directors General of Police and Inspectors General of Police at New Delhi

Patil, Shivraj, Union Home Minister 6/45

Unlawful Activities (Prevention) Act, The, Act No. 37 of 1967. . . . . 10/67

Terrorism – Military Role

Armed Forces (Special Powers) Act, The, Act 28 of 1958 9/63

Terrorism – Policy

An Overview on India-Pakistan Relations, Indian Ministry of External Affairs (PAI Division). 3/23

Armed Forces (Special Powers) Act, The, Act 28 of 1958 . . . . 9/63

India, European Union Joint Declaration against International Terrorism 21/213

India's Country Report, November 30, 2004

Pathak, D.K. 1/1

Parliament Resolution on Jammu and Kashmir, Indian Parliament Resolution. 13/105

Prevention of Terrorism (Repeal) Ordinance, The, President of India . . . 16/175

Prevention of Terrorism Act, The, Act No. 15 of 2002. . . . . 15/141

Prevention of Terrorism Ordinance, The, No. 9 of 2001

Narayanan, K.R.; Jain, Subhash C., President; Secretary to the Government of India 14/107

Prime Minister's Address to the Nation on the Mumbai Attacks

Singh, Dr. Manmohan, Prime Minister of India. 8/61

Report of India's Mission to the UN on Small Arms and Light Weapons 27/367

South Asian Association for Regional Cooperation Convention (Suppression of Terrorism) Act, The, Act No. 36 of 1993 . . . . 12/99

Speech of Prime Minister Dr. Manmohan Singh, Speech of the Prime Minister at Conference of Directors General of Police and Inspectors General of Police at New Delhi

Singh, Dr. Manmohan, Prime Minister of India. 7/55

Speech of Union Home Minister Shivraj Patil, Speech of the Union Home Minister at Conference of Directors General of Police and Inspectors General of Police at New Delhi

Patil, Shivraj, Union Home Minister 6/45

Terrorist and Disruptive Activities (Prevention) Act, Act No. 28 of 1987 (Amended by Act 43 of 1993). 11/79

Unlawful Activities (Prevention) Act, The, Act No. 37 of 1967. . . . . 10/67

Unlawful Activities (Prevention) Amendment, The, No. 29 of 2004 . . . . . 17/177

Doc/Pg

Weapons of Mass Destruction and Their Delivery Systems (Prohibition of Unlawful Activities) Act, Act No. 21 of 2005
Viswanathan, T.K., Secretary to the Government of India 18/195

Terrorism – Threat Assessment

Muslims, Terrorism and Rise of The Hindu Right in India, The Australian National University: Strategic and Defence Studies Centre, Working Paper No. 389
Gordon, Sandy 34/449

Terrorist Incidents

Prime Minister's Address to the Nation on the Mumbai Attacks
Singh, Dr. Manmohan, Prime Minister of India. 8/61

Terrorist Organizations

India's Country Report, November 30, 2004
Pathak, D.K. 1/1
International Terrorism in South Asia, Congressional Research Service Report, RS21658
Kronstadt, K. Alan, Specialist, Foreign Affairs, Defense and Trade Division, Congressional Research Service 28/377
Kashmir Conflict and its Global Reach, The, Intelligence and Terrorism Information Center at the Center for Special Studies (C.S.S) Report
Zuckerbrot-Finkelstein, Bluma 36/497
Lashkar-e-Tayyiba
Ruddock, Philip, Australian Attorney General 35/491
Prevention of Terrorism Act, The, Act No. 15 of 2002. . . . . 15/141
Prevention of Terrorism Ordinance, The, No. 9 of 2001
Narayanan, K.R.; Jain, Subhash C., President; Secretary to the Government of India 14/107
Social Network Analysis of Terrorist Organizations in India, Institute for Defence Studies and Analysis, India, IDSA Report, 2004, November 30, 2003
Basu, Aparna, Fellow, GN Ramachandran Genome Informatics Knowledge Centre Institute of Genomics and Integrative Biology (at TCGA) 2/13
Typologies and Open Source Reporting on Terrorist Abuse of Charitable Operations in Post-Earthquake Pakistan and India, U.S. Treasury 30/393
Unlawful Activities (Prevention) Amendment, The, No. 29 of 2004 . . . . . 17/177

Doc/Pg

United Nations – Security Council Resolutions

India's 2001 Counter-Terrorism Report to the UN, UN Security Council Resolution S/2001/1278

Greenstock, Jeremy; Pal, Satyabrata, Chairman, Counter-Terrorism Committee; Chargé d'affaires a.i. of the Permanent Mission of India to the United Nations 22/215

India's 2002 Counter-Terrorism Report to the UN, UN Security Council Resolution S/2002/883

Greenstock, Jeremy; Nambiar, V. K., Chairman, Security Council Committee; Permanent Representative of India to the United Nations 23/283

India's 2003 Counter-Terrorism Report to the UN, UN Security Council Resolution S/2003/452

Arias, Inocencio F.; Nambiar, V. K., Chairman, Security Council Committee; Permanent Representative of India to the United Nations 24/311

India's 2004 Counter-Terrorism Report to the UN, UN Security Council Resolution S/2003/452

Konuzin, Alexander V.; Nambiar, V. K., Chairman, Security Council Committee; Permanent Representative of India to the United Nations 25/321

India's 2007 Counter-Terrorism Report to the UN, UN Security Council Resolution S/2007/196

Arias, Inocencio F.; Sen, Nirupam, Chairman, Security Council Committee; Permanent Representative of India to the United Nations 26/347

Kashmir: The True Story, Indian Ministry of External Affairs 4/29

Weapons of Mass Destruction

Lahore Declaration, The

Vajpayee, Atal Behari; Sharif, Muhammad Nawaz, Prime Minister of the Republic of India; Prime Minister of the Islamic Republic of Pakistan 20/211

Weapons of Mass Destruction and Their Delivery Systems (Prohibition of Unlawful Activities) Act, Act No. 21 of 2005

Viswanathan, T.K., Secretary to the Government of India 18/195

www.ingramcontent.com/pod-product-compliance
Ingram Content Group UK Ltd.
Pitfield, Milton Keynes, MK11 3LW, UK
UKHW051048150926
475595UK00005B/172